Springer Proceedings in Business and Economics

D1810688

Springer Proceedings in Business and Economics brings the most current research presented at conferences and workshops to a global readership. The series features volumes (in electronic and print formats) of selected contributions from conferences in all areas of economics, business, management, and finance. In addition to an overall evaluation by the publisher of the topical interest, scientific quality, and timeliness of each volume, each contribution is refereed to standards comparable to those of leading journals, resulting in authoritative contributions to the respective fields. Springer's production and distribution infrastructure ensures rapid publication and wide circulation of the latest developments in the most compelling and promising areas of research today.

The editorial development of volumes may be managed using Springer Nature's innovative EquinOCS, a proven online conference proceedings submission, management and review system. This system is designed to ensure an efficient timeline for your publication, making Springer Proceedings in Business and Economics the premier series to publish your workshop or conference volume.

This book series is indexed in SCOPUS.

Pantelis Sklias · Persefoni Polychronidou ·
Anastasios Karasavvoglou · Victoria Pistikou ·
Nikolaos Apostolopoulos
Editors

Business Development and Economic Governance in Southeastern Europe

13th International Conference on
the Economies of the Balkan and Eastern
European Countries (EBEEC), Pafos, Cyprus,
2021

 Springer

Editors
Pantelis Sklias
Neapolis University Pafos
Paphos, Cyprus

Anastasios Karasavvoglou
Department of Accounting and Finance
International Hellenic University
Kavala, Greece

Nikolaos Apostolopoulos
University of Peloponnese
Tripoli, Greece

Persefoni Polychronidou
Department of Economics
International Hellenic University
Serres, Greece

Victoria Pistikou
Democritus University of Thrace
Komotini, Greece

ISSN 2198-7246   ISSN 2198-7254 (electronic)
Springer Proceedings in Business and Economics
ISBN 978-3-031-05353-5   ISBN 978-3-031-05351-1 (eBook)
https://doi.org/10.1007/978-3-031-05351-1

This Springer imprint is published by the registered company Springer Nature Switzerland AG
The registered company address is: Gewerbestrasse 11, 6330 Cham, Switzerland

Preface

Due to endogenous and exogenous forces, the only constant in the complex world of business and economy is continuous change and development. New ideas, novelty in products, technology development, new regulations, changes in environment, behaviour changes and other novelties in everyday life alters the economy on daily basis. Perpetual growth and evolvement of all participants have been modelling business and public sector to today's level of the systems. The few past decades' have been highly turbulent, and it could be expressed by two phenomena's; first one is crisis, and other one is changing economic environment due to the digital transformation. Business performance analysis in these days is more complex and demanding that ever before. Risk management and performance analysis because of pace of changes require new knowledges and implementations of new economics models. Global-level changes, tensions and issues like political, health, environmental, technological are influencing shift of paradigms in world economy. Europe is not an island, and changes are influencing to its business and economic landscape. Some changes are endogenous, like Brexit; some are exogenous like "America First" politics, SARS-COV-2, etc. All these changes are unquestionably being changing and challenging business development and economic governance in Europe.

Thus, this volume encompasses manuscripts with focus on assessments of the business development and economic governance in Europe, with the particulate interest to the Central and Southeastern European countries. The original perspective of the authors, researchers and practitioners, on the issue and utilized complex quantities and qualitative models, delivers firm ground for quality scientific conclusions and recommendations for further discussions. The majority of the researchers that this volume gathers have affiliation of higher education and research institutions from Central and Southeastern Europe.

The international conference "Economies of the Balkan and Eastern European Countries (EBEEC)", through its twelve previous editions, has become a recognized forum where the knowledge and experiences gained by academics specialized in economics and business in the region of Central and Southeastern Europe are exchanged, debated and validated. Besides that, the results of the EBEEC conference are numerous publications disseminated to the scientific public and practitioners all over the world. In this effort, substantial assistance and contribution come from renowned publishers such as Springer.

The 13th International Conference "Economies of the Balkan and Eastern European Countries" was organized jointly in Cyprus (Pafos) by Neapolis University Pafos and Department of Economics and Accounting of the International Hellenic University, on 14–16 May 2021. The aim of the conference was to gather scientists and practitioners' that will present academic papers and to exchange theoretical and empirical results on contemporary issues in economy with specific focus in business development and economic governance in Central and Southeastern European countries. Due to the epidemic situation with SARS-CoV-2 and numerus restrictions regarding travelling, the conference was held online. The conference brought together more than 100 manuscripts and by more than 150 authors from 20 countries from Europe and all over the world. A broad range of issues—Greek political economy; recession; generalized trust; sustainability; emerging economies; multinational enterprises; statistical arbitrage; entrepreneurship education; innovation policy; social cooperative enterprise (SCE); etc.—have been discussed at the conference and in the resulting published manuscripts.

This volume as one of the publications resulting from the **13th International Conference "Economies of the Balkan and Eastern European Countries" (EBEEC)—Pafos, Cyprus, May 2021**, has a goal to present to the worldwide audience new and original research and conclusions in a specific field of business development and economic governance in Europe. The volume includes 25 selected manuscripts based on their quality and originality arranged and presented at the 13th EBEEC conference in Pafos, Cyprus. The book consists of two parts. Part One focuses on **Public Administration/Governance and the Economies of Southeastern Europe**. Part Two unfolds the subject of **Business Growth and Development in Southeastern Europe**. The entire manuscript selection process was managed by the board of editors in compliance with the highest standards and best practice guidelines on publishing ethics, paying special attention to issues regarding plagiarism, peer review, objectivity, funding, privacy and conflict of interest. All selected manuscripts have gone through the peer review process and carefully edited. Research ideas and applied quantitative methods indicate that scientists emerging from Central and Southeastern Europe are developing new worthy of attention knowledge and conclusions in this field. This is the result of changing nature of the economy in Central and Southeastern European countries and merits attention in increasing the scientific quality work. Selected papers are independent and do not constitute joint research; their appearance in the volume is aimed to present analogues topics in the field of economy and business and to attract the attention of scientific public and also practitioners.

Part One of the edited volume opens with a paper written by **Prof. Pantelis Sklias** (*Neapolis University Pafos, Cyprus*), **Spyros A. Roukanas** (*University of Piraeus, Greece*) and **Georgios Galatsidas** (*University of the Aegean*). As described in their paper, the strict austerity policy that was imposed on Greece by the Tripartite Support Mechanism (EC, ECB and IMF) had unforeseen and unprecedented macroeconomic and social effects. There can be no doubt that the fiscal stability programme was originally designed to facilitate the overall improvement of the Greek economy's macroeconomic situation, emphasizing on the stabilization of budget deficits and the containment of public debt as necessary conditions for both Greece's return to capital markets and restarting economic growth in the country. Ten years later, the question is to what extent the macroeconomic targets of reducing the public debt and the budget deficit, as well as the ultimate goal of achieving economic growth, have been realized (or not)? This paper is an attempt to systematically document the course of Greek Political Economy during 2010–2019. More specifically, this paper discusses macroeconomic aggregates (economic growth, public debt, public deficit, unemployment, employment and the labour force) with the ultimate goal of evaluating the economic policies of the tripartite support mechanism. The study of macroeconomic indicators shows that ten years after the programme's implementation the overall macroeconomic situation of the Greek economy has not improved (with the exception of the public deficit), while key indicators (such as the public debt and economic growth) have worsened, further aggravating labour market conditions, and as a result, the Greek economy is in a much worse macroeconomic position as compared to May 2010.

The second paper of the volume, authored by **Nalleli Patricia Bolaños Pérez and Edgar J. Saucedo-Acosta** (*University of Veracruz, Xalapa, Mexico*), aims to investigate the causal relationship between generalized trust, as well as income inequalities in 23 economies belonging to the Organization for Economic Cooperation and Development from 2000 to 2019. In this study, we use the application of a fully modified least squares model and the canonical correlation regression estimator. In addition, the unit root and co-integration test are applied before applying the Granger causality test. The findings show that there is a bidirectional relationship between social capital and income inequality.

The manuscript prepared by **Grazia Dicuonzo, Francesca Donofrio, Simona Ranaldo** (*University of Bari Aldo Moro, Italy*) explains how, in the last decade, corporate reporting has undergone a radical transformation, adding sustainability reporting to traditional financial reporting. The Barnier Directive (2014/95/EU) introduced into European law the obligation for large public-interest entities to prepare and publish a non-financial statement. This document must contain information relating to the environment, the social sphere, employee matters, respect for human rights, and the fight against active and passive corruption, aimed at ensuring an understanding of the company's activities, performance, results and impact. Indeed, to date, managers consider it necessary to adopt a holistic approach, considering both financial and non-financial aspects, to ensure the protection of the creation of corporate value. On April 2021, the European Commission adopted a proposal of Corporate Sustainability Reporting Directive (CSRD), aiming at improving sustainability reporting in order to contribute to the transition towards a fully sustainable and inclusive economic and financial system. In this context, the topic of sustainability reporting has become relevant for companies. This paper reviews the main frameworks and standards developed by international standards available to companies, investigating the level of adoption by a sample of European listed companies.

The following paper arranged by **M. Giusti** (*University of Florence, Florence, Italy*), **N. Persiani** (*University of Florence, Florence, Italy*), **M. De Luca** (*Centre of Global Health of Tuscany Region, Florence, Italy*) and **J. M. Caldes** (*Centre of Global Health of Tuscany Region, Florence, Italy*) explores how in the last years, with the affirmation of the Theory of Change (ToC—Connel and Kunisch, 1998), a lot of tools for the evaluation of projects having social relevance have been developed. The need to measure their impact has led to leave the use of traditional qualitative measurement instruments joints for quantitative tools, which calculate the effectiveness of the resources employed and the generated impact by social project (Anderson, 2006). Among them, recently, it has paid attention on the Social Return on Investment (SROI—Lingane et Olsen, 2004), a model to account for created value.

It includes not only the return of investments but also the benefits for the broader public in the social, economic and environmental spheres.

The research aim is to verify and calculate SROI as a valid tool to measure the impact generated by social projects in transitional countries, especially those of health international cooperation.

Indeed, the economic quantification of the SROI rate appears as an important element to improve reporting and accountability both to the lender and the users.

The case study has been identified as appropriate methodology for conducting this research (Yin, 2003; Eisenhardt, 1989). The project "Introducing Health Information System (IHIS): a modern approach to transparency and accountability in the Albanian public health" conducted by the Tuscany Region resulted relevant for the involvement of different actors and its action in a transition country as Albania. This project was realized from 2014 to 2016 using financing from IADSA (Italian–Albanian Debt for Development Swap Agreement) to support the Albanian government in the NHS technological and accountant development. Now, it is possible to adequately observe the generated impact 5 years after the conclusion of IHIS project.

The necessary data for the calculation of SROI were collected by desk analysis of project's documents and reports and the conduction of interviews and focus groups to a specimen of involved stakeholders.

Results show the good capability of SROI to quantitatively evaluate the impact produced by a health international cooperation project, also if complex and articulated as that studied. In particular, the SROI rate of this project is 9.4, an optimal rate (for 100€ invested, the project generated an economic impact of 940€). Therefore, it is demonstrated the optimal use of the allocated resources obtaining a strong effectiveness impact in the Albanian healthcare system and on the network of involved stakeholders. Another important aspect is the reinforcement of results dissemination in the society, for the simplicity and easy comprehension of the SROI rate, and the internal restitution promoted by SROI analysis. So, SROI proves as a good instrument both to measure and to share the economic value of generated impact.

Charalampos Chrysomallidis (*Neapolis University Pafos, Cyprus*) examines the operation of Monetary Union and its implications for less competitive Eurozone member states, including Greece, is examined. In this analysis, impact of fiscal and pandemic crises on economy is also taken into account. The article examines initiatives and proposals for making the MU resembling more to EMU under the

the creation of a new value added. A permanent increasing of this one may be only achieved by innovation activities. This methodological vision is important in identifying the current economic problems of the Balkan and Eastern European countries, as it can propose answers at the question how a low- and middle- income countries can significantly increase the value of their national product and narrows the gap in GDP per capita against developed countries.

The manuscript authored by **Ioannis Tsoukalidis** (*Domi Development PC, Greece*), **Antonios Kostas and Anastasios G. Karasavvoglou** (both of them from *International Hellenic University, Greece*), explains how Social Cooperative Enterprises (SCEs) in Greece are legal entities under private law. They operate on the basis of the relevant provisions of the law 4430/2016 as in force. The main objectives of SCEs are the socioeconomic inclusion, the re-integration in terms of employment and the overall social impact of their activities. This article attempts to proceed with the ex-ante evaluation of the operation of a newly established SCE in North Greece and risk assessment to sets of basic parameters that alter negatively, compared to a "classical form" of privately owned enterprise, of the same type of business. In order to do so, nine (9) basic parameters of control have been selected, to evaluate the resilience of a SCE and juxtapose it with the respective resilience of "classical form" private enterprise. Those parameters were organized in three (3) sets, and three (3) different simulations within a period of five (5) years ahead were performed, for negative shift of each set, in order to finally estimate the sustainability risks—resilience, as well as financial income and social impact. Conclusions of simulations as the ones illustrated in this article are of high importance for prospective social entrepreneurs, as they raise awareness of risks, helping them to be better prepared in case those risks become reality.

Author **Katerina Lyroudi** (*Hellenic Open University, Greece*) describes how innovation enhances corporate value and offers the underlying company a new competitive advantage, strategic and financial benefits and potential for survival and future growth. As a proxy for innovation, we use the expenditures in research and development (R&D) and the intangible assets of the company following the relevant literature. This paper focuses on the European markets. The objective of the paper is to investigate first whether R&D expenditures and intangible assets affect the value of the underlying company, and if they do so, in what way and second whether they affect the performance of the company. Our sample consists of the companies in the information technology (IT) industry in Europe, the most innovative industry. We apply several regression models to test our hypotheses. Our results indicated a positive relation between the innovative investments as proxied by the research and development expenses and the intangible assets with the firm's value. However, regarding the company performance as measured by the ROA and ROE, our results rejected our hypothesis since we found a negative relation between the innovation variables and the profitability ratios as performance variables.

Part Two of the edited volume opens with a paper written by **Ermira H. Kalaj** (*University of Shkodra "Luigj Gurakuqi", Albania*), which focuses on the analyses of financial obstacles facing small and medium enterprises in Albania. Using data from 2019 Enterprise Surveys (ES), we try to give answers to questions related to financial patterns that characterize Albanian enterprises. The survey was a shared project of the European Bank for Reconstruction and Development (EBRD), the European Investment Bank (EIB) and the World Bank Group (WBG); the data are collected in Albania between January and May 2019. The objective of the survey is to better understand firms experience in the private sector. Collected data are based on firms' experiences and perception of the environment in which they operate.

The data are stratified in three levels for Albania: industry, enterprise size and region. The stratification according to the industry was completed as follows: manufacturing—combining all the relevant activities, retail and other services. Moreover, 2019 Albanian ES was based on the following size stratification: small (5–19 employees), medium (20–99 employees) and large (100 or more employees). Regional stratification was done across three regions: Northern Albania comprising Dibër, Durrës, Kukës, Lezhë, Shkodër, Central Albania comprising Tirana and Elbasan and Southern Albania comprising Berat, Fier, Gjirokastër, Korçë and Vlorë.

To analyse financial obstacles and factors affecting on them, we estimate the ordered probit model where the dependent variable corresponds to the survey question: "How much of an obstacle: access to finance?" While the vector of independent variables is composed by enterprise characteristics such as firm size, ownership structure, legal status and region. Moreover, dummy variables are used to capture firm's technological capability and gender ownership.

Empirical results show that financial obstacles tend to be more significant for smaller enterprises, operating not in the central area of the country, and female ownership means more challenges in the financial markets. Additionally, lack of financial challenges has a steadily constructive impact on the productivity of SMEs.

According to the next paper of the volume, authored by **Marian Mair, Thomas Dilger, Christian Ploder and Reinhard Bernsteiner** (*The Institute of Economics, Croatia*), the basic concept of dynamic pricing (DP) has been around for a long time (e.g. gas station prices). It is now commonly known as an algorithm-based automatic price adjustment tool on e-commerce platforms (e.g. flight tickets or hotel prices) to maximize profit. Through the invention and implementation of the electronic shelf label (ESL) technology in stationary retail, DP is based on time or demand. It creates new opportunities for the physical contribution channel. This potential is also the focus of this study by precisely dealing with the recognition and impact of DP with ESL technology on consumers' purchasing decisions in stationary grocery stores. Our literature review includes current DP, ESL technology, price behaviour and price fairness. According to the first review, no single experiment on ESLs in combination with DP in stationary grocery stores and only a few general studies on ESLs exist. Thus, an experimental design is proposed to research customers' post-purchase reaction/acceptance of ESLs in stationary grocery stores and customers' recognition and perception (perceived price fairness) of DP adjustment strategies. Participants purchase twice an ethnically defined shopping cart in a supermarket by applying ESLs, whereby the second time, the prices of several products from the shopping list are slightly increased. The goal of the between-participants post-test-only control-group experiment design is to identify the technology's potential for stationary grocery stores. Equity theory deals with price fairness and is used as the primary consumer behaviour model for price adjustments. The results depict a design for experimental research on DP with ESL technology. The system should function as a pre-study and discussion base for further research on this topic. A draft of the experimental setting (instruction sheets, evaluation plan, digitally designed survey) is already provided as a basis for further improvements. With the proposed execution plan, third parties can further test the experiment on feasibility and applicability in the described experimental setting, by usage of technology (virtual reality and augmented reality) or on different industries or other groups.

The next paper, prepared by **Sofia Karagiannopoulou, Paris Patsis and Nikolaos Sariannidis** (*all from the University of Western Macedonia, Greece*), details how in September of 2014 ECB decides the beginning of the first Quantitative Easing (QE) programme called Asset-Backed Securities Purchase (ABSPP) and Covered Bond Purchase programme (CBPP), in order to face the financial crisis. The next programme was the Public Sector Purchase Programme (PSPP) on 9 March 2015. Finally, on 18 March 2020, the ECB started the third programme called Pandemic Emergency Purchase Programme (PEPP). The goal of this study is to explore the impact of QE programmes on the stock market of Athens, considering the fact that Greece was the only European country to participate only in the third programme. Using daily data from 1/9/2014 to 22/1/2021, three GARCH (1,1) models with dummy variables are constructed to incorporate different QE programmes. In addition, 10-year bond, gold and DAX are used in order to isolate systematic international factors. The empirical results show that the first QE programme has decreased the stock prices, the findings of the second QE programme are not statistically important, while the third programme has a positive effect on the stock market. The paper concludes that Greek participation on the QE programme played an important role in the stock market and suggests that other researchers investigate the methods in which Greece can utilize the positive climate after the end of PEPP.

Authors **Georgios A. Deirmentzoglou** (*Neapolis University Pafos, Cyprus*) **and Evangelos A. Deirmentzoglou** (*University of Piraeus, Greece*) analyse the electronic commerce (e-commerce) industry. E-commerce has shown to be a critical driver of economic development and has the ability to boost efficiency and productivity in many countries. In the last years, e-commerce has seen rapid growth, especially during the pandemic of COVID-19. Specifically, Greece saw an increase in the number of Internet users who made online purchases and the total revenues of e-commerce transactions. Despite this growth, Greece still has a slow pace of digital transformation compared to other countries of the European Union. The purpose of this paper was to discuss the future of e-commerce in Greece and investigate the factors of the external macroenvironment that can be an opportunity or a threat to Greek e-tailing. PEST analysis was used to examine the political, economic, socio-cultural and technological factors that are related to the digital transformation of Greek retail stores. The analysis showed that the e-tailing industry is facing significant threats, but at the same time, it can take advantage of the opportunities created by the external environment. Although there is a trend towards the digital transition of retailing, the state should support both entrepreneurs and consumers.

In the following manuscript prepared by **Daniel Dragičević, Maja Nikšić Radić and Maja Buljat** (*University of Rijeka, Croatia*), a framework for the migration–tourism–terrorism nexus has been established and the main areas of current research have been highlighted. Bibliometric analysis was applied to the WOS database for the period from 2001 to 2021. The research implemented a three-tiered approach that identified relevant articles in the area of terrorism and tourism (TT) (138), migration and tourism (MT) (103) and migration, tourism and terrorism (MTT) (2). In addition to the citation and co-authorship analysis, this study analysed the co-occurrence of keywords. The results show that the USA, UK and China are the most prolific countries, while Tourism Economics, Tourism Management and Annals of Tourism Research are the most relevant journals in the field. The co-keyword analysis identified four distinct research areas for TT and three for MT. At the end of the paper, possible future research directions for each area are clearly indicated and the limitations of this study are highlighted.

Authors **Besa Ombashi** (*University College Bedër, Albania*), **Denita Cepiku** (*University of Rome Tor Vergata via Columbia, Rome*) and **Niccolò Persiani** (*University of Florence, Italy*) analyse the dynamics of implementation of public–private partnership (PPP) in the healthcare sector considered as opportunities for countries in transition, enhancing the case of Albania considered as a typical Balkan transition country of the post-Soviet era. When the course of two decades has almost been completed, the changes that countries in transition are facing are significant and have transformed the way of the economic environment. In transitioning or developing economies, despite the potential for PPP arrangements to finance and develop public projects, the use of PPPs has been slow and limited (Yang et al., 2013).

Currently, Albania boasts a portfolio of more than 222 PPP, 186 in energy with the rest in transport, health, environment and agriculture. As in the focus of the article, there is an overview of the four PPP in the healthcare sector considering one out of four as the case study based on the importance as well as the changes and needs during COVID-19.

The article will highlight a need to adopt a long-term strategy in the field of health care as well as applicable standards for the monitoring of the implementation procedures.

The healthcare sector in a typical Balkanic transition country, that aspires for European Union membership, such as Albania, was considered as a case study in the research because in the health care were introduced reforms aim to improve the public health system, the quality of care provided, and to reduce out-of-pocket healthcare expenses and the application of PPP in this sector were considered as part of this reforms and their success.

The case study is based on the data collected from the analysis of the contracts signed between the parties; different reports, interviews and the documentation collection with regard to the management of this contract are going to be used.

During the pandemic moment, the implementation of these contracts became even more important for a country facing a global emergency regarding health care when these contracts were seen as a way of innovation in the management of public services.

The next paper, written by **Valentina Diana Rusu and Angela Roman**(*both from Alexandru Ioan Cuza University of Iasi, Romania*), aims to examine the relationship between the way small and medium enterprises are financed in the first years of existence and their performance. Thus, they wish to determine whether the debt structure of these enterprises plays an important role in obtaining performance.

In order to achieve the purpose of the paper, they perform an econometric analysis by choosing a sample of small and medium enterprises from the CEE countries in their first years of existence. Given the fact that start-ups are considered enterprises in the first five years of life, the analysis period considered is 2015–2019. As a method of analysis, they use the panel data technique considering as dependent variables a set of indicators that measure the performance of enterprises and as independent variables indicators that expresses the degree of indebtedness of enterprises. The data for this analysis are obtained from the financial statements of the companies accessed through the AMADEUS Bureau van Djik database. The results of their research show that the way in which the SMEs financing decisions are based plays a significant role in achieving performance. The use of short- and long-term debt can stimulate the performance of enterprises, but an increased gearing ratio hampers this performance. These results can be useful for decision-makers because they emphasize the need for them to focus on formulating policies that facilitate access to finance for SMEs in the first years of life, thus generating an increase in their performance with positive effects at the level of general economy.

The paper provided by **Sofia Daskou, Andreas Masouras and Anastasia Athanasoula Reppa** (*all from Neapolis University Pafos*) presents a conceptualization of the utility of Service Dominant Logic (SDL) in theoretically underpinning the value co-creation process that emerges from the interactions and relationships of place visitors with local resource integrators of destinations. Under the SDL of marketing, service becomes the ontological content of the place brand and a fundamental mechanism of the exchange of place-branded products. The work is based on Vargo and Lusch (2008) premise, that service is the fundamental basis of exchange, and builds an argument about how operant resources can be deployed by place marketers, as a source of competitive advantage to sustain loyalty to place visitors. It proceeds to explain how place marketers (i.e. hospitality services, tourist attractions, etc.) co-create value with place visitors (customers) to generate effects that stimulate visitor loyalty and build the place brand. The relationships that develop between the customers and place marketers are embedded in a service ecosystem, which appreciates the phenomenologically determined perceptions of value of the parties and stimulate place visitors repeat custom. The paper argues in favour of the integration of the roles of the customers and service suppliers in the formation of a value output, which becomes input in the identity of a place.

In an article co-authored by **Dimitra Ntertsou** (*Panteion University of Social and Political Sciences, Greece*), **Christos Galanos** (*Agricultural University of Athens, Greece*) and **Konstantinos Liapis** (*Panteion University of Social and Political Sciences, Greece*), the authors aim to assess tax regime similarities among Eurozone countries in the field of personal income tax, given that human capital is highly mobile and thus affected by the design of a country's tax code. Using information on the central government personal income tax rates and thresholds, available on the OECD tax database, this article employs dendrograms to present similarities of tax regimes and clustering of homogeneous Eurozone countries for four different years (2003–2008–2013–2018), in order to capture the effects of the 2008 economic crisis in the design of personal income tax systems. Their findings suggest a great degree of divergence in the design of personal income tax systems, especially regarding the degree of progressivity as well as top income brackets and marginal rates. It is interesting to observe how clusters of groups of countries with similar tax regimes are differentiated through time. Most of the literature, when comparing different tax regimes, focuses on tax revenues and average tax burdens. The value of this research stems from the fact that it provides a similarity analysis, based on the actual design of the tax schedule. Results can be indicative of the degree of convergence in Eurozone countries, thus providing tax authorities with a transparent methodology to assess the level of fiscal harmonization.

Authors **Giannoula Florou** and **Aikaterini Tsisinou** (*International Hellenic University, Greece*) discuss taxation as a basic revenue source for a state. In this paper, they present the essential characteristics of Greek taxation system. They analyse the taxes from different income categories, from business taxes and non-business taxes, from different Greek regions. They compare revenue data of the year 2019 with corresponding revenue data from the year 2011, before the economic crisis. The aim is to determine how the economic crisis influenced the Greek taxation system and its efficiency. They present their findings and proposals for optimal taxation.

The study by **Marinela Chamzallari** (*International Hellenic University, Greece*), **Antonios Chantziaras** (*International Hellenic University, Greece* and *Durham University, United Kingdom*) and **Christos Grose** (*International Hellenic University, Greece*) investigates the impact of the COVID-19 external shock on the stock return volatility of global firms. Using a sample of 30,516 firms, accounting for 60% of listed firms globally, scattered across 63 countries, we evidence that COVID-19 cases (fatalities) have a positive and significant impact on stock return volatility of global firms, measured at different estimation intervals (windows of 30, 60, 90, 180 and 250 days). In particular, a one standard deviation increase in COVID-19 cases (fatalities) is associated with 0.79% (0.86%) increase in firm volatility. Additionally, we inform that the effect of COVID-19 is amplified for companies from Oceania and Asia. Our insights are advantageous to a wide spectrum of stakeholders, including managers, market participants and policy-makers.

The aim of the paper by **Victoria Pistikou** (*Neapolis University Pafos, Cyprus*) is to assess the tendency and dynamics of Turkey's economic relations with selective countries in Africa. The research question is whether these economic ties rely upon economic or political incentives and to what degree. Current literature examines Turkish economic relations focusing on China, the Western Balkans, the Gulf and the Middle East, while little has been said about Turkey's rising role in Africa as an economic power. In addition, most of the studies approach this issue from a geostrategic perspective rather than the economic one. In order to answer the research question, it is necessary to examine the correlation between macroeconomic and political variables in order to assess whether high levels of Turkish economic connectivity with African states emerge as a result of market operation or emerge as a consequence of political goals or is a combination of both of them. From 2000 onwards, I will examine the dynamics and the tendances of Turkish economic relations with selective African countries in terms of indicators including trade relations, FDIs, development and humanitarian assistance. I will then assess to what extent those international economic relations tendances coincide with Turkish political and geostrategic considerations.

Hoping that the paper selection included in the volume confirms the research quality standards needed for addressing the complex issue of the **Business Development and Economic Governance in Southeastern Europe** and offers insightful look at the changing economic and business landscape, we leave to the readers the final assessment of their quality, as well as of their ability to disseminate new approaches and ideas that may be further used by academics, practitioners and public decision-makers alike.

Paphos, Cyprus   Pantelis Sklias
Serres, Greece   Persefoni Polychronidou
Kavala, Greece   Anastasios Karasavvoglou
Komotini, Greece   Victoria Pistikou
Tripoli, Greece   Nikolaos Apostolopoulos

Contents

Public Administration/Governance and the Economies of Southeastern Europe

Greek Political Economy in the Post-crisis Period 2010–2019

Pantelis Sklias, Spyros A. Roukanas, and Georgios Galatsidas

Abstract The strict austerity policy that was imposed on Greece by the Tripartite Support Mechanism (EC, ECB, and IMF) had unforeseen and unprecedented macroeconomic and social effects. There can be no doubt that the fiscal stability programme was originally designed to facilitate the overall improvement of the Greek economy's macroeconomic situation, emphasising on the stabilisation of budget deficits and the containment of public debt as necessary conditions for both Greece's return to capital markets and restarting economic growth in the country. Ten years later, the question is to what extent the macroeconomic targets of reducing the public debt and the budget deficit, as well as the ultimate goal of achieving economic growth, have been realised (or not)? This paper is an attempt to systematically document the course of Greek Political Economy during 2010–2019. More specifically, this paper discusses macroeconomic aggregates (economic growth, public debt, public deficit, unemployment, employment, and the labour force) with the ultimate goal of evaluating the economic policies of the Tripartite Support Mechanism. The study of macroeconomic indicators shows that, ten years after the programme's implementation, the overall macroeconomic situation of the Greek economy has not improved (with the exception of the public deficit), while key indicators (such as the public debt and economic growth) have worsened, further aggravating labour market conditions, and as a result the Greek economy is in a much worse macroeconomic position as compared to May 2010.

P. Sklias
Neapolis University Pafos, 2 Danais Avenue, 8042 Pafos, Cyprus
e-mail: p.sklias@nup.ac.cy

S. A. Roukanas
Department of International and European Studies, University of Piraeus, G. Lampraki Str, 18534 Piraeus, Greece
e-mail: sroukana@unipi.gr

G. Galatsidas (✉)
Department of Financial and Management Engineering, University of the Aegean, Mytilene, Greece
e-mail: g_galatsidas@yahoo.gr

Keywords Greek political economy · Unemployment · Employment · Labour
force · Recession · Effects of the adjustment programmes

1 Introduction

In May 2010, Greece was placed under the supervision of the Tripartite Support
Mechanism (European Commission, European Central Bank, and the International
Monetary Fund), in order to deal with the financing difficulties that it started to face
in money and capital markets, as a result of the downgrades of its credit rating by
rating agencies. Greece's entry into the Tripartite Support Mechanism ensured that
the country would be able to finance its overdue debt obligations, conditional on
its placement under fiscal supervision and surveillance, in order to ensure the more
effective realisation, among other things, of the macroeconomic targets of reducing
the public deficit and **public** debt. The realisation of the aforementioned targets was,
according to the prevailing view of the Tripartite Support Mechanism, a prerequisite
for the country to regain its credit rating and return to the capital markets as soon as
possible, as well as for restarting economic growth (Sklias and Maris 2014: 468–472;
Panagiotarea 2017: 187–191). The achievement of the targets would be ensured—
also according to the prevailing view of the Support Mechanism—by a fiscal adjustment process, which, among other things, provided for institutional reforms, the
promotion of fiscal consolidation, as well as tough restrictive policies, i.e. it was an
"invasive cure" that would lead to internal devaluation. The individual policies of this
"cure" were specified in the Memorandums of Understanding, and their implementation was a prerequisite for any disbursement of funds (Kotios and Pavlidis 2012:
222–228; Marangos 2020). However, the implementation of the "bailout" programme
for the Greek economy did not only fail to produce the expected results in terms of
public debt management and containment, but also had a devastating effect on the
real economy.[1] Under this lens, we are attempting to investigate both the macro-
conomic situation, and the situation of the real economy, as it has developed up to
2019, following ten years of the implementation of the economic policies prescribed
by the Support Mechanism in the Greek economy (Appendix 2).

In order to tackle this dual objective, we will have to answer the following question:
how did Greece's public debt and budget deficit evolve during the period from 2010
to 2019 (during the ten years when the economic policies prescribed by the "Support

---

[1] Krugman argues that the Greek depression "has devastated Greece just about as much as defeat
in total war devastated imperial Germany" (Krugman 2015). Moreover, it is worth mentioning the
paper by Sklias et al. (2018) titled: "Was the Great Depression of 1929 harsher than the Greek
Depression?", which makes a comparative evaluation of the consequences of the Great Depression
of 1929 on the US economy and the Greek fiscal crisis on the Greek economy, studying how each
crisis affected the evolution of key macroeconomic aggregates of the corresponding country, such
as overall income loss, GDP, debt, deficit, unemployment, stock exchange index, duration of the
recession, and the time required for the recovery of the aforementioned macroeconomic indicators.
The study concludes that the recent Greek depression has been harsher than the Great Depression
of 1929.

Mechanism" were imposed on the Greek economy). Some additional questions that we attempt to answer in this paper and, what is more, reveal the situation of the real economy are: How much did the Greek economy's GDP shrink during this period? How did the unemployment rate, employment, and the labour force evolve? Can we claim that the reduction of the unemployment rate during 2014–2019 is due to the improvement of the real economy or should we also investigate other factors? What is the effect of the contraction of the labour force (because of emigration) on the aforementioned drop in the unemployment rate? Is there a positive correlation between the reduction of the unemployment rate and the increase in sustainable and high-quality employment in the Greek economy?

As we can see from the aforementioned questions, the focus of this paper is to assess the macroeconomic results from the implementation of memorandum-related economic policies in the Greek economy. Macroeconomic results are approached through quantitative documentation. More specifically, this means that we examine the evolution of the public debt and budget deficits during the period 2009–2019. Moreover, we are attempting to study the extent of the recession experienced by Greece, as well as the situation in the labour market during the period under review, by examining the evolution of the following macroeconomic aggregates over time: the total output (GDP) of the economy; the unemployment rate; employment; the number of the unemployed; and the labour force. In addition, we attempt to study the negative repercussions of the mass emigration of high-added-value human resources on both the economy and its productive specialisation. Finally, we examine the qualitative dimensions of the new jobs created in the past few years, as well as whether they ensure the Greek economy's specialisation in high-added-value industries. The ultimate goal is to highlight the problem faced by the Greek economy and, consequently, to demonstrate whether it is necessary to implement a plan to restructure the productive base of the economy, alongside the requisite fiscal adjustment policies that are being pursued.

From a methodological standpoint, successfully approaching the above multifactor study requires an interdisciplinary approach. More specifically, we utilise various disciplines—political economy, international economic relations, European political economy, and economics—in order to understand the complex contemporary structures of the Greek political economy during the period 2010–2019. The key contribution of political economy lies in the admission that economics is a highly restrictive social science, since it tries to understand modern economy within a strictly "mathematised" framework. As pointed out by Hadjiconstantinou, the mechanistic approach to the workings of the economy apparently has certain limitations (1998, p. 45–46), especially within the internationalised economic environment in which it must operate, and the various components of which (economic, political, social, business, etc., relationships) are increasingly complex and interdependent, and interact with each other, therefore they must be also assessed in order to reach as objective conclusions as possible.

Moreover, as stressed above, from a methodological standpoint, this paper aims at providing answers based on quantitative documentation. Under this lens, we analyse the evolution of macroeconomic aggregates over time, and, in particular, the public debt and budget deficit, unemployment, employment, and the labour force, in relation with the corresponding fluctuations of the economy's total output (GDP) during the period 2010–2019. Moreover, we calculate indicators used as proxies for the performance of the macroeconomic aggregates under review. In addition, in order to ensure the more comprehensive understanding of the subject, we also perform an analysis of the above macroeconomic aggregates for the time period preceding the manifestation of the fiscal crisis (2000–2009), with the aim of making comparisons between these two successive time periods and draw conclusions.

This position of this paper is that Greece has seen an unprecedented (in peace time) contraction of total output (GDP), and, by extension, of employment, along with a surge in unemployment and an irreversible loss of human resources (primarily high value-adding labour force), because of migration abroad during the ten-year period 2010–2019 (following Greece's entry into the support mechanism). All the above, represented the price paid for the effective reduction of budget deficits, while, instead of being harnessed, public debt as a percentage of GDP increased as compared to the year 2009. That said, the most unfavourable effect lies in the real risk of mortgaging Greece's future growth prospects, which is compounded by the obsolescence, and consequent emigration and loss, of high-added-value human resources. This means that Greece is at risk of being trapped in the category of economies characterised by low skills, low wages, and by extension, specialisation in low-added-value products.

The structure of the rest of the essay is the following: The next section analyses the findings of the study on the evolution of macroeconomic aggregates and, more specifically, the Greek economy's public debt and budget deficit, GDP, employment, unemployment, and labour force, during the precursor period from 2000 (the eve of Greece's entry in the EMU) to 2009 (Greece's entry into the support mechanism). The third section of our paper focuses on the same macroeconomic aggregates, albeit for the period following Greece's entry into the support mechanism (2010–2019). The paper is completed with the conclusions and the answers to the above research questions.

2   From Emu to the Support Mechanism: The Period of Euphoria for the Greek Economy, 2000–2009

The beginning of the period (2001–2009) is marked by the pre-accession processes for Greece's entry in the EMU, an objective that was viewed by the vast majority of both the Greek political system, and the Greek society, as a top priority.[2] This period

---

[2] There is no doubt that, during the pre-accession stage, there was a coincidence of opinion regarding the expected benefits (Kotios, 2000; De Graw 2000; Kotios and Pavlidis 2012: 203); however, the debate that took place in Greece was dominated by arguments in favour of EMU membership, while the challenges that go together with potential opportunities are almost totally disregarded (Thygessen 1990; Kotios 1997; 2000; Kotios and Pavlidis 2012: 204–205). Despite efforts to exaggerate the benefits, there were sober scientific voices, both in Greece, and abroad, who pointed out that Greece's accession to the EMU was also a major challenge, which carried serious risks (Thygessen 1990;

ends with Greece's entry into the Tripartite Support Mechanism. In this section, we will examine the evolution of data and findings pertaining to Greece's: (a) economic growth, public debt, and budget deficit; and (b) employment, unemployment rate, and labour force, with the ultimate purpose of evaluating the situation of the Greek Economy during the period under review.

2.1 Greece's Fiscal Position and Economic Growth During 2001–2009

In this subsection, we will study Greece's fiscal position and economic growth during the period under review. To this end, column A of Table 1 presents the size of the annual gross domestic product (GDP) at constant 2015 prices (in bn euros). Moreover, the findings in column B show the year-on-year percentage change in GDP (the economy's growth or recession rate). The analysis of the data shows that, in the sub-period 2001–2007, the performance of the Greek economy is positive, with high growth rates, and more specifically, the average annual rate of change (the average of annual economic growth rates) is estimated at 4.06%. However, in 2008, along with the onset of the global financial crisis, Greece also entered a recession, with negative growth rates of −3.4% and −4.29% for that year and 2009, respectively. At this point, it is worth pointing out that the average economic growth rate for the entire period 2001–2009 stands at 2.30%.

Columns C and D of Table 1 refer to the budget deficit. More specifically, column C presents the annual fiscal result at current prices (billion euros), as derived from the database of the European Commission (2020). Moreover, the findings of column D show the annual fiscal result as a percentage of GDP at current prices. The study of the data presented in columns C and D shows that the fiscal result was negative in all years of the period 2001–2009. Moreover, we can see many significant year-on-year increases of budget deficits (in absolute terms). In contrast, the annual budget deficit as a percentage of GDP did not grow at the same rate. Indeed, despite the fact that the budget deficit rose, in absolute terms, during the first sub-period (from 5.74 billion euros in 2001 to 15.61 billion euros in 2007), it did not increase as a

---

Kotios 1997, 2000; Kotios and Pavlidis 2012: 204–205). The emergence and intensity of these challenges had to do both with the condition of the Greek economy at the time of accession [both its fiscal condition (public debt and budget deficit) and its condition as regards competitiveness], which is closely linked to its ability to cope with the demands of the new competitive environment of the enlarged market (Feldstein 1998; Kotios and Pavlidis 2012: 205). Therefore, objective researchers stressed that the final outcome would be, to a great extent, determined by the national economic policies implemented in regard to both the above issues, i.e.: a) proper fiscal management, and b) the improvement of competitiveness through the development and differentiation of the Greek economy's productive base. It is a fact that Greece's EMU membership did not, in its own right, ensure that the above issues were efficiently dealt with, but instead aggravated any pre-existing problems (Kotios and Pavlidis 2012). This is also due to the weaknesses of the Economic Governance of the EMU (for more information on this, see: Hazakis 2014; Kotios et al. 2012; Kotios and Pavlidis 2012).

Table 1 Growth-development, budget deficit, public Debt 2001–2009

Year	Growth		Fiscal deficit			Public debt			
	(A) GDP at constant 2015 prices (€ bn)	(B) Y–o–y Change (%)	(C) Annual deficit at constant prices (€ bn)	(D) Annual deficit to GDP ratio (%)	(E) Annual debt as a percentage of GDP (%)	(F) Y–o–y percentage change (%)	(G) Public debt in absolute terms (at constant prices, € bn)	(H) Y–o–y percentage change (%)
2001	189.21	4.1	−5.74	−5.47	107.08	2	163	10
2002	196.64	3.9	−8.32	−6.02	104.86	−2.12	171.4	5.1
2003	208.03	5.8	−9.85	−7.83	101.46	−3.3	181.5	5.9
2004	218.56	5.1	−14.01	−8.83	102.87	1.38	199.3	9.8
2005	219.87	0.6	−12.33	−6.19	107.39	4.39	214.4	7.4
2006	232.3	5.65	−12.95	−5.95	103.61	−3.55	225.7	5.5
2007	239.9	3.27	−15.61	−6.71	103.11	−0.49	239.9	6.3
2008	239.1	−0.34	−24.63	−10.18	109.42	6.12	264.8	10.4
2009	228.81	−4.29	−35.98	−15.15	126.74	15.83	301.1	13.7

Source Columns A, C, D, E and G, data from the European Commission 2020. Columns F and H, author's calculations

percentage of GDP, but remained more or less unchanged at 7%-8% throughout this period. Therefore, while budget deficits increased year-on-year in absolute terms, the budget deficit as a percentage of GDP remained **stable up to 2007 at almost the same levels which enabled Greece to become a member of the EMU.**[3] It is worth noting that this happened because, during the same period, economic growth was strong, as shown in columns A and B, thus absorbing the increase of budget deficits in absolute terms. In contrast to the first sub-period, in 2008–2009 the annual budget deficit reached alarmingly high levels both in absolute terms, and as a percentage of GDP. More specifically, we can see that, during the second sub-period, the year-on-year increase of the budget deficit in absolute terms stands at almost 70%. Budget deficit as a percentage of GDP also soared to 10.18% and 15.15% in 2008 and 2009, respectively.

The remaining columns of Table 1 (E, F, G, H) present data pertaining to Greece's public debt. More specifically, they show the following: column G presents the public debt in absolute terms as given in the database of the European Commission (2020); column H presents the annual percentage change of the public debt as an absolute number; column E presents the public debt as a percentage of GDP; and column F presents the annual change of public debt as a percentage of GDP. The data shown in these columns (E, F, G, H) reveal that public debt as an absolute number was incessantly growing year-on-year throughout the entire period, and the growth rate varies from 5 to 10%, with the exception of the year 2009, when public debt increased by 14% as compared to the previous year. In contrast, public debt as a percentage of GDP remained almost stable at 101–109% throughout the entire period, despite the persistent increase in public debt in absolute terms, thus corroborating that economic growth contributes to the stabilisation of debt as a percentage of GDP. The only exception was the year 2009, when the debt to GDP ratio jumped to 126%.

2.2 Employment, Labour Force, Number of the Unemployed, and Unemployment Rate in Greece During 2001–2009

As we have already seen, this period is marked by strong economic growth (Table 2), as average year-on-year GDP growth exceeded the average for the EU-16 (Anastasatos 2009: 4). In this overall context of economic progress, the unemployment rate remained low, also showing a slight downward tendency (Table 2). Indeed, at the beginning of this period (2001), the unemployment rate stood at 10.8%, while in 2008 and 2009, it stood at 7.8% and 9.6%, respectively. Methodologically, though, our paper is not confined to the study of the unemployment rate, because this does not shed enough light on additional aspects of employment, thus altering the objectivity of the results.

---

[3] This does not imply complacency as regards the effort to rationalise public spending during the first sub-period.

Table 2 Labour force, employment, unemployment, and the unemployment rate, 2001–2009

Year	Quarter	Total labour force	Employed	Unemployed	Unemployment rate (%)	Average annual unemployment rate	GDP at constant 2015 prices (€ bn)	Year-on-year change (%)
2001	1st	4739.0	4206.7	532.3	11.2	10.8	189.21	4.1
	2nd	4,716.9	4223.7	493.2	10.5			
	3rd	4707.6	4225.9	481.7	10.2			
	4th	4678.6	4152.2	526.3	11.2			
2002	1st	4707.4 4,170.3	4170.3	537.1	11.4	10.4	196.64	3.9
	2nd	4756.6	4282.2	474.5	10.0			
	3rd	4782.6	4311.8	470.9	9.8			
	4th	4783.6	4295.5	488.1	10.2			
2003 4th	1st	4804.6	4303.4	501.2	10.4	9.8	208.03	5.8
	2nd	4819.7	4366.1	453.6	9.4			
	3rd	4839.9	4388.3	451.6	9.3			
	4th	4839.0	4354.9	484.2	10.0			
2004	1st	4888.5	4330.3	558.2	11.4	10.6	218.56	5.1
	2nd	4917.0	4410.0	507.0	10.3			
	3rd	4916.0	4416.1	499.9	10.2			
	4th	4916.5	4401.7	514.8	10.5			
2005	1st	4912.6	4395.2	517.4	10.5	10.0	219.87	0.6
	2nd	4937.4	4455.5	481.9	9.8			
	3rd	4947.6	4461.0	486.5	9.8			
	4th	4950.8	4462.5	488.4	9.9			

(continued)

Table 2 (continued)

Year	Quarter	Total labour force	Employed	Unemployed	Unemployment rate (%)	Average annual unemployment rate	GDP at constant 2015 prices (€ bn)	Year-on-year change (%)
2006	1st	4970.4	4481.9	488.5	9.8	9	232.3	5.65
	2nd	4972.2	4531.5	440.7	8.9			
	3rd	4988.9	4568.0	420.9	8.4			
	4th	4971.4	4528.6	442.8	8.9			
2007	1st	4970.7	4511.6	459.1	9.2	8.4	239.90	3.27
	2nd	4980.9	4572.4	408.5	8.2			
	3rd	4994.1	4595.8	398.3	8,0			
	4th	4983.9	4576.4	407.5	8.20			
2008	1st	4985.7	4567.2	418.6	8.4	7.8	239.1	−0.34
	2nd	5003.9	4637.3	366.7	7.3			
	3rd	5003.5	4639.6	364.0	7.3			
	4th	4597.9	5000.1	402.2	8.0			
2009	1st	5022.3	4545.6	476.7	9.5	9.6	228.81	−4.29
	2nd	5040.2	4584.6	455.6	9.0			
	3rd	5063.2	4585.2	477.9	9.4			
	4th	5037.2	4508.6	528.6	10.5			

Source Columns 3, 4, 5, and 6, data from ELSTAT (2018, 2019). Columns 7 and 6, author's calculations. Column 8, data from the European Commission (2019)

To this end, it is deemed necessary to thoroughly examine the evolution of the labour force, and the number of the employed and the unemployed in absolute terms, in order to provide a fuller and more objective assessment of the situation in the labour market and, to a certain extent, in the real economy. As a matter of fact, Greece's total labour force rose from 4739.0 thousand in 2001 to 5037.2 thousand in 2009, i.e. increased by 298,000. There was an almost equal increase in the number of those employed during the same period, from 4206.7 thousand to 4508.6 thousand, i.e. 302,000 more people had jobs in 2009, as compared to 2001. The number of the unemployed over the same period was reduced by 121,000. So, the central finding of the above analysis is that the dynamics of employment growth was such to make it possible for the number of the unemployed to go down and the unemployment rate to be contained, despite the growth of Greece's labour force (Appendix 1).

The findings presented in Table 2 (columns 8, 9) show the Greek economy's GDP in billion euros, as well as the annual percentage change in GDP (growth rate), and were found in the Website of the European Commission (2019). The third column of the same table shows the size of Greece's total labour force. The fourth column informs us about the total number of the employed, the fifth column shows the total number of the unemployed, and the sixth column demonstrates the unemployment rate, which is the ratio of the number of the unemployed (column 5) to the total size of the labour force (column 3). The research of employment data was made on the database of the Hellenic Statistical Authority (ELSTAT). Overall, the data presented in this table show that there is a consistently negative correlation between changes in GDP and the unemployment rate, whereas there is a positive correlation between economic growth and employment (labour as a factor of production) (Appendix 3).

Based on the above and given the proportionate relationship between changes in GDP and employment, we still have to explore whether there is a causal relationship between economic growth and labour (via labour productivity). In order to answer this question, we will explore whether the growth of per capita GDP can be attributed to labour productivity.

The findings of research by Sidiropoulos (2016) show that there is no causal relationship between economic growth and labour (via labour productivity). More specifically, the economic growth experienced by Greece during the said period was not accompanied by any increase in labour productivity.[4] In order to approach the issue with greater precision, we will study the evolution of these two macroeconomic aggregates, i.e.: (a) per capita income, and (b) the growth of labour productivity in Greece, compared to the other countries of the eurozone. As mentioned above, Greece's high economic growth rate led to an increase in the country's per capita GDP and to its convergence with its partners in the EU. Actually, between 2000 and 2009, Greece's gross per capita income increased by 32%, while the corresponding increases were 11% in France, 16% in Germany, 2% in Italy, and 10% in Portugal. In addition, for the first time since 1981, Greece's living standard, measured in terms of

---

[4] The fact that the growth of incomes in Greece outpaced labour productivity growth acted as a mechanism that led to unsustainable economic growth.

private consumption, exceeded that of the EU-15, rising to 107.9% of the eurozone average in 2008 (Sidiropoulos 2016: 309–310).

Given that all the aforementioned countries have a common currency, this rise in Greek incomes could only be sustainable if labour productivity grew faster than in the other countries, thus justifying the fact that wages in Greece grew faster than in the other countries of the eurozone. However, this is not verified by the facts. The productivity of one hour of labour increased by 26% in Greece during 2000–2009, as compared to 20% in France, 18% in Germany and Portugal, and 3% in Italy. Thus, we can conclude that the growth of productivity in Greece was not sufficient to justify such a large rise in incomes (Sidiropoulos 2016: 309–310), casting doubt on the sustainability of the growth of GDP, as well as employment.[5]

Indeed, this boom, which led to a slow but steady decline of unemployment, is apparently reversed in 2008, as a result of the global financial crisis of 2007–08, when the economy entered a recession. In fact, as shown by the data of Table 2, whereas up to 2007 the economy had been steadily growing, starting in 2008 growth is negative at -0.34%, further falling to −4.29% in 2009 (Table 1). Negative GDP growth caused unemployment to explode. As a matter of fact, during the same period, the unemployment rate increased as GDP fell (Appendix 3), rising from 7.8% in 2007 to 8.4% in 2008 and 9.6% in 2009 (Table 2).

All the above lead us to the conclusion that, during the period under review, Greece maintained high growth rates (with the exception of the years 2008 and 2009).[6] Moreover, fiscal aggregates—debt and deficit—as a percentage of GDP remained at stable, albeit high, levels throughout the entire sub-period 2001–2007, making it, nonetheless, possible for Greece to join the EMU. That said, economic euphoria is ended in 2007, and from 2008 onwards we do not only see negative growth rates, but also a deterioration of the fiscal situation, which culminated in 2009. All this caused a succession of economic events (such as the downgrading of the country's credit rating, and the increase of borrowing rates), which set in motion the procedures for Greece's entry into the Tripartite Support Mechanism. The purpose for that was to provide the Greek economy with a liquidity injection, as well as with technocratic support for the improvement of its macroeconomic performance and the promotion of economic growth, as necessary conditions for social prosperity. The crucial question here is to what extent was this specific target met? In order to answer this question, in the next section we will try to study the evolution of Greece's aggregate income, public debt, and budget deficit, as well as the real situation in the labour market from 2010 to 2019.

---

[5] More detailed interpretations of the long-term development of growth rates and investigations of the causal relationships can be found in many studies (Christodoulakis 2009; Sklias et al. 2017; Dimeli 2010; Bosworth and Kollintzas 2002; Stournaras and Albani 2008, etc.).

[6] It should also be noted that Greece's growth rates exceeded the average for the 16 member-states of the eurozone in most of the years under review, exceeding even the growth rates of Germany and France, as seen by the comparative analysis of the macroeconomic performance of EMU countries. (Eurostat in Roukanas 2011: 227).

3   From the Support Mechanism to the Period of Persistent Recession and High Unemployment, 2010–2019

Greece's entry into the Support Mechanism in 2010 (as a result of the onset of the fiscal crisis in the Greek economy) ushered in a period of recession, which lasted from 2010 to 2019. Indeed, following the outbreak of the global financial crisis of 2007/08, Greece was faced with high public debt and budget deficit levels, which stood at approximately 127% and 15.5% of GDP, respectively, in 2009 (Table 1). Greece's resulting fiscal position triggered the immediate reaction of rating agencies, as shown by the consecutive downgrades of its credit rating (Schizas 2014). This immediately led to the increase of Greece's borrowing rate, which, in turn, was reflected on an increase in borrowing costs. This rendered Greece's borrowing in international markets prohibitive, leading to the country's exclusion from the markets. In such cases and based on international experience, it is considered advisable for the International Monetary Fund to intervene (Sklias and Maris 2014).

The above events gave rise to an intense debate on whether Greece could, or should, exit the eurozone (Galatsidas et al. 2015). In this case, and given the lack of prior experience, there was uncertainty regarding the consequences of such an option, which, according to many, could prove disastrous both for Greece and the eurozone[7] (Koutsoukis and Roukanas 2014; Kotios and Pavlidis 2012; Kotios et al. 2012). The option that was finally selected was the establishment of the Tripartite Support Mechanism—which consists of the European Commission (EC), the European Central Bank (ECB) and the International Monetary Fund (IMF)—with the purpose of supporting the Greek economy.

Following this intervention, Greece signed Memorandums of Understanding, thus receiving a series of bailout packages, which included bilateral loans from the above institutions, in order to cover its current borrowing requirements. In return, Greece had to undergo an internal devaluation in order to adjust its current account balance. Another prerequisite for Greece was fiscal consolidation, which would lead to a balanced budget. According to the views of the Tripartite Support Mechanism, both the adjustment of the current account and the fiscal consolidation of the Greek economy were necessary conditions for containing the increase in public debt, and boosting competitiveness, thus bringing the country back on the track of economic recovery (GDP growth). The above policies were accompanied by institutional reforms and an attempt to modernise the economy, under the technical supervision and guidance of the Tripartite Support Mechanism, as part of the overall effort to boost economic growth (Panagiotarea 2017; Galatsidas et al. 2015). At this point, the question is whether the targets of reducing the public debt and the budget deficit were achieved during the period 2010–2019, and how did GDP and the unemployment rate evolve? Also, how much did the labour force decrease because of emigration? We

---

[7] This argument also takes into account the fact that Portugal, Ireland, Italy, and Spain, which had equally large public debt or deficit to GDP ratios, saw their macroeconomic position deteriorate as a result of the economic developments of 2007/08.

will try to answer these questions by analysing the available data from the database of the European Commission and the Hellenic Statistical Authority (ELSTAT).

3.1 Greece's Fiscal Position and Growth During 2010–2019

In this section, we will study the evolution of the same macroeconomic aggregates during the period 2010–2019. First, we will examine the changes in the budget deficit during the period under review. It is a fact that Greece's entry into the Tripartite Support Mechanism (2010) led almost immediately to the reduction of the annual budget deficit, both in absolute terms, and as a percentage of GDP at current prices. The following years until the end of the reference period (2019) not only did see the gradual decrease of the annual deficit as a percentage of GDP below the safe 3% limit (Stability and Growth Pact of the Maastricht Treaty), but also the creation of fiscal surpluses in absolute terms. This is not an exaggeration since, by observing the data of Table 2, columns C and D, we can see that the budget deficit fell from 15.14% of GDP in 2009 to −11.29% in 2010 and −10.47% in 2011, further falling to −3.58% by 2014, while in the following years up to 2019 Greece managed to produce fiscal surpluses.[8] Therefore, we can safely conclude that during the period when Greece was under the supervision and technical support of the Tripartite Support Mechanism, and the prescribed economic policies were implemented, the high budget deficit was efficiently dealt with.

As regards the evolution of public debt during the same period (2010–2019), in columns E, F, G, and H of Table 1, we can see that public debt as a percentage of GDP rose from 129% in 2009 to 147% in 2010 and 175% in 2011. In 2012, however, public debt as a percentage of GDP registered a slight[9] drop to 161% of GDP, while in the following years until 2019 it remained more or less stable at 180% of GDP. So, we can see that the public debt, which stood at 129% of GDP in 2009 (being instrumental to triggering the fiscal crisis and leading to Greece's entry into the Tripartite Support Mechanism), jumped to 180.51% of GDP ten years later. In absolute terms, public debt rose from 301 billion euros in 2009 to 331 billion euros in 2019. In summary, it is worth noting that during Greece's ten-year stay under the supervision of the Tripartite Support Mechanism we can see a disproportionately large increase of the public debt to GDP ratio (by 50%) as compared to the increase in public debt in absolute terms (by 10%), which is attributed to the persistent recession brought on the economy as a result of austerity policies.

---

[8] Primary surpluses are not an end in themselves in an economy; on the contrary, the existence of a manageable deficit for investment activities and, by extension, the managed maintenance of moderate debt levels is necessary for financing sustainable economic growth in deficit countries and, consequently, has a positive effect on the sustainable reduction of the debt to GDP ratio (Sidiropoulos 2009; Krugman 2011; Kazakos et al. 2016: 51; Wolfson 1994: 221; Gelos et al. 2004: 4). However, the occrrence of the problem was due to the high debt level (Cecchetti et al. 2011) and the way this debt was utilised (Cohn 2009).

[9] This is attributed to the "insufficient" loan haircut.

The research done regarding the course of the recession from 2010 to 2019 shows that the negative growth rates of −0.34% for the year 2008 and −4.29% for the year 2009 that resulted from the global financial crisis surged to −5.5% and −10.2% in 2010 and 2011, respectively, following the onset of the debt crisis and Greece's entry into the Tripartite Support Mechanism. In 2012, recession remained high and, in particular, stood at −6.1%. In the following years and up to 2015, recession slowed down, albeit without being reversed, while the Greek economy could not enter a steady course of sustainable growth (as shown by European Commission data). Based on the above, in 2010–2019 Greece lost almost 25% of its GDP (income) for the year 2008 (see Table 3). In other words, an entire decade passed with absolutely no economic progress; on the contrary, there was an income loss that will take some time to be restored, in order for the economy to return to 2008 income levels. The dynamics of the recession drag down employment and cause the unemployment rate to surge, also dealing an irreversible blow to Greece's labour force, as shown in the following analysis (Appendix 2).

3.2   Employment, Labour Force, Number of the Unemployed, and Unemployment Rate in Greece During 2010–2019

As regards the evolution of the unemployment rate in 2010–2019, we can indeed see that at the beginning of the period (the year 2010) the unemployment rate stands at 12.7%, slightly increased as compared to 2008 and 2009 and inversely related to the trend of GDP. In 2011 (and after the Support Mechanism was activated and the prescribed adjustment measures were implemented), the unemployment rate shot up by 5.2%, to almost 17.9%. Then, and for the next two years, the situation in the labour market deteriorated; more specifically, in 2012 the unemployment rate stood at 24.4% and in 2013 peaked at 27.5%, registering year-on-year increases of 6.5% and 3.1%, respectively. In 2014, there was a slight decrease in the unemployment rate for the first time since the onset of the crisis; however, it remained very high, at 26.5%, as shown by ELSTAT data (Table 4) (Appendix 1).

The unemployment rate continued to decrease steadily after 2014 and until the end of the period under review. More specifically, in 2017 and 2019, the unemployment rate stood at 21.5% and 17.24%, respectively (see Table 4). It begs the question, however, of whether this decrease in the unemployment rate (from 27.5 to 19.3%) resulted from the creation of new, sustainable, high-added-value jobs or is, to a great extent, attributed to other factors (such as the reduction of the Greek economy's labour force, emigration, and so forth). In order to answer this question, we will try to thoroughly examine the evolution of the number of the unemployed, employment, and the labour force in absolute terms for the entire period 2010–2019, as well as for the sub-period 2014–2019 in particular, when the unemployment rate was reduced. We will also explore additional parameters related to the qualitative features of new jobs—such as flexible employment, subsidised job creation programmes, labour flexibility, undeclared work in conjunction with the fines imposed for uninsured labour—as well as the way all the above factors help paint a fictitious picture of Greece's unemployment rate.

Based on an analysis of ELSTAT data for the period 2010–2019, we can see that the number of the unemployed in 2010 stood at 638.75 thousand. This number kept rising up to 2013, when it peaked at 1330 thousand jobless people, i.e. two and a half times more than in the year 2010, and more than three times as much as in the year 2008. Then, from 2014 onwards there is a gradual decrease in the number of the unemployed until the year 2019, when it falls to 811.5 thousand. Despite this reduction, however, the total number of the unemployed remains high in 2019, almost one and a half times as high as in 2010 and twice as high as in 2008 (from 387.79 thousand to 811.5 thousand) (Tables 3and 4). The persistence of high unemployment numbers for a decade implies the obsolescence of large parts of Greece's human and material productive capacity (and/or vice versa).

In 2010, the number of the people employed in the Greek economy stood at 4389.5 thousand, markedly down from 2008 and 2009, when it stood at 4610 thousand and 4555 thousand, respectively. After 2010 and up to 2015, employment continued to shrink—owing to the contraction of the economy's productive base, as shown by GDP growth—until it reached the lowest point, at 3610 thousand, in 2015. That said, from the following year (2016) and up to 2019, there is a slight increase in the number of the employed. More specifically, in 2016 they rose to 3673 thousand, while in 2019, they rose to 3894.6 thousand. In practical terms, however, the economy has failed to restore employment to 2008 and 2010 levels, (i.e. to 4610.5 thousand and 4389.5 thousand, respectively) (Tables 3 and 4).

As regards the size of Greece's labour force, Table 4 shows that its decline started immediately after the implementation of the fiscal adjustment programme and continued unabated throughout 2010–2019. More specifically, in 2009 and 2010, the labour force stood at 5040 thousand and 5028 thousand, respectively, while by 2019, it fell to 4706.5 thousand, meaning that 322,000 workers are not any more included in Greece's labour force.

It is obvious that, apart from its impact on the growth process (analysed below), the overall decrease in the absolute size of the labour force was also instrumental to keeping the unemployment rate at low levels in recent years (Appendix 1). More specifically, the fact that 322 thousand persons (Table 2) are not included in the country's labour force, means that they do not affect the ELSTAT measurements used to calculate the unemployment rate. Moreover, these persons are also not included in the total number of the unemployed. This, however, means that the unemployment rate seems to decrease faster than new job creation during the said period. This fact corroborates the argument that these two aggregates are inversely, albeit not proportionately, related, in other words the reduction of the unemployment rate does not imply an equal increase in the number of jobs. Therefore, the decrease in the unemployment rate appears to be larger than it would be, had a part of the labour force not migrated abroad (Appendix 1). In any case, any increase of Greece's labour force equal to the number of citizens who migrated abroad, given the current situation in

Table 3 Growth-development, budget deficit, public debt 2010–2019

Year	Growth-development		Fiscal deficit		Public debt			
	(A) GDP at constant 2015 prices (€ bn)	(B) Y–o–y Change (%)	(D) Annual deficit at constant prices (€ bn)	(E) Annual deficit to GDP ratio (%)	(E) Annual debt as a percentage of GDP (%)	(F) Y–o–y percentage change (%)	(G) Public debt in absolute terms (at constant prices, € bn)	(H) Y–o–y percentage change (%)
2010	216.28	−5.5	−25.31	−10.47	147.49	16.37	330.6	9.8
2011	194.33	−10.2	−21.28	−9	175.22	18.79	356.2	7.71
2012	180.56	−7.1	−16.95	−13.23	161.94	−7.6	305.1	−14.3
2013	175.61	−2.7	−23.77	−8.83	178.43	10.17	320.5	5
2014	176.84	0.69	−6.36	−3.58	180.23	1	319.6	−0.28
2015	176.11	−0.41	−9.95	−5.65	177.01	−1.73	311.7	−2.5
2016	175.25	−0.49	0.95	0.54	180.8	2.14	315	1.05
2017	177.49	1.26	1.29	0.73	179.21	−0.88	317.5	0.79
2018	180.26	1.54	1.84	1.02	186.24	3.92	334.7	5.42
2019	183.61	1.82	2.8	1.52	180.51	3.13	331.1	−1.9

Source Columns A, C, D, E and G, data from the European Commission (2020). Columns F and H, author's calculations

Table 4 Labour force, employment, unemployment, and the unemployment rate, 2010–2018

Year	Quarter	Total labour force	Employed	Unemployed	Unemployment rate (%)	Average annual unemployment rate	GDP at constant 2015 prices (€ bn)	Annual Change (%)
2010	1st	5046.2	4446.0	600.2	11.9	12.7	216.28	−5.5
	2nd	5041.1	4436.5	604.6	12.0			
	3rd	5029.8	4398.0	631.9	12.6			
	4th	4999.3	4278.5	720.8	14.4			
2011	1st	4965.1 4,165.5	4165.5	799,6	16.1	17.9	194.33	−10.2
	2nd	4939.8	4124.2	815.6	16.5			
	3rd	4924.2	4040.8	883.5	17.9			
	4th	4915.5	3886.9	1028.6	20.9			
2012	1st	4904.1	3785.0	1119.1	22.8	24.4	190.39	−6.1
	2nd	4892.9	3729.9	1163.0	23.8			
	3rd	4886.3	3668.0	1218.4	24.9			
	4th	4877.0	3597.0	1279.9	26.2			
2013	1st	4840.2	3504.2	1336.0	27.6	27.5	184.22	0.7
	2nd	4862.9	3535.0	1327.9	27.3			
	3rd	4854.0	3533.7	1320.3	27.2			
	4th	4817.1	3479.9	1337.2	27.8			
2014	1st	4826.0	3483.7	1342.3	27.8	26.5	176.84	0.69
	2nd	4819.2	3539.1	1280.1	26.6			
	3rd	4816.3	3586.9	1229.4	25.5			
	4th	4781.1	3535.3	1245.9	26.1			

(continued)

Table 4 (continued)

Year	Quarter	Total labour force	Employed	Unemployed	Unemployment rate (%)	Average annual unemployment rate	GDP at constant 2015 prices (€ bn)	Annual Change (%)
2015	1st	4777.0	3504.4	1272.5	26.6	24.9	176.11	−0.41
	2nd	4805.7	3625.5	1180.1	24.6			
	3rd	4831.6	3671.1	1160.5	24.0			
	4th	4816.3	3641.7	1174.7	24.4			
2016	1st	4801.4	3606.3	1195.1	24.9	23.5	175.25	−0.49
	2nd	4814.7	3702.6	1112.1	23.1			
	3rd	4829.3	3736.7	1092.6	22.6			
	4th	4772.6	3648.6	1124.0	23.6			
2017	1st	4774.0	3659.3	1114.7	23.3	21.5	177.49	1.26
	2nd	4808.0	3791.4	1016.6	21.1			
	3rd	4793.8	3823.7	970.1	20.2			
	4th	4743.2	3736.3	1006.8	21.2			
2018	1st	4725.0	3723.8	1001.2	21.2	19.3	180.26	1.54
	2nd	4766.4	3860.4	906.0	19.0			
	3rd	4766	3894.2	871.8	18.3			
	4th	4714.80	3833.7	881.1	18.7			
2019	1st	4695.7	3796.9	899	19.1	17.24	183.61	1.82
	2nd	4742	3943.8	797	16.8			
	3rd	4726.1	3953.6	772	16.3			
	4th	4662.5	3884.1	778	16.7			

Source Columns 3, 4, 5, and 6, data from ELSTAT (2018, 2019). Columns 7 and 6, author's calculations. Column 8, data from the European Commission (2019)

the labour market (employment opportunities), would reveal the real unemployment rates.

In order to get a better understanding of this interdependence between the labour force/number of the employed and the unemployment rate, it suffices to compare the relative figures for the years 2011 and 2018, which show very similar unemployment rates of 17.9% and 19.3%, respectively. Initially, the number of the employed in these two years stood at 4053 thousand and 3827 thousand, respectively, i.e. there were 225 thousand fewer employed persons (jobs) in 2018 as compared to 2011. However, the number of the unemployed in 2018 is increased by 33 thousand as compared to 2011. The size of the labour force[10] during the same period was reduced (as a result of emigration), and there are 234 thousand fewer citizens in Greece. Therefore, whereas the change of the unemployment rate between 2018 and 2011 stood at 1.4%, the number of the employed fell by 225 thousand, and the number of the unemployed rose by 33 thousand (Table 4). Therefore, the above show that the reduction of the total size of the labour force (by 234 thousand persons) also plays a key role in containing the unemployment rate for the year 2018 at 2011 levels. In this context, we realise that the fact that the unemployment rate is the same in those two years does not imply that employment (or the productive base) is also the same.

Based on the above, it is easy to infer that the reduction of the unemployment rate since 2014 can also be attributed to the contraction of the labour force, whereas it should, to the greatest extent possible, result from the creation of new sustainable jobs.[11] With this argument as our starting point, we will try to expand our research, approaching the issue (of the reduction of the unemployment rate) under the lens of new job creation. In this context, the question is whether we can argue that the reduction of the unemployment rate by 8 percentage points in 2018 (as compared to 2014) and its restoration to 2011 levels implies progress as far as employment and the real economy are concerned? In the following paragraphs, we will try to answer this question, i.e. whether there is a relationship between the reduction of the unemployment rate and real progress in the field of employment. In general, conventional wisdom says that a decrease of the unemployment rate is not consistent with an economy that experiences recession or weak growth.

More specifically, in an attempt to provide a more thorough answer to the above question, it is worth studying economic theory and, in particular, Okun's law, in conjunction with international experience. According to the above, the study of the relationship between employment and growth points to a 1% change (decrease) in unemployment as a result of an opposite change in GDP by approximately 2% (Blaunchard 2002; Christopoulos 2003). In the case of Greece, the Okun coefficient for the period 2001–2014 stands at −0.31, meaning that every increase/decrease in total output (real GDP) by 1% leads to a decrease/increase in unemployment by

---

[10] At this point we will take into account the size of the labour force, given that the unemployment rate and the number of the employed are examined in relation to the total labour force.

[11] The same conclusion is drawn by a SEV study on Greece's labour force, which, in particular, finds that: "a large part of the decrease in the unemployment rate is linked with the negative change in the size of the labour force" (SEV 2018:3).

0.31%. Alternatively, we could say that a 1% change in unemployment is linked to an opposite change in GDP by 3.18% and vice versa. During the period of the Greek economic crisis (2008–2014), in particular, the Okun coefficient was equal to −0.2 (Petrakis 2014). That said, what really happened in Greece during the recession years was that the decrease in unemployment was either disproportionate to changes in GDP, or even moved to the opposite direction. As a matter of fact, despite the fact that Greek GDP in 2018 is, more or less, at the same level with that of 2012, unemployment is down by almost five percentage points (see Table 4).

On the other hand, we must point out that job creation since 2014 is a reality and contributes to the reduction of the unemployment rate, as demonstrated by ELSTAT data (Table 2) and determined by our analysis of the number of the employed. Certain questions are, nonetheless, raised regarding the quality and sustainability of new jobs. According to the SEV report, the new jobs that were created in the Greek labour market between 2014 and 2017 are mostly related to low-wage employment, primarily in commerce and catering, thus being symptomatic to the economy's specialisation in low-added-value and low-wage sectors (SEV 2018: 7).

In relation with the above, by expanding our research we can also see that job creation during the period 2014–2018 is, in fact, due to a combination of factors, which have very little do to with the growth of sustainable employment. First, the reduction of undeclared work by almost 10% in the last four years, according to data by the Ministry of Labour—which is attributed to the increase in the relevant fines from 500 euros to 10,500 euros[12] since 2013—means that the increase in recruitment does not actually reflect new job creation in the economy. In other words, undeclared workers, who officially appeared as unemployed in the database of the Labour Inspectorate, were in fact employed, albeit their retrospective hiring is counted as a new job in ELSTAT measurements.[13] Therefore, the shift from undeclared to declared work is a de facto "grey area" as regards real employment metrics; however, it is counted as new job creation in the data of the Manpower Employment Organization and the ERGANI system, as well as in other ELSTAT measurements, thus altering the number of actual new jobs and providing a distorted picture of employment and, by extension, of the unemployment rate (Kostoula 2019).

Second, job creation is facilitated by the proliferation of employment boosting programmes subsidised by the Ministry of Labour—as part of implementing a wider countercyclical economic policy for fighting unemployment. It is true that this procedure removes unemployed individuals from the relevant lists and moves them to subsidised jobs, albeit for a limited time period. On the other hand, new job subsidisation programmes do not require workers to remain in their positions for a significant time period after the subsidy is terminated (OAED 2019), raising questions about the sustainability of these specific jobs.

---

[12] Pursuant to Law 4144/2013 and Joint Ministerial Decision 27,397/122/19/08/2013.

[13] This inconsistency in statistical measurements occurs because new hiring forms do not include the question whether a person had been working legally or illegally under their previous work status, while there are almost no truthful responses to this specific question as part of the Manpower Survey regarding new jobs.

Third, the factors that contributed to the decrease of unemployment include flexible forms of employment—a key priority of the "adjustment programmes". According to ERGANI statistics, full-time work was the dominant form of employment in the Greek labour market, representing almost 67.7% up to 2015. However, the situation tends to change since 2016–2017, as the number of part-time jobs increased, to the expense of full-time work. As a matter of fact, full-time work accounted for less than half of new hiring announcements for the year 2018 (45.66%) (SEV 2018: 6). However, it is worth noting that the contribution of flexible forms of employment to the reduction of unemployment does not indicate an economy that has recovered from the crisis and has a productive base capable of creating high-added-value and sustainable jobs.[14]

At this point, it is worth noting that a crucial factor for generating sustainable jobs (and, by extension, sustainable growth) is the ability to maintain a ratio of approximately 1 new job in internationally tradable to three new jobs in non-internationally tradable goods and services sectors (Ioannou et al. 2013: 40–45, 2017: 62–72). In the case of the Greek Economy, the ratio of new jobs in each of the two sectors was almost 1–5 (jobs in internationally tradable goods to jobs in non-internationally tradable goods) during the period of euphoria (2001–2009). In 2014–2017, employment in the internationally tradable goods sector rose by 13%, a percentage that is almost 10 percentage points short of the increase in the non-internationally tradable goods sector (SEV 2018: 10). Therefore, the key issue is not only the extent of economic growth or the quantitative increase of jobs, but also the quality of these jobs, which, surely, cannot be determined by employment in commerce and catering, but, on the contrary, is determined to a great extent by the Greek economy's ability to capture a place in the global division of labour, emphasising on high-added-value sectors.[15]

At this point, we will revisit the issue of the contraction of the labour force and its implications for the Greek economy. It is a fact that 322,000 workers are not any more included in Greece's labour force (Table 4). What is really important is that most of them migrated abroad, a substantial percentage of almost 70% being tertiary education graduates and 51% belonging to the crucial 25–45 age group, according to research carried out by KPMG and the Hellenic Federation of Enteprirse (SEV) (Lakasas 2018; SEV 2020: 1). As regards the latter, it is telling that the share (percentage) of employed persons aged 25–44 in Greece's total labour force seems to subside. In order to explain this, we referred to a study carried out by SEV on the basis of data from the ERGANI labour information system, regarding the distribution of jobs per age group, which shows that, up to the year 2014, the largest share of total jobs (approximately 60%) is held by people aged 25–44. However, this share seems to fall by five percentage points in the sub-period 2014–2017. At the same time, there is a significant increase in the percentage participation of workers aged 44 + (in the total labour force), along with a smaller increase in the share of employed

---

[14] The same conclusion is drawn from the study of the data concerning the monthly earnings of new jobs (SEV 2018).

[15] See the study by Sklias et al. (2017), on the quality and sustainability of the Greek economy's growth during the boom period.

persons under the age of 24 (in the total labour force). In absolute terms, the largest increase concerns the age group 44+ (by 163,889 new jobs, or 36.14%) (SEV 2018: 5). The above findings confirm the impact of the brain drain phenomenon on the labour force, as regards both tertiary education graduates and people belonging to the highly productive 25–44 age group.

Apart from that, questions are also raised regarding the capability of Greece's productive base to absorb the workers that emigrated and offer them employment in the same specific specialties, given the absence of a strategic plan for the differentiation of the Greek Economy towards high-added-value industries. This inability not only makes it difficult to repatriate scientific personnel, but also deprives the Greek economy from high value-added human resources. All the above effortlessly lead us to the conclusion that Greece's total labour force and, in particular, its most highly-skilled, productive and value-adding segment, suffered irreparable damage[16] in the period 2019–2018.

It is worth noting that the contraction of high-added value human resources undermines the development of the Greek economy. Indeed, the emigration of Greek scientists and practitioners implies that Greece has squandered financial resources and highly productive factors of production, since the cost of the investment made by the Greek state in the training and education of its human resources[17] is, in fact, given away for free to the host countries, along with the expected benefits from high-added value labour, which is a key ingredient of sustainable growth.

In this vein, and taking into account the technological and productive shifts occurring worldwide, Greece is at real risk of being trapped in the category of low-skill economies and, by extension, of building a productive base characterised by low-added value products (SEV 2018: 1). In fact, as regards the same issue, the European Commission, in a report on the Greek economy, stresses that trends in total factor productivity, in conjunction with the contraction of the labour force, undermine Greece's economic growth in the long term (European Commission 2017).

The above analysis shows that from 2010 to 2018 the Greek economy saw a substantial contraction of GDP, by almost 25%. At the same time, the unemployment rate surged to almost 26–27% up to 2013. Already in 2014, there is a drop in the unemployment rate, but this is to a great extent a statistical effect, which does not reflect the actual conditions prevailing in Greece's labour market and real economy. This can be easily understood by the following: first, we can see that the labour force was reduced by 504,000 persons (mostly tertiary education graduates) as a result of migration abroad, which has a downward effect on the unemployment rate. Second, certain parameters are neglected, which are related to the quality and sustainability of new jobs, such as flexible forms of employment, subsidised work

---

[16] The same conclusion is reached by the paper by Alderman et al. (2015), titled "Is Greece Worse Off Than the U.S. During the Great Depression?".

[17] According to a study by the Ministry of Education, titled "Higher Education Strategy in Greece, 2016–2020", expenditure per tertiary education student stands at 3571 euros per annum, without factoring in the cost incurred in other educational levels, which is also estimated in a study by S. Papaefthimiou at 1347 euros per annum per primary and secondary education student (Lakasas 2018).

programmes, the legitimisation of undeclared work since 2013, the level of remuneration of the new jobs, and the distribution of new jobs among the sectors of the
Greek economy, with commerce and catering enjoying the largest share. In addition,
remember that the current distribution of new jobs between internationally tradable
and non-internationally tradable goods remains unchanged at the pre-crisis ratio of
1–5, whereas the necessary ratio for achieving sustainable economic growth and, by
extension, sustainable jobs, is 1–3. Moreover, the economy's growth rates do not
justify the reduction in unemployment experienced by the Greek economy, always
in accordance with Okun's law and international experience.

4 Conclusions

The above analysis demonstrated that the implementation of the fiscal adjustment
programme turned the public debt crisis of 2010 into a widespread crisis with
very serious consequences for growth. This is not an exaggeration since the Greek
economy's gains in terms of GDP and employment during the period 2000–2009
were completely lost during the subsequent period 2010–2019. At the same time, in
the same period we can see a surge in the unemployment rate, and the loss of high-
added-value human resources because of the migration of young scientists abroad.
This means that Greece is at risk of being trapped in the category of low-added-value
economies, thus undermining the future growth of the Greek Economy.

On the other hand, there has, indeed, been a decrease of the unemployment rate
in recent years, which is nonetheless based on uncertain foundations. There is no
doubting the legitimacy of all unemployment-reducing policies, direct or indirect.
What is needed, however, is not to reduce the statistical figures regarding unemployment, but to increase the number of sustainable jobs by pursuing sustainable
growth, instead of returning to the same outdated growth model that prevailed until
2008. Finally, the fact that the target of reducing the public debt was not achieved
is considered to be very important, as, more specifically, Greece's debt, both as a
percentage of GDP, and in absolute terms, is higher than in the first period.

Therefore, the central finding of our macroeconomic analysis is that Greece is
not only facing the negative consequences from the failure of the fiscal adjustment
programme, which was acknowledged by the IMF, but also that this programme has
undermined the country's future prospects. A key prerequisite for Greece to exit the
crisis and achieve sustainable growth, but also for mitigating the cost of adjustment,
is to prepare and promote a new productive model for the Greek economy, aimed
at the production of quality products and high-added-value services, with a view to
accessing international markets and attracting investment. Moreover, further questions are raised by the fact that no provision was made for the change of the country's
existing productive model through specific and decisive government interventions.

Starting from the above position, we must stress that whoever attributes the
crisis only to misfortune, underestimates their (collective or individual) potential
and focuses on the problems, instead of the solutions. Apart from its other negative

effects, a crisis is also a bringer of progress, as it may turn out to be an opportunity for change for both people and countries. This is based on the fact that creativity is also born out of hardship. Moreover, periods of crisis also give rise to ingenuity, discoveries, and major strategic solutions. The real crisis for both people and countries lies in the unwillingness to fight to get over it and the lack of will to find outlets and solutions. Also, we should not forget that we do not try to change the situation when we keep on repeating the same mistakes.

Appendix

In order to ensure the uninterrupted flow of this study, it is deemed useful to make a critical approach of the concepts of the business cycle and economic crises in this Appendix. We will also attempt to examine the theoretical framework concerning the response of the unemployment and employment variables to the various phases of the business cycle the economy goes through. Moreover, it is imperative to define the concepts of employment, unemployment, and the labour force, in order to ensure the more comprehensive understanding of the paper.

Appendix 1: The Concepts of Employment, Unemployment, and the Labour Force

The population can be divided into two broad categories: (1) the *economically active* population includes the persons who are capable of work and, at the same time, want to work, i.e. those who have a job and are called "employed", and those without a job, albeit in search for work, who are called "unemployed". Both subgroups comprise the total labour force of an economy; (2) the *economically inactive* population, which comprises people who are incapable for work (young children, the elderly, people with ill health, and soldiers), as well as those who are not willing to work (idle). From the above, we deduce that the sum of the employed and unemployed is equal to the labour force. Labour force = Unemployed + Employed (Fig. 1) (Lixourgiotis 2013).

Fig. 1 Labour force. *Source* Data compiled by the author

The status of employed persons is referred to as employment. In general, the term "employment" defines the status of all factors of production when they are actively involved in the productive process. More specifically, as regards the factor of production called "labour", employment is defined as the form of using human resources in economic activities. In contrast, the concept of unemployment describes the status of people available of work who, nonetheless, cannot find paid employment that corresponds to their specialisation and skills (Petrinioti 1999).

As regards the above, it is worth clarifying that any persons who do not belong in the labour force despite being capable of work, are not counted as unemployed. Moreover, persons who are capable for work are not counted as unemployed if they do not want to work (Lianos and Benos 2013).

Unemployment is calculated as an absolute figure, for example: thousands of unemployed. However, the importance of this figure depends on the size of the labour force at any given time. Therefore, the need to include the labour force variable in unemployment measurements suggests that unemployment should be measured as a percentage (%) of the labour force. Based on the above, the unemployment rate is the ratio of the number of the unemployed to the total labour force (unemployment rate = unemployed persons/labour force or unemployment rate = unemployed persons/[employed + unemployed]) (Fig. 2a, b) (Prodromidis 1994).

The unemployment rate may change because of changes in either the absolute size of unemployment (i.e. the number of the unemployed) or the size of the labour force, or because both figures have changed (albeit, at different rates). Therefore, the reduction of the unemployment rate (a fraction) is not only the result of a reduction in the number of the unemployed (the numerator of the fraction), but also of the total reduction of the denominator of the fraction, i.e. the labour force pool or the rate of change of each figure relative to the other. The size of the labour force is affected by various factors, for example, the economically inactive part of the population that decides to seek employment and joins the economically active population (labour force), migration flows, etc. (Papavasiliou 2000).

At this point, it should be stressed that employment and the unemployment rate are not two aggregates that function as communicating vessels, in other words a reduction of the unemployment rate does not imply the creation of an equal number of jobs and an equal decrease in the absolute number of the unemployed. Moreover, changes in both employment and unemployment are interactively related to changes in the total output (GDP) of the economy (Dedousopoulos 2000).

Appendix 2: Business Cycle and Economic Crises

It is a fact that total output and production do not follow a linear and stable course, albeit fluctuate and go through boom (GDP growth) and bust (GDP contraction) phases. The concept of the business cycle aims inter alia at highlighting and analysing the various phases that total output goes through (boom-bust-slowdown-depression-stagnation-recovery) (Krugman 2008).

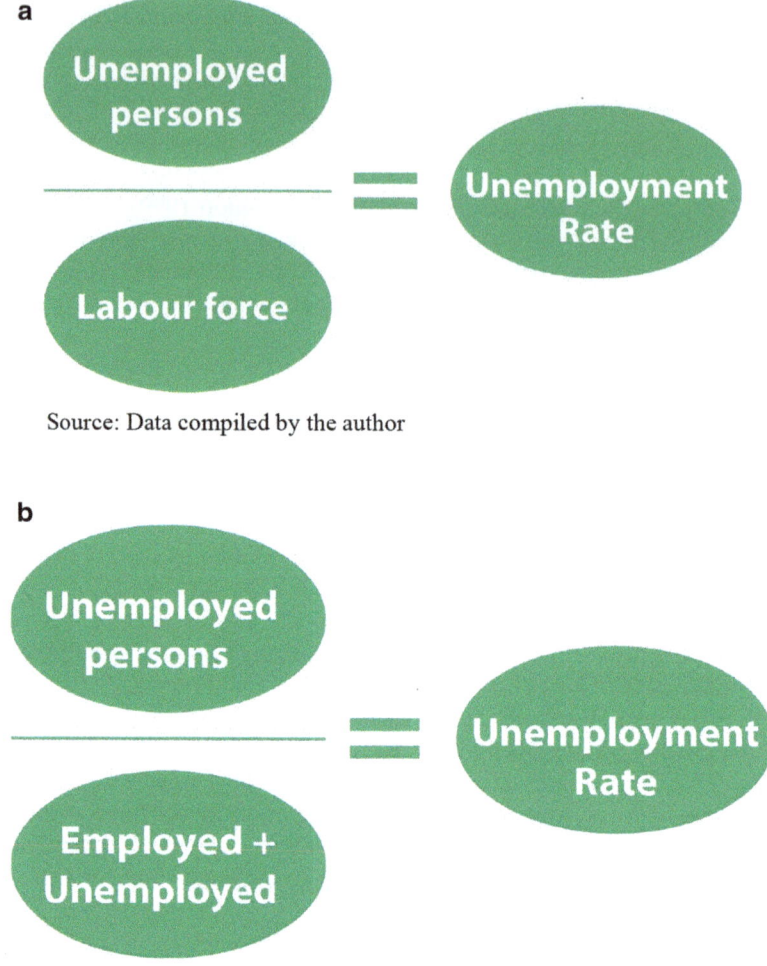

Source: Data compiled by the author

Source: Data compiled by the author

Fig. 2 a Unemployment rate. *Source* Data compiled by the author. **b** Unemployment rate. *Source* Data compiled by the author

The business cycle, as defined by Mitchell, comprises four phases (recovery, prosperity, crisis, and depression-stagnation). For practical purposes, we define the trough of the business cycle, i.e. the stagnation phase, as the first phase. After the economy has passed this phase, it enters a phase of fast improvement, which is called recovery. This is followed by a possible additional expansion of economic activity that constitutes the phase of prosperity. This phase is interrupted by the manifestation of the crisis, which is followed by a downward trend in total output. Therefore, an economic crisis is the event that causes the economy to alternate between various phases of the business cycle and, more specifically, interrupts the prosperity phase

Fig. 3 Business cycle.
Source Data compiled by the
author

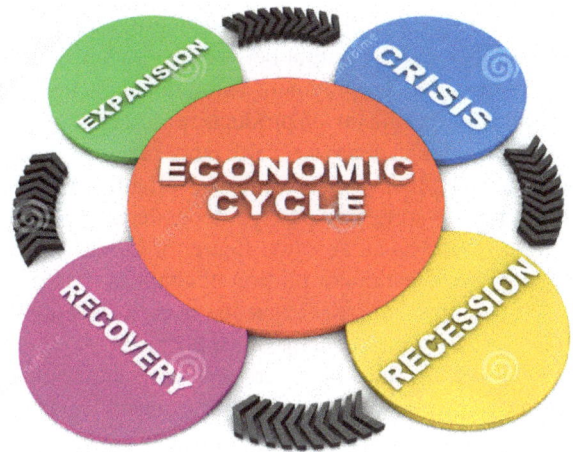

and ushers the economy in the depression phase (Cited in Howard 1991: 7–11). The term "depression" describes a deep and protracted downturn of economic activity and, by extension, a contraction of the economy's GDP (for at least two or more consecutive quarters) (Fig. 3) (Knoop 2008: 60). Based on the above analysis, it is easy to conclude that Economic Crisis theories try to highlight the factors that interrupt the ascending phase of the business cycle and, in particular, analyse the parameters that lead to the emergence of the crisis during a specific time period (Knoop 2004: 27).

Appendix 3: Response of Macroeconomic Variables in Relation to GDP Changes During the Phases of the Business Cycle

A factor that will help us understand the concept and operation of the business cycle is the examination of the behaviour (response) of key macroeconomic variables in relation to GDP changes that occur during the various phases of the business cycle. Admittedly, there are certain macroeconomic variables that increase or decrease when GDP increases or decreases, respectively. Typical examples of such variables include consumption, investment, employment, etc., and the term "procyclical" is used to describe them. On the contrary, the term "countercyclical" indicates a negative correlation between the variable and changes in GDP. More specifically, the value of the variable increases when GDP decreases (and vice versa), one such example being unemployment. Finally, there is the acyclical variable category, which has no consistent correlation with changes in GDP (Knoop 2004: 15).

Unemployment is, in fact, one of the macroeconomic aggregates that exhibit anticyclical behaviour during the business cycle. This inherent characteristic means that these specific macroeconomic aggregates move to the opposite direction to the alternations of total output between boom and bust phases (Howard 1991: 16–17).

As far as the employment variable is concerned, tt is also worth noting that the changes in this factor of production during a recession are much larger and more pronounced than changes in any other factor of production (Howard 1991: 16–17), a fact meaning that employment is a variable directly related to the course of the real economy. Despite this passive dependence between labour and aggregate output, labour (either as an absolute figure, or in terms of its productivity) may in its own right determine a major portion of changes in total output (Sidiropoulos 2016:245–246), demonstrating the existence of an interactive relationship between changes in GDP and labour as a factor of production.

Mentioning the key macroeconomic variables related to the business cycle is important because some of them are used by economists for predicting the cycle by approximation, as well as for evaluating the behaviour of the business cycle and its effects on the real economy. Moreover, understanding crises, the business cycle, and the economy's cyclical behaviour is necessary for exploring the consequences of crises on the economy.

References

Alderman et. Al (2015), *Is Greece Worse Off Than the U.S. During the Great Depression?* Available at: https://www.nytimes.com/interactive/2015/07/09/business/international/is-greece-worse-off-than-the-us-during-the-great-depression.html [accessed November 25, 2019].

Anastasatos T., 2009. *"Towards a new Greek growth model:* investment and extroversion" (in Greek), Eurobank Research: Economy and Markets

Blaunchard, O., 2002. *Macroeconomics.* N. Jersey: Prentice Hall

Bosworth, B., and Kollintzas Tr., 2002. Economic Growth in Greece: Past Performance and Future Prospects", in R. Bryant, N. Garganas and G. Tavlas (eds.), Greece's Economic Performance and Prospects, Athens: Bank of Greece /Washington: The Brookings Institution. 189–236.

Cecchetti S. et. al, 2011. The real effect of debt, Bank for international settlements. Working paper No 352.

Christodoulakis, N., 2009. Ten years of EMU: convergence divergence and new policy priorities. *The Hellenic Observatory LSE.* Paper No 22.

Christopoulos, D., 2003 *The relationship between output and unemployment: Evidence from Greek regions.* Review Economic Design 83(3):611–620

Cohn, T., 2009. Global Political Economy Theory and Practice, Gutemberg, Athens.

De Grauwe, P., 2000. The Economics of Monetary Integration, 4th ed., Oxford.

Dedousopoulos, A. 2000. *Theories of Unemployment, The Crisis in the Labour Market: Regulation-Flexibilities-Deregulation* (in Greek), Volume One. Athens: Typothito.

Dimeli S., 2010. *Macroeconomic aggregates and growth rates of the Greek economy* (in Greek), Athens: Athens University of Economics and Business.

ELSTAT, 2018. *Labour force* December 2018, available at: https://www.statistics.gr/el/statistics/-/publication/SJO02/2018-M12. [accessed January 5, 2020].

ELSTAT, 2019. *Labour force* December 2019, available at: https://www.statistics.gr/el/statistics/-/publication/SJO02/2019-M12. [accessed January 5, 2020].

European Commission, 2017. *Compliance Report. The Third Economic Adjustment Programme for Greece.* Available at: http://media.enikonomia.gr/data/files/157709_63374349dd-a9e2b4c074eb 7274.pdf [Accessed November 29, 2019].

European Commission, 2019. Annual Macro-economic Database (AMECO). Available at: http:// eu.economy_finance/ameco//user/serie/SelectSerie.cfm. [accessed October 5, 2019].

European Commission, 2020. Annual Macro-economic Database (AMECO). Available at: http:// eu.economy_finance/ameco//user/serie/SelectSerie.cfm. [accessed October 5, 2020].

Feldstein, M., 1998. Asking for Trouble. The Single Currency Will Lead to Regional Conflict, not Economic Efficiency, TIME, January.

Galatsidas G, Roukanas S., and Sklias P., 2015. The institutional and "developmental" course of the Greek Economy following its entry into the Tripartite Support Mechanism. In the Minutes to the International Scientific Conference Economies of the Balkan and Eastern Europe Countries (EBEEC), 8–10 May 2015, Kavala, Greece.

Gelos, et. al. 2004. Sovereign borrowing by developing countries: what determines market access? IMF Working Paper 04/221, IMF Washington, DC.

Hadjiconstantinou G. Th. 1998. In the Bonds of Fabled Economic Paradigm (Realising the Transformation and Understanding Complexity), (in Greek), Athens: Ellinika Grammata.

Hazakis, K. 2014. The economic governance crisis in the euro zone and its implications for the management of Greece's public debt in S. Roukanas & P. Sklias, eds. 2014. *The Greek Political Economy, 2000–2015. From EMU to the Support Mechanism* Athens: Livanis Publications.

Howard, S., (1991), The business cycle. Growth and crisis under capitalism, New Jersey: Princeton University Press.

Ioannou, D. and Ioannou, Chr. 2013. *Greece: Victim of Austerity or "Dutch Disease"?* (in Greek) Foreign Affairs, The Hellenic Edition, Issue 18: 40–54.

Ioannou, D. and Ioannou, Chr., 2017. *The fundamental asymmetry of the Greek Economy (in Greek), Greek Economic Outlook,* KEPE, Issue 33:63- 72.

Kazakos P. *et. al.,* 2016. *Greece's public debt* (in Greek). Athens: Papazisis Publications.

Knoop, T., 2004. Recessions and Depressions. Understanding Business Cycles. Westport: Greenwood Praeger Publishers.

Knoop T., 2008. *Modern financial macroeconomics. Panics, crashes and crises,* Oxford: Blackwell publishing.

Kostoula, B., 2019. *How unemployment is reduced in Greece. "Technical" reduction: reduction of registered unemployment without increase in full-time employment (in Greek).* Naftemporiki newspaper Available at: https://www.naftemporiki.gr/finance/story/1447155/pos-meionetai-i-anergia-stin-ellada [Accessed January 5, 2020].

Kotios A., Pavlidis G., 2012. International Economic Crises: Systemic or Policy Crises? (in Greek), Athens: Rosili Publications.

Kotios A., 1997. The two sides of the EMU (in Greek). EVROPAIKI PAROUSIA monthly publication on Europe, December.

Kotios A., 2000. Greece in the euro area – from nominal to real convergence (in Greek) in Zoning, Urban Planning, and Regional Development, Scientific Yearbook for the Tenth Anniversary of the Department of Planning and Regional Development of the University of Thessaly, Volos, p. 341–365.

Kotios, A, Galanos G, Roukanas S., 2012. "The Greek crisis and the crisis of the euro zone's governance system" (in Greek), *Research Papers*, 18(1) 1–26.

Koutsoukis, N.S. and Roukanas, S., 2014. The GrExit paradox, Procedia Economics and Finance, Vol. 9, p. 24–31.

Krugman, P., 2008. *The Return of Depression Economics and the Crisis of 2008,* (Greek translation by Ariadne Alavanou), Athens: Kastaniotis

Krugman, P., 2011. End this Depression Now! (Translated in Greek by Tina Theou), Athens: Polis Publications.

Krugman, P., 2015. *"Weimar and Greece, Continued"*. The New York Times, February 15, 2015, available at https://krugman.blogs.nytimes.com/2015/02/15/weimar-and-greece-continued/

Lakasas, A. 2018. "The Brain Drain Costs 15.3 bn" (in Greek). *Kathimerini* newspaper. Available at: https://www.kathimerini.gr/946827/article/epikairothta/ellada/153-dis-to-kostos-toy-brain-drain [Accessed April 13, 2020].

Law 4144/2013 "Combating delinquency at the Social Security and at the labour market and other provisions within the competence of the Ministry of Labour, Social Security and Welfare" Available at: https://www.taxheaven.gr/law/4144/2013 [Accessed 02 March 2020].

Lianos P. and Benos E., 2013. *Macroeconomic Theory and Policy (in Greek).* Athens: Benou.

Lixourgiotis, I. 2013. *Personal Labour Relations* (in Greek). Athens: Nomiki Vivliothiki.

Marangos, J., 2020 *The Troika's conditionalities during the Greek financial crisis of 2010–2014: the Washington Consensus is alive, well, and here to stay.* European Journal of economics and economic policies: intervention.

OAED, 2019. *New Job Subsidisation Programmes (in Greek).* Available at: http://www.oaed.gr/anoikta-programmata [Accessed March 25, 2020].

Panagiotarea, E., 2017. It is true that the eurozone did not act in solidarity. in D. Katsikas, K. Filinis and M. Anastasatou, eds 2017. UNDERSTANDING THE GREEK CRISIS. Answers to key questions about the State, Economy, and Europe (in Greek).

Papavasiliou, Ch. 2000. *The European Employment Strategy* (in Greek). Athens:

Petrakis, P. 2014. *On unemployment (in Greek).* Available at: http://www.indeepanalysis.gr/analyseis/arthra/gia-thn-anergia [Accessed 22 March, 2020].

Petrinioti, X. 1999. *Labour Markets, Economic Theories, and Research* (in Greek). Athens: Papazisis Publications.

Prodromidis, K. 1994. *Economic Policy Theory* (in Greek). Athens: Benou.

Roukanas S., 2011. European Political Economy and Competitiveness in the crisis age *in the minutes to the INTERNATIONAL CONFERENCE ON INTERNATIONAL BUSINESS,* 19–21 May 2011, Thessaloniki

Schizas, P. 2014. *The Greek debt crisis and the effect of CDSs* in S. Roukanas & P. Sklias, eds. 2014. *The Greek Political Economy, 2000–2015. From EMU to the Support Mechanism* Athens: Livanis Publications.

SEV, 2018. ERGANI Data on the Minimum Wage (in Greek). *Economy and Business.* Available at: http://www.sev.org.gr/Uploads/Documents/51680/Special%20Report%20ERGANI_21.11.2018.pdf [Accessed March 20, 2020].

SEV, 2020. *How we will get from the drain drain to the brain gain* (in Greek). Economy and Business. Available at: https://www.sev.org.gr/Uploads/Documents/52684/Final_SR_Brain_Drain.pdf [Accessed March 5, 2020].

Sidiropoulos M., 2009. Should Greece eradicate its public debt? (in Greek), [online] Available at: https://sidiropoulos.wordpress.com/2009/02/10/%cf%80%cf%81%ce%ad%cf%80%ce%b5%ce%b9-%ce%b7-%ce%b5%ce%bb%ce%bb%ce%ac%ce%b4%ce%b1-%ce%bd%ce%b1-%ce%b5%ce%be%ce%b1%ce%bb%ce%b5%ce%af%cf%88%ce%b5%ce%b9-%cf%84%ce%bf-%ce%b4%ce%b7%ce%bc%cf%8c%cf%83%ce%b9/

Sidiropoulos M., 2016. *"Economic policy impetus to post-EMU Greece's economic growth"* in S. Roukanas & P. Sklias, eds. 2014. *The Greek Political Economy, 2000–2015. From EMU to the Support Mechanism* Athens: Livanis Publications.

Sklias P. and Maris G., 2014. *Greece's entry into the Support Mechanism* in S. Roukanas & P. Sklias, eds. 2014. *The Greek Political Economy, 2000–2015. From EMU to the Support Mechanism* Athens: Livanis Publications.

Sklias P., Roukanas S. and Galatsidas G. 2017. *Greek Political Economy in a Period of Economic Crisis: the need to design a state growth strategy (in Greek), in the minutes to the PEDiS scientific conference title "Greece and the European Union at the Crossroads of Crucual Developments: Policies, Strategic Choices, and Prospects"* (Loutraki, December 6–8, 2013), www.academu.edu/41350184/Βιβλίο_Συνόψεων_3ου_Συνεδρίου_ΠΕΔιΣ_2017.

Sklias P., Roukanas S. and Galatsidas G. 2018. Was the Great Depression of 1929 harsher than the Greek Depression? *in the Minutes to the 14th International Scientific Conference* of the Economic

Society of Thessaloniki, titled: Social, Economic and Curent Policy Issues, 29 November- 01 December 2018, Thessaloniki.

Stournaras G. and Albani M., 2008, Greek Economy after the Crisis: In Search of a New Growth Model (in Greek), Athens: AUEB publications.

Thugesen, N., 1990. The Benefits and Costs of Currency Unification. In: H. Siebert, Ed. 1990. The Completion of the Internal Market, Kiel Institute of World Economics, Tubingen: Mohr-siebeck, pp. 347–385.

Wolfson, M., 1994. Financial Crises: Understanding the Postwar Experience, N.Y: M.E. Sharpe.

Social Capital and Income Inequality in OECD Countries: Causality Evidence

Nalleli Patricia Bolaños Pérez and Edgar J. Saucedo-Acosta

Abstract Social capital has declined in both developments and in other developing economies, while income inequality has tended to increase. Recent studies show the correlation between social capital and income inequalities, while few studies analyse the direction of causality at a macro level. This paper aims to investigate the causal relationship between generalised trust, as well as income inequalities in 23 economies belonging to the Organisation for Economic Cooperation and Development (OECD) from 2000 to 2019. In this study, we use the application of a fully modified least squares model (FMOLS) and the canonical correlation regression estimator (CCR). In addition, the unit root and cointegration test is applied before applying the Granger causality test. The findings show that there is a bidirectional relationship between social capital and income inequality.

Keywords Inequality · Generalised trust · Granger causality test

JEL Classification Codes D31 · CO1 · 057

1 Introduction

The role that income inequalities have played on social capital has been of great interest in a variety of studies for some time (Knack and Keefer 1997; Putnam 2000). Recent research has been developed in a large number of European countries (Clark 2015; De Blasio and Nuzzo 2012; d'Hombres et al. 2013; Ferragina 2013; Iglič et al. 2020; Parente 2019) but less in the combination of economies with heterogeneous characteristics, where attention should be paid to the countries of The Organisation

N. P. Bolaños Pérez
Management and Accounting Faculty, University of Veracruz, Xalapa, Mexico

N. P. Bolaños Pérez · E. J. Saucedo-Acosta (✉)
Economics and Social Higher Studies Research Institute, University of Veracruz, Xalapa 91190, Mexico
e-mail: esaucedo@uv.mx

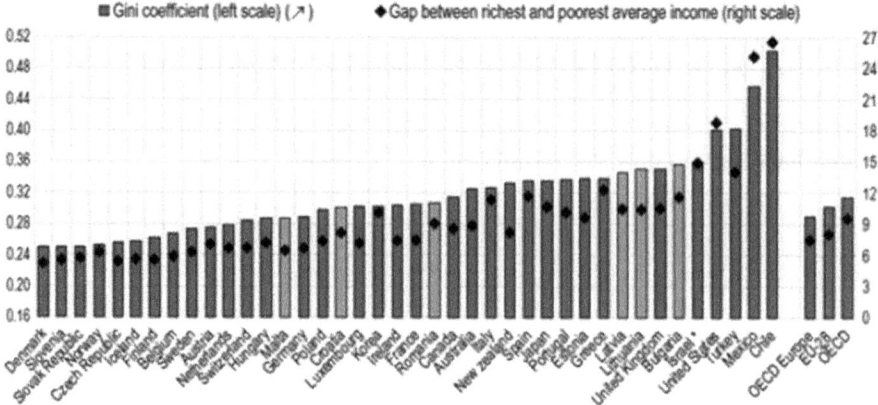

Fig. 1 Level of income inequality by country. *Source* The Organisation for Economic Cooperation and Development (OECD 2014)

for Economic Cooperation and Development (OECD), not only due to academic demand, but also because of the constant increases in wage gaps that occur in societies, and which are increasingly more perceptible by the inhabitants of an economy (OECD 2015).

Cohen and Ladaique (2018) argue that economic inequalities present different patterns and have increased in the last three decades, this is reflected in the Gini index. In the 80s an increase in inequalities began to be seen and by the 2000s the wage gap became ever greater, thus ensuring that the economies of Asia, Eastern Europe and Latin America have the highest indices of income inequality (Dabla-Norris et al. 2015) Gasparini and Lustig (2012) (see Fig. 1). This has led various scholars on the subject to consider that the main driver of income inequalities is due to the gap that exists between wages (Piketty 2014; Stiglitz 2012). In most OECD countries, the causal factors for the increase in wage gaps correspond to the fact that the wages of the best-paid workers rise at a faster rate than the wages of those in the lowest deciles, along the same lines, annual hours have decreased for people with lower wages and increased for workers with higher wages. Furthermore, the arrival of globalisation, constant technological changes and the transformation of the labour market require a workforce with skills in technology and finance (Atkinson 2016; Milanovic 2017; Piketty 2014). Wage differences are one of the main obstacles to building trust within societies. With the rise in wages being increasingly skewed towards the top deciles, social capital has a minimal probability of increasing.

The relationship between both variables has been debated in various investigations, without reaching a consensus. The literature shows us that the countries which enjoy greater wage equalities and high trust among their inhabitants, allow the creation of environments where economic transactions are adequately developed because those involved participate by developing more honest behaviour. Also in these scenarios, political institutions function correctly, societies can recover quickly from economic crises, as well as at an individual level, social capital allows citizens to be more intelligent, enjoy better health, be happy and have fair and stable democratic systems (Dai et al. 2018; Obert et al. 2018; Putnam 2000).

In contrast, some studies show that there is an inversely proportional relationship between the variables, creating stratified societies, with an unfair distribution of resources, psychosocial effects and collective action problems among the population (Steijn and Lancee 2011; Uslaner and Brown 2005).

Furthermore, the results of other studies coincide in the null relationship between income inequalities and generalised trust (Leigh 2006; Geys and Murdoch 2008). From empirical studies, there are not many investigations that can visualise the direction of causality between wage gaps and generalised trust. Gustavsson and Jordahl (2008) present a step forward in the causal link between these variables, considering the possible existence of a causal relationship between them. In this research, they apply a panel data with fixed effects for different Swedish states, there was a four-year analysis period, and their findings consider that economic inequalities are negatively related to trust and that people located in the middle of income distribution trust-less. However, we consider that their results are questionable due to the short period of analysis and the econometric model used. The studies have not focused on the analysis of bidirectionality for the countries that make up the OECD. The increasing trends of income inequalities together with the decrease in social capital, lead us to the interest of this study to empirically investigate the relationship between the variables. Therefore, the following research question arises; what is the nature of the causal relationship between income inequalities and generalised trust in OECD countries? We mainly believe that the study contributes to the current literature by considering the heterogeneous nature of OECD countries in the framework of causality proposed by Dumitrescu and Hurlin (2012). We analyse panel data for the period 2000 to 2019 for 23 OECD economies. The causality results suggest a bidirectional relationship between income inequalities and social capital.

The study is structured as follows: Sect. 2 is the literature review; Sect. 3 demonstrates the econometric methodology and data sources for the study. Section 4 shows the empirical results, while Sect. 5 presents the discussion and conclusion.

2 Literature Review

Economic inequalities are linked to a variety of effects that are detrimental within societies (Costa Font et al. 2014; Graafland 2018; Norris et al. 2015; Piketty 2014), in this sense, studies have shown that attitudes and behaviours related to social cohesion are affected when resource distribution is inclined towards a certain segment, which is known as inequality in a society (Buttrick 2017).

Uslaner and Brown (2005) argue that perceptions and beliefs about how resources are distributed in societies and how they should be allocated equitably determine the distribution of trust within societies. Uslaner and Brown (2005) claim that if resources in a work or social context are distributed unevenly, people who are at the lowest levels of the distribution and those who are at the highest levels will feel that they do not have shared purposes. For example, if this arises in the workplace context when workers consider that there are stratospheric wage gaps between positions that are at the same hierarchical level and that wages are assigned by relationship factors and not based on merit with respect to their work performance, employees experience a decrease in trust among their colleagues and in general in their work environment. In other words, the perception they observe increases their degree of distrust, this may be because they do not possess all the real information on income, but the imperfect information they have leads them to suppose that there is such a wage discrepancy.

Likewise, it has been argued that income inequalities affect social capital from a stratification perspective (Steijn and Lancee 2011). This approach considers that when there is an increase in wage inequalities, social segmentation coexists, causing people with high incomes to have different living conditions, that is, they live in exclusive areas, study in private universities and belong to different networks, etc. When these events occur, trust between different social levels is damaged; usually, each social stratum tends to trust actors of the same economic level (Doob 2015; Schneider et al. 2018). This also happens when people from different social strata meet sporadically; intergroup differences arise between both parties, which is further aggravated by the lack of trust that can occur between them.

Regarding the relationship of social capital and income inequalities, studies have shown the importance of trust with macro-social, economic and political aspects (Álvarez-Botas and González 2021; Ayob 2018; Foster and Frieden 2017). Considering the theory about trust, cooperation and collective action problems at a micro and macro level (Carballo et al. 2014; Gavrilets 2015; Ostrom and Ahn 2003), the relationship of social capital and income inequalities can be studied (Bergh and Bjørnskov 2014). In this sense, trust and cooperation have been explained from the classic analysis, the prisoner's dilemma proposed by Axelrod (1980) (See Table 1).

Table 1 shows that the participants have three options: (a) both players cooperate, (b) one player cooperates and the other does not cooperate, or (c) neither player cooperates. The result of individual interactions within the game produces negative results, on the other hand, if both parties decide to cooperate, the result is positive for those involved. Although, at first glance it seems that the most optimal option is the cooperation of the parties involved, this does not happen in real life, since it is unknown whether the other participant will opt for cooperation; This leads to trust playing a relevant role for cooperation to occur. The cooperation resulting from trust (social capital) will help the actors to make efficient use of resources, allowing them to solve collective action problems (Koutsou et al. 2014; Bandiera et al. 2005; Vugt and Cremer 1999).

Table 1 The prisoner's dilemma

	Cooperate	Defect
Cooperate	3.3	0.5
Defect	5.0	1.1

Source Extracted from Axelrod (1980)

In particular, in business, some of the conflicts that arise revolve around labour relations between workers, administrators and managers. If workers perceive selfish, opportunistic behaviour among the actors, it will generate mistrust, which will prevent them from cooperating and solving problems that may involve aspects related to work and wages. This fact of non-cooperation will generate unequal distributional consequences.

In addition, from a macro perspective, the theory proposed by Aristotle (2005) which shows the existence of the three social classes, opened up the problems of collective action in redistribution, followed by recent theories such as Korpi's resource theory (2018), which highlights the relevance of the cohesion between the working class and the middle class to produce egalitarian distributive results.

Ultimately, the relationship between social capital and income inequalities can be supported by the existing literature. In Fig. 2, it is shown that the effect of income inequalities implies a change in social capital, whereas the effect of social capital causes a change in income inequalities. The unidirectional relationship is studied more exhaustively, proving the existence of bidirectional causal relationships between the two variables.

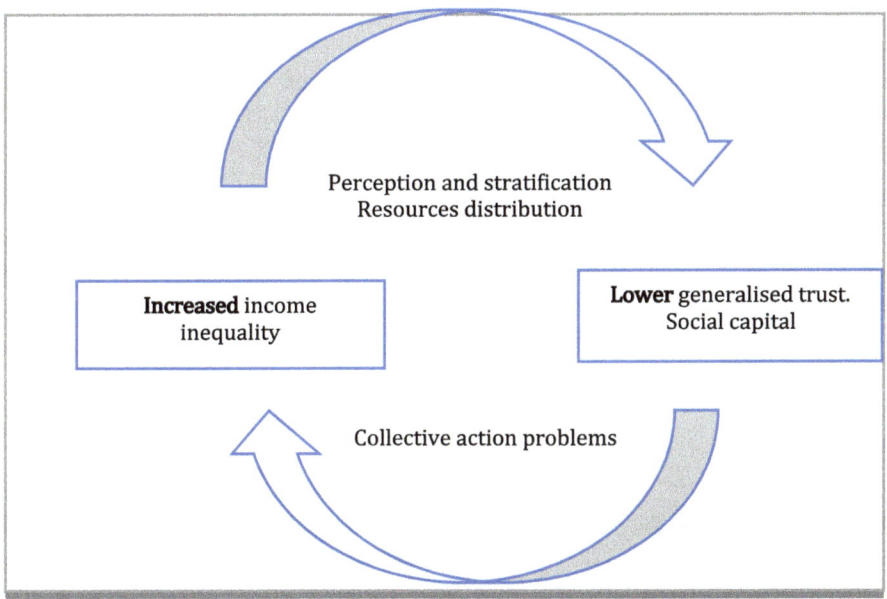

Fig. 2 Relationship between income inequalities and social capital

2.1 *Empirical Research Studies*

Few studies consider the inverse causal relationship between income inequalities and trust. In this sense, Alesina and La Ferrara (2002) showed that societies with high levels of trust can improve their economic aspects for the benefit of the poorest. Gustavsson and Jordahl (2008) conducted an investigation in Swedish counties, through quantile income regressions, where they took trust as an explanatory variable, finding that people who are in the 10th and 90th percentiles have higher incomes and high confidence. Along these lines Bergh and Bjørnskov (2014), analysed 104 countries in 2000 and 2006, applying a model of structural equations. The objective of their research was to demonstrate the causal relationship between welfare states, generalised trust and economic equality. Their findings showed that social trust enables countries to maintain welfare states and high welfare states reduce income inequalities, however; this does not happen the other way around (Table 2).

Other studies, applied at intraregional levels, analyse this causal relationship. In this way, Shen and Bian (2018), carried out their study in a national sample in China, in the labour context. Their aim was to demonstrate the causal effect of social capital on income through the Poisson regression model. Their causality analysis was based on the classification of three groups, which were considered based on their formal and informal relationship channel, confirming that the group with the highest social capital (formal and informal) has a higher salary income.

Yang and Xin (2020), developed an individual and intraregional research in China through temporal analysis and the Granger causality test and found that income inequality has an effect on the decrease in interpersonal trust, however, interpersonal trust had no effect on income inequalities. To support the debate between income inequalities and social trust (social capital), it is relevant to develop a long-term analysis, as well as to perform causality tests. This methodology remains unusual in the empirical analysis of these variables. Therefore, the panel data analysis was developed for a set of 23 OECD economies.

3   Data

The annual data for the study cover the period from 2000 to 2019. The research is applied in 23 economies of the Organisation for Economic Cooperation and Development (OECD 2020) (see Table 3).

Table 4 shows the data set used in the study: Generalised trust (GT) Gini index (Gini), Trade (ExImp), GDP per capita (GDP_pc) and Education (EDU). The missing data were calculated through simple imputation using the regression model for each of the economies (Cañizares et al. 2004).

4   Methodology

The objective of the research is to determine the existence of causality between income inequalities and social capital; therefore, the study is based on unit root tests, panel cointegration, the application of a fully modified least squares model (FMOLS), the canonical correlation regression estimator (CCR) and a panel causality test.

When considering the cross-section time-series data, unit root tests were applied to determine if the variables were stationary. First, the order of integration of the variables is tested, then if the integration of the variables is of order I (1), the cointegration test of the analysis variables is carried out. Finally, the panel causality test is applied, in order to identify the direction of causality between the variables.

Table 2 Empirical studies on causality

Authors	Sample	Database	Methodology	Results
Gustavsson and Jordah (2008)	Swedish counties 1994–1998	Swedish Election Studies and longitudinal database LINDA data on trust from the 1994 and 1998 Swedish Election Studies	Linear regressions for our cross-sectional and panel samples. 2SLS estimates	Finding that inequalities in disposable (rather than gross) income are negatively related to trust
Bergh and Bjørnskov (2014)	104 countries Between 2000 and 2006	• Standardised world income inequality database by Solt (2009). • World Values Survey • AfroBarometer • Asian Barometer, East Asian Barometer, LatinoBarometro and the Arab Barometer-Gallup	Structural equation model	Trust facilitates welfare state policies that may reduce net inequality, this decrease in inequality does not increase trust
Shena and Bian (2018)	5894 adult urbanites, 18–69 years old, randomly selected through a stratified probability sampling strategy (2003)	Chinese General Social Survey	Poisson regression model. OLS estimations	Social capital has a causal effect on income

(continued)

Table 2 (continued)

Authors	Sample	Database	Methodology	Results
Yang and Xin (2020)	Study 1—141 studies (N = 64,853) found that Chinese college students' scores on the Interpersonal Trust Scale decreased 0.54 SD from 1998 to 2016. Study 2 Data of 11,783 Chinese individuals from 31 provinces using multistage stratified random sampling. (2010)	Chinese general social survey the national bureau of statistics of China	• Cross-temporal meta-analysis • Cross-regional analysis	More income inequality perceived the local government to be less trustworthy and, in turn, reported lower levels of interpersonal trust

Source Own elaboration

Table 3 Study countries

OECD Countries
Austria, Belgium, Chile, Colombia, Czech Republic, Denmark, Estonia, Finland, France, Germany, Hungary, Ireland, Mexico, Netherlands, Norway, Poland, Portugal, Slovenia, Spain, Sweden, Switzerland, United Kingdom and United States.

Source Own elaboration

The unit root tests applied in the study were Levin et al. (2002), Im et al. (2003), Harris and Tzavalis (1999) and Fisher (1932).

The results of the unit root tests accept the null hypothesis regarding the existence of a unit root for the four variables: Generalised trust, Gini index, GDP per capita and Education. Subsequently, the cointegration tests of Pedroni (2004) and Westerlund (2007) were applied. Liu et al. (2019) and Pedroni (2004) suggest that the cointegration tests of Pedroni, Kao and Westerlund can be used when variables are cointegrated of order I (0) and order I (1). Therefore, in this research we applied the Pedroni cointegration test and Westerlund cointegration test, both tests combine statistics calculated for each individual in the panel.

To analyse the variables of income inequality and social capital, we applied the fully modified least squares (FMOLS) cointegration regression estimator proposed by Phillips and Hansen (1990) and the canonical correlation regression estimator (CCR) proposed by Park (1992). Both estimators are obtained by calculating the regressors and regressand, and subsequently applying the OLS procedure. FMOLS and CCR

Table 4 Study variables

Variable	Description	Data source
Generalised trust (GT)	Percentage of trust between people	Latinobarometro European Social Survey
Gini Index (Gini)	Distribution of income in the family market	Standardised Global Income Inequality Data (SWIID)
Trade (ExpImp)	Measured in million USD, as percentage of GDP for net trade and also in annual growth for exports and imports	The Organisation for Economic Cooperation and Development (OECD)
GDP_per capita (GDP_pc)	Gross domestic product converted to international dollars using purchasing power parity rates	World Development Indicators
Education (EDU)	Mean years of schooling	Human Development Reports

Source European Social Survey (2020); Human Development Reports (2020); Latinobarometro, (2020); Organisation for Economic Cooperation and Development (2020), The ICTWSS (Visser, 2016) and World Development Indicators (2020), processed and elaborated by authors

are suitable panel tests, which include heterogeneous integration. According to Wang and Wu (2012), the FMOLS estimator is obtained with the regressand transformation.

$$y_t^+ = y_t - \hat{\omega}_{12}\hat{\Omega}_{22}^{-1}\hat{\upsilon}_{2t} \tag{1}$$

where $\hat{\upsilon}_{1t}$ is the residual of the cointegration equation estimated by OLS, and $\hat{\upsilon}_{2t}$ are the differenced residuals of regressor equations or the residuals of the differenced regressor equations.

The FMOLS estimators and their covariance are given by

$$\hat{\theta} = \left[\left[\begin{matrix}\widehat{\beta}\\ \widehat{\gamma_1}\end{matrix}\right]\right] = \left[\left[\sum_{t=1}^{T} z_t z_t'\right]\right]\left[\left[\sum_{t=1}^{T} z_t y_t^+ - T\left(\begin{matrix}\lambda_{12}^{+\prime}\\ 0\end{matrix}\right)\right]\right] \tag{2}$$

$$\text{Var}\left(\hat{\theta}\right) = \hat{\omega}_{1.2}\left[\left[\sum_{t=1}^{T} z_t z_t'\right]\right] \quad \hat{\omega}_{1.2} = \hat{\omega}_{11} - \hat{\omega}_{12}\hat{\Omega}_{22}^{-1}\hat{\omega}_{21} \tag{3}$$

where $\hat{\lambda}_{12}^+ = \hat{\lambda}_{12} - \hat{\omega}_{12}\hat{\Omega}_{22}^{-1}\hat{\Lambda}_{22}$ are called bias-correction terms $z_t = \left(x_t', d_{1t}'\right)'.\hat{\omega}_{1.2}$ is the estimate of the LRCOV of μ_{1t} conditional on μ_{2t}.

Therefore, the equation that represents the FMOLS study model is the following:

$$CG_{ti} = \beta_0 + \beta_{1ti} + \beta_2 Gini_{ti} + \beta_3 GDPpc_{ti} + \beta_4 Edu_{ti} + \mu_{ti} \tag{4}$$

The equation considers a constant and a time trend.

The CCR estimator is obtained through the following transformation (Wang and Wu 2012):

$$y_t^+ = y_t - \left\{ \hat{\Sigma}^{-1} \hat{\Lambda}_2 \tilde{\beta} + \begin{pmatrix} 0 \\ \hat{\Omega}_{22}^{-1} \hat{\omega}_{21} \end{pmatrix} \right\}' \hat{\mu}_t \tag{5}$$

$$x_t^+ = x_t - \left(\hat{\Sigma}^{-1} \hat{\Lambda}_2 \right)' \hat{\mu}_t \tag{6}$$

where $\hat{\Lambda}_2 = \left(\hat{\Lambda}_{12}, \hat{\Lambda}_{22}' \right)' . \tilde{\beta}$ is a consistent estimator of β.

The following equation represents the study model for the CCR estimator:

$$CG_t = \beta_0 + \beta_1 Gini_t + \beta_2 GDPpc_t + \beta_3 Edu_t + \mu_t \tag{7}$$

After applying the FMOLS and CCR cointegration regression, the direction of causality between the variables was analysed, to do this, the panel causality test proposed by Dumitrescu and Hurlin (2012) was used. This test considers that the coefficients are different in the cross-sections, therefore, bivariate regressions are run for individual cross-sections and the average of the statistical tests are taken as the panel representation.

5 Results

5.1 Unit Root Test

This paper analyses the relationship between social capital (generalised trust), the Gini index, GDP pc, education (average number of years of education) and the causality among them. It was estimated whether social capital, Gini index, GDP pc and education have a unit root. Then, the cointegration test, the Fully Modified OLS and the Canonical Cointegrating Regression were applied followed finally by the panel Granger causality test.

Table 5 shows the Leven et al. (2002) test for unit root. The Gini index is not

Table 5 Panel unit test of Levin et al. (2002) for Gini Index, Social Capital, GDP pc and education

Variables	Level (Wt, bar)	1st difference
Gini index	−1.2430 (0.1069)	−2.1755 (0.0148) **
Social capital	−2.0794 (0.0188)	−10.5755 (0.0000) ***
GDP pc	3.0390 (0.9988)	−1.5199 (0.0643) *
Education	−5.1776 (0.000)	0.9104 (0.8187)

Note ***$p < 0.01$, **$p < 0.05$ and *$p < 0.1$ are the levels of significance, respectively

Table 6 Panel unit test of Im et al. (2003) for Gini index, social capital, GDP pc and education

Variables	Level (Wt, bar)	1st difference
Gini Index	0.8164 (0.7929)	−4.6313 (0.0000)***
Social capital	−0.7776 (0.2184)	−9.1899 (0.0000)***
GDP pc	3.4627 (0.9997)	−6.6793 (0.0000)***
Education	−1.5791 (0.0572)	−9.0842 (0.0000)***

Note ***$p < 0.01$, **$p < 0.05$ and *$p < 0.1$ are the levels of significance, respectively

Table 7 Panel unit test of Harris-Tzavalis (1999) for gini index, social capital, GDP pc and education

Harris-Tzavalis (1999) unit root test	Level		1st difference	
Variables	Rho			
	Statistic	*p*-value	Statistic	*p*-value
Gini Index	0.9847	0.1694	0.4115	0.0000***
Social capital	0.9791	0.0947	−0.4577	0.0000***
GDP pc	1.0070	0.6697	0.4039	0.0000***
Education	0.9899	0.2627	-0.0625	0.0000***

Note ***$p < 0.01$, **$p < 0.05$ and *$p < 0.1$ are the levels of significance, respectively

stationary at level so this variable has one-unit root. Social capital and GDP pc also have one-unit root and education are stationary at levels.

Table 6 shows the Im et al. (2003) test for unit root. The Gini index, Social Capital, GDP pc and education are not stationary at levels and these variables have one-unit root.

Table 7 shows the Harris-Tzavalis test for unit root. The Gini index, Social Capital, GDP pc and education are not stationary at levels and these variables have one-unit root.

Table 8 shows the Fisher-type test for unit root. The Gini index has one-unit root, Social Capital is stationary at levels and GDP pc and education have one-unit root.

Overall, it can be said that the four variables have one-unit root because the majority of the tests show that these variables are not stationary at levels. In the next section, the cointegration test will be applied.

5.2   Panel Cointegration Tests

Table 9 shows the cointegration test of Pedroni (2004). This test indicates that the variables of Eq. 1 are cointegrated. According to the Modified Phillips-Perron test, Phillips-Perron test and Augmented Dickey-Fuller test, all the variables of Eq. 1 are cointegrated.

Table 8 The fisher-type panel unit test (Choi 2001) for Gini index, social capital, GDP pc and education

Fisher-type (Choi 2001) unit root test			Level		1st difference	
			Statistic	p-value	Statistic	p-value
Gini Index	Inverse chi-squared (46)	P	38.3811	0.7801	105.3408	0.0000***
	Inverse normal	Z	1.4272	0.9232	−5.0949	0.0000***
	Inverse logit t (119)	L*	1.5401	0.9369	−5.3586	0.0000***
	Modified inv. chi-squared	Pm	−0.7943	0.7865	6.1867	0.0000***
Social capital	Inverse chi-squared (46)	P	115.1512	0.0000***	392.9233	0.0000
	Inverse normal	Z	−4.6681	0.0000***	−15.9552	0.0000
	Inverse logit t (119)	L*	−5.3781	0.0000***	−22.6072	0.0000
	Modified inv. chi-squared	Pm	7.2095	0.0000***	36.1693	0.0000
GDP pc	Inverse chi-squared (46)	P	42.5291	0.6184	122.4185	0.0000***
	Inverse normal	Z	0.3847	0.6498	−6.5100	0.0000***
	Inverse logit t (119)	L*	0.2846	0.6118	−6.6734	0.0000***
	Modified inv. chi-squared	Pm	−0.3619	0.6413	7.9672	0.0000***
Education	Inverse chi-squared (46)	P	67.9418	0.0193	134.6942	0.0000***
	Inverse normal	Z	−1.2330	0.1088	−5.9147	0.0000***
	Inverse logit t (119)	L*	−1.7557	0.0409	−6.6633	0.0000***
	Modified inv. chi-squared	Pm	2.2876	0.0111	9.2470	0.0000***

Note ***$p < 0.01$, **$p < 0.05$ and *$p < 0.1$ are the levels of significance, respectively

Table 10 shows the cointegration test of Westerlund (2007). According to the variance ratio, Social capital, Gini index, GDP pc and education are cointegrated.

Table 9 Panel cointegration test of Pedroni (2004)

Pedroni test (2004)		
	Statistic	p-value
Modified phillips-perron t	3.0404	0.0012***
Phillips-perron t	−12.4558	0.0000***
Augmented dickey-fuller t	−13.7756	0.0000***

Note ***p < 0.01, **p < 0.05 and *p < 0.1 are the levels of significance, respectively

Table 10 Panel cointegration test of Westerlund (2007)

Westerlund test		
	Statistic	p-value
Variance ratio	−2.9729	0.0015***

Note ***p < 0.01, **p < 0.05 and *p < 0.1 are the levels of significance, respectively

Table 11 Fully modified ordinary least squares (Social capital as dependent variable)

Variable	Coefficient	p-value
Gini index	−1.067799	0.006 ***
GDP pc	0.0005867	0.000***
Education	−0.0499649	0.975
R-squared	0.4485591	
Adj. Squared	0.4437006	

Note ***p < 0.01, **p < 0.05 and *p < 0.1 are the levels of significance, respectively

5.3 Results of Panel FMOLS and Causality

Table 11 shows the results of the Fully Modified Ordinary Least Squares of Eq. 1. According to this table, the Gini index negatively impacts on Social capital, because the coefficient is −1.06 and is significant. GDP pc positively impacts on Social capital, but the coefficient is small (0.0005) and significant. Education is not significant, and the R2 is 0.44.

Table 12 indicates the results of the Canonical Cointegration Regression of Eq. 1. The results are similar to Table 11 because the Gini index and GDP pc are significant, and the coefficient of the former is higher. Education is not significant and the R2 is 0.54.

Table 13 shows the Panel Granger Causality test. This table indicates that Social Capital impacts on the Gini index, but the Gini index also affects Social Capital. Thus, there is bidirectionality between these variables. GDP pc and Education have influence on Social Capital.

Table 12 Canonical cointegrating regression (social capital as dependent variable)

Variable	Coefficient	p-value
Gini index	−1.291109	0.002***
GDP pc	0.0005955	0.000***
Education	−0.7878758	0.633
R-squared	0.541157	
Adj. Squared	0.5381317	

Note ***$p < 0.01$, **$p < 0.05$ and *$p < 0.1$ are the levels of significance, respectively

Table 13 The results of panel granger causality

Dumitrescu and Hurlin (2012) Granger non-causality test results	Z-bar	
	Wald statistic	Valor p
Social capital does not Granger cause Gini	2.7904	0.0053***
Gini does not Granger cause social capital	3.9819	0.0001***
GDP pc does not Granger cause Social capital	11.6154	0.0000***
Social capital does not Granger cause GDP pc	1.5185	0.1289
Education does not Granger cause social capital	8.3254	0.0000***
Social capital does not Granger cause education	−0.0312	0.9751

Note ***$p < 0.01$, **$p < 0.05$ and *$p < 0.1$ are the levels of significance, respectively

6 Conclusions and Discussion

This paper aimed to estimate the relationship and the causality between social capital and inequality, GDP pc and education. The results show that there is bidirectionality between social capital and inequality because generalised trust impacts Gini index and the Gini index affects generalised trust. Education and GDP pc affect social capital, but social capital does not cause Education and GDP pc, therefore, in this case, there is no bidirectionality.

The results are in line with our argument because inequality affects generalised trust, due to the fact that higher levels of wage gaps give expectations that the system is unfair and the workers have no confidence in the rest of society. But also, low levels of social capital induce higher inequality because people do not consider the rest of society when doing their activities and labour unions are weak when the social capital of the community is low. Overall, our argument considered the bidirectionality between social capital and inequality and the findings of this paper confirmed this relationship.

Most of the studies focus on the effect of social capital on inequality or vice versa (Gustavsson and Jordah 2008; Bergh and Bjørnskov 2014; Shena and Bian 2018; Yang and Xin 2020). Those studies used structural equations, cross-temporal meta-analysis, the Poisson regression model and panel samples, and they found a negative relationship between social capital and inequality. We also found a negative relationship between these variables. However, the main difference between our paper and the others is that we find a bidirectional relationship between wage gaps and generalised trust.

The main weakness of the paper is that we only included OECD countries, of which the majority are developed countries. If we had included more developing countries the results could have been different, but many developing countries do not have enough data for all the variables.

Many research questions could emerge from our findings, but we consider that future research should be focused on the bidirectionality between social capital and inequality in developing countries, mainly in Latin America because it is the region with the highest levels of inequality in the world.

Our findings could be applied to public policies because if a national government promotes a policy to reduce inequality, it also impacts social capital, which means that trust in the rest of society will increase.

References

Alesina A. and La Ferrara, E., 2002. Who trusts others? Journal of Public Economics, [online] 85(2), pp. 207–234. Available at: https://www.sciencedirect.com/science/article/abs/pii/S00472 72701000846.

Álvarez-Botas, C. and González, V.M., 2021. Does trust matter for the cost of bank loans? Journal of Corporate Finance, [online] 66, p. 101791. Available at: https://doi.org/10.1016/j.jcorpfin.2020. 101791.

Aristóteles, 2005. La política. Madrid: Akal.

Atkinson, A.B., 2016. Desigualdad. ¿Què podemos hacer?. Primera ed. Mèxico: Fondo de Cultura Económica.

Axelrod, R., 1980. Effective Choice in the Prisoner's Dilemma. Journal of Conflict Resolution, [online] 24(1), pp. 1–25. Available at: https://doi.org/10.1177/002200278002400101.

Ayob, A.H., 2018. Diversity, Trust and Social Entrepreneurship. Journal of Social Entrepreneurship, [online] 9(1), pp. 1–12. Available at: https://doi.org/10.1080/19420676.2017.1399433.

Bandiera, O., Barankay, I. and Rasul, I., 2005. Cooperation in collective action. Economics of Transition, [online] 13(3), pp. 473–498. Available at: https://doi.org/10.1111/j.1468-0351.2005. 00228.x.

Bergh, A. and Bjørnskov, C., 2014. Trust, welfare states and income equality: Sorting out the causality. European Journal of Political, [online] 35, pp. 183–199. Available at: https://doi.org/ 10.1016/j.ejpoleco.2014.06.002

Buttrick, N.R., 2017. The psychological consequences of income inequality. The psychological consequences of income inequality, (January), pp. 1–12.

Cañizares, M., Barroso, I. and Alfonso, K., 2004. Datos incompletos: una mirada crítica para su manejo en estudios sanitarios. Gaceta sanitaria, [online] 18(1), pp. 58–63. Available at: https:// doi.org/10.1016/S0213-9111(04)72000-2

Carballo, D.M., Roscoe, P. and Feinman, G.M., 2014. Cooperation and Collective Action in the Cultural Evolution of Complex Societies. Journal of Archaeological Method and Theory, 21(1), pp. 98–133.

Clark, A.K., 2015. Rethinking the Decline in Social Capital. American Politics Research, 43(4), pp. 569–601.

Choi, I. 2001. Unit root tests for panel data. Journal of International Money and Finance 20: 249–272.

Cohen, G. and Ladaique, M., 2018. Drivers of Growing Income Inequalities in OECD and European Countries. In: C. Palgrave Macmillan, ed., Reducing Inequalities. pp. 31–43.

Costa Font, J., Hernandez Quevedo, C. and Jimenez Rubio, D., 2014. Economics and Human Biology Income inequalities in unhealthy lifestyles in England and Spain. Economics and Human Biology, 13, pp. 66–75.

d'Hombres, B., Leandro, E. and Webwer, A., 2013. Multivariate analysis of the effect of income inequality on health, social capital, and happiness Multivariate analysis of the effect of income inequality on health, social capital, and happiness. 978-92-79-35414-4

Dabla-norris, E., Kochhar, K., Ricka, F., Suphaphat, N. and Tsounta, E., 2015. Causes and Consequences of Income Inequality: A Global Perspective. International Monetary Fund.

Dai, T., Jiang, S., Sun, A., Wu, S. and Dai, T., 2018. Inequality and Social Capital: How Inequality in China's Housing Assets Affects People's Trust Inequality and Social Capital: How Inequality in China's Housing Assets Affects People's Trust. Emerging Markets Finance and Trade, [online] 00(00), pp. 1–14. Available at: https://doi.org/10.1080/1540496X.2018.1516637.

De Blasio, D.G. and Nuzzo, G., 2012. Questioni di Economia e Finanza. [online] Italia. Available at: https://www.bancaditalia.it/pubblicazioni/qef/2012-0116/index.html.

Doob, C.B., 2015. Desigualdad social y estratificación social en la sociedad estadounidense. Routledge.

Dumitrescu, E.I. and Hurlin, C., 2012. Testing for Granger non-causality in heterogeneous panels. Economic Modelling, [online] 29(4), pp. 1450–1460. Available at: https://doi.org/10.1016/j.econmod.2012.02.014.

Europan Social Survey, E., 2020. Data Base. [online] European Social Survey. Available at: https://www.europeansocialsurvey.org/data/themes.html?t=media.

Ferragina, E., 2013. The socio-economic determinants of social capital and the mediating effect of history: Making Democracy Work revisited. International Journal of Comparative Sociology, 54(1), pp. 48–73.

Fisher, R.A., 1932. Statistical Methods for Research Workers. 4th ed. Edinburgh: Oliver and Boyd.

Foster, C. and Frieden, J., 2017. Crisis of trust: Socio-economic determinants of Europeans' confidence in government. European Union Politics, [online] 18(4), pp. 511–535. Available at: https://doi.org/10.1177/1465116517723499.

Gasparini, L. and Lustig, N., 2012. Oxford Handbooks Online The Rise and Fall of Income Inequality in Latin America. In: The Oxford Handbook of Latin America Economics. Oxford University Press Inc, pp. 1–26.

Gavrilets, S., 2015. Collective action problem in heterogeneous groups. Philosophical Transactions of the Royal Society B: Biological Sciences, [online] 370(1683). Available at: https://doi.org/10.1098/rstb.2015.0016.

Geys, B. and Murdoch, Z., 2008. How to make head or tail of 'bridging' and 'bonding'?: addressing the methodological. The British Journal of Sociology, [online] 59(3), pp. 436–452. Available at: https://openresearch-repository.anu.edu.au/bitstream/1885/43276/2/DP511.pdf.

Graafland, J., 2018. Economic Freedom, Income Inequality and Life Satisfaction in OECD Countries. Journal of Happiness Studies, 19(7), pp. 2071–2093.

Gustavsson, M. and Jordahl, H., 2008. Inequality and trust in Sweden: Some inequalities are more harmful than others ☆. Journal of Public Economics, 92, pp. 348–365.

Harris, R.D.F. and Tzavalis, E., 1999. Inference for unit roots in dynamic panels where the time dimension is fixed. Journal of Econometrics, [online] 91(2), pp. 201–226. Available at: https://www.sciencedirect.com/science/article/abs/pii/S0304407698000761.

Human Development Report, U., 2020. Database. [online] Human Development Report. Available at: http://hdr.undp.org/en/data.

Iglič, H., Rözer, J. and Volker, B.G.M., 2020. Economic crisis and social capital in European societies: the role of politics in understanding short-term changes in social capital. European Societies, pp. 1–37.

Im, K.S., Pesaran, M.H. and Shin, Y., 2003. Testing for unit roots in heterogeneous panels. Journal of Econometrics, [online] 115(1), pp. 53–74. Available at: https://www.sciencedirect.com/science/article/abs/pii/S0304407603000927.

Knack, S. and Keefer, P., 1997. Does Social Capital Have an Economic Payoff? A Cross-Country. Quarterly Journal of Economics, [online] 112(4), pp. 1251–1288. Available at: http://www.jstor.org/stable/2951271 Accessed:.

Korpi, W., 2018. The democratic class struggle. Routledge.

Koutsou, S., Partalidou, M. and Ragkos, A., 2014. Young farmers' social capital in Greece: Trust levels and collective actions. Journal of Rural Studies, [online] 34, pp. 204–211. Available at: http://dx.doi.org/https://doi.org/10.1016/j.jrurstud.2014.02.002.

Latinobarómetro, 2020. Database. [online] Latinobarómetro. Available at: http://www.latinobarometro.org/lat.jsp.

Leigh, A., 2006. Centre for Economic Policy Research Trust, Inequality, and Ethnic Heterogeneity. The Australian National University, [online] (511), pp. 1–20. Available at: https://openresearch-repository.anu.edu.au/bitstream/1885/43276/2/DP511.pdf.

Levin, A., Lin, C.F. and Chu, C.S.J., 2002. Unit root tests in panel data: Asymptotic and finite-sample properties. Journal of Econometrics, [online] 108(1), pp. 1–24. Available at: https://www.sciencedirect.com/science/article/abs/pii/S0304407601000987.

Liu, H., Fan, J., Zhou, K. and Wang, Q., 2019. Exploring regional differences in the impact of high energy-intensive industries on CO_2 emissions: Evidence from a panel analysis in China. Environmental Science and Pollution Research, [online] 26(25), pp. 26229–26241. Available at: https://doi.org/10.1007/s11356-019-05865-w.

Milanovic, B., 2017. Desigualdad mundial. Un nuevo enfoque para la globalizaciòn. Primera ed. Mèxico: Fondo de Cultura Económica.

Norris, E.D., Kalpana, K., Suphaphiphat, N., Ricka, F. and Evridiki, T., 2015. Causes and Consequences of Income Inequality: A Global Perspective. International Monetary Fund, [online] pp. 1–39. Available at: https://www.elibrary.imf.org/doc/IMF006/22594-9781513555188/22594-9781513555188/Other_formats/Source_PDF/22594-9781513544373.pdf.

Obert, P., Theocharis, Y. and Deth, J.W. Van, 2018. Threats, chances and opportunities: social capital in Europe in times of social and economic hardship. Policy Studies, [online] 0(0), pp. 1–19. Available at: https://doi.org/10.1080/01442872.2018.1533109.

Organization for Economic Co-operation and Development, O., 2015. In It Together: Why Less Inequality Benefits All. Paris: OECD Publishing.

Organization for Economic Co-operation and Development, O., 2020. Database. [online] OECD. Available at: https://data.oecd.org/.

Ostrom, E. and Ahn, T.K., 2003. Una perspectiva del capital social desde las ciencias sociales: capital social y acción colectiva. Revista Mexicana de Sociología, [online] 65(1), pp. 155–233. Available at: http://www.scielo.org.mx/scielo.php?pid=S0188-25032003000100005&script=sci_abstract.

Parente, F., 2019. Inequality and social capital in the EU regions: a multidimensional analysis. Regional Studies, Regional Science, [online] 6(1), pp. 1–24. Available at: https://www.bancaditalia.it/pubblicazioni/qef/2012-0116/index.html.

Park, J.Y., 1992. Canonical cointegrating regressions. Econometrica 60.

Pedroni, P., 2004. Panel cointegration: Asymptotic and finite sample properties of pooled time series tests with an application to the PPP hypothesis. Econometric Theory, [online] 20(3), pp. 597–625. Available at: www.jstor.org/stable/3533533.

Phillips, P.C. and Hansen, B.E., 1990. Statistical Inference in Instrumental Variables Regression with I (1) Processes. The review of Economic Studies, [online] 57, pp. 99–125. Available at: https://academic.oup.com/restud/article-abstract/57/1/99/1610097.

Piketty, T., 2014. El capital en el siglo XXI. México: Fondo de cultura ecocómica.

Putnam, R., 2000. Bowling Alone: America's Declining Social Capital. New York: Simon & Schuster paperbacks.

Schneider, D., Hastings, O.P. and LaBriola, J., 2018. Income Inequality and Class Divides in Parental Investments. American Sociological Review, [online] 83(3), pp. 475–507. Available at: https://doi.org/10.1177/0003122418772034

Shen, J. and Bian, Y., 2018. The causal effect of social capital on income: A new analytic strategy. Social Networks, [online] 54, pp. 82–90. Available at: https://doi.org/10.1016/j.socnet.2018.01.004.

Solt, F., 2016. The Standardized World Income Inequality Database. Social Science Quarterly, [online] p.24. Available at: https://fsolt.org/papers/solt2016_pre.pdf.

Steijn, S. and Lancee, B., 2011. Does income inequality negatively affect general trust? Gini, growing inequalities impacts, [online] pp. 1–40. Available at: https://core.ac.uk/download/pdf/6273040.pdf.

Stiglitz, J.E., 2012. El precio de la desigualdad. El 1% tiene lo que el 99% necesita. Taurus.

Uslaner, E.M. and Brown, M., 2005. Inequality, trust, and civic engagement. American Politics Research, [online] 33(6), pp. 868–894. Available at: https://doi.org/10.1177/1532673X04271903#articleCitationDownloadContainer.

Vugt, M. Van and Cremer, D. De, 1999. Leadership in Social Dilemmas: The Effects of Group Identification on Collective Actions to Provide Public Goods. Journal of Personality and Social Psychology, [online] 76(4), pp. 587–599. Available at: https://psycnet.apa.org/record/1999-10970-006.

Wang, Q. and Wu, N., 2012. Long-run covariance and its applications in cointegration regression Qunyong. Stata Journal, [online] 12(3), pp. 515–542. Available at: https://doi.org/10.1177/1536867X1201200312.

Westerlund, J., 2007. Testing for error correction in panel data. Oxford Bulletin of Economics and Statistics, [online] 69(6), pp. 709–748. Available at: www.jstor.org/stable/3533533.

World Development Indicators, W., 2020. Database. [online] World Development Indicators. Available at: https://datacatalog.worldbank.org/dataset/world-development-indicators.

Yang, Z. and Xin, Z., 2020. Income inequality and interpersonal trust in China. Asian Journal of Social Psychology, 23(3), pp. 253–263.

The Jungle of Sustainability Frameworks and Standards: Evidence from European Listed Companies

Grazia Dicuonzo, Francesca Donofrio, and Simona Ranaldo

Abstract In the last decade, corporate reporting has undergone a radical transformation, adding sustainability reporting to traditional financial reporting. The Barnier Directive (2014/95/EU) introduced into European law the obligation for large public-interest entities to prepare and publish a non-financial statement. This document must contain information relating to the environment, the social sphere, employee matters, respect for human rights, and the fight against active and passive corruption, aimed at ensuring an understanding of the company's activities, performance, results, and impact. Indeed, to date, managers consider it necessary to adopt a holistic approach, considering both financial and non-financial aspects, to ensure the protection of the creation of corporate value. On April 2021, the European Commission adopted a proposal of Corporate Sustainability Reporting Directive (CSRD) aiming at improving sustainability reporting in order to contribute to the transition towards a fully sustainable and inclusive economic and financial system. In this context, the topic of sustainability reporting has become relevant for companies. This paper reviews the main frameworks and standards developed by international standards available to companies, investigating the level of adoption by a sample of European listed companies.

Keywords Framework · International standard setter · Sustainability · Reporting

JEL Classification Q56 · M10 · G30

This chapter represents the results of a joint research project carried out by the three authors. However, the various paragraphs of the paper are divided as follows: paragraphs 1 "Introduction", 2.1 "A preliminary overview", 2.2 "Global Reporting Initiative", 2.3 "Sustainability Accounting Standards Board" and 6 "Conclusion" G. Dicuonzo; paragraph 2.4 "Carbon Disclosure Project", 2.5 "Climate Disclosure Standards Board", 3 "Literature review" and 4 "Methodology" F. Donofrio; paragraphs 2.6 "Task Force on Climate-related Financial Disclosures", 2.7 "International Integrated Reporting Council", 4 "Methodology" and 5 "Results and discussion" S. Ranaldo.

G. Dicuonzo · F. Donofrio (✉) · S. Ranaldo
Department of Economics, Management and Business Law, University of Bari Aldo Moro, Largo Abbazia di Santa Scolastica n. 53, 70124 Bari, Italy
e-mail: francesca.donofrio@uniba.it

1   Introduction

Companies' focus on sustainability is growing steadily and nowadays it is the most important factor to ensure a competitive advantage. The United Nations' Sustainable Development Goals (SDGs) are guiding companies in integrating sustainability measures into their operations and business models. With the development and—totally voluntary—adherence of organisations to different frameworks (Mauro et al. 2020; Nawaz and Koç 2018; Raza et al. 2019), legislation is also increasingly focusing on the disclosure of non-financial information in order to meet the growing demand for transparency from all stakeholders (Aras and Crowther 2008; Girella et al. 2019; Vaz et al. 2016). At the European level, Directive 2014/95/EU (NFRD) on non-financial and diversity information, requires companies to disclose information on social and human rights, the environment, anti-corruption, and diversity policies on the composition of management and supervisory boards by large companies and groups and public-interest entities (Makarenko 2017). Recently, the European Commission has published a proposal of Corporate Sustainability Reporting Directive (CSRD) with the aim to improve information on sustainability issue and to amend the existing reporting requirements of the NFRD.

Disclosure and measurement of sustainability performance are now considered a fundamental part of effective business management, essential to maintaining customers and stakeholder confidence in the business (Aras and Crowther 2008; Badia et al. 2019a). In this regard, sustainability reporting is a process of collecting and disclosing non-financial data on a company's performance, including environmental, social, labour, and ethical issues, while setting sustainability measures, indicators, and targets based on the company's strategy (Deloitte 2015; Makarenko 2017; Pranugrahaning et al. 2021). However, the complexity surrounding sustainability reporting has made it difficult to develop a comprehensive and unified solution for corporate reporting. To this end, five leading organisations in sustainability and integrated reporting (CDP, CDSB, GRI, IIRC, and SASB) have co-published a shared vision of the elements needed for more comprehensive corporate reporting along with a joint statement of intent to drive towards this goal (CDP; CDSB; GRI; IIRC; SASB 2020a). In order to achieve this goal, the five organisations have committed to working with key players, including IOSCO, IFRS, the European Commission, and the International Business Council of the World Economic Forum (CDP; CDSB; GRI; IIRC; SASB 2020b).

Based on these premises, it is clear that the topic of sustainability reporting is becoming highly relevant in the field of corporate responsibility (Girella et al. 2019). This paper reviews the main frameworks developed by international standard setters and other organisations. Furthermore, by adopting the methodology of content analysis, this work investigates the level of adoption of different sustainability frameworks and standards by companies listed in the Eurostoxx 50, and it explores the level of accuracy and depth of the information disclosed.

The article is structured as follows: Sect. 2 presents the review of the main frameworks and standards that support sustainable reporting, which have been developed over time; Sect. 3 presents the literature review; Sect. 4 describes the sample and methodology; Sect. 5 shows the results of the empirical analysis; finally, Sect. 6 discusses the conclusions, implications, and future lines of research.

2 Sustainability Standards and Frameworks

2.1 A Preliminary Overview

Today, there are several guidelines for providing sustainability information. As is well known, companies do not have financial responsibilities alone, as they must, above all, operate in a socially responsible manner. In particular, we talk about organizational sustainability that, according to the triple bottom line (TBL) perspective, includes three components represented by the natural environment, society, and economic performances (Elkington 2004). According to this approach, in addition to focusing on economic performance, companies must also engage in activities that positively affect the environment and society. In other words, as defined by the European Commission, corporate social responsibility means the ability of companies to integrate "*on a voluntary basis social and environmental concerns into their business operations and their interaction with their stakeholders*" (Commission of The European Communities 2001). Among the initiatives that guide the sustainability performance measurement process and the relative disclosure, the Global Reporting Initiative (GRI), the Sustainability Accounting Standards Board (SASB), the Carbon Disclosure Project (CDP), and the Climate Disclosure Standards Board (CDSB) define the frameworks and standards for sustainability reporting, including climate-related reporting, together with the recommendations of the Task Force on Climate-related Financial Disclosures (TCFD). Finally, IIRC provides the integrated reporting framework that links sustainability reporting to financial and other capital reporting (Coulson et al. 2015). The following paragraphs analyse these frameworks in detail (Fig. 1).

Fig. 1 New corporate reporting. *Source* Author elaboration

2.2 Global Reporting Initiative

The Global Reporting Initiative (GRI) is a non-profit organisation, founded in 1997 with the aim of creating a useful support system for reporting on the sustainable performance of organisations of all sizes, encompassing all sectors and countries in the world.

GRI's mission is to make sustainability reporting a widespread practice for all organisations, helping them apply sustainability reporting through guides and tools. It is based on extensive networking, involving thousands of professionals and organisations from many sectors, constituencies, and regions. Over the years, the work and importance of GRI has been progressively developed, as evidenced by the evolution of the 'sectoral' standards produced.

First published in 2000, the GRI Guidelines (G1) provided the first global framework for sustainability reporting. In 2002, GRI launched the first update of the Guidelines (G2). As demand and acceptance for GRI reporting continued to grow, the guidelines were expanded and improved, leading to G3 (2006) and G4 (2013). In 2016, GRI moved from preparing guidelines to establishing (by the Global Sustainability Standards Board—GSSB) the first global standards for sustainability reporting (GRI Standards), which saw a reorganisation of the content of the previous GRI G4 Guidelines, taking on a crucial role in sustainability reporting. The standards provide information on how to prepare a sustainability report.

This information is outlined in the 100 Series of Universal Standards (Global Reporting Initiative 2016), which outlines both the Reporting Principles for defining the content of the report (Stakeholder Inclusivity, Sustainability Context, Materiality, and Completeness) and the Reporting Principles for defining the quality of the report (Accuracy, Balance, Clarity, Comparability, Reliability, and Timeliness). The other two universal standards, GRI 102—General Disclosures and GRI 103—Management Practices, help provide information on the organisational context, as well as on reporting and management practices. The GRIs are divided into four series (Global Reporting Initiative 2020): GRI 100—Universal Standards; GRI 200—Economic Issues; GRI 300—Environmental Issues; and GRI 400—Social Issues. However, the flexibility of the GRI allows only certain standards, or parts of their content, to be used for reporting specific information.

2.3 Sustainability Accounting Standards Board

The Sustainability Accounting Standards Board (SASB) is a not-for-profit organisation, founded in 2011 by Jean Rogers. Investors, lenders, insurance underwriters, and other providers of financial capital are increasingly attuned to the impact of environmental, social, and governance (ESG) factors on the financial performance of companies, driving the need for standardised reporting of ESG data.

Specifically, the SASB's stated mission is to set out industry-specific disclosure standards on ESG topics which facilitate communication between companies and investors on information that is financially relevant and useful for decision-making. This must be relevant, reliable, and comparable information among companies on a global basis.

SASB operates with a set of core principles that guide its approach to setting standards, as defined in its Conceptual Framework. These principles are as follows: (i) global applicability of sustainability disclosures; (ii) financial materiality; and (iii) standard-setting approach (sector-specific, evidence-based, and market-informed). With particular regard to the sector-specific approach, the SASB has developed a unique set of standards for each sector. Finally, SASB identifies qualitative and quantitative metrics, indications of alignment with other standards, such as GRI and CDP, or with frameworks, procedures, or regulations from other national and international organisations that can improve the reporting of the standard.

2.4   Carbon Disclosure Project

The Carbon Disclosure Project (CDP) is an international non-profit organisation that promotes one of the most important reporting systems in the private sector. The CDP encourages companies and governments to reduce their greenhouse gas emissions in order to protect water security and deforestation, providing its users with data and an overview of the risks and opportunities related to these issues. For example, section C.2 of the CDP framework, entitled "risks and opportunities", provides for the disclosure of information regarding the potential positive impacts on an organisation of efforts to mitigate and adapt to climate change, or the negative impacts of climate change on an organisation, resulting for example from extreme weather events.

Through the provision of distributing questionnaires to companies, cities, states, and regions, in full or minimized versions, depending on the size and activity of the company, organisations disclose their strategies for measuring emissions and managing environmental risks. The questionnaire is structured into fourteen modules, plus one module presented only to organisations that are responding to an explicit request from a client. These modules are Introduction, Governance, Risks and Opportunities, Business Strategy, Targets and Performance, Emissions Methodology, Emissions Data, Emissions Breakdown, Energy, Additional Metrics, Verification, Carbon Pricing, Engagement Strategies, and Sectoral Approach. At the end of each year, the CDP publishes the score achieved by each member organisation, ranging from a level 'A' ("Leadership") to a level 'D' ("Disclosure").

2.5 Climate Disclosure Standards Board

The Climate Disclosure Standards Board (CDSB) is an international consortium of not-for-profit organisations, consisting of nine NGOs committed to establishing a global corporate reporting model for environmental and climate information. The CDSB seeks to standardise the reporting of environmental information by unifying the most widely accepted and tested reporting approaches that are emerging around the world. The CDSB Framework has been prepared in line with financial reporting objectives and approaches offered by other organisations, integrating these with environmental and climate change information.

The first CDSB Framework, the Climate Change Reporting Framework, was published in 2010, and it focused on the effects of climate change—in terms of risks and opportunities—on business strategy and financial performance. In 2013, the CDSB decided to expand the scope of the framework beyond climate change and greenhouse gas (GHG) emissions, also incorporating environmental information and natural capital. Since its initial publication in 2015, the CDSB Framework has been refined and updated to better meet the needs of the market. The latest update of the CDSB Framework (CDSB 2019) was in December 2019.

The framework contains seven principles or guiding principles to be applied in the determination, preparation, and presentation of all environmental information reported in accordance with the twelve reporting requirements. These principles define the environmental information that must be reported, and, for each of them, there is a threshold prescribed by the regulatory authorities to which the organisation itself adheres. Based on this framework, the CDBS aligns with financial reporting standards, as well as IASB principles and proposals, regulatory references, and guidelines from national and international organisations (CDSB 2020).

2.6 Task Force on Climate-Related Financial Disclosures

In the field of corporate reporting, the establishment of the Task Force on Climate-related Financial Disclosures (TCFD) is of great help to investors, lenders, and insurers to appropriately assess risks and opportunities with a unique climate focus. It consists of 32 international members, a broad audience of professionals and experts from the financial and insurance sectors, large non-financial corporations, accounting and consulting firms, and rating agencies.

Established in 2015 by the Financial Stability Board (FSB), at the request of the G20 Finance Ministers and Central Bank Governors, the TCFD aims to develop mutually consistent voluntary disclosures and recommendations on climate-change-related financial risks. It is an important resource for integrating corporate disclosures, aligning with investors' expectations and needs with respect to physical, liability, and transition risks.

The Task Force encourages all organisations, according to their sectors, to implement its recommendations outlined in the 2017 Final Report (TCFD 2017). The recommendations, supported by the seven principles for effective disclosure (TCFD 2017), are divided into four thematic areas: governance, strategy, risk management, and metrics.

2.7 International Integrated Reporting Council

The International Integrated Reporting Council (IIRC) is a global body that has established an International Integrated Reporting Framework suitable for all types of organisations, with the intention of determining how value is created over time. By describing the links between strategy, governance, performance, and prospects of the company, the reports demonstrate the value creation process of the company. In addition, these reports describe how capital transformation is influenced by the performance of business activities, as well as the realisation of outputs, the interaction of internal and external factors, the way they are managed, and the impact on the organisation in the short, medium, and long term.

The relationships and resources of the company affect its ability to continue its business and to create value over the short, medium and long term. These resources are called 'capital' in the Framework, and they are divided into financial, manufactured, intellectual, human, and social and relationship categories.

In order to prepare an integrated report, it is essential to give detailed information on different factors that influence the ability to create value. The company's business model is shaped not only by its internal organisation, but also by its interaction with the external environment and the resulting risks and opportunities. In particular, among the factors that influence the external environment, the new IIRC framework (IIRC 2021) highlights: stakeholder needs and interests; macro and micro economic conditions; market forces; technological change; social issues; environmental issues (e.g. climate change, loss of ecosystems and resource scarcity), the legislative environment and the political environment. Value creation, therefore, is influenced by a set of factors that impact the company's business with varied intensity and that can be facilitated through the materiality matrix. A factor is said to be material when it substantially influences the company's ability to create value in the reference period. The identification of such a factor makes it possible to avoid information overload, and making the value management process more robust.

3 Literature Review

The growing concern of consumers and stakeholders, regarding the social and environmental impact of companies' actions, has driven forward the interest of companies towards the focus on Corporate Social Responsibility (CSR) (Lokuwaduge and

Heenetigala 2017). In truth, the problem of measuring Corporate Social Responsibility, according to the "Triple Bottom Line" or "People, Planet, Profit" approach (Elkington 1997), referring to companies' ability to harmonize their efforts to be economically viable, ecologically sound, and socially responsible, dates back to the 1990s. Subsequently, the concept of CSR moved toward a "stakeholder model," becoming the overall goal of companies to meet the legal, ethical, social, and environmental expectations of stakeholders (Badia et al. 2019b; Raynard and Forstater 2002). Specifically, some studies revealed that companies with better CSR performance are also the most attentive to stakeholder expectations. In business management systems, attention to stakeholders has become crucial for companies and often the development of positive relationships with these actors can bring increased value to the firm (Renneboog et al. 2008). In fact, for several years now, there has been an exponential increase in consumers' awareness of the importance of their respective purchasing choices, focusing more on production systems and values conveyed by the brand (Najah and Jarboui 2013).

Essentially, for these reasons, more and more companies are combining financial reporting with non-financial reporting, highlighting the company's performance with reference to ESG practices and, therefore, regarding environmental, social, and governance aspects (Tarmuji et al. 2016). At the regulatory level, institutions, such as the Global Reporting Initiative (GRI) or the International Integrated Reporting Council (IIRC), along with standard-setters, such as the Sustainability Accounting Standards Board (SASB), have developed guidelines for required information included in corporate reporting.

The directive issued by the European Union (2014/95/EU) made non-financial disclosure mandatory for the largest European companies as of January 1, 2017, in order to ensure a minimum level of disclosure (La Torre et al. 2018). The choice of introducing rules that promote corporate transparency—to allow stakeholders to have a wider set of information to support their decision-making processes—is related to the fact that, by itself, corporate self-regulation could generate information asymmetries (Hess 2007) as well as induce the overestimating of irresponsible actions (Lopatta et al. 2016). In this regard, some studies have shown that while the European directive will lead to an increase in CSR activities, it is not guaranteed to reduce levels of corporate social irresponsibility (Jackson et al. 2020).

The tools available to companies to ensure greater disclosure transparency on these issues are substantiated by frameworks and standards (e.g., OECD Guidelines for Multinational Enterprises, Global Reporting Initiative—GRI Guidelines) that provide guidance in the preparation of this disclosure (Aureli et al. 2019). However, the presence of different types of recommendations and requirements governing non-financial disclosure limits the comparability of statements (European Commission 2017). Among other critical findings, the NFRD does not provide a precise definition of non-financial information, merely presenting examples of "non-financial information" as well as references to their rather generic interpretation (Haller et al. 2017). This, in addition to making the issue of mandatory or voluntary reporting unclear (Doni et al. 2019), confuses stakeholders' perceptions about the meaning of non-financial information disseminated (Stubbs and Higgins 2018).

Since the effectiveness of regulatory intervention is closely linked to its degree of specification (Baldwin et al. 2011), the effectiveness of the disclosure process could be compromised (Bini et al. 2017). At the same time, the introduction of a mandatory reporting system could lead companies to produce qualitatively poor non-financial statements, while remaining compliant with current regulations (Doni et al. 2019). In other words, the use of a standardized reporting system does not preclude that an increase in the number of disclosures is matched by an increase in the quality of the information disclosed—there remains a risk that some of the specific information required may not be applicable to the specific business sector (Brown et al. 2009).

With respect to the quality of non-financial disclosure, it is often difficult to measure (Venturelli et al. 2019). Initially, the concept of quality was associated with the quantity of information communicated, accepted as an effective proxy for quality; subsequently, the notion of quantity and quality were referred to indiscriminately (Beretta and Bozzolan 2008; Marston and Shrives 1991). Nevertheless, the disclosure of non-financial information is the tool through which the company manages to satisfy a broader category of stakeholders, other than investors, by providing insights regarding the overall strategy (Du and Yu 2020). In addition, non-financial disclosure not only increases the accuracy of analysts' forecasts, but it also influences the financial performance of firms (Dawn et al. 2002). This increase in financial performance can also be attributed to improving employee well-being as a result of CSR implementation, thereby fostering greater productivity (Edmans 2011).

Finally, other studies have shown that CSR disclosure is valued by the stock market, representing an opportunity for firms to also communicate future prospects and their commitment to the market (Benlemlih et al. 2020).

In light of the above considerations, there is a clear need to understand the level of adoption of the various sustainability frameworks and standards developed over time. More precisely, also based on the letter of intent signed in September 2020 by the five international leading organisations in sustainability and integrated reporting, the convergence of companies towards a single framework or standard for sustainability is desirable.

In this sense, our study intends to answer the following research question:

RQ: *Which frameworks, standards or guidelines are companies adopting for sustainability reporting?*

4 Methodology

The analysis focuses on companies belonging to the EURO STOXX 50 (see Appendix A). We have chosen the Euro Stoxx 50 index for two main reasons. First of all, the Euro Stoxx 50 is the most widely used index in the literature (Brechmann and Czado 2013; Chen et al. 2018). Secondly, it replicates the performance of the 50 largest capitalization companies in the Eurozone.

The index includes the most highly regarded European institutions operating in different sectors (Chart 1): technology (14%), consumer cyclicals (20%), basic materials (8%), consumer non-cyclicals (12%), utilities (10%), healthcare (6%), financial (16%), real estate (2%), and industrial (12%).

As of 30 October 2020, 16% of the index is represented by ASML Holding NV, LVMH Moët Hennessy, Louis Vuitton, and Linde plc, which are the largest holdings in the EURO STOXX 50. In order to achieve our research goal, a quantitative analysis was conducted to summarize the adoption level of a sustainability standard framework by companies belonging to Euro Stoxx50.

Adopting the content analysis approach, we analysed all official documents of Euro Stoxx 50 companies on sustainability reporting and disclosure in 2020 (Annual Report, Integrated Report, Sustainability Report, Climate Change Report, etc.; see Table 1) in order to understand the progress of adoption of the different sustainability frameworks developed over time. Content analysis is a systematic and guided technique for analysing information contained in textual data (Mayring 2000). There are several types of content analysis, including quantitative and qualitative methods, whose common element concerns the systematic categorization of textual data, giving a comprehensive meaning (Huberman and Miles 1994).

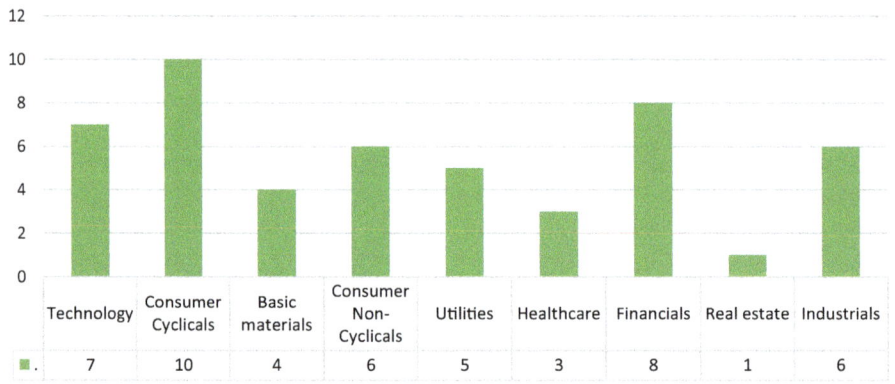

	Technology	Consumer Cyclicals	Basic materials	Consumer Non-Cyclicals	Utilities	Healthcare	Financials	Real estate	Industrials
▪.	7	10	4	6	5	3	8	1	6

Chart 1   Number of analysed companies by sector. *Source* Author processing

Table 1   Source of documents

Document type	No
Annual report	34
Integrated report	8
Sustainability report	5
Non-financial statement	1
NA for 2020	2
Total	50

Source Author processing

In other words, the method of content analysis has been defined as "a way to systematize the understanding of the text," or as "the application of scientific methods to document evidence." The best-known definition is provided by Krippendorff (2004): the content analysis method represents a "research technique aimed at making valid and replicable inferences by third parties to the contexts of their use." The analysis involves a classification of the text units into categories, developed through eight consequential phases:

1. definition of the categories used to encode the text;
2. definition of the recording units (e.g., words, phrases, or themes);
3. preliminary test of a small sample;
4. evaluation of the reliability of the coding;
5. revision of the coding rules;
6. possible repetition of steps 3, 4, and 5 to ensure a satisfactory level of reliability;
7. text encoding;
8. assessment of the reliability achieved.

Through the analysis of the documents available on the analysed companies' websites, 11 of them contained no information on sustainability reporting. More precisely, although all the companies in the sample state that they pay attention to sustainability and that their strategy is oriented towards protecting and safeguarding the environment, these 11 companies make no specific reference to the framework used for sustainable reporting. Furthermore, for 2 of the analysed companies, sustainability reports for the year 2020 are not available. Thus, our final sample consists of 37 companies.

Initially, we analysed the sustainability frameworks and standards adopted by each company. Specifically, on the basis of existing literature, we identified the following initiatives: GRI, SASB, CDP, CDSB, TCFD, and IIRC; each benchmark is valued 1, for each framework, in the case of adoption by companies. The following section describes the results of our analysis.

5 Results and Discussion

As previously mentioned, 37 companies—belonging to nine different sectors—were examined (as stated earlier, 13 companies were excluded due to lack of information). The companies examined adopt different sustainable reporting standards, individually or in combination. Considering the adoption of the frameworks and standards individually, 31 of the sampled companies (84%) adopt the GRI guidelines; 16 companies (43%) follow the SASB; 12 companies (32%) participate in the CDP; 18 companies (49%) follow the TCFD; and finally, 6 companies (16%) prepare their annual report following the IIRC framework. It is important to note that none of the companies in the sample follow the standards set by the Climate Disclosure Standards Board. Conversely, 84% of the examined companies adopt GRI. This percentage can be justified by the fact that GRI can be used to compare organisational

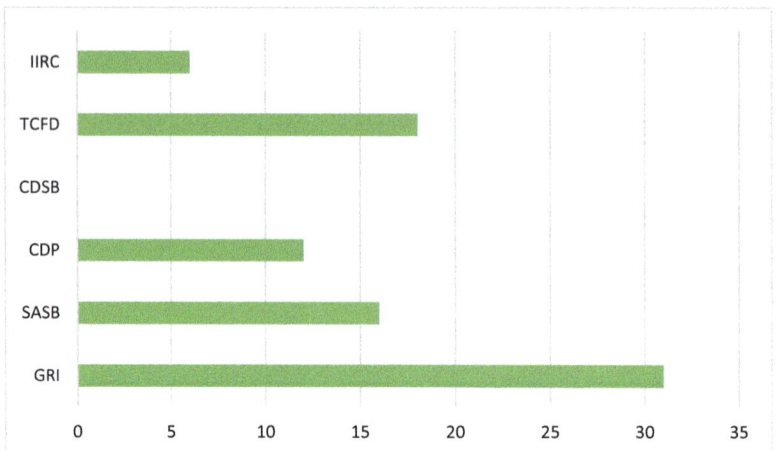

Chart 2 Adoption of each framework by companies. *Source* Author processing

performance with laws, regulations, codes, performance standards, and voluntary initiatives, demonstrating organisational commitment to sustainable development, and then comparing organisational performance over time. In addition, the relevance of GRIs is justified by the external assurance provided in GRI Disclosure 102–56. This assurance consists of activities designed to publish conclusions about the quality of the report and the information it contains to increase decision-makers' confidence in the accuracy and reliability of the information reported (Chart 2).

Furthermore, of the 31 companies that adopted the Global Reporting Initiative, 15 also publish additional sustainability information according to the specific requirements of the Sustainability Accounting Standards Board; 9 companies participate in the Carbon Disclosure Project; 14 companies use the evaluation guidelines of the Task Force on Climate-related Financial Disclosures; and 3 companies adopt the model of the International Integrated Reporting Council.

A high percentage of companies (49%) also chose to align climate-related disclosures, including risks, opportunities, governance, objectives, and scenario analysis, according to the guidance of the Task Force on Climate-related Financial Disclosures (TCFD) as part of the CDP report. For example, ASML Holding N.V. measures its progress in reducing emissions by monitoring the outcomes of three key performance indicators in this regard, participating in the annual evaluation of the Carbon Disclosure Project (CDP). Notably, the company in question achieved a score of "C" in the most recent CDP Climate Change 2020 assessment, corresponding to the industry's average level.

Clearly, the analysis shows that companies are leaning toward the adoption of multiple sustainability frameworks in order to (i) ensure full compliance with ethical principles, according to which a company is concerned, to have minimal impact on the world around it, while (ii) responding to real evolving market trends and, consequently, stakeholders needs.

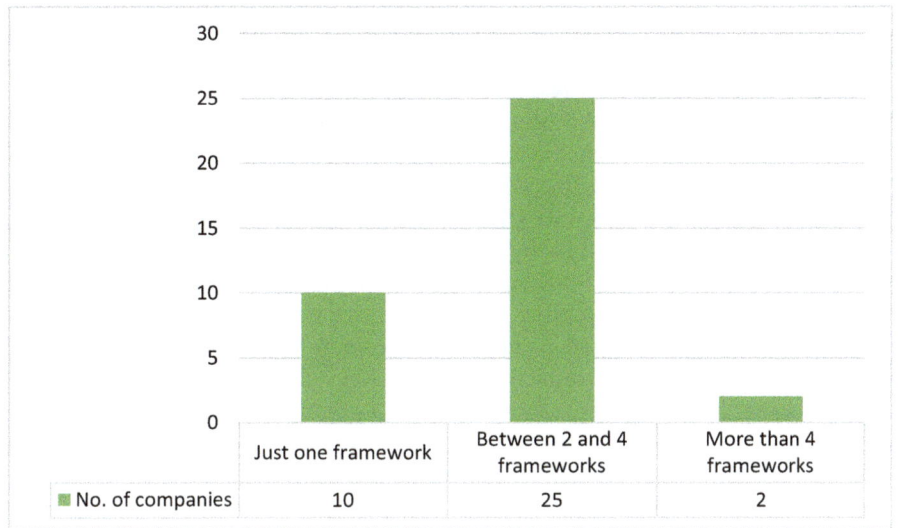

Chart 3 Number of frameworks adopted by each company. *Source* Author processing

The following graph shows the number of sustainable reporting frameworks adopted by each company in the sample (Chart 3).

Only 10 of the considered companies adopt a single framework. Specifically, 8 companies (Siemens Ag, Essilorluxottica, Vonovia Se, Volkswagen Ag, Amadeus It Group S.A., BMW Ag, ENI S.p.A., and Anheuser-Busch Inbev) have decided to adopt the GRI guidelines for sustainable disclosure; 1 company (Danone) participates in the Carbon Disclosure Project; and 1 company (Koninklijke Philips N.V.) prepares its annual report according to the IIRC framework.

Among companies adopting a single framework, 3 operate solely in the Consumer Non-cyclicals sector or in the Consumer Cyclicals sector, while the Healthcare, Real Estate, Technology, and Utilities sectors only have one company each operating.

Findings also reveal that 25 companies adopt between 2 and 4 sustainability frameworks. Among these, the most common combination is the adoption of GRI guidelines and SASB recommendations. This is justified by the fact that the GRI guidelines and the SASB together could offer companies and their stakeholders a comprehensive view of how companies can create value for shareholders and, at the same time, also help to create the conditions for sustainable development. These frameworks and standards, although designed for different purposes, are complementary. Indeed, GRI examines the company's impact on the world, and SASB examines the impact of the world on the company. In particular, 14 companies adopt two types of frameworks, and, among these, 5 operate in the Financial sector, 1 in the Consumer Non-cyclicals sector, 1 in the Utilities sector, 1 in the Healthcare sector, 2 in Consumer Cyclicals sector, 1 in the Technology sector, 2 in the Industrial sector, and 1 in the Basic Material sector.

Of the firms using 3 frameworks, 3 companies operate in the Technology sector, 1 in the Utilities sector, 1 in the Basic Material sector, 1 in the Consumer Cyclicals sector, and 1 in the Consumer Non-cyclicals sector.

Only 3 companies adopt 4 frameworks, with 2 companies operating in the Industrial sector (Schneider Electric Se and Vinci) and 1 operating in the Utilities sector (Iberdrola, S.A.). Finally, 2 of the selected companies adopt 5 different frameworks, reporting according to GRI, SASB, CDP, TCFD, and IR standards (SAP SE, operating in the Technology sector, and BASF SE, operating in the Basic Material sector).

From the analysis of SAP SE and BASF SE reports, in response to increasing regulatory pressure for a reporting standard for environmental, social, and governance criteria, and as recommended by the Greenhouse Gas Protocol and CDP, SAP SE actively seeks the best available quality and standards that support renewable energy projects, meeting robust criteria in terms of environmental integrity, stakeholder inclusiveness, reporting, and verification. For example, BASF's report has been based on GRI guidelines and standards since 2003, then applying the "Comprehensive" option since their 2017 report. The company has been active in the International Integrated Reporting Council (IIRC) since 2014 and has outlined the circular economy programmes and projects as well as adopting plans to reduce CO_2 emissions. In addition, the company issued its first green bond in 2020, gaining recognition from analysts and investors regarding the quality of financial market communications issued by the company.

In this sense, the results allow us to state that the use of different types of frameworks and standards is aimed at improving the quality of disclosure, which also involves obtaining recognition and awards, while improving the corporate image. At the level of sectoral analysis, no specific sector dominates among companies that adopt 4 or 5 frameworks. This evidence does not allow us to identify a correlation between the sector the firm belongs to and the number of adopted executives.

Finally, among the companies adopting GRI guidelines, we analysed which specific GRIs they adopt. The following figure (Fig. 2) shows the level of adoption of each GRI standard by the selected companies. As mentioned above, 31 companies adopt the GRI guidelines. In order to report correctly, three universal standards must be met. For specific topics, however, there is no obligation to comply with all of them. Clearly, the more topics there are, the more complete the report is, but the number of principles and disclosures to which an organisation complies depends on its material topics. Material topics are defined as "those topics that reflect the organisation's significant economic, environmental, and social impact or that have a profound effect on the assessments and decisions of stakeholders," the identification of which is described in the methodological note, as well as deriving from the application of the specific series of disclosures and references to GRI 103 for general disclosures on management methods.

With regard to universal standards, on the one hand, in all documents reviewed we highlighted the reference to the GRI-101 standard. This is justified by the fact that GRI 101 (Foundation) applies to any organisation that wishes to use the GRI Standards to report on its economic, environmental, and/or social impacts. Furthermore, in 25 of the analysed reports there is a specific reference to the adoption of GRI 102, with

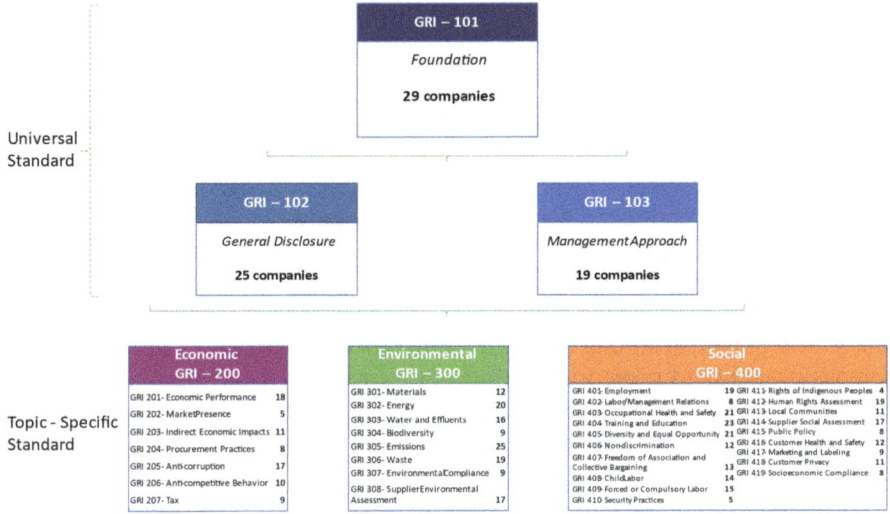

Fig. 2 Analysis of 2016 GRI standards. *Source* Author processing

19 referencing adoption to GRI 103. In other words, GRI 102 (General Disclosures) sets reporting requirements on contextual information about an organisation and its sustainability reporting practices, and GRI 103 (Management Approach) sets reporting requirements on the approach used by an organisation to manage a material issue.

Regarding the specific part, each organisation has its own material themes, the title of which may coincide with, or be very similar to, that of the GRI principles and from each of which derives the application of one or more principles and disclosures of the specific series, referencing GRI 103 for disclosures on how to precisely manage these material themes. In relation to the Topic-Specific Standards, the standard belonging to 200, 300, and 400 series are used to report information on an organisation's impacts related to economic, environmental, and social issues. For the Economic series, the most widely adopted Standards are Economic Performance (GRI 101), Market Presence (GRI 202), Indirect Economic Impacts (GRI 203), Procurement Practices (GRI 204), Anti-corruption (GRI 205), and Anti-competitive Behaviour (GRI 206). The most widely used standards in the Environmental series (GRI 300) are GRI 302 and 303 (Energy; Water and Effluents), GRI 305 (Emissions), and GRI 306 (Waste).

Finally, regarding the social sphere, the standards most used by the companies in the sample are GRI 403, 404, and 405. Of particular interest is the result for GRI 403 (Occupational Health and Safety), which sets out the reporting requirements for occupational health and safety. This standard is effective for reports published on or after 1 January 2021; however, since 2018 (year of issue), GRI has encouraged early adoption. An examination of the results shows that 21 out of 31 companies have already adopted this standard for the 2020 report.

6 Conclusion

The disclosure and measurement of sustainability performance in recent years has become fundamentally important. It is a new aspect of all-encompassing corporate reporting, one that increasingly needs to be reported and measured if it is to be accredited and consolidated in practice. Such an approach requires not only reporting financial, environmental, social, and governance results through a single tool, but also directing the company's work towards a new approach to "integrated thinking."

After the European Directive on "Non-financial Information" was issued, it seems clear that—with what can be defined as a real leap forward imposed by the legislation—Corporate Reporting has increasingly taken on the task of describing the company's ability to relate to its stakeholders, integrating economic and financial performance with ESG performance. Over time, different frameworks and standards have been developed to support sustainable corporate reporting. Most recently, in September 2020, CDP, CDSB, GRI, IIRC, and SASB co-published a shared vision of the elements required for more comprehensive corporate reporting.

Given the importance of non-financial reporting, together with the complexity and variety of the different frameworks and standards developed over time, the European Commission has entrusted the European Financial Reporting Advisory Group (EFRAG) with the development of new sustainability standards, requesting consistency with the European Green Deal and the existing legal framework in Europe. This paper, after analysing the existing literature on sustainability reporting and the main frameworks developed by international standards, investigated the level of adoption of different sustainability frameworks by companies listed in the Stoxx 50.

From our analysis, the most widespread standards are those of the Global Reporting Initiative (GRI). The results clearly show that companies are moving towards the adoption of multiple sustainability frameworks in order to (i) ensure full compliance with ethical principles, according to those a company may have the least possible impact on the world around it; additionally, (ii) the principles respond to real evolving market trends and, consequently, stakeholders needs. In 2020, two of the analysed companies jointly adopted the guidelines developed by GRI, CDP, IIRC, and SASB, as well as the recommendations of the Task Force on Climate-related Financial Disclosures. In light of the "Statement of Intent to Work Together Towards Comprehensive Corporate Reporting," co-published in September 2020 by CDP, CDSB, GRI, IIRC, and SASB, these two companies are certainly the most advanced in the convergence process, with respect to the examined sample. The analysis by industry does not show a correlation between the sector to which the company belongs and the number of adopted frameworks. Finally, in relation to the focus on specific GRI standards adopted by companies, it is possible to state that the degree of adoption is certainly higher for the 200 (Economic) and 300 (Environmental) series, while being less relevant for the Social series (400), with the exception of some specific standards.

The sustainability reports and, specifically, the reporting of environmental and social performance information are steadily increasing in organisations around the world. At the same time, companies are paying more and more attention to the process of securing reports to meet stakeholder expectations in terms of transparency and the information's integrity.

Our results have several important implications for both practitioners and scholars. First, this study can be used by investors to obtain information regarding the degree to which different frameworks and standards are being used, thereby also understanding firms' orientation towards sustainable disclosure. In this respect, investors and professionals could make their decisions and base their assessment in a more informed way, having evidence regarding the integration of sustainability issues into the business and its decision-making processes. At the same time, this study could stimulate companies that are less attentive to sustainable disclosure, pushing them to integrate more of their disclosure in this sense, while also highlighting the potential benefits in terms of improving corporate image and reputation.

Among the possible future developments of research, the analysis of the convergence towards the different types of frameworks through the analysis of a larger sample certainly represents an interesting study. In this way, it would be possible to have a more extensive view of the level and quality of communication of non-financial information, finally identifying the most widely used framework. In addition, future studies could analyse the accuracy level of the information provided.

The recent proposal of a Corporate Sustainability Reporting Directive by the European Commission represents a first step toward an integration of different recommendations and requirements on disclosure about sustainability, offering a wide space for future research on this issue.

Appendix A: Euro Stoxx 50

No	Country	Company	No	Country	Company
1	Netherlands	ASML HOLDING N.V	26	Netherlands	KONINKLIJKE PHILIPS N.V
2	France	LVMH MOËT HENNESSY	27	France	KERING SA
3	Germany	SAP SE	28	Germany	DEUTSCHE POST AG
4	Germany	LINDE PLC	29	France	AXA
5	Germany	SIEMENS AG	30	France	SAFRAN
6	France	TOTAL SE	31	France	DANONE
7	France	SANOFI	32	France	ESSILORLUXOTTICA
8	Germany	ALLIANZ SE	33	Italy	INTESA SANPAOLO S.P.A
9	France	L'ORÉAL	34	Germany	MUENCHENER RUECKVERSICH

(continued)

(continued)

No	Country	Company	No	Country	Company
10	France	SCHNEIDER ELECTRIC SE	35	France	PERNOD RICARD
11	Spain	IBERDROLA, S.A	36	Germany	VONOVIA SE
12	Italy	ENEL S.P.A	37	Germany	VOLKSWAGEN AG
13	France	AIR LIQUIDE	38	Netherlands	ING GROEP N.V
14	Germany	BASF SE	39	Ireland	CRH PLC
15	Germany	BAYER AG	40	Spain	INDUSTRIA DE DISEÑO TEX
16	Germany	ADIDAS AG	41	Finland	KONE OYJ
17	France	AIRBUS SE	42	Germany	DEUTSCHE BÖRSE AG
18	Netherlands	ADYEN N.V	43	Netherlands	AHOLD DELHAIZE N.V
19	Germany	DEUTSCHE TELEKOM AG	44	Ireland	FLUTTER ENTERTAINMENT P
20	Germany	DAIMLER AG	45	Spain	AMADEUS IT GROUP, S.A
21	France	BNP PARIBAS	46	France	ENGIE
22	Belgium	ANHEUSER-BUSCH INBEV	47	Germany	BMW AG
23	France	VINCI	48	France	VIVENDI SE
24	Netherlands	PROSUS N.V	49	Italy	ENI S.P.A
25	Spain	BANCO SANTANDER, S.A	50	Finland	NOKIA OYJ

References

Aras, G. and Crowther, D. (2008), 'Governance and sustainability: An investigation into the relationship between corporate governance and corporate sustainability', *Management Decision*, Vol. 46 No. 3, pp. 433–448.

Aureli, S., Magnaghi, E. and Salvatori, F. (2019), 'The Role of Existing Regulation and Discretion in Harmonising Non-Financial Disclosure', *Accounting in Europe*, Taylor & Francis, Vol. 16 No. 3, pp. 290–312.

Badia, F., Dicuonzo, G., Petruzzelli, S. and Dell'Atti, V. (2019a), 'Integrated reporting in action: mobilizing intellectual capital to improve management and governance practices', *Journal of Management and Governance*, Vol. 23 No. 2, pp. 299–320.

Badia, F., Dicuonzo, G., Petruzzelli, S. and Dell'Atti, V. (2019b), 'The Role of Stakeholder Engagement in the Measurement, Management, and Reporting of Intellectual Capital: A Qualitative Analysis on Integrated Reporting Practices', *Qualitative Research in Intangibles, Intellectual Capital and Integrated Reporting Practices. Opportunities, Criticalities and Future Perspectives*, pp. 41–63.

Baldwin, R., Cave, M. and Lodge, M. (2011), *Understanding Regulation: Theory, Strategy, and Practice*, Oxford University Press, Oxford.

Benlemlih, M., Ge, J. and Zhao, S. (2020), 'Undervaluation and non-financial information: Evidence from voluntary disclosure of CSR news', *Journal of Business Finance and Accounting*, pp. 1–49.

Beretta, S. and Bozzolan, S.J. (2008), 'Quality versus Quantity: The Case of Forward-Looking Disclosure.', *Account. Audit. Financ.*, Vol. 23, pp. 333–376.

Bini, L., Dainelli, F. and Giunta, F. (2017), 'Is a loosely specified regulatory intervention effective in disciplining management commentary? The case of performance indicator disclosure', *Journal of Management and Governance*, Springer US, Vol. 21 No. 1, pp. 63–91.

Brechmann, E.C. and Czado, C. (2013), 'Risk management with high-dimensional vine copulas : An analysis of the Euro Stoxx 50', Vol. 342, pp. 307–342.

Brown, H.S., de Jong, M. and Levy, D.L. (2009), 'Building institutions based on information disclosure: lessons from GRI's sustainability reporting', *Journal of Cleaner Production*, Vol. 17 No. 6, pp. 571-580.

CDP; CDSB; GRI; IIRC; SASB. (2020a), *Statement of Intent to Work Together Towards Comprehensive Corporate Reporting*.

CDP; CDSB; GRI; IIRC; SASB. (2020b), *Open Letter to Erik Thedéen, Director General of Finansinspektionen, Sweden, Chair of the Sustainable Finance Task Force of the International Organization of Securities Commissions (IOSCO)*.

CDSB. (2019), 'CDSB Framework', No. June, p. 43.

CDSB. (2020), 'Application guidance for About the Climate Disclosure Standards Board', No. July.

Chen, Y., Mantegna, R.N., Pantelous, A.A. and Zuev, M. (2018), *A Dynamic Analysis of S & P 500 , FTSE 100 and EURO STOXX 50 Indices under Different Exchange Rates*.

Commission Of The European Communities. (2001), *GREEN PAPER: Promoting a European Framework for Corporate Social Responsibility*.

Coulson, A.B., Adams, C.A., Nugent, M.N. and Haynes, K. (2015), 'Exploring metaphors of capitals and the framing of multiple capitals: Challenges and opportunities for <ir>', *Sustainability Accounting, Management and Policy Journal*, Vol. 6 No. 3, pp. 290–314.

Dawn, J., Bodonik, P. and Dhaliwal, J. (2002), 'Supporting the e-Business Readiness of Small and Medium-Sized Enterprises: Approaches and Metrics', *Internet Research*, Vol. 12 No. 2, pp. 139–195.

Deloitte. (2015), *Non-Financial Reporting*.

Doni, F., Bianchi Martini, S., Corvino, A. and Mazzoni, M. (2019), 'Voluntary versus mandatory non-financial disclosure', *Meditari Accountancy Research*, Vol. 28 No. 5, pp. 781–802.

Du, S. and Yu, K. (2020), 'Do corporate social responsibility reports convey value relevant information? Evidence from report readability and tone.', *Journal of Business Ethics*, pp. 1–22.

Edmans, A. (2011), 'Does the Stock Market Fully Value Intangibles? Employee Satisfaction and Equity Prices.', *Journal of Financial Economics*, Vol. 101 No. 3, pp. 621–640.

Elkington, J. (1997), *Cannibals with Forks. The Triple Bottom Line of 21st Century Business*, Capstone Publishing Ltd., Oxford, UK.

Elkington, J. (2004), 'Enter the triple bottom line.', *Henriques, A., Richardson, J. (Eds.), The Triple Bottom Line: Does It All Add Up?*, pp. 1–16.

European Commission. (2017), 'Communication from the commission, guidelines on non-financial reporting (methodology for reporting non-financial information) (2017/C 215/01)'.

Girella, L., Zambon, S. and Rossi, P. (2019), 'Reporting on sustainable development: A comparison of three Italian small and medium-sized enterprises', *Corporate Social Responsibility and Environmental Management*, Vol. 26 No. 4, pp. 981–996.

Haller, A., Link, M. and Groß, T. (2017), 'The Term "Non-financial Information"—A Semantic Analysis of a Key Feature of Current and Future Corporate Reporting', *Accounting in Europe*, Vol. 14 No. 3, pp. 407–429.

Hess, D. (2007), 'Social reporting and new governance regulation: The prospects of achieving corporate accountability through transparency.', *Business Ethics Quarterly*, Vol. 17 No. 3, pp. 453–476.

Huberman, A.M. and Miles, M.B. (1994), 'Data management and analysis methods', *Handbook of Qualitative Research*, Thousand Oaks, CA: Sage.

IIRC. (2021), *<IR> Framework*.

Jackson, G., Bartosch, J., Avetisyan, E., Kinderman, D. and Knudsen, J.S. (2020), 'Mandatory Non-financial Disclosure and Its Influence on CSR: An International Comparison', *Journal of Business Ethics*, Springer Netherlands, Vol. 162 No. 2, pp. 323–342.

Krippendorff, K. (2004), *Content Analysis. An Introduction to Its Methodology*, edited by Publications, S., Sage Publications.

Lokuwaduge, C.S.D.S. and Heenetigala, K. (2017), 'Integrating Environmental, Social and Governance (ESG) Disclosure for a Sustainable Development: An Australian Study', *Business Strategy and the Environment*, Vol. 26 No. 4, pp. 438–450.

Lopatta, K., Buchholz, F. and Kaspereit, T. (2016), 'Asymmetric information and corporate social responsibility.', *Business and Society*, Vol. 55 No. 3, pp. 458–488.

Makarenko, I. (2017), 'Public companies non-financial reporting and audit in Ukraine: challenges and prospects', *Accounting and Financial Control*, Vol. 1 No. 1, pp. 32–38.

Marston, C.L. and Shrives, P.J. (1991), 'The use of disclosure indices in accounting research: A review article.', *Br. Account. Rev.*, Vol. 23, pp. 195–210.

Mauro, S.G., Cinquini, L., Simonini, E. and Tenucci, A. (2020), 'Moving from social and sustainability reporting to integrated reporting: Exploring the potential of Italian public-funded universities' reports', *Sustainability (Switzerland)*, Vol. 12 No. 8, p. 3172.

Mayring, P. (2000), 'Qualitative content analysis.', *Forum on Qualitative Social Research*, Vol. 1 No. 2.

Najah, A. and Jarboui, A. (2013), 'Non-Financial Disclosure and Value Creation through Consumer Satisfaction in France', *Journal of Academic Finance*, Vol. 1, pp. 1–14.

Nawaz, W. and Koç, M. (2018), 'Development of a systematic framework for sustainability management of organizations', *Journal of Cleaner Production*, Elsevier Ltd, Vol. 171, pp. 1255–1274.

Pranugrahaning, A., Donovan, J.D., Topple, C. and Masli, E.K. (2021), 'Corporate sustainability assessments: A systematic literature review and conceptual framework', *Journal of Cleaner Production*, Elsevier Ltd, Vol. 295, p. 126385.

Raynard, P. and Forstater, M. (2002), *Corporate Social Responsibility. Implications for Small and Medium Enterprises in Developing Countries*, United Nations Industrial Development Organization, Vienna, Austria.

Raza, J., Liu, Y. and Usman, M. (2019), 'Corporate social responsibility commitment of small-to-medium enterprises and organizational competitive differentiation: Stakeholder pressure, market orientation, and socioeconomic context effects', *Journal of Public Affairs*, Vol. 19 No. 2, pp. 1–11.

Renneboog, L., Horst, J.T. and Zhang, C. (2008), 'Socially responsible investments: Institutional aspects, performance, and investor behavior.', *Journal of Banking and Finance*, Vol. 32, pp. 1723–1742.

Stubbs, W. and Higgins, C. (2018), 'Stakeholders' perspectives on the role of regulatory reform in integrated reporting', *Journal of Business Ethics*, Vol. 147 No. 3, pp. 489–508.

Tarmuji, I., Maelah, R. and Tarmuji, N.H. (2016), 'The Impact of Environmental, Social and Governance Practices (ESG) on Economic Performance: Evidence from ESG Score', *International Journal of Trade, Economics and Finance*, Vol. 7 No. 3, pp. 67–74.

TCFD. (2017), 'Recommendations of the Task Force on Climate-related Financial Disclosures', *Launch at the Tate Modern*, No. December, pp. 1–6.

La Torre, M., Sabelfeld, S., Blomkvist, M., Tarquinio, L. and Dumay, J. (2018), 'Harmonising non-financial reporting regulation in Europe: Practical forces and projections for future research.', *Meditari Accountancy Research*, available at: https://doi.org/10.1108/MEDAR-02-2018-0290.

Vaz, N., Fernandez-Feijoo, B. and Ruiz, S. (2016), 'Integrated reporting: an international overview', *Business Ethics*, Vol. 25 No. 4, pp. 577–591.

Venturelli, A., Caputo, F., Leopizzi, R. and Pizzi, S. (2019), 'The state of art of corporate social disclosure before the introduction of non-financial reporting directive: a cross country analysis', *Social Responsibility Journal*, Vol. 15 No. 4, pp. 409–423.

The Social Return on Investment (SROI) for Evaluation of the Impact in International Cooperation Health Project in Albania: A Case Study

Martina Giusti, Niccolò Persiani, Michele De Luca, and Maria Josè Caldes

Abstract In the last years with the affirmation of the Theory of Change (ToC—Connel and Kunisch in New approaches to evaluating community initiatives 2:1–16, Connell and Kubisch, New Approaches to Evaluating Community Initiatives 2:1–16, 1998), a lot of tools for the evaluation of projects having social relevance have been developed. The need to measure their impact has led to leave the use of traditional qualitative measurement instruments joints for quantitative tools, which calculate the effectiveness of the resources employed and the generated impact by social projects (Anderson in The community builder's approach to Theory of Change, Anderson, A.A., (2006). The community builder's approach to Theory of Change.). Among them, recently it is paid attention on the Social Return on Investment (SROI—Lingane and Olsen in California management review 46:116–135, Lingane and Olsen, California Management Review 46:116–135, 2004), a model to account for created value. It includes not only the return of investments but also the benefits for the broader public in the social, economic and environmental spheres. The research aim is to verify and calculate SROI as a valid tool to measure the impact generated by social projects in transitional countries, especially those of health international cooperation. Indeed, the economic quantification of the SROI rate appears as an important element to improve reporting and accountability both to the lender, the gesture and the users. The case study has been identified as appropriate methodology for conducting this research (Yin 2003; Eisenhardt in Academy of Management Review 14:532–550, Eisenhardt, Academy of Management Review 14:532–550, 1989). The project 'Introducing Health Information System (IHIS): a modern approach to transparency and accountability in the Albanian public health' conducted by the Tuscany Region resulted relevant for the involvement of different actors and its action in a transition

M. Giusti · N. Persiani (✉)
Department of Experimental and Clinic Medicine, University of Florence, Florence, Italy
e-mail: niccolo.persini@unifi.it

M. Giusti
e-mail: martina.giusti@unifi.it

M. De Luca · M. J. Caldes
Centre of Global Health of Tuscany Region, Florence, Italy
e-mail: michele.deluca@meyer.it

© The Author(s), under exclusive license to Springer Nature Switzerland AG 2022
P. Sklias et al. (eds.), *Business Development and Economic Governance in Southeastern Europe*, Springer Proceedings in Business and Economics,
https://doi.org/10.1007/978-3-031-05351-1_4

country as Albania. This project was realized from 2014 to 2016 using financing from IADSA (Italian Albanian Debt for Development Swap Agreement) to support the Albanian government in the NHS technological and accountant development. Now it's possible to adequately observe the generated impact 5 years after the conclusion of IHIS project. The necessary data for the calculation of SROI was collected by desk analysis of project's documents and reports and the conduction of interviews and focus groups to a specimen of involved stakeholders. Results show the good capability of SROI to quantitatively evaluate the impact produced by a health international cooperation project, also if complex and articulated as that studied. In particular, the SROI rate of this project is 9.4, an optimal rate (for 1.00€ invested, the project generated an economic impact of 9.40€). Therefore, it is demonstrated the optimal use of the allocated resources obtaining a strong effective impact in the Albanian health care system and on the network of involved stakeholders. Another important aspect is the reinforcement of results dissemination in the society, for the simplicity and easy comprehension of the SROI rate and the internal restitution promoted by SROI analysis. So SROI proves as a good instrument both to measure and to share the economic value of generated impact.

Keywords Social projects · Impact · Evaluation tools · International cooperation · SROI · Health

JEL Classification H43 · H51 · I15

1 Introduction

About 20 years ago, the criteria for planning and evaluating the effectiveness of social projects changed with the affirmation of the Theory of Change (Connel and Kubisch 1998). It shifted attention from obtained results (outputs) to context of action, process and outcomes. All steps of the project acquired value, rather than just its goals, enforcing the involvement of stakeholders, who gave their contribution to realize the change.

The Theory of Change (ToC) guided the passage from a qualitative analysis of the results, descriptive and focused on the achievement of outputs, to a quantitative assessment, which has paid attention on the generated impact in the medium-long term and on the sustainability of the intervention (Fullbright-Anderson, Kubisch and Connell 1998).

In particular, the international cooperation immediately adhered to the ToC to be able to develop social projects, where the generated impact was adequately measured and the sustainability was controlled through the economic valorization of objective indicators. Before until, in fact, a significant portion of the produced impact did not contribute to the social value of an international cooperation project (Jackson 2013). Between possible contexts of action of international cooperation, this need was stronger in the field of health. Indeed, the generated impact corresponds to better or worse outcomes in terms of care and well-being for the involved realities, as well as to a better or worse ability of the interventions' promoters to meet the specific needs (De Silvia et al. 2014).

To respond to the new measurement's necessities, a lot of tools were developed for the detection and quantitative calculation of the produced impact. Among these, SROI (Social Return on Investments) has the greatest diffusion due to its specific characteristics. It is an economic index capable of measuring the extra-financial value obtained at the end of a project, verifying if there is more value compared to the invested resources for the realization of the project itself. SROI rate shows for each economic unit invested how many were produced through the promoted intervention (Lingane and Olsen 2004). In the health international cooperation projects, SROI could be a valid instrument to support the estimation of the generated impact and the activities of reporting and sharing of generated social return with the community and all engaged stakeholders (SHs) (Millar and Hall 2013).

Aim of this study is to verify the possible application and effectiveness of SROI for the quantification of economic impact generated by health international cooperation projects, especially if they are realized in transitional countries. The objective quantification of the impact generated in these countries is important for the strong resonance, that has these interventions; indeed, benefits are absolute in terms of improving the general living conditions of these countries, especially with projects for health care and promotion and guarantee.

To achieve this scope, the case study was considered the most adequate methodology. The project 'Introducing Health Information System (IHIS): a modern approach to transparency and accountability in the Albanian public health' was identified as significant case study. Tuscany Region carried it out between 2014 and 2016 with the purpose to preserve and develop the health of the Albanian population by increasing efficiency, maximizing the productivity of the service and rationalizing the use of resources.

This paper is structured as follows. The literature review investigates the state of art about the evaluation of social projects, focusing on quantitative tools and on the health care sector in international cooperation. After it's reported the used method with the presentation of the selected case study. Below the passages for the SROI rate calculation are shown and discussed. Finally, there are conclusions, limits and possible developments of the research.

2 Literature Review

The Theory of Change (ToC) is a programming, monitoring and evaluation model of social projects that aim to ensure the sustainability of the achieved results over time by focusing on the duration of the initiated change (Anderson 2006). The advent of ToC revolutionized the reference paradigm for the evaluation of social projects, infantizing the role of the incisiveness of the projects in the reference contexts carried out in any field of action and anywhere in the world. This approach promotes the sustainable social development because it favours impact assessment, which is not limited only to the analysis of the achieved results (outputs) but also includes the examination of the path, its corrections and the created social value by project at its end and in the following period (Jackson 2013). The examination of its effectiveness occurs through stakeholders' engagement (Sullivan and Stewart 2006). The growth, the strengthening or the effective reorganization of a social setting cannot ignore its economic sustainability and the generation of a positive impact of the realized intervention, which is the improvement of the social conditions of the subjects belonging to the entire supply chain. These characteristics make this theory particularly suitable for the development, implementation and evaluation of international cooperation projects (Stein and Valters 2012; Mayne 2015). Indeed, these initiatives are always finalized to generate a lasting social value in the reality of intervention and to ensure its sustainability in the medium to long term.

Given the importance attached to the impact, numerous qualitative and quantitative instruments were developed for its measurement and monitoring (Maas and Liket 2011; Gibbon and Dey 2011). Both types of tools are widely used in the evaluation of social projects in relation to the information that we want to have or the type of communication we want to adopt. In fact, quantitative and qualitative evaluation are two sides of the same process which, only together, offer a complete analysis of the phenomenon under examination. Nevertheless, the use of quantitative approaches in the evaluation of social projects prevailed since they offer objective and more expendable information in reporting on the use of the allocated economic resources, the achieved effects (outputs), the dissemination of the reached objectives (Black 1998; Moody, Littlepage and Paydar 2015) and the generate impact (outcomes) (Cloqueel-Ballester et al. 2006), which is not just a perception but a real evaluative indicator.

Between the validated tools for the quantitative analysis of the impact, the SROI has had the greatest diffusion because it is able to summarize in an easy and comprehensible economic index the value of social return.

SROI rate indicates for each economic unit invested, how many were generated by realized intervention (Arvidson et al. 2013; Krlev, Muenscher and Muelbert 2013; Banke-Thomas et al. 2015). The same WHO ascribed SROI as reference model for calculating the produced social value by intervention of health care delivery and promotion (Hamelmann et al. 2017; Dyakova et al. 2017). It is contextualized in the improvement of the use of structured Health Impact Assessment plan, with which it was redefined the issued guidelines for the evaluation of international health cooperation projects. The quantification of the generated impact is a keystone in preparation, control and estimation of developed projects (WHO, Regional office for Europe – 2016 and 2018).

Following the WHO recommendations, studies on the effectiveness of health prevention and promotion interventions used SROI to calculate the generated impact. This approach is applied especially in the evaluation of projects promoted by National Healthcare Systems (Deeming et al. 2017; Macaulay et al. 2018; Ricciuti and Bufalini 2019). At government level, in fact, there is a strict adherence to the international health guideline as an indispensable prerequisite for the accreditation, consolidation and validation of the activities carried out. But the use of SROI is not so widespread in the evaluation of international health cooperation projects, although in the field of intervention it is the same (Goudet et al. 2018). However, international cooperation operates through different channels and interfaces with different evaluation and control institutions so, necessarily, the guidelines and the procedures for validating the effectiveness of the processes conducted change. Here, the achieved impact is qualitatively assessing but not measured quantitatively (Ferrarini and Sjöberg 2010; D'Hombres et al. 2010), as disclosed in the WHO recommendations.

There is a full adherence to the monitoring, reporting and evaluation protocols proper to social design, that provide for full compliance with other criteria and parameters compared to purely sanitary ones.

This discrepancy is particularly significant in low-middle-income countries, where there are a lot of healthcare projects favoured by international health cooperation to support the establishment, management and promotion of health systems (Oketch, McCowan and Schendler 2014). While in low-income countries they are predominantly humanitarian projects, in order to directly meet urgent health needs of users, which can determine their lives or deaths, capacity and institution building projects are carried out in middle-income countries to create the conditions to provide adequate support for the strengthening and development of fragile, non-performing and poor quality but presented health systems (Hill et al. 2012).

Focusing on the transition countries of the Balkan area, we observe the application of the second type of international health cooperation interventions. They are more complex and articulated projects, which involve the government structure of the country and usually generate a more radical and lasting impact on the reality of intervention by acting directly on the decision-making level. Nevertheless, this approach needs time to manifest itself and to be perceived. Before Bredenkamp and his research group on the health expenditure (Bredenkamp, Mendola and Gragnolati 2011) and after Jakonljevic and colleagues on the performance of Balkan health care systems (Jakonljevic et al. 2017) have studied social projects for introduction and development of new managerial policies in transitional countries, like those developed by international health care in similar countries. Impact measurement is totally omitted at the end of the carried-out initiatives.

To the best of our knowledge, no similar papers have been found in literature on the evaluation of the socio-health projects' effectiveness carried out in the Balkan transitional countries (Kutzin et al. 2010), either by local institutions or by international health cooperation, which evaluates quantitatively the impact generated by this type of social projects. Therefore, it is appropriate to fill this lack of information.

3 Method

The case study (Yin 2012; Eisenhardt 1989) was identified as the most appropriate method for conducting the present research to measure the impact of health international cooperation projects in transition country of Balkan area.

Given the methodology, we looked for the tool for the quantitative measurement of impact. The Social Return On Investment (SROI) was chosen according to the recommendations of WHO, for which SROI is the reference evaluation approach for the objective measurement of impact in the field of action of socio-health projects, also those promoted by international cooperation. The research group studied SROI analysis to know the phases of its application and the information necessary for its calculation. This made it possible to determine the following selection criteria for the choice of a suitable and significant project as case study:

- project developed in a transition country of Balkan area;
- project developed interesting health care or/and prevention or/and promotion;
- project completed for at least 3 years to be able to observe its impact;
- availability of relative documentation project;
- possibility to contact all the SHs engaged in the project.

The identification of the case study project took place through the regional institutional realities present throughout the Italian territory, that deal with health international cooperation and had carried out projects in the Balkan area with all the selection criteria previously defined. It was decided to interface with regional rather than national realities dedicated to international cooperation at governmental level, such as AICS (Italian Agency for Development Cooperation) or DGCS (Directorate-General for Development Cooperation), to have few bureaucratic passages and to have a direct contact with the people promoters and conductors of the possible selected project. Among the Italian regional institutions engaged in this specific activity, the Global Health Centre (GHC) of the Tuscany Region was chosen as the reference reality. Since its inception in 2002, this centre has always worked with the Balkan countries for the close diplomatic relations, that have linked Tuscany to the Balkan region since the 70s. GHC was contacted to understand if they were developed projects with the defined characteristics in the last years and if they are able to share with the research group reports and documentation related to a possible project. GHC presented to us the project 'Introducing Health Information System (IHIS): a modern approach to transparency and accountability in the Albanian public health'. This project was conducted in Albania between 2014 and 2016 and aimed to create the financial, operative and managerial conditions to improve the Albanian health care system by increasing efficiency, maximizing productivity in services and rationalizing the use of resources. Having found the utmost willingness to collaborate by the GHC and the satisfaction of all the criteria by the proposed project, this was chosen as a significant case study of this paper.

Data for the SROI calculation were collected by desk analysis of the administrative-accounting documentation of the studied project, while the SHs outcomes were collected by conducting semi-structured interviews with the reference members of each class of stakeholder.

At the end of SROI analysis, an email was sent to the subjects previously interviewed to share obtained results and to invite them to their assessment in online meeting for the next week. One week after, all the invited participated in the online focus group. The effectiveness of SROI analysis and its strengths and weaknesses, opportunities and threats offered by the employment of SROI were discussed together. Information for filling the SWOT analysis matrix and opinions were taken through the content analysis of the unwinding of the recorded focus group.

4 Case Study: Introducing Health Information System (IHIS): A Modern Approach to Transparency and Accountability in the Albanian Public Health

After a long period of transition from the previous Soviet totalitarian regime, in recent years Albania has undergone a strong development with the consolidation of its economy (Tomaszewski and Świadek 2017). Its continuous economic-financial growth has generated greater well-being in the population and pushed the government to start a season of reforms aimed at offering greater and better services to create a new state welfare and to adapt the country to European standards for the possible entry of Albania into the European Union (OECD 2019).

In years following the fall of the Soviet Regime, Albania launched especially a profound reform of the healthcare sector. The Ministry of Health has issued a strategic plan with three main lines of intervention:

a. decentralization;
b. creation of a public insurance fund to increase healthcare spending;
c. introduction of an accreditation system of the quality in the national health realities (Ministry of Health of the Republic of Albania 1993).

In time, these objectives were reaffirmed in the documents 'Long-term Strategy for the Development of the Albanian Health System 2004' and 'National Strategy for Development and Integration 2007–2013'. The institution building about the Albanian healthcare system is supported prevalently by health international cooperation, coming from Italy. Indeed, there is a strong collaboration between these two countries consequently the massive movement migration of the 90th from Albania to Italy (King and Vullnetari 2003). Tuscany Region is particularly committed because it hosts the bigger Albanian community in Italy (Rossi et al. 2010; Taddei et al. 2014; Aledort et al. 2016). In this field of action, the project 'Introducing Health Information System (IHIS): a modern approach to transparency and accountability in the Albanian Public Health' was promoted by the Tuscany Region, through its operative institute Global Health Centre (GHC), in collaboration with Albanian Ministry of Health and financed with IADSA (Italian Albanian Debt for Development Swap Agreement) resources with an amount equal to 61,627,926.00 ALL (corresponding to 439.289, 51€). The principal aim of the IHIS projects was the reorganization of the financing system of the Albanian National Healthcare through the introduction of DRGs, supported by the implementation of a HIS software and the training of the personnel involved, to create the condition to support Albanian health service

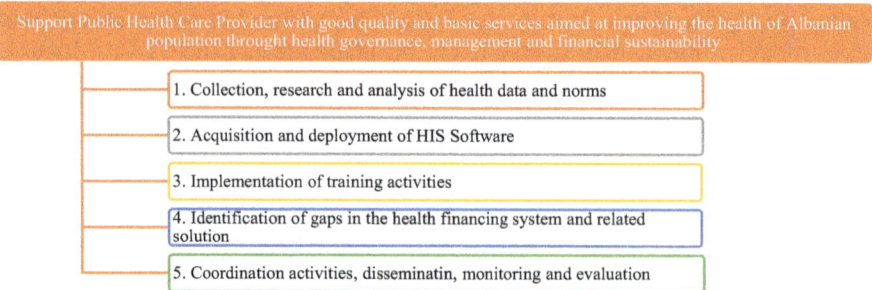

Fig. 1 Activities of the project 'Introducing Health Information System (IHIS): a modern approach to transparency and accountability in the Albanian public health

providers in improving and preserving the health of the Albanian population through good governance, proper management and financial sustainability. The project lasted 24 months, from November 2014 to December 2016 and was articulated in five activities (Fig. 1).

The major partners involved in the execution of these actions were: (a) the Foundation of Lady of Good Council (FLC), as local support for the intervention; (b) the five Italian teachers of the Italian NHS engaged to support the context analysis and the government guidelines writing and to provide training; (c) the 200 professionals of the four pilot hospitals (University Hospital 'Shefqet Ndroqi', Neurology Hospital, Paediatric Hospital in Tirana and Durres Regional Hospital), who adequately trained have contributed to the operational implementation of the procedures at local level.

According to research group, this project is a significant case study for assessing the possible application and effectiveness of the SROI, as a tool for measuring economic impact of health cooperation projects, for three principal reasons:

- An adequate period of time has elapsed since its conclusion (now 5 years) for which it is possible to adequately quantify the impact generated by the same;
- Its development in international health cooperation context, for which a significant social impact is expected not only in terms of quality and effectiveness of the Albanian health system (direct consequences on the health of citizens) but also for the affirmation and accreditation of project promoters and partners in the international panorama;
- The involvement both of members of government level (Ministry of Health) and of the professionals of the managerial dimension of the Albanian Health Care services.

The project did not create new structures but supported the public health service with technical tools and knowledge to better carry out the functions, that they had been tasked by law and, at the same time, strengthen their capacities as administration structures in realizing health services.

5   Results and Discussion

Most of the needed elements for the SROI analysis (Fig. 2) were recovered easily a posteriori by desk analysis of all documents (project planning, application for access to funding, five periodic technical reports for monitoring the maintenance of the route, costs reporting, final report) relating to the IHIS project made available to us by the GHC. Therefore, it was possible to reconstruct the field of action, to quantify inputs and outputs and to analyze the realized activities. The identification of who participated as stakeholders in the studied project and, especially, their selection was particularly important because their outcomes directly determined the impact and its punctual measurement, without introducing significant errors of over or underestimation.

We included in the SROI analysis only the following SHs, strictly committed in execution of the project:

- Global Health Centre as institutional promoter of the project;
- Albanian Ministry of Health (MoH), which worked in partnership with GHC;
- Foundation of Lady of Good Council (FLC), local partner, who is the perpetrator of the intervention;
- Engaged Italian teachers/researchers;
- A specimen of 12 trainers of about 120 students (three for each of the four involved hospitals).

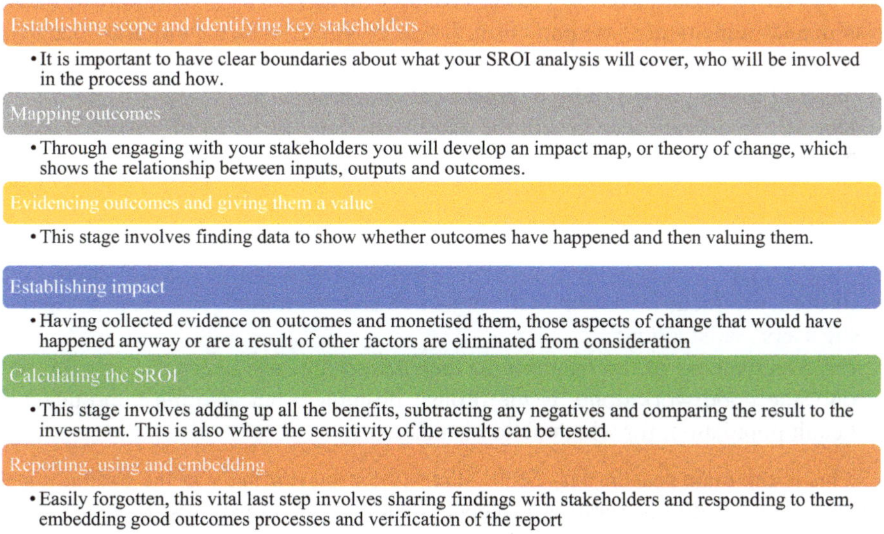

Establishing scope and identifying key stakeholders
- It is important to have clear boundaries about what your SROI analysis will cover, who will be involved in the process and how.

Mapping outcomes
- Through engaging with your stakeholders you will develop an impact map, or theory of change, which shows the relationship between inputs, outputs and outcomes.

Evidencing outcomes and giving them a value
- This stage involves finding data to show whether outcomes have happened and then valuing them.

Establishing impact
- Having collected evidence on outcomes and monetised them, those aspects of change that would have happened anyway or are a result of other factors are eliminated from consideration

Calculating the SROI
- This stage involves adding up all the benefits, subtracting any negatives and comparing the result to the investment. This is also where the sensitivity of the results can be tested.

Reporting, using and embedding
- Easily forgotten, this vital last step involves sharing findings with stakeholders and responding to them, embedding good outcomes processes and verification of the report

Fig. 2 Phases of SROI analysis

Moreover, semi-structured interviews were conducted with the reference members of each SHs group both to collect SHs outcomes and to validate the data obtained by desk analysis. We asked the respondents to indicate:

1. what inputs were used in the project and what outputs were obtained in order to validate the data collected from the desk analysis;
2. what outcomes were and how long they would last;
3. how much the SROI would be, after explaining them its calculation mechanism, to compare the obtained with the supposed SROI rate;
4. the promotion of actions for results dissemination.

In addiction were applied also coefficients to purify the final economic impact value from the influence of outcomes, that would have occurred in any case regardless of the intervention (deadweight and displacement) or attributable to actions carried out in parallel (attribution) and to account for their exhaustion in time (drop-off). Hence, we proceed to SROI rate calculation as the ratio between the current value of the impact and the value of the inputs (Table 1).

The SROI rate stood at 9.40. Every 1.00€ invested in the IHIS project generated 9.40€, with a return of +940%. This index immediately shows the strong impact and the social generativity, that the IHIS project has had. That SROI rate (9.40) indicates that all SHs involved, including the Albanian Ministry of Health and the health professionals, shared and used well the available resources (material, experts' competencies and acquired knowledge) to optimize the achievement of objectives but also something more. Albania with the support of GHC has been able to plan the total reorganization of the informative and financial system of national health system and implement some parts of it. It was promoted also the cultural change of the thinking of the health professionals through the sharing of experiences and the managerial training realized by international cooperation.

During the online focus group, the SROI was considered by all involved actors (promoters, partners, consultants and users of IHIS project) the most effective tool for measuring the social value generated by all kinds of health international cooperation projects, also complex such as that examined in this study. The added value of SROI lies in:

•   its ability to focus attention on the objective and economic quantification right of the users' satisfaction;
•   the effectiveness of the response to their specific health needs, recognizing not only the good work done by the project promoters but also the importance of health population, for which action is taken.

This is the main reason why SROI should be used routinely in the evaluation of international health cooperation projects. WHO's indications must be extended to those bordering realities of health, such as international cooperation projects, where the focus is always on improving or restoring global health. There is a significant and general underestimation of the economic social return, which is believed to be approximately half of the actual impact evaluated. It considerably conditions both all the actions of restitution, utilization and integration within the group of SHs and the

Table 1 SROI analysis IHIS project

SH	Outcome	Index	Financial proxy	Valorisation (€)	Deadweight, attribution and drop-off (%)	Impatto	Anno	Impatto—deadweight—attribuzione	Rate 5% 2017
Tuscany Region. Interview with dr. Michele De Luca	Start of a strong collaboration with the Albanian healthcare	The Improvement of Emergency Medical Services in the Coastal Area (IEMSCA)	Financing by AICS/Italian Embassy: 587,647.37€ (30%)	€ 176,294.21	10%–10%–10%	€ 142,798.31	2017	€ 115,666.63	€ 706,084.83
		Reinforcing Primary Health Care in Vau i Dejës Municipality (PHCINVID)	Financing by AICS/Italian Embassy: 502,634.97€ (35%)	€ 175,922.24	10%–10%–10%	€ 175,922.24	2017	€ 142,497.01	**2018**
		GoI/MoH/12/2015 project—Local Training for the health professionals of the cardiac surgery unit of UCCK with the Kosovo MoH for technical assistance during the construction of a cardiological network	Financing by AICS: 225,620.00€ (35%)	€ 78,967.00	10%–10%–10%	€ 78,967.00	2018	€ 63,963.27	€ 718,957.22
		Provision of Technical Assistance Services to Albanian Public Health Institutions for the improving of the Emergency—Urgency Health System in Coastal Areas". Rif. OJ/S83—29/04/2019 -198180—2019—EN/CIG 7885040CD7	Financing by AICS: 679,000.00€ (30%)	€ 203,700.00	10%–10%–10%	€ 203,700.00	2020	€ 164,997.00	**2019**
	Increase of competences in engaged operators	Participation to advanced course about health development cooperation	Valorisation of a course: about 2500.00€	€ 7,500.00	25%–25%–10%	€ 7,500.00	2017	€ 4218.75	€ 650,504.00

(continued)

Table 1 (continued)

SH	Outcome	Index	Financial proxy	Valorisation (€)	Deadweight, attribution and drop-off (%)	Impatto	Anno	Impatto—deadweight—attribuzione	Rate 5% 2017
Albanian MoH and its institutions. Interview with dr. Edmond Ahdjieri	Improvement in data analysis in the PHCP	N° realized reports by trainers	Cost of consultancy for the realization of each report: 10,000 €	€ 50,000.00	15%–25%–20%	€ 50,000.00	2017	€ 31,875.00	**2020**
	Improvement in healthcare delivery in facilities (financing, management, …)	N° approved guidelines to apply, realized in IHIS projects, by Albanian government	Cost of consultancy for the application of each guideline: 10,000 €	€ 70,000.00	15%–25%–20%	€ 70,000.00	2017	€ 44,625.00	€ 1.133.107,78
		N° Checklist to implement with digital procedures	Cost of consultancy for the improvement of each checklist: 10,000 €	€ 20,000.00	15%–25%–20%	€ 20,000.00	2017	€ 12,750.00	**2021**
	Start of a strong collaboration with the RT	The Improvement of Emergency Medical Services in the Coastal Area (IEMSCA)	Financing by AICS/Italian Embassy: 587,647.37€ (60%)	€ 352,588.42	10%–10%–10%	€ 285,596.62	2017	€ 231,333.26	€ 1,014,005.85

(continued)

Table 1 (continued)

SH	Outcome	Index	Financial proxy	Valorisation (€)	Deadweight, attribution and drop-off (%)	Impatto	Anno	Impatto—deadweight—attribuzione	Rate 5% 2017
		Provision of Technical Assistance Services to Albanian Public Health Institutions for the improving of the Emergency—Urgency Health System in Coastal Areas". Rif. OJ/S83—29/04/2019 –198180—2019—EN/CIG 7885040CD7	Financing by AICS: 679,000.00€ (60%)	€ 407,400.00	10%–10%–10%	€ 407,400.00	2020	€ 329,994.00	**Total**
Foundation Our Lady of Good Counsel. Interview with: dr. Laura Yzeiraj	Growth and strengthening of the relationships' network with Tuscany realities	N° financed scholarships	Financing by Florence South Rotary: 30,000.00€ (20%)	€ 6,000.00	10%–10%–10%	€ 6,000.00	2020	€ 4,860.00	€ 4,129,173.50
		The Improvement of Emergency Medical Services in the Coastal Area (IEMSCA)	Financing by AICS/Italian Embassy: 587,647.37€ (10%)	€ 58,764.74	10%–10%–10%	€ 47,599.44	2017	€ 38,555.55	**Actual value**
		GoI/MoH/12/2015 project—Local Training for the health professionals of the cardiac surgery unit of UCCK with the Kosovo MoH for technical assistance during the construction of a cardiological network	Financing by AICS: 225,620.00€ (10%)	€ 22,562.00	10%–10%–10%	€ 22,562.00	2018	€ 18,275.22	€ 3,689,883.99

(continued)

Table 1 (continued)

SH	Outcome	Index	Financial proxy	Valorisation (€)	Deadweigh, attribution and drop-off (%)	Impatto	Anno	Impatto—deadweight—attribuzione	Rate 5% 2017
									Input value
		Provision of Technical Assistance Services to Albanian Public Health Institutions for the improving of the Emergency—Urgency Health System in Coastal Areas". Rif. OJ/S83—29/04/2019—198180—2019—EN / CIG 7885040CD7	Financing by AICS: 679,000.00€ (10%)	€ 67,900.00	10%–10%–10%	€ 67,900.00	2020	€ 54,999.00	
Teachers/Researchers from Italian Nation Healthcare System. Focus group (Taiti F., Romolini A., Biancalanci A., Galani C.)	Professional growth	Improvement of capabilities to manage and teach in a foreign country	Cost of advanced course on this subject with experiences abroad: about 2500€	€ 12,500.00	25%–25%–10%	€ 12,500.00	2017	€7,031.25	€ 439,289.51
		N° following experiences in IC	Cost of similar voyagers: about 500€ (5 voyages)	€ 37,500.00	10%–15%–10%	€ 37,500.00	2017	€ 28,687.50	**Rate SROI**
		N° research grants	Research grant: 19,367.00€	€ 19,367.00	20%–20%–10%	€ 19,367.00	2017	€ 12,394.88	**9.40**
				€ 19,367.00	20%–20%–10%	€ 19,367.00	2018	€ 12,394.88	
				€ 19,367.00	20%–20%–10%	€ 19,367.00	2019	€ 12,394.88	
		Technological instruments	PC: 2000€	€ 6,000.00	10%–50%–30%	€ 6,000.00	2017	€ 2,700.00	
Focus group with 30 trainers	More knowledge, skills and abilities	N° organized training courses	Cost of course on the topic: 300€	€ 60,000.00	25%–25%–15%	€ 60,000.00	2017	€ 33,750.00	

sharing of the results obtained from the project with the entire civil community. The SROI demonstrates to be a tool for the economic quantification of the impact that is powerful and simple, thanks to its excellent communicability and easy to understand, which provide the basis for an effective communication and promotion campaign for the initiative developed by projects promoters and its closers collaborators.

Possible positive and negative aspects, opportunities and difficulties given by integration of SROI analysis in the usual monitoring and evaluation process were collected and reported in the SWOT analysis matrix (Fig. 3).

Starting from opinions acquired during the focus group, three reflections were developed.

In first instance, most of the variables used for the SROI analysis were the same monitored at each stage of the intervention by project's developers, according to the international guidelines on social planning and its evaluation. Certainly, it looks favourably on the use of SROI over other models for the economic quantification of the impact generated because it does not require the use of more resources. With the structuring of a wider reporting system, which integrates usual data with few additional information for SROI calculating, it permits to carry out easily a more serious objective check and measurement of the social return. The calculation of the SROI requires only one more passage with the re-contact of the SHs after a

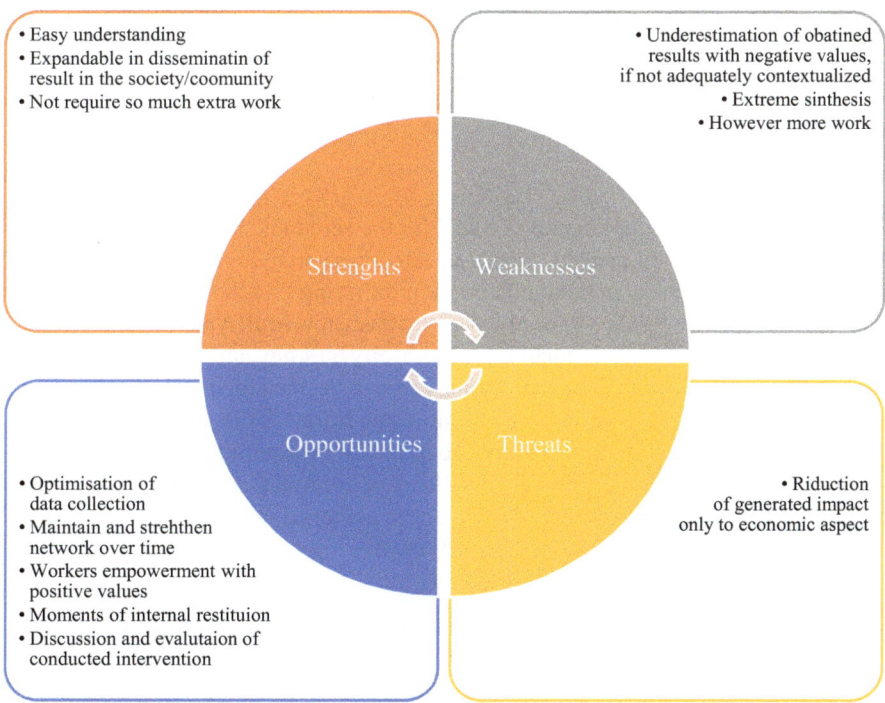

Fig. 3 SWOT analysis of SROI analysis application

medium-long period to question them about direct and indirect benefits attained by project. This point can be read as additional work but also as a good opportunity to maintain the network of relationships and contacts over time, a fundamental aspect of international cooperation.

Indeed, the second aspect has related the need to integrate the evaluation of outcomes at the end of the project with the measurement of the impact later. It is almost never done, although it allows the complete representation of the opening scenario thanks to the realized project. Yet this specific compliance should even be a monitoring and evaluation criteria for the accreditation of institutional and private organizations engaged and the recognition of their effectiveness. Moreover, making explicit the impact achieved and generated by a socially relevant project, such as one of international cooperation, is very important motivational lever acting on all SHs, which is absolutely focusing on.

The third and final consideration concerns the need both to external and internal restitution, utilization and integration of outputs, outcomes and impact. In international cooperation, particularly in the health field, is as important to carry out the intervention as to promote it, making its effects known not only to professionals throughout the community. Return and dissemination measures are often directed to society without, however, creating similar moments of sharing with the working group itself. SROI analysis during the outcomes mapping offers the opportunity to put all together for a collegial moment of dialogue, analysis and comparison of the entire process and the influencing variables, after having settled experience.

6   Conclusions

Result obtained by the application of SROI for the economic measurement of impact generated in a complex project, as the selected case study, is surprisingly positive in terms of effectiveness in data collection, monitoring of activities carried out and evaluation of impact. SROI will be always used from now in all types of health international cooperation projects (humanitarian, capacity building and institution building) to measure the generated impacts, especially in middle-long time after the conclusion of intervention for the presence of favourable conditions for its application.

SROI is powerful and simple, thanks to its excellent communicability and understanding, which provide the basis for an effective communication and promotion; it supports the internal sharing and discussion on achieved outputs and outcomes and the external dissemination of the obtained results.

Positive specific aspects of SROI rate are:

- A wider collection of project variables thanks to the involvement of all stakeholders;
- The integration of objective and subjective impact evaluation for its complete description;

- The promotion of return moments, even after years, to strengthen bonds that can be worn out over time and/or to encourage the development of new projects.

The limits of this study are the lack of application of the SROI analysis to more health international cooperation projects, with different action levels, always carried out in transitional countries but located in a different region.

Future developments will be the SROI application to other similar projects and, if the effectiveness will be confirmed, we will proceed with the results generalization and, maybe, with the submission of new integrated impact evaluation guidelines.

References

Aledort, L.M., De Luca, M., Caldes Pinilla, M.J., Zanobini, A., Carli, S., Godo, A., Manastirliu, O., Kolaj, G., Caja, T. and Neziri, V., (2016). Hemophilia Lend-Lease Program in Italy Successfully Meets Albania Factor Needs.

Anderson, A.A., (2006). The community builder's approach to Theory of Change.

Arvidson, M., Lyon, F., McKay, S. and Moro, D., (2013). Valuing the social? The nature and controversies of measuring social return on investment (SROI). *Voluntary sector review, 4*(1), pp.3–18.

Banke-Thomas, A.O., Madaj, B., Charles, A. and van den Broek, N., (2015). Social Return on Investment (SROI) methodology to account for value for money of public health interventions: a systematic review. *BMC public health, 15*(1), pp.1–14.

Black, T.R., (1998). *Doing quantitative research in the social sciences: An integrated approach to research design, measurement and statistics.* Sage.

Bredenkamp, C., Mendola, M. and Gragnolati, M., (2011). Catastrophic and impoverishing effects of health expenditure: new evidence from the Western Balkans. *Health policy and planning, 26*(4), pp.349–356.

Cloquell-Ballester, V.A., Cloquell-Ballester, V.A., Monterde-Diaz, R. and Santamarina-Siurana, M.C., (2006). Indicators validation for the improvement of environmental and social impact quantitative assessment. *Environmental Impact Assessment Review, 26*(1), pp.79–105.

Connell, J.P. and Kubisch, A.C., (1998). Applying a theory of change approach to the evaluation of comprehensive community initiatives: progress, prospects, and problems. *New approaches to evaluating community initiatives, 2*(15–44), pp.1–16.

De Silva, M.J., Breuer, E., Lee, L., Asher, L., Chowdhary, N., Lund, C. and Patel, V., (2014). Theory of change: a theory-driven approach to enhance the Medical Research Council's framework for complex interventions. *Trials, 15*(1), pp.1–13.

Deeming, S., Searles, A., Reeves, P. and Nilsson, M., (2017). Measuring research impact in Australia's medical research institutes: a scoping literature review of the objectives for and an assessment of the capabilities of research impact assessment frameworks. *Health research policy and systems, 15*(1), pp.1–13.

D'Hombres, B., Rocco, L., Suhrcke, M. and McKee, M., (2010). Does social capital determine health? Evidence from eight transition countries. *Health economics, 19*(1), pp.56–74.

Dyakova, M., Hamelmann, C., Bellis, M.A., Besnier, E., Grey, C.N.B., Ashton, K., Schwappach, A., Clar, C (2017). Investment for health and well-being: a review of the social return on investment from public health policies to support implementing the Sustainable Development Goals by building on Health 2020 Health Evidence Network synthesis report 51, *WHO, Regional Office for Europe*, ISBN 978 92 890 5259 7;

Eisenhardt, K.M., (1989). Building theories from case study research. *Academy of management review, 14*(4), pp.532–550.

Ferrarini, T. and Sjöberg, O., (2010). Social policy and health: transition countries in a comparative perspective. *International Journal of Social Welfare*, *19*, pp.S60–S88.

Fullbright-Anderson, K., Kubisch, A.C. and Connell, J.P., (1998). New approaches to evaluating community initiatives: Theory, measurement, and analysis.

Gibbon, J. and Dey, C., (2011). Developments in social impact measurement in the third sector: scaling up or dumbing down?. *Social and Environmental Accountability Journal*, *31*(1), pp.63–72.

Goudet, S., Griffiths, P.L., Wainaina, C.W., Macharia, T.N., Wekesah, F.M., Wanjohi, M., Muriuki, P. and Kimani-Murage, E., (2018). Social value of a nutritional counselling and support program for breastfeeding in urban poor settings, Nairobi. *BMC public health*, *18*(1), pp.1–14.

Hamelmann, C., Turatto, F., Then, V., Dyakova, M. (2017). Social return on investment: accounting for value in the context of implementing Health 2020 and the 2030 Agenda for Sustainable Development. Discussion Paper. *WHO Regional Office for Europe*. Investment for Health and Development. Copenhagen;

Hill, P.S., Dodd, R., Brown, S. and Haffeld, J., (2012). Development cooperation for health: reviewing a dynamic concept in a complex global aid environment. *Globalization and Health*, *8*(1), pp.1–6.

Jackson, E.T., (2013). Interrogating the theory of change: evaluating impact investing where it matters most. *Journal of Sustainable Finance & Investment*, *3*(2), pp.95–110.

Jakovljevic, M., Arsenijevic, J., Pavlova, M., Verhaeghe, N., Laaser, U. and Groot, W., (2017). Within the triangle of healthcare legacies: comparing the performance of South-Eastern European health systems. *Journal of medical economics*, *20*(5), pp.483–492.

King, R. and Vullnetari, J., (2003). Migration and development in Albania.

Krlev, G., Münscher, R. and Mülbert, K., (2013). Social Return on Investment (SROI): state-of-the-art and perspectives—a meta-analysis of practice in Social Return on Investment (SROI) studies published 2002–2012.

Kutzin, J., Cashin, C., Jakab, M. and World Health Organization, (2010). *Implementing health financing reform: lessons from countries in transition*. World Health Organization. Regional Office for Europe.

Lingane, A. and Olsen, S., (2004). Guidelines for social return on investment. *California management review*, *46*(3), pp.116–135.

Maas, K. and Liket, K., (2011). Social impact measurement: Classification of methods. In *Environmental management accounting and supply chain management* (pp. 171–202). Springer, Dordrecht.

Macaulay, B., Roy, M.J., Donaldson, C., Teasdale, S. and Kay, A., (2018). Conceptualizing the health and well-being impacts of social enterprise: a UK-based study. *Health Promotion International*, *33*(5), pp.748–759.

Mayne, J., (2015). Useful theory of change models. *Canadian Journal of Program Evaluation*, *30*(2).

Millar, R. and Hall, K., (2013). Social return on investment (SROI) and performance measurement: The opportunities and barriers for social enterprises in health and social care. *Public Management Review*, *15*(6), pp.923–941.

Ministry of Health of the Republic of Albania (1993). A new policy for the health care sector in Albania. Tirana.

Ministry of Health of the Republic of Albania (2004). The long term strategy for the development of the Albanian Health System. Tirana.

Moody, M., Littlepage, L. and Paydar, N., (2015). Measuring social return on investment: Lessons from organizational implementation of SROI in the Netherlands and the United States. *Nonprofit Management and Leadership*, *26*(1), pp.19–37.

OECD (2019), Regions in Industrial Transition: Policies for People and Places, *OECD Publishing*, Paris.

Oketch, M., McCowan, T. and Schendel, R., (2014). The impact of tertiary education on development: A rigorous literature review.

Republic of Albania, National Council of Ministers (2008). National strategy for Development and Integration 2007–2013. NSDI, Tirana.

Ricciuti, E. and Bufali, M.V., (2019). The health and social impact of Blood Donors Associations: A Social Return on Investment (SROI) analysis. *Evaluation and program planning*, *73*, pp.204–213.

Rossi, E., Di Stefano, M., Baccetti, S., Firenzuoli, F., Verdone, M., Facchini, M., Stambolovich, V., Viña, M.P. and Caldés, M.J., (2010). International cooperation in support of homeopathy and complementary medicine in developing countries: the Tuscan experience. *Homeopathy*, *99*(4), pp.278–283.

Stein, D. and Valters, C., (2012). Understanding theory of change in international development.

Sullivan, H. and Stewart, M., (2006). Who owns the theory of change? *Evaluation*, *12*(2), pp.179–199.

Taddei, A., Gori, A., Rocca, E., Carducci, T., Piccini, G., Augiero, G., Festa, P., Assanta, N., Ricci, G. and Murzi, B., (2014). Telemedicine network for early diagnosis and care of heart malformations. In *The International Conference on Health Informatics* (pp. 268–271). Springer, Cham.

Tomaszewski, M. and Świadek, A., (2017). The impact of the economic conditions on the innovation activity of the companies from selected Balkan states. *Economic research-Ekonomska istraživanja*, *30*(1), pp.1896–1913.

WHO, Europe (2016). WORKING TOGETHER FOR BETTER HEALTH AND WELL-BEING Promoting Intersectoral and Interagency Action for Health and Well-being in the WHO European Region. High-level Conference 7–8 December 2016, Paris, France. *World Health Organization Regional Office for Europe*. Copenhagen.

WHO, Europe (2018). WHO European Office for Investment for Health and Development Biennial report 2016–2017. Edited by Nicole Satterley. *WHO European Office for Investment for Health and Development*. Copenhagen

Yin, R.K., (2012). Case study methods.

The Transformation of EU'S MU to a Real EMU as a Need for Addressing Crises

Charalampos Chrysomallidis

Abstract More than a decade has passed since the outbreak of deficit crisis in Greece, and the question that arose was whether Greek economy was stabilised—at least until the COVID-19 pandemic. On the other hand, economic prospects in Europe are related—up to a point—to next steps in European integration, especially those dealing with the transformation of Monetary Union (MU) into a real Economic and Monetary Union (EMU). This correlation may be crucial for 'peripheral' Eurozone member states. For the purposes of the article, the operation of Monetary Union and its implications for less competitive Eurozone member states, including Greece, is examined. In this analysis impact of fiscal and pandemic crises on economy is also taken into account. The article examines initiatives and proposals for making the MU resembling more to EMU under the pressure of recent crises, concluding that a potential evolution of existing architecture of the Eurozone seems to be necessary, in order to avoid similar asymmetric shocks and crises in the future.

Keywords Greece · Eurozone · Crisis · Growth · European integration · Fiscal union

JEL Classification F45 · H77 · P16

1 Introduction

Economic crisis of 2010s and impact of COVID-19 pandemic on economy have been major challenges that EU, and particularly Eurozone, should confront with; as member states have been affected by these developments. However, peripheral EU member states—that used to be known as 'cohesion countries' in the 1990s—have been affected in a more negative way, at the same time that are mostly dependent

C. Chrysomallidis (✉)
Department of Economics and Business, Neapolis University Paphos, 2 Danais Ave, Paphos, Cyprus
e-mail: c.chrysomallidis@nup.ac.cy

on decisions taken at the EU level, due to the fact that their economies are more vulnerable, they have less competitive productive capacities, etc.

The remainder of the paper is structured as follows: at first, we present theoretical background on economic integration, as well as economic reality for a peripheral EU member state within the Eurozone, examining Greece as a case study. The last section—before article's final remarks—analyses the need for transforming MU into a real EMU, relating potential reforms in the existing architecture of Eurozone, as potential next steps in European integration, to the prosperity in all Eurozone member states and their ability to address (future) crises.

2   Theoretical Background

The article relies on the classical approach of economic integration that may take various forms, such as free trade area, customs union, common market, monetary union and economic union. According to the main, introductory argumentation of static analysis, liberalisation of trade and the absence of barriers to mobility of factors of production, are key elements for increasing prosperity in economy. The benefits of creating a monetary union are related to reduction of transaction costs and uncertainty, due to lower exchange rate risk, while prices, among similar goods and factors of production, converge. Synthesis of many individual national economies leads to the establishment of a single, larger market that proves to be more competitive and more efficient in economic terms, under some critical preconditions, as it contributes to optimisation of resource allocation, improved ability for redistributing wealth and economy's growth at full employment level (Georgakopoulos and Christou 1992). However, competition makes weaker economic actors leave market; thus, big in size enterprises are favoured, either expanding their existing activities or through mergers and acquisitions. Therefore, adopting competition policy is a critical prerequisite for common markets, in order to avoid oligopolistic conditions.

In macroeconomic terms, a country and its economy may also face negative effects, as a result of its membership in any sort of economic union; thus, distribution of costs and benefits may vary among countries. In fact, it is expected that economies that will be benefited most from the creation of an integrated larger market, will be those having the largest and most competitive companies. Since some of the countries that participate in common market may have to deal with higher losses than benefits, transfer of resources and payments from countries that derive benefits to those that face the main losses is justified, according to theory. Beyond ensuring union's cohesion, the aim of this transfer is to contribute to productive and structural modernisation of recipient countries, in terms of infrastructure, human capital, technological level, etc., so as to enforce their growth potential, making, thus, easier real convergence among all member states' economies (Korres et al. 2010). On the other hand, being a member of an economic union implies that participating country loses some degrees of sovereignty and independence in exercising economic and public policy, although the range of that loss—mainly in trade, monetary, or even broadly, economic policy—depends on the level of union's institutionalisation (Giannakopoulos 1994; Theodoropoulos 2001).

On the whole, does economic integration fit all countries and all possible combinations of collaboration? The answer is definitely no. According to theory, high transport costs—that prevent price equalisation among countries—as well as serious differences in other parameters, both economic and non-economic, such as cultural factors and income level may be regarded as disincentives for establishing an economic union among some countries. Other crucial factors that should be examined, in order to assess, *ex ante,* whether participation of a country in (some kind of) economic union would be beneficial or not, refer to main characteristics not only of potentially participating economies (productive structure, divergence in production cost, transport cost, similar or not levels of income, etc.), but also of the union itself (size, tariffs' height, trade with third countries before the establishment of the union, etc.) (Georgakopoulos and Christou 1992; Pournarakis 1996).

In the case of Eurozone, (optimistic) analyses predicted that the cost of abandoning national currencies would be relatively low, as impact of independent monetary policies had been already rather limited. In addition, any cost for participating in EU's monetary union could be offset by the benefits that would result finally from it (Busetti et al. 2006; Mongelli 2008). However, several scholars and economists have expressed their doubts about the potential success of monetary union in EU, right from the beginning. Actually, the main objections were based on Optimum Currency Area (OCA) approach and the so-called 'Mundell's argument'. According to it, there was no evidence that EU constituted an optimum currency area, apparently on the basis of heterogeneity of national productive structures among EU member states, low price and wage flexibility and modest labour mobility (De Grauwe 2001). This position, which was documented right from the beginning, namely the launch of Economic and Monetary Union (EMU) reached the conclusion that some countries that would participate in EMU may suffer a loss of prosperity per se (De Grauwe 1994). Furthermore, Krugman and Obstfeld (2003) argued that EMU does not include the necessary degree of economic integration, bearing thus probably higher costs than benefits for some participating countries (Frankel and Rose 1996; Crespo-Cuaresma et al. 2005). In response to these analyses, and according to the viewpoint that prevailed at last, the operation of monetary union, by itself, would be able to reduce or curb structural differences, observed initially among member states, leading gradually to real convergence in terms of productivity and growth rates in all Eurozone countries (Bayoumi and Eichengreen 1996; Barbosa and Alves 2011).

On the other hand, according to theory of economic integration, potential sources of Eurozone's destabilisation may be asymmetries in the following—mostly interdependent—factors: demand disruptions, relevant trade disturbances, the inability of building a genuine European labour market, low money circulation in peripheral EU countries (e.g. due to economy's downturn), etc. These phenomena are directly related to different productive structures that are observed in participating economies; thus, the more asymmetric the 'shocks' and disturbances are, the more useful it would be to follow a national, independent monetary policy. Moreover, as integration goes on, differences in terms of productive specialisation deepen in practice, increasing the potential (negative) impact of asymmetric disorder among member states (Pelagidis 2012). In this case, it would be expected that less competitive economies would be at a disadvantage.[1] Adjustment cost will depend on effectiveness of 'correction' mechanisms. But, if they do not exist (as in the case of Eurozone), the 'demand-hit' state will be forced to reduce domestic circulation of money, mainly by reducing wages, provoking eventually economic recession (Pelagidis 2017).

3 Peripheral Countries and the Eurozone. Examining Greece as a Case Study

In good days, namely during the first decade of common currency's circulation, converging money costs among Eurozone member states was translated into low-interest rates in all participating countries. However, this has led to 'loss of fiscal discipline', and higher consumption mainly in peripheral and less competitive economies, leaving aside the need for structural reforms; the Greek case being a typical example of that. This was translated into expansion of consumer demand (and not higher investment) in the 2000s, both from public and private sectors (Fig. 1), thanks to increased borrowing, leading to twin deficits, in government budget and current account balance. These became even higher due to financial crisis of 2008. In this context, one may assume that the outburst of some sort of economic crisis in Greece was inevitable; the main issue was when that would happen and for what reason.

As a matter of fact, Walters warned back in 1990 that if a single level of nominal interest rates prevailed throughout the monetary union, this would lead to high consumption and investment boom that would destabilise weaker economies. Thus, '(m)uch as Walters (1990) *had forecast, the countries at the periphery of the eurozone saw booms in construction spending (Ireland, Spain), consumption spending (Portugal) and government spending (Greece), as the cost of borrowing for households, firms and governments came down. Their spending booms were financed by large capital flows from the monetary union's core to its periphery, and they were reflected in equally large current account deficits for the eurozone periphery and surpluses for the core. When doubts arose in 2009-10 about the sustainability of the process, those capital flows came to a sudden stop, imparting a destabilising asymmetric shock. The clear implication, emphasised by Walters, was that this asymmetric shock was intrinsic to the operation of the monetary union'* (Eichengreen 2014: 3).

Thus, Eurozone peripheral countries sharing—by and large—common characteristics (e.g. less competitive productive capacities, more clientelistic political systems, rather inefficient public administrations and public sector covering a quite large part of national economic activity) have not taken advantage during the 2000s of the possibilities that sound and stable macroeconomic environment—attributed to common currency-offered, being trapped in financial crises, of greater or lesser intensity (Maravegias and Katsikas 2017). At the same time, core countries of the Eurozone were taking steps to boost further their competitiveness. The consequence of these

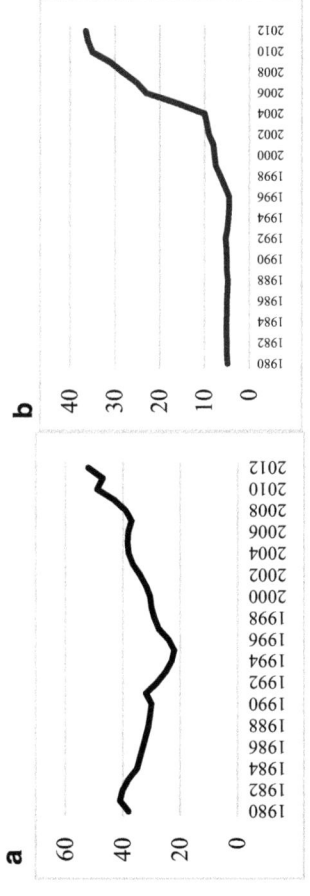

Fig. 1 a, b Loans to enterprises and households in Greece (as % of GDP). *Source* Bank of Greece (elaborated data)

opposite practices was the development of centrifugal dynamic among the Eurozone member states, in the wake of the financial crisis (Petrakis et al. 2013).

Under these circumstances, one should bear in mind a structural characteristic of EMU the fact that the European Central Bank (ECB) is not able to meet simultaneously all conflicting needs arising from different Eurozone member states. This means that EMU is unable to cope with demand disruptions, due to the way that it was initially designed. After the outburst of financial crisis of 2008 and fiscal crisis in some Eurozone member states, there were simultaneously two disturbing situations: Economic turbulence—due to global financial crisis and structural productive and economic weaknesses of South-European countries—was combined with the locked exchange rate and price inflexibility for domestic products. This has led further to serious loss of competitiveness, and exports' decrease; thus, the most vulnerable Eurozone countries had to face high deficits in trade balance, too (Maravegias 2015).

Having in mind the above-mentioned characteristics of the Eurozone, as well as serious structural differences among its member states, internal devaluation was chosen as the main adjustment instrument for all countries that agreed for a bail-out programme with their lenders. Although this could be regarded initially as rational, in economic terms, it has contributed to a situation where economy was trapped to deeper recession, making adjustment difficult for member states with fiscal problems. In the Greek case, the fact that necessary reforms and relevant policy means were not adequately implemented deteriorated further socio-economic conditions (Wolff 2018).

4   The Impact of Fiscal Crisis and Covid-19 Pandemic on Greek Economy

When examining some exploratory positions of International Monetary Fund (IMF) that were produced in March 2010, namely after the outbreak of financial crisis in Greece, but before the agreement for the first bail-out programme, it is interesting to note that IMF confirms the 'peripherality' hypothesis for Greek economy, recognising failures of domestic economic policy and admitting indirectly that participation in the Eurozone deteriorated conditions for economy, according to *ex-post* analyses (Ignatiou 2015). IMF's analysis refers also to the ineffectiveness of fiscal policy, as there has been a significant increase in spending and fiscal deficits, just before the outbreak of crisis, in the late 2000s (Figs. 2 and 3).

As already mentioned, according to mainstream economics, it is necessary under these circumstances to reduce money circulation in economy, via internal devaluation. Interestingly, the IMF itself had predicted to some extent, from the beginning, the negative consequences of this policy for Greek economy, but there were no easy solutions under such demanding circumstances. Actually, the IMF expected that

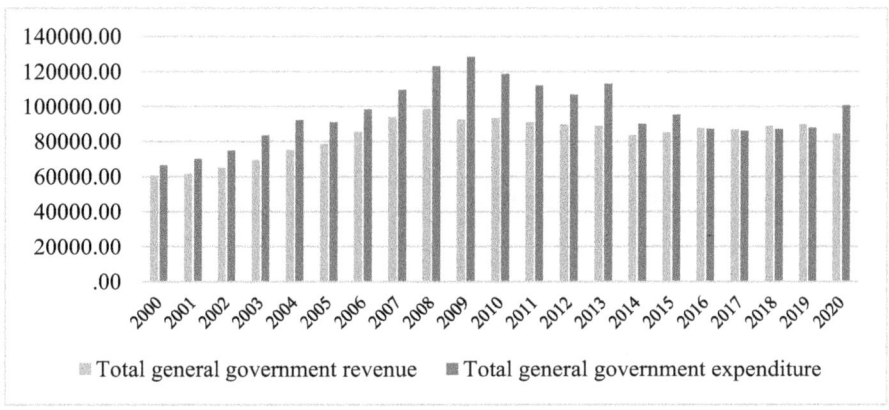

Fig. 2 Public revenues and expenditure in Greece (million €). *Source* Eurostat (gov_10a_main)

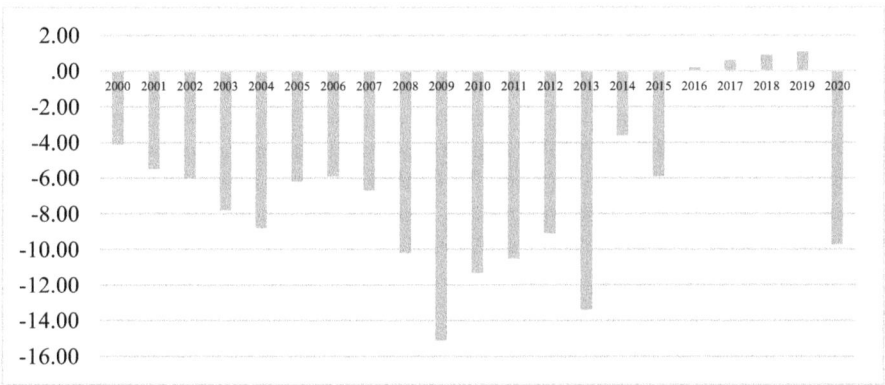

Fig. 3 Deficit of general government in Greece (as % of GDP). *Source* Eurostat (gov_10dd_edpt1)

there would be a 'deflationary scenario', according to which GDP would decline for several years. Domestic expenditure, (and tax revenues, too) would decrease, affecting negatively the debt/GDP ratio (actually, debt/GDP ratio's evolution is presented in Fig. 4). Therefore, fiscal adjustment should be realistic and relatively mild; otherwise, domestic demand was expected to shrink sharply, deepening further recession. IMF's analysis predicted that debt to GDP ratio would reach 150% by 2013, while deficit would be lower than 3% in 2014. During discussion of the IMF Board on the adoption of the Greek bail-out program, it was supported that Greek debt would be viable in the medium term, although there were significant doubts even for that (Ignatiou 2015; Wolff 2018).

Greek governments were definitely responsible for delays in implementing reforms; and in practice, government's failures and country's urgent financing needs made the final program and its conditions 'hard, difficult and painful', as it was

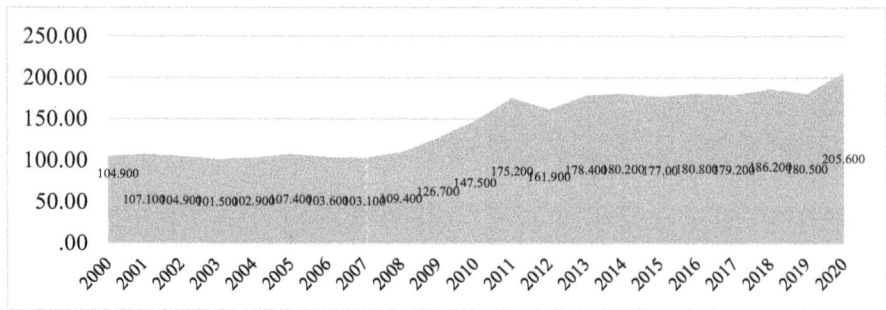

Fig. 4 General government debt ratio in Greece (as % of GDP). *Source* Eurostat (gov_10dd_edpt1)

described by the IMF, having to deal at the same time with low competitiveness, poor public finances and pressure to the banking and financial sector (Ignatiou 2015; Maravegias 2015).

Recession trap in the Greek case may be attributed—according to economic theory—to the following sequence: wage cuts and high taxation lead to lower demand and consumption and secondly to reduction in savings, affecting negatively investment and production, while high uncertainty (e.g. increased risk of unemployment) contributes to cash holding. All this happens rationally for each economic individual, separately, but the ultimate outcome can be described as a gathering of self-acting rationalists, whose decisions and actions lead to severe collapse of total demand, deepening further crisis (Christodoulakis 2012).

Finally, economy seemed to be stabilised after 2016, approximately at the levels of the late 1990s. In terms of investment, there is significant decline, which ranged from −23.4% (in 2012) to −4.4% (in 2014), following also two years of constant reductions (2010 and 2011) (Bank of Greece 2015, 2017). Stabilisation was achieved in 2015, as well as a slight increase in 2016 (around 1.5%), but references to existing 'investment gap' or 'investment deficit' in the country are repeated (PWC 2017; SEV and Deloitte 2018).

In EU, other countries, such as Ireland, Cyprus, Portugal, Spain, Latvia and Hungary, suffered severely from consequences of the 2008 financial crisis, but all returned to growth, although they still face difficulties, for instance in terms of national income distribution and inequality. As a matter of fact, social adaptation has been violent in some of them (e.g. Ireland and Cyprus), as adjustment cost has been high for citizens, but even in these cases GDP has already surpassed pre-crisis level. In other words, although other countries had also to deal with crisis's consequences, they achieved recovery, at least in some areas of economic activity and national production (Chrysomallidis and Maravegias 2017). On the contrary, Greece needed more than 7 years to stabilise its economy at around 80% of its pre-crisis GDP. From this aspect, Greek crisis was the most intense and lasting, having the most serious, negative impact on economy, at the same time that it proved to be the most complicated in political terms; thus, political turbulence[2] was added to tenuous economic conditions. Exiting crisis was bound with a slight return to economic

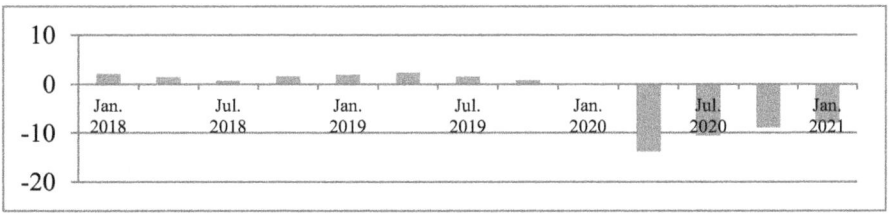

Fig. 5 Rates of economic growth in Greece, in the COVID-19 era (as % of GDP). *Source* https://tradingeconomics.com/greece/gdp-growth-annual

growth. From 2017 to 2019 rates of economic growth were limited to 0.5–1.5% of GDP, proving that those economists, who argued that economy has accumulated unexploited resources and potential during crisis that would contribute to higher rates of economic growth (more than 2.5–3.0% of GDP), right after exiting crisis, were wrong.

However, it was proved that things could go even worse, as COVID-19 pandemic emerged, hitting societies and economies globally (OECD 2020a). Data show the severe impact that this particular crisis and relevant policy measures (e.g. lock-down) had on Greek economy, for instance in terms of rates of economic growth (Fig. 5) and balance of payments of the general government, which is a crucial indicator for Greek debt in the post-fiscal crisis era. Negative impact in macroeconomic terms is highlighted also in previous figures (Figs. 2, 3 and 4). According to several analyses, economies like the Greek one have been mostly affected by the pandemic, as they depend significantly on demand from abroad, being among the less competitive EU member states (Barbier-Gauchard et al. 2020; Barro et al. 2020; HFC 2020; Sidiropoulos 2020). Moreover, conditions in the pandemic era have led to income loss in Greece, particularly in regions, where employment is heavily dependent on tourism industry, as well as for specific categories of employees and non-standard workers, such as self-employed and part-time employed individuals (OECD 2020b; Zavras 2021). Thus, Greece has experienced a prolonged economic recession, and the COVID-19 pandemic is slowing down its recovery efforts, while economic impact may be more severe than that of fiscal crisis, deteriorating further citizens' professional life, economic activities, personal life and well-being (Papanikos 2020; Vatavali et al. 2020).

5 Next Steps in European Integration as a Defining Parameter for Eurozone Economies' Prospects

Under these conditions, and before the emergence of COVID-19 crisis, could be a country's exit from the Eurozone, a solution? Several analysts have described such a scenario and its possible implications for the Greek case at the peak of crisis (from 2012 to 2015), but also for other countries (e.g. Italy), too. Different analyses agree that adopting a national currency would have major negative consequences for society and economy, due to the definitely severe devaluation of the new currency. That would contribute only slightly to improvement of domestic products' competitiveness, deteriorating dramatically living standards of Greek society (Valinakis et al. 2014; Maravegias 2015).

However, as long as EMU's structure remains the same, any negative economic juncture will probably lead to new asymmetric shocks that will affect peripheral Eurozone economies, testing not only their strengths but also Eurozone's limits. This implies that these countries continue to live under the fear of a next crisis, even if it seems that their economies have been stabilised.

The fact that Eurozone is still a monetary union (MU) and not a real EMU is actually the main point of criticism for its current form (Gros 2017; Sawyer 2017). According to that viewpoint, there is the need for Monetary Union's evolution, integrating some features of fiscal union. For this purpose, there have been several proposals, trying to face imbalances of Eurozone, as it stands now. One of the most holistic solutions is to replicate the mechanism met in federal systems and countries for providing income distribution among different regions. A well-known example of this practice is the so-called *Finanzausgleich* in Germany. However, implementing a similar system among the Eurozone countries would entail a significant increase in EU budget's resources and a severe transfer of money from national to supranational level, in parallel with the establishment of a kind of European budgetary authority; these options seem today to be rather unrealistic.

Other proposals focus indicatively on: (i) unification of bond market for Eurozone member states (an idea that implies some kind of debt consolidation), (ii) elimination of competition among countries on the basis of tax differentiation, favouring a tax union and tax harmonisation among member states, (iii) promotion of a truly unified European labour market that would contribute to some absorption of economic disruptions and (iv) the continuing process of integration that would lead probably to a political union, by attributing key national competencies to supranational level (Pelagidis 2012; Maravegias 2015).

On the other hand, according to De Grauwe (2013), the ECB should enrich its role and activities, combining features that will be closer to what was known as the old model of national central banks, since the absolutely stabilising element of an economy, the lender of last resort, does not exist anymore for Eurozone member states. In addition, Eurozone should introduce mechanisms to secure implementation of symmetrical fiscal policies among its member states; thus, a degree of centralisation of fiscal policy will allow better overview of fiscal conditions and coordination of fiscal policies followed in each member state. Economic policy will combine in that way distinct, but supplementary fiscal measures that would serve at the same time different needs in Eurozone member states. Eichengreen (2014) comes to similar conclusions since the operation of banking union, the integration of fiscal union with distributional consequences within the EMU, as well as the preparation and operation of a mechanism for restructuring probably member states' debts are regarded to be the prerequisites for a sustainable monetary union.

In practice, the banking union proposal that was presented by the European Commission, itself seems more realistic, although the degree of implementation varies considerably when examining different versions of this particular undertaking. However, Demertzis and Wolff (2018) argue that after Eurogroup's agreement on reform of the EMU[3], banking union continues to suffer from a missing European Deposit Insurance System, as well as from a lack of clarity on how the roles between national treasuries, the European Stability Mechanism, the Single Resolution Board (SRB) and the ECB are divided in bank resolution, failing finally to serve financial stability. In any case, though, building a resilient banking union would reduce or at least curb some of the disruptions that the Eurozone has suffered from time to time, especially those that arise from national banking systems.

In this context, other advanced proposals refer to creating the post of European Minister of Economy and Finance, the introduction of Capital Markets Union, the establishment of a financial instrument for structural reform support, being integrated in the European Semester process, the introduction of National Competitiveness Authorities coordinated by the Commission, the introduction of a European Fiscal Board to assist national fiscal councils, etc. (European Commission 2015, 2017).

On the other hand, the prospect of turning the ESM into a European Monetary Fund may be also considered to be a first 'firefighting' initiative to avoid the extent of similar crises in the future. Although this measure is regarded as one of the most nation-friendly solutions, at least for those member states that bear the greatest burden of lending countries in bail-out programmes, it is not certain that the EMF will be established, as that would imply that most prosperous countries may be indirectly fiscally equalised with the rest Eurozone member states, within a potentially binding European fiscal federation. In other words, '(t)*he more a preventive approach can be reinforced, the less recourse is needed to euro-level emergency measures, the greater will be the confidence that such measures can be introduced without risking "moral hazard"*' (Watt and Watzka 2018: 16).

When relevant discussion refers to the next Multi-annual financial framework (MFF) and the probable need for additional tools, that would contribute to EMU's sound operation, it should be clear that certain functions (cross-country risk-sharing and counter-cyclical stabilisation) can be performed only through fiscal instruments in a monetary union, and these functions should not be mixed with the budget of the whole EU. Actually, in the MFF proposal, Eurozone compartment includes a Reform Support Programme (RSP) and a European Investment Stabilisation Function (EISF), but these are characterised as '… *an attempt at political fudge, promoted by those who fear that economically sounder instruments might be impossible to agree politically*' (Andor 2018: 17). Thus, out of the three key functions of public finance (allocation, redistribution and stabilisation) it is primarily stabilisation that provides a rationale for the debate on a so-called Eurozone budget (Wolff 2017), while counter-cyclical potential in the existing EU budget remains very small (Rinaldi and Núñez Ferrer 2017).

On the other hand, in the case of dealing with pandemic's effects on European economies, and as a result of the need to increase public spending for mitigating negative results of pandemic on households and especially the business sector, a crucial discussion has started in EU about the need to make European Central Bank eligible to purchase public debt of countries that take up loans, due to COVID-19, the establishment of a recovery fund, as well as activation of the general escape clause of the Stability and Growth Pact (Boitani and Tamborini 2020; De Grauwe 2020; Wyplosz 2020; Tooze 2020). To some extent, critical decisions have been made by the EU, at the same time that—even under crisis conditions, trying again to deal with emergency circumstances—these developments continue to cultivate further— indirectly and rather hesitantly, though—an evolving framework for fostering further integration on the grounds of economic policy and governance.

In any case, the need for transforming MU into a real EMU is still here, being of great importance for Eurozone, as a whole, but mostly for peripheral Eurozone countries, as an EMU with a new architecture would give them the ability to face more efficiently any future economic asymmetric turbulence. The practice of rescuing Eurozone member states' economies in the period 2010–2016 was imposed mainly on the basis of the only available adjustment mechanism at that time[4]. During the new crisis, EU seems again to react to face demanding challenges, without having already operated a crisis management mechanism. At least, this time, crisis has more symmetrical impact and results. Therefore, it is vital to enrich architecture and operation of the Eurozone with other elements, too, beyond emergency decisions, having in mind that Eurozone still fails to converge booms and busts among different, but more and more interdependent, economies.

6   Conclusions

Starting point for our analysis has been the thesis that economic prospects in Europe are related—up to a point—to next steps in European integration, especially those dealing with the transformation of MU into a real EMU. The reason for that was that after the fiscal crisis of 2009–2016 and the pandemic crisis that emerged in Europe in 2020, this correlation proves to be crucial for Eurozone economies, especially the 'peripheral' ones. For the purposes of the article, the operation of Monetary Union and its implications for less competitive Eurozone member states, including Greece, was examined, referring also impact of fiscal and pandemic crises on Greek economy that is presented as a case study of peripheral EU member state.

Previous analysis has highlighted the fact that a crucial condition—amongst others—for making participation in the Eurozone sustainable and more advanta- geous not only for Greece but for other member states that share similar political and economic characteristics, is transforming Eurozone to an Economic and Mone- tary Union. This kind of political decision would indicatively imply comprehen- sive control of fiscal policies in different member states, requiring at the same time symmetry and complementarity between them. In other words, crises and the need to deal with them indicate the need to combine monetary and fiscal policy in a way that goes beyond economic policy at the national level. Moreover, the provision of fiscal compensation among countries could be regarded as a next step towards a deeper and more substantial fiscal union. However, these options are unlikely to be agreed and implemented, at least in the near future in EU, as a potential agreement for the future of Eurozone faces the challenge of choosing between economically prudent and appropriate solutions on the one hand, and politically acceptable solutions, on the other (Pisani-Ferry 2013). However, Van Rompuy et al. (2012) mentioned—profoundly as a generic idea without referring to the exact way to achieve this—that major steps towards a Banking Union, Fiscal Union and Political Union were needed, within the foreseeable future, to avoid operating issues within the EMU framework.

In any case, Eurozone crisis was the result firstly of economic and political failures in some countries (mostly in Greece) and secondly of major economic and structural differences among its member states, combined with the existing architecture of Eurozone. As Rodriguez (2017) mentioned, the challenge, now, is to re-establish economic and social cohesion in EU, making it again one of the main objectives of European integration, since stabilisation objective by itself maybe not enough. These issues could come in parallel to emergency conditions that emerged due to COVID-19 pandemic, as well as the discussion about the goals of sustainable development in Europe towards 2030.

Notes

1. Within the existing framework of Eurozone, when an EMU member state faces a positive demand disorder, another (actually, the less competitive one) will face a negative one. In this case, the former will have to cope with trade surplus, but the latter with trade deficit.
2. Five national elections took place in Greece between 2009 and 2015.
3. Eurogroup report to Leaders on EMU deepening, 4 December 2018, available at https://www.consilium.europa.eu/el/press/press-releases/2018/12/04/eurogr oup-report-to-leaders-on-emu-deepening/pdf (accessed 23 December 2011).
4. According to Patterson and Amati (1998), mechanisms of adaptation within a MU may be related either to market or institutional mechanisms. In the first case, the adjustment concerns wage and price flexibility, and labour and capital mobility. On the other hand, institutional mechanisms are related to automatic transfers (probably according to fiscal federalism), allowing direct transfer of resources among different regions, member states, etc.

References

Andor, L. (2018). Resources for a prosperous Europe. Redesigning the EU Budget on a progressive way. *Friedrich Ebert Stiftung WISO Diskurs,* No. 18.

Bank of Greece (2015). Financial Stability Review. *Bank of Greece, November-December 2015,* Vol. 165.

Bank of Greece (2017). Financial Stability Review. *Bank of Greece, November-December 2017,* Vol. 177.

Barbier-Gauchard, A. et al. (2020). Towards a more resilient European Union after the COVID-19 crisis. *Bureau d'Économie Théorique et Appliquée—BETA*, Working paper n° 2020—33.

Barbosa, J.R. and Alves, R.H. (2011). Divergent Competiveness in the Eurozone and the Optimum Currency Area Theory. *FEP Working Paper,* No. 436.

Barro, R. et al. (2020). The Coronavirus and the Great Influenza Epidemic Lessons from the "Spanish Flu" for the Coronavirus's Potential Effects on Mortality and Economic Activity. *CESifo Working Papers,* No. 8166/2020.

Bayoumi, T. and Eichengreen, B. (1996). Ever Closer to Heaven? An Optimum-Currency-Area Index for European Countries. *European Economic Review,* 41(3), 761—770.

Boitani, A. and Tamborini, R. (2020). Crisis and reform of the Eurozone. Why do we disagree? A reflection paper on the North-South divide. *Friedrich Ebert Stiftung.*

Busetti, F. et al. (2006). Inflation convergence and divergence within the European Monetary Union. *European Central Bank Working Paper Series,* No. 574.

Christodoulakis, N. (2012). *Economic theories and crises. Histories of rationalism and imprudence.* Kritiki, Athens.

Chrysomallidis, C. and Maravegias, N. (2017). European Integration and the Greek Economy: Greece at the Core or on the Periphery of Europe? *Region & Periphery Scientific Review,* 6—7, 71—97.

Crespo-Cuaresma, J. et al. (2005). Growth, Convergence and EU Membership. *Austrian National Bank Working Paper,* No. 2005-62.

De Grauwe, P. (1994). *The Economics of Monetary Integration.* Oxford University Press, Oxford.

De Grauwe, P. (ed.) (2001). *The political economy of monetary union.* Edward Elgar, Cheltenham.

De Grauwe, P. (2013). Design failures in the Eurozone: Can they be fixed? *LSE 'Europe in Question' Discussion Paper Series LEQS Paper,* No. 57/2013.

De Grauwe, P. (2020). The Need for Monetary Financing of Corona Budget Deficits. https://doi.org/10.1007/s10272-020-0885-1.

Demertzis, M. and Wolff, G. (2018). Providing funding in resolution: Unfinished business even after Eurogroup agreement on EMU reform. *Bruegel Blog,* available at http://bruegel.org/2018/12/providing-funding-in-resolution-unfinished-business-even-after-eurogroup-agreement-on-emu-reform/

Eichengreen, B. (2014). The eurozone crisis: the theory of optimum currency areas bites back. *Notenstein Academy White Paper Series.*

European Commission (2015). Completing Europe's Economic and Monetary Union. *Report by Jean-Claude Juncker in close cooperation with Donald Tusk, Jeroen Dijsselbloem, Mario Draghi and Martin Schulz.*

European Commission (2017). Communication from the Commission to the European Parliament, the European Council, the Council and the European Central Bank. A European Minister of Economy and Finance. *COM(2017) 823 final.*

Frankel, J. and Rose, A. (1996). The Endogeneity of the Optimum Currency Area Criteria. *Economic Journal,* 109, 1009—1025.

Georgakopoulos, T. and Christou, G. (1992). *Lectures on theory of economic integration.* Stamoulis, Athens.

Giannakopoulos, N. (1994). *International trade.* Stamoulis, Athens.

Gros, D. (2017). The Commission's views on strengthening the Euro area: Barking up the wrong tree? *CEPS Commentary,* available at https://www.ceps.eu/publications/commissions-views-strengthening-euro-area-barking-wrong-tree

HFC (2020). Analysing macroeconomic provisions regarding the 2021 State Budget. *Hellenic Fiscal Council.*

Ignatiou, M. (2015). *Troika.* Livanis, Athens.

Korres, G. et al. (2010). *Economic of European integration,* Stamoulis, Athens.

Krugman, P. and Obstfeld, M., 2003. *International economics: Theory and policy.* Pearson Education Inc, Boston.

Maravegias, N. (2015). *The promise… of growth in Greece.* Papazisis, Athens.

Maravegias, N. and Katsikas, D. (2017). Crisis in Southern European countries and failures of the Eurozone: The case of Greece. In: A. Kontis and S. Verny (eds), *European Integration, Crises and Future Perspectives*. Papazisis, Athens, 372—390.

Mongelli, F.P. (2008). European economic and monetary integration, and the optimum currency area theory. *European Economy Economic Papers,* No. 302.

OECD (2020a). OECD Economic Outlook—No. 107. *Organisation for Economic Co-operation and Development.*

OECD (2020b). *Regional Policy for Greece Post-2020.* OECD Publishing, Paris.

Papanikos, G. (2020). The impact of the COVID-19 pandemic on Greek tourism. *Athens Journal of Tourism*, 7(2), 87—100.

Patterson, B. and Amati, S. (1998). Adjustment to asymmetric shocks. *European Parliament Economic Affairs Series Directorate-General for Research Working Paper*, ECON 104, 09-98.

Pelagidis, T. (2012). European economic and monetary integration in the context of globalization. In: N. Maravegias and M. Tsinisizelis (eds), *New European Union: 50 years.* Themelio, Athens, 316—341.

Pelagidis, T. (2017). Why is economy's recovery anaemic? *I Kathimerini,* 13 November.

Petrakis, P. et al, 2013. *European economics and politics in the midst of the crisis. From the outbreak of crisis to the fragmented European Federation.* Springer, London.

Pisani-Ferry, J. (2013). The politics of moral hazard. *Bruegel blog,* available at http://bruegel.org/2013/03/the-politics-of-moral-hazard/

Pournarakis, E. (1996). *International Economics. An introductory analysis,* Athens University of Economics and Business Publications, Athens.

PWC (2017). From recession to anaemic growth. *PWC Greece,* available at https://www.pwc.com/gr/en/publications/greek-thought-leadership/investments-greece.pdf

Rinaldi, D. and Núñez Ferrer, J. (2017). Towards an EU budget with an effective stabilisation function. *FIRSTRUN research papers,* available at http://www.firstrun.eu/files/2017/04/EU-Budget-Stabilisation-Function-FirstRun-v3-1.pdf

Rodriguez, M.J. (2017). *Europe is still possible—Political adventures in the 21st century*. Paper presented at the 15th International Globelics Conference. Athens, Greece, 11–13 October.

Sawyer, M. (2017). *Can the Euro be saved?* Polity, Cambridge.

SEV and Deloitte (2018). Toolkit for accelerating productive investment. *Hellenic Federation of Enterprises,* available at http://www.sev.org.gr/Uploads/Documents/50906/0_Investment_Toolkit_handbook_19_4.pdf

Sidiropoulos, M. (2020). What can Central Banks do to address the Covid-19 crisis. *unpublished paper.*

Theodoropoulos, S. (2001). *Development and prospects of European economic integration.* Stamoulis, Athens.

Tooze, A. (2020). Light in the tunnel or oncoming train? Available at: https://www.socialeurope.eu/light-in-the-tunnel-or-oncoming-train

Valinakis, G. et al. (2014). *Exiting crisis. Feasible alternative proposals.* Papazisis, Athens.

Van Rompuy, H. et al. (2012). Towards a genuine Economic and Monetary Union. Available at https://www.consilium.europa.eu/media/23818/134069.pdf

Vatavali, F. et al. (2020). Impact of COVID-19 on Urban Everyday Life in Greece. Perceptions, Experiences and Practices of the Active Population. *Sustainability*, 12, https://doi.org/10.3390/su12229410.

Walters, A. (1990). *Sterling in Danger*. Fontana, London.

Watt, A. and Watzka, S. (2018). Overcoming Euro area fragility. *IMK Macroeconomic Policy Institute*, IMK Report 139, available at https://www.boeckler.de/pdf/p_imk_report_139_2018.pdf

Wolff, G. (2017). Eurozone or EU budget? Confronting a complex political question. *Bruegel blog*, available at http://bruegel.org/2017/06/eurozone-or-eu-budget-confronting-a-complex-political-question/

Wolff, G. (2018). Griechenland braucht einen Neuanfang. *Bruegel blog,* available at http://bruegel.
    org/2018/07/griechenland-braucht-einen-neuanfang/
Wyplosz, C. (2020). A Covid test for Europe. Available at: https://www.fuw.ch/article/a-covid-test-
    for-europe/
Zavras, D. (2021). A cross-sectional population-based study on the influence of the COVID-19
    pandemic on incomes in Greece. *AIMS Public Health,* 8(3), 376–387.

MNEs Institutional Entrepreneurship: The Effect on Corruption. An Analysis of Emerging Economies

Xanthippe Adamoglou, Vasiliki Kounnou, Yannis Hajidimitriou, and Dimitris Kyrkilis

Abstract This paper examines the impact MNEs exert on the corruption level of emerging economies. The research employs the institutional entrepreneurship theory. It is hypothesized that, in emerging economies, MNEs presence reduces the level of corruption. Furthermore, it is hypothesized that the faster the rate of increase of the number of MNEs in the country, the faster the increase of pervasive corruption level. The sample consists of seventeen emerging economies. The period of analysis extends from 2012 to 2019. The fix effect model has been applied to the panel dataset to test the model hypotheses. Results indicate that MNEs presence reduces the level of corruption in the said host emerging economies. On the contrary, the hypothesis that the higher the rate of increase of the number of MNEs in the host emerging economies, the higher the level of pervasive corruption in such economies is not supported.

Keywords Multinational enterprises · Corruption · Institutional entrepreneurship · Emerging economies · Foreign direct investment

X. Adamoglou (✉) · V. Kounnou
University of Macedonia, Thessaloniki, Greece
e-mail: adamoglou@uom.edu.gr

V. Kounnou
e-mail: vasi14nou@uom.edu.gr

Y. Hajidimitriou
International Business, University of Macedonia, Thessaloniki, Greece
e-mail: Hajidm@uom.edu.gr

D. Kyrkilis
Economics, University of Macedonia, Thessaloniki, Greece
e-mail: kyrkilis@uom.edu.gr

© The Author(s), under exclusive license to Springer Nature Switzerland AG 2022   109
P. Sklias et al. (eds.), *Business Development and Economic Governance in Southeastern Europe*, Springer Proceedings in Business and Economics,
https://doi.org/10.1007/978-3-031-05351-1_6

1 Introduction

Research on Multinational Enterprises (MNEs) international expansion is well established in International Business (IB) literature (Stopford and Wells 1972; Ellis 2000). Much of this research has related corruption with Foreign Direct Investment (FDI) activity (Habib and Zurawicki 2002; Doh et al. 2005; Rodriguez et al. 2005; Uhlenbruck et al. 2006), illustrating both positive (Cuervo-Cazurra 2006) and negative (McGuinness and Demirbag 2012) impact of FDI activity on corruption.

Such endeavors have been particularly supported by the institutional theory (North 1990; Scott 1995), and, more specifically, new organizational institutionalism. Researchers have linked variations in pressure for internal and external legitimacy with variations in FDI activity (Davis et al. 2000; Chan and Makino 2007) producing, however, inconclusive results. A possible explanation for these results is that new organizational institutionalism, due to its emphasis on how organizational forms and practices are shaped by their environments (Hotho and Pedersen 2012), has been trapped into what is called "embedded agency" (Seo and Creed 2002). Embedded agency refers to the "tension between institutional determinism and agency" (Battilana et al. 2009, p. 67), implying that firms must conform and adapt to institutional pressures if they wish to gain legitimacy within any organizational field (García-Cabrera and Durán-Herrera 2016, p. 1). Consequently, using this aspect of institutional theory to explore the relationship between corruption and FDI activity is misleading, as Birkinshaw and Morrison (1995) point out.

In parallel, a new emerging strand of literature (Crouch 2005; Hancké and Goyer 2005; Streeck and Thelen 2005; Kwok and Tadesse 2006) has emphasized the other side of the coin, i.e., how MNEs agency affect the establishment and change of institutions. These endeavors have been mainly directed to emerging economies (Robertson and Watson 2004; Collins et al. 2009) and expressed either through the new comparative institutional reasoning (Saka-Helmhout and Geppert 2011), or from a strategic (Robertson and Watson 2004) or management (Collins and Uhlenbruck 2004; Collins et al. 2009) perspective. However, this substantial field of research has presented paucity, since it has yet to spell out answers to a key question, i.e., the agency of MNEs (Battilana and D'Aunno 2009; Saka-Helmhout and Geppert 2011) on corruption under the interpretation of institutional entrepreneurship reasoning.

Indeed, the institutional background of entrepreneurship (Segerstrom et al. 1990; Baumol 1993) has paid particular attention to the correlation of institutions (North 1990) with growth (Romer 1990; Temple 1999) and economic policies (Barro 1991). However, less interest has been drawn to answering the question of how MNEs instigate changes to the corruption level of a host country. This is why the research at hand proceeds to fill this gap in the relevant literature by examining how MNEs affect the corruption level in emerging economies. To do so, the paper addresses two research questions: First, it investigates the positive influence MNEs exert on corruption levels in emerging economies. Second, following Robertson and Watson (2004), it investigates whether the rate of increase of the number of MNEs in the host emerging economies affects the level of corruption in the said countries.

This research differs from previous literature in three distinctive ways: First, it employs institutional entrepreneurship reasoning to provide a rich analysis of how MNEs shape the corruption level in emerging economies. Second, it illustrates the positive aspect of such a relationship, i.e., how MNEs presence reduces the corruption level in the emerging economy, providing clear insight. Third, it emphasizes the conceptualization of institutional change as a necessary and important mechanism that underscores the agency of MNEs on corruption (Robertson and Watson 2004).

The choice of institutional entrepreneurship reasoning, herein, emerges as useful and appropriate because it involves two necessary elements for this analysis to take place: institutional entrepreneurs and institutional change. Institutional entrepreneurs refer to change agents or actors (organizations or groups of organizations, or individuals or groups of individuals) (Fligstein 1997; Garud et al. 2002; Greenwood et al. 2002; Maguire et al. 2004) initiating institutional changes in the host country. Institutional change refers to the transformation of existing or the establishment of new institutions (DiMaggio 1988; Battilana et al. 2009) in the host country. In other words, it refers to changes that emanate from the everyday and contemporary behavior of individuals but concludes with the transformation of the field-level logic (Smets et al. 2017).

Emerging economies are also excellent research settings since they are characterized by insufficient and immature institutions (Peng 2003; Dieleman and Sachs 2008), due to the changing nature of the local economic, institutional, and business environment (Meyer and Peng 2005). Therefore, these economies seem to be easily influenced by MNEs entrepreneurship (Alon and Rottig 2013) which contributes to the incremental creation of new institutional stability, e.g., "the newly legitimated characteristics of an emerging institutional framework" (Chung and Beamish 2005, p. 36).

The paper makes a series of key contributions to the existing body of literature: **First**, it reverses the dominant question that prevails in relevant literature examining the relationship from a different perspective, i.e., MNEs impact on corruption in emerging economies. This way, the paper offers new insights concerning the criteria by which the approach of such a relationship has been examined so far.

Second, this study acknowledges the significance of the agency theory and new comparative institutionalism reasonings. It also acknowledges the issues derived from agency theory, i.e., the differences (Andreas et al. 2012), or else, the conflict of interest (Mallin et al. 2015) between boards of directors and shareholders. Thus, this research departs from the dominant conceptual settings, employing the reasoning of institutional entrepreneurship. Such a theory offers a more integrative and holistic perspective than agency in that it mixes agency and institutional theory, thereby stressing institutions as important factors that both constrain and enable the choice of actors (Hoffman and Ventresca 2002; Thornton and Ocasio 2008; Ang et al. 2014). Furthermore, the theory illustrates the potential role MNEs might play as change agents in the host institutional setting. Last, the paper examines whether institutional entrepreneurship theory can be applied to very different contexts, such as the impact of MNEs presence on host institutional settings.

Third, this research illustrates the dynamic nature of the relationship discussed because it underlines the change emerging from the interaction of MNEs and corruption, rather than emphasize the impact of FDI on corruption (Robertson and Watson 2004). **Fourth,** this study effectively responds to calls by scholars (Westney 1993; Battilana et al. 2009; Cantwell et al. 2010; Hotho and Pedersen 2012) that the relationship between MNEs and institutions has to break away from the "given" perspective of embedded agency, bringing to the fore the more active institutional entrepreneurship.

Our paper's hypotheses are empirically tested using a sample of seventeen emerging economies. The dataset comes from World Bank (https://data.worldbank.org/indicator/BX.KLT.DINV.CD.WD) and the econometric testing method applied is the fix effect model. The period of analysis extends from 2012 to 2019. The structure of the rest paper rest is as following: The next section reviews the relevant literature. The research hypotheses are developed and formulated. The Regression Model Specification section describes and applies the model that the hypotheses are tested. Methodology describes and analyzes the sample data and variables utilized when applying the econometric testing. Empirical analysis and results section presents the econometric results derived from the empirical application of the model. Discussion, conclusions, limitations, and prospects for future research section develops on results, conclusions, conceptual, managerial implications, and avenues for future research.

2   Literature Review and Conceptual Framework

Corruption is considered a key factor apparent in almost all societies, albeit, at different degrees (Collins et al. 2009). Scholars have offered various definitions (Rose-Ackerman 1978; Uhlenbruck et al. 2006; Cuervo-Cazzurra 2006; Kwok and Tadesse 2006; Lee and Oh 2007) involving various conceptual aspects, such as institutional and transaction-specific (Rodriguez et al. 2005) (for an extensive review see Bahoo et al. 2019). This study uses the most widely used definition of government/public corruption, i.e., abuse (or misuse) of public power for private benefit (Bardhan 1997; Rodriguez et al. 2005; Uhlenbruck et al. 2006), and distinguishes corruption as pervasive and arbitrary. Pervasive corruption refers to the systematic and predictable (Demirbag et al. 2010) way corruption takes place in a given country or, else, it reflects "the average likelihood of encountering bribery requests in the business interactions" (Lee and Oh 2007, p. 98). Arbitrary corruption refers to the "degree of uncertainty and precariousness associated with public sector corruption" (Uhlenbruck et al. 2006, p. 403).

The research, herein, emphasizes the pervasive type, because, contrary to the arbitrary one, it is a more multidimensional, dynamic, and socially evaluated behavior, closely linked with institutions (McGuinness and Demirbag 2012) of the host country. This argument is based on North's (1990) reasoning, which asserts that pervasive corruption represents the social capital aspect of corruption apparent in three types of social exchanges: personalized social exchange, i.e., the cognitive aspect of society; impersonal social exchange, i.e., normative aspect; and impersonal social exchange with third-party enforcement.

Following this line of thought, a large part of corruption literature (McGuinness and Demirbag 2012) has revolved around the impact of corruption on MNEs activities across various host countries. The institution-based perspective of MNEs strategy (Peng 2002, 2003) has prevailed, providing crucial explanations for why corruption transaction costs take place, why resources are transformed in a particular way, and how organizations evolve (Saka-Helmhout and Geppert 2011). Institutions, in this domain, are perceived as prime actors in the international business game, since host countries' regulatory rules affect MNEs location decisions (Meyer and Nguyen 2005) and entry mode choices (Brouthers 2002; Dikova and van Witteloostuijn 2007; Cuervo-Cazurra and Gene 2008). The success of MNE strategies depends on specific types of host institutions, such as the degree of market development (Lee and Beamish 1995) or distance from the home country (Ghemawat 2001).

However, this institution-based reasoning tends to overlook two critical aspects of MNE expansion: First, the potential role MNEs play in the host institutional setting and, second, potential interactions MNEs may have with the host institutional setting. To remedy this issue, scholars have illustrated the role MNEs play in the configuration of the institutional environment of the host country (Collins and Uhlenbruck 2004; Robertson and Watson 2004; Kwok and Tadesse 2006). These endeavors proceeded from the "hard" (economic) perspective (Shleifer and Vishny 1993; Wei 2000), the "soft" perspective (Wines and Napier 1992; Robertson et al. 2002), the national culture perspective and, finally, the strategic perspective that is the product of mixing the hard and soft perspectives (Robertson and Watson 2004).

The dominance of the strategic perspective took place through exclusively stressing the aid of the agency theory (Collins and Uhlenbruck 2004; Collins et al. 2009), the executives' perspective on corruption (Collins and Uhlenbruck 2004; Collins et al. 2009) and cross-country analyses. However, to the best of our knowledge, no analysis has so far directly addressed the relationship of MNEs and institutions using institutional entrepreneurship reasoning. Institutional entrepreneurship reasoning revolves around the way firms could influence institutions or governments (Child et al. 2012) because some firms are able to do this through building up political capital (Frynas et al. 2006). However, others may induce significant changes to levels of competition by collectively mobilizing economic and institutional agents around a cause or business model (Rodriguez et al. 2005).

Therefore, given that the aim of this paper is to examine how MNE investments influence the corruption level of an emerging economy, this research differentiates itself from pertinent literature presented above by employing institutional entrepreneurship reasoning. As a derivative of institutional theory (Karademir and Yaprak 2012), institutional entrepreneurship is considered the product of the reconciliation of two main paradigms/reasonings of IB literature: Agency and Institutional theory (Battilana et al. 2009; Saka-Helmhout and Geppert 2011). In this sense, institutions are not perceived only as constraints on MNE activity (Meyer and Rowan 1975; Hotho and Pedersen 2012). Instead, institutions are also perceived as "toolkits for actors that may influence actors' cognition and actions in important and often unconscious ways" (Battilana et al. 2009, p. 73). In other words, institutions arise as important factors that both constrain and enable the choice of actors (Hoffman and Ventresca 2002; Thornton and Ocasio 2008; Ang et al. 2014). Besides, MNEs are perceived as key factors that may influence and interact with the host institutional environment they invest in Battilana et al. (2009).

In this framework, MNEs entering an emerging host institutional setting are often subjected to transaction costs, namely, corruption (Doh et al. 2005). To overcome corruption costs and maintain legitimacy (Hotho and Pedersen 2012), MNEs develop strategies that respond to the needs of local institutions (Meyer 2001; Battilana et al. 2009; Saka-Helmhout and Geppert, 2011). These strategies are the product of MNEs international operations in multiple, different, and often conflicting institutional environments (Kostova et al. 2008) around the world. MNEs develop interactions shaped by various institutions outside the firm, so as to generate different internal capabilities (strategies or strategic responses) and foundations used (Hall and Soskice 2001; Whitley 2007) in similar host institutional settings. As a corollary, MNEs accept that they may approach institutions as both enabling and constraining factors (Bruton and Ahlstrom 2002). At the same time, MNEs may also express their agency to address risks derived from uncertainties in the host institutional setting, such as corruption costs.

Considering the conceptual reasoning presented above, the research at hand proceeds to examine the impact the presence of MNEs exerts on corruption in an emerging economy, as well as the impact of the rate of increasing number of MNEs on the corruption level that exists in emerging economies. This is done by formulating and testing two hypotheses.

3 Development of Hypotheses

In a business environment where corruption is pervasive, corruption tends to become the dominant business practice in local businesses (Kwok and Tadesse 2006). Essentially, corruption becomes an integral part of the regulative institutions of the host country (Doh et al. 2005; Uhlenbruck et al. 2006) "and both parties of the transaction would take it for granted" (Kwok and Tadesse 2006, p. 770). However, scholars (Kwok and Tadesse 2006; McGuinness and Demirbag 2012) have stressed that, when dealing with corrupt government officials, MNEs may be reluctant to negotiate based on corruption terms. This takes place because MNEs are accountable to their internal legitimacy (Madhok and Liu 2006), their home country (Stinchcombe 1965; Walsh 1995), and the international business community (Cantwell et al. 2010). Internal legitimacy bans negotiations and transactions with corrupt institutions. Home country regulations and international community impose restrictions and severe sanctions on corrupt transactions (DiMaggio and Powell 1983). In this direction, the U.S. Foreign Corrupt Practices Act of 1977, or the more recent 2010 UK Bribery Act (McGuinness and Demirbag 2012), as well as transnational agreements, such as the Organization for Economic Co-operation and Development (OECD) (Demirbag et al. 2010; Wood and Demirbag 2015), were mobilized to legislate against corruption motivated by a number of scandals involving contentious payments by U.S. and UK firms to overseas government officials (Kwok and Tadesse 2006; McGuinness and Demirbag 2012). These acts prohibit MNEs from engaging in corrupt practices when they deal with the host country, from entering into corrupt contracts, or from acquiring illegal business advantages (Cuervo-Cazurra 2006). Consequently, under such regulatory pressures from home country and international business community, MNEs are reluctant to take part in corrupt transactions (Kwok and Tadesse 2006).

In parallel, many host countries are motivated to align themselves with these regulative pressures, since they perceive that attracting MNEs acts as a necessary ticket that enables them to get access to and legitimacy within the bigger and global business environments MNEs derive from. Therefore, the more such host countries attract more MNEs, the more likely it would be for them to enhance their international reputation (Kwok and Tadesse 2006). In this setting, host countries are eager to apply institutional changes that redefine their corruption regulative mechanisms and prevent the emergence of corruption. The outcome of such institutional changes is that they prohibit the rise of corruption in the host country. Thus, following this line of thought, it is hypothesized that:

Hypothesis 1: The more MNEs an emerging economy attracts, the more likely it is that the pervasive corruption level decreases in the host economy.

However, a major part of the relevant literature illustrates that corruption does not always act as expected. Instead, it is argued that businesses are frequently involved in corrupt activities despite the fact that they are aware of these activities have adverse consequences for society as a whole (Collins et al. 2009). The underlying reason for this behavior is that MNEs are equipped with advanced knowledge derived from their international transactions, particularly through a vast international network that makes them develop effective corrupt practices when dealing with various host countries (Collins et al. 2009).

In doing so, MNEs develop and transfer sophisticated practices of managing corruption in the host country they invest in. Such strategies familiarize and simultaneously "contaminate" (Kwok and Tadesse 2006, p. 786) local firms and host governments with corruption, thus, increasing the level of pervasive corruption in the host country (Collins and Uhlenbruck 2004; Uhlenbruck et al. 2006). Therefore, the increasing number of MNEs means a larger amount of foreign currency flowing into the country and, subsequently, the expansion of opportunities for corruption (Kwok and Tadesse 2006).

This is especially important for MNEs that use long-term investments in the host country (Collins et al. 2009). In order to address risks of unpredictable changes in government regulations (Henisz and Williamson 1999) and obtain official government approvals for potentially lucrative public contracts, MNEs take part in lobbying practices, which are also defined as corrupt (Levy and Spiller 1994). More specifically, the zest of foreign investors to enter the market may allure them (Robertson and Watson 2004; Kwok and Tadesse 2006) to participate in long contracts with local governments, which also increases the level of corruption in the host country (Smarzynska and Wei 2000). Yet this becomes more potent when MNEs are increasingly entering specific markets.

In order to effectively capture the conceptualization of institutional change, herein, the paper, following Robertson and Watson (2004), employs the notion of the rate of increase of MNEs numbers in the host country. Researchers (Jones 1991; Getz and Volkema 2001; Robertson and Watson 2004) argue that a rapid increase in FDI contributes to higher levels of corruption in host emerging economies. In particular, it is supported that an abrupt rise in MNEs presence in the host country "by definition represents a higher amount of foreign money flowing into the country, and hence a higher level of opportunities for corruption" (Robertson and Watson 2004, p. 388). For instance, in the case of Turkey, the corruption perception index (CPI) compiled by Transparency International, tells the story most sharply (Acemoglu and Ucer 2015). For instance, in the period 2002–2007, in which Turkey was at the peak of attracting MNEs, the CPI showed strong signs of high corruption. More particularly, in the period 2002–2003 Turkey's clean position fell from the 64th to the 77th position. Similarly, according to Robertson and Watson (2004), Ecuador, for instance, has experienced a resurgence of economic growth and an influx of FDI. "Yet, corruption went up" (Robertson and Watson 2004, p. 388). This resurgence was accompanied by the phenomenon of "Ecuador's 2001 corruption 'clean' score dropping by 13%, and the country falling from 74 to 79th place in the overall rankings" (Robertson and Watson 2004, p. 388). Therefore, considering the examples described above, it is noted that the rapid increase of MNEs presence in emerging economies leads to higher levels of pervasive corruption. Thus, it is hypothesized that:

Hypothesis 2: The faster the rate of increase in the number of MNEs in emerging economies, the higher the level of pervasive corruption in such economies.

4 The Regression Model Specification

The fix effect model has been applied to the panel dataset of 136 observations to test the model hypotheses. The Hausman test was applied to the model and the results indicated that the Fixed Effect model is more appropriate for rejecting the null hypothesis for random effect. The Fixed Effect model can deal with the issue of unobserved heterogeneity (Liargovas and Skandalis 2010) and its general form is expressed as follows:

$$Y_{it} = f(\text{FDI, GDP, schooling, political stability, government effectiveness}) \quad (1)$$

Next, logarithmic transformation is applied for the variables of the model except for foreign direct investment inflows ratio, to reduce data variability and make data comply with normal distribution (Robert and Casella 2010). Thus, following the general form (1), the two model equations for this study are specified as:

$$\mathbf{Model\ 1}:\ \ln \text{Cor}_{it} = a_i + \beta_1 \text{FDI}_{it} + \beta_2 \ln \text{GDP}_{it} + \beta_3 \ln \text{Pol}_{it}$$
$$+ \beta_4 \ln \text{Gov}_{it} + \beta_5 \ln \text{EDUC}_{it} + u_{it} \qquad (2)$$

$$\mathbf{Model\ 2}:\ \ln \text{Cor}_{it} = a_i + \beta_1 \Delta \text{FDI}_{it} + \beta_2 \ln \text{GDP}_{it} + \beta_3 \ln \text{Pol}_{it}$$
$$+ \beta_4 \ln \text{Gov}_{it} + \beta_5 \ln \text{EDUC}_{it} + u_{it} \qquad (3)$$

where in lnCor is the variable of corruption for country i and year t. FDI_{it} is inward Foreign Direct Investment flows as a share of GDP for country I in year t. Also, $\ln \text{GDP}_{it}$ is the variable for Gross Domestic Product per capita in constant 2010 US dollars for country i and year t. Furthermore, $\ln \text{Pol}_{it}$, $\ln \text{Gov}_{it,}$ and $\ln \text{EDUC}_{it}$ are variables for political stability and absence of violence, Government Effectiveness, and Education for country i and year t, respectively. Additionally, ΔFDI_{it} equals to the percentage of FDI flow change. Multiple regression coefficients $\beta_1, \beta_2, \beta_3, \beta_4,$ and β_5 of the independent variables (slope) indicate the percentage change in the dependent variable, namely corruption, for a one-percent change in the independent variables of the model. Lastly, u_{it} is the model error term incorporating the unobserved characteristics.

5 Methodology

The above-mentioned hypotheses are tested using secondary data which were collected from a sample of seventeen emerging economies, and more particularly, Argentina, Brazil, China, Colombia, Egypt, India, Indonesia, Kenya, Mexico, Pakistan, the Philippines, the Federation of Russia, Serbia, Thailand, Turkey, Ukraine, and Venezuela. The choice of such countries was based on the argument that the Goldman Sachs group initially coined in 2001 the name of BRIC countries to group, under this abbreviation, the more dynamic emerging economies in the international market: Brazil, Russia, India, and China (Wilson and Purushothman 2003). Dynamic means that despite these countries are characterized as medium-income, they present rapid-growth opportunities for MNEs by applying liberalization strategies as the main toolkit for achieving their development path (Hoskisson et al. 2000). Ten years later, in 2011, the same group proposed a new abbreviation, namely MIST, to talk about the economies of Mexico, Indonesia, South Korea, and Turkey (Roughneen 2011). Relevant recently, BRIC and MIST countries are recognized as most dynamic (Mahasi and Wanjiru 2015). Therefore, the paper employs Brazil, the Federation of Russia, India, China, Mexico, Indonesia, and Turkey as an appropriate baseline sample, supplementing it with further medium-income emerging economies to strengthen the sample size and, consequently, its validity. The period of analysis extends from 2012 to 2019.

5.1   The Dependent Variable

The examination of the relationship between MNEs and pervasive corruption in this paper differs from that of prior researchers in that corruption, herein, is the dependent variable, rather than the independent one. Data concerning pervasive corruption are derived from the Transparency International agency (https://www.transparency.org/en/cpi/2020/index/nzl), a widely respected international corruption consultancy. At this point, it is important to underline that the CPI has been criticized (Budsaratragoon and Jitmaneeroj 2020) because it compiles data from various surveys and, subsequently, it cannot be considered reliable for measuring corruption change. However, this study, following Robertson and Watson (2004), Uhlenbruck et al. (2006), and Kwok and Tadesse (2006), employs the CPI to approach pervasive corruption as its validity in this aspect appears to be high (Volkema and Chang 1998; Husted 1999). Furthermore, this study, following Husted (1999), Getz and Volkema (2001), and Robertson and Watson (2004), inverts the 0 to 100 scale by subtracting each country's score from 100, so that 100 indicates the most corrupt country and 0 the least corrupt one.

5.2   The Independent Variable

The independent variable of this study is examined in relation to: (a) MNEs presence in the host country and (b) the impact the change in the number of the MNEs exerts on the corruption level of the host country. Considering the former, this research, following Kwok and Tadesse (2006), emphasizes not the actual number of MNEs in the host country, but instead, the FDI activity MNEs undertake in the host country. The dataset for inward FDI is drawn from the World Bank database (https://data.worldbank.org/indicator/BX.KLT.DINV.CD.WD). Considering the latter, Robertson and Watson (2004) have argued that there are three FDI change variables that capture a picture of this relationship: the linear, the V-shaped, and the U-shaped. This paper employs the linear one to depict the notion of the rate of increase in the number of MNEs in the host country. This is because it emphasizes on the impact of inward FDI, rather than the total sum of outward and inward FDI on corruption.

5.3   Control Variables

5.3.1   Control for Development

To explore the impact of MNEs on the corruption level in emerging economies, the model is qualified for any influence specific country characteristics might exert on the relationship between inward FDI and corruption. Following Habib and Zurawicki

(2002) and Uhlenbruck et al. (2006), GDP per capita in PPP is included as an appropriate broad proxy for economic development. GDP per capita in PPP is measured in constant dollars and adjusted for the price level. Scholars (Abed and Davoodi 2002; Brautigam and Knack 2004) have shown that higher levels of growth are associated with lower corruption, since high levels of national income may have been brought about by institutional development that leads to containing corruption. Therefore, it is expected that an increase in GDP per capita reduces the level of corruption. Data for GDP per capita in PPP are derived from the Word Bank database (https://data.worldbank.org/).

5.3.2 Control for Education

Education is one of the most important variables related to corruption (Hotho and Pedersen 2012). Education, as a societal institution, often develops in an interdependent and mutually reinforcing way (Hall and Soskice 2001; Hotho and Pedersen 2012) with corruption. This takes place because well-developed education systems contribute to the transformation of societies and to higher development associated with lower corruption, including the perception of corruption (Kwok and Tadesse 2006). As a corollary, education is related to corruption formation and is expected to have a negative relationship with corruption, that is, higher levels of education lead to lower corruption in the host country (Kwok and Tadesse 2006). Education is approached through the enrollment in secondary education. More particularly, it refers to the ratio of total secondary enrollment, regardless of age. Secondary education completes the provision of basic education that began at the primary level and aims at laying the foundations for lifelong learning and human development, by offering more subject- or skill-oriented instruction using more specialized teachers (https://data.worldbank.org/indicator/SE.SEC.ENRR?end=2020andstart=2020andview=map). The data are drawn from the World Bank database (https://data.worldbank.org/topic/4).

5.3.3 Control for Institutional Influences

To control for the regulative institutional influences of the host country, two variables are used: Political stability and absence of violence (terrorism), as well as government effectiveness. Asongu and Nwachukwu (2015) argues that a host environment characterized by political instability boosts confidence about less impunity and corruption control because resources allocated to the fight against corruption may not be optimal. Moreover, in the absence of such impunity from corruption, political instability further increases corruption. Therefore, it is expected, herein, that political stability reduces corruption.

In the same vein, Jadhav (2012) supports that the increase in government effectiveness decreases the level of corruption since this indicator reflects the quality of civil and public services and the extent of their autonomy from political pressure.

Besides, a higher degree of government effectiveness indicates a lower degree of corruption (Kaufmann et al. 2010). It is, therefore, expected that there is a negative relationship between government effectiveness and corruption.

Data on political stability and absence of violence (terrorism), as well as government effectiveness, are drawn from Worldwide Governance Indicators (WGI) (https://info.worldbank.org/governance/wgi/) of the World Bank. This database reports aggregate and individual governance indicators from over 200 countries and territories over the period 1996–2019. In this framework, political stability and absence of violence (terrorism) refer to perceptions of the likelihood of political instability and/or politically motivated violence, including terrorism (Worldwide Governance Indicators 2021). Government effectiveness reflects perceptions of the quality of public services, the quality of civil service and the degree of their independence from political pressures, the quality of policy planning and implementation, and the credibility of the government's commitment to such policies (Worldwide Governance Indicators 2021).

At this point of the analysis, however, it is important to illustrate that for ease of interpretation, and in line with Luu et al. (2018), the values of political stability and government effectiveness are rescaled by subtracting each country's score from 100. As a result, the new scale runs from 0 to 100 with higher values corresponding to worse outcomes concerning corruption.

6 Empirical Analysis and Results

6.1 Descriptive Statistics and Correlation Matrix

According to the descriptive statistics (see Table 1), there is a significant variation in the corruption perception index ranging from 50.00 to 97.00 across countries. In

Table 1 Descriptive statistics

Variable	Mean	S.D.	Minimum	Maximum
Dependent variable				
Corruption	66.10	7.012	50.00	97.00
Independent variable				
FDI as share of GDP	2.3121	1.489	−0.4054	8.293
ΔFDI inflows	4.8270	126.30	−1148.3	407.05
GDP per capita	7410	6130	1137	28,832
Political stability	79.27	13.80	44.76	99.06
Government effectiveness	52.87	15.45	28.37	95.67
Schooling	88.28	15.45	47.96	120.7

Source EVIEWS 9. Authors' design, 2021

Table 2 Correlation matrix

	Corruption	FDI as share of GDP	GDP per capita	Government effectiveness	Political stability	Schooling	ΔFDI inflows
Corruption	1	−0.2979	−0.2727	0.6304	0.2750	−0.2876	−0.1130
FDI as share of GDP	−0.2979	1	−0.0402	−0.2747	−0.4322	0.2058	0.0672
GDP per capita	−0.2727	−0.0402	1	−0.2833	−0.1475	0.5157	0.0790
Government effectiveness	0.6304	−0.2747	−0.2833	1	0.3532	−0.4134	−0.1517
Political Stability	0.2750	−0.4322	−0.1475	0.3532	1	−0.2362	−0.1524
Schooling	−0.2876	0.2058	0.5157	−0.4134	−0.2362	1	0.0125
ΔFDI inflows	−0.1130	0.0672	0.0790	−0.1517	−0.1524	0.0125	1

Source EVIEWS 9. Authors' design, 2021

addition, the corruption perception index is negatively correlated with the inward FDI flows at constant 2010 US dollars as a share of GDP and similarly is negatively correlated with the percentage change of FDI inflows (ΔFDI) (see Table 2).

6.2 Unit Root Tests, Regression Analysis and Diagnostics Tests

To examine the relationship between corruption and the extent of inward FDI, we control for other potential country influences. This paper applies panel least square regression using Fixed Effect estimation. However, before results are presented, a number of tests are applied. The first test applies two-panel unit root tests and examines the robustness of results, or else, whether results lack economic significance (Wooldridge 2015). In particular, the first test involves a panel unit root test that examines whether the series of the model is stationary or contains a unit root (Wooldridge 2015). The second-panel unit root tests applied in the model refer to the Levin-Lin and Chu (LLC) and Im Pesaran and Shin (IPS). This tests whether the null hypothesis has a unit root or not. Interpreted together, these two tests can be summarized as follows: the p-value is less than 0.01 and 0.10 at significance levels of 1% and 10%, respectively. This means that the null hypothesis is rejected and the alternative one for stationarity accepted (see Table 3). Furthermore, the unit root test was applied in level including both the individual intercept term (a_{it}) with trend and individual intercept term (a_{it}) without trend in the test equation. Last, an automatic selection for lag length, based on the Schwarz Info Criterion, has been used for selecting the optimum number of lags.

Table 3 Panel unit root test results

Test		
Variables	LLC	IPS
LnCor	−7.82993 (0.0000)*	−3.82616 (0.0000)*
FDI	11.0418 (0.0000)*	−5.14248 (0.0000)*
ΔFDI	−1.1191 (0.0000)*	−2.1191 (0.0000)*
LnGDP	−4.69786 (0.0000)*	−3.55875 (0.0000)*
LnPOL	−7.54850 (0.0000)*	−1.38809 (0.0826)***
LnGOV	−5.07693 (0.0000)*	−2.47902 (0.0000)*
LnEDUC	−5.84589 (0.0000)*	−5.12049 (0.0000)*

*Significant at 1% level
**Significant at 5% level
***Significant at 10% significance level
EVIEWS 2009

With this aim in view, we present the panel data results of our regression models in Table 4, in which all equations were well specified with significant Wald chi-square values (at $p < 0.01$ and $p < 0.1$). To verify our arguments in Hypothesis 1, we first introduce the direct effect of MNEs presence in Model 1. Next, in order to verify

Table 4 Results of panel linear regression—fixed effect specification

Model	(1)	(2)
Variables		
FDI	−0.688150***	–
ΔFDI	–	0.000841826
LnGDP	−0.000160154***	−0.000123565***
LnPOL	0.0174116	0.0138184
LnGOV	0.255003*	0.268471*
LnEDUC	−0.0200814	−0.0324121
Adjusted-R^2	0.727206	0.727833
F-statistic	16.57370	16.48229
Prob (*F*-statistic)	0.000000	0.000000

*Significant at 1% level
**Significant at 5% level
***Significant at 10% level
EVIEWS 2009

Hypothesis 2, which refers to the rate of change of FDI inflows, we introduce the linear raw percentage change of FDI inflows.

Proceeding with the results of the regression of models (1) and (2), the fit of the model is examined (Table 4). Adjusted-R^2 equals 0.726728 and 0.727833, respectively, implying that 72% of the variation of the output variables is explained by independent variables and models are statistically significant Prob (F-statistic $=$ 0.000) at the 1% level. Thus, it is indicated that the models at hand have very strong explanatory power. In particular, inward FDI flows at constant 2010 US dollars as a share of GDP in the model (1) have a negative sign ($\beta = -0.688150$) and are statistically significant at 10% level of significance ($p = 0.0526$). However, in model (2) the percentage change of FDI inflows (ΔFDI) has a positive sign ($\beta = 0.000841826$) contrary to model (1), but it is not statistically significant at any level of significance ($p = 0.8627$).

Next, the model was tested for the presence of autocorrelation through the application of the Wooldridge test, which examines the null hypothesis for no first-order autocorrelation. Results have indicated that there is no autocorrelation, failing to reject the null hypothesis ($F (1.1) = 5.32571$, p-value $= 0.260313$). This means that the variables of the model do not have first-order autocorrelation.

Concerning the control variables, the coefficients of *GDP per capita and government effectiveness* emerge are statistically significant except for political stability and education in models (1) and (2). As expected, in both models GDP per capita is negatively correlated ($\beta = -0.000160$, $\beta = -0.000123$) with the level of corruption, implying that an increase in GDP per capita in constant 2010 US dollars decreases the level of corruption. Education has a positive effect ($\beta_5 = -0.0200814$ for model 1 and $\beta_5 = -0.0324121$ for model 2) on pervasive corruption (because of rescaling), albeit not statistically significant. Political stability is shown to have a positive effect ($\beta_3 = 0.0174116$ for model 1 and $\beta_3 = 0.0138184$ for model 2) on pervasive corruption (because of rescaling), even if it is not statistically significant for both models. Government effectiveness, as expected, has a positive effect ($\beta_4 = 0.255003$ for model 1 and $\beta_4 = 0.268471$ for model 2) (because of rescaling) on pervasive corruption and it is statistically significant at 1% level for both models (1) and (2). This implies that as government effectiveness improves, pervasive corruption decreases.

Concerning the hypothesis testing based on empirical results, it is shown that Hypothesis 1 is validated. Model 1 shows significant negative effect of MNEs presence on the pervasive corruption level of an emerging economy, which provides support for Hypothesis 1. This means that the higher the number of MNEs investing in an emerging economy, the more likely it is for pervasive corruption to decrease in the said emerging economy. On the contrary, Hypothesis 2, *"The faster the rate of increase in the number of MNEs in emerging economies, the higher the level of pervasive corruption in such economies"* is not supported. This takes place since the variable ΔFDI is found to be not statistically significant for any level of corruption. A possible explanation is that this paper has paid attention to a specific type of corruption (pervasive) which may be subject to different dynamics domains in which the focal activity is not inherently illegal (Spencer and Gomez 2011). Another possible explanation derives from the fact that despite we introduce seventeen emerging economies, there are still missing values that negatively affect our final dataset.

7 Discussion, Conclusions, Limitations, and Prospects for Future Research

Institutional literature has made a lot of progress in explaining the impact of corruption on the MNEs internationalization process. However, this reasoning has been trapped within the argument of embedded agency, producing inconclusive results. In this sense, our study aims to examine the conditions that enable institutionally-embedded actors to engage in strategic actions and, more particularly, how MNEs shape the level of corruption in emerging economies. This study employs the institutional entrepreneurship reasoning as an appropriate derivative of institutionally based reasoning capable of approaching the following: First, institutions as important factors that both constrain and enable the choice of actors in host economies. Second, MNEs as key factors that may influence and interact with their host institutional environment.

The paper investigates two specific research questions, namely, the positive impact MNEs have on the corruption level of emerging economies, and the impact the rate of increase of the number of MNEs exerts on the levels of corruption in the host country. The context of this analysis is emerging economies. Such economies are characterized by insufficient and immature institutions that tend to be easily influenced by MNEs entrepreneurship and the notion of institutional change.

This paper makes a series of key contributions to relevant literature: **First**, it brings to the forefront the substantial, albeit neglected, relationship of the impact MNEs exert on corruption in emerging economies. This way the research offers new insights into the criteria by which the approach of the said relationship has been perceived so far. **Second**, this study acknowledges the key role of the agency theory and new comparative institutionalism reasonings in examining the relationship between corruption and FDI attraction. It also recognizes that the agency theory has many disadvantages in the way it approaches the said relationship, i.e., there are differences between boards of directors and shareholders or, else, there is conflict of interest between them. Therefore, this paper departs from previously dominant conceptual settings, employing the reasoning of institutional entrepreneurship which offers a more integrative and holistic perspective than agency and new comparative institutionalism in that it combines agency and institutional theory. Furthermore, institutional entrepreneurship reasoning illustrates whether the institutional entrepreneurship theory can be applied in different emerging institutional contexts. **Last**, this study effectively responds to calls in literature (Westney 1993; Battilana et al. 2009; Cantwell et al. 2010; Hotho and Pedersen 2012) supporting that the relationship between MNEs and institutions has to break away from the conventional perspective of embedded agency, bringing to the forefront the more active institutional entrepreneurship.

Specifically, our results confirm Hypothesis 1, that is, MNEs may decrease the corruption level in emerging economies since MNEs are limited by home and international regulations that forbid them to negotiate using corrupt government practices. In parallel, it is indicated that such regulations entail another positive ramification. They encourage host countries to align with international regulations, which gives them access to and legitimacy in the bigger and global business environments, which the MNEs derive from. Therefore, host countries are eager to apply institutional changes that make them redefine their corruption regulating mechanisms and prevent the emergence of corruption. This finding is in line with Kwok and Tadesse (2006) empirical study concluding that MNEs' presence decreases the level of corruption in the host economy.

Hypothesis 2 that the rising rate of growth of the number of MNEs increases pervasive corruption in the host country was not confirmed. Such results contrast those by Robertson and Watson (2004) who validate the said hypothesis. This finding may arise from our consideration of the specific domain of corruption, which may be subject to different dynamics domains in which the focal activity is not inherently illegal (Spencer and Gomez 2011).

Furthermore, a possible explanation in this direction is that MNEs may realize that the use of corrupt practices may induce greater unpredictability and higher costs in business operations (Kaufmann and Wei 1999; Wei 1997). Indeed, in a study across 73 countries, Kaufmann and Wei (1999) found that a firm's payment of bribes corresponded with more management time wasted with government bureaucrats and a higher cost of capital. Thus, instead of facilitating business operations, MNEs operating in environments where corruption is prevalent may well notch lower economic efficiency. In this sense, MNEs may decide not to transfer to and apply corrupt practices in the host emerging economy, thereby, not increasing the level of corruption in the said economies.

Considering the control variables, GDP per capita and government effectiveness emerge as significant ones and with the sign expected, validating the direct effect of GDP per capita and government effectiveness on corruption. This means that an increase in GDP per capita and government effectiveness reduces the level of corruption in the host country, as Abed and Davoodi (2002), Brautigam and Knack (2004), and Jadhav (2012) have argued. On the contrary, education and political stability emerge as insignificant control variables, not confirming any direct impact on corruption.

However, it is important to stress that the variables of education and political stability, also examined under the lens of interaction terms of FDI, emerge again as insignificant ones. These findings are contrary to the results found by Kwok and Tadesse (2006), who found that the beneficial effects of education on corruption are higher in countries with higher FDI levels. A possible explanation for this divergence derives from the fact that this study included fewer observations than the study of

Kwok and Tadesse (2006). What's more, variability in the selection of countries concerning those two studies may play a role in this divergence in results.

Overall, our results validate the two main aspects of institutional entrepreneurship reasoning. First, institutions do not exclusively act as constraints that produce costs. On the contrary, they may act as enabling factors and produce positive changes. What is demonstrated, in particular, is that institutional incompatibilities, such as corruption, are likely to trigger actors' reactions to redefine existing institutional arrangements if these hinge on unsupportive coordination structures (Saka-Helmhout and Geppert 2011). Second, MNEs may also act as institutional entrepreneurs or, else, MNEs can be regarded as organizers of economic activity (Dunning and Lundan 2008) that have a role in a range of environmental, social, poverty-related, and human rights issues (Kolk and van Tulder 2010). Therefore, the institutional change process seems to require the participation of MNEs as institutional entrepreneurs, similar to what is proposed by institutional entrepreneurship reasoning. This aspect also underlines that MNEs do not always consider institutions as a framework that needs to be taken for granted. Instead, MNEs may regard institutions as a bundle "of resources to be tapped into in order to solve their coordination problems and to develop specific capabilities" (García-Cabrera and Durán-Herrera 2016, p. 2).

The results presented above illustrate a number of conceptual and managerial implications. In conceptual terms, it is indicated that MNEs do not just accept the institutional context in which they take place but, under certain circumstances, may lead to important new directions in IB domain (Phillips et al. 2009). Researchers could draw on the extensive research on institutional entrepreneurship "to develop deeper understanding of the conditions under which MNEs engage in this kind of activity and the factors that will make their attempts at institutional entrepreneurship more likely to succeed" (Phillips et al. 2009, p. 346). In this sense, attention is shifted toward a more agentic view of MNEs, which in turn, challenges a number of assumptions and models in the IB domain and has the potential of bringing important aspects of MNE activity more clearly into focus (Phillips et al. 2009).

The ramifications of our arguments are not only clustered as conceptual ones. They extend to include managers, as well. MNEs should realize that they "may affect sustainable development through a much wider variety of mechanisms than those traditionally distinguished" (Dunning and Fortanier 2007, p. 40). In particular, MNEs should become increasingly aware of their role in promoting various strategies for the image-building process they are engaged in Dunning and Fortanier (2007; Spencer and Gomez 2011). This can and does have important implications for the effects FDI has on growth. As with the passive effects of investments, the active role of MNEs in fostering the reduction of corruption also illustrates other potential active effects MNEs may cause in their host institutional environment, such as environmental, health and safety, and employment practices of an MNE and its affiliates. In this direction, Fortanier and Kolk (2007) have shown that approximately 70 percent of the largest 250 firms worldwide actively promote workforce diversity and equal opportunity, good working conditions, and effective training schemes. A similar number of firms are addressing climate change issues and direct greenhouse gas emissions. "Labor rights, such as collective bargaining and freedom of association, are recognized and implemented by one-third of all firms" (Dunning and Fortanier 2007, p. 545). Consequently, the active roles of MNEs related to CSR activities undertaken within the MNE and its affiliates, and those engaged in by organizations associated with the MNEs, merit more research attention.

Although this research offers a cohesive conceptual model for institutional entrepreneurship in relevant IB literature, our model can only be considered as a first exploratory step toward conceptualizing and examining institutional entrepreneurship in the field of IB. This implies that there are further areas to which the relationship between MNEs and corruption can be applied. One potential direction includes the examination of the impact of MNEs entry mode strategies on the corruption level in the host country. This research may also expand to involve the conceptualization of distance, examining the influence of institutional, geographic, and economic distance on corruption in the host country. Last but not least, the replication of our analysis using different data samples and various contexts of analysis, such as developed economies, would enhance the validity of the present results.

References

Abed, G., and Davoodi, H. (2002). *Challenges of Growth and Globalization in the Middle East and North Africa*. Washington, DC: International Monetary Fund.

Acemoglu, D., and Ucer, M. (2015). The Ups and Downs of Turkish Growth, 2002–2015: Political Dynamics, the European Union and the Institutional Slide. *NBER Working Paper No. 21608*, Issued in October 2015.

Alon, I., and Rottig, D. (2013). Entrepreneurship in emerging markets: New insights and directions for future research. *Thunderbird International Business Review*, 55(5), pp. 487–492.

Andreas, J., Raap, M., and Wolff, M. (2012). Determinants of director compensation on two-tier systems: Evidence from German panel data. *Review of Managerial Science*, 6 (1), pp. 33–79.

Ang, S. H., Benischke, M. H., and Doh, J. P. (2014). The interactions of institutions on foreign market entry mode. *Strategic Management Journal*, 36(10), pp. 1536–1553.

Asongu, S., and Nwachukwu, J.C. (2015). A Good Turn Deserves Another: Political Stability, Corruption and Corruption-Control, *AGDI Working Paper, No. WP/15/039*.

Bahoo, S., Alon, I., and Paltrinieri, A. (2019). Corruption in international business: A review and research agenda, *International Business Review*, 29(4), pp. 1–24.

Bardhan, P. (1997). Corruption and Development: A Review of the Issues, *Journal of Economic Literature* 35, pp.1320–46.

Barro, R. (1991). Economic growth in a cross-section of countries. *Quarterly Journal of Economics*, 106(2), pp. 407–444.

Battilana, J., and D'Aunno, T. (2009). Institutional work and the paradox of embedded agency. In T. Lawrence, et al. (Eds.), Institutional work: Actors and agency in institutional studies of organizations (pp. 31–58). Cambridge: Cambridge University Press.

Battilana, J., Leca, B., and Boxenbaum, E. (2009). How Actors Change Institutions: Towards a Theory of Institutional Entrepreneurship. *The Academy of Management Annals*, 3(1), pp. 65–107.

Baumol, W. (1993). Formal entrepreneurship theory in economics: Existence and bounds. *Journal of Business Venturing*, 8, pp. 197–210.

Birkinshaw, J. M., and Morrison, A. (1995). Configurations of strategy and structure in subsidiaries of multinational corporations. *Journal of International Business Studies*, 26, pp. 729–754.

Brautigam, D. A., and Knack. S., (2004). Foreign Aid, Institutions, and Governance in Sub Saharan Africa. *Economic Development and Cultural Change*, 52(2), pp. 255–85.

Brouthers, K. D. (2002). Institutional, cultural and transaction cost influences on entry mode choice and performance. *Journal of International Business Studies*, 33, pp. 203–221.

Bruton, G., and Ahlstrom, D. (2002). An institutional view of China's venture capital industry: Explaining the differences between China and the West. *Journal of Business Venturing*, 17, pp.1–27.

Budsaratragoon, P., and Jitmaneeroj, B. (2020). Reform priorities for prosperity of nations: The Legatum Index. *Journal of Policy Modeling*, 70 (6), pp. 67–85.

Cantwell, J., Dunning, J.H., and Lundan, S.M. (2010). An evolutionary approach to understanding international business activity: The co-evolution of MNEs and the institutional environment. *Journal of International Business Studies*, 41(4) pp. 567–586.

Chan, C.M., and Makino, S. (2007). Legitimacy and multi-level institutional environments: Implications for foreign subsidiary ownership structure. *Journal of International Business Studies*, 38(4), pp. 621–638.

Child, J., Rodrigues, S.B., and Tse, K.K.–T. (2012). The dynamics of influence in corporate co-evolution. *Journal of Management Studies, 49(7)*, 1246–1273.

Chung, C.C., and Beamish, P.W. (2005). The impact of institutional reforms on characteristics and survival of foreign subsidiaries in emerging economies. *Journal of Management Studies*, 42(1) pp. 35–62.

Collins, J., and Uhlenbruck, K. (2004). How Firms Respond to Government Corruption: Insights from India. *Academy of Management Proceedings*, A1–A6.

Collins, J., Uhlenbruck, K., and Rodriguez, P. (2009). Why firms engage in corruption: A top management perspective. *Journal of Business Ethics*, 87, pp. 89–108.

Crouch, C. (2005). *Capitalist Diversity and Change: Recombinant Governance and Institutional Entrepreneurs*. Oxford: Oxford University Press.

Cuervo-Cazurra, A. (2006). Who cares about corruption?. *Journal of International Business Studies,* 37, pp. 807–822.

Cuervo-Cazurra, A., and Gene, M. (2008). Transforming disadvantages into advantages: Developing-country MNEs in the least developed countries. *Journal of International Business Studies*, 39, pp. 957–979.

Davis, P.S., Desai, A.B., and Francis, J.D. (2000). Mode of International Entry: An Isomorphism Perspective. *Journal of International Business Studies*, 31(2), 239–258.

Demirbag, M., Sunil S., and Kamel, M. (2010). Country Image and Consumer Preference for Emerging Economy Products: The Moderating Role of Consumer Materialism. *International Marketing Review*, 27 (2), pp. 141–163.

Dieleman, M., and Sachs, W. M. (2008). Coevolution of institutions and corporations in emerging economies: How the Salim group morphed into an institution of Suharto's crony regime. *Journal of Management Studies*, 45, pp. 1274–1300.

Dikova, D., and Witteloostuijn, A. (2007). Foreign direct investment mode choice: entry and establishment modes in transition economies. *Journal of International Business Studies,* 38, pp. 1013–1033.

DiMaggio, P.J. (1988). Interest and agency in institutional theory. In L.G. Zucker (Eds), Institutional patterns and organizations: Culture and environment: pp. 3-22. Cambridge, MA: Ballinger.

DiMaggio, P., and Powell, W. (1983). The Iron cage revisited: institutional isomorphism and collective rationality in organizational fields. *American Sociological Review,* 48(2), pp. 147–160.

Doh, J., Rodriguez, P., Uhlenbruck, K., Collins, J., and Eden, L. (2005). Coping with corruption in foreign markets. *Academy of Management Executive,* 17(3), pp. 114–127.

Dunning, J. H., and Fortanier, F. (2007). Multinational enterprises and the new development paradigm: consequences for host country development. *Multinational Business Review*, 15(1), pp. 25–46.

Dunning, J. H., and Lundan, S.M. (2008). Institutions and the OLI Paradigm of the Multinational Enterprise. *Asia Pacific Management*, 25(4), pp. 573–593.

Ellis, P. (2000). Social ties and foreign market entry. *Journal of International Business Studies,* 31(3), 443–469.

Fligstein, N. (1997). Social skill and institutional theory. *American Behavioral Scientist*, 40, pp. 397–405.

Fortanier, F., and Kolk, A. (2007). On the economic dimensions of CSR: Exploring Fortune Global 250 reports. *Business and Society*, 46, pp. 457–478.

Frynas, J.G., Mellahi, K., and Pigman, G.A. (2006). First mover advantages in international business and firm-specific political resources. *Strategic Management Journal*, 27, pp. 321–345.

García-Cabrera, A., and Durán-Herrera, J.J. (2016). MNEs as institutional entrepreneurs: a dynamic model of co–evolution process. *European Management Journal*, 12(3), pp. 1–14.

Garud, R., Jain, S., and Kumaraswamy, A. (2002). Institutional entrepreneurship in the sponsorship of common technological standards: the case of Sun Microsystems and Java. *Academy of Management Journal*, 45(1), pp. 196–214.

Getz, K. A., and Volkema, R. J. (2001). Culture, perceived corruption, and economics: A model of predictors and outcomes. *Business and Society*, 40, pp. 7–30.

Ghemawat, P. (2001). Distance Still Matters: The Hard Reality of Global Expansion. *Harvard Business Review*, 9, pp. 137–147.

Greenwood, R., Suddaby, R., and Hinings, C.R. (2002). Theorizing change: The role of professional associations in the transformation of institutional fields. *Academy of Management Journal*, 45(1), pp. 58–80.

Habib, M., and Zurawicki, L. (2002). Corruption and foreign direct investment. *Journal of International Business Studies*, 33(2), pp. 291–307.

Hall, P., and Soskice, D. (2001). *Varieties of Capitalism: The institutional foundations of competitive advantage*. Oxford: Oxford University Press.

Hancké, B., and Goyer, M. (2005). Degree of freedom: Rethinking the institutional analysis of economic change. In G. Morgan, R. Whitley, and E. Moen (Eds), Changing capitalisms? Institutional change and systems of economic organization: pp. 53–77. Oxford: Oxford University Press.

Henisz, W., and Williamson, O. (1999). Comparative Economic Organization—Within and Between Countries. *Business and Politics*, 1(3), pp. 261–277.

Hoffman, A.J., and Ventresca, M.J. (2002). *Organization, Policy, and the Natural Environment: Institutional and Strategic Perspectives*. Stanford University Press: Stanford, CA.

Hoskisson, R.E., Eden, L., Chung, L., and Wright, M. (2000). Strategies in Emerging Economies. *The Academy of Management Journal*, 43(3), pp. 249–267.

Hotho, J., and Pedersen, T. (2012). Beyond the rules of the game: Three institutional approaches and how they matter for inter- national business. In M. Demirbag, and C. Wood (Eds), Handbook of institutional approaches to international business: 366–368. Cheltenham, UK: Edward Elgar.

Husted, B.W. (1999). Wealth, culture, and corruption. *Journal of International Business Studies*, 30(2), pp. 339–360.

Jadhav, P. (2012). Determinants of foreign direct investment in BRICS economies: Analysis of economic, institutional and political factor. *Social and Behavioral Sciences*, 37, pp. 5–14.

Jones, J. (1991). Earnings Management During Import Relief Investigations. *Journal of Accounting Research*, 29(2), pp. 193–228.

Karademir, B., and Yaprak, A. (2012). The co-evolution of the institutional environments and internationalization experiences of Turkish internationalizing firms. In G. Wood and M. Demirbag (Eds.), *Handbook of Institutional Approaches to International Business* (pp. 236–273). Cheltenham, UK, and Northampton, USA: Edward Elgar.

Kaufmann, D., and Wei, S. J. (1999). Does 'Grease Money' Speed Up the Wheels of Commerce?. NBER Working Paper, 7093.

Kaufmann, D., Kraay, A., and Mastruzzi, M. (2010). Response to 'What do the Worldwide Governance Indicators Measure?. *European Journal of Development Research*, 22, pp. 55–58.

Kolk, A., and Van Tulder, R. (2010). International business, corporate social responsibility and sustainable development. *International Business Review*, 19, pp. 119–125.

Kostova, T., Roth, K., and Dacin, M.T. (2008). Institutional theory in the study of multinational corporations: a critique and new directions. *Academy of Management Review*, 33, pp. 994–1006.

Kwok, C.C.Y., and Tadesse, S. (2006). The MNC as an Agent of Change for Host-Country Institutions: FDI and Corruption. *Palgrave Macmillan Journals*, 37(6), pp. 767–785.

Lee, C., and Beamish, P.W. (1995). The characteristics and performance of Korean joint ventures in LDCs. *Journal of International Business Studies*, 26(3), pp. 637–654.

Lee, S.-H., and Oh, K. (2007). Corruption in Asia: Pervasiveness and arbitrariness. *Asia Pacific Journal of Management*, 24(1), pp. 97–114.

Levy, B., and Spiller, P.T. (1994). The Institutional Foundations of Regulatory Commitment: A Comparative Analysis of Telecommunications Regulation. *The Journal of Law, Economics, and Organization*, 10(2), pp. 201–246.

Liargovas, P. G., and Skandalis, K. S. (2010). Factors affecting firms' performance: The case of Greece. *Global Business and Management Research: An International Journal*, 2(2), pp. 184–197.

Luu, H.N., Nguyen, N.M., Ho, H.H., and Nam, V. (2018). The effect of corruption on FDI and its modes of entry. *Journal of Financial Economic Policy*, 11 (2), pp. 232–250.

Madhok, A., and Liu, C. (2006). A co-evolutionary theory of the multinational firm. *Journal of International Management*, 12, pp. 1–21.

Maguire, S., Hardy, C., and Lawrence, T.B. (2004). Institutional entrepreneurship in emerging fields: HIVIAIDS treatment advocacy in Canada. *Academy of Management Journal*, 47, pp. 657–79.

Mahasi, J., and Wanjiru, R. (2015). Risk Control versus Risk Management in the Context of an Active Management: The Emerging Market Alternative. *International Journal of Econometrics and Financial Management*, 3 (4),142–150.

Mallin, C., Melis, A., and Gaia, S. (2015). The remuneration of independent directors in the UK and Italy: An empirical analysis based on agency theory. *International Business Review*, 24, 175–186.

McGuinness, M., and Demirbag, M. (2012), The multinational enterprise, institutions and corruption. In G. Wood and M. Demirbag (Eds.), Handbook of institutional approaches to international business (pp. 274–296). Cheltenham/Northhampton: Edward Elgar.

Meyer, K. E. (2001). Institutions, transaction costs, and entry mode choice in Eastern Europe. *Journal of International Business Studies*, 32(2), pp. 357–365.

Meyer, K. E., and Nguyen, H. V. (2005). Foreign investment strategies and sub-national institutions in emerging markets: Evidence from Vietnam. *Journal of Management Studies*, 42(1), pp. 63–93.

Meyer, K. E., and Peng, M. W. (2005). Probing theoretically into Central and Eastern Europe: Transactions, resources, and institutions. *Journal of International Business Studies*, 36(6), pp. 600–621.

Meyer J., and Rowan B. (1975). Institutionalized organizations: formal structure as myth and ceremony. *American Journal of Sociology*, 83, pp. 340–363.

North, D. C. (1990). *Institutions, institutional change and economic performance.* Cambridge: Cambridge University Press.

Peng, M. W. (2002). Towards an institution-based view of business strategy. *Asia Pacific Journal of Management*, 19(2/3), pp. 251–267.

Peng, M. W. (2003). Institutional transitions and strategic choices. *Academy of Management Review*, 28(2), pp. 275–296.

Phillips, N., Tracey, P., and Karra, N. (2009). Rethinking institutional distance: strengthening the tie between new institutional theory and international management. *Strategic Organisation*, 7(3), pp. 339–348.

Robert, C. P., and Casella, G. (2010). *Introducing Monte Carlo Methods with R Solutions to Odd-Numbered Exercises.* Springer, New York.

Robertson, C.J., and Watson, A. (2004). Corruption and Change: The Impact of Foreign Direct Investment. *Strategic Management Journal*, 25(4), pp. 385–396.

Robertson, C.J., Crittenden, W., Brady, M., and Hoffman J. (2002). Situational ethics across borders: a multicultural examination. *Journal of Business Ethics*, 38(4), pp. 327–338.

Rodriguez, P., Uhlenbruck, K., and Eden, L. (2005). Government corruption and the entry strategies of multinationals. *Academy of Management Review*, 30(2), pp. 383–396.

Romer, P.M. (1990). Endogenous Technological Change. *Journal of Political Economy*, 98 (5), pp. 71–102.

Rose-Ackerman, S. (1978). The economics of corruption. *Journal of Public Economics*, 4(2), pp. 187–203.

Roughneen, S. (2011). After BRIC comes MIST, the acronym Turkey would certainly welcome. *The Guardian*. https://www.theguardian.com/global-development/poverty-matters/2011/feb/01/emerging-economies-turkey-jim-oneill. (Accessed: 27 April 2021).

Saka-Helmhout, A., and Geppert, M. (2011). Different forms of agency and institutional influences within multinational enterprises. *Management International Review*, 51, pp. 567–92.

Scott, W. R. (1995). *Institutions and organizations*. Thousand Oaks, CA: Sage.

Segerstrom, P.S., Anant, T.C.A., and Dinopoulos, E. (1990). A Schumpeterian Model of the Product Life Cycle. *American Economic Review*, 90 (5), pp. 1077–1091.

Seo, M., and Creed, W.E.D. (2002). Institutional contradictions, praxis, and institutional change: a dialectical perspective. Academy of Management Review, 27, pp. 222–247.

Shleifer, A., and Vishny, R. (1993). Corruption. *Quarterly Journal of Economics*, 108, pp. 599–618.

Smarzynska, B.K., and Wei, S.J. (2000). Corruption and composition of foreign direct investment: Firm-level evidence. WORKING PAPER 7969.

Smets, M., Morris, T., and Greenwood, R. (2017). From practice to field: A multilevel model of institutional change. *Academy of Management Journal*, 55 (4), pp. 877–904.

Spencer, J., and Gomez, C. (2011). MNEs and corruption: The impact of national institutions and subsidiary strategy. *Strategic Management Journal*, 32 (3), pp. 280–300.

Stinchcombe, A.L. (1965). Social structure and organizations In J. G. March (Eds), Handbook of Organizations: 141–193. Chicago: Rand McNally.

Stopford, J., and Wells, L. (1972). *Managing the multinational enterprise: Organization of the firm and ownership of the subsidiaries*. New York: Basic Books.

Streeck, K., and Thelen, K. (2005). *Beyond Continuity: Institutional Change in Advanced Political Economies*. Oxford: Oxford University Press.

Temple, J. (1999). The new growth evidence. *Journal of economic Literature,* 37(1), pp. 112–156.

Thornton, P.H., and Ocasio, W. (2008). Institutional logics. In R. Greenwood, C. Oliver, K. Sahlin, and R. Suddaby (Eds), The SAGE handbook of organizational institutionalism: pp. 99–129. London: Sage.

Transparency International (2001). Corruption Perceptions Index 2001, Transparency International. Available at https://www.transparency.org/en/cpi/2019/index/nzl [Accessed 25 April 2021].

Uhlenbruck, K., Rodriguez, P., Doh, J., and Eden, L. (2006). The impact of corruption on entry strategy: Evidence from telecommunication projects in emerging economies. *Organization Science*, 17(3), pp. 402–414.

Volkema, R.J., and Chang, S. (1998). Negotiating in Latin America: What we know (or think we know) and what we would like to know. *Latin American Business Review*, 1(2), pp. 3–25.

Walsh, J.P. (1995). Managerial and organizational cognition: Notes from a trip down memory lane. *Organization Science*, 6, pp. 280–32.

Wei, S.J. (1997). Why is corruption so much more taxing than tax? Arbitrariness kills. NBER Working paper #6255. National Bureau of Economic Research, Cambridge, MA.

Wei, S.J. (2000). How taxing is corruption on international investors?. *Review of Economics and Statistics*, 82, pp. 1–11.

Westney, D. E. (1993). *Institutionalization theory and the multinational corporation, Organization theory and the multinational corporation*. New York: St Martin's Press.

Whitley, R. (2007). *Business Systems and Organizational Capabilities: The Institutional Structuring of Competitive Competences*. University Press Scholarship Online.

Wilson, D., and Purushothman, R. (2003). Dreaming with BRICs: The Path to 2050. *Global Economics Paper*, 99, Goldman Sachs, New York.

Wines, W.A., and Napier, N. (1992). Toward an understanding of cross-cultural ethics: A tentative model. *Journal of Business Ethics*, 11, pp. 831–41.

Wood, G.T., and Demirbag, M. (2015). Business and society on the transitional periphery: Comparative perspectives. *International Business Review*, 24(6), pp. 917–920.

Wooldridge, J.M. (2015). *Introductory Econometrics: A Modern Approach.* USA: South-Western, Cengage Learning.

Worldwide Governance Indicators. (2021). The Worldwide Governance Indicators (WGI) project. Available at https://info.worldbank.org/governance/wgi/ [Accessed 25 April 2021].

World Bank (2021). World Development Indicators. Available at https://data.worldbank.org> [Accessed 25 April 2021a].

World Bank (2021). World Development Indicators. Available at https://info.worldbank.org/govern ance/wgi/Home/Reports>. [Accessed 25 April 2021b].

Innovation and Skills Requirements in Post-transition Economies

Valerija Botrić

Abstract Innovators are more likely to ensure strong foundations for economic growth and contribute positively to employment. Yet, one of the important innovation inputs is the continuous upgrading of the innovating enterprise human capital. Innovative firms are more likely to report having problems finding adequate skills on the job market. Previous studies have established that innovative firms require a workforce with modern, higher-order skills, that are frequently unavailable on the local labour market. This leads to more specific training requirements for the innovating firms. Based on the most recent The World Bank Enterprise Survey dataset, the paper explores different aspects of inadequate human capital on innovation propensity in post-transition societies. Specifically, the impact of the inadequately educated workers, provision of on-the-job training and the share of high-skill workers on firm innovation propensity are analysed. In addition to firm characteristics, the paper explores aspects of the managers' human capital, such as years of experience and gender of the top manager. Analysis confirms differences between innovating and non-innovating firms and differences between countries belonging to the Central and South-European region compared to the Commonwealth of Independent States region.

Keywords Innovation · Post-transition economies · Human capital

JEL Classification O30 · J24

1 Introduction

The role of human capital has long been acknowledged as an important factor for both innovation and economic growth, even during the early phases of industrialization (Cinnirella and Streb 2017). However, most of the research has been

V. Botrić (✉)
The Institute of Economics, Zagreb, Trg J. F. Kennedy 7, 10000 Zagreb, Croatia
e-mail: vbotric@eizg.hr

© The Author(s), under exclusive license to Springer Nature Switzerland AG 2022
P. Sklias et al. (eds.), *Business Development and Economic Governance in Southeastern Europe*, Springer Proceedings in Business and Economics,
https://doi.org/10.1007/978-3-031-05351-1_7

focused on developed economies, and in policy-oriented discussions, it is implicitly assumed that transition societies would follow similar patterns. The transition process involved significant changes in the demand for new skills that were not supported by previous education and training systems (Mulliqi et al. 2019). While there is little doubt that education systems in these countries went through significant changes, the open question remains to what extent reformed educational systems were able to support the development of the post-transitional societies in this context of abrupt structural changes. The data consistently shows lagging of innovation output in post-transition societies (Božić 2020), which is at odds with the socialist legacy of substantial innovation input (Kotz 2002). This is also evident for European post-transition countries, whose catching up process has been additionally supported by the EU accession. According to the latest Eurostat Innovation Scoreboard indicators for the year 2019, most of the countries belonged to the group of modest (Bulgaria, Montenegro, North Macedonia, Poland, Romania and Serbia) or moderate innovators (Czechia, Croatia, Hungary, Lithuania, Latvia, Slovakia and Slovenia). Only Estonia reached the qualification of the strong innovator (https://interactivetool.eu/EIS/EIS_2.html#d).

Transition economies have completely restructured their innovation systems through transformation from planned to market economies. However, few global aspects affect the scope of the national level transformations. First, the effects of the recent global economic crisis significantly reduced innovation activity of transition countries enterprises (Friz and Günther 2020), mostly related to the global credit crunch episode that especially affected projects perceived to be risky, i.e. projects innovative enterprises frequently engage in. Second, the liberalization and accession to the European Union correlated with increased brain drain from the Central and Eastern Europe (Loukil 2017). This put additional pressure on the innovating firms to find adequate human resources for their business endeavours.

Previous literature has established that innovators, to a greater extent, perceive inadequate human resources as an important obstacle for their business (World Bank Group 2015). However, higher skills are not in demand only by innovators; the upskilling is a broader phenomenon (Bogliacino et al. 2018) related to the fast technological changes. For the European post-transition economies, the proximity of the labour markets of advanced European economies could imply larger skills shortages on the local labour markets. In the case of skills shortages, innovative firms are more likely to struggle to attract workers with desired characteristics as well as to maintain optimal levels of human capital.

The paper offers recent evidence on different aspects of skills requirements for the innovating and non-innovating firms in post-transition societies. The results imply that innovators are different to non-innovating firms when it comes to demand for human capital. Additionally, differences between firms in Central and South-European (CESEE) economies and Commonwealth of Independent (CIS) states have been established.

The paper adopts the following structure. The next section briefly presents relevant literature. Section 3 presents data sources and the estimation strategy, while Sect. 4 discusses the results. The last section summarizes the main conclusions.

2 Literature Review

The transition process brought severe changes, not only for the economic structures but also for many aspects of the society, including the educational system. In one of the examples from early transition periods, Barro and Lee (2001) documented decreases in the proportion of the population without schooling or with only primary education and increases in the proportion of the population who completed secondary education, the magnitude being significantly higher in the CEECs as compared to the CIS. The average educational attainment has, subsequently, increased.

The transition was also associated with severe changes in the economic structure, marked by pronounced deindustrialization (Kuttor and Hegyi-Kéri 2014), affecting the structure of labour demand. The demand for skills depends on the structure of the economy. For example, while both the manufacturing and service sectors might be facing upskilling (and have benefits of higher shares of university graduates in the society), high-end manufacturing will also be in need of highly skilled workers from a relatively narrow set of disciplines, i.e. STEM graduates (Durazzi 2019). Service sector upskilling could be related to the changes in the demand for a broader set of workers' technological advances. This affects the educational system in a very specific way. The literature subsequently acknowledges the existence of a 'race' between the increasing demand for high skills due to the introduction of technologies across the sectors of the economy and the supply of skills in the labour market (Goldin and Katz 2008). Due to profound changes in the economic structure, the effect might be more severe in a transition economy.

Innovation literature is traditionally focused on manufacturing firms (Crowley 2017), while the service sector was considered an adopter of technology and subsequently less innovative in general (Evangelista 2000). However, recent evidence reveals specific patterns of innovation in the service sector firms (Audretsch et al. 2020; Tether 2005). Subsequently, skills demand in service sector is also more likely to shift towards high interpersonal and, in particular cognitive skills, such as problem-solving or analytical skills (Durazzi 2019). It remains relatively unexplored what effects of labour demand upskilling has on the innovative behaviour of service sector firms.

In addition to increased demand for specific skills, technology change is frequently labour-saving (Staccioli and Virgillito 2021) and could lead to decrease of specific skills demand, thus making them obsolete. There is some evidence that the employment impact of technology is more challenging for emerging countries (World Bank 2017). Thus, the so-called technology unemployment is increasing in post-transition societies. Krzywdzinski (2017) argues that this is not strictly related to the changes in adopted process technologies but more to the institutional framework within a country. Indeed, labour market institutions and their relative slow adjustments to the market economy attracted much attention from scholars. For example, Lehmann and Muravyev (2012) confirmed that labour market institutions significantly affect labour market outcomes in transition economies.

Studies have suggested that innovative firms, in general, grow faster and are more likely to expand their employment than non-innovative ones, regardless of industry, size or other firm characteristics (Pianta 2018). Also, innovative firms are more likely to demand high-skilled labour. Friz and Günther (2020) claim that firms where most employees hold a university degree have 40% higher propensity to innovate in comparison with firms that do not have university-trained employees. These results suggest that innovation knowledge is impersonated in skilled workers (Paunov 2012). For innovative firms to reach their potential, the availability of highly skilled workers is crucial.

The essential human capital for innovation activity can exist within a firm, could be obtained on the labour market or if not, it might be necessary to provide additional training to the firm's employees. When a firm provides training with the aim to increase the knowledge of the workforce and enable them to obtain new skills, the learning process itself can lead to new product development (Beugelsdijk 2008; Laursen and Foss 2003). Cinnirella and Streb (2017) suggest that different types of human capital available within a firm might play different roles in production and innovation activities. While it is necessary to ensure the ongoing production processes with the existing levels of human capital, for the innovation output higher levels or increases in human capital are necessary (Capozza and Divella 2019). On-the-job training is one of the methods to increase the existing fir level of human capital. Nazarov and Akhmedjonov (2012) confirm that in the case of transition economies on-the-job training increases a firm's ability to innovate.

The quality of management is crucial for a firm's performance. A firm's human capital might even to a greater extent depend on the manager's skills because the manager makes innovation decisions (Crowley and Bourke 2018). Foreign-owned companies innovate more in transition countries than local firms (Radosevic and Ciampi Stancova 2018; Gorodnichenko and Schnitzer 2013). This is partially related to the quality of managers they provided, in particular in the early phases of transition when local managers were still not familiar enough with the market mechanisms. The question remains whether this is still the case in the post-transition phase, when more multinational companies rely on local management structures. Another important concern is that the primary interest of foreign direct investment in the early stages of transition was to benefit from the relatively inexpensive labour force. This is at odds with the goal of attracting more talented workers and foreign ownership might not have been directly related to innovativeness at the firm level. Thus, it could be the case that through increased EU mobility, high-skilled workers were attracted by companies in the advanced EU economies, while foreign companies attracted remaining talent within the post-transition economies.

Different stages of transition also play an important role when it comes to the perceived inadequacy of the workforce skills. Rutkowski (2007) argues that early phases of transition were not critical in that respect, but the firms' have realized the issues since the beginning of the 2000s. Early phases of transition were marked by the relative abundance of readily available workforce, due to the previously widespread phenomenon of hidden unemployment. The introduction of the market mechanisms thus created large open unemployment, and the firms did not perceive labour short-ages. However, other business cycle episodes also play a significant role in determining the perceived skills shortages. For example, Kupets (2016) suggests that in the aftermath of the global financial crisis there was a decline in the number of transition economies in which employers identified workforce skills as one of the top three major obstacles for doing business, from 11 of 29 countries in 2008/2009 to five countries in 2013/2014. Kupets (2016) attributes this finding directly to the impacts of the global financial crisis, which affected the availability of skilled workers and made other obstacles relatively more important. Although many aspects of innovation-human capital have been previously explored in the literature, the evidence suggests that the relationship can be time-specific.

The analysis in the present paper is focused on post-transition economies in the aftermath of the global financial effects. Since many forces shaped the interaction between human resources and innovation activity, it might not be possible to disentangle the specific causal relationships. However, by providing recent evidence, the analysis aims to set the ground for further research efforts.

3 Data and Methodology

The empirical analysis in the paper relies on the World Bank data from Enterprise Survey (https://www.enterprisesurveys.org/en/enterprisesurveys). This is a firm-level survey based on face-to-face interviews with managers containing information on a wide range of standard firm characteristics. The sample does not include companies that are ruled by government price regulations and state-owned enterprises. It contains firms both in the manufacturing and service sector. The survey is carried out in waves, with a few year gaps between the observations. The balanced panel data for the period 2009–2019 has been used, and thus, the sample contains only that information where the enterprise has been included in the sample in all three periods (2009, 2013 and 2019 wave). The aim of the paper is to analyse Central and Southeastern European (CESEE) and Commonwealth of Independent States (CIS) post-transition countries. Based on the data availability, in CESEE we include Albania, Bosnia and Herzegovina, Bulgaria, Croatia, Czechia, Estonia, Kosovo, Latvia, Lithuania, North Macedonia, Poland, Serbia and Slovenia. In CIS countries, we include Armenia, Georgia, Kyrgyz Republic, Moldova, Tajikistan and Uzbekistan.

We first turn attention to the question of differences in workforce characteristics between innovators and non-innovators in the most recent year of observation (2019). According to the information from the survey, the innovating firm is defined as the one that introduced new products or services to the market over the period of last 3 years.[1] The data is presented in Table 1. The definition of all the variables used in

---

[1] The dataset does not enable detection of other types of innovation (process, marketing and organizational innovation) that would be in accordance with the Oslo Manual. The questionnaire does include questions related to innovation input (R&D). However, innovation input does not necessarily

Table 1 Differences between innovators and non-innovators in CESEE and CIS

	CESEE		CIS	
	Innovator	Non-innovator	Innovator	Non-innovator
Labour regulations major or very severe obstacle	8.5	7.4	7.1	4.7
Inadequately educated workforce major or very severe obstacle	20.3	18.5	34.5	19.7
Additional education of employees	42.0	29.9	36.3	19.9
Production workers additional education	65.0	60.1	28.5	33.6
Percentage of temporary full-time employees	8.6	7.4	19.5	15.9
Percentage of full-time production workers in total	69.7	72.5	73.3	74.5
Percentage of high-skill production workers in total	40.9	39.8	51.9	45.6
Labour cost percentage of sales	30.9	26.1	18.0	30.2

Source Enterprise Survey

the analysis is presented in Table 3 in the Appendix.

The data in Table 1 confirms previous findings from the literature that innovators to a larger degree perceive labour regulations as an important obstacle for their business (Blind 2012), even though the percentage of firms reporting this as an important issue is relatively small. Innovators also more frequently find that the workforce is inadequately educated (Rapini et al. 2017) and they are compelled to provide additional training to their employees. However, it seems that employers in CESEE countries are more likely to provide training for production workers compared to employers in CIS countries. This does not necessarily imply that the skill gap is larger in CESEE. It could be the case that employers in CESEE are more willing to provide training in order to ensure the competitiveness of their firms.

Employers in CIS countries are also more willing to rely on temporary workers. In both country groupings, innovating firms are more likely to have higher shares of temporary employees. The data does not, however, reveal whether temporary workers belong to the group of high-skill or low-skill workers, which can have important consequences for the long-term innovation propensity, depending on the predominate structure of the innovation sector. Specifically, Kleinknecht et al. (2014) claim that in the case of a 'routinised' innovation regime, high shares of low-paid temporary workers have a negative impact on the probability that firms invest in R&D. Thus, the increased reliance on flexible labour is correlated with less innovation (Hoxha and

---

lead to innovation output, and it is highly expected that firms with R&D as innovation input would require another type of human capital, also an input in the innovation process. The information on R&D cannot be confirmed by alternative sources and the responses to the new product or service question were considered more relevant for the analysis in the present paper.

Kleinknecht 2020). Firms require a constant pool of R&D capable human capital in order to ensure innovation output. The contrary is found if the dominant form of innovation is through a 'garage business' regime, where temporary work has no effect on innovation output. The studies also consistently find that workers hired under temporary contracts are paid less than those with a permanent position (Booth et al. 2002). Thus, a relatively higher prevalence of temporary work in innovating companies might suggest that the intent is not to compete on the market with the quality of (innovative) product, but with the product price (obtained through reduced costs of inputs). This is consistent with countries being followers in innovation, and the innovative products being more frequently new to the local market and not radically new.

In order to provide additional insight, we investigate whether the firm propensity to innovate in the analysed economies is related to human capital. Specifically, we estimate the following equation:

$$
\begin{aligned}
\text{inno}_{i,j} = {} & \alpha + \beta_1 \text{lab\_ edu}_{i,j} + \beta_2 \text{lab\_ regulations}_{i,j} + \beta_3 \text{edu\_ prod}_{i,j} \\
& + \beta_4 \text{emp\_ prodhigh}_{i,j} + \beta_5 \text{relative\_ lcost}_{i,j} \\
& + \beta_6 \text{small}_{i,j} + \beta_7 \text{large}_{i,j} + \beta_8 \text{female\_ manager}_{i,j} \\
& + \beta_9 \text{man\_ experience}_{i,j} + \beta_{10} \text{foreign}_{i,j} \\
& + \beta_{11} \text{manufacture}_{i,j} + \beta_{12} \text{export\_ direct}_{i,j} \\
& + \beta_{13} \text{EU}_{i,j} + \beta_{14} \text{CIS}_{i,j} + \epsilon_{i,j}
\end{aligned}
$$

Previous findings in the literature have guided the choice of the independent variables. Innovating firms to a larger extent complain about the labour regulations and inadequacy of existing workforce qualifications. Related to that, we further explore whether innovation propensity is related to the training provided to full-time production workers, the share of high-skill production workers or relative share of labour cost. Based on previous discussions, the assumption is that innovation propensity will be positively associated with the first two indicators, while the expected sign on the relative labour cost is not a priori clear. Specifically, we assume that innovating firms will more likely employ higher shares of highly skilled production workers and that their innovative orientation would require providing additional on-the-job training. Baldwin and Johnson (1996) documented that more innovative firms offer formal and informal training than less innovative firms.

The size of the enterprise is of particular importance in post-transition economies. Previous studies have established that small and very large firms have the highest innovation propensities (Tether 1998). Large firms invest more in in-house R&D activities, while small are focused on activities providing immediate solutions to critical problems (Corsten 1987; Santoro and Chakrabarti 2002). Specifically, in the case of transition economies, literature has established that firm size is an important predictor for innovation propensity (Seker 2009).

Extant findings show that presence in foreign market leads to more innovation (Criscuolo et al. 2010). This is partially related to access to a wider pool of business ideas. But, the entrance to the international market also enhances access to larger concentrated markets, which stimulates firms to persist in their effort to maintain internal innovation activities (Love and Roper 2002). In the case of transition economies, however, Bahl et al. (2021) argue that the relationship between innovation and internationalization is negative.

Innovation remains a risky undertaking (Leiponen and Helfat 2010), making the role of innovative firm managers crucial. To emphasize this, variable capturing managers years of experience in the sector is included in the specification. It is assumed that if the manager is more familiar with a specific sector, the innovation activity within a firm will be organized more efficiently. The literature is somewhat inconclusive on the role of female managers. While some studies find that female managers attribute more risk to innovative projects (Millward and Freeman 2002), others suggest that female board representation is associated with greater innovative success (Chen et al. 2018). The evidence on transition countries is relatively scarce, so a dummy variable taking value 1 if a firm has a female manager is included in the specification.

A few additional dummy variables are also included in the specification. Since the sample contains both manufacturing and service sector enterprises, a dummy variable taking value 1 if a firm operates in the manufacturing sector is included as a control. A dummy variable taking value 1 is included if a firm is operating in a country that is an EU member, to capture possible common markets effects. Finally, since the preliminary analysis suggested differences between CESEE and CIS countries, a dummy variable taking value 1 if a firm is operating in one of the CIS countries is included in the specification.

We are interested in the average partial effects of the variables and not the coefficients. Since heteroskedasticity is a potential problem due to different firm responses across the countries, we estimate a correlated random effects model. Thus, in addition to specified variables, we include time-constant variables as well as time dummies in the specification. Preliminary data analysis shows that there is no innovation persistence in the sample. Since we focus on average partial effects, we utilize a pooled probit. The average partial effects are presented in the following section, while the probit estimates are presented in Table 4 in the Appendix.

4   Results and Discussion

Since the analysis is performed on the balanced sample, only the firms participating in all three waves are included, and consequently, the size of the sample is relatively small. Subsequently, the results in Table 2 should be considered as an indication and not a firm conclusion on the relationships explored in this paper.

Before discussing the results, it has to be noticed that many of the innovation propensity determinants identified in the literature were not confirmed by this dataset.

Table 2 Factors of innovation propensity

	Average partial effect (standard error)
lab_edu	−0.024 (0.121)
lab_regulations	0.085 (0.124)
edu_prod	0.002** (0.001)
emp_prodhigh	0.105 (0.180)
relative_lcost	0.380 (0.295)
small	−0.021 (0.101)
large	0.219*** (0.077)
female_manager	−0.217* (0.113)
man_experience	0.009 (0.006)
foreign	−0.213** (0.097)
manufacture	−0.076 (0.119)
exports_direct	−0.001 (0.003)
EU	−0.050 (0.097)
CIS	0.010 (0.112)

Source Author's estimates based on Enterprise Survey

This can be attributed to the heterogeneity of such a small sample. The heterogeneity can be identified in the differences between CIS and CESEE groups, but also differences between the countries within a group, as well as differences within a specific country. In addition to intrinsic characteristics of the firm, firm innovation propensity is influenced by specific policy measures that have not been addressed in this paper. This issue deserves attention in future research efforts. Another source of heterogeneity is related to the period under the analysis, which is the aftermath of the global economic crisis. The countries in the sample were not equally affected by the crisis (Bayar et al. 2021; Dombi and Grigoriadis 2020), and the length of the crisis has been different as well as policy responses. To try to reduce the problem of small sample, the same equation has been estimated with an unbalanced sample (results not presented, but available from the author upon request), and there were no substantial differences in the signs or the levels of significance of the estimated partial effects.

Results in Table 2 suggest that large enterprises are significantly more likely to have innovative output in the analysed period. Since the analysed period begins directly with the 2008–2009 global economic crisis, it seems that the large enterprises were resilient enough to continue their innovation activity. This is consistent with previous findings, as Botrić and Božić (2017) suggest that larger and innovative firms are more likely to apply for financing in post-transition economies in the aftermath of the global financial crisis. Thus, it could be the case that in the context of the global credit crunch, larger firms did manage to obtain the necessary capital to fund their innovative activities.

On the other hand, it is frequently assumed that foreign ownership is positively associated with innovation. The results based on this sample do not corroborate such assumptions. It could be the case that during the analysed period foreign firms were more risk-averse than domestic firms, who in their struggle to survive did manage to have innovation activity. Another possible explanation is related to the notion that the actual impact of foreign ownership depends on specific firm strategy (Jankowska et al. 2021). Thus, a more detailed investigation into this matter is needed in future research.

When it comes to skills requirement, only variable capturing training of production workers is positively associated with the innovation propensity. This would suggest that in the analysed period the supply of labour was probably relatively high on the market, and firms did not to a greater extent perceived labour market regulations or education of the labour force in general as the important obstacle for their business activity. This is consistent with skills shortages literature that suggests counter-cyclical country-specific dynamics of skills shortages mediated by other labour market characteristics (Brunello and Wruuck 2021). The relative abundance of labour would be particularly evident at the beginning of the analysed period that coincides with the aftermath of the financial crisis.

Regardless, it seems that innovators in post-transition economies recognize the need to provide additional training to their employers, in order to maintain and improve their competitive position on the market. This is in accordance with findings that training of employees is especially important in post-transition countries that generally lag behind those in developed countries in terms of innovation performance and level of technology (Božić 2020). Furthermore, Petreski (2021) argues that negative effects can be traced only to low-skilled industries, while workers in high-skilled industries were not negatively affected by the increased integration of transition economies into global value chains. Subsequently, it could be argued that education and training provide benefits for both employers and employees.

Managers' experience in this dataset is not a significant predictor for innovation propensity. However, having a female manager is negatively associated with innovation propensity. This suggests that in the post-transition economies, where the share of female managers is still relatively low, firms with female managers are predominately found in non-innovative segments of the economy. The reasons for such findings should be further explored. It could be the case that there are specific obstacles for firms with female managers—for example, access to finance—that could be alleviated with specific policy measures.

It is also interesting to note that neither belonging to European Union nor CIS creates a significant influence on the propensity to innovate. This would suggest that although there are substantial institutional differences among the analysing countries, and in some cases, they are considered institutional barriers, innovative firms tend to overcome them and continue their business efforts. Although such findings are encouraging, this does not suggest that there is no need for innovation-friendly reforms of institutions within specific countries. The reason is that the magnitude of the innovation effect could be additionally supported if innovation is attainable to more entrepreneurs. Since the analysed countries are still lagging in innovation activity in general, it is evident that there is an important potential for further support to innovative firms.

5 Conclusions

Based on the recent The World Bank Enterprise Survey dataset, the paper explores different aspects of inadequate human capital on innovation propensity in post-transition societies. The paper's main contribution is that it presents previously seldom analysed aspects of human capital and discusses their correlations to the innovation propensity of post-transition firms. By disaggregating post-transition countries in two groups, it further enables the identification of the most important human capital constraints the innovating firms are encountering in each group of countries.

The descriptive analysis finds differences between innovating and non-innovating firms, but also differences between countries belonging to the Central and South-European region compared to the countries belonging to the Commonwealth of Independent States region. Innovating firms to a larger degree perceive labour regulations as an important obstacle for their business and more frequently find that workforce is inadequately educated. While in both groups of countries innovators are more likely to provide additional training to their employees, employers in CESEE countries are more likely to provide training for production workers in comparison with employers in CIS countries. A somewhat puzzling finding is that innovating firms have higher shares of temporary employees. This could be potentially problematic for the innovation output in the longer run, as it suggests that innovating firms are not relying on their inner human capital for persistence in innovation activity. This is an issue that should also be raised in policy discussions aimed at supporting innovating firms in post-transition economies.

The empirical analysis investigated both effects of employers' and managers' human capital on firm innovation activity. While managers' human capital was not a significant predictor for innovation propensity, for workers there is a positive association between innovation propensity and training of production workers. Overall, it can be concluded that human capital is not a strong predictor for innovation activity of firms in post-transition societies, predominately because they are facing more important business constraints. However, it has been confirmed that innovators are more likely to provide additional training to their employees. The question is whether this could be attributed to the inadequate educational systems or the inability of firms to attract and appropriately employ the available talent. Regardless, the overall position of the analysed countries in the European innovation map suggests that existing human resources should be put to better use in order to enhance the innovation activity of the firms.

Such issues should be explored in the future with more extensive datasets. It is also acknowledged that different economic sectors, based on their intrinsic phases of development and subjected to specific business cycles, play very specific roles in the overall skills demand within a country. The present analysis should be supplemented by further disaggregation to accommodate the specific economic sector characteristics.

Appendix

See Tables 3 and 4.

Table 3 Definition of variables

Variable	Description	Average (standard deviation)
inno	= 1, if introduce new products/services over last 3 years	0.41 (0.49)
lab_edu	= 1, if inadequately educated workforce major or very severe obstacle	0.22 (0.41)
lab_regulations	= 1, if labour regulations major of very severe obstacle	0.07 (0.25)
edu_prod	= share of full-time production workers received formal education in last fiscal year	53.17 (38.38)
emp_prodhigh	= share of high-skill production workers in total	0.43 (0.39)
relative_lcost	= share of labour cost in sales	0.27 (1.28)
small	= 1, if a firm has 5–19 employees	0.38 (0.49)
large	= 1, if a firm has more than 100 employees	0.20 (0.40)
female_manager	= 1, if top manager female	0.20 (0.40)
man_experience	= number of years top manager works within the firm sector	18.91 (10.83)
foreign	= 1, if manufacturing firm	0.07 (0.25)
manufacture	= 1, if had direct exports	0.35 (0.48)
exports_direct	= 1, if percentage of foreign capital in firm ownership higher than 51	39.11 (35.82)
EU	= 1, if a country is an EU member	
CIS	= 1, if a country belongs to the CIS	

Table 4 Innovation propensity estimates

Variable	Estimated coefficients (standard error)
constant	4.076*** (1.455)
lab_edu	−0.107 (0.545)
lab_regulations	0.382 (0.551)
edu_prod	0.00907** (0.00447)
emp_prodhigh	0.472 (0.809)
relative_lcost	1.702 (1.341)
small	−0.0938 (0.455)
large	0.979*** (0.366)
female_manager	−0.970* (0.514)
man_experience	0.0408 (0.0265)
foreign	−0.951** (0.457)
manufacture	−0.339 (0.533)
exports_direct	−0.00257 (0.0131)
EU	−0.223 (0.437)
CIS	0.0434 (0.500)
m(lab_edu)	0.709 (0.982)
m(lab_regulations)	1.467 (1.582)
m(emp_prod)	−6.262*** (2.079)
m(emp_prodhigh)	2.662* (1.468)
m(relative_lcost)	−2.004 (1.706)
m(female_manager)	1.261* (0.740)

(continued)

Table 4 (continued)

Variable	Estimated coefficients (standard error)
m(man_experience)	−0.058* (0.035)
m(export_direct)	0.006 (0.014)
Y2013	−0.964** (0.409)
Y2019	−1.046* (0.572)
$N = 106$	
Wald chi^2 = 42.33**	
Pseudo $R^2 = 0.32$	

*** p<0.01, ** p<0.05, * p<0.1
Source Author's estimates based on Enterprise Survey

References

Audretsch, D.B., Kritikos, A.S., Schiersch, A. (2020) Microfirms and innovation in the service sector. Small Business Economics, 55(4): 997–1018.

Bahl, M., Lahiri, S., Mukherjee, D. (2021). Managing internationalization and innovation tradeoffs in entrepreneurial firms: Evidence from transition economics. Journal of World Business, 56(1): 101150.

Baldwin, J. R., Johnson, J. (1996) Business strategies in more- and less-innovative firms in Canada. Research Policy, 25(6): 785–804.

Barro, R. J., Lee, J.-W. (2001) International data on educational attainment: Updates and implications. Oxford Economic Papers, 53(3): 541–563.

Bayar, Y., Borozan, D., Gavriletea, M.D. (2021) Banking sector stability and economic growth in post-transition European Union countries. Finance & Economics, 26(1): 949–961.

Beugelsdijk, S. (2008) Strategic human resource practices and product innovation. Organization Studies, 29(6): 821–847.

Blind, K. (2012) The influence of regulations on innovation: A quantitative assessment for OECD countries. Research Policy,41(2): 391–400.

Bogliacino, F., Guarascio, D., Cirillo, V. (2018) The dynamics of profits and wages: technology, offshoring and demand. Industry and Innovation, 25(8): 778–808.

Booth, A. L., Francesconi, M., Frank, J. (2002) Temporary jobs: Stepping stones or dead ends? The Economic Journal, 112(480): F189–F213.

Botrić, V., Božić, Lj. (2017) Access to finance – innovation relationship in post-transition, EBEEC Conference Proceedings, The Economies of Balkan and Eastern Europe Countries in the Changed World, KnE Social Sciences, pp 28–41.

Božić, Lj. (2020) Sources of Business Growth at Different Levels of Innovativeness: Case of Firms in EU Countries. Managing Global Transitions: International Research Journal, 18(2): 127–145.

Brunello, G., and Wruuck, P., 2021. Skill Shortages and Skill Mismatch in Europe: A Review of the Literature. Journal of Economic Surveys, 35(4): 1145–1167.

Capozza, C., Divella, M. (2019) Human capital and firms' innovation: evidence from emerging economies. Economics of Innovation and New Technology, 28(7): 741–757.

Chen, J., Leung, W., Evans, K.P. (2018) Female board representation, corporate innovation and firm performance. Journal of Empirical Finance, 48: 236–254.

Cinnirella, F., Streb, J. (2017) The role of human capital and innovation in economic development: evidence from post-Malthusian Prussia. Journal of Economic Growth, 22(2): 193–227.

Corsten, H. (1987) Technology transfer from universities to small and medium-sized enterprises-an empirical survey from the standpoint of such enterprises. Technovation, 6(1): 57–68.

Criscuolo, C., Haskel, J. E., Slaughter, M. J. (2010) Global engagement and the innovation activities of firms. International Journal of Industrial Organization, 28(2): 191–202.

Crowley, F. (2017) Product and service innovation and discontinuation in manufacturing and service firms in Europe. European Journal of Innovation Management, 20(2): 250–268.

Crowley, F., Bourke, J. (2018) The influence of the manager on firm innovation in emerging economies. International Journal of Innovation Management, 22(3): 1850028.

Dombi, Á., Grigoriadis, T. (2020) State history and the finance-growth nexus: Evidence from transition economies. Economic Systems, 44(1): 100738.

Durazzi, N. (2019) The political economy of high skills: higher education in knowledge-based labour markets. Journal of European Public Policy, 26(12): 1799–1817.

Evangelista, R. (2000) Sectoral patterns of technological change in services. Economics of Innovation and New Technology, 9(3): 183–222.

Friz, K., Günther, J. (2020) Innovation and economic crisis in transition economies. Bremen Papers on Economics and Innovation, No. 2014.

Goldin, C., Katz, L. F. (2008) The race between education and technology: The evolution of U.S. educational wage differentials, 1890 to 2005. NBER Working Papers, No. 12984.

Gorodnichenko, Y., Schnitzer, M. (2013) Financial constraints and innovation: Why poor countries don't catch up. Journal of the European Economic Association, 11(5): 1115–1152.

Hoxha, S., Kleinknecht, A. (2020) When labour market rigidities are useful for innovation. Evidence from German IAB firm-level data. Research Policy, 49(7): 104066.

Jankowska, B., Götz, M., Tarka, P. (2021) Foreign subsidiaries as vehicles of industry 4.0: The case of foreign subsidiaries in a post-transition economy. International Business Review, 30(6): 101886.

Kleinknecht, A., van Schaik, F.N., Zhou, H. (2014) Is flexible labour good for innovation? Evidence from firm-level data. Cambridge Journal of Economics, 38(5): 1207–1219.

Kotz, D.M. (2002) Socialism and innovation. Science & Society, 66(1): 94–108.

Krzywdzinski, M. (2017) Automation, skill requirements and labour-use strategies: high-wage and low-wage approaches to high-tech manufacturing in the automotive industry. New Technology, Work and Employment, 32(3): 247–267.

Kupets, O. (2016) Skill mismatch and overeducation in transition economies. IZA World of Labor, No. 2016:224.

Kuttor, D., Hegyi-Kéri, A. (2014) Reasons or effects of the deindustrialization in Visegrad countries. Journal of Global Strategic Management, 8(1): 93–100.

Laursen, K., Foss, N. (2003) New human resource management practices, complementarities, and the impact on innovation performance. Cambridge Journal of Economics, 27(2): 243–263.

Lehmann, H., Muravyev, A. (2012) Labour market institutions and labour market performance: what can we learn from transition countries? Economics of Transition, 20(2): 235–269.

Leiponen A., Helfat C.E. (2010) Innovation objectives, knowledge sources, and the benefits of breadth. Strategic Management Journal, 31(2): 224–236.

Loukil, K. (2017) Technological innovation in Central and Eastern Europe: what's the contribution of innovation policy? The Economics and Finance Letters, 4(1): 1–8.

Love, J. H., Roper, S. (2002) Internal versus external R&D: A study of R&D choice with sample selection. International Journal of the Economics of Business, 9(2): 239–255.

Millward, L.J., Freeman, H. (2002) Role expectations as constraints to innovation: the case of female managers. Communication Research Journal, 14(1): 93–109.

Mulliqi, A., Adnett, N., Hisarciklilar, M. (2019) Human capital and exports: A micro-level analysis of transition countries. The Journal of International Trade & Economic Development, 28(7): 775–800.

Nazarov, Z., Akhmedjonov, A. (2012) Education, on-the-job training, and innovation in transition economies. Eastern European Economics, 50(6): 28–56.

Paunov, C. (2012) The global crisis and firms' investments in innovation. Research Policy, 41(1): 24–35.

Petreski, M. (2021). Has globalization shrunk manufacturing labor share in transition economies? Journal of Comparative Economics, 49(1): 201–211.

Pianta, M. (2018) Technology and employment: twelve stylized facts for the digital age. The Indian Journal of Labour Economics, 61: 189–225.

Radosevic, S., Ciampi Stancova, K. (2018) Internationalising smart specialisation: Assessment and issues in the case of EU new member states. Journal of the Knowledge Economy, 9(1): 263–293.

Rapini, M.S., Chiarini, T., Bittencourt, P.F. (2017) Obstacles to innovation in Brazil: the lack of qualified individuals to implement and establish university-firm interactions. Industry and higher Education, 31(3): 168–183.

Rutkowski, J. (2007) From the shortage of jobs to the shortage of skilled workers: Labor markets in the EU new member states. IZA Discussion Paper, No. 3202.

Santoro, M., Chakrabarti, A. (2002) Firm size and technology centrality in industry-university interactions. Research Policy, 31(7): 1163–1180.

Seker, M. (2009) Importing, exporting and innovation in developing countries. The World Bank Policy Research Working Paper, No. 5156.

Staccioli, J., Virgillito, M.E. (2021) Back to the past: the historical roots of labor-saving automation. Eurasian Business Review, 11(1): 27–57.

Tether, B. S. (1998) Small and large firms: Sources of unequal innovations? Research Policy, 27(7): 725–745.

Tether, B. S. (2005) Do services innovate (differently)? Insights from the European innobarometer survey. Industry and Innovation, 12(2): 153–184.

World Bank (2017) Trouble in the making? The future of manufacturing-led development. Washington D.C.: The World Bank.

World Bank Group, (2015) Skills Gaps and the Path to Successful Skills Development: Emerging Findings from Skills Measurement Surveys in Armenia, Georgia, FYR Macedonia, and Ukraine. World Bank Report, No. ACS14318.

Managing Labor Relations in Greek Hospitals—A Nursing Approach

Tsimpida Dialechti, Chris A. Grose, and Michael A. Talias

Abstract Conflicts are one of the most difficult problems healthcare executives have to deal with, while education on their effective management is of the utmost importance. They can be observed among the personnel of the same or a different service, either to peers or superiors, to the patients and their family environment, as well as the doctors of the institution. A hospital, being a complex organization, with heterogeneity in the skills, tasks or responsibilities of the workforce, often manages such conflicts through communication skills the administrative personnel acquires. The purpose of this study is to investigate the causes and effects of conflicts among nurses' working relations as well as their interaction with other healthcare professionals in Greek Hospitals. An effort is made to compare the sample between the public service and the private sector and to explore the effectiveness of how nurses manage conflicts. In contrast to other studies, public and private sector hospital employees appear to have a similar stance toward conflicts and the ways to overcome the stress they cause. To resolve them, they mainly use a consensual style of solving while avoiding conflict at work.

Keywords Conflict resolution in health care · Nursing community · Hospital conflicts · Conflict management

JEL Classification Codes · M10 · M12

T. Dialechti (✉)
RN, MSc Health Management, Faculty of Economics and Management, Open University of Cyprus, Nicosia, Cyprus
e-mail: dialechti23@yahoo.gr

C. A. Grose
International Hellenic University, Thermi, Greece

M. A. Talias
Healthcare Management Postgraduate Program, Open University of Cyprus, Nicosia, Cyprus

151
P. Sklias et al. (eds.), *Business Development and Economic Governance in Southeastern Europe*, Springer Proceedings in Business and Economics, https://doi.org/10.1007/978-3-031-05351-1_8

1 Introduction

Conflicts are one of the most difficult problems executives face in health sector, while training is considered necessary for their proper and effective management (Anderson 2009). They are often observed among staff members of the same or different service, either subordinates or supervisors, with patients and their environment as well as the doctors of the institution. Any organization that manages human resources is prone to conflicts; an   institution, being a complex organization, having heterogeneity in the responsibilities and skills of the workforce, often manages conflicts through the various communication skills of the management (Brown et al. 2011). As the proper functioning of the organization is the most important goal for an administration, some factors are required for its implementation (Borou and Korakidi 2013). Indicative such factors include the intraprofessional cooperation of the staff, the adequacy of knowledge of the health professionals and the communication (De Dreu et al. 2008). When high-demand nursing specialties began to emerge, role conflict and ambiguity became apparent in the nursing industry in the mid-1990 in countries such as Australia and the UK. The phenomenon had already appeared in the 1960s and 1970s in the USA in the field of specialized nurses (Tarrant and Sabo 2010).

The international literature offers various definitions regarding the concept of conflict (Conflict), but in which there are related and similar elements. According to Flanagan and Runde (2009) "conflict is the opposition or disagreement between individuals, groups, or ideas." Furumo (2009) considers conflict to be the presence of a difference, difference of opinion, or interest.

Describing and categorizing conflict can be done in several ways. Some of those include cognitive or emotional conflict, work or relationship conflict, combat or defense, chaos or conflict relationship, in or out of group conflict, virtual or non-virtual group conflict, competitive or disruptive conflict and functional or dysfunctional conflict (Filley 1975).

According to Spyrakis and Spyrakis (2008), the classification of conflicts and where they take place, through the structure of an organization or a company, has as follows:

- Hierarchical conflicts (between hierarchy levels),
- Functional conflicts (between different parts or functions of the organization chart),
- Conflicts between staff and line executives and
- Conflicts between formal and informal organizational structure.

A precondition for the conflict resolution is to find the sources and causes that lead to its creation (Guastello 2008). In the literature, three categories are identified: individual factors, interpersonal factors and organizing factors (Papanis 2011). Conflict management is helping individuals or groups who disagree to adopt an effective and equitable process of dealing with it (Guttman 2009). However, it must be separated by the definition of conflict resolution, where its goal is to minimize or end the conflict (Guttman 2009).

Management begins by deciding when and if one should intervene. Depending on the people involved and the intensity of the conflict, there is intervention with a positive or negative outcome (Fountouki et al. 2009). For example, if there are two people and the intensity is insignificant, there may be no intervention. However, if the conflict is large and the intervention has been delayed, then the situation is likely to get out of control, as the outcome may be detrimental to the people involved (Mele 2007). Also, it is noticeable that, if two people are given the opportunity to resolve a dispute on their own, then their ability to handle future disputes develops and improves (Sullivan and Phillip 2005). However, if there are negative consequences, the intervention of the boss is considered necessary (Flanagan and Runde 2009). Proper conflict management depends directly on many factors, of which the most important ones are the environment, the culture of the organization and the variation of the personalities of the people involved (Moore 2014; Swarnsburg and Swarnsburg 1999).

Common yet effective conflict resolution techniques are demonstration of leadership, third-party intervention and the staff's adherence to protocols (Montana and Charnov 2005). It is worth mentioning that direct communication as an individual strategy can be effective in maintaining a functional environment.

Filley (1975) identifies three strategies depending on the outcome of the conflict:

(a)   *win–lose,*
(b)   *lose–lose and*
(c)   *win–win.*

Negotiation presupposes that the situation is solvable and both parties are willing to give something; the climate should be good and supportive, there should be trust and good communication between the parties in-between the negotiation process (Sourtzi 2012). An important step in conflict management is to assess the situation. The first person to be involved from the administrative side is seen as the leader as his role is important in resolving the conflict (TKI 2018). Quite often, the two parties who disagree turn to the leader for a solution. A good tactic on their part is to encourage him to resolve the dispute without involving anyone else while maintaining a supportive spirit (Papanis 2011). The purpose of the intervention of the leader is to restore peace and increase productivity through the process of conflict resolution. Management, leadership skills, active communication and a climate of positive negotiation are required (Rahim 2011). Job satisfaction was investigated in Spain, in a public hospital with a sample of 270 health professionals, where the models of management and organizational conflicts were documented (Sureda et al. 2018). In a survey in Pakistan, hospital workers choose methods such as commitment, integration, compromise and finally avoidance as reasons of choice of work (Khalid and Fatima 2016).

For the needs of the paper, the public and the private sectors of the wider area of Larissa were studied equally. Young staff work in the private sector with a few years of service, avoiding conflicts during the shift. About half of the staff consider the issue of the conflict to be very serious and at least once have requested a change of department due to their poor management with the rest of the staff of the hospital or clinic. Collaboration is the dominant role as a management style by nurses, while many choose complex styles, e.g., compromise and cooperation.

The rest of the paper contains in Sect. 2 the research methodology and data, the results and the discussion in Sect. 3 and concluding remarks in Sect. 4.

2 Research Methodology and Data

Following the analysis in the previous section, the purpose of the dissertation is to investigate the causes and effects of conflicts between nurses' employment relationships, as well as their interaction with other health professionals in Greek Hospitals. An attempt is made to compare the sample between the public and private sectors and to investigate the effectiveness of the way nurses manage conflicts. Furthermore, the relationship between conflict management style through a special questionnaire (TKI) and the characteristics of individuals is recorded, as the various parameters of public and private sector are related.

The research questions to be answered by this paper are the following:

✓   Can labor conflicts be identified or not?
✓   After being categorized according to their characteristics, what are the reasons causing them?
✓   What is the frequency of conflicts on hospital premises and between which working groups?
✓   How effective is the way in which hospital employees manage conflicts?
✓   Are health professionals trained toward conflict resolution by hospital management or/and a conflict management program?

In order to answer the research questions, qualitative research was selected. The paper tries to explore the views of the sample by the use of qualitative variables: a methodology chosen by most researchers studying the phenomenon of conflict management. The main criterion for selecting the sample of institutions was the accessibility and the number of nurses in employment. For the purposes of this study, the international model with a mixed questionnaire including the Thomas–Kilmann conflict instrument (TKI) was used. This questionnaire is considered to be the first in finding conflict resolution methods and has been widely used internationally in recent decades.

The short structured questionnaire (TKI, Kilmann Diagnostics 2018) consists of 30 closed-ended questions per pair. For each pair, the respondent chooses either A or B. Each pair of sentences is designed so that there is parity in terms of the socially desirable result. The tool identifies five (5) conflict management styles:

- *Avoidance (turtle)*
- *Retreat (teddy bear)*
- *Compromise (fox)*
- *Competition (shark) and*

Graph 1 Distribution of samples in different hospitals and sectors

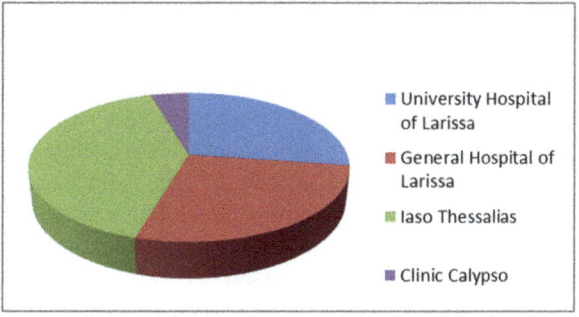

- University Hospital of Larissa
- General Hospital of Larissa
- Iaso Thessalias
- Clinic Calypso

- *Collaboration (owl).*

The questionnaire is also available electronically in many languages, but for the needs of the present research, it was translated into Greek from English and vice versa by people who have excellent knowledge of Greek and English and with previous experience in translating research tools. The translators were independent of each other, and it was checked that the back translation was similar to the original one. The questionnaire used Likert scale and closed-type questions with the aim of collecting quality data. The total filling time did not exceed 15 min. The questions fully covered the research questions of the study and included issues of demographic type, frequency of conflicts, administrative role, peer solidarity and job satisfaction.

The research was carried out in the following hospitals: Larissa Regional University Hospital, Larissa General Hospital, Iaso Thessaly Private Hospital and Kalypso Private Clinic. A total of 440 questionnaires were distributed in the various departments of hospitals, open and closed, in March 2018, and were collected on March 31, 2018 (Graph 1). The sampling method had random sampling elements since the participants were randomly selected. For the correct observance of the rules, written permission was requested from the four institutions with a Letter of Assurance of License, submission of a research protocol.

In each department, the set of questionnaires was accompanied by an information letter to the head of department, while all employees had access. The letter included general information of the researcher, contact details, goals and objectives, as well as the research questions. They were handed over to the head of each department by the researcher and returned by the head to the same. They were placed in a prominent place in the department or office, available for completion. Since the supervisor has a key position for the smooth completion of the sample collection process, it was decided that he/she would be responsible for informing the staff about the survey and not giving the questionnaires to the staff himself/herself.

Participation was optional and voluntary in order to ensure the objectivity of the answers. Participants were fully informed of the aims and objectives of the research, with an introductory note before the distribution form questions began, so that there could be consensus and confirmation that all ethical procedures would be followed. However, the supervisor responsible for informing staff about the questionnaire is a critical factor in the process, while many times employees are forced to participate in the research against their will or not to give objective answers (Mercouris 2008). In the present work, an attempt was made to ensure the representativeness of the sample in terms of the size of both the public and the private sectors.

Out of the 440 questionnaires distributed, 320 were answered eventually completed. It should be noted that there were a number of 15 questionnaires where that were considered incomplete and they were not included in the response rate of the study. The response rate reached 73%. Tables 1 and 2 present the study response and the hospital response of each institution separately. Data analysis was performed with SPSS v.23 software. The questionnaires, after being coded, were registered in the software in order to analyze the data and draw conclusions. Descriptive statistics and comparison–correlation indices of two quality variables were used for the analysis.

The following were used in more detail:

- Frequencies, frequency tables, graphs, position measures and percentages for the presentation of demographic data,
- The x2 method for the correlation and analysis of variables (qualitative variables).

The analysis was performed with a minimum acceptable 95% confidence interval of $p < 0.05$.

Table 1 Study response of the hospitals—public and private sectors

Hospital	Distribution	Response	Response (%)
University Hospital of Larissa	120	60	**50**
General Hospital of Larissa	120	90	**75**
Iaso Thessalias	180	160	**89**
Clinic Calypso	20	10	**50**
Total	**440**	**320**	73

Table 2 Study response percent of the hospitals—public and private sectors

	Frequency	Percent	Valid percent	Cumulative percent
University Hospital of Larissa	60	18.8	18.8	18.8
General Hospital of Larissa	90	28.1	28.1	46.9
Iaso Thessalias	160	50.0	50.0	96.6
Clinic Calypso	10	3.1	3.1	100.00
Total	320	100.0	100.0	

3 Results and Discussion

This section presents questionnaire results attempting to investigate the various characteristics of the sample but also its relation toward conflict in public and private sectors. The study population consisted of nurses, men and women, of all levels and transporters of the four investigated institutions of public and private sectors. Age ranged between 18 and 65 years (see Graph 2). According to Table 3, women make up 85% (272) of the sample, compared to men with 15% (48). As depicted in Table 4, 41.3% (132) of the population is between 31 and 40 years old, followed by 24.7% (79) under 30 years old. Continuing on with the demographics and sample characteristics married men and women are the largest percentages with 53.1% of the sample (Table 5), single is 34.4% (110), while divorced another 33 people from the

Graph 2 Demographic data of sample

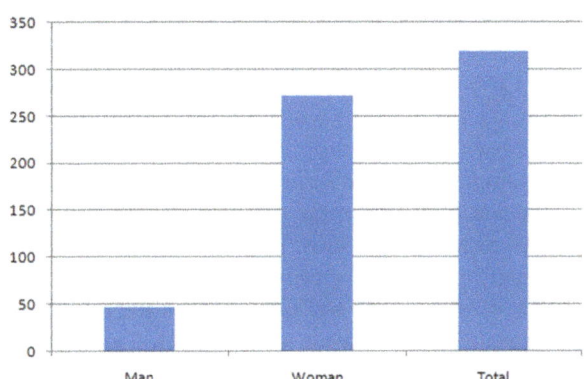

Table 3 Gender frequency table data of sample

	Frequency	Percent	Valid percent	Cumulative percent
Man	48	15.0	15.0	15.0
Woman	272	85.0	85.0	100.0
Total	320	100.0	100.0	

Table 4 Age frequency table data of sample

	Frequency	Percent	Valid percent	Cumulative percent
<30	79	24.7	24.7	24.7
31–40	132	41.3	41.3	65.9
41–50	69	21.6	21.6	87.5
51–60	39	12.2	12.2	99.7
>60	1	0.3	0.3	100.0
Total	320	100.0	100.0	

Table 5 Marital status frequency table of sample

	Frequency	Percent	Valid percent	Cumulative percent
Married	170	53.1	53.1	53.1
Unmarried	110	34.4	34.4	87.5
Divorced	33	10.3	10.3	97.8
Other	7	2.2	2.2	100.0
Total	320	100.0	100.0	

total population. In the same table, one can observe those with and without children (44.1% have 1–2 children and no children 46.6% of the sample).

Most of the answers to the questionnaire came from nurses that constitute 76.9% of the sample (246), another 10% (32) obstetricians/midwives and 8.4% (27) supervisors. Regarding the level of education, 48.8% (156) people have a diploma in technological education, while another 20.9% (67) hold a secondary education degree and 11.6% (37) have a master's degree. In the attempt to compare the public–private sector, 43.1% (138) of women work in the private sector and 41.9% (134) in the public sector representing, therefore, a fairly balanced sample. For the remaining total sample of both male and female participants, 10% are employed in the private sector and only 5% in the public sector (Table 6). From the staff working in the private sector, 22.2% have less than 5 years of service, while the total figure with less than 5 years of service is 29.1%. This is followed by 6–10 years of work, 23.1% (74) with 16.6% (56) and 6.6% (21) in the private and public sectors, respectively. More than 21 years of service is indicated in 18.1% (58) of the sample (Table 7).

Table 8 reports results with respect to conflicts per se. Conflicts are common in 43.8% (140) of the sample in hospital wards, with 24.7% (79) reported by the private and 19.1% (61) in the public sector. Conflicts in the health sector are quite common, according to 24.7% (79) of the sample, with 12.2% in the private sector and 12.5% in the public sector. Occasionally states only 2.5% of the study sample. According to the frequency tables of conflicts between groups, it is stated that conflicts between nurses occur frequently and quite often in 37.8% and 21.6% of cases, respectively. In addition to colleagues, they come into conflict with other people from other professional groups because communication is close and demanding. It is reported that

Table 6 Gender frequency and employment sector table

Employment sector			
	Private	Public	Total
Man count	32	16	48
% of total	10.0%	5.0%	15%
Woman count	138	134	272
% of total	43.1%	41.9%	85.0%
Total count	170	150	320
% of total	53.1%	46.9%	100.0%

Table 7 Table of frequencies percentages of years of service and employment sector

Employment sector			Private	Public	Total
Years of service	<5	Count	71	22	93
		% of total	22.2%	6.9%	29.1%
	6–10	Count	53	21	74
		% of total	16.6%	6.6%	23.1%
	11–15	Count	23	27	50
		% of total	7.2%	8.4%	15.6%
	16–20	Count	11	34	45
		% of total	3.4%	10.6%	14.1%
	>21	Count	12	46	58
		% of total	3.8%	14.4%	18.1%
Total		Count	170	150	320
		% of total	53.1%	46.9%	100.0%

Table 8 Conflict frequency—employment sector cross tabulation

			Private	Public	Total
Conflict Frequency	Never	Count	4	4	8
		% of total	1.3%	1.3%	2.5%
	Rarely	Count	45	34	79
		% of total	14.1%	10.6%	24.7%
	Often	Count	79	61	140
		% of total	24.7%	19.1%	43.8%
	Quite often	Count	30	40	79
		% of total	12.2%	12.5%	24.7%
	Almost always	Count	3	11	14
		% of total	0.9%	3.4%	4.4%
Total		Count	170	150	320

in Cyprus health professionals often clash with superiors (56.2%) (Pitsillidou et al. 2018). Among nurses and doctors, they occur often with a rate of 34.1% (109) and quite often with a rate of 21.3% (68). They occur rarely among nurses and patients in 46.3% (148) of the sample. Another 30% of the sample reported that conflicts occur often between nurses and ward attendants. Almost half of the sample (49.7%) stated that conflicts between patients are rare, while another 52.5% considered the same for conflicts between patients and attendants. A further 53.1% reported no conflicts between attendants and patients.

A very high proportion of the sample (77.5%) has not been informed of any program by the administration of the institution with 40.6% (130) coming from the private and 36.9% (118) from the public sector, respectively. Only 22.5% seem to have been informed in some way of any such program existing within the hospital premises, almost equally distributed between the public and private sectors. A department change due to the frequent occurrence of collisions seems to have been requested by 19.4% of the sample while four out five have remained in the same department. In the pertinent literature, the percentage is very low (Moisoglou et al. 2014). This fact is in agreement with the work of Rousou and Pavlakis (2009).

As reported in Table 9, combinedly 76.9% of the population characterize the issue of conflicts very serious. Stress appears to be caused in over 75% of the sample. In this, context satisfied with their work despite such occurrences is 59.4% (190) with 32.2% (103) coming from the private sector and 27.2% (87) from the public (Table 10). 36.3% (116) of the population appear to be aware of what is expected of them at work. Frequent harassment is reported by 20.3% (65) of the sample with 13.1% (42) from the private and 7.2% (23) from the public sector.

In Graph 3, we see that only 77%, more specifically 12.5% (40) of the private and 10% (32) of the public, are aware of some kind of conflict management program.

Freedom of decision at work is a sentiment shared by 48.8% (156) of the study population, in contrast to 51.2% (164) who work within set duties. Seventy percent (224) of the sample state that they have the opportunity to talk to their superiors, with 36.6% (117) working in the private sector and 33.4% (107) in the public sector. Peer support is experienced quite often by 36.9% (118) of the sample and almost ever-present by a percentage of 22.5% (72). Of the sample surveyed, 44.1% stated that they often have respect from their colleagues, while 33.8% often receive clear

Table 9 Severity of conflict management

		Frequency	Percent	Valid percent	Cumulative percent
Valid	Not at all	4	1.3	1.3	1.3
	A little bit	12	3.8	3.8	5.0
	Enough	58	18.1	18.1	23.1
	Very	87	27.2	27.2	50.3
	Very much	159	49.7	49.7	100.0
	Total	320	100.0	100.0	

Table 10 Table of job satisfaction frequencies and employment sector percents—private and public

Employment sector			
	Private	Public	Total
Job satisfaction YES Count % of total	103 32.2%	87 27.2%	190 59.4%
Job satisfaction NO Count % of total	67 20.9%	63 19.7%	130 40.6%
Total Count % of total	170 53.1%	150 46.9%	320 100.0%

Graph 3 Total conflict
management
information—yes or no

instructions from their superiors. They seem to have enough encouragement from their leader often in 34.1% (109) of the sample. Clear work schedules are received by 30.3, and 29.4% of the population has the opportunity to discuss problems almost always. Graph 4 represented that collaboration according to TKI with 47.5% (153) wins a dominant role in the style of conflict management. The percentages are in the line with the international literature (TKI, Kilmann Diagnostics 2018). The following are: the compromise style with 9.4% (30), the competitive style with 7.2% (23), the avoidance style with 5.9% (19) and finally the compliant style with 4.7% (15).

Thomas–Kilmann conflict management profiles are 5 (five). In the present study, from the analysis of the results, combinations of management styles emanate as analytically mentioned in Table 11. 47.8% (153) of the population of employees

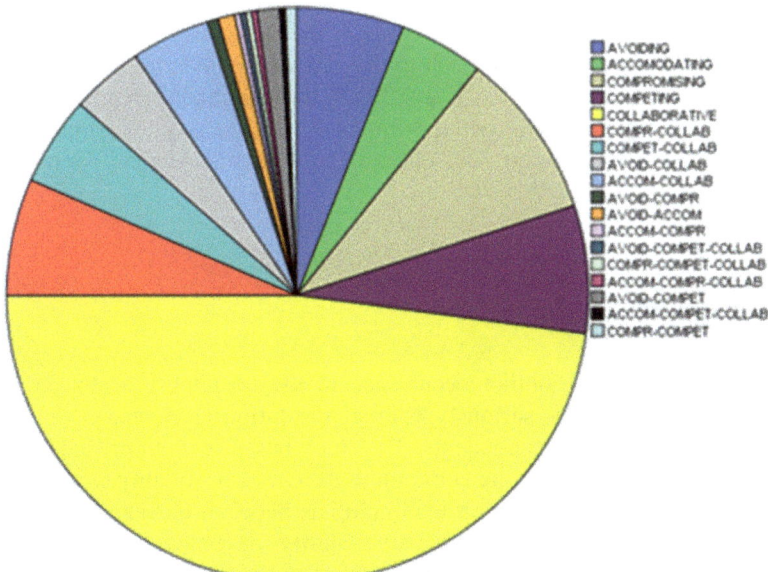

Graph 4 Total management by Thomas–Kilmann pie-profiles

Table 11 Management frequencies of profiles according to Thomas–Kilmann

	Frequency	Percent	Valid percent	Cumulative percent
Avoiding	19	5.9	5.9	5.9
Accomodating	15	4.7	4.7	10.6
Compromising	30	9.4	9.4	20.0
Competing	23	7.2	7.2	27.2
Collaborative	153	47.8	47.8	75.0
Compr-collab	21	6.6	6.6	81.6
Compet-collab	16	5.0	5.0	86.6
Avoid-collab	13	4.1	4.1	90.6
Accom-collab	14	4.4	4.4	95.0
Avoid-compr	2	0.6	0.6	95.6
Avoid-accom	3	0.9	0.9	96.6
Accom-compr	1	0.3	0.3	96.9
Avoid-compet-collab	1	0.3	0.3	97.2
Compr-compet-collab	1	0.3	0.3	97.5
Accom-compr-collab	1	0.3	0.3	97.8
Avoid-compet	4	1.3	1.3	99.1
Avoid-compet-collab	1	0.3	0.3	99.4
Compr-compet	2	0.3	0.3	100.0
Total	320	100.0	100.0	

seem to adopt a cooperative approach in the case of conflicts in their work. Out of that 25% work in the private sector and 22.8% in the public sector. This finding is followed by the style of compromise with 9.4% with the style of retreat is chosen by 4.7%. The particular sector differences in conflict management approaches are found in Graph 5.

4   Conclusion

This paper investigates conflict occurrence in the hospitality sector in Greece. It further delves into how seriously conflict resolution is viewed by individuals comprising the sample of respondents. The study based on both private and public sector data finds that conflicts are common in the Greek hospitality sector. Conflicts between nurses are more common than conflicts between nurses and doctors and nurses and the public. However, the vast majority view such conflicts as serious calling for relevant training on the methods of optimal conflict resolution. Such programs though rarely exist according to the examined sample.

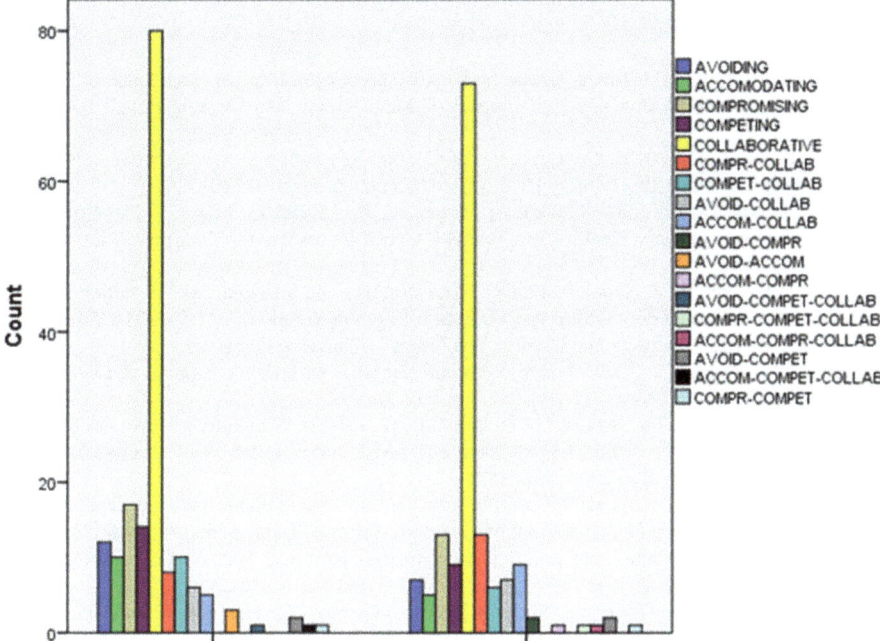

Graph 5 TKI and employment sector—private or public

It appears that the majority of respondents adopt a cooperative approach toward resolving conflicts and only one out of 10 and one out of 20 choose compromise and retreat as a corrective measure. The results are in line with international findings, and these findings on the one hand highlight personnel's ability to satisfactorily manage situations but underline the need to develop intra-hospital mechanisms toward the optimal treatment of similar incidents. However, it appears that contrary to the international evidence, both public and private sector hospital employees choose cooperation as the main tool for the resolution of disputes, whereas internationally evidence shows that this is clearly the case only in the case of private hospitals.

Since the quality of the delivered hospital services is closely related to the level of cooperation and the adoption of sound dispute resolution, the need to adopt mechanisms of immediate and fair treatment of such occurrences is imminent. Future studies should focus toward the more focused and systematic study of conflicts in different hospitality settings so as to investigate further the characteristics that could potentially differentiate the employees' approach to conflict in different settings.

References

Anderson, M. (2009). "The role of group personality composition in the emergence of task and relationship conflict within groups." Journal of Management and Organization, USA, 15(1), 82–96.

Borou, A. Korakidi, D. (2013). "Investigation of Conflict Resolution Strategies between Nurses in Public Hospitals", Interdisciplinary Health Care, Volume 5, Issue 3, 120–129.

Brown, J., Lewis, L., Ellis, K., Stewart, M., Freeman, T., Kasperski, M.J. (2011). "Conflict on Interprofessional Primary Health Care Teams – Can it be resolved?", Interprof Care, 25 (11), 4–10.

De Dreu, C., Kluwer, E., & Nauta, A. (2008). "The structure and management of conflict: Fighting or defending the status quo. Group Processes & Intergroup Relations", 11(3), 331–353.

Filley, A. C. (1975). "Interpersonal Conflict resolution", Glenview, Foresman.

Flanagan, T., & Runde, C. (2009). "How teams can capitalize on conflict. Strategy & Leadership", San Francisco, USA.

Fountouki, A., Gatzelis, Th., Pantas, D., Theofanidis, D., (2009). "The Interprofessional Cooperation of the nurse in the working environment of a provincial hospital", To Vima tou Asklipiou, Volume 8, Issue 4, Oct-Dec 2009, 336–352.

Furumo, K. (2009). "The impact of conflict and conflict management style on deadbeats and deserters in virtual teams". The Journal of Computer Information Systems, 49(4): 6673.

Guastello, S. (2008). "Chaos and conflict: Recognizing patterns. Emergence: complexity and organization", 10(4): 1–9.

Guttman, H. (2009). "Conflict management as a core competency for HR professionals. People and Strategy", USA, 32(1): 32–39.

Khalid, S., & Fatima, I. (2016). "Conflict types and conflict management styles in public and private hospitals", Pakistan Armed Forces Medical Journal, 66(1), 122–126.

Mele, D, (2007). "Ethics in Management: Exploring the contributions of Mary Parker Follett", International Journal of Public Administration, 30 (4).

Mercouris, Anastasios (2008). "Nursing Services Administration", Athens: Ellin Publications, (17), 271–280.

Moisoglou, I., Panagiotis, P., Galanis, P., Siskou, O., Maniadakis, N., & Kaitelidou, D. (2014). "Conflict Management in a Greek Public Hospital : Collaboration or Avoidance?" International Journal of Caring Sciences, 7(1), 75–82.

Montana, P. & Charnov, B. (2005). "Management", Athens: Klidarithmos Publications.

Moore, C. (2014). "The Mediation Process Practical Strategies for Resolving Conflict", John Wiley & Sons, San Fransisco.

Papanis, E. (2011), "Internet Consulting and Communication", Athens: Kyriakidis Publications.

Pitsillidou, M., Farmakas, A., Noula, M., & Roupa, Z. (2018). "Conflict management among health professionals in hospitals of Cyprus". Journal of Nursing Management, 26, 953–960.

Rahim, M. (2011), "Managing Conflicts in Organizations", USA, Transaction Publishers.

Rousou, E., Pavlakis, A., (2009). "Evaluation of conflicts between doctors and nurses in the Departments Accidents and Emergencies of public hospitals in Cyprus", Cyprus Nursing Chronicles, 12 (1): 36–50.

Sourtzi, P. (2012). "Nursing Staff Aging and Work - Challenge for Health Care Services", Nursing, Volume 51, Issue 3, 239–241.

Spyrakis, G. & Spyrakis, Ch. (2008), "Conflict Management in Organizations: From Conflict Resolution to Conflict Management", Administrative Briefing, January 2008 Issue, 44: 32–50.

Sullivan, E. & Phillip, D. (2005). "Effective Leadership and Management in Health Services", Athens: Giourdas Publications, (9), 133–139.

Sureda, E., Mancho, J., & Sesé, A. (2018). "Psychosocial risk factors, organizational conflict and job satisfaction in Health professionals : A SEM model", Annals of Psychology, 35(1), 106–115.

Swarnsburg, R. & Swarnsburg, R. (1999). "Introductory Management and Leadership for Nurses, Second Edition", Toronto, Canada, Managing Conflict 23, 591–607.

Tarrant, T., Sabo, E. C. (2010). "Role conflict, Role ambiguity, and Job satisfaction in Nurse Executives", Nursing Administration Quarterly, 34 (1), 72–82.

TKI, Kilmann Diagnostics. (2018). http://www.kilmanndiagnostics.com/overview-thomas-kil mann-conflict-mode-instrument-tki. Accessed 3/1/2018.

Statistical Arbitrage Using Cointegration and Principal Component Analysis Approach

Oleksandr Bartkoviak, Viktor Shpyrko, Oleksandr Chernyak, and Yevgen Chernyak

Abstract Two approaches to model-driven statistical arbitrage in the most liquid equities tradable on the NYSE and NASDAQ are studied in the article. Cointegration and PCA analysis were used in the research. In both strategies, we are developing contrarian trading signals, which then are back-tested through period of 2016–2020 with 4-h frequency and 2019–2020 with 1-h frequency data. Back-testing of the strategies through growing market of 2016–2019, and global sell-off at beginning of 2020 is the main contribution of the research. Both strategies demonstrated consistent returns, with lower than the broad market drawdowns. While Sharpe ratio of the strategies may be considered quite low at 0.49 for PCA-based approach, it outperformed both long- and short-only proxies. Lower than broad market downturn through sell-off period, and consistent median returns for both strategies were observed.

Keywords Statistical arbitrage · PCA · Cointegration · Ornstein-Uhlenbeck process

JEL Classification C02 · C55 · C53

O. Bartkoviak (✉) · V. Shpyrko · O. Chernyak · Y. Chernyak
Taras Shevchenko National University of Kyiv, 90a, Vasilkivska str., Kyiv 03022, Ukraine
e-mail: alexander.bartkoviak@gmail.com

V. Shpyrko
e-mail: viksh@bigmir.net

O. Chernyak
e-mail: chernyak@univ.kiev.ua

1   Introduction

In this article we are researching statistical arbitrage strategies—the term includes spectrum of statistical and model-driven investment and trading strategies. Essentially statistical arbitrage refers to exploration of the market assets pricing inefficiencies in similar assets. Arbitrage opportunity is generally measured by:

- Similarity of the mispriced assets, which may be evaluated using number of methods, while the most effective is widely considered to be cointegration degree;
- Mispricing opportunity, with one, or several, similar assets, diverging from historical corridor.

Arbitrageur may seek returns in several possible applications, which employ number of common features, such as:

- The strategy is rules-based, with trading signals generation as a model output, and cannot include special situations of any kind, or be based solely on fundamental analysis;
- Trading signals are generated based on the model output, and are systematic;
- Trading book should be market-neutral, with close-to-zero beta, in order to generate returns despite changing market conditions.

Statistical arbitrage is aimed at the making many bets with the positive expected return, across diversified universe of assets, aiming at the achieving low-volatility strategy, and generation of market-neutral beta. Holding periods may vary from seconds to more than a month, depending on the exposure, risk aversion, and market conditions.

Since statistical arbitrage is similar and may be considered as derivative of pairs-trading. Generally, pairs-trading relies on the trading of two stocks, or stock against ETF, other instruments; which exhibits some kind of correlation, or may have similar operational characteristics.

If stock A and stock B operate in the same sector (UPS and FedEx, etc.) expected returns should track each other, after adjustments. Consequently, we can model the system as:

$$\frac{dA_t}{A_t} = \alpha dt + \beta \frac{B_t}{B_t} + dX_t \tag{1}$$

where X_t being mean-reverting process, and is a cointegration residual, which is used for determination of stock relations. Thus, leading to the conclusion that after controlling for beta, long-short portfolio is poised to oscillate in proximity to some statistical equilibrium. Thus, the model explores market's overreaction on some events, which occur and provoke stock to diverge from the equilibrium, being temporarily over-, underpriced in line with mean-reversion theory (Hong and Stein 1999). In order to capture positive return, arbitrageur will employ contrarian strategy, when one would go long 1 share (or in the currency value) of stock A, and short β shares, proportional to the coefficient of the regression (or in the currency value) of stock B, expecting valuations to revert back to equilibrium.

Statistical arbitrage exploration may also employ model based on the residuals of the assets pool. Mean-reverting mispricing of two securities is vastly modeled as a stochastic mean-reverting process using Ornstein-Uhlebeck process (Maller et al. 2009):

$$dX_t = k(m - X_t) + \sigma W_t \qquad (2)$$

where k is a mean-reversion speed; m—mean; σ—volatility; W_t—Brownian motion.

While pairs-trading represents simpler strategy, in order to capture more diversification and positive return, statistical arbitrage book, as a rule, includes trading group of stocks against another group of stocks, or ETFs (Gatev 2006). The book will be formed performing cointegration analysis using applicable sector benchmarks, e.g., indexes or ETFs. Statistical arbitrage book will form a market-neutral pairs-trades based on the X_t explanation of the stocks being over-, under- or fairly-valued relative to the factors, which will elaborate on the systematic stock return. The strategy employs holding a stock long, short against contrarian ETF, or other collection of stocks, positions. Therefore, portfolio will be market-neutral, formed from long, short positions in the most effective securities with respect to the arbitrageur objectives.

Key objective of the paper is exploration of the agility of the statistical arbitrage strategy and its ability to outperform traditional long-, short-only strategies and broad market through growing market of 2016–2019, and sell-off of the beginning of 2020. The paper will be focused on employing cointegration analysis (Hassler 2016) and PCA analysis (Denis 2020) as a tool for formulating beta-neutral portfolio formed with selected companies with valuation of more than 100 billion USD, and with average daily trading volume of more than 1 million shares (Quotes information).

Structure of the paper consists of: Sect. 2, where we study formation of market-neutral books and market-neutrality as such, through two different methods. First approach employs principal components analysis, which derives risk factors for the correlation matrix of U.S. equity market, which as such represents long-short portfolios in market segments. Second approach uses cointegration analysis based on the Engle-Granger 2-step approach (Lee and Lee 2014). This approach derives tradable pairs using augmented Dickey-Fuller test (Dahlberg and Jansson 1993), and ordinary least squares estimate (Montana et al. 2007).

In Sect. 3 we are elaborating on the construction of the model and trading signals, through statistical estimation of the mean-reverting process X_t for each stock based on the 4 h trading frequency, based on the lookback periods evaluations, simulating practical algorithmic trading decision-making process. We are also exploring 2019–2020 period closer, using 1-h frequency data, and elaborating on the performance of the strategy further on.

In Sect. 4 we are back testing before said trading strategies, and evaluating effectiveness of the strategies in relation to the broad market and long-, short-only strategies.

In Sect. 5 we are reconciling research results and present conclusions derived from the back-testing. In Sect. 6 we are weighing possible future development of the research.

2 Market-Neutrality and PCA, Cointegration Approach

As noted above, statistical arbitrage portfolio seeks a limited exposure to the market risks, hence returns are directed toward minimization of the correlation with the market.

Returns of the universe of stocks will be recorded as $\{R_i\}_{i=1}^{N}$ over one trading day, F will constitute market return (e.g., SPY). Thus, each return for each stock from our universe will be modeled as a regression:

$$R_i = \beta_i F + \tilde{R}_i \tag{3}$$

Stock returns will be decomposed into systematic parts, or components, $\beta_i F$; $\tilde{R}_i$ represents uncorrelated components. We can elaborate said model into multi-factor one, with m systematic factors representing benchmark returns:

$$R_i = \sum_{j=1}^{m} \beta_{ij} F_j + \tilde{R}_i \tag{4}$$

Further deepening, we will denote market-neutral trading portfolio exposure in each stock as $\{I_i\}_{i=1}^{N}$ and model portfolio betas:

$$\overline{\beta}_j = \sum_{i=1}^{N} \beta_{ij} I_i = 0, \quad j = 1, 2, \ldots, m \tag{5}$$

Consequently, market-neutral portfolio, with betas close to zero will be uncorrelated with broad market, noted above as market portfolio; with factors, which are directing the market, and will correspond to:

$$\sum_{i=1}^{N} I_i \tilde{R}_i = \sum_{j=1}^{m} \left[\sum_{i=1}^{N} I_i \tilde{R}_i \right] F_j + \sum_{i=1}^{N} I_i \tilde{R}_i \tag{6}$$

Previous research evaluated approximate number of factors, which drive market returns at $m \in [10; 20]$ (Avellaneda and Lee 2008).

Market-neutral portfolios are traditionally formed using several approaches, while in this paper we are focusing on cointegration and principal components analysis approaches.

a. Cointegration Analysis Using Engle-Granger 2-Step Approach

The approach was introduced by Engle and Granger for estimation of the equilibrium relations between non-stationary time series. Two non-stationery time series are deemed to have long-run equilibrium when linear combination of them is stationary. The process consists of two-step approach:

- First step uses augmented Dickey-Fuller test, which determines appropriate lag length with Akaike Information Criterion (Akaike 1973):

$$\Delta Z_t = \beta_0 + \beta_1 t + \delta Z_{t-1} + \sum_{i=1}^{k} \phi_i \Delta Z_{t-i} + \varepsilon_t \tag{7}$$

- Null hypothesis of the test constitutes that the spread Z_t unit-root process, while alternative constitutes stationarity of the process.
- Second step verifies if residual series is stationary using OLS regression:

$$\hat{\varepsilon}_t = y_t - \beta_0 - \beta_1 x_t \tag{8}$$

In accordance with the approach, residual series is to be stationary. Result of the analysis evaluates if $\hat{\varepsilon}_t$ is a stationary process, and therefore deviation from the equilibrium ensures mean-reversion of the process.

b. Principal Components Analysis Approach

PCA-approach uses historical share-price data of the given number of stocks N, through given lookback period M. Representing the stock return data for given date t_0, with lookback period $M + 1$ through following matrix:

$$R_{ik} = \frac{S_{i(t_0-(k-1)\Delta t)} - S_{i(t_0-k\Delta t)}}{S_{i(t_0-k\Delta t)}}, \quad k = 1, \ldots, M, \ i = 1, \ldots, N, \tag{9}$$

where S_{it} represents stock i price at time t, and $\Delta t = 1/252$ as trading days amount dummy. While in order to smooth more volatile stocks we will produce formula for standardized returns:

$$Y_{ik} = \frac{R_{ik} - \frac{1}{M}\sum_{k=1}^{M} R_{ik}}{\sqrt{\frac{1}{M-1}\sum_{k=1}^{M}(R_{ik} - \overline{R}_i)^2}} = \frac{R_{ik} - \overline{R}_i}{\overline{\sigma}_i} \tag{10}$$

And correlation matrix defined by:

$$\rho_{ij} = \frac{1}{M-1}\sum_{k=1}^{M} Y_{ik}Y_{jk} \tag{11}$$

Small data under analysis and relative long estimation window may represent unnecessary historical economic data, and therefore period for the model testing should be adjusted. Agile way to analyze data and derive sense from the given datasets is Principal Components Analysis, as it produces higher degree of explanation for the data. For this approach we consider eigenvectors. Ranking eigenvalues of the empirical correlation matrix in decreasing order:

$$N \geq \lambda_1 > \lambda_2 \geq \lambda_3 \geq \ldots \geq \lambda_N \geq 0$$

Further developing our PCA model, we denote eigenvectors as:

$$v^{(j)} = (v_1^{(j)}, \ldots, v_N^{(j)}), \quad j = 1, \ldots N$$

Analysis of the said vector may reveal that there are few numbers of eigenvalues, which can deviate from the spectrum. While those values are out of spectrum, relations between significant and noise eigenvalues may still be unclear. Therefore, two approaches can be employed: variable number of eigenvectors may be taken into analysis scope, with sum of retained eigenvalues exceeding percentage of the correlation matrix trace; second approach constitutes a fixed number of eigenvalues in order to derive the factors.

If $\lambda_1, \ldots, \lambda_m$, with $m < N$, then for each index j eigenportfolio should be considered, with investment amount in each of the stocks described as:

$$I_i^{(j)} = \frac{v_i^{(j)}}{\overline{\sigma}_i}$$

Consequently, returns are:

$$F_{jk} = \sum_{i=1}^{N} \frac{v_i^{(j)}}{\overline{\sigma}_i} R_{ik} \quad j = 1, 2, \ldots, m \tag{12}$$

Therefore, returns of each stock from the investment universe may be decomposed as a projection of the m factors and a residual. Deepening into PCA-approach, we are using set of derived risk factors for decomposition of returns.

Eigenvectors may be interpreted through association of the dominant vector with previously defined market portfolio, with all coefficients $v_i^{(1)}$, $i = 1, 2, \ldots N$ positive, and, consequently, weights $I_{(i)}^1 = \frac{v_i^{(1)}}{\overline{\sigma}_i}$ are inversely proportional to the volatility of the stocks.

On the other hand, other eigenvectors are deemed to be negative in order to be orthogonal to $v^{(i)}$, while shape-analysis will be an approximation to the Latin America sovereign bond yields analysis (Scherer and Avellaneda 2002). Further ranking we define as:

$$v_{n_1}^{(2)} \geq v_{n_2}^{(2)} \geq \ldots v_{n_{MN}}^{(2)}$$

Through further analysis, we are recognizing that generally neighboring positions, which represent stocks, or companies, are operating in the same industry, or sector, with gradual decline of coherence when endeavoring further into analysis. Therefore, the eigenportfolio is interpreted as long-short positions in the chosen stock universe.

3 Trading Models and Signal Generation

a. Two-Step Engle-Granger Approach-Based Model

Noting that the strategy in development is poised to be market-neutral, we need to reach optimal allocation of assets, with beta being in close proximity to zero. In the first approach, which, as previously established, will employ cointegration analysis we selected pairs, which are tradable within needed system. Further development is based on the Engle-Granger 2-step approach: through second section we described said approach, which uses augmented Dickey-Fuller test if all series are cointegrated in the same order, while second step deploys OLS analysis in order to check if residuals are stationary.

Further, we need to detect trading signals for our strategy, which will be based on the set of trading decision rules, designed for entering and closing positions in our long, short portfolios. Initial step is to determine z-score, which describes distance to the long-term mean standard deviation, or equilibrium—basically how far the stock has deviated from the determined equilibrium, and calculated as:

$$Z_t = \frac{\varepsilon_t - \mu_i}{\sigma_\varepsilon} \tag{13}$$

where $\varepsilon = P_t^l - \gamma P_t^s$ is a spread between the shares, and σ_ε is equilibrium variance.

Rules will be based on the said deviation of the z-score, with the expected mean-reversion:

- Open long position when $Z_i < -\bar{s}_{lo}$;
- Open short position when $Z_i > \bar{s}_{so}$;
- Close long position when $Z_i > -\bar{s}_{lc}$;
- Close short position when $Z_i < \bar{s}_{sc}$.

If we open the trade, we are acquiring one dollar worth of securities, and selling β_i dollars of the corresponding stock, and vice-versa based on predetermined cutoffs, which were determined based on the previous studies (Avellaneda and Lee 2008), and defined as:

- $\bar{s}_{lo} = 1.25$—opening long position, when z-score is smaller than defined negative value;
- $\bar{s}_{so} = 1.25$—opening short position, when z-score is larger than defined value;

- $\bar{s}_{lc} = 0.50$—closing long position, when z-score is larger than defined negative value;
- $\bar{s}_{sc} = 0.75$—closing short position, when z-score is smaller than defined value.

Cutoffs are determining level of deviation from equilibrium, and thus are detecting abnormal moves in the stock price, which is expected to return to the equilibrium.

Model is based on the bid, ask price, and volume, in order to effectively capture market inefficiencies in the pricing of the assets.

b. **PCA-Based Model**

Second model, which is based on the PCA analysis approach, employs relative pricing model and based on the historical pricing of the securities, denoting prices as $S_i(t), \ldots, S_N(t)$. With previously introduced multi-factor models, we implying that returns are in line with stochastic differential equation:

$$\frac{dS_i(t)}{S_i(t)} = \alpha_i dt + \sum_{j=1}^{N} \beta_{ij} \frac{dI_j(t)}{I_j(t)} + dX_i(t) \tag{14}$$

Assuming that model encompass mean-reverting price fluctuation in relation with the industry and have systematic deviation from the sector, we are assuming trading strategy, which is based on the stocks which are, following employed factor analysis, exhibiting deviation from the equilibrium, In order to capture it we developed parametric model for process $X_i(t)$ using Ornstein-Uhlebeck stationary process (Maller et al. 2009):

$$dX_i(t) = k_i(m_i - X_i(t))dt + \sigma_i dW_i(t), \quad k_i > 0 \tag{15}$$

where $\alpha_i, k_i, m_i, \sigma_i$ are specific parameters, and have slow variation relating to the Brownian-motion increments $dW_i(t)$ in the period of the model (Mörters and Peres 2010).

The process is auto-regressive, with lag 1 (AR-1 model), and $dX_i(t)$ has conditional mean described as:

$$E\{dX_i(t)|X_i(s), s \le t\} = k_i(m_i - X_i(t))dt \tag{16}$$

Endeavoring further into the model, we describe $X_i(t)$ process equilibrium probability as normal:

$$E\{X_i(t)\} = m_i, \ \text{Var}\{X_i(t)\} = \frac{\sigma_i^2}{2k_i} \tag{17}$$

Returns of the market-neutral portfolio is defined as:

$$\alpha_i dt + k_i(m_i - X_i(t))dt \tag{18}$$

where parameter k_i is time-scale characteristic for mean-reversion:

$$\tau_i = \frac{1}{k_i} \tag{19}$$

And assumed to be equal to half of the 60-day period mentioned beforehand, or $k > 252/30 = 8.4$.

Models signals employ slightly different approaches, with:

$$\sigma_{eq,i} = \frac{\sigma_i}{\sqrt{2k_i}} \sigma_i \sqrt{\frac{\tau_i}{2}} \tag{20}$$

And Z-score defined as:

$$Z_i = \frac{X_i(t) - m_i}{\sigma_{eq,i}} \tag{21}$$

Cutoffs will be maintained as prior, at:

- Open long position when $Z_i < -\bar{s}_{lo}$
- Open short position when $Z_i > \bar{s}_{so}$
- Close long position when $Z_i > -\bar{s}_{lc}$
- Close short position when $Z_i < \bar{s}_{sc}$

Entering the trade when z-score exceeds 1.25 in absolute value we are capturing abnormality of the stock's dynamic, and closing the trades when price is returning to the long-term equilibrium.

In Fig. 1 we observe deviation through both rapidly growing market period of 2016–2019, and after coronavirus triggered sell-off. As we can see, periods of

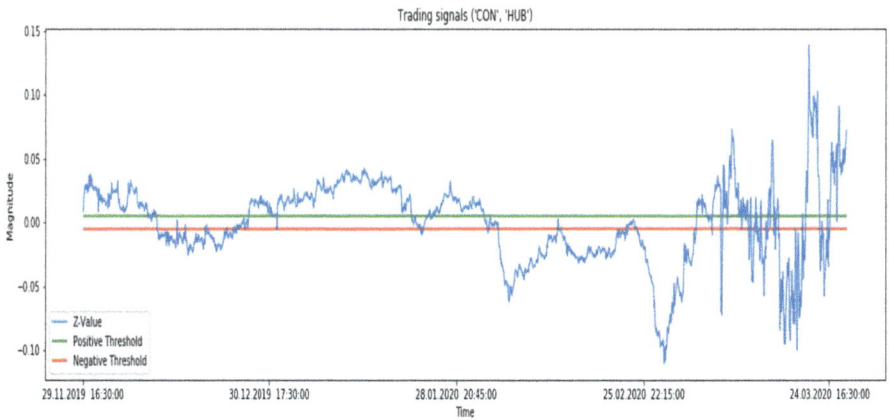

Fig. 1 Trading signals

the market disruptions are especially difficult for value capturing, and therefore adjustable changes of the rules may be in order. We will elaborate on this in the following sections.

4   Strategies Back-Testing

For strategies back-testing was created universe of 65 stocks, which are tradable on the NYSE and NASDAQ exchanges. Stock-picking criteria included market capitalization of more than 100 billion USD, trading volume of more than 1 million shares per day in order to simulate short-term trading of leveraged positions. As a proxy of long-only strategies we chose to utilize return of Long S&P500 ETF (TIC: SPY), and short-only—return of inverse ETF ProShares Short S&P500 (TIC: SH) (Quotes information).

Historical scope included 2016–2020, with 4-h frequency in order to capture the most active trading periods: first and last trading hours, and price deviations, which occur through trading day. Transaction cost per trade was assumed at five basis points, incorporating price slippage, which was presumed to be almost completely mitigated due to high-liquidity of the chosen securities. Testing of the 2019–2020 period was conducted on the 1-h frequency data through said period.

We assumed $5\times$ leveraged strategy, based on the available market instruments in order to obtain such trading leverage, and with possibility to increase it up to $10\times$ through available instruments (e.g., CFDs) (Huang and Martin 2018).

a.   Two-Step Engle-Granger Approach Model Back-Testing

Back-testing of the cointegration analysis-based strategy was conducted using dataset with a lookback period till 2016, with 4-h frequency data.

Cointegration tests were performed for all possible pairs in the dataset, based on the bid and ask prices and volume. After conducting above described 2-step approach, top 25 tradable pairs were obtained for further development of the market-neutral portfolio with respect to the industries exposure diversification of the book (Fig. 2).

Further endeavoring into the back testing, we calculated thresholds for each tradable pair in order to generate profit from trading of each pair, calculating estimation of the stock's equilibrium relations through z-score, with respect to the dynamic hedge ratio, which is assumed to follow random walk:

$$\gamma_t = \gamma_{t-1} + \omega_t \tag{22}$$

Based on the calculated hedge ratio, we improved our trading rules, and conducted back-testing of the strategy. Strategy Profit and Loss statement are presented below (Fig. 3).

Strategies performance in relation to the long-, short-only strategies proxies demonstrate superior return of the employed statistical arbitrage model, with

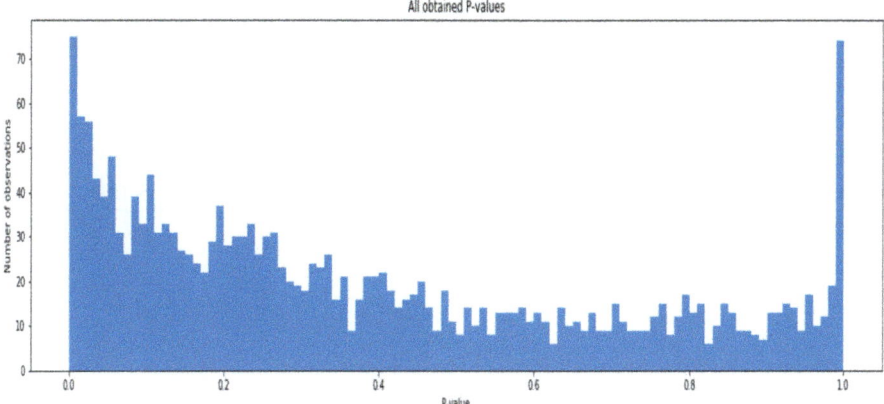

Fig. 2 *P*-values of the all possible pairs

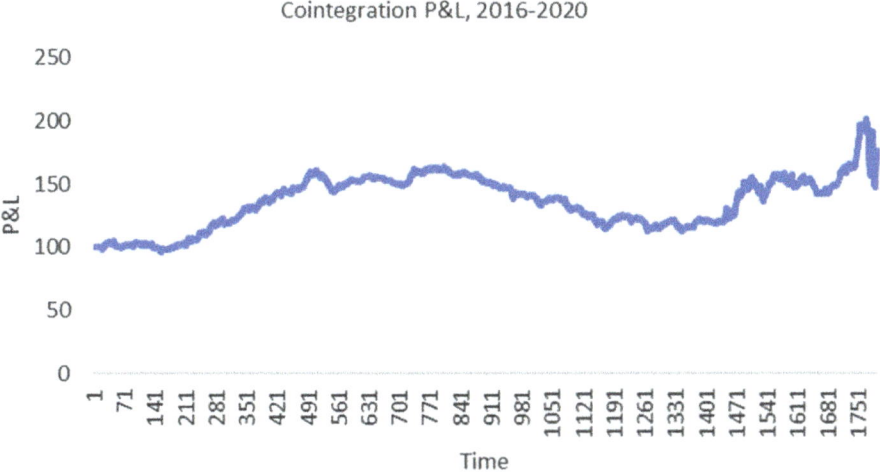

Fig. 3 Profit and loss statement for cointegration-based strategy

back-tested portfolio demonstrated superior returns and lesser drawdowns (Table 1).

b. PCA-Approach Model Back-Testing

Back-testing of our PCA-based strategy was based on the same universe of stocks, with previously noted changes in relation to 2-step based approach. We assumed our Profit and Loss for our portfolio to be:

$$P_{t+\Delta t} = P_t + \sum_{i=1}^{N} I_{it} R_{it} + \sum_{i=1}^{N} I_{it}/S_{it} - \sum_{i=1}^{N} \left| I_{i(t+\Delta t)} - Q I_{it} \right| \mathrm{SL},$$

Table 1 Cointegration-based strategy against proxies

	Cointegration-based strategy	Long-only proxy	Short-only proxy
Cumulative return, %	56.85	26.95	−283.92
Maximum drawdown, %	−14.41	−11.59	−33.34
Maximum return, %	9.95	8.67	28.32
Median return, %	0.02	0.05	−0.36

Source Author analysis

$$I_{it} = P_t \lambda_t \tag{23}$$

where P_{it} value of the i stock trade at time t in USD, R_{it}—stock return in period $(t, t + \Delta t)$, with $\Delta t = 1/252$, S_{it} price of the stock i at time of trade t and SL $=$ 0.005—slippage. $I_{it} = P_t \lambda_t$ implies factor λ_t, which introduces proportionality of the trading activities, which in accordance adjusts leveraged exposure in the new trades.

Back-testing goes back to 2016 and is based on the 4-h frequency trading data. Back-testing employed previously defined trading rules, and trading signals are defining our trading activities as such, with continuous portfolio adjustments in order to retain minimum market correlation and capture deviations of the chosen stocks from long-term equilibrium. In order to hedge our portfolio, we employed diversified exposure in respect to stocks sector and hedging with index.

Results of our back-testing presented below (Fig. 4).

PCA-based strategy demonstrated outstanding performance in relation to long-, short-only strategies proxies, and cointegration-based model, employing stronger test for market-neutral portfolio construction. Demonstrated superior return of the

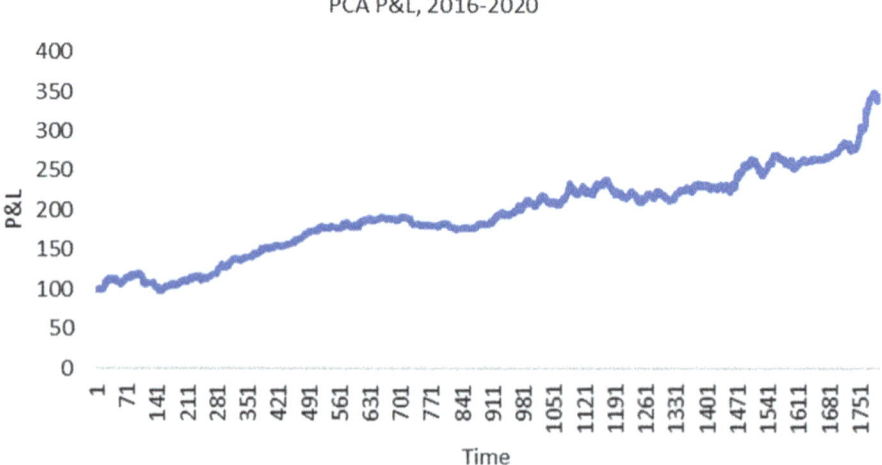

Fig. 4 Profit and loss statement for PCA-based strategy

Table 2 PCA-based strategy against proxies

	PCA-based strategy	Long-only proxy	Short-only proxy
Cumulative return, %	123.34	26.95	−283.92
Maximum drawdown, %	−5.07	−11.59	−33.34
Maximum return, %	5.77	8.67	28.32
Median return, %	0.06	0.05	−0.36

Source Author analysis

PCA-based statistical arbitrage model, with back-tested portfolio demonstrated better returns and lesser drawdowns (Table 2).

c. **PCA-Approach Back Testing of the End of 2019–2020**

While growing market of 2019 presented high-opportunity for macro-, and quant-funds, rapid correction of the market in beginning of 2020 led to heavy losses and several bailouts. Some of this fund, for example, Renaissance Technology, employ, among others, statistical arbitrage strategies, and experienced 15% losses.

Similar situation occurred in 2007 when quant-funds experienced strong draw-downs. Later the period was reproduced by Avellaneda and Lee (2008).

We analyzed PCA-based strategy through 2019, while the market was continu-ously growing, economy already started to give signs of unbalance, with stock market demonstrating increased multiples, till 2020 when the most rapid sell-off occurred, correcting S&P500 from an all-time high by 10% in 6 days, and decreasing further to current bottom of 2.174.

For back testing of our strategy through 2019–2020 we used 1-h frequency data in order to capture volatility increase at the beginning of 2020 while using the same universe of stocks (Fig. 5).

We can observe that our strategy demonstrated drawdown in the beginning of 2020 while recovering rapidly, and demonstrating high-performance through the period of highest volatility in Mar–Apr 2020 (Table 3).

5 Conclusion

We presented two systematic-based approaches to the construction of market-neutral portfolio, with the main objective of capturing returns through 2016–2019 growing market; and through the sharpest global sell-off, during which S&P500 decreased from an all-time high, down to 2.174 in one month, with the heaviest losses incurred by oil producers due to crude oil price decrease. Meanwhile, market's volatility index VIX has surged up to record high of 82.69 basis points, surpassing level of 2008 record of 80.74 (Quotes information).

Fig. 5 Profit and loss statement for PCA-based strategy 2019–2020

Table 3 PCA-based strategy against proxies, 2019–2020

	PCA-based strategy	Long-only proxy	Short-only proxy
Cumulative return, %	76.34	3.03	−3.14
Maximum drawdown, %	−19.84	−10.94	−9.25
Maximum return, %	7.88	9.06	11.51
Median return, %	0.02	0.06	−0.10

Source Author analysis

Presented strategies employ cointegration and PCA-based analysis, decomposing returns of the securities in systematic and idiosyncratic components. Through development of the strategies were constituted superiority of the PCA-based approach, and need for optimization of number of factors employed by the strategy. Number of factors, employed for development of the statistical arbitrage model may vary anywhere from 10 to 30 but basically should maximize ability to explain variance of the correlation matrix. In order to maximize effectiveness of the model, variable number of factors may be used, with highest number during lowest volatility, with benchmark being VIX index; and lowest during increased and peaked volatility, as one, that was seen during recent sell-off.

Employed strategies were found to exhibit lesser maximum drawdowns than the broad market, and perform well through both growing and decreasing markets. PCA-based strategy, which employed factors or stock returns explanation performed considerably better, and demonstrated Sharpe ratio of 0.49; moreover, number of positive return days outpaced negative, with 972 positive return days, and 725 in the negative zone. During research, we found that statistical arbitrage strategies perform well during most volatile periods, which can be explained by number of factors employed by the strategy, against necessary levels during low-volatility periods. Consequently, necessity of more than 25 factors, leads to worse returns, when 15 factors can explain less than 50% of variance (Avellaneda and Lee 2008).

Finally, demonstrated Profit and Loss statements represented in the same manner, and during similar market conditions period as in research of Avellaneda and Lee (2008), enforces statement, that market-neutral arbitrage strategy, if produced correctly, may ensure better returns, and enhance trading performance through lesser, and more volatile period, as well as growing and decreasing markets, exploiting pricing inefficiencies (Do and Faff 2010).

6 Future Work

Further development of the research should include several enhancements for the explored model. Longer-holding position, if applicable, should be adjusted for ex-dividend dates, and dividends payment periods. On the fundamental side, further factors may be deployed, such as analyst ratings increase, earnings expectations, and possible effect of the earnings surprise on the position. While in our research volume has not been included in the formation of the mean-reversion signals, it should be explored as a necessary adjustment for their development and considered when entering and exiting positions, as well as slippage case by case review. In order to increase accuracy, new models should be based on the higher-frequency data, of more than 5 min.

Model performance should also be explored from the perspective of different methods, such as exploration of the possible ways to introduce Hidden Markov Model for regime change (Yuan 2016), (Grunwald et al. 1996).

Statistical arbitrage application in the field of derivatives, such as options trading (Hull 2012), credit derivatives market (Mengle 2007), (Cserna and Imbierowicz 2008) and fixed-income securities, also represents a vast filed for the application and improvement of the statistical arbitrage model, in order to increase returns with respect to the higher risk or explore possible hedging of the equity positions.

References

Maller, Ross & Müller, Gernot & Szimayer, Alexander. (2009). *Ornstein–Uhlenbeck Processes and Extensions*. https://doi.org/10.1007/978-3-540-71297-8_18.
Hassler, Uwe. (2016). *Cointegration Analysis*. https://doi.org/10.1007/978-3-319-23428-1_16.

Denis, Daniel. (2020). *Principal Component Analysis*. https://doi.org/10.1002/9781119549963. ch10.

Quotes information, https://finance.yahoo.com/. Last accessed 03 Oct 2020

Lee, Hyejin & Lee, Junsoo. (2014). More powerful Engle–Granger cointegration tests. *Journal of Statistical Computation and Simulation*. 85. 1-18. https://doi.org/10.1080/00949655.2014. 957206

Dahlberg, M. & Jansson, Per. (1993). *On the Autoregressive Correction of the Augmented Dickey-Fuller Test.*

Montana, Giovanni & Triantafyllopoulos, Kostas & Tsagaris, Theodoros. (2007). *Flexible Least Squares for Temporal Data Mining and Statistical Arbitrage. Expert Systems with Applications.* 36. 2819-2830. https://doi.org/10.1016/j.eswa.2008.01.062.

Avellaneda, Marco & Lee, Jeong-Hyun. (2008). *Statistical Arbitrage in the U.S. Equities Market. Quantitative Finance.* 10. 761–782. https://doi.org/10.2139/ssrn.1153505.

Akaike, H. (1973). Information theory and an extension of the maximum likelihood principle. In B. N. Petrov & B. F. Csaki (Eds.), *Second International Symposium on Information Theory*, (pp. 267–281). Academiai Kiado: Budapest.

Scherer, K. P. and Avellaneda, M., All for one and one for all? A principal component analysis of Latin American brady bond debt from 1994 to 2000. *International Journal of Theoretical and Applied Finance*, 2002, Vol. 5, No. 1, 79–106.

Mörters, P., & Peres, Y. (2010). Brownian Motion (Cambridge Series in Statistical and Probabilistic Mathematics). *Cambridge: Cambridge University Press.* https://doi.org/10.1017/CBO 9780511750489

Huang, Zhe & Martin, Franck. (2018). Pairs trading strategies in a cointegration framework: backtested on CFD and optimized by profit factor. *Applied Economics.* 51. 1–17. https://doi.org/10. 1080/00036846.2018.1545080

A unified view of linear AR(1) models G.K. Grunwald, R.J. Hyndman and L.M. Tedesco June 1996

Yuan, Yuan and Mitra, Gautam, Market Regime Identification Using Hidden Markov Models (September 18, 2016). https://doi.org/10.2139/ssrn.3406068

An improved pairs trading strategy based on switching regime volatility Marco Bee Department of Economics and Management, University of Trento Giulio Gatti Department of Economics and Management, University of Trento July 27, 2015

S. Hogan, R. Jarrow, M. Teoc, and M. Warachka. Testing market efficiency using statistical arbitrage with applications to momentum and value strategies. *Journal of Financial Economics*, 73:525–565, 2004.

J. C. Hull. Options, Futures, And Other Derivatives. Pearson, 8th edition, 2012.

E. Gatev, W. N. Goetzmann, and K. G. Rouwenhorst. Pairs trading: Performance of a relative-value arbitrage rule. *Review of Financial Studies*, 19:797–827, 2006

Mengle, D., 2007. Credit derivatives: an overview. *Economic Review, Federal Reserve Bank of Atlanta, issue Q4*, 1–24.

Cserna, B., Imbierowicz, B., 2008. How efficient are credit default swap markets? An empirical study of capital structure arbitrage based on structural pricing models. *Working Paper, Goethe University Frankfurt.*

Hong H and Stein JC. (1999) A Unified Theory of Underreaction, Momentum Trading, and Overreaction in Asset Markets. *Journal of Finance* 54(6): 2143–2184.

Do B and Faff R. (2010) Does Simple Pairs Trading Still Work? *Financial Analysts Journal* 66(4): 1–13.

Assessing Relationship Between Entrepreneurship Education and Business Growth

Stavros Kalogiannidis⊙**, Efstratios Loizou, Katerina Melfou, and Olympia Papaevangelou**

Abstract This research focused on establishing the relationship between entrepreneurship education and business growth. Young entrepreneurs in a Greek township of Kozani were engaged to establish whether skills acquired through entrepreneurship education are essential in driving business growth. A self-administered questionnaire was utilized to collect data from a sample of 150 young entrepreneurs. Results confirmed that entrepreneurship education equips the youth with necessary skills to innovative new business ideas and achieve desired business growth. The results further revealed entrepreneurship education doubles is a viable method for the growth of competent entrepreneurs in different countries across the world. The study recommended that townships should consider having a more personalized training and development plan strategy to enhance entrepreneurship education in Greece thereby achieving business growth for different startups.

Keywords Entrepreneurship education · Entrepreneurship training · Business growth

S. Kalogiannidis (✉)
Department of Regional and Cross Border Development, University of Western Macedonia, Kozani, Greece
e-mail: stavroskalogiannidis@gmail.com

E. Loizou
Department of Regional Development and Cross Border Studies, University of Western Macedonia, 50100 Kozani, Greece
e-mail: eloizou@uowm.gr

K. Melfou
Department of Agriculture, School of Agricultural Sciences, University of Western Macedonia, Terma Kontopoulou, 53100 Florina, Greece
e-mail: kmelfou@uowm.gr

O. Papaevangelou
Ministry of Education, Kozani, Greece

1   Introduction

Entrepreneurship is among the most powerful driver of the world economy and it has become relevant in offering employment for the many young jobless people across the world. Many institutions of high learning across the globe have responded to the increased need for entrepreneurship skills among young graduates by introducing different entrepreneurship courses in institutions' curriculum. Greece is no different since most institutions in the country are currently offering different entrepreneurship study programs starting from lower levels of education (Siakas et al. 2016).

Kakouris (2016) indicates that the current levels of job scarcity in Greece whereby several traditional industries are not employing the high number of young graduates which has kept them jobless and financially constrained. Furthermore, the increased business uncertainties in the world due to pandemics such as Covid-19 have increased the need for more creativity and innovation for business survival (Kalogiannidis and Chatzitheodoridis 2021). Recent studies confirm that possession of skills through entrepreneurship education is among the best ways of addressing the large numbers of unemployed graduates in most countries across the world (Hernández-Sánchez et al. 2019). Skill and abilities attained from entrepreneurship education programs have enabled millions of youth to engage in different small business startups thereby creating jobs and consequently addressing the problems of high unemployment among young graduates.

Grecu and Denes (2017) indicated that developed countries have in the recent decades experienced an upsurge concerning the uptake of entrepreneurship among students and young professionals. This is mostly attributed to the increase in the number of institutions venturing into different entrepreneurship programs or courses. Probably this is the reason why most countries in other parts of world have embraced or acknowledged entrepreneurship as a tool or mechanism to tackle the issue of unemployment which is common among the youth in Greece (Siakas et al. 2016).

Kotsios and Mitsios (2013) indicate that majority of young people in Greece live in relatively average standards of living as compared to the employed class. The high levels of unemployment among the youth have increased the levels of crime in most countries and low esteem among the youth which has resulted in a negative outlook on life among the victims of unemployment. The persistence of high levels of unemployment among the youth is a threat to the future generation since it could yield a financially constrained or poor generation thereby affecting the future global economy.

The relevance of entrepreneurial skills in starting up and successfully managing businesses across the world cannot be downplayed. Sánchez et al. (2017) confirm that most entrepreneurs across the world have utilized their creativity to innovate and find solutions to the financial problems of the current modern through creating great businesses. This, in the long run, has solved other problems such as high crime rate since most youth are now occupied with different business ventures.

Hernández-Sánchez et al. (2019) further confirm that entrepreneurs have the capacity to innovate new technologies, products, or services, to satisfy the different needs of society. The knowledge acquired from the different entrepreneurship courses equips entrepreneurs with several problem-solving skills that are applicable to transforming the socioeconomic landscape of the world (Chatzitheodoridis et al. 2013). Transformation is mostly possible through the general creation and general exploitation of several lucrative opportunities in the global market (Loizou et al. 2019).

1.1 Purpose of the Study

This study focuses on establishing the relationship that exists between entrepreneurship education and business growth, particularly in Greece.

1.2 Specific Objectives

- To establish the influence of entrepreneurship education on the ability to do business
- To explore the role of entrepreneurship education in the business growth
- To determine whether entrepreneurial skills are catalyst for business success

1.3 Research Question

- What is the relationship between entrepreneurship education and business growth?

1.4 Significance of the Study

The study will contribute to the existing knowledge concerning the relevance of entrepreneurship education in business growth. This knowledge is very important, especially in the current dynamic and highly competitive world that requires people to possess creative and innovative skills to venture into different business startups.

2   Literature Review

2.1   Entrepreneurship Education and Training

Several academicians and researchers have had varying descriptions and interpretations of entrepreneurship education (Grecu and Denes 2017; Hernández-Sánchez et al. 2019). A section of researchers has described entrepreneurship as an art and science of finding solutions to socioeconomic problems of the global world. Other researchers and academicians have interpreted entrepreneurship as a process that gives people an opportunity to gain unique skills and abilities to recognize several opportunities that cannot be recognized by other people. Such skills and knowledge enable people to grow in area of self-esteem, creativity, effective decision making, and creativity, among others (Kotsios and Mitsios 2013; Siakas et al. 2016).

According to Fenton and Barry (2011), entrepreneurship education is described as the intentional involvement of an educator through different entrepreneurial-based qualities and teaching skills in the life of a learner, enabling the latter to gain essential skills for use in business growth and development. Siakas et al. (2016) argue that the design of entrepreneurship education is made in such a manner that enables the learner to gain an attitude of creativity that enables such learners to set up or operate personal entrepreneurial or business ventures instead of employment in either private or public organizations.

According to Sánchez et al. (2017), entrepreneurship education is essential in empowering the youth to their potential in starting and managing business. The ability to sustain a new business venture for a relatively long period of time requires the person to possess the key essentials of entrepreneurship that majorly include; creativity, innovation, and invention. Gwija et al. (2014) suggest that the major objective of entrepreneurship education is to build highly innovative and creative thinking among different learned and consequently mold them into great entrepreneurs or business proprietors.

2.2   Areas of Entrepreneurship Education

Raposo and do Paço (2011) indicate that entrepreneurship education is associated with two major areas that include; entrepreneurship education that tackles the different issues of production and transfer of expertise in the field, and that which addresses learning experience and the development of skills and values. A study conducted by Kakouris (2016) clearly stated the different methods or techniques used in the field of entrepreneurship education and these majorly revolve on the student and research consulting services. Boldureanu et al. (n.d.) also explain the different strategies used in entrepreneurship education which majorly include; images, practical work, and writing business plans as well as collaborating or working with experienced entrepreneurs, among other strategies. Liñán (2007) also suggested that learners can gain essential entrepreneurship knowledge through attending business seminars, listening to guest speakers, attending entrepreneurship workshops, and reading different books about entrepreneurship.

Most scholars have suggested that more focus on entrepreneurship education be directed to the key attributes of entrepreneurship education and training instead of only business education since the former gives a wider range of knowledge concerning business startups and business growth (Fenton and Barry 2011; Gwija et al. 2014; Kakouris 2016). Entrepreneurship education is largely is a lifelong learning process that is comprised of five phases that include; basics, knowledge of skills, creative applications, startup, and growth. These phases are considered fundamental in starting up and managing businesses (Grecu and Denes 2017).

2.3 Relevance of Entrepreneurship Education

Entrepreneurship is considered a very essential tool for socioeconomic growth since it plays a very key role in transforming the mindsets of people in society thereby rendering them great entrepreneurs (Kotsios and Mitsios 2013). A study by Siakas et al. (2016) noted that entrepreneurship training is very important for people intending to startup companies since it equips them with the necessary skills for business growth and sustainability. Sánchez et al. (2017) indicate that most industrialized economies such as the United States acknowledge the value of entrepreneurship education in economic growth of a country. This is based on the fact that it influences the emergence of various industries owing to the highly creative and innovative entrepreneurs in such countries (Kotsios and Mitsios 2013). Enhancing the value of entrepreneurship in a country requires active participation of different stakeholders in both the private and public sectors. These sectors may include; the entrepreneurship educators, government institutions, senior entrepreneurs, learners, and different business proprietors, among others. According to Grecu and Denes (2017), entrepreneurship training equips learners with several managerial competencies that are necessary for successful business ventures. Entrepreneurship is associated with several knowledge areas that cut across; management of small business startups, project management skills, and emotional intelligence skills, among others, and these play a key role in the management of business or entrepreneurial ventures (Gwija et al. 2014).

3 Methodology

3.1 Research Design

The quantitative study was based on a descriptive research methodology that helped to gain a deeper insight into the area of entrepreneurship education and business growth, with major emphasis on the selected townships of Greece.

3.2 Target Population

The study targeted that different young entrepreneurs in the selected townships of Greece and these were selected since it was assumed that they have experience in applying the different aspects of entrepreneurship education to manage businesses.

3.3 Sample Size and Sampling Technique

Sampling design is defined as research plan that clarifies how different cases are selected as a sample for a particular study. The study was based on sample of 150 young entrepreneurs hat were selected from the township of Kozani, Greece using simple random sampling.

3.4 Data Analysis

Data collected using the questionnaire was edited to remove any inconsistencies, summarized, and consequently coded to make it ready for analysis using SPSS. Interpretation of descriptive statistics was done based on the percentages and frequencies obtained after analysis. Correlation analysis was used to establish the relationship between entrepreneurship education and business growth at 0.01 level of significance.

3.5 Ethical Considerations

Different ethical requirements were put into consideration for this study. First and foremost informed consent was obtained from the participants before engaging the, in the process of data collection. This was aimed at avoiding any form of bias in the process of data collection. Participants were also assured of maximum confidentiality of the information provided.

4 Analysis and Results

This section presents the different results of the study obtained after analyzing using SPSS. Demographic characteristics of respondents are presented in Table 1 and interpreted based on their percentage distribution.

Results in Table 1 show that majority of the respondents (78%) were male and only 22% were female. Concerning the age bracket, slightly more than half of the respondents (52%) were between 26 and 32 years, 22% were above 32 years, 18% were below 20 years and the least number of respondents (8%) were between 20 and 25 years. Concerning level of education, more than half of the respondents (64%) had diplomas, 20% had bachelor's degrees, 10% had certificates and only 6% were master's degree holders. In regard to their individual business ventures, majority of respondents (34%) were in the Food and beverages service sector, 26%

Table 1 Demographic characteristics

Characteristic	Frequency	Percentage (%)
Sex		
Male	117	78
Female	33	22
Age bracket		
Below 20 years	27	18
20–25 years	12	8
26–32 years	78	52
Above 32 years	33	22
Level of education		
Certificate	15	10
Diploma	96	64
Bachelor	30	20
Masters	9	6
Business venture		
Food and beverages service sector	51	34
Manufacturing and production	33	22
Agribusiness	39	26
Others	27	18
Years of the business		
Less than 1 year	21	14
1–3 years	96	64
3–5 years	24	16
Above 5 years	9	6
Total	**150**	**100**

Source Survey (2021)

were in agribusiness, 22% were in Manufacturing and production and the remaining 18% were involved in other business ventures. Concerning years spent in business, majority of respondents (64%) had spent 1–3 years, 16% had spent 3–5 years, 14% had spent Less than 1 year and the least number of respondents (6%) had spent above 5 years.

4.1 Descriptive Analysis

The descriptive analysis focused on addressing the different research questions of the study as presented below.

Concerning the influence of entrepreneurship education on the ability to engage in businesses among the youth, majority of the participants (46%) disagreed with the fact that they had based on entrepreneurship education and training to startup businesses, 32% strongly agreed that entrepreneurship education and training had helped them make business startups whereas the least number of respondents (6) strongly disagreed with the statement as presented in Table 2.

The results in Table 2 are in line with the findings of Raposo and do Paço (2011) who indicated that the ability to start up and consequently manage businesses is not only among the entrepreneurship or business students but also among students offering other courses. Gwija et al. (2014) suggested that there need to incorporate the different aspects of entrepreneurship across all academic disciplines to instill this knowledge in students across academic disciplines. This is considered very important based on the fact that in Greece, many business students lack the necessary technical and creative skills to innovate new forms of businesses or new products and services. Creativity and innovation capabilities are considered the most essential attributes of a competent entrepreneur, which can be acquired through entrepreneurship education and training. However, this training should majorly be practical and not entirely theoretical since innovation and creativity go along with practicality. Research indicates that global entrepreneurs such as Bill Gates of Microsoft and Mark Zuckerberg of Facebook, among many others applied more of their technical than theoretical knowledge to innovate new services and products that are being utilized across the world (Gwija et al. 2014).

Table 2 Participant's response concerning influence of entrepreneurship education on the ability to do business

Response	Frequency	Percentage (%)
Strongly agree	48	32
Agree	27	18
Disagree	69	46
Strongly disagree	6	4
Total	**150**	**100**

Source Survey (2021)

The study was also concerned with establishing the perceptions of the participants about the general role or relevance of entrepreneurship education and training in the business growth and the descriptive statistics are presented in Table 3.

From Table 3, more than half of the respondents (74%) strongly agreed that entrepreneurship education plays a very big role in business growth and the least number of respondents (26%) agreed with the same notion. No respondent either disagreed or strongly disagreed with the notion that entrepreneurship education plays a role in the business growth. The results clearly indicate that achieving the desired business growth requires the proprietors to apply the different techniques or skills acquired through entrepreneurial training or entrepreneurship courses. These results are in line with Hernández-Sánchez et al. (2019) who confirmed that entrepreneurship education equips people with the necessary knowledge and techniques to run successful business ventures. Gwija et al. (2014) also indicated that despite that entrepreneurship education does not necessarily succeed in businesses run by entrepreneurs, it increases the chances of business growth. Countries that have embraced entrepreneurship education have registered an increase in the number of successful business startups, especially in agricultural sector (Kontogeorgos et al. 2017a, b).

The study also sought establish whether entrepreneurial skills are a catalyst concerning the success of businesses and the results are presented in Table 4.

From Table 4, majority of the respondents (76%) Strongly agreed that entrepreneurial skills are catalyst for the success of a business, 20% agreed while only (4%) disagreed. These findings justify the fact that the participants considered

Table 3 Perceptions concerning role of entrepreneurship education in the business growth

Response	Frequency	Percentage (%)
Strongly agree	111	74
Agree	39	26
Disagree	0	0
Strongly disagree	0	0
Total	**150**	**100**

Source Survey (2021)

Table 4 Whether entrepreneurial skills are catalyst for business success

Response	Frequency	Percentage (%)
Strongly agree	114	76
Agree	30	20
Disagree	6	4
Strongly disagree	0	0
Total	**150**	**100**

Source Survey (2021)

skills acquired through entrepreneurship education as vital competencies for business growth. Fenton and Barry (2011) indicates that most developed economies have acknowledged the relevance of entrepreneurship education in economic growth since it helps in nurturing a group of highly skilled, innovative, and creative entrepreneurs.

Sánchez et al. (2017) also indicate that several entrepreneurship ventures have continued to emerge in developing countries owing to the increased uptake of entrepreneurship education by learners. This, therefore, indicates that in absence of entrepreneurship education, it may become very hard for entrepreneurs to gain desirable business or entrepreneurial competencies to successfully manage businesses (Kalogiannidis 2021).

4.2   Correlation Analysis

Correlation analysis was conducted in order to achieve the major objective of the study which was to establish the relationship between entrepreneurship education and business growth and the results are presented in Table 5.

After the cross-tabulation and analysis, it was established that there is a significant positive relationship between entrepreneurship education and business growth ($r = 0.361^{**}$, $n = 60$, $p = 0.000$). The results clearly show that the different aspects of entrepreneurship education that include; knowledge acquisition, entrepreneurial skills acquisition, innovative mind, and business passion, among many aspects, have a great influence on the successful growth of a business in Greece.

5   Conclusion

The study focused on establishing the relationship that exists between entrepreneurship education and business growth, particularly in Kozani, Greece. The study established a positive correlation between entrepreneurship education and business growth

Table 5 Correlation between entrepreneurship education and business growth

		Entrepreneurship education	Business growth
Entrepreneurship education	Pearson Correlation	1	0.361[a]
	Sig. (2-tailed)		0.000
	N	150	150
Business growth	Pearson Correlation	0.361[a]	1
	Sig. (2-tailed)	0.000	
	N	150	150

[a]Correlation is significant at the 0.01 level (2-tailed)

which confirmed that the different attributes of entrepreneurship education are so essential for successful business ventures. The literature review revealed that the relevance of entrepreneurship education and training in business growth is much based on the knowledge, skills, and techniques that the learners acquire through such education or training, which are replicated in their individual business ventures. The study also revealed that entrepreneurship education is a great catalyst for business success hence ought to be emphasized by different countries such as Greece to encourage successful business ventures among the youth.

This justified the need for strategic measures to enhance the engagement of the youth in different entrepreneurial activities most especially those youth that have acquired some formal entrepreneurship training from colleges or universities. This can only be achieved if entrepreneurs good and convincing business plans obtain necessary financial and mentoring assistance from different providers and public stakeholders.

6   Recommendations

It is important to foster the entrepreneurship culture among the youth to enable them succeed in different business startups. Some youth could possess the necessary skills and creativity but lack the proper formal education to enable the, to apply their creativity or skills in venturing into meaningful businesses. Therefore, support strictures from the government and the private sector are needed to encourage the youth enroll for entrepreneurship education,

Customized and highly affordable short entrepreneurial courses can be introduced in Kozani and other townships in Greece to enable the youth to obtain formal education in entrepreneurship education. This could stimulate high interest to enroll for a higher qualification and consequently become more competent to run different business ventures.

6.1   Areas for Future Research

The current focus on establishing the relationship between entrepreneurship education and business growth but did not clearly how entrepreneurship education can be improved to enhance its influence on business venture startups. Therefore, more research is needed about the strategies to improve entrepreneurship education and training in education institutions.

References

Boldureanu, G., Alina, M., Bercu, A., Boldureanu, D., & Bedrule-grigorut, M. V. (n.d.). *Sustainability-12-01267*. 1–33.

Fenton, M., & Barry, A. (2011). The Efficacy of Entrepreneurship Education: Perspectives of Irish Graduate Entrepreneurs. *Industry and Higher Education, 25*(6), 451–460. https://doi.org/10.5367/ihe.2011.0069.

Chatzitheodoridis, F., Michailidis, A., Theodosiou, G., & Loizou, E. (2013). Local cooperation: A dynamic force for endogenous rural development. In *Balkan and Eastern European Countries in the Midst of the Global Economic Crisis* (pp. 121–132). Physica, Heidelberg.

Grecu, V., & Denes, C. (2017). Benefits of entrepreneurship education and training for engineering students. *MATEC Web of Conferences, 121*, 1–7. https://doi.org/10.1051/matecconf/201712112007.

Gwija, S. A., Eresia-Eke, C., & Iwu, C. G. (2014). The Link between Entrepreneurship Education and Business Success: Evidence from Youth Entrepreneurs in South Africa. *Journal of Economics, 5*(2), 165–175. https://doi.org/10.1080/09765239.2014.11884993.

Hernández-Sánchez, B. R., Sánchez-García, J. C., & Mayens, A. W. (2019). Impact of Entrepreneurial Education Programs on Total Entrepreneurial Activity: The Case of Spain. *Administrative Sciences, 9*(1), 25. https://doi.org/10.3390/admsci9010025.

Kakouris, A. (2016). Exploring entrepreneurial conceptions, beliefs and intentions of Greek graduates. In *International Journal of Entrepreneurial Behaviour and Research* (Vol. 22, Issue 1). https://doi.org/10.1108/IJEBR-07-2014-0137.

Kalogiannidis, S. (2021). Role of Revenue Mobilisation in the Growth and Development of Economy: A Case Analysis of Greece. *Research in World Economy, 12*(2), 63. https://doi.org/10.5430/rwe.v12n2p63.

Kalogiannidis, S., & Chatzitheodoridis, F. (2021). Impact of Covid-19 in the European Start-ups Business and the Idea to Re-energise the Economy. *International Journal of Financial Research, 12*(2), 55. https://doi.org/10.5430/ijfr.v12n2p55.

Kontogeorgos, A., Sergaki, P., & Chatzitheodoridis, F. (2017a). An assessment of new farmers' perceptions about agricultural cooperatives. *Journal of Developmental Entrepreneurship, 22*(01), 1750003.

Kontogeorgos, A., Pendaraki, K., & Chatzitheodoridis, F. (2017b). Economic crisis and firms' performance: empirical evidence for the greek cheese industry. *Revista Galega de Economía, 26*(1), 73–82.

Kotsios, P., & Mitsios, V. (2013). Entrepreneurship in Greece: A Way Out of the Crisis or a Dive In? *Research in Applied Economics, 5*(1). https://doi.org/10.5296/rae.v5i1.3142.

Liñán, F. (2007). The role of entrepreneurship education in the entrepreneurial process. *Handbook of Research in Entrepreneurship Education, Volume 1: A General Perspective*, 230–247.

Loizou, E., Karelakis, C., Galanopoulos, K., & Mattas, K. (2019). The role of agriculture as a development tool for a regional economy. *Agricultural Systems, 173*, 482–490.

Raposo, M., & do Paço, A. (2011). Entrepreneurship education: relationship between education and entrepreneurial activity. *Psicothema, 23*(3), 453–457. http://www.ncbi.nlm.nih.gov/pubmed/21774900.

Sánchez, J. C., Ward, A., Hernández, B., & Flores, J. (2017). Entrepreneurship Education: State of the Art. *Propósitos y Representaciones, 5*(2), 401–473.

Siakas, K., Albulescu, C. T., Draghici, A., & Tamasila, M. (2016). *S tudents ' entrepreneurial potential and the role of entrepreneurial education - A Comparative study between Romania and Greece. January.*

Innovation Policy to Solve Convergence Challenge for the Eastern European and Balkan Countries

Iurii Bazhal

Abstract This study is aimed to analyze the economic development processes in the Balkan and Eastern European economies concerning convergence problem. It is shown that both during the transitive period and after the global economic crisis these countries failed to substantially improve their economic situation under criterion of GDP per capita in comparison with developed countries. This paper presents analysis that demonstrates importance to engage methodological approaches based on J. Schumpeter's theory of economic development, where innovations play a crucial role in solving convergence challenges. The main feature of Schumpeter's theory of innovations in this context is their ability to independently create added value in the economic system of the country, that is, to act as a separate factor of economic growth. Significances of such theoretical vision to build the effective economic policy in the Balkan and Eastern European countries are demonstrated by the main publications on the processes of market transformation of post-socialist countries, when in many cases ignore innovations as separate important factor of successful economic growth. Experts and politicians of these countries mostly oriented on the neoclassical recipes. Focusing on economic policies to modernize productions that operate in traditional competitive markets is ultimately hampering the creation of a new value added. A permanent increase of this one may be only achieved by innovation activities. This methodological vision is important in identifying the current economic problems of the Balkan and Eastern European countries, as well as can propose answers the question how a low and middle-income countries can significantly increase the value of their national product and makes narrow the gap in GDP per capita against developed countries.

Keywords Schumpeter's theory of economic development · Convergence problem · Innovation policy · Smart growth · Middle income trap · Catch-up policy

Jel Classification O11 · 030 · O38

I. Bazhal (✉)
Head of Economics Department, National University of Kyiv-Mohyla Academy, 2 Skovorody Str., Kyiv 04655, Ukraine
e-mail: bazhal@ukma.edu.ua; ibazhal@gmail.com

© The Author(s), under exclusive license to Springer Nature Switzerland AG 2022
P. Sklias et al. (eds.), *Business Development and Economic Governance in Southeastern Europe*, Springer Proceedings in Business and Economics,
https://doi.org/10.1007/978-3-031-05351-1_11

1 Introduction

The analysis of economic development processes in emerging economies of the Balkan and Eastern European Countries, both during the transitive period and after the global great recession, shows that these countries failed to substantially improve their economic situation by the criterion of GDP per capita in comparison with developed countries. Such situation has been causing many crisis phenomena in these countries, as well as sharply actualizes conceptual discussions about the methodological approaches to overcoming these tendencies and enabling to ensure long run economic development. Standard recommendations on the factors of economic growth from adherents of neoclassical theory have not brought a positive result for the transitive countries. Such processes are subject of many analyses from a variety of theoretical and practical angles, but in this article, we will focus on the situation when the convergence processes emerging economies have been fading and stopping.

Preservation of such situation may lead to the economic and politic crises in all countries that have got of similar mode. The Europe has got analogous state after the global financial and economic crisis of 2008–2009. The similar processes have developed due to continuation or saving the situation of economic disparity between "North" and "South" countries, as well as countries of Western and Eastern Europe. The forecasts about the automatic economic convergence the European Union economies have not been to come true. Why was it happened? Why the global financial and economic crisis stopped the economic growth of many European countries? This article tries to give some analytical answers this question and suggests certain economic policy measures to overcome this situation in the Balkans and the East European economies.

It is important to recognize the "Schumpeter's innovations" must be considered as a special factor for economic growth that generates the increasing the aggregated added value of a country separately from the processes related to productivity growth of the existing traditional manufacturing resources. In this sense such factor becomes main determinant of the successful Catch-up processes. The Schumpeter's methodological approach allows substantiating the possibility of accelerated economic development of a country without historically formed resource limitations. Such scenario can be implemented only with innovation-driven growth.

2 Literature Review

There are several research publications analyzed this situation for different countries. They found that such economic mode means first a stop in the economic development of those countries that pursue a policy of economic growth but after a certain successful period this tendency slow down and the gap of welfare against developed countries ceases to narrow down. Such paradox arose for many economies. In the scientific literature, this situation was called "The middle-income trap" (MIT) by

Gill and Kharas (2007). Traditionally such problem has been discussed concerning to countries with low GDP per capita (Im and Rosenblatt 2013). In recent times it has been appeared in the fundamental investigations about it for more successful countries (Lee 2013; Gill and Kharas 2015; Word Bank 2017). This problem has been appeared in Asia region (Pruchnik and Zowczak 2017), for the countries of Central and Eastern Europe (Galgoczi and Drahokoupil 2017), and for the Visegrad countries (Golonka et al. 2015). This is also directly related to the Economies of the Balkans and Eastern European Countries, including Ukraine (EBRD 2018). The variance in countries income may be rather large, but the common feature is preservation of the existing welfare gap against the developed countries (The middle-income trap 2017).

The conceptual review of existing approaches to explanation of the MIT mode has been given by authors of this category (Gill and Kharas 2015) as well as Kamil Pruchnik and Jakub Zowczak (Pruchnik and Zowczak 2017). According to the World Bank's classification that was taking as main criterion the Gross National Income (GNI) per capita and used the World Bank Atlas method, in 2013 the groups of countries was classified as following: Low-income economies are those with a GNI per capita of $1045 or less; Middle-income economies are with this indicators between ($) 1045 and 12,746 (divided at Lower middle-income and Upper middle-income economies) with average as middle income of $4125; High-income economies are of $12,746 or more (World Bank 2015). In 2016 the World Bank considered countries with upper and middle incomes as US $7650 to US $19,800 at PPP (World Bank 2017). Michael Spence has suggested criterion to recognize the middle-income economies in diapason of 5000–10,000 US$ GDP per capita at PPP (Spence 2011).

Methodological difficulties in solving the problem of slowing down the processes of convergence of middle-income countries rightly have been associated with an underestimation in mainstream economic theories of the importance of the development in these countries of the innovation processes. Today the practical disadvantage of neoclassical approach is reflected in the inability of the orthodox theorists to explain such acute issues as "the productivity paradox" (McKinsey and Company 2018; OECD 2018) and "the middle-income trap" (Albuquerque 2007; Kim and Nelson 2000; Kohli et al. 2011; Lee 2013; Lee and Malerba 2017). The gap between the productivity levels of emerging and developed countries has significantly escalated over recent decades during which the gap widened in many cases instead of narrowing as it was supposed by the neoclassical theory. Another weakness of this theory is associated with ignoring the crucial meaning of structural technological change in production systems of these countries. According to the Neo-Schumpeterian approaches, the Balkan and Eastern European countries to overcome MIT must elaborate economic policy with main priorities of the developing the perspective innovation ICT and biotechnologies. To ensure such strategy, it is very important to be creating efficient National innovation systems (Chaminade et al. 2018).

Considering our topic there is the interesting book about trends in economic convergence in the New EU member states from post-socialist Central and Eastern Europe countries (Gorzelak 2019). Although this research finds the positive regional trends in the real convergence processes in those countries it is still difficult to consider these tendencies as the stable in long run. Further in our article it will be demonstrated.

We can also mention a recently published the meaningful collective work of known economists that considers the technological upgrading as key factor of economic catch-up processes on all level of management—the countries, separated sectors, for the global value chain as well as for the technological paradigm concept and the sustainable development (The Challenges 2021).

The known researcher in the innovation processes and policy Radosevic (2020) pays attention to the methodology of setting priorities for the innovation policy in the emerging and catching up economies, which are elaborated with an indexing method. Such policy must support the generation and diffusion of new products, processes, as well as service, diffusion, demand, absorptive capacity, and linkages in the innovation system.

The useful approach to solve convergence issues is contained in the latest study on the issue of catching and convergence for the Korean and US firms during the 1990s, the 2000s, and 2010s. Authors demonstrate findings that there are certain convergence processes on the Korean firms that become more profitability and the less growth oriented (Im and Lee 2021).

The current methodological problems with implementation of the EU flagman innovation policy named "smart specialization strategy" discuss in fundamental article of Foray et al. (2021) that considers designing an innovation policy which builds the innovators' networks for structural technological change including innovation ecosystem of a regional economy.

3 Theoretical Framework

It should be noted that the findings of many studies conducted on the MIT problem, including those presented earlier, are almost unanimous—the MIT situation is associated with low intensity and efficiency of innovative processes. Such generalizations are based mainly on empirical analysis. However, we can explain the economic nature of this phenomenon also by theoretical background based on J. Schumpeter's theory of economic development.

Our research (Bazhal 2017) has shown that the main feature of Schumpeter's theory of innovations in this context is their ability to independently create added value in the economic system of the country, that is, to act as a separate factor of economic growth. This means that the whole value of innovative products is contributing to GDP growth. If the country's economy is functioning without innovations or their quantity is limited, then such economy, according to Schumpeter, will not grow, but will only reproduce those amounts of added value that were earlier.

For the conceptual positioning of economic systems with innovative development and without it, Schumpeter introduced, respectively, two categories of economic models of countries with names "Dynamics" and "Statics". Proceeding from this methodological approach, we can assume—if a country develops on the model "Statics" (weak innovation processes), then it falls into the trap of middle income.

Recognizing the innovation in quality of main driving force of economic growth has led to apply the modern Neo-Schumpeterian approach as basic theoretical background of two EU strategies in twenty-first century (Rodrigues 2002). These programs have determined the crucial role of the innovation structural policy in dynamic economic development of EU countries (European Commission 2010). On this methodological way it is very important to clear distinguish the innovation industries and traditional ones to economic policy be supporting innovation activities recognizing them as the main factor of the dynamic economic growth. This attitude stipulates the necessary creating of social and economic demands on building of the strong innovation policy with the dynamic structural changes in economy.

In first edition of Schumpeter's fundamental book (Schumpeter 1934) he called "innovation" as a "new combination" that are no predictable. According to this theory the long-term economic growth is depended on scale of creating new production structures of economy with using prospective innovation technology. The existing technological structure of economy supports statically processes of general equilibrium, but rank of development, according to Schumpeter, has been caused by successful innovation activities.

Such methodological platform had become fruitful theoretical basis for adherents of The Neo-Schumpeterian approach in explanation the nature of innovation development (Elgar Companion to Neo-Schumpeterian Economics 2007; Dosi 2012). In contrast to the neoclassical approach, in which economic models were built based on events and indicators that reflect past processes to outline the trends by extrapolation, Neo-Schumpeterian have been trying to predict the future economic landscape which was not existing in the previous period but will be caused by current and future innovation technologies.

The Neo-Schumpeterian approach has elaborated theoretical and applied concept of technological paradigms. The main policy application of this concept is that if the country wants to be rich it must develop economy on progressive technologies belong to current and future technological paradigms. Today such technologies represent ICT and biotechnologies.

4 The Convergence Processes in the Balkans and East European Economies

In principle, the Balkans and East European economies can be attributed to middle-income countries and therefore to them it can be applied in the methodological and political findings of the concept of "the middle-income trap" (MIT). The standard quantitative criterion of the country's GDP level, by which it can be classified as the middle-income country is not yet defined.

The difficulty in comparing the size of these criteria is due to a different method-ology for calculating the indicators of a national product, which are used by different authors. As noted, the World Bank uses the indicator Gross National Income (GNI) per capita that is calculated under the World Bank Atlas method, i.e., in current US dollars; Michael Spence uses the PPP methodology to estimation; it is often such analyses are applying the relative indicators, for example a comparison to the United States level; the using of international dollars (the Geary-Khamis dollar) method in calculations is also popular among analytics to establish various benchmark years for international comparisons in time-series. In our analysis we will use the most "nat-ural" indicator of an economy state—GDP per capita in current US dollars, which has minimal artificially calculated components and eliminates impacts of inflation that arise due to changes in the exchange rates of national currencies.

To provide a statistical illustration of the MIT problem in the Balkans and Eastern European countries, we used the data from the World Development Indi-cators database (indicator code NY.GDP.PCAP.CD). The international comparisons of these indicators for the transition and post-crisis period 1991–2019 presented by two diagrams. The comparison of countries classified as a group of the middle-income countries (Lower middle income, Middle income, Upper middle income), and countries that are grouped according to the regional geographic locations—the Central Europe and the Baltic, which include Bulgaria, Croatia, Czech Republic, Estonia, Hungary, Latvia, Lithuania, Poland, Romania, Slovak Republic, Slovenia, shown in Fig. 1. Second diagram shows the comparison of mentioned group with taxon of the Balkan and Eastern European Countries (Fig. 2).

For our analysis it is necessary to consider these two diagrams simultaneously to make their analytical collation. Although the structures of the groups «European Union», «The Central Europe and the Baltics», and «The Balkan and Eastern Europe»

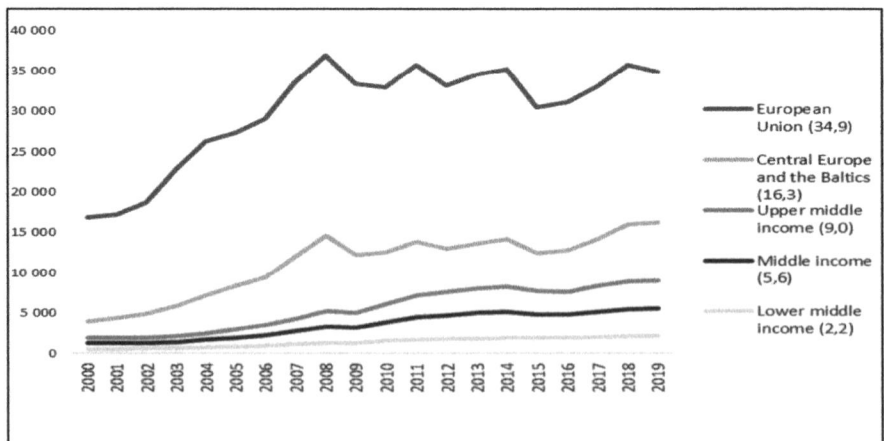

Fig. 1 GDP per capita the selected groups of countries (current $, legend—in brackets $thousands, 2019). *Source* own representation from The World Bank national accounts data, and OECD National Accounts data (https://data.worldbank.org/indicator/NY.GDP.PCAP.CD)

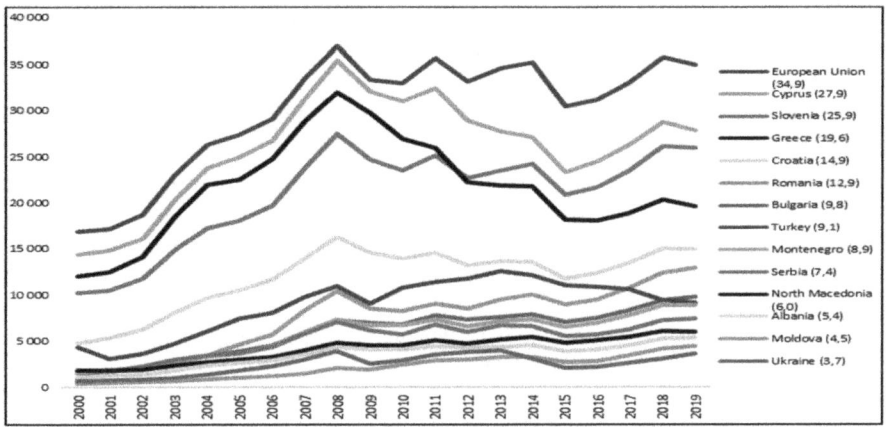

Fig. 2 GDP per capita of the South Eastern European Countries and European Union (current $, legend—in brackets $thousands, 2019). *Source* own representation from The World Bank national accounts data, and OECD National Accounts data (https://data.worldbank.org/indicator/NY.GDP.PCAP.CD)

are partly duplicated, the data presented can give an idea of the comparative trends of the GDP per capita dynamics concerning the selected regions and separated countries.

Figure 1 clearly demonstrates the existence of a stable status quo regarding the characteristics of the GDP per capita gap between the represented groups of countries. The period analyzed was the time of transition from the command-administrative to the market economy for the countries of the Baltic, Central, and Eastern Europe. During this period, many other developing countries have been experimented with implementation of neoliberal recipes of economic policy.

The GDP gaps for the considered countries in principle were not declined. This can be considered one of the basic signs of the presence of the MIT effect. No significant convergence processes changes occurred in this area over the past years, neither in comparison between the countries of the European Union as a whole and the Central Europe and the Baltics countries, nor between different groups of countries classified as middle-income category. It is interesting to note that such picture is demonstrated despite many countries have moved from one group to another. For example, almost all the Central Europe and the Baltics after 2004 became EU countries. This means that the economic rank of each selected group was determined by the stable institutional models of these groups, that is, the specific properties of economic systems and policies.

Figure 1 also identifies the problem of MIT under the criterion for the actual cessation of economic growth after a certain successful dynamic period. In our example, these are periods before and after the economic crisis of 2008–2009. Prior to this, these economies grew in principle synchronously, keeping the proportion of the GDP per capita gap between them, but after the crisis, this growth practically stopped in all more developed countries. Although during the post-crisis period the recovery of more successful economies have taken place, but almost all of them did not exceed the level of GDP per capita in 2008. The economies classified as "the middle-income countries" had a certain steady dynamic of development, but their growth rates were neither sufficient to allow them reducing the gap in the level of GDP per capita against developed countries, nor leave the category of "middle income". However, this picture reflects the processes of not all countries that are members of the groups represented. Some of them successfully solved the task of transitioning to a higher league of such economic competitions. Why did it happen? This will be discussed following in this article after a more detailed disposition for the Balkan and Eastern European countries is presented.

Figure 2 presents in more detail the Balkan and Eastern European countries and, in comparison, an aggregate group of EU countries. One can see that only two countries from eastern region were able to get closer to the average figures of the European Union and enter the group of developed countries by GDP per capita: Greece and Croatia. These successes took place before the crisis (2008–2009), but after this achievement the indicator of the welfare of the country has fallen and it became possible to talk about these countries can be getting into a state of MIT.

According to methodology of The Global Competitiveness Index from the Davos World Economic Forum the countries must introduce the innovation-driven economic policy (Innovation-driven Stage) if they have reached the level of GDP per capita of 17,000 US dollars. Such benchmark was established in 2005, but until now it remains the same (The World Economic Forum 2006, 2017). This situation means that the welfare gap between developed countries and developing countries has not become perceptibly lesser. Only three countries of considered region are above such criterium (Cyprus, Slovenia, and Greece). This assumption can be used to explain convergence problems in the countries presented in Figs. 1 and 2.

5   Innovations as Solving of Convergence Problem

Following to the Schumpeter's approach, economic category of "innovation" appears as the separate driving force of economic growth, and is acting as the isolated factor, separated from the traditional aggregate factors of production used in neoclassical macroeconomic analysis (Aghion 2010; Aghion and Howitt 2009). These are such production factors as Capital, Labour, and Total Factor Productivity. Using Schumpeterian approach, we could explain some paradoxical weaknesses attitudes of the orthodox neoclassical economic theory for revealing the nature of the new phenomena of modern economics. Especially, it regards to the problem of MIT.

The Schumpeter's theory of economic development (Schumpeter 1934) proves that the Statics type of economy with a traditional structure of production without the innovation structural changes inevitably leads to a financial and economic crisis, since in this case there is no real development. In addition, such an economy cannot significantly increase the welfare of the country. Focusing on economic policies to modernize productions that operate in traditional competitive markets is ultimately hampering the creation of a new value added. A steady increase in national income (value added) can only be achieved through permanent innovation. This methodological vision is important in identifying the current economic problems of the Balkan and Eastern European countries, as well as can get answer the question how a low and middle-income countries can significantly increase the value of their national product and the growth rate that makes narrow the gap in per capita GDP.

Speaking of the lack of attention to the innovation model of economic development in the Balkan and Eastern European countries, we must also take in consideration that such model had not been recommended practically by authoritative analysts as a model of transition economy. In the main generalizing publications on the processes of market transformation of post-socialist countries, innovation processes as a separate important factor of successful economic growth are practically not mentioned, and the main priorities in politics were put to neoclassical recipes for the achievement of financial stabilization, privatization, and the attraction of foreign investments (without accentuation on the innovation component of such investments). Examples include works (Roland 2000; World Bank 2002; Kolodko 2011; Aslund 2012), as well as the recommendations of the International Monetary Fund in providing loans. This, of course, had a very strong methodological influence on the conceptual foundations of the formation of socio-economic policies of these countries. The exceptions here are Slovenia and Estonia, which immediately after independence started successfully implement an innovative development model. Unfortunately, very weak influence on the formation of real policies in transition economies had works, which contained detailed recommendations for the activation of innovation policy (Radosevic 1999; Piech and Radosevic 2006; World Bank 2010; Carayannis 2013; Phelps 2013).

Innovative countries have a larger volume of nominal GDP due to larger volumes of innovative products, which leads to a higher level of GDP per capita. However, the problems with this indicator in the post-crisis period, in our opinion, are also associated with a decrease in innovation activity in these countries. As it is mentioned on the beginning of this article the paradigmatic Schumpeter's economic invention is that innovation influences economic development as isolated production factor. It acts independently from other production factors which create added value in the country's macroeconomic system, i.e., innovations have an attribute of directly ensuring economic growth. In this case all value volume of the innovation products is a contribution to GDP growth. That is why innovation countries are economically developed countries. Contrary developing countries as a rule have reached GDP only on a middle level.

The analysis has shown the economic policy of the Catch-up mode becomes successful if it is based on the building of an innovation knowledge economy. The peculiarity of such policy is the focus on the development of new high-tech industries that did not exist before. In this sense, such a policy is less dependent on the traditional productions and has significant methodological differences from the principles of the neoclassical industrial policy, which focuses on the modernization of existing enterprises. In essence, an innovative development model is aimed at the formation of smart economy, the main feature of which is the creation of an innovative specialization of the region, which will provide it with dynamic economic growth. This policy can be implemented even in a depressed region, since it must primarily rely on the creation of a new innovative potential, which was almost never existed. An important resource of such an economy is knowledge. Therefore, it provides for the advanced development of the intellectual and human capital of the region.

The historical method of research also shows convincingly that countries became rich when their economy had mainly built on the resource basis of the current techno-logical paradigm (Neo-Schumpeterian approach). When the technological paradigm was changing even the successful states to remain in the group of developed coun-tries must had been correspondingly changing according to requirements of the new technological paradigm. In most of the Balkan and Eastern European countries such structural adjustments unfortunately have not been enough. Moreover, there are weak innovations potential in these countries to ensure the effectiveness of such structural policy in economies. The orientation of economic policy mainly on the moderniza-tion of existing production, albeit on an innovative basis, cannot create resources to overcome MIT.

The analysis of the innovative development of the Eastern European and Balkan Countries with the help of the European Innovation Scoreboard shows that all of them have significantly lower values of innovation activity indicators than the corre-sponding EU average indices. It demonstrates with the example of two parameters: SII—Summary Innovation Index, and Sales impact of the new-to-market innovations and the new-to-firm innovations as a percentage of turnover (European Innovation Scoreboard 2020). The first indicator is a synthetic characteristic of all parameters of innovation activity of the evaluated countries, and the second directly demonstrates the finale result of the innovation cycle: its commercialization. Figure 3 shows the value of these indicators in 2019 in the form of relative values of the share of the parameter for an individual country in relation to the European average (EU).

The comparative analysis of the innovation potential of the Eastern European and Balkan Countries shows that these economies significantly lose competitiveness comparing to the average European level. Only Cyprus and Slovenia have got a rank of approximately like of EU structure of innovation potential. We can recognize this fact as approval for the innovation theory of Schumpeter because Slovenia has reached the group of old European countries by indicator of GDP per capita. It may be indicative if compare the rank of considered countries by GDP per capita with their rank by indexes of SII and Sales impact. It is also testifying to conceptual fruitful of Schumpeter's theory. The same picture we can observe if will compare other indicators of innovation potential the Eastern European and Balkan Countries to the similar average meanings of European Union.

The issue of the identification in the main factor of economic development is very important to explain systemic economic problems and find the recipes for their solution. Historical analysis shows that, despite the huge variety of the forms of socio-economic processes, primary directions of the economic policy of a country have been determined based on a limited list of characteristics. A striking example of the practical implementation of the ideas of Schumpeter's theory is the Europe 2020 Strategy (European Commission 2010), where the priority of economic development is "Smart growth—developing an economy based on knowledge and innovation".

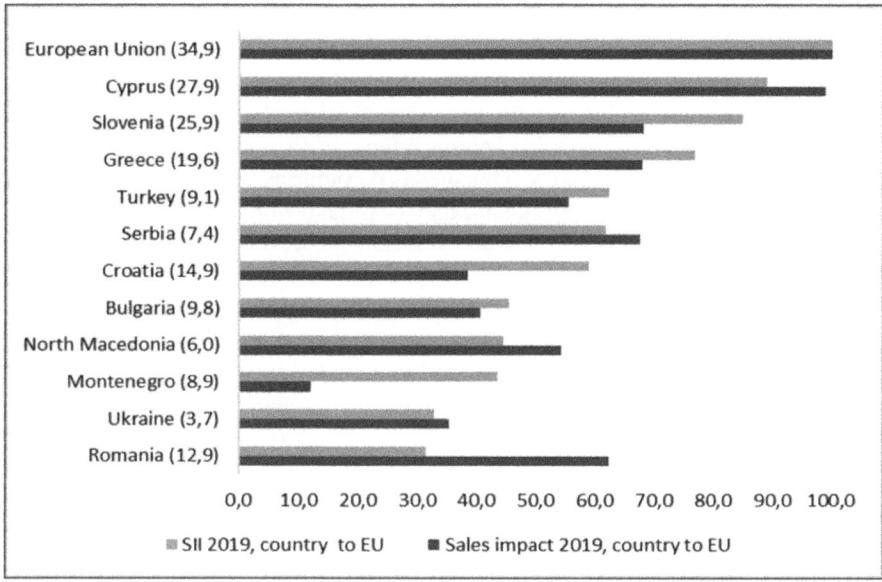

Fig. 3 Comparison selected innovation indicators of the Balkan and Eastern European economies as fractions of EU indices (% to EU), 2019, in brackets—$thousands GDP per capita in current prices (ranking of countries by SII). *Source* European Innovation Scoreboard (2020). Luxembourg: Publications Office of the European Union, 2020—Annex F, G

This was the strategy that posed the innovation policy as main priority to ensure "smart growth" in the economies of all EU countries.

Efficiency of "the Catch-up" policies depends on creating a productive regional innovation ecosystem that will organically unite all stakeholders in frame of generating innovations. This cooperation is fitted to be supported at the state level by creating the appropriate institutions that could help the interaction between big, medium, and small companies, Universities, and the government research and authorities' organizations. Appropriate incentives for innovators should be applied comprehensively for a cluster manufacturing system, considering spin-off effects from joint development and implementation of innovations.

Analysis showed that existing problem of failure in convergence policy has been forming due to the lack of the strong innovation policy. There has been an unjustified methodologic drift from the basic conceptual guidelines of the Europe 2020 Strategy to the traditional Ricardian paradigm of market competitive advantages, i.e., focusing on the existing structure of production in the country, region. Such approaches that spontaneously formed under the influence of market forces need to be supported and strengthened through innovation. On this sense the policy of "smart growth" becomes especially relevant to ensure the radical innovation structural technological changes. The other part of this strategy is a building of the innovation potential of universities which have ability to become as core part of "triple helix" system.

The University innovation ecosystems successfully ensure the achievement of the innovation result, i.e., the commercialization of the academic and technological achievements. The necessity of using the methodology in building smart innovation economy to overcome problems with convergence for the Balkan and Eastern European countries is actual because this approach focuses on managing future economic processes that may not exist today. This means if countries keep a focus on an innovative model of economic development, they can make a breakthrough in economic growth, regardless of the existing resource base that has developed historically. In this case such countries could overcome the negative inheritance of underdevelopment based on existing production factors and competitive advantages.

It is necessary to create and develop a new resource base that will ensure the emergence of innovations. The neoclassical approach directly preserves the historical preconditions for development, when in the recommendations on the economic policy for developing countries, the emphasis is on increasing the productivity or efficiency of the use of available resources. It is important to recognize the "Schumpeter's innovations" must be considered as a special factor for economic growth that generates the increasing the aggregated added value of a countries.

6 Conclusions

Presented analysis illustrated standpoint that Schumpeter's theory explains the MIT to which many emerging economies have come. This "trap" is the focusing of economic policy on increasing the output of traditional industries, even if it was concerning to the labor productivity growth. Such policy does not create a powerful intellectual resource for dynamic long-run development in the Balkan and Eastern European countries. The Schumpeterian theoretical vision gives new understanding of the nature of the required economic reforms in these countries. It is very important to understand the economic reforms not as the repair or modernization of the given economic situation, but as progressive innovation technological change that will push a further progress.

The necessity of using the methodology of an innovation economy to overcome MIT in the Balkan and Eastern European countries is because this approach focuses on managing future economic processes that may not exist today. This means if countries keep a focus on an innovation model of economic development, they can make a breakthrough in economic growth, regardless of the existing resource base that has developed historically. In this case such countries could overcome the negative inheritance of underdevelopment based on existing production factors and competitive advantages. It is necessary to create and develop a new resource base that will ensure the emergence of innovations.

The building of an innovation model of economic growth must become the main policy measure for countries that have got into the MIT. This is because innovative products can directly provide the highest GDP growth, as well as be reaching it through increasing the own share of global markets for innovation products. It is in these markets that less developed countries have a chance to increase their presence. According to our previous research, the structure of traditional international markets is steady, and it is very difficult to change it in their favor for the emerging countries. The implementation of the innovation model of economic development in the Balkan and Eastern European countries require considerable efforts are requested the significantly strengthen of all components of the innovation cycle: science, education, innovative technological R & D, technology transfer, state support for innovative enterprises, and international cooperation in these areas. International cooperation of the countries of the region for the formation of its effective smart specializations can become an important resource.

When forming the common regional innovation policy of the Balkan and Eastern European countries, it is important to draw attention to the applying the "Triple Helix" model of the innovation cycle management of the cooperative innovation efforts. This model will help to overcome the shortcomings of the linear system of management of the innovation process that are associated with the institutional disjunct of the stages of innovation cycle. Such an outdated linear model also limits possible regional cooperation in the field of generation of scientific and technological innovations and the formation of regional smart specializations. This model is also more suitable for the use of a variety of government support tools for innovative processes. This is because the goal of such support can be focused on the final innovation result.

References

Aghion P (2010) Schumpeterian growth and growth policy design. *Economic Growth*. Ed by Durlauf S N, and Blume L E The New Palgrave Economics Collection. Palgrave Macmillan, 229–36.

Aghion P, Howitt P W (2009) *The Economics of Growth*. The MIT Press.

Albuquerque E (2007) Inadequacy of technology and innovation systems at the periphery. *Cambridge Journal of Economics*, 31, 669–690.

Aslund A (2012) How Capitalism Was Built: The Transformation of Central and Eastern Europe, Russia, the Caucasus, and Central Asia. 2nd Edition. Cambridge: Cambridge University Press.

Bazhal I (2017) *The Political Economy of Innovation Development: Breaking the Vicious Cycle of Economic Theory*. New York: Springer Nature, Palgrave Macmillan.

Carayannis EG Ed (2013) *The Innovation Union in Europe: A Socio-Economic Perspective on EU Integration*. Cheltenham UK, Northhampton MA USA: Edward Elgar Publishing.

Chaminade C, Lundvall B-A, and S Haneff (2018) *Advanced Introduction to National Innovation Systems*. Edward Elgar Publ. Cheltenham, UK.

Dosi G (2012) *Economic organization, industrial dynamics and development: Selected essays*. Sant'Anna School of Advanced Studies, Pisa, Italy.

EBRD 2018 *Transition Report 2017–18: Sustaining Growth*. European Bank for Reconstruction and Development.

Elgar Companion to Neo-Schumpeterian Economics (Elgar original reference) Ed H Hanusch and A Pyka (2007). Elgar Pbl.

European Commission (2010) *Europe 2020: A strategy for smart, sustainable, and inclusive growth* COM (2010). Brussels.

European Innovation Scoreboard 2020 (2020) Luxembourg: Publications Office of the European Union.

Foray D, Eichler M, Keller M (2021) Smart specialization strategies—insights gained from a unique European policy experiment on innovation and industrial policy design. *Review of Evolutionary Political Economy* 2:83–103.

Galgoczi B and J Drahokoupil ed (2017) *Condemned to be left behind? Can Central and Eastern Europe emerge from its low-wage model?* ETUI Brussels.

Gill I and Kharas H (2007) An East Asian Renaissance: Ideas for Economic Growth. Washington DC: World Bank.

Gill I S and Kharas H (2015) *The Middle-Income Trap Turns Ten. Policy Research Working Paper No. 7403. Development Policy Department*, World Bank.

Golonka M, et al (2015) *Middle-Income Trap in V4 Countries? Analysis and Recommendations.* Kosciuszko Institute, Visegrad Fund.

Gorzelak G (Ed) (2019) Social and Economic Development in Central and Eastern Europe. Stability and Change after 1990. Routledge. London.

Im, B, Lee K (2021) From Catching Up to Convergence of the Latecomer Firms: Comparing Behavior and Innovation Systems of Firms in Korea and the US. *J. Open Innov. Technol. Mark. Complex. 2021 7 191.*

Im F G and D Rosenblatt (2013) Middle-Income Traps: A Conceptual and Empirical Survey. *Policy Research Working Paper No. 6594.* Washington, DC: World Bank.

Kim L, Nelson R R (Eds) (2000) *Technology, Learning, and Innovation: Experiences of Newly Industrializing Economies.* Cambridge: Cambridge University Press.

Kohli H S, A Charma and A Sood eds (2011) Asia 2050: Realizing the Asian. SAGE Publications Pvt. Ltd.

Kolodko G W (2011) 20 Years of Transformation: Achievements, Problems and Perspectives. *European Political Economic and Security Issues.* New York: Nova Science.

Lee K (2013) Schumpeterian Analysis of Economic Catch-up: Knowledge, Path-Creation, and the Middle-Income Trap. Cambridge University Press.

Lee K, Malerba F (2017) Catch-up cycles and changes in industrial leadership: Windows of opportunity and responses of firms and countries in the evolution of sectoral systems. *Research Policy,* Volume 46, Issue 2: 338–351.

McKinsey & Company (2018) *Outperformers: High-growth emerging economies and the companies that propel them.* The McKinsey Global Institute.

OECD (2018) *OECD Compendium of Productivity Indicators 2018.* OECD Publishing, Paris.

Phelps E S (2013) *Mass Flourishing: How Grassroots Innovation Created Jobs, Challenge, and Change.* Princeton, N.J.: Princeton University Press.

Piech K and Radosevic S eds (2006) *The knowledge-based economy in Central and East European countries: countries and industries in a process of change.* Palgrave Macmillan: Basingstoke, UK.

Pruchnik K and J Zowczak (2017) Middle-income trap: review of the conceptual framework. *ADBI Working Paper Series No.760.* Asian Development Bank Institute.

Radosevic S (1999) *International technology transfer and catch-up in economic development.* Edward Elgar Publishing.

Radosevic S (2020) Benchmarking innovation policy in catching up and emerging economies: methodology for innovation policy index. *UCL Centre for Comparative Studies of Emerging Economies Working Papers Series 2020/1.* London, UK.

Rodrigues M J ed (2002) *The new knowledge economy in Europe – A strategy for international competitiveness and social cohesion,* with the collaboration of R. Boyer, M. Castells, G. Esping-Andersen, R. Lindley, B.A. Lundvall, L. Soete, M. Telò and M. Tomlinson. Cheltenham, UK and Northampton, MA. USA:Edward Elgar.

Roland G (2000) *Transition and Economics: Politics, Markets, and Firms.* Cambridge, Mass. London: The MIT Press.

Schumpeter J (1934) *Theory of economic development: An inquiry into profits, capital, credit, interest, and the business cycle.* Cambridge, MA: Harvard University Press.

Spence M (2011) *The Next Convergence. The Future of Economic Growth in a Multispeed World.* New York, Farrar, Straus and Giroux.

The Challenges of Technology and Economic Catch-up in Emerging Economies Ed by Jeong-Dong Lee, Keun Lee, Dirk Meissner, Slavo Radosevic, Nicholas Vonortas. (2021). Oxford University Press.

The middle income traps (2017) Chapter 5: Governance for growth. *World Development Report 2017: Governance and the Law.* Washington, DC: The World Bank, 157–163.

The World Economic Forum (2006) *The Global Competitiveness Report 2006-2007.* The World Economic Forum, Palgrave Macmillan.

The World Economic Forum (2017) *The Global Competitiveness Report 2017–2018.* World Economic Forum, Geneva, Switzerland.

World Bank (2002) *Transition—The First Ten Years: Analysis and Lessons for Eastern Europe and the Former Soviet Union.* The World Bank: Washington, D.C.

World Bank (2010) *Innovation policy: a guide for developing countries.* The World Bank: Washington, D.C.

World Bank (2015) *World Development Indicators 2015.* The World Bank: Washington, D.C.

World Bank (2017) *World Development Report 2017: Governance and the Law.* The World Bank: Washington, D.C., 157–163.

Evaluation of the Operation of a Social Cooperative Enterprise and Comparison with an 'Ordinary' Enterprise of the Private Sector in Greece

Ioannis Tsoukalidis, Antonios Kostas, and Anastasios G. Karasavvoglou

Abstract Social Cooperative Enterprises (SCEs) in Greece are legal entities under private law. They operate on the basis of the relevant provisions of the Law 4430/2016 as in force. The main objectives of SCEs are the socioeconomic inclusion; the re-integration in terms of employment, and the overall social impact of their activities. This article attempts to proceed with the ex-ante evaluation of the operation of a newly established SCE in North Greece and risk assessment to sets of basic parameters that alter negatively, compared to a 'classical form' of privately-owned enterprise, of the same type of business. In order to do so, nine (9) basic parameters of control have been selected, to evaluate the resilience of an SCE and juxtapose it with the respective resilience of 'classical form' private enterprise. Those parameters were organised in three (3) sets and three (3) different simulations within a period of five (5) years ahead were performed, for negative shift of each set, in order to finally estimate the sustainability risks—resilience, as well as financial income and social impact. Conclusions of simulations as the ones illustrated in this article are of high importance for prospective social entrepreneurs, as they raise awareness of risks, helping them to be better prepared in case those risks become reality.

Keywords Social cooperative enterprise (SCE) · 'Classical form' private enterprise · Ex-ante evaluation · Comparison · Business simulation

JEL Classification L31. Social entrepreneurship · E17. Forecasting and simulation: models and applications

I. Tsoukalidis (✉)
Domi Development PC, 133 Omonias Street, 65403 Kavala, Greece
e-mail: yiannis@domikoinep.gr

A. Kostas · A. G. Karasavvoglou
International Hellenic University, Agios Loukas, 65404 Kavala, Greece
e-mail: antonios_kostas@yahoo.gr

A. G. Karasavvoglou
e-mail: akarasa@af.ihu.gr

1 Introduction and Brief Review

Social Cooperative Enterprises (SCEs) in Greece are private legal entities and operate on the basis of the provisions of the Law 4430/2016 as in force, replacing former Law 4019/2011. The shareholders can be individuals or legal entities, with the latest not exceeding the 1/3 of the members. According to Law 4430/2016, SCEs in Greece are civil cooperatives (under the Law 1667/1986) with the statutory aim of collective and social benefit and have commercial character. The types of SCEs in Greece according to Law 4430/2016 are: (1) the SCEs for Integration (divided into two subcategories: (i) the SCEs for Vulnerable Groups' Integration and (ii) the SCEs for Special Groups' Integration); (2) The Limited Liability Social Cooperatives (LLSCs) of Article 12 of Law 2716/1999 (they function as SCEs for Integration) and (3) the SCEs for Collective and Social Benefit. The activities of SCEs have a social purpose and their main objectives are: (a) socioeconomic inclusion; (b) re-integration in terms of employment and (c) overall social impact of their activities. In comparison with 'classical form' private enterprises, they are based on an alternative organisation of production, distribution and reinvestment relations, founded on the principles of democracy, equality, solidarity and collaboration and with respect for individuals and the environment. Moreover, they include profit distribution rules in their statute (Law 4430/2016) and they prioritise: (a) the development of activities for collective and social benefit and (b) the use of a democratic decision-making structure based on the rule of 'one member, one vote,' independent of each member's level of engagement.

According to Borzaga et al. (2020), the SCEs in 2019 in Greece was 1148 (107 per million of inhabitants). Of those, according to Varvarousis and Tsitsirigkos (2019) the 984 (85.71%) were SCEs for Collective and Social Benefit (that generate 'sustainable activities' or provide 'social services of broad interest'), while the vast majority of those SCEs are new legal entities, at an early stage of development, with needs for financial support (funding) as their ordinary income sources are insufficient to cover their needs. Kostas et al. (2017, 2018), identified significant barriers and obstacles for SCEs development at the legislative, financial and administrative levels, including legal, taxation, shareholders' provided work, funding and others.

The approach of this article is the preliminary evaluation of the operation of a relatively new SCE, established in North Greece, their resilience for several negative changes of basic parameters and the comparison with a 'classical form' private enterprise that operates in the same type of business. Such exercise is estimated to be critical for aspiring social entrepreneurs since it raises risk awareness, allowing them to be better prepared if those dangers materialise.

2 Methodology

We selected an SCE in North Greece, established in late 2019, few months before the novel coronavirus outbreak. It produces goods from recycled materials, handcrafts, ceramics, jewelleries, decoration items, etc. It also provides services for public events such as Christianism of children and others, organises scientific and cultural—art events, etc. Its principles are the promotion of social benefit through the production of goods and providing of services of collective and social purpose, with the priority to people over capital, the supporting to members or the community and, in parallel, the use of its profits for the development of employment and sustainable expansion of its activities. In the first months of its operation, until the first strict lockdown for the prevention of the spread of the novel coronavirus, the SCE managed to have a robust team, be equipped and hosted with sponsoring and undertaking some small projects.

With the business simulation games in mind (Schröder and Ciucan-Rusu 2012; Barišić and Prović 2014), applied in the science of management and the education process of managers in Business Schools (e.g. (i) Harvard Business to Business Marketing Simulation; (ii) University of Leicester (Business Simulation); (iii) University of Kent (Business Simulation); University of Leeds (Business Simulation)), we prepared a testing simulation based on nine (9) basic parameters of control that were selected, to evaluate the resilience of an SCE and juxtapose it with the respective resilience of 'classical form' private enterprise that runs similar activities. Those parameters were organised in three (3) sets and three (3) different scenarios within a period of five (5) years ahead were deployed (simulation), for negative shift of each set, in order to finally estimate the sustainability risks—resilience, as well as financial income and social impact of the two different types of enterprises.

Each parameter had received a sensitivity weight, based on interviews with stakeholders, the principles and interests of the selected SCE, bibliography, type of business, region of activities, the approach of methodology of Quality Function Deployment (Tsoukalidis et al. 2009) and experience.

2.1 Model of Simulation

The selected parameters for the preliminary assessment and simulation are:

- P_1: Active participation of the members of the SCE in decisions' making;
- P_2: Work of the members of the SCE, in the SCE;
- P_3: Work of non-members of the SCE, in the SCE;
- P_4: Existence of concrete roles among members;
- P_5: (i) bargaining power of buyers/profit margin; (ii) bargaining power of suppliers; (iii) existing rivalry; (iv) threat of new entrants and (v) threat of substitute products or services;
- P_6: Exogenous factors;
- P_7: Available financials/credit line(s);
- P_8: Available technological resources;
- P_9: Distribution of financial resources in Marketing.

P_1 and P_4 are based on the findings of Varvarousis and Tsitsirigkos (2019: 58), according to which, in most SCEs in Greece democratic control is of high importance, with 82% making decisions through general assemblies, 76% decides collectively for labour and roles, 74% has active participatory role, 66% has frequent meetings of all members and 66% organises targeted actions for the local community.

P_5 consists of the five (5) basic forces of Porter (1979, 2008), referring to the competition analysis, used to support defining the strategy of an enterprise.

P_6 covers any other force that could affect significantly an enterprise (e.g. technological accident, war, pandemic, etc.)

The performance and development of the SCE and a 'classical form' private enterprise with similar activities are evaluated, for negative changes in different sets of parameters (scenarios), followed by comparison of the reaction of each type of entity. More specifically, for each scenario, some basic parameters are changing negatively, while the others do not fluctuate or alter slightly, not affecting practically the behaviour of the legal entities under evaluation. Conclusions are then extracted, regarding the viability, the income and the social impact, for both cases (SCE and 'classical form' private enterprise).

The sensitivity weights of the selected parameters are as follows (Table 1).

Calculations refer to the overall negative change of the system, affected by the cumulative variations of the basic parameters:

$$\Delta P = \sum_{t=1}^{t=9} \Delta P_t \cdot PW_t$$

while especially for P (five forces of Porter), we have:

$$\Delta P_5 = \sum_{t=1}^{t=5} \Delta PP_t \cdot PPW_t$$

The variations ΔP_k of the basic control parameters (P_k) are identified by the 7-point Likert scale as:

$$\forall k \in [1, 9], \Delta P_k = A; \text{ where } A \in [1, 7]; \{k, A\} \in \mathbb{N}$$

and the variations ΔPP_n of the basic control parameters (PP_n) are identified by the 7-point Likert scale as:

$$\forall n \in [1, 5], \Delta PP_n = A; \text{ where } A \in [1, 7]; \{n, A\} \in \mathbb{N}$$

where the values for each parameter vary from 1 (little negative change) to 7 (very negative change).

Table 1 Sensitivity weights of the selected parameters and justification

P_k	PW_k	Justification		
P_1	10%	Important parameter, as justified by literature as it is a key element that differentiates SCEs from the 'classical form' of private enterprises		
P_2	15%	Important parameter, as the work of the shareholders, is a crucial element of the decision to participate in an SCE		
P_3	3%	Includes the work of non-shareholders of the SCE, in case of additional needs (e.g. specialties) or close relatives of shareholders of the SCE, etc.		
P_4	10%	Important parameter, as the actual distinctive roles (e.g. in charge of the production, in charge of sales, etc.), in correlation with the democratic operation (P_1), are key elements of successful development of an SCE		
		PP_n	PPW_n	Justification
P_5	30%	(i)	40% (12%)	The existence of a satisfactory market for the products and/or services of an SCE allows margins for development
		(ii)	10% (3%)	The bargaining power of suppliers could control the cost of the products and/or services (e.g. in case a supplier is in an advantageous position, the competitiveness risk for SCE could be high)
		(iii)	15% (4.5%)	The balance of rivals in the market (e.g. an enormous number of competitors could cause a high risk for the competitive position of the SCE)
		(iv)	10% (3%)	The easy and relatively non-expensive entrance of new rivals in the market of reference
		(v)	25% (7.5%)	The risk of the reference market to react to new substitutes of the provided products and/or services of the SCE
P_6	10%	The exogenous parameters, although not frequently presented, could play a role for the development of an SCE, or even its collapse		
P_7	12%	Depending on the type of activities of the SCE, if there are significant requirements for capital (e.g. investment capital; working capital), this parameter could play significant role for the development of an SCE		
P_8	7%	Depending on the type of activities of the SCE, if there are significant requirements for technological resources/equipment, those should be available in order not to weaken the position of the SCE in the competition		

(continued)

Table 1 (continued)

P_k	PW_k	Justification
P_9	3%	The promotion of the products and/or services of an SCE is a crucial element of development. The right time plan and the improvement of distribution of resources for that purpose could be elements of viability and development

Table 2 Estimation of the possibilities of the degree of a change

1	2	3	4	5	6	7
35%	25%	18%	12%	6%	3%	1%

We make the assumption that very negative changes in the basic control parameters have very few possibilities to occur. More specifically, we make the following assumptions (Table 2).

Each Scenario simulation of operations runs through the respective algorithm of random selection, based on the above distribution, for 10,000 (ten thousand) times and the mean value is calculated for five (5) years ahead.

The final calculations are made as per the specific contribution of each parameter.

2.2 Sets of Simulation (Scenarios)

We deploy simulation for three (3) different sets of parameters that change (3 scenarios), as follows:

Scenario1 (Table 3)

Scenario2 (Table 4)

Scenario 3 (Table 5)

2.3 The Algorithm

For each scenario, the algorithm iterates 10,000 times. In each iteration, an independent random numbers' generator produces a value (negative alteration) for each basic parameter, from 1 to 7, taking in the consideration the probability for the respective degree of variation. Then, the algorithm calculates the average value (degree of negative alteration) and the contribution of each parameter as per its sensitivity weight. Next, the overall value of negative alteration for the SCE is calculated for the parameters of the scenario that are assumed being in the status of change. Following, for the same conditions (simulation values), the respective value of negative alteration

Table 3 Changes for the parameters of Scenario 1

P_k	PW_k	Change		
P_1	10%	Yes		
P_2	15%	Yes		
P_3	3%	No		
P_4	10%	Yes		
		PP_n	PPW_n	Change
P_5	30%	(i)	40% (12%)	No
		(ii)	10% (3%)	No
		(iii)	15% (4.5%)	No
		(iv)	10% (3%)	No
		(v)	25% (7.5%)	No
P_6	10%	No		
P_7	12%	No		
P_8	7%	No		
P_9	3%	No		

Table 4 Changes for the parameters of Scenario 2

P_k	PW_k	Change		
P_1	10%	No		
P_2	15%	No		
P_3	3%	No		
P_4	10%	No		
		PP_n	PPW_n	Change
P_5	30%	(i)	40% (12%)	Yes
		(ii)	10% (3%)	Yes
		(iii)	15% (4.5%)	Yes
		(iv)	10% (3%)	Yes
		(v)	25% (7.5%)	Yes
P_6	10%	No		
P_7	12%	No		
P_8	7%	No		
P_9	3%	No		

is calculated for the 'classical form' private enterprise based on the degree of the scenario parameters' contribution in this case.

Table 5 Changes for the parameters of Scenario 3

P_k	PW_k	Change		
P_1	10%	No		
P_2	15%	No		
P_3	3%	No		
P_4	10%	No		
		PP_n	PPW_n	Change
P_5	30%	(i)	40% (12%)	No
		(ii)	10% (3%)	No
		(iii)	15% (4,5%)	No
		(iv)	10% (3%)	No
		(v)	25% (7.5%)	No
P_6	10%	Yes		
P_7	12%	Yes		
P_8	7%	No		
P_9	3%	No		

3 Results

The deployment of the algorithm provided the following results:

3.1 Scenario 1

$$\{(\Delta P_1)^2 \cdot (\Delta P_2)^2 \cdot (\Delta P_4)^2 > 0\},$$
$$\Delta P_3 = \Delta P_5 = \Delta P_6 = \Delta P_7 = \Delta P_8 = \Delta P_9 = 0$$

The deployment of the algorithm for 10,000 (ten thousand) times, with the general and special assumptions, gives a coefficient of variation of **0.846** for the case of the SCE.

In the case of a 'classical form' private enterprise only the parameter P_4 has a significant impact on the performance of the entity, while the parameter P_2 has a minor impact, not more than 10% of the respective case of the SCE.

'classical form' private enterprise Versus SCE sensitivity:

$$P_{1\,\text{private}} = 0.00 \cdot P_{1\,\text{SCE}}$$
$$P_{2\,\text{private}} = 0.10 \cdot P_{2\,\text{SCE}}$$
$$P_{4\,\text{private}} = 1.00 \cdot P_{4\,\text{SCE}}$$

The deployment of the algorithm for 10,000 (ten thousand) times, with the general and special assumptions, gives a coefficient of variation of **0.266** for the case of the 'classical form' private enterprise.

We conclude that the sensitivity in the negative change of the set of basic parameters P_1, P_2, P_4 in the case of SCE, is higher compared to the 'classical form' private enterprise, by 2.18 times (3.18 times the sensitivity of 'classical form' private enterprise). This means that for SCEs the degree of risk is significantly higher compared to the 'classical form' private enterprise.

3.2 Scenario 2

$$\{(\Delta P_5)^2 > 0\},$$
$$\Delta P_1 = \Delta P_2 = \Delta P_3 = \Delta P_4 = \Delta P_6 = \Delta P_7 = \Delta P_8 = \Delta P_9 = 0$$

The deployment of the algorithm for 10,000 (ten thousand) times, with the general and special assumptions, gives a coefficient of variation of **0.730** for the case of the SCE.

In the case of a 'classical form' private enterprise, the parameter P_5 has also a significant impact on the performance of the entity. Moreover, the impact of negative variations of the basic parameter P_5 is more intensive for a 'classical form' private enterprise, which has a pure for-profit approach, compared to an SCE which in many cases is satisfied in viability conditions with relatively small margin for profit. According to Parker (2021) the margin of gross profit ((sales − production cost)/sales) could have large diversions for different types of business, while, according to Schorn (2016) the net profit margin is on average between 10.5 and 18.3%. Based on market prices and the assumption that SCEs can survive with an average profit margin of 10%, while the private enterprises wouldn't wish to fall below the average 25%, we assume an increased average weight by 15% for the 'classical form' private enterprise.

'classical form' private enterprise Versus SCE sensitivity:

$$P_{5\,\text{private}} = 1.15 \cdot P_{5\,\text{SCE}}$$

The deployment of the algorithm for 10,000 (ten thousand) times, with the general and special assumptions, gives a coefficient of variation of **0.831** for the case of the 'classical form' private enterprise.

We conclude that the sensitivity in the negative change of the set of basic parameter P_5 in the case of 'classical form' private enterprise, is higher compared to the SCE, by 0.13 times (1.13 times the sensitivity of SCE). This means that for SCEs the degree of risk is slightly lower compared to the 'classical form' private enterprise.

3.3   Scenario 3

$$\{(\Delta P_6)^2 \cdot (\Delta P_7)^2 > 0\},$$
$$\Delta P_1 = \Delta P_2 = \Delta P_3 = \Delta P_4 = \Delta P_5 = \Delta P_8 = \Delta P_9 = 0$$

The deployment of the algorithm for 10,000 (ten thousand) times, with the general and special assumptions, gives a coefficient of variation of **0.534** for the case of the SCE.

In the case of a 'classical form' private enterprise, the parameters P_6 and P_7 have also a significant impact on the performance of the entity.

P_6 has a relatively increased impact on a 'classical form' private enterprise in comparison to an SCE. Based on market prices and the assumption that SCEs can survive with an average profit margin of 10%, while the private enterprises wouldn't wish to fall below the average 25%, we assume an increased average weight by 15% for the 'classical form' private enterprise.

P_7 has less impact, while the 'classical form' private enterprises according to Kostas et al. (2017, 2018) they have in general easier access to funding sources. Thus we assume the average weight to be 40% of the SCE.

'classical form' private enterprise Versus SCE sensitivity:

$$P_{6\,private} = 1.15 \cdot P_{6\,SCE}$$
$$P_{7\,private} = 0.40 \cdot P_{7\,SCE}$$

The deployment of the algorithm for 10,000 (ten thousand) times, with the general and special assumptions, gives a coefficient of variation of **0.394** for the case of the 'classical form' private enterprise.

We conclude that the sensitivity in the negative change of the set of basic parameters P_6 and P_7 in the case of SCE is higher compared to the 'classical form' private enterprise, by 0.35 times (1.35 times the sensitivity of 'classical form' private enterprise). This means that for SCEs the degree of risk is higher compared to the 'classical form' private enterprise.

3.4   Summarised Simulation Results

In the following Table 6 and the respective Fig. 1, we present the simulation results for all three (3) scenarios and the comparative correlation of an SCE and a 'classical form' private enterprise allows inferences for the resilience of each one, in alteration of different sets of parameters.

Table 6 Summarised simulation results and comparison between SCE and 'classical form' private enterprise

	Scenario 1	Scenario 2	Scenario 3
SCE	0.846	0.730	0.534
'classical form' private enterprise	0.266	0.831	0.394
CSE $\frac{SCE}{\text{'classical form' private enterprise}}$	3.180	0.878	1.355
More robust entity	'classical form' private enterprise ++++++	SCE ++	'classical form' private enterprise +++

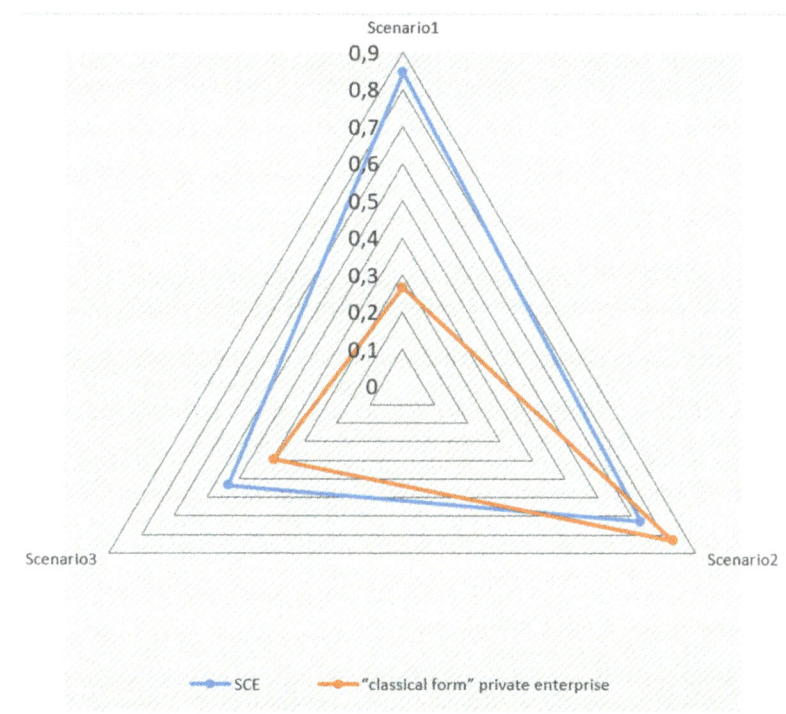

Fig. 1 Resilience of SCE and 'classical form' private enterprise in the three different scenarios

4 Conclusions

The evaluation is completed with the conclusions about the viability, the income of the involved entities and the respective social impact, for the two different types of legal entities. The results are interpreted as follows: (i) SCEs are more sensitive in break of their fundamental principles (Scenario 1) and the negative changes of the exogenous environment and needs for funding (Scenario 3), while they are more resilient than the 'classical form' private enterprises in the competition (Scenario 2). (ii) The income of the members of an SCE follows the pattern of its response behaviour in each of the scenarios. (iii) Social Impact is a key characteristic of SCEs. The risk of its sustainability means also risk for negative consequences for its social impact actions. Therefore, it is advisable that in special cases, that the SCE is exposed to risks, to pursue the optimal correlation between 'actions' and 'social impact', without elimination of the social actions, as those would allow the approach to existing and new customers.

As the weights of the control parameters could differ for different types of business or the country/region where activities are performed, it would be interesting to test the presented the simulation model in different environments and industries.

When sufficient historical data for the operation of SCEs are available, it would be interesting to proceed with comparison of the actual evolution in time of the two different types of enterprises and the ex-ante evaluation results of the simulation model (for the same parameter data).

References

Barišić, A.F., & Prović, M. (2014). Business simulation as a tool for entrepreneurial learning. The role of business simulation in entrepreneurship education. *Education for Entrepreneurship - E4E*, 4(2), 97–107.

Borzaga, C., Galera, G., Franchini, B., Chiomento, S., Nogales, R., & Carini, C. (2020). Social Enterprises and their Ecosystems in Europe. Comparative synthesis report. European Union. Publications Office of the European Union: Luxembourg. http://www.bollettinoadapt.it/wp-con tent/uploads/2020/04/KE0220042ENN.en_.pdf. Accessed 2 May 2021.

Kostas, A., Tsoukalidis, I., Karasavvoglou, G.A., Polychronidou, P., & Tsourgiannis, L. (2017). The barriers for the development of the Social Cooperative Enterprises in Greece. In A.G. Karasavvoglou, S. Goić, P. Polychronidou & P. Delias (Eds), *Economy, Finance and Business in Southeastern and Central Europe, Proceedings of the 8th International Conference on the Economies of the Balkan and Eastern European Countries in the Changing World (EBEEC)* (pp. 513–522). Springer Proceedings in Business and Economics. Springer Publication: Cham. https://doi.org/10.1007/978-3-319-70377-0_35

Kostas, A., Tsoukalidis, I., & Karasavvoglou, G.A. (2018). Social Cooperative Enterprises in Greece: The transition from the Law 4019/2011 to the Law 4430/2016. A process without a "road map". In A.G. Karasavvoglou, P. Polychronidou, A. Śliwiński, K. Łyskawa & M. Janowicz-Lomott (Eds), *Proceedings of 10th International Conference: The Economies of the Balkan and the Eastern European Countries in the changing world - EBEEC 2018* (pp. 48–58). http://ebeec. ihu.gr/documents/oldConferences/EBEEC_2018_Proceedings.pdf

Law 4430/2016 (2016). Social and Solidarity Economy and development of its entities and other provisions. https://www.e-nomothesia.gr/kat-oikonomia/nomos-4430-2016.html. Accessed 3 May 2021.

Parker, T. (2021). What's a Good Profit Margin for a New Business?. Investopedia. https://www.inv estopedia.com/articles/personal-finance/093015/whats-good-profit-margin-new-business.asp. Accessed 15 May 2021.

Porter, M.E. (1979). How Competitive Forces Shape Strategy. *Harvard Business Review*, 57(2), 137–145.

Porter, M.E. (2008). The Five Competitive Forces that Shape Strategy. *Harvard Business Review*, 86(1), 78–93.

Schorn, D. (2016). The 5 private industries with the highest profit margins. CBC News [Online]. https://www.cbsnews.com/news/the-5-private-industries-with-the-highest-pro fit-margins. Accessed 9 February 2021.

Schröder, H.P., & Ciucan-Rusu, L. (2012). Business Simulation. *Conference Best Entrepreneurship 2012,* Tirgu Mures, Romania. https://www.researchgate.net/publication/280387309_Business_ Simulation. Accessed 12 January 2021.

Tsoukalidis, I., Karassavoglou, A., Mandilas, A., & Valsamides, S. (2009). Application of Quality Function Deployment on an Alternative Transportation System (Paratransit System). *European Research Studies, Vol XII,* Issue (2), 131–148.

Varvarousis, A., & Tsitsirigkos, G. (2019). Social Enterprises and their Ecosystems in Europe. Country report: Greece. European Union. Publications Office of the European Union: Luxembourg.

The R&D Effect on Firm Value in the Information Technology Industry

Katerina Lyroudi

Abstract Innovation enhances corporate value and offers the underlying company a new competitive advantage, strategic and financial benefits and potential for survival and future growth. As a proxy for innovation, we use the expenditures in research and development (R&D) and the intangible assets of the company following the relevant literature. This paper focuses on the European markets. The objective of the paper is to investigate first whether R&D expenditures and intangible assets affect the value of the underlying company and if they do so, in what way and second whether they affect the performance of the company. Our sample consists of the companies in the information technology (IT) industry in Europe, the most innovative industry. We apply several regression models to test our hypotheses. Our results indicated a positive relation between the innovative investments as proxied by the research and development expenses and the intangible assets with the firm's value. However, regarding the company performance as measured by the ROA and ROE, our results rejected our hypothesis since we found a negative relation between the innovation variables and the profitability ratios as performance variables.

Keywords Market value · Innovation · Book value · Earnings · R&D expenses · Intangibles

Jel Classification G30 · M4 · O30

1 Introduction

Innovation enhances corporate value and offers the underlying company a new competitive advantage, strategic and financial benefits and potential for survival and future growth. According to Mauboussin and Kawaja (1999), the value of a company can be estimated as the present value of all the future free cash flows it will generate.

K. Lyroudi (✉)
Hellenic Open University, Patra, Greece
e-mail: lyrkat@gmail.com; lyroudi.aikaterini@ac.eap.gr

Therefore, the more innovative a company is, the more future free cash flows are expected to be generated. As a proxy for innovation, we use first the expenditures in research and development (R&D) and second the intangible assets of the company following the relevant literature (Griliches 1984; Sher and Yang 2005; Cho and Pucik 2005).

The concept of research and development (R&D) defines the various activities that the underlying department of a company is conducting and realizes in order to create new products or discover solutions to problems or improve existing products. If a company has its own R&D department, it incurs the relative expenses and if the research results in specific products/solutions, it creates intellectual property or intellectual capital such as patents or copyrights.

In general, the literature is rich regarding this issue of innovation for the USA, Canada, Australia, India, China and other Asian markets, as it will be presented in the next section. However, there is not enough literature to our knowledge regarding the companies in Europe and this issue of innovation. Therefore, this paper by examining this subject for a sample of European companies enriches the relevant literature and covers this gap. The objective of this paper is to investigate whether innovation (as measured by the company's R&D expenses and its intangible assets) affects the value and performance of the underlying company in a sample of information technology enterprises listed in the European stock exchanges that comprise the EuroSTOXX 600 index and those IT companies listed in the Greek stock exchange. First it presents the concept of R&D and the incurring expenses as intangible assets and some aspects on the tax and accounting laws regarding the R&D expenditures and intangible assets.

The contribution of this paper to academicians is the new light and information that we get in exploring the innovation effects on the firm value for a sample of high technological companies in Europe. The results will shed more light on this issue for practitioners and company stakeholders as well as policymakers in regard to the investments in innovation. For instance, it will be clearer to investors whether it will be a good, profitable decision to invest in innovation and in terms of policymakers, whether governments should encourage firms to innovate by providing motivations such as direct R&D government subsidies or tax incentives.

In order to achieve our goal the paper is structured as follows: The next section presents some accounting aspects regarding the R&D expenditures and intangibles and the relative review of literature. The third section describes the data, the methodology and the testable hypotheses. The fourth section analyses the results, and the last section contains a summary and concluding remarks.

2   Literature Review

The concept of research and development (R&D) contains the various activities that a company is involved with and realizes so that it can: (a) create new products, or processes or services. As products are considered formulas, inventions, pilot models, computer software and techniques; (b) discover solutions to problems and/or (c) improve existing products or services [Frascati Manual (2002) OECD]. Intangible assets can be defined as business assets that have no physical form and are distinguished in two types: those that are purchased and those that are internally generated. If a company has its own R&D department, it incurs the relative expenses, and if the research results in specific products/solutions, it creates intellectual property or intellectual capital such as patents or copyrights which will create future probable economic benefits to the enterprise. There are national laws that treat the accounting of R&D expenses and intangible assets such as the International Financial Reporting Standards (IFRS) and the US-GAAP. These systems of reporting have differences. However, the discussion of the differences is beyond the scope of this study.

There is rich literature on the relation of firm value and innovation for the markets of the USA, Canada, Australia, India, China, Taiwan and other Asian markets, but few studies for European markets. Grilishes and Mairesse (1984) for a sample of 133 large U.S. firms for the period 1966–1977 analyzed the relationship between output, employment, and physical and R&D capital and found a strong positive relationship between firm productivity and the level of its R&D investments.

Johnson and Pazderka (1993) for a sample of the Canadian market companies, listed on the Toronto stock exchange, tested the hypothesis that the market gave a positive value on the research and development spending of firms as an indicator of expected profitability and growth. The empirical results showed a positive, statistically significant relationship between the R&D expenditures and the market value of the firms. These results implied that "investment in R&D is a rational allocation of resources".

Mairesse and Hall (1996) compared the contribution of R&D expenses to the firm's productivity for the French and the US manufacturing companies in the 1980s. They used the GMM method to control for both sources of estimation bias and found that the contribution of R&D expenses to sales productivity growth had declined during the 1980s, and this decline was higher for the US firms than for the French ones.

Lev and Sougiannis (1996) addressed the capitalization, amortization and value-relevance of R&D since the GAAP mandated the full expensing of R&D in the financial statements for USA firms. They adjusted the reported earnings and book values of their sample firms for the R&D capitalization and found that investors placed value to such adjustments since they found a positive relation between the R&D capital and the stock returns of the underlying companies. This implied that either R&D-intensive firms were systematically mispriced by the market, or investors required a compensation for the extra-market risk that is associated with R&D investments.

Abrahams and Sidhu (1998) investigated the extent to which R&D expenses improve the association between accounting-based measures of firm performance and capital market returns for a sample of Australian companies listed on the Australian Stock Exchange (ASX). Their results indicated that capitalized R&D on the balance sheets had a significant positive information effect on the firms' value (stock prices).

Ho et al. (2005) examined for a sample of USA companies whether firm spending on innovation as measured by research and development (R&D) expenditures and marketing, as measured by advertising expenses, are yielding positive returns in terms of share price performance. So, the authors examined the relationship between firm performance and the intensity of their investments in R&D and advertising expenses for 40 years from 1962 to 2001. They found that investment in R&D had a positive effect on the one-year stock market performance for the manufacturing companies but not for the non-manufacturing ones. On the other hand, the non-manufacturing companies showed a positive effect of advertising expenses on their stock market performance.

Lin and Chen (2005) for 78 US technology companies examined the relationship between technology portfolio strategies and five R&D performance measures, from 1976 to 1995. Their results indicated that large firms have more advantages for technological innovation due to better exploitation of synergy effects of their technology portfolios, compared to smaller companies.

Sher and Yang (2005) investigated the effect of R&D clustering on innovation and thus on firm competitiveness for the Taiwanese integrated circuit (IC) industry. They found that higher R&D intensity and higher R&D manpower were positively related to firm performance as measured by the return on assets ratio (ROA).

Harhoff (2006) found that since the early 1980s patent rights as a type of innovation have become important resources for companies to build and maintain their value. Greenhalgh and Rogers (2006) found that companies that filed for patents in the European patent office had on average higher R&D expenditures and this led to higher company value compared to those that filed in the UK patent office.

De Meyer and Garg (2006) examined the concept of innovation in the corporate world in selected Asian countries, such as China, Thailand, Indonesia, India, Korea, Singapore and Taiwan, since there are differences in some aspects versus the western world's (including Japan) equivalent viewpoint. They found that in the above Asian countries except Taiwan, the management's view regarding innovation was interpreted more as cost reduction policies than new value creation. Possibly because they had a limited understanding of marketing and there was a lack of employees with quality training. However, in Taiwan, the situation was similar to the western world companies, because the engineering capability and the financing of innovations were of high quality, since most of the scientists employed were educated and had worked in the USA for a time and were familiar with the western world's view of innovation and innovation processes. That made Taiwan an example for imitation in order to succeed in adopting innovation to promote their company's growth.

Hall et al. (2009) distinguished the R&D expenses in three categories: those directed toward invention of new methods of production to improve the quality or decrease the production costs and called them process R&D, those directed towards the creation of new goods and improved products (intermediate or final) called product R&D and those that depend on the source of funds as private or public. They found that R&D investments increased productivity and created spillovers "Pecuniary" and "Non-pecuniary" to other firms by the knowledge that is disseminated.

Beld (2014) for a sample of publicly listed firms in Belgium, Luxembourg and the Netherlands examined the effect of research and development (R&D) expenditures on the companies' performance. The latter, measured by the return on assets (ROA), was found to be positively affected by the research and development (R&D) expenditures.

Warusawitharana (2015) for the non-financial USA companies taken from the compustat database examined whether the firms' investment in research and development (R&D) to generate innovations had a positive effect on their underlying profitability and firm value. The results indicated that the R&D expenditures had an economically and statistically significant impact on profits and firm value.

VanderPal (2015) investigated the R&D impact on the company value for a sample of 103 US listed companies for the period 1979–2013. His results indicated a positive relationship between R&D expenses and equity, revenue and ROA and a negative relationship with ROE.

Jaisinghani (2016) investigated the impact of R&D expenses on the profitability of a sample of Indian companies in the pharmaceutical sector for the period 2005–2014. They used the variable Rand D intensity as the ratio of R&D expenses to sales and found that there exists a positive relationship between R&D intensity and performance for the Indian pharmaceutical Industry, with performance being proxied by two measures of profitability, the ratios return on assets and return on sales.

Bouaziz (2016) for the BIST technology index companies in the Istanbul stock exchange concluded that there is no relation between R&D expenses and firm performance for the period 2010–2014. Similar conclusions were reached by Xu et al. (2016) for 79 listed energy companies on the Shanghai Stock Exchange regarding the effect of R&D investments on the current firm performance. However, they found a positive two-year lagged effect of R&D activities on company performance.

Wang et al. (2017) found that R&D investments create additional value for the underlying companies when there are interactions with IT investments in several industry sectors for China.

Guo et al. (2018) examined the effect of R&D expenditures on the firm's future performance for a sample of Chinese companies from another perspective. This perspective was the strategic position of each firm. They distinguished two group of firms, those that adopt a product differentiation strategy and those that adopt a cost leadership strategy. Their results indicated that regarding the former group the R&D spending had a positive effect on the firm's future performance measured by the ROA, the ROE and Tobin's Q ratio. Regarding the latter group they found that the above relationship was not linear and resembled an inversed U-shape curve. The firms that follow a cost leadership strategy have as their crucial competitive advantage their efficiency. They keep tight cost controls and apply aggressive pricing and economic scale maximization to defeat their competitors. For this group of companies, excessive spending in R&D activities is not acceptable because it violates their principle of strict cost control. They invest in R&D up to the point to design products for large-scale production. Based on this approach, only a specific level of R&D expenditures affects positively the firm's future performance.

Regarding the European markets Almeida et al. (2019) found that R&D investments influenced positively the firm's performance measured by sales and operating profit. Chen et al. (2019) examined this issue for Taiwanese semiconductor industry companies and found that R&D investments had a positive and one-year lagged effect on the companies' performance. Firm size was also significant in affecting positively the business performance. Zhu and Huang (2012) for the Chinese listed information technology (IT) companies found also that R&D expenditures had a one-year lagged positive effect on the firm performance.

Dimitropoulos (2020) examined the impact of intangibles on financial performance by examining the impact of the R&D investments on the profitability of Greek firms especially during the sovereign debt crisis for the period 2003–2016. He used panel regression analysis and the results indicated that R&D investments and expenses affected negatively the sample firms' profitability before the crisis, while during the crisis from 2011 to 2016 those companies that managed to sustain or increase their R&D investments improved their profitability. This finding is important because it indicated that during a period of scarcity of external financing and financial uncertainty, R&D investments could be a vital tool for the sustainability and growth of the companies.

More recent studies like Tung et al. (2021) for the listed companies of the developing economy of Vietnam, for the period 2010–2018, found that R&D expenditures/investments had positive effects on revenues, profits, the return on assets (ROA) and the return on equity (ROE).

However, there are some studies that have investigated this inconsistency in the empirical results of the R&D effect on firm performance. As early as 2010 Yang et al. (2010) for a sample of Taiwanese companies, both high-tech and non-high-tech manufacturing firms found that the disparities in the literature regarding the R&D expenses and performance relation are due to the fact that it is not a linear relation. They suggested a three stage S-curve model to cover these disparities in the pertinent literature. Their data analysis confirmed this model and the non-linearity of the relation. The slope was negative at low levels (stage 1), positive at medium levels (stage 2) and negative again at high levels (stage 3) of R&D investments/expenditures, forming an S-curve model. More recently, Vrontis and Christofi (2019) after reviewing systematically pertinent articles on this issue concluded that the effect of R&D activities on business performance has a multi-disciplinary nature and that is why the empirical results are not clear and more research is required. Finally, Boiko (2021) reviewed the academic articles from 1980 to 2020 on this issue, the impact of R&D activities on company performance and concluded that there are contradictory results; therefore, more research needs to be done in terms of theory and methodology, to be able to identify the various factors that influence this relationship, applying several methodological approaches also to double check the findings.

3   Data, Testable Hypotheses and Methodology

3.1   Data and Variables

The focus of this study is the firms in the information technology industry, which is generally considered the most growing and innovative industry. The reason for selecting this sector is that the information technology industry is the fastest growing industry in the twenty-first century, and its products and services are used by most individuals and organizations. Our sample, after we deleted those observations that did not have data for our selected variables for certain years, is consisted of all the information technology companies listed in the European stock markets and are part of the EuroSTOXX 600 index (a total number of 87 firms) and all the information technology companies listed in the Greek stock exchange (a total number of 17 firms). All the data was collected from the Thomson EIKON database. The final sample consisted of 104 companies of the European Information Technology industry. This industry sector has the code number 45 in the Global Industry Classification Standard (GICS). Specifically, there are three IT industry groups with the relative codes, such as 4510 Software and Information Technology Services, 4520 Technology Hardware and Equipment and 4530 Semiconductors and Semiconductor Equipment. The time period examined is from 2000 to 2019. The year 2020 is the year of the global health crisis of the COVID-19 pandemic, and it has caused a severe negative economic impact to all the markets and companies around the world. Therefore, we excluded this year 2020 in order to avoid contamination of our results by this crisis, although we had data for enough European companies to perform our tests, but no data for the Greek firms.

The variables used are: the market value of equity as a proxy for firm value based on Warusawitharana (2015); the R&D expenses following VanderPal (2015) and Dimitropoulos (2020) and the ratio of R&D divided by sales for size adjustment according to Ho et al. (2005) and Jaisinghani (2016) as the first proxy for firm innovation investments; the intangible assets and the ratio of intangible assets divided by total assets as the second proxy for firm innovation investments according to Bolek and Lyroudi (2017); the return on assets (ROA) and the return on equity (ROE) as the two proxies for company performance according to VanderPal (2015); the size as control variable measured by total assets, following Richard et al. (1991) and Kumar and Warne (2009), actually the logarithm of total assets. We considered only the variable of size from other firm characteristic variables because according to Dang et al. (2017) firm size is commonly used as an important, fundamental firm characteristic in corporate finance empirical research in various topics according to Rajan and Zingales (1995), Frank and Goyal (2003), Moeller et al. (2004), Klapper and Love (2004), Shubita and Alsawalhah (2012), Vijh and Yang (2013), Gabaix et al. (2014), and others. Furthermore, in many studies, it is observed a "size effect", whereby this variable is a significant explanatory variable of the dependent variable the underlying study is investigating. Dang et al. (2017) have also found that in most studies the coefficients of firm size measures from regression analyses are robust in sign and statistical significance. Therefore, we followed this line of thought and tried to test for a "size effect". Larger companies may perform better because they are able to take advantage of scale economies and are able to have access to more resources and better bargains according to Asimakopoulos et al. (2009) and Lee (2009). Furthermore, Schimke and Brenner (2014) for 1000 European companies found that the positive relationship of R&D activities on turnover growth depended strongly on firm size and industry sector. In this aspect regarding innovation, the variable of size should matter, and this is what this study is investigating with the third testable hypothesis.

Regarding the profitability ratios that measure the company performance we follow the determination of Jose et al. (1996), since we have companies from different countries and different taxation systems. Therefore, instead of earnings after taxes in the numerator for both ratios as is the classical approach, we use for the ROA the ratio of earnings before interest and taxes (EBIT) to total assets, and for the ROE, we use the ratio of earnings before taxes (EBT) to equity capital.

3.2 Testable Hypotheses

Based on the relevant literature we discussed above, in order to achieve our objectives, we test the following hypotheses. Specifically:

According to Abrahams and Sidhu (1998) for the Australian market, Greenhalgh and Rogers (2006) for selected European firms and Wang et al. (2017) for Chinese firms higher R&D expenses lead to higher company value, and hence, we have formulated our first testable hypothesis:

H1: The R&D expenditures and the intangible assets as proxies of innovation in a company are expected to increase the value of the underlying company.

Based on Sher and Yang (2005) for the Taiwaneses IC industry firms, the study of Beld (2014) for firms in Belgium, Luxemburg and the Netherlands, Warusawitharana (2015) and VanderPal (2015) for USA firms and Jaisinghani (2016) for Indian Pharmaceutical firms, which found that R&D expenses were positively related to firm performance as measured by the return on assets (ROA), we have formulated our second testable hypothesis:

H2: The R&D expenditures and the intangible assets as proxies of innovation in a company are expected to increase the performance of the underlying company as measured by the ROA and ROE indicators.

Lin and Chen (2005) for the US technology companies found a size effect, since large firms had more advantages for technological innovation compared to smaller firms. The same result was found by Chen et al. (2019) for Taiwanese semiconductor companies, since the larger the company, the greater is the exposure to R&D and the more innovative products and services can be produced. This can lead to gaining more market share and more firm growth. Thus, based on these studies, we have formulated our third testable hypothesis:

H3: The size of a company is expected to affect positively the innovation effect (from R&D expenses and from intangible assets) on the firm value and on the company performance.

3.3 Methodology

In order to investigate our testable hypotheses, we apply correlation analysis with the Pearson correlation coefficient and multiple regression analysis, using the following models for all the years together cross-sectionally:

$$\text{Value of firm}_{it} = a_1 + b_1 \text{RD}_{it} + b_2 \text{Size}_{it} + e_{it} \tag{1}$$

$$\text{Value of firm}_{it} = a_1 + \gamma_1 \text{Intangibles}_{it} + \gamma_2 \text{Size}_{it} + e_{it} \tag{2}$$

$$\text{Performance of firm}_{it} = a_1 + b_1 \text{RD}_{it} + b_2 \text{Size}_{it} + e_{it} \tag{3}$$

$$\text{Performance of firm}_{it} = a_1 + \gamma_1 \text{Intangibles}_{it} + \gamma_2 \text{Size}_t + e_{it} \tag{4}$$

The models 3 and 4 that examine the effect of the explanatory variables on the company's performance are run twice, one whereby the performance is proxied by the return on assets, (ROA) and the other whereby the performance is proxied by the return on equity (ROE).

4 Empirical Results

Table 1 presents the descriptive statistics of our variables. Table 2 depicts the Pearson correlation coefficients between our selected variables for the whole examined period.

Based on the Pearson correlation coefficients in Table 2, the ratio of intangible assets to sales is negatively and significantly related to the R&D expenses, the

Table 1 Descriptive statistics

	N	Minimum	Maximum	Mean	Std. deviation
RandD	1704	−158,000,000	46,640,000,000	1,766,523,969.60	6,896,148,584.98
RDS	1704	−0.02966	9.52611	0.19494260436	0.50009
Intangibles	1704	0	27,619,000,000	529,331,410.12	2,369,124,363.95
INTANGA	1704	0.00000	0.85911	0.12503	0.14288
MV	1704	0.00000	927,887,993,560	21,232,680,614.201	81,011,405,118.226
ROA	1704	−21.41935	0.73608	−0.01306	0.58481
ROE	1704	−181.47368	24.14545	−0.24464	4.83763
Size	1704	11.03489	26.40534	19.52978	2.35231

Source Authors' results based on the statistical analysis

Table 2 Pearson correlation coefficients

	R&D	Intangibles	MV	Size	RDS	INTANGA	ROA	ROE
R&D	1							
Intangibles	0.817[**]	1						
	0.000							
MV	0.609[**]	0.381[**]	1					
	0.000	0.000						
Size	0.572[**]	0.498[**]	0.368[**]	1				
	0.000	0.000	0.000					
RDS	−0.016	−0.27	−0.045	−0.068[*]	1			
	0.640	0.435	0.186	0.047				
INTANGA	−0.145[**]	0.005	−0.029	−0.166[**]	0.114[**]	1		
	0.000	0.833	0.229	0.000	0.001			
ROA	0.032	0.053[*]	0.051[*]	0.197[**]	−0.477[**]	−0.229[**]	1	
	0.355	0.027	0.031	0.000	0.000	0.000		
ROE	0.021	0.017	0.023	0.096[**]	−0.238[**]	−0.066[**]	0.083[**]	1
	0.532	0.478	0.323	0.000	0.000	0.006	0.000	

Source Authors' results based on the statistical analysis. **Correlation is significant at the 0.01 level (2-tailed). *Correlation is significant at the 0.05 level (2-tailed)

company size, the return on assets (ROA) and the return on equity (ROE). On the other hand, the variable of intangible assets is positively and significantly related to the R&D expenses, the market value of the company, the size of the company and the ROA.

4.1 Effect of Innovation (by R&D and Intangibles) on Firm Value

We reported in Table 3 only the empirical results of the OLS regression analyses of those models that had the best explanatory power, regarding the influence of the variable R&D expenses in two forms, as is (R&D) and as a ratio of R&D to sales (RDS) and the influence of intangible assets, along with the other explanatory variable (size) on the company's market value (MV). We checked for autocorrelation, and in all reported models, we have positive autocorrelation since the Durbin and Watson (DW) statistic is less than 2.

Regarding the independent variable R&D expenses for the whole examined period, the results in Table 3, model 1 indicates that the coefficient of the explanatory variable R&D is statistically significant and positive (beta coefficient = 5.199 and t-test = 14.496). This implies that the R&D expenditures affect significantly and positively the market value of the information technology firms in Europe. This

Table 3 Regression analysis for innovation effect on market value

Models dependent: MV Independent variables	Beta coef	t-test	Sign	R^2	D–W
1. Constant	−1.319E+11			0.413	0.524
R&D	5.199*	14.496	0.000		
Size	7,487,950,418*	7.818	0.000		
2. Constant	−2.814E+11			0.267	0.468
RDS	−1,567E+9	−0.345	0.730		
Size	1.541E+10*	17.515	0.000		
3. Constant	−1.491E+11			0.188	0.325
Intangible assets	9.189*	10.396	0.000		
Size	8,465,267,114*	9.460	0.000		

Source Authors' results based on the statistical analysis
*Statistical significance at the 1% level
**Statistical significance at the 5% level
***Statistical significance at the 10% level

result is consistent with our first hypothesis and the studies of Johnson and Pazderka (1993), Abrahams and Sidhu (1998), Ho et al. (2005), Harhoff (2006) and VanderPal (2015). Model 2 depicts the effect of the R&D expenses to sales ratio (RDS) on the firm value. This effect is negative but not significant statistically (beta coefficient = −1.567E+9 and t-test = −0.345), so we rely on model 1 for the examination of our first hypothesis.

Regarding the independent variable intangible assets for the whole examined period, the results in Table 3, model 3 indicates that the coefficient of the explanatory variable intangible assets is statistically significant and positive (beta coefficient = 9.189 and t-test = 10.396). This implies that intangible assets affect significantly and positively the market value of the information technology firms in Europe supporting our first hypothesis. The control variable size is significant and positively related to the market value of the company in any of the three models, supporting our third hypothesis and consistent to Lin and Chen (2005). The implication of this result is that large companies have more advantages for technological innovation, since they have better access to more sources of financing to support these investments. More innovation in products and services can lead the underlying company to better competitive advantages and more market share, hence more sales, more revenues and higher growth potential. All these lead to higher market value.

Table 4 Regression analysis for innovation effect on performance—ROA

Models dependent: ROA Independent variables	Beta coef	t-test	Sign	R^2	D–W
1. Constant	−0.465			0.042	0.973
R&D	−0.3962E−12*	−2.654	0.008		
Size	0.024*	5.994	0.000		
2. Constant	−0.242			0.267	0.468
RDS	-0.234*	-15.630	0.000		
Size	0.015*	5.087	0.000		
3. Constant	−0.709			0.127	0.911
Intangible assets	−1.174E−11	−3.763*	0.000		
Size	0.036	11.542*	0.000		
4. Constant	−0.480			0.103	0.940
IntangA	−0.368	−8.207*	0.000		
Size	0.027	9.803*	0.000		

Source Authors' results based on the statistical analysis
*Statistical significance at the 1% level
**Statistical significance at the 5% level
***Statistical significance at the 10% level

Table 5 Regression analysis for innovation effect on performance—ROE

Models dependent: ROE Independent variables	Beta coef	t-test	Sign	R^2	D–W
1. Constant	−1.160			0.042	0.973
R&D	−9.456E−12***	−1.710	0.088		
Size	0.057*	3.892	0.000		
2. Constant	−0.692			0.068	1.772
RDS	−0.424*	−6.937	0.000		
Size	0.037*	3.164	0.002		
3. Constant	−5.744			0.117	1.947
Intangible assets	−1.027E−1	−1.767***	0.077		
Size	0.282	4.789*	0.000		
4. Constant	−4.2210			0.119	1.949
IntangA	−1.728	−2.040**	0.041		
Size	0.213	4.109*	0.000		

Source Authors' results based on the statistical analysis
*Statistical significance at the 1% level
**Statistical significance at the 5% level
***Statistical significance at the 10% level

4.2 Effect of Innovation (by R&D and Intangibles) on Firm Performance

Tables 4 and 5 depict only the empirical results of the OLS regression analyses of those models that had the best explanatory power, regarding the influence of the variable R&D expenses in two forms, as is (R&D) and as a ratio of R&D to sales (RDS) and the influence of intangible assets, along with the explanatory variable size on the company's performance, measured by the return on assets (ROA) and the return on equity (ROE) respectively. We checked for autocorrelation, and in some reported models, we have positive autocorrelation since the Durbin and Watson (DW) statistic is less than 2.

Regarding the independent variable R&D expenses for the whole examined period, the results in Table 4, model 1 indicates that the coefficient of the explanatory variable R&D is statistically and significantly negative (beta coefficient $= -0.3962E-12$ and t-test $= -2.654$). The same relation is observed in model 2 where we have the ratio of R&D expenses to sales (beta coefficient $= -0.234$ and t-test $= -15.630$) as independent variable. This implies that the R&D expenditures affect significantly and negatively the performance as measured by the profitability ratio ROA of the information technology firms in Europe. This result is inconsistent with our second hypothesis and the studies of Sher and Yang (2005), Ozdemir et al. (2012), Beld (2014), VanderPal (2015), Warusawitharana (2015) and Jaisinghani (2016). However, this negative relation is reported also by Dimitropoulos (2020) for Greek listed firms whereby R&D investments and expenses affected negatively the sample firms' profitability before the economic crisis of 2010.

Regarding the independent variable intangible assets for the whole examined period, the results in Table 4, models 3 and 4 indicate that the coefficient of the explanatory variable intangible assets is statistically and significantly negative (beta coefficient $= -1.174E-11$ and t-test $= -3.763$) in model 3 and (beta coefficient $= -0.368$ and t-test $= -8.207$) in model 4. This implies that the intangible assets affect significantly and negatively the performance as measured by the profitability ratio ROA of the information technology firms in Europe, rejecting our second hypothesis.

The control variable size is significant and positively related to the performance of the company as measured by the return on assets ratio (ROA) in any of the 4 models, supporting the third hypothesis. The implication of this result as we stated above is that large companies have more advantages for technological innovation, since they have better access to more sources of financing to support these investments. More innovation in products and services can lead the underlying company to better competitive advantages and more market share, hence more sales, more revenues and higher growth potential. All these lead to better performance.

Table 5 reports the effect of innovation on the return on equity, ROE and performance measure. Regarding the independent variable R&D expenses for the whole examined period, the results in model 1 indicate that the coefficient of the explanatory variable R&D is statistically significant and negative (beta coefficient $= -9.456E-12$ and t-test $= -1.710$). The same relation is observed in model 2 where we have the ratio of R&D expenses to sales (beta coefficient $= -0.424$ and t-test $= -6.937$). This implies that the R&D expenditures affect significantly and negatively the performance as measured by the profitability ratio ROE of the information technology firms in Europe. This result is inconsistent with our second hypothesis and the studies of Sher and Yang (2005), Ozdemir et al. (2012) and Beld (2014). However, our result is consistent with VanderPal (2015) who found a negative relation of R&D and performance measured by the ROE for US companies.

Regarding the independent variable intangible assets for the whole examined period, the results in Table 5, models 3 and 4 indicate that the coefficient of the explanatory variable intangible assets is statistically and significantly negative (beta coefficient $= -1.027\mathrm{E}-1$ and t-test $= -1.767$) in model 3 and (beta coefficient $= -1.728$ and t-test $= -2.040$) in model 4. This implies that the intangible assets affect significantly and negatively the performance as measured by the profitability ratio ROE of the information technology firms in Europe, but not so strong as in the case of the ROA performance measure, rejecting also our second hypothesis. The control variable size is significant and positively related to the performance of the company in any of the 4 models, supporting the third hypothesis as we have explained above.

In general, the proxy variables for innovation (R&D expenses and intangible assets) both have a negative impact on firm performance for the information technology companies in Europe, as measured by the ROA and the ROE ratios in contrast to our second hypothesis. This result implies that the higher the R&D expenses or the investment in intangible assets, the lower is the firm's profitability for this sector. One explanation could be the fact that the level of R&D expenses exceeds the optimal level for the companies of this sector and that is why it has a negative impact on profitability. Furthermore, R&D investments in the information technology sector have higher risk because these companies have to do continuous, extensive and rigorous research to achieve uniqueness in their products and services and gain market share, but not all research projects can result in marketable products. Hence, this higher risk involved, especially in the information technology sector, could dominate future benefits, and it has to be compensated by the investors by higher required returns, which are translated into higher costs for the underlying company. So, more investments in R&D mean higher costs which lead to lower profitability, hence the negative relation we found between the investment in innovation and company performance.

5   Conclusions

This study focuses on information technology firms in Europe to explore the innovation effects on firm value. The paper found a positive relation between the innovative investments as proxied by the research and development expenses and the intangible assets with the firm's value. However, regarding the company performance as measured by the ROA and ROE, our results rejected our hypothesis since we found a negative relation between the innovation variables and the profitability ratios as performance variables. One explanation could be the fact that the level of R&D expenses exceeds the optimal level for the companies of this sector and that is why it has a negative impact on profitability. Another explanation could be the higher risk involved in this sector's R&D and innovation investments which leads to higher costs and decreases the profits.

Future research could concentrate on the relation between the number of patents granted as another innovation proxy and the R&D expenditures to investigate whether the number of granted patents improves the R&D performance of a company, and the company's performance in general. It could examine also for all European companies the hypotheses tested in the present paper that focused only on the information technology (IT) firms and investigate whether there are any differences among the various industries regarding these issues, as the more recent literature suggests based on Vrontis and Christofi (2019) and Boiko (2021). The same hypotheses can also be examined for other developed and developing countries to get more insights for academicians, investors and policymakers about the significance of innovation in the company's survival and growth and the factors affecting it, since innovation is important for companies in terms of strategic, organizational, behavioral, knowledge, legal, economic and business perspectives.

References

Abrahams, Tony and Sidhu, Baljit K. (1998). The Role of R&D Capitalisations in Firm Valuation and Performance Measurement. *Australian Journal of Management,* 23(2), 169–183. The University of New South Wales.

Almeida, Carlos Alano Soares de , Corso, Jansen Maia Del, Rocha, Leonardo Andrade, Silva, Wesley Vieira da and Veiga, Claudimar Pereira da. (2019). Innovation and Performance: The Impact of Investments in R&D According to the Different Levels of Productivity of Firms. *International Journal of Innovation and Technology Management, 16(5),* https://doi.org/10.1142/S02198770 19500366

Asimakopoulos, I., Samitas, A., and Papadogonas, T. (2009). Firm-specific and Economy Wide Determinants of Firm Profitability: Greek Evidence Using Panel Data. *Managerial Fina*nce, 35(11), 930–939.

Beld, B. (2014). The Effects of R&D Investment on Firm Performance. *4th IBA Conference , University of Twente, Enschede, the Netherlands*, p 9.

Boiko, K. (2021). R&D activity and firm performance: mapping the field. *Management Review Quarterly,* https://doi.org/10.1007/s11301-021-00220-1

Bolek, Monika and Lyroudi, Katerina. (2017). Do Intangibles Influence the Market Rate of Return? Panel Data Analysis of the NewConnect Market in Warsaw. *European Scientific Journal,* 13(1), 12–28.

Bouaziz, Zied (2016). The Impact of R&D Expenses on Firm Performance: Empirical Witness from the Bist Technology Index. Journal of Business Theory and Practice 4(1):51, https://doi.org/10.22158/jbtp.v4n1p51

Chen, Tsung-chun, Guo, Dong-Qiang, Chen, Hsiao-Min and Wei, Tzu-ti. (2019). Effects of R&D intensity on firm performance in Taiwan's semiconductor industry. *Economic Research-Ekonomska Istraživanja, 32(1),* 2377-2392 . https://doi.org/10.1080/1331677X.2019.1642776

Cho, H. J., & Pucik, V. (2005). Relationship Between Innovativeness, Quality, Growth, Profitability, and Market Value. *Strategic Management Journal,* 26(6), 555–575.

Dang, Chongyu, Li, Zhichuan (Frank) and Yang, Chen. (2017). Measuring Firm Size in Empirical Corporate Finance. Journal of Banking & Finance, 59p. Forthcoming, Available at SSRN: https://ssrn.com/abstract=2345506 or https://doi.org/10.2139/ssrn.2345506. https://doi.org/10.2139/ssrn.2345506

De Meyer, A. and Garg, S. (2006). What is Different About Innovation in Asia? *Economic and Management Perspectives on Intellectual Property Rights,* ed. PALGRAVE MACMILLAN, NY, USA, ch 7, 151–170.

Dimitropoulos, Panagiotis E. (2020). R &D investments and profitability during the crisis: evidence from Greece. *R&D Management,* 50(5), 587–598. https://doi.org/10.1111/radm.12424

Frank, M.Z. and Goyal, V.K.. (2003). Testing the pecking order theory of capital structure. *Journal of Financial Economics,* 67(2), 217–248.

Frascati Manual (2002), OECD.

Gabaix, X., Landier, A. and Sauvagnat, J. (2014). CEO pay and firm size: An update after the crisis. *The Economic Journal,* 124(574), 40–59.

Greenhalgh, Chr. and Rogers, M., (2006). EPO Patents and a Low Level of Competition Improve Market Valuation, *Economic and Management Perspectives on Intellectual Property Rights,* ed. PALGRAVE MACMILLAN, NY, USA, ch 2, 40–57.

Griliches, Zvi (1984). a chapter in *R&D, Patents, and Productivity,* pp 1–20 from National Bureau of Economic Research, Inc.

Griliches, Z. and Mairesse, J. (1984). Output and R&D at the firm level. *R&D, Patent and Output,* 339–374, University of Chicago Press.

Guo, B., Wang, J. & Wei, S.X. R&D spending, strategic position and firm performance. *Front. Bus. Res. China* 12, 14 (2018). https://doi.org/10.1186/s11782-018-0037-7

Hall, Bronwyn H., Mairesse, Jacques and Mohnen, Pierre. (2009). Measuring The Returns To R&D. *Working Paper 15622, NATIONAL BUREAU OF ECONOMIC RESEARCH 1050 Massachusetts Avenue Cambridge, MA 02138,* https://www.nber.org/system/files/working_papers/w15622/w15622.pdf

Harhoff, Dietmar. (2006). The Battle for Patent Rights. *Economic and Management Perspectives on Intellectual Property Rights,* ed. PALGRAVE MACMILLAN, NY, USA, ch 1, 21–39.

Ho, Yew Kee, Keh, Hean Tat and Ong, Jin Mei. (2005). The Effects of R&D and Advertising on Firm Value: An Examination of Manufacturing and Nonmanufacturing Firms. *IEEE Transactions on Engineering Management,* 52(1), 3–14.

Jaisinghani, Dinesh. (2016). Impact of R&D on profitability in the pharma sector: an empirical study from India. *Journal of Asia Business Studies,* 10(2), 194–210. https://doi.org/10.1108/JABS-03-2015-0031

Johnson, Lewis D. and Pazderka, Bohumir. (1993). Firm value and investment in R&D. *Managerial and Decision Economics,* 14(1), 15–24.

Jose Manuel L., Lancaster Carol, Stevens J.L. (1996). Corporate Returns and Cash Conversion Cycles. *Journal of Economics and Finance,* 20(1), 35–48.

Klapper, Leora F. & Love, Inessa. (2004). Corporate governance, investor protection, and performance in emerging markets. *Journal of Corporate Finance,* 10(5), 703–728. Elsevier.

Kumar, S., & Warne, D. (2009). Parametric Determinants of Price-Earnings Ratio in Indian Capital Markets. *The IUP Journal of Applied Finance,* 15(9), 63–82.

Lee, J. (2009). Does Size Matter in Firm Performance? Evidence from US Public Firms. *International Journal of the Economics of Business,* 16(2), 189–203.

Lev, B. and Sougiannis, T. (1996). The capitalization, amortization, and value - relevance of R & D. *Journal of Accounting and Economics,* 21(1), 107–138. https://doi.org/10.1016/0165-4101(95)00410-6

Lin, B-W. and Chen, J-S. (2005). Corporate technology portfolios and R&D performance measures: a study of technology intensive firms. *R&D Management* 35(2), 157–170. https://doi.org/10.1111/j.1467-9310.2005.00380.x

Mairesse, J. and Hall, B. H. (1996). Estimating the productivity of research and development in France and united states manufacturing firms: An exploration of simultaneity issues with

GMM, In Wagner K., and B. van Ark, eds., *International Productivity Comparisons (Amsterdam, North-Holland)*, 285–315.

Mairesse, Jacques and Siu. Alan K. (1984). An Extended Accelerator Model of R&D and Physical Investment. *R&D, Patents and Productivity*, edited by Zvi Griliches. Chicago: Univeristy of Chicago Press.

Mairesse, J. and Hall, B.H. (1996) "Estimating the Productivity of Research and Development: An Exploration of GMM Methods Using Data on French & United States Manufacturing Firms*", No 5501, NBER Working Papers from National Bureau of Economic Research, Inc* Published as *International Productivity Differences, Measurement and Explanations,* van Ark, Bart and Karin Wagner, eds., Amsterdam: Elsevier Science, 1996. Published as *"Le productivite de le recherche et developpement des entreprisesindutrielles aux Etats-Unis et en France: une exploration des biasessimultaneite par le methode des moments generalises," Economie et Prevision*, no. 126 (1996). https://www.nber.org/system/files/working_papers/w5501/w5501.pdf

Mauboussin, M.J. and Kawaja, S. G. (1999). Atoms, Bits and Cash. *Credit Suisse First Boston Corporation Report,* 1–29.

Moeller, S.B., Schlingemann, F.P. and Stulz, R.M. (2004). Firm size and the gains from acquisitions. *Journal of Financial Economics*, 73(2), 201–228.

Ozdemir, H., Karan, M., Arslan-Ayaydin, O. And Ulucan, A. (2012). How is the Firm Performance Related with R & D Innovations?. *Presentation at the 2012 Multinational Finance Society 19th Annual Conference, June 24th-27th 2012*, in Kracow, Poland, p. 12.

Rajan, R.G. and Zingales, L.. (1995). What do we know about capital structure? Some evidence from international data. *The Journal of Finance*, 50(5), pp.1421–1460.

Richard, L.C. Lewis, P. F. and Michael, J.S. (1991). Factors Affecting Price Earnings Ratios and Market Values of Japaneses Firms. *Financial Management*, 20(4), 68–79.

Schimke, A., Brenner, T. (2014). The role of R&D investments in highly R&D-based firms. *Studies in Economics and Finance*, 31:3–45

Sher, J. Peter and Yang, Phil. (2005). The Effects of Innovative Capabilities and R&D Clustering on Firm Performance: the Evidence of Taiwan's Semiconductor Industry. *Technovation,* 25(1), 33-43. https://doi.org/10.1016/S0166-4972(03)00068-3

Shubita, F., and Alsawalhah, M. (2012). The Relationship between Capital Structure and Profitability. *International Journal of Business and Social Science*, 3(16), 104–112.

Tung, Le Thanh and Binh, Quan Minh Quoc. (2021). The impact of R&D expenditure on firm performance in emerging markets: evidence from the Vietnamese listed companies. *Asian Journal of Technology Innovation*.https://doi.org/10.1080/19761597.2021.1897470

VanderPal, Geoffrey A. (2015). Impact of R&D Expenses and Corporate Financial Performance. *Journal of Accounting and Finance,* 15(7), 135–149.

Vijh, A.M. and Yang, K. (2013). Are small firms less vulnerable to overpriced stock offers? *Journal of Financial Economics,* 110(1), 61–86.

Vrontis D., Christofi, M. (2019). R&D internationalization and innovation: a systematic review, integrative framework and future research directions. *Journal of Business Research,* https://doi.org/10.1016/j.jbusres.2019.03.031

Wang, Yu, Wang, Tie-nan and Li, Xin (2017). Does R&D create additional business value through IT?. *Chinese Management Studies,* 11(2), 194-208.https://doi.org/10.1108/CMS-04-2016-0084

Warusawitharana, Missaka, (2015). Research and development, profits, and firm value: A structural estimation. *Quantitative Economics*, 6(2), 531–565.

Xu,Jian, Sim, Jae-Woo and Jin, Zhenji (2016), Research on the Impact of R&D Investment on Firm Performance and Enterprise Value Based on Multiple Linear Regression Model and Data Mining, International Journal of Database Theory and Application, vol. 9 (11):305–316, https://doi.org/10.14257/ijdta.2016.9.11.27

Yang KP, Chiao YC, Kuo CC. (2010). The relationship between R&D investment and firm profitability under a three-stage sigmoid curve model: evidence from an emerging economy. *IEEE Transactions on Engineering Management,* 57(1), 103–117.https://doi.org/10.1109/TEM.2009. 2023452

Zhu, Z., Huang, F. (2012). The effect of R&D investment on firms' financial performance: evidence from the Chinese listed IT firms. *Modern Economy,* 3(8), 915–919.

Business Growth and Development
in Southeastern Europe

Investigating Financial Challenges Facing Enterprises: Evidence from Albania

Ermira H. Kalaj

Abstract This paper focuses on the analyses of financial obstacles facing small and medium enterprises in Albania. Using data from 2019 Enterprise Surveys (ES) we try to give answers to questions related to financial patterns that characterise Albanian enterprises. The survey was a shared project of the European Bank for Reconstruction and Development (EBRD), the European Investment Bank (EIB), and the World Bank Group (WBG), the data are collected in Albania between January and May 2019. The objective of the survey is to better understand firms experience in the private sector. Collected data are based on firms' experiences and perception of the environment in which they operate. The data are stratified in three levels for Albania: industry, enterprise size, and region. The stratification according to the industry was completed as follows: Manufacturing—combining all the relevant activities, Retail, and Other Services. Moreover, 2019 Albanian ES was based on the following size stratification: small (5–19 employees), medium (20–99 employees), and large (100 or more employees). Regional stratification was done across three regions: Northern Albania comprising Dibër, Durrës, Kukës, Lezhë, Shkodër, Central Albania comprising Tirana and Elbasan, and Southern Albania comprising Berat, Fier, Gjirokastër, Korçë, and Vlorë. To analyse financial obstacles and factors affecting on them we estimate the Ordered Probit model where the dependent variable corresponds to the survey question: "How much of an obstacle: access to finance?". Whilst the vector of independent variables is composed by enterprise characteristics such as firm size, ownership structure, legal status, region, etc. Moreover, dummy variables are used to capture firm's technological capability, and gender ownership. Empirical results show that financial obstacles tend to be more significant for smaller enterprises, operating not in the central area of the country, and female ownership means more challenges in the financial markets. Additionally, lack of financial challenges has a steadily constructive impact on the productivity of SME-s.

Keywords Financial access · Firm behaviour · Ordered probit

E. H. Kalaj (✉)
University of Shkodra "Luigj Gurakuqi", Shkodër, Albania
e-mail: ermira.kalaj@unishk.edu.al

© The Author(s), under exclusive license to Springer Nature Switzerland AG 2022
P. Sklias et al. (eds.), *Business Development and Economic Governance in Southeastern Europe*, Springer Proceedings in Business and Economics,
https://doi.org/10.1007/978-3-031-05351-1_14

JEL Classification G51 · D21 · C31

1   Introduction

The study of enterprise financing represents a topic of great interest both for policy makers and researchers. External financing is important to enterprises because of its contribution in the formation of new businesses, and allows existing businesses in expansion of operations, innovation, and new staff. The tactical use of financial instruments, such as loans and investments, is important to the success of enterprises.

According to the theory, enterprise operation can be hindered by many factors, including lack of finance, corruption, and legal instability. However, one of the most important obstacles to enterprise growth in developing countries seems to be the lack to access to finance. Therefore, it is substantial to further investigate on financial obstacles and factors that contribute to these challenges faced by Albanian enterprises (Becchetti and Trovatto 2002; Angelini and Generale 2005; Baumol 2010).

The economy of Albania has experienced some important structural changes over the last decade. Internal migration led to a shift from agriculture towards industry and service sector, contributing enterprises development in different economic sectors. Small and Medium enterprises account for about 70% of formal, non-agricultural employment in the private sector (OECD 2019). Regardless of this shift, agriculture remains one of the largest and most important sectors in Albania. Albania's enterprises face several challenges such as poor infrastructure, market limitations, and limited access to credit and grants which delay faster development of enterprises.

The purpose of this article is to explore the obstacles and challenges facing Albanian enterprises. The literature review regarding the main topics is summarized in the Sect. 2 of the article. Section 3 presents the methodology and the data base used in the study. In Sect. 4 empirical results are reflected and the Sect. 5 discusses the findings.

2   Literature Review

There is a large body of empirical literature on the microeconomic analyses on financial obstacles of enterprises. According to Hashi (2001) the growth of small and medium enterprises in Albania has been disadvantaged by a variety of barriers created, directly or indirectly, by the state. Fiscal restrictions particularly high rate of taxes and contributions, financial constraints and the institutional environment have been some of the major barriers. These barriers have encouraged many enterprises to conduct some or all their activities in the informal sector of the economy.

The analysis of Xheneti and Bartlett (2012) offers important insights of the environment of entrepreneurship in a post-communist context. Apart from the firm's characteristics inadequate information, and corruption, explain the discrepancy in enterprises growth. Older entrepreneurs grow faster indicating unsatisfied aspirations during communism as well as their access to wider professional, social, and possibly also political connections. The positive effect of corruption on firm's growth suggests that an ability to handle with a corrupt environment has been a necessary entrepreneurial skill during a period of chaotic social and institutional changes that have characterized transition in Albania.

Using a firm level survey database involving 54 different countries, Thorsten et al. (2005) investigate the influence of financial, legal, and corruption problems on firms' growth rates. The authors analyse if these factors hinder growth depends on firm size. It is consistently the smallest firms that are most constrained. Financial and institutional development undermines the constraining effects of financial, legal, and corruption obstacles and it is again the small firms that benefit the most. They found a weak relation between firms' perception of the quality of the courts in their country and firm growth. They also give evidence that the corruption of bank officials hinders firm growth.

Thorsten et al. (2008) investigate how financial and institutional development affects financing of large and small firms, using a database covering 48 countries. Their database covers a variety of financing sources, including leasing, supplier, development, and informal finance. According to the empirical results small firms and firms in countries with poor institutions use less external finance, in particular bank finance. Moreover, small firms do not use excessively more leasing, or trade finance compared with larger firms, so these financing sources do not compensate for lower access to bank financing of small firms. They also find that larger firms more easily expand external financing when they are constrained than small firms.

Using data for 34,342 firms from 90 developing countries, the study of Asiedu et al. (2013) evaluates the determinants of firms' financing constraints and appraises whether female-owned firms are more financially constrained than male-owned firms. Their study focuses to gender as a determinant of access to finance. The results show that female-owned firms in Sub-Saharan Africa are more likely to be financially constrained than male-owned firms, but there is no gender gap in other developing regions.

Moscalu et al. (2020), using the data on SMEs' access to finance aggregated at the country level for the largest 11 euro area countries during 2009–2015. The data are taken from the European Central Bank/Survey on the Access to Finance of Enterprises (ECB/SAFE). The results suggest that financing constraints hamper SMEs' growth and that the effect is stronger for perceived, rather than actual, financing constraints. They also found that the reduction in financing constraints is crucial in the transmission channel from banking markets integration to growth.

Analysing survey data and qualitative evidence from a sample of Albanian manufacturing firms (Kalaj 2015) examines the scale and consequences of corruption and tax evasion at the enterprise level, discussing costs and benefits from an entrepreneur's perspective. The empirical results show that manufacturing firms operating in an environment in which tax evasion is more prevalent are more likely to experience demands for bribes from corrupt officials. Regression analysis shows that tax evasion is a matter of degree and that it is not limited to small and medium-sized enterprises: even quite large firms recognize the hiding part of their sales from the tax authorities. Furthermore, the data predict that corruption and tax evasion are more likely to occur when the principal owner is male rather than female.

Since financial constraints to enterprises have important implication for economic and social development of Albania, our study will investigate financial obstacles facing small and medium enterprises.

3 Data and Methodology

In this paper we use data from 2019 Enterprise Surveys (ES) and focus on financial patterns that characterize Albanian enterprises. The survey was a shared project of the European Bank for Reconstruction and Development (EBRD), the European Investment Bank (EIB), and the World Bank Group (WBG), the data are collected in Albania between January and May 2019. The objective of the ES is to contribute the understanding of what firms experience in the private sector. Collected data are based on firms' experiences and enterprises' perception of the environment in which they operate.

The data are stratified in three levels for Albania: industry, establishment size, and region. Industry stratification was completed as follows: Manufacturing—combining all the relevant activities, Retail, and Other Services. Moreover, 2019 Albanian ES was based on the following size stratification: small (5–19 employees), medium (20–99 employees), and large (100 or more employees). Regional stratification was done across three regions: Northern Albania comprising Dibër, Durrës, Kukës, Lezhë, Shkodër, Central Albania comprising Tirana and Elbasan, and Southern Albania comprising Berat, Fier, Gjirokastër, Korçë, and Vlorë.

As we can notice from Fig. 1, around 34% of medium size enterprises identify access to finance as a major constraint in their activity. Moreover, exporter enterprises, intended as firms that export 10% or more of their sales seem to identify access to finance as a major constraint. Issues related to access to finance are more evident in the case of manufacturing sector if compared to service sector.

To analyse financial obstacles and factors affecting on them we estimate the Ordered Probit Model where the dependent variable corresponds to the survey question: "How much of an obstacle: access to finance?". The five possible answers are: no obstacles, minor obstacles, moderate obstacles, major obstacles, very severe obstacles. Data on Table 1 show that around 45% face moderate, major, or severe obstacles. Therefore, we evaluate as appropriate using the Ordered Probit Model (Greene 2012). We estimate the following equation:

$$y_i = \beta_1 + \beta_2 X_i + \varepsilon_i \tag{1}$$

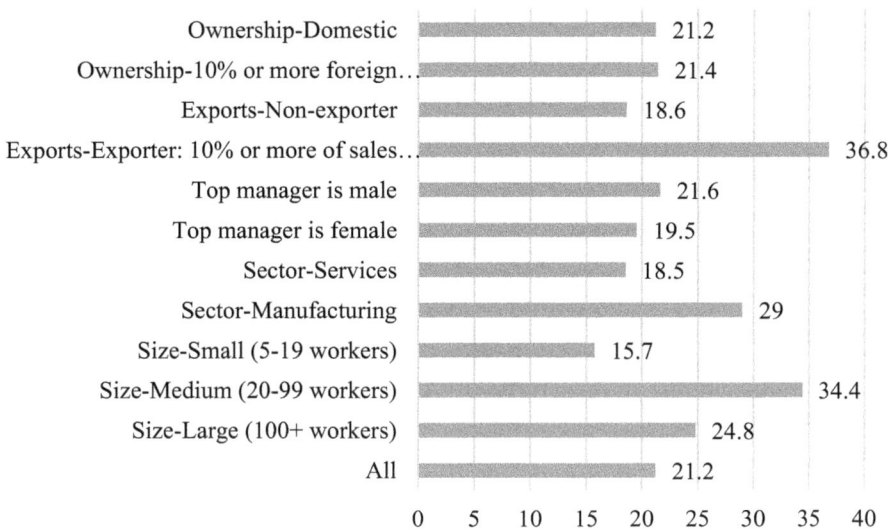

Fig. 1 Percentage of firms identifying access to finance as a major constraint

Table 1 Responses of firms related to access to finance

How much of an obstacle: access to finance	Freq	Percentage	Cum
Don't know (spontaneous)	7	1.86	1.86
No obstacle	121	32.10	33.95
Minor obstacle	80	21.22	55.17
Moderate obstacle	109	28.91	84.08
Major obstacle	36	9.55	93.63
Very severe obstacle	24	6.37	100.00
Total	377	100.00	

where y_i is the measure of financial constraint of firm i which is categorical and takes values from 0 to 4, X_i is a vector of independent variables is composed by enterprise characteristics such as firm size, ownership structure, legal status, region, etc.

Following the study of Asiedu et al. (2013) we use a second measure of financial obstacles which is dichotomous, meaning y_i equals one if a firm responded that access to finance is moderate, major, or very severe obstacles and zero otherwise. Using this dependent variable, we run a Probit Model to further investigate the access to finance patterns.

4 Empirical Results

We begin by estimating Eq. (1) as an Ordered Probit Model. The results about the Ordered Probit Regression are reported in Table 2. We notice that the impact of the

Table 2 Ordered probit regression by region

	North Albania	Central Albania	Southern Albania
How much of an obstacle: Access to finance			
Small	0.192	0.521	0.0164
	(0.68)	(1.78)	(0.06)
Medium	−0.121	0.475	0.288
	(−0.43)	(1.60)	(0.99)
Manufacturing	0.215*	0.282*	0.450
	(2.68)	(2.14)	(1.67)
Service	−0.0343	0.253	0.463
	(−0.12)	(1.07)	(1.65)
Sole proprietorship	−0.702	−0.0406	−0.0936
	(−1.87)	(−0.16)	(−0.32)
Foreign owned	−0.147	−0.257	−0.267
	(−0.44)	(−0.73)	(−0.57)
Exporter	0.0641	0.575*	0.0310
	(0.25)	(2.37)	(0.12)
Female owned	−0.264	0.106	0.0601
	(−0.98)	(0.47)	(0.21)
cut1			
Constant	−0.170	0.300	−0.476
	(−0.53)	(0.97)	(−1.52)
cut2			
Constant	0.297	0.835**	0.309
	(0.94)	(2.66)	(1.00)
cut3			
Constant	0.945**	1.649***	1.592***
	(2.94)	(5.03)	(4.73)
cut4			
Constant	1.649***	2.044***	2.292***
	(4.62)	(6.00)	(6.05)
Observations	118	130	122

t statistics in parentheses
$^*p < 0.05$, $^{**}p < 0.01$, $^{***}p < 0.001$

independent varies by region. The coefficient for small firms is positive for the three regions but not statistically significant. However, this result gives evidence on the fact that small firms are more likely to be financially constraint than medium firms in the northern part of the country.

According to the regression results manufacturing and firms engaged in exports are more likely to face obstacles to finance if compared to service or non-exporting firms. Results are statistically significant. This effect is more significant in magnitude in the central area of the country. This may be related with the fact that most enterprises operate in the central part of the country mainly in the cities of Durrës and Tirana.

Firms that are sole proprietorship and foreign owned are less financially constraint if compared to other firms. However, coefficients are not statistically significant and further investigation is needed. The interesting result is that there is no gender gap in the access to finance. Female ownership does not mean more financial obstacles if compared to men ownership. Sometimes maybe a question of female self-selection in not preferring to use external financial sources.

To check for robustness of the results we run the logit model using the dichotomous dependent variable of financial obstacles. Regression results still hold for the manufacturing and firms engaged in exports.

5 Discussions and Conclusions

In this paper we investigate on the factors affecting enterprises that face financial obstacles. We use Ordered Probit Model for the ordinal dependent variable relying on the survey question: "How much of an obstacle: access to finance?". Manufacturing and exporting firms are more likely to face obstacles to finance if compared to service or non-exporting firms. Results are statistically significant, but the magnitude is higher in the central area of the country. The estimation is still robust when we use Logit Model.

Quite interesting is the lack of gender gap in access to finance. Female ownership does not mean more financial obstacles if compared to men ownership. However, it needs further investigation to capture if self-selection patterns exit.

There are a number of reasons showing that finance promotes growth and firm-level productivity. Financial constrains lead firms to give up on profitable investment opportunities, which may reduce their efficiency.

The present paper contributes to the body of literature related with the role of finance in the efficiency of Albanian enterprises. Paper's contribution remains mainly in investigating this fundamental aspect. We focus on the role of the most important variables. Empirical results may help in policy formulation oriented toward public and private schemes that reduce financial obstacles to enterprises.

References

Angelini, P. & Generale, A., 2005. *Firm Size Distribution: Do Financial Constraints Explain It All?*. Working paper no. 549, Banca D'Italia.

Asiedu, E., Kalonda-Kanyama, I., Ndikumana, L. & Nti-Addae, A., 2013. Access to Credit by Firms in Sub-Saharan Africa: How Relevant Is Gender?. *American Economic Review,* 103(3), pp. 293–97.

Ayyagari, M., Beck, T. & Demirgüç-Kunt., A., 2007. Small and Medium Enterprises across the Globe. *Small Business Economics,* 4(29), pp. 415–34.

Baumol, W. J., 2010. *The Microtheory of Innovative Entrepreneurship.* Princeton: Princeton University Press.

Becchetti, L. & Trovato, G., 2002. The Determinants of Growth of Small and Medium Sized Firms. The Role of the Availability of External Finance. *Small Business Economics,* 4(19), pp. 291–306.

Greene, W. H., 2012. *Econometric Analysis (Seventh ed.).* Boston: Pearson Education.

Hashi, I., 2001. Financial and Institutional Barriers to SME Growth in Albania: Results of an Enterprise Survey.. *Economic Policy in Transitional Economies,* p. 221–238.

Kalaj, E., 2015. Doing Business with Corruption: An Enterprise Empirical Analysis. *SEER: Journal for Labour and Social Affairs in Eastern Europe,* pp. 83–91.

Moscalu, M., Girardone, C. & Calabrese, R., 2020. SME's Growth under Financial Constraints and Banking Markets Integration in the Euro Area. *Journal of Small Business Management,* 4(58), pp. 707–746.

OECD, 2019. *Small Business in Transition Economies,* Paris: OECD.

Thorsten, B., Demirguç-Kunt, A. & Maksimovic, V., 2005. Financial and Legal Constraints to Growth: Does Firm Size Matter?. *Journal of Finance,* 60(I), pp. 137–77.

Thorsten, B., Demirgüç-Kunt, A. & Maksimovic, V., 2008. Financing patterns around the world: Are small firms different?. *Journal of Financial Economics,* 89(3), pp. 467–487.

Xheneti, M. & Bartlett, W., 2012. Institutional constraints and SME growth in post-communist Albania.. *Journal of Small Business and Enterprise Development.,* 19(4), pp. 607–626.

The Recognition and Impact of Dynamic Pricing with ESL Technology on the Purchase Decision of Consumers in Stationary Grocery Stores: Current Findings and Experiment

Marian Mair, Thomas Dilger, Christian Ploder, and Reinhard Bernsteiner

Abstract The basic concept of dynamic pricing (DP) has been around for a long time (e.g., gas station prices). To maximize profit, it is now commonly known as an algorithm-based automatic price adjustment tool on eCommerce platforms (e.g., flight tickets or hotel prices). DP is based on time or demand through the invention and implementation of the electronic shelf label (ESL) technology in stationary retail. It creates new opportunities for the physical contribution channel. This potential is also the focus of this study by precisely dealing with the recognition and impact of DP with ESL technology on consumers' purchasing decisions in stationary grocery stores. Our literature review includes current research on DP, ESL technology, price behavior, and price fairness. According to the first review, no single experiment on ESLs combined with DP in stationary grocery stores, and only a few general studies on ESLs exist. Thus, an experimental design is proposed to research customers' post-purchase reaction/acceptance of ESLs in stationary grocery stores and customers' recognition and perception (perceived price fairness) of DP adjustment strategies. Participants purchase twice an ethnically defined shopping cart in a supermarket by applying ESLs, whereby the second time, the prices of several products from the shopping list are slightly increased. The goal of the between-participants post-test-only control-group experiment design is to identify the technology's potential for stationary grocery stores. Equity theory deals with price fairness and is used as the primary consumer behavior model for price adjustments. The results depict a design for experimental research on DP with ESL technology. The system should function as a pre-study and discussion base for further research on this topic. A draft of the experimental setting (instruction sheets, evaluation plan, digitally designed survey) is already provided as a basis for further improvements. With the proposed execution plan, third parties can further test the experiment on feasibility and applicability in the described experimental setting by using technology (virtual reality, augmented reality) or on different industries or other groups.

M. Mair · T. Dilger (✉) · C. Ploder · R. Bernsteiner
MCI-Management Center Innsbruck, 6020 Innsbruck, Austria
e-mail: thomas.dilger@mci.edu

© The Author(s), under exclusive license to Springer Nature Switzerland AG 2022   253
P. Sklias et al. (eds.), *Business Development and Economic Governance in Southeastern Europe*, Springer Proceedings in Business and Economics,
https://doi.org/10.1007/978-3-031-05351-1_15

1 Introduction

Dynamic pricing (DP) is generally defined as a planned approach of price strategy by a supplier to dynamically change its individual price targets at any time within the sales process to respond to changes in demand, supply, competition, and other external factors like the weather (Klein and Steinhardt 2008). This price strategy is prevalent by expiring offers like airline flights, hotel rooms, and limited capacity, where the value of a unit in shortage increases. Other popular application areas are retail, electricity (Dütschke and Paetz 2013), or the taxi industry (McAfee and Velde 1978). Due to the development of technology and the focus on online retail, individual price adjustment has gained more attention and importance in recent years. Companies are continually trying to find the optimal pricing policy to generate profit, which requires a precise observation of consumers' pricing behavior. The development of algorithms, in particular, has made it possible to recognize demand changes quickly and adapt prices to the economic circumstances of a company in real-time without high costs and effort. This development also allows a different definition of DP:

> Dynamic pricing is the process of using information-age tools, such as big data and algorithms, to adjust prices based on new information over periods during which output is fixed. (Woodcock 2018)

DP has been researched for more than 25 years (Woodcock 2018). The idea of DP is not new, for example, seasonal pricing of winter jackets and beachwear, adjusted gas prices through rush hours (holiday season), or membership discounts (Ochs et al. 2019). However, its popularity increased significantly in recent years and is supported by a wide range of business communities, such as marketing, computer science, economics, operations research, and management (OR/MS) (Boer 2015).

The method can reach new dimensions and unfulfilled potential (Ochs et al. 2019). Especially since it is possible to collect and process a large amount of customer data (big data), companies can analyze these data to derive the optimal price strategy in real-time (Reinartz et al. 2017). This method can predict the consumers' willingness to pay with relatively little effort (Tillmann and Vogt 2018). For some business models, this type of pricing policy has become indispensable. It is used particularly frequently in eCommerce, but also stationary retail already takes advantage of DP methods in contributing membership cards (Boer 2015), apps, or mobile payment methods (Tillmann and Vogt 2018). In Germany online, around 40% of the retailers use DP as a pricing method, while in stationary retail, only about 12% take this approach. In general, over 65% of the consumers see DP as unfair (Reinartz et al. 2017).

With DP, companies can reach higher margins (profit optimizing) but also risk higher competition. The extent of price differentiation is limited by competition, arbitrage opportunities, customer information, and consumers' perception of fairness (Reinartz et al. 2017). However, one problem that is becoming increasingly apparent is that more and more companies are using DP as a method of pricing policy, as pricing is flexible, individual per product, and uses customer-specific data. As a result, the markets lose transparency, and more customers find themselves in problematic situations, as they pay different amounts for identical goods or services (Tschunko 2015). This approach is now returning to supermarkets using electronic shelf labels (ESLs) to avoid the costs and effort of adjusting prices and the risk of incorrect labeling on the shelves. There is much potential in this new pricing method in stationary retail (Garaus et al. 2016).

This new approach in stationary grocery stores is also the focus of this research. Since this topic is current, the motivation is to review which potential and risks ESLs in combination with DP could have and how consumers will perceive and react to it. By explaining price fairness theory, the goal is to design an experiment that can measure ESL technology's acceptance and applicability. This leads us to the following research question:

> To what extent is an experimental design that researches the consumer perception and recognition of dynamic pricing in combination with ESL technology in stationary retail feasible?

To avoid confusion, it has to be stated that this study, due to the Covid-19 pandemic, has not been carried out yet and is displaying all necessary documents and a detailed execution plan on how to carry out the proposed study.

2   Equity Theory

It is critical to set a theoretical method for consumer-related outcomes to observe how new technologies like DP interact with consumer behavior. Price fairness is still a very young theory, and its theoretical derivation occurs in literature in the dissonance theory, the theory of justice, and the equity theory (Koschate 2002). We have chosen the equity theory for further usage in discussing the experiment because it has its roots in social psychology and deals with the sense of justice in social exchange processes involving two parties, which demonstrates the relationship between buyer and seller (Adams 1965; Homans 1974; Walster, Berscheid, Walster 1978, as cited in Koschate, 11). Price fairness can be defined in this theory as cognition and emotion connected to the perception of price fairness of the consumer toward the price supplier. It is based on expectations and experiences and refers to the whole behavior of the price supplier in the life cycle of a product. For that reason, it can be seen as a part of price satisfaction (Diller 2008). The core questions of the equity theory are twofold: (1) What do individuals perceive as fair? (2) How do individuals react when the social exchange process is perceived as unfair? (Adams 1965; Homans 1974; Walster, Berscheid, Walster 1978, as cited in Koschate, 11).

To better understand the price experience of consumers, Diller (2008) created a three-dimensional classification scheme for price experience, which is displayed in Fig. 1.

The first dimension is the trigger of price experience. It describes which price element (gross/net price, discount, etc.) or price circumstance (price reward, pricing system, etc.) creates the emotion. The second dimension is the direction of price

Fig. 1 A classification
scheme for price experience
own illustration translated of
15

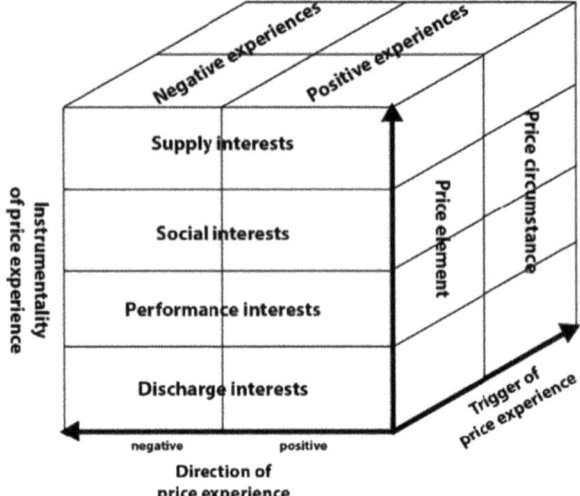

experience, which explains if the feeling is positive (joy, pride, etc.) or negative (anger, disappointment). The last dimension is the instrumentality of price experience, which shows price interests relevant to the price experience. A distinction is made between supply, social, performance, and discharge interests. Considering this scheme, every price experience can be characterized, making it easier for the retailer to understand the price reaction of customers (Diller 2008).

3 Consumer Behavior Toward Dynamic Pricing Methods

More companies are using DP strategies based on their effectiveness. Huckemann and Dinges (1998) show that a percent increase in price raises operating profits by an average of 11.1%, while a one percent reduction in variable costs leads to an average profit increase of only 7.8%. A factor to be taken into account is the perception of consumers. Grewal et al. (2004) study shows that price fairness and trust are closely related, especially if a consumer paid a higher price for the same product, which lowers the price fairness as well as benevolence trust and (re)purchase intentions (Fig. 2). Consumer perception of offering new customers lower prices to increase the customer base decreases trustworthiness toward a company (Grewal et al. 2004; Garbarino and Maxwell 2010).

The three studies from Weisstein et al. (2013) show that price-disadvantaged consumers' negative perception of DP (price fairness, trust, and repurchase intention) can be reduced by using the right price policy.

If consumers perceive the price as unfair, each one can respond differently. The reaction can lead to a change in attitude, an increase in comparative search behavior, hostile (electronic) word-of-mouth, complaints, boycott, and reprisal to revenger non-repurchase, non-purchase, or resistance. The most harmful resistance behavior can

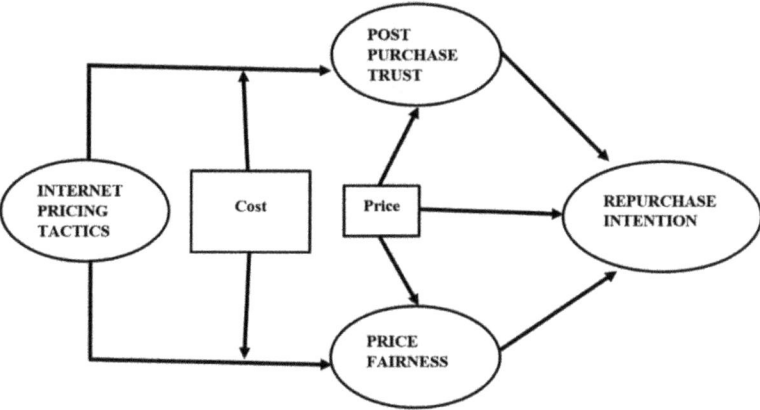

Fig. 2 Relationship between trust, price fairness, and repurchase intention own illustration of 17

be triggered by hurting moral principles, the vendor's behavior that seems ethically unacceptable, or differences between the communicated price and actual price (Ayadi et al. 2017).

4 Dynamic Pricing in Stationary Retail

The topic of electronic shelf labels (ESLs) is relatively new for the scientific world even though the technology has existed since the 1990s (Soutjis et al. 2017). The papers existing about ESLs are explaining the latest technology or superficially researching consumer perception. Additionally, many papers explain ESLs technically as well as showing potential designs on stable and long-lasting frameworks (Suh et al. 2018). However, no papers investigate the consumer acceptance and perception of ESLs and their effects on consumers (Garaus et al. 2016). However, this research focuses on the technology itself and its potential with DP in stationary grocery stores.

4.1 Potential of ESL in the Retail Market

The technology for ESL has been available for a long time, but since the cost for technology dropped and the connection with DP is possible, the trend and growth will be expected soon. A report of the PR Newswire (Newswire 2019a, b) expected a CAGR (compound annual growth rate) of around 25% or $2 billion by 2024 in the Europe ESL market and the industry research estimates a growth of over 15% (Research and Market 2017). The reason is the decrease in technology costs and the improvement in displays, which makes it look like the numbers and letters are printed with ink. Additionally, the "click and collect" trends significantly switch to ESLs in stationary retail (Newswire 2019b). That ESLs are more in direction also shows REW by equipping 1,500 stores in 2018 (Elsbeck 2018), and Media-Saturn more than 1000 in 2016 (Flier 2016). Other stores, which are planning to digitalize its stores with ESLs are Anhold (Flier 2019a), Lidl, Rossman, Aldi Süd, Bartels-Langness, Bauhaus as well as Fressnapf (Flier 2019b).

4.2   Resistance to ESLs

Technology makes everything more flexible with online shopping and touch screen information, making it more accessible to consumers (Krafft and Mantrala 2010). Consumers in the US also get more sophisticated and knowledgeable because more than 40% of consumers inform themselves about a product before going into the shops. That also results in the need of consumers to get offered more individual goods (Krafft and Mantrala 2010). Other studies argue that a standardized price tag design will reduce the consumers' price sensitivity because it will mute the salience of prices (Soutjis et al. 2017).

DP in retail stores by using ESLs confronts the store as well with the topic of price discrimination. Now a store can charge different prices for different times of the day and price higher through peak consumer frequencies. It is also possible to adjust the price to specific consumer groups (e.g., depending on age) by categorizing them according to the time of visiting the store, which reminds about gas station prices (Krafft and Mantrala 2010). Coca-Cola experimented by pricing its products in vending machines depending on the day, the outside temperature, and the amount of stock in the vending machine. The report in the Wall Street Journal (Hays 1999) of this experiment faced widespread outrage, which led to the company denying the experiment (Hays 1999).

An interview study of 261 supermarket shoppers by Solomon, Deeter-Schmelz (Solomon and Deeter-Schmelz 2015) investigates the consumer's attitude toward new technology in the retail business in the form of ESL. Prior studies focus more on benefits on stores and less on consumer reaction. Prices are for 72% of the consumers a primary concern during the shopping process. The interviews show a positive response from ESLs on the consumer side, mainly because of more accrued retail pricing at the shelf labels and the cashier. Surprisingly, the participants did not think that the price with ESL would rise. Worries on retailers' side are that the technology of ESL is an expensive tool to implement. However, it can be a competitive advantage in the grocery industry, which amortizes in the long run. The limitation of the study is the timing because they only ask people at a new store, and only three aisles were utilized with ESLs. (Solomon and Deeter-Schmelz 2015).

5 Experimental Design

In the grocery retail industry, the trend to eCommerce already exists, whereby the in-store digitalization is not yet very advanced (Theuvsen et al. 2013). We propose an experiment based on the gathered literature by answering the following research question:

> To what extent is an experimental design that researches the consumer perception and recognition of dynamic pricing in combination with ESL technology in stationary retail feasible?

A qualitative field experiment with a between-participants design, in particular, a "between-participants posttest-only control-group design", will be applied. The experiment is designed for 50 participants, which will be randomly divided into two groups. One group gets a treatment ("experimental group") that the other group does not get ("control group") and compares the two groups. That is also called a completely randomized design, which is necessary for achieving equivalence (Fig. 3), especially with a small group of 50 people (Christensen et al. 2014). Additionally to the post-test measurement of the experiment, the participant will take part in a classic survey to expand the research to find out about the perception toward price fairness.

The experiment is built on the three most prominent criteria for evaluating business research—reliability, replication, and validity. This experiment provides reliability, which ensures that quantitative analysis can be repeated and has stable measurements. A field experiment survey design is the best fit to test in-store pricing behavior and provides the internal and external measurement and ecological validity, especially since an actual experiment tends to be very valid in its results (Bryman and Bell 2011).

5.1 Experimental Research Design

The in-store experiment takes place in a restricted area in a physical store, where ESLs are already implemented. Currently, ESLs are already used in retail stores but

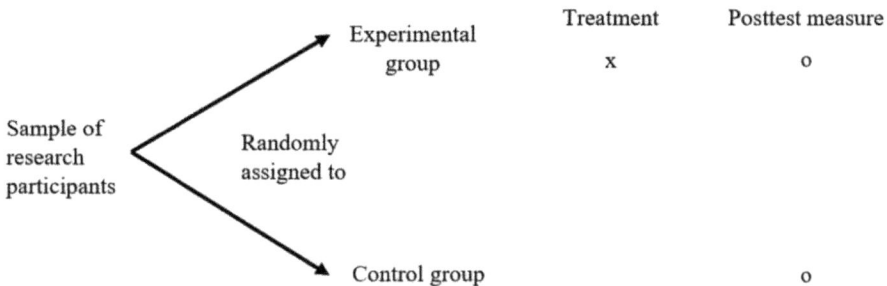

Fig. 3 Between-participants posttest-only control-group design intention own illustration of 33

are not connected to DP algorithms (McKenzie and Taylor 2016). The idea of this experiment is based on an experiment of Coca-Cola, where they changed the prices in vending machines based on demand peaks and the outside temperature (Hays 1999). This basic concept can be transformed into an indoor setting, where prices in grocery stores increase based on demand peaks (time), inventory level, loyal customer status, and product condition (perishable goods). The experiment's goal is to determine their perception of ESLs toward price fairness based on the equity theory and if customers recognize the price change.

5.2 Hypotheses Formation

To answer the research question and set a goal for the experiment, the following hypotheses (Fig. 4) are developed.

The null hypotheses H0, H2, and H3 always assume that there is no significant correlation. The alternative hypotheses H1, H4–H9, marked with a "+", suggest differently. On the one hand, hypotheses are newly created and formulated; on the other hand, cited from existing related literature, which is listed below and illustrated in Table 1.

In addition to the sources already mentioned, the hypotheses were derived by Ratchford (2014), Garbarino and Lee (2003), Haws and Bearden (2006), Morgan and Hunt (1994), Evanschitzky et al. (2007), and Mak et al. (2012) to depict a holistic picture of the hypotheses to be explored. This, in turn, favors a better understanding of the related scientific topics of the experiment. It is not only important to understand how and when a consumer recognizes the price changes, but also the post-purchase reaction in form of perception and behavior.

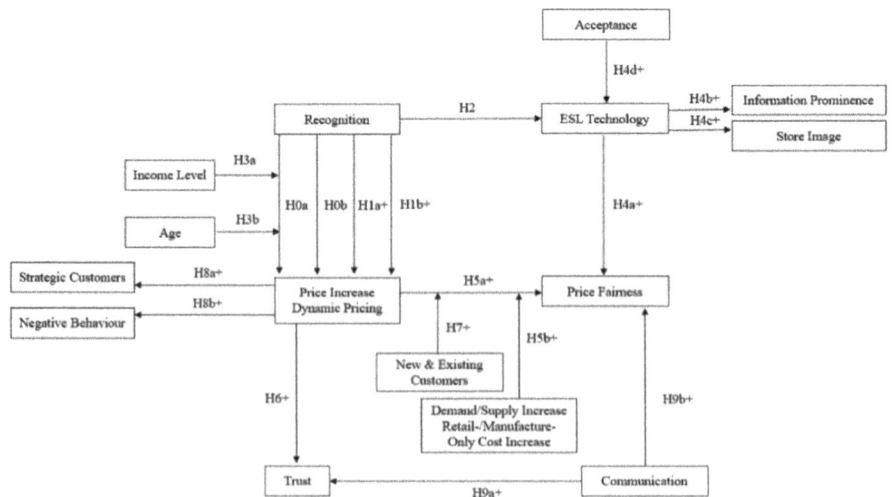

Fig. 4 Context of the hypotheses

Table 1 Hypotheses

Recognition	**H0a** *Customers do not recognize a price change in the overall amount of the shopping cart* **H0b** *Customers cannot identify the products, which were affected by price adjustments* **H1a+** *Minor price changes on products up to 2€ (Change A) are more likely to be recognized than minor price changes on products above 2€ (Changes C)* **H1b+** *Larger price changes on products up to 2€ (Changes B) are more likely to be recognized than lager price changes on products above 2€ (Changes D)* **H2** *The ESL technology is not recognized by the customers* **H3a** *Customers in a higher income level do not recognize price changes because they are less price sensitive* **H3b** *Older customers do not recognize price changes compared to younger customers*
ESL Technology	**H4a+** *ESLs does negatively influence price fairness perceptions* (*Based on* Garaus et al. 2016) **H4b+** *"ESLs enhance price information prominence"* (Garaus et al. 2016, 3689) **H4c+** *"ESLs positively influence store image perceptions"* (Garaus et al. 2016, 3690) **H4d+** *Customers accept ESL technology*
Perception	**H5a+** *The higher the price increase, the lower the perceived price fairness* (*Translated from* Evanschitzky et al. (2007)) **H5b+** *"A price increase given a demand increase, a supply decrease, or a retailer-only cost increase will be perceived as more unfair than a price increase given a channel or manufacturer-only cost increase"* (Ratchford 2014, 346) **H6+** *"Exposure to a dynamic pricing event will reduce mean overall trust"* (Garbarino and Lee 2003, 502) **H7+** *Higher prices paid by existing customers relative to new customers triggers stronger negative price fairness judgements than higher prices paid by new customers relative to existing customers* (*Based on* Haws and Bearden (2006))
Behavior	**H8a+** *Exposure to a dynamic pricing event increases the number of strategic customers* **H8b+** *Exposure to a dynamic pricing event encounters rejection complains, negative word of mouth, search for alternatives, decrease satisfaction, and purchase intention*
Communication	**H9a+** *"There is a positive relationship between communication and trust"* (Morgan and Hunt 1994, 26) **H9b+** *Credible communication has a positive influence on the perceived price fairness* (*Translated from* Evanschitzky et al. (2007)

5.3 Shopping Cart

Table 2 reflects the shopping cart of the experiment in an Austrian grocery store environment and product choices. Therefore, the experiment contains 37 products and goods, which are part of the shopping cart weighted according to the consumer price index (CPI) (Austria 2020). The 37 products include products of daily use, which can be bought in a supermarket, including non-food products like cosmetics. For the experiment, the size of the shopping card is around 75€ (gross) for a two-person household. This price is between two data collections with an average expensive

Table 2 Shopping cart own illustration based on 43 & 44

No	VPI Code	VPI Weight	Product	Unit	Single Price	Amount	Price (gross)
1	000100	0.08960	Pizza Margherita, frozen	1 Piece	3.25 €	2	6.50 €
2	000600	0.17135	Mixed bread	1 kg	2.43 €	0.5	1.22 €
3	001900	0.05150	Rice (long grain)	1 kg	1.19 €	1	1.19 €
4	002000	0.05784	Flour (wheat)	1 kg	0.86 €	1	0.86 €
5	002100	0.09301	Pasta Penne	1 kg	0.80 €	2	1.60 €
6	002600	0.14078	Minced meat, beef	1 kg	6.88 €	0.5	3.44 €
7	003600	0.06346	Pork tenderloin	1 kg	11.07 €	0.5	5.54 €
8	004800	0.10694	Chicken breast meat	1 kg	7.17 €	0.5	3.59 €
9	005661	0.07752	Whole milk	1 L	1.13 €	1	1.13 €
10	006200	0.12901	Fruit yoghurt	1 Piece	0.49 €	4	1.96 €
11	006500	0.20908	Eggs, barn keeping, size M	1 Piece	0.24 €	10	2.40 €
12	006700	0.12381	Gouda (wrapped)	1 kg	6.27 €	0.25	1.57 €
13	007300	0.17973	Tea butter	250 g	2.26 €	1	2.26 €
14	007800	0.05338	Sunflower oil	1 L	2.47 €	1	2.47 €
15	008500	0.13461	Apples	1 kg	1.62 €	0.5	0.81 €
16	009200	0.10628	Bananas	1 Piece	0.39 €	4	1.56 €
17	010700	0.05393	Cucumber	1 Piece	1.05 €	1	1.05 €
18	010800	0.05005	Regional carrots	1 kg	1.62 €	0.5	0.81 €
19	011400	0.15062	Tomatoes	1 kg	1.93 €	1	1.93 €
20	011700	0.05305	Onions	1 kg	1.58 €	0.5	0.79 €
21	011800	0.09940	Potatoes	1 kg	1.34 €	2	2.68 €

(continued)

Table 2 (continued)

No	VPI Code	VPI Weight	Product	Unit	Single Price	Amount	Price (gross)
22	013000	0.03824	Jam	1 kg	2.13 €	0.45	0.96 €
23	013200	0.06362	Fine crystal sugar	1 kg	1.06 €	1	1.06 €
24	014100	0.57700	Vinegar	1 L	1.34 €	1	1.34 €
25	014200	0.07263	Black tea in infusion bag	1 Piece	0.10 €	25	2.50 €
26	014300	0.25906	Bean coffee (ground)	1 kg	4.58 €	0.5	2.29 €
27	014800	0.16298	Mineral water	1 L	0.26 €	6	1.56 €
28	015200	0.14289	Orange juice	1 L	1.18 €	1.5	1.77 €
29	015800	0.26690	White wine, glass bottle, quality wine	1 L	5.32 €	1.5	7.98 €
30	016300	0.33513	Botteld beer (glass)	0.5 L	1.38 €	6	8.28 €
31	047500	0.09177	Dishwashing detergent	1 L	3.80 €	1	3.80 €
32	047900	0.18237	Liquid detergent	1 Washcycle	0.15 €	35	5.25 €
33	099200	0.08150	Hair shampoo	100 ml	0.59 €	2.5	1.48 €
34	100000	0.07408	Toothpaste	75 ml	1.25 €	1	1.25 €
35	100400	0.10763	Showergel	100 ml	0.40 €	10	4.00 €
36	100500	0.07008	Toilet paper	1 Piece	0.26 €	15	3.90 €
37	100600	0.05748	Tissues	100 Pieces	0.50 €	1	0.50 €
					Total Price		93.28 €

Fig. 5 Electronic shelf label design

shopping card of 89.36€ (gross) (Delapina 2020) and an average cheap shopping card of 55.34€ (gross) (Knotzer and Delapina 2018). Additionally, current product trends like sustainability, organic, vegan, or vegetarian products have been considered (Sevelius 2019), making the average cart more expensive. Selecting the 37 products, the statistic by Statista (Statista 2019) was very helpful by showing preference for groceries in Austria.

5.3.1 Price Determination

To determine the price, the highest price in the data collection of Knotzer and Delapina (2018), and Delapina (2020) got compared with average product prices at a local supermarket (shop.mpreis.at) in Innsbruck, Austria. The price is made up of the average of all three price collections. The whole data collection is published in the appendix (Appendix 1). In Table 2, the "Single Price" column shows the average price of the three compared prices. In the experiment and the shopping cart, the product will be displayed without a brand name to avoid prejudices and preferences of brands. To better understand Fig. 5, line 22 will be described in further detail. The "VPI Code" 013000 shows the sequence code of jam, and "VPI Weight" offers the share of jam to the total shopping cart of the CPI by Austria (2020). "Unit" and "Single Price" show that jam costs 2.13€ per kilogram, and the column "Amount" illustrates how many units will be bought of a particular product (0.45 for jam means a glass of 450-g). The "Gross Price" then refers to the column "Amount", which means 450-g jam costs 0.96€.

5.3.2 Ethnic Shopping Cart Refinement for Austria

Austria is very diverse related to religion, migration, and attitude to life. Considering the different ethnic groups in Austria and their bias, the shopping cart will be refined for the experiment. Literature has shown other motives for food taboos/bias

(Meyer-Rochow 2009). Therefore, it will be categorized into four reasons: *religion, addiction, intolerance,* and *attitude toward life.* Statista (2020) shows that the four most prominent religions are Catholic, Orthodox, Muslim, and Evangelical. Muslim is the only religion with existing food taboos on pork, meat, and alcohol (Battour et al. 2011). Alcohol and tobacco are also the two products with the highest *addiction* potential in Austria (Anzenberger et al. 2019; Ecker and Brem 2020). As a result, the shopping cart will be refined by deleting numbers 7 (pork tenderloins), 29 (white wine), and 30 (bottled beer).

Furthermore, the most common food *intolerances* are lactose, histamine, fructose, and gluten (Statista 2014). Since this would reduce the number of products in the shopping cart significantly, the food intolerances are not leading to an elimination of products but to an additional question in the survey to filter them out in the analysis. Therefore, an extra column with food information about allergies has been added (Table 3). The same thing applies to the *attitude of life,* which refers to customers on a vegetarian or vegan diet. Estimated around 750,000 Austrian are vegetarian, and around 80,000 are vegan (Statista 2018). Table 3 shows the refined shopping cart with the deleted products and extra information for food intolerances and life attitudes.

5.4   Determination of Price Adjustments

The idea of the experiment is first to let the participants go through the shop and buy the products for the price specified in Table 3. In the second run, the prices (independent variable) will increase according to different factors, called the treatment. Before that, it is necessary to find out how many products of the shopping cart should receive a price increase, that the participants have the chance to recognize a price adjustment. Therefore, a pre-study would be ideal, where at the beginning, 50% of the products (17) are receiving price changes to see if people recognize the difference. If they do, the experiment needs at least 17 price adjustments to reach a valid result. Otherwise, it has to be more.

To determine between minor and large price changes by lower- and higher-priced products, it is necessary to define two groups with a range. Starting with the price level, looking at the shopping cart, it appears that the prices are low for each unit or package in grocery stores. An analysis of the existing shopping cart of Table 3 shows that 15 products out of 34 are above 2€ for a package or unit (Appendix 2). Therefore 2€ will be the separation between low and high price levels (Table 4). 22 out of the 34 products (65%) will receive a price adjustment for this experimenting about the level of price changes a study by Zelleken and Dellbrügge (2000) shows that price increases up to 5.6%, or those that remain below a price threshold, do not trigger an adverse reaction to the quantity of food sold. Pre-calculation shows that with randomizing percentages, the total cart value only increases by around 4€ if the divider between minor and significant changes is 6% (Appendix 3). The experiment should show a more substantial difference in cart value. Therefore, the percentage

Table 3 Ethnic refined shopping cart own illustration based on 43 & 44

No	VPI Code	VPI Weight	Product	Allergeis and Nutrition	Unit	Single price	Amount	Price (gross)
1	000100	0.08960	Pizza Margherita, frozen	Gluten	1 Piece	3.25 €	2	6.50 €
2	000600	0.17135	Mixed bread	Gluten	1 kg	2.43 €	0.5	1.22 €
3	001900	0.05150	Rice (long grain)		1 kg	1.19 €	1	1.19 €
4	002000	0.05784	Flour (wheat)	Gluten	1 kg	0.86 €	1	0.86 €
5	002100	0.09301	Pasta Penne	Gluten	1 kg	0.80 €	2	1.60 €
6	002600	0.14078	Minced meat, beef	Non-Vegan, Non-Vegetarian	1 kg	6.88 €	0.5	3.44 €
	~~003600~~	~~0.06346~~	~~Pork tenderloin~~	~~Non-Vegan, Non-Vegetarian~~	~~1 kg~~	~~11.07 €~~	~~0.5~~	
7	004800	0.10694	Chicken breast meat	Non-Vegan, Non-Vegetarian	1 kg	7.17 €	0.5	3.59 €
8	005661	0.07752	Whole milk	Non-Vegan, Lactose	1 L	1.13 €	1	1.13 €
9	006200	0.12901	Fruit yoghurt	Non-Vegan, Lactose	1 Piece	0.49 €	4	1.96 €
10	006500	0.20908	Eggs, barn keeping, size M	Non-Vegan, Lactose	1 Piece	0.24 €	10	2.40 €
11	006700	0.12381	Gouda (wrapped)	Non-Vegan, Lactose, Histamine	1 kg	6.27 €	0.25	1.57 €
12	007300	0.17973	Tea butter	Non-Vegan, Lactose	250 g	2.26 €	1	2.26 €
13	007800	0.05338	Sunflower oil		1 L	2.47 €	1	2.47 €
14	008500	0.13461	Apples	Fructose	1 kg	1.62 €	0.5	0.81 €
15	009200	0.10628	Bananas		1 Piece	0.39 €	4	1.56 €
16	010,700	0.05393	Cucumber		1 Piece	1.05 €	1	1.05 €
17	010800	0.05005	Regional carrots		1 kg	1.62 €	0.5	0.81 €
18	011400	0.15062	Tomatoes	Histamine	1 kg	1.93 €	1	1.93 €
19	011700	0.05305	Onions		1 kg	1.58 €	0.5	0.79 €
20	011800	0.09940	Potatoes		1 kg	1.34 €	2	2.68 €

(continued)

Table 3 (continued)

No	VPI Code	VPI Weight	Product	Allergeis and Nutrition	Unit	Single price	Amount	Price (gross)
21	013000	0.03824	Jam		1 kg	2.13 €	0.45	0.96 €
22	013200	0.06362	Fine crystal sugar		1 kg	1.06 €	1	1.06 €
23	014100	0.57700	Vinegar		1 L	1.34 €	1	1.34 €
24	014200	0.07263	Black tea in infusion bag		1 Piece	0.10 €	25	2.50 €
25	014300	0.25906	Bean coffee (ground)		1 kg	4.58 €	0.5	2.29 €
26	014800	0.16298	Mineral water		1 L	0.26 €	6	1.56 €
27	015200	0.14289	Orange juice	Fructose, Histamine	1 L	1.18 €	1.5	1.77 €
	~~015800~~	~~0.26690~~	~~White wine, glass bottle, quality wine~~	~~Histamine~~	~~1 L~~	~~5.32 €~~	~~1.5~~	
	~~016300~~	~~0.33513~~	~~Bottled beer (glass)~~		~~0,5 L~~	~~1.38 €~~	~~6~~	
28	047500	0.09177	Dishwashing detergent		1 L	3.80 €	1	3.80 €
29	047900	0.18237	Liquid detergent		1 Washcycle	0.15 €	35	5.25 €
30	099200	0.08150	Hair shampoo		100 ml	0.59 €	2.5	1.48 €
31	100000	0.07408	Toothpaste		75 ml	1.25 €	1	1.25 €
32	100400	0.10763	Showergel		100 ml	0.40 €	10	4.00 €
33	100500	0.07008	Toilet paper		1 Piece	0.26 €	15	3.90 €
34	100600	0.05748	Tissues		100 Pieces	0.50 €	1	0.50 €
						Total Price		71.48 €

Table 4 Types and levels of price change

	Change A	Change B	Change C	Change D
Products	≤2 €	≤2 €	>2 €	>2 €
Changes	Minor	Large	Minor	Large
Changes %	≤12%	12–25%	≤12%	12–25%

was doubled to a maximum of 12% for minor changes and for large changes to a maximum of 25% (rounded double of 12%), which leads to the following definition of groups in Table 4.

The experiment only focuses on price increases to see a straightforward price distinction. In a follow-up experiment, possible dependencies on price reductions can be tested. Table 5 shows the determination of the adjusted prices for the second round. To explain the table in further detail, sunflower oil (number 13) is taken as an example. The left part of the table until the column headline "<2€" is ident in Table 4. HIGH means the package or unit per measurement price is above 2€. A formula for randomization in Excel chooses randomly 11 HIGH and 11 LOW products out of the cart for which a price change is made, which can be seen in the column "Price Increase" with YES. Next, it got randomly assigned which product receives a minor (0–12%) or a significant (12–25%) price increase seen in column "Minor/Large". In the column "Increase in %", a random percentage within the range of the previously selected price increase group (Table 4) is created. Sunflower oil is minor, which shows an increase of 12%. "Reason" explains the reason for a price increase. In the case of sunflower oil, the demand increases because of a different purchase timing and a loss of discount because of a missing loyal card. 2.77€ shows the single increased price of 2.47€ by 12%. This is an increase of 0.30€ which results in a total price for 1 L of 2.77€. In total, the shopping cart increased 8.60€ from 71.48€ to 79.94€. The price increase is ideal because it stays within the 70€ range, so it is not that easy for customers to recognize the price difference.

5.5 Experiment Execution

The last part is experimenting by combining all preparation work made above into one experiment. The execution is provided as detailed as possible since this research offers the design in the form of a pre-study.

The total amount of participants are 50 people. People are randomly assigned to the treatment group (30 people) or the control group (20 people), which is 40% out of all participants. The first step of the experiment is to hand out the "Part I—Introduction" paper (Appendix 4) to the participants, which explains the simulated situation. They also got a shopping list based on Table 3 to know which products to buy. Figure 5 shows an ESL, how it can look in the experiment with name, region, stock counter, stock lamp (green), barcode, price inclusive VAT, and price per unit.

Table 5 Price adjustments with a divider by 12%

No.	VPI Code	VPI Weight	Product	Unit	Single Price	Amount	Price (gross)	>2.4	Price Increase	Minor-Large	Increase in %	Reason	Adj. Single Price	Increase in €	New Price (gross)	Price Ch.	Min./Lag
1	000100	0.08960	Pizza Margherita & mass	1 Piece	3.25 €	2	6.50 €	HIGH	YES	Minor	9%	Demand (Time), Inventory Level	3.54 €	0.59 €	7.08 €	2	2
2	000600	0.17135	Mixed bread	1 Kilogram	2.43 €	0.5	1.22 €	-	NO	-	-	-	-	-	1.22 €	1	2
3	001900	0.05150	Rice (long grain)	1 Kilogram	1.19 €	1	1.19 €	LOW	YES	Minor	10%	Demand (Time), No-Loyal Card	1.31 €	0.12 €	1.31 €	1	2
4	002000	0.05784	Flour (wheat)	1 Kilogram	0.86 €	1	0.86 €	LOW	YES	Large	25%	Demand (Time)	1.08 €	0.22 €	1.08 €	1	2
5	002100	0.09391	Pasta Penne	1 Kilogram	0.80 €	2	1.60 €	-	NO	-	-	-	-	-	1.60 €	1	2
6	002600	0.14078	Minced meat, beef	1 Kilogram	6.88 €	0.5	3.44 €	HIGH	YES	Large	22%	Demand (Time)	3.39 €	0.76 €	4.20 €	2	2
7	004800	0.10694	Chicken breast meat	1 Kilogram	7.17 €	0.5	3.59 €	HIGH	YES	Large	19%	Demand (Time)	3.53 €	0.68 €	4.27 €	2	2
8	005661	0.07752	Whole milk	1 Litre	1.13 €	1	1.13 €	LOW	YES	Large	16%	Demand (Time)	1.31 €	0.18 €	1.31 €	1	2
9	006200	0.12901	Fruit yoghurt	1 Piece	0.49 €	4	1.96 €	-	NO	-	-	-	-	-	1.96 €	1	2
10	006900	0.32908	Eggs, from keeping, size M	75 Pieces	0.24 €	10	2.40 €	HIGH	YES	Minor	25%	Demand (Time)	0.30 €	0.55 €	3.00 €	1	2
11	006700	0.12381	Gouda (wrapped)	1 Kilogram	6.27 €	0.25	1.57 €	-	NO	-	-	-	-	-	1.57 €	2	2
12	007900	0.19973	Sea butter	250 Gram	2.36 €	1	2.36 €	HIGH	YES	Minor	8%	Demand (Time)	2.44 €	0.13 €	2.57 €	2	2
13	007800	0.05338	Sunflower oil	1 Litre	2.47 €	1	2.47 €	HIGH	YES	Minor	12%	Demand (Time), No-Loyal Card	2.75 €	0.30 €	2.77 €	1	2
14	008500	0.13461	Apples	1 Kilogram	1.62 €	0.5	0.81 €	-	NO	-	-	-	-	-	0.81 €	1	2
15	009700	0.10628	Bananas	1 Piece	0.39 €	4	1.56 €	HIGH	YES	Large	21%	Demand (Time)	0.47 €	0.33 €	1.38 €	1	2
16	010700	0.05395	Cucumber	1 Piece	1.05 €	1	1.05 €	-	NO	-	-	-	-	-	1.05 €	2	2
17	010800	0.05065	Regional carrots	1 Kilogram	1.62 €	0.5	0.81 €	-	NO	-	-	-	-	-	0.81 €	1	2
18	011400	0.15062	Tomatoes	1 Kilogram	1.93 €	1	1.93 €	LOW	YES	Large	24%	Demand (Time)	2.39 €	0.46 €	2.39 €	2	2
19	011700	0.05305	Onions	1 Kilogram	1.58 €	0.5	0.79 €	LOW	YES	Large	21%	Demand (Time)	1.91 €	0.17 €	0.96 €	2	2
20	011800	0.09840	Potatoes	1 Kilogram	1.34 €	2	2.68 €	LOW	YES	Large	14%	Demand (Time), Inventory Level	1.53 €	0.38 €	3.06 €	1	2
21	013000	0.03624	Jam	1 Kilogram	1.13 €	0.45	0.96 €	-	NO	-	-	-	-	-	0.96 €	2	2
22	013200	0.06362	Fine crystal sugar	1 Kilogram	1.06 €	1	1.06 €	-	NO	-	-	-	-	-	1.06 €	1	2
23	014100	0.57700	Vinegar	1 Litre	1.34 €	1	1.34 €	-	NO	-	-	-	-	-	1.34 €	2	2
24	014200	0.07268	Black tea in infusion bag	1 Piece	0.10 €	25	2.50 €	HIGH	YES	Large	22%	Demand (Time), No-Loyal Card	0.12 €	0.53 €	3.00 €	1	2
25	014300	0.25906	Bean coffee (ground)	1 Kilogram	4.58 €	0.5	2.29 €	HIGH	YES	Large	24%	Demand (Time), Inventory Level	5.68 €	0.55 €	2.84 €	2	2
26	014800	0.16295	Mineral water	1 Litre	0.26 €	6	1.56 €	-	NO	-	-	-	-	-	1.56 €	2	2
27	015200	0.14289	Orange juice	1 Litre	1.18 €	1.5	1.77 €	LOW	YES	Minor	7%	Demand (Time), Inventory Level	1.26 €	0.12 €	1.89 €	1	2
28	047500	0.89177	Dishwashing detergent	1 Litre	3.80 €	1	3.80 €	HIGH	YES	Minor	6%	Demand (Time), Inventory Level	4.03 €	0.23 €	4.03 €	1	2
29	047900	0.18237	Liquid detergent	1 Wash-cycle	0.15 €	35	5.25 €	HIGH	YES	Large	22%	Demand (Time)	0.18 €	1.16 €	6.30 €	1	2
30	099200	0.06150	Hair shampoo	100 Millilitre	0.59 €	2.5	1.48 €	LOW	YES	Minor	10%	Demand (Time)	0.65 €	0.15 €	1.63 €	2	2
31	099400	0.07408	Toothpaste	75 Millilitre	1.25 €	1	1.25 €	LOW	YES	Minor	10%	Demand (Time)	1.38 €	0.13 €	1.38 €	1	2
32	100400	0.19763	Grocery pail	1 Piece	0.40 €	10	4.00 €	-	NO	-	-	-	-	-	4.00 €	2	2
33	100500	0.07008	Toilet paper	1 Piece	0.26 €	15	3.90 €	HIGH	YES	Large	20%	Demand (Time)	0.31 €	0.76 €	4.65 €	2	2
34	100600	0.05748	Tissues	100 Pieces	0.50 €	1	0.50 €	LOW	YES	Minor	5%	Demand (Time)	0.53 €	0.03 €	0.53 €	2	2
						Total Price	71.48 €							8.69 €	79.94 €		

=WENN(L>"2.0";".";WENN(M="Minor";RUNDEN(ZUFALLSZAHL()*11-1;0)/100;RUNDEN(ZUFALLSZAHL()*11+13;0)/100))   =ZUFALLSBEREICH(1;2)

The prices are also based on product 17 in Table 3. After checking out the products, the participants will receive a receipt, found in Appendix 5.

The participants do not know anything about the topic because it would influence the result. To keep it that way, after the first purchase, they get a small questionnaire (Appendix 6) handed out, where they have to answer questions and calculate the VAT of products. In the appendix, the results are included as well. This should deflect the participants that they do not think about price changes. There is another introduction for part three (Appendix 7), where they have to go shopping again for the same products. The shopping list got randomized for another deflection. This time the prices for the treatment group change compared to the first round based on the column "Adj. Single Price" in Table 5. After the participants get all the products and checked out, they will get a receipt again (Appendix 8), and they are done with the physical part. The last part of the experiment consists of a survey (evaluation plan in Appendix 9). The survey will be displayed on a tablet because the survey will be collected by soscisurvey.de for quicker and easier analysis (Appendix 10). The questions and answers are self-developed by achieving the goal to answer the hypotheses. For the appropriate Likert scale, Bruner (2019) was taken into account.

5.6   Proposed Pilot Test

Due to the detailed execution planning, the next step is a pilot phase. Due to the ongoing Covid-19 pandemic, a first pilot test is not possible until the publication of this article. That is because, especially in food retail, too strict security precautions are given. Thus an execution at a supermarket chain is not possible even after inquiries on our part. Nevertheless, execution planning could also be carried out with the help of augmented reality or virtual reality. For this setting, we are currently in the test phase of a mixed reality setting using the Microsoft HoloLens 2.[1]

5.7   Limitations

Delimitations of the paper were the focus only on the B2C market. Furthermore, the size of the focus group was limited to 50 people. Additionally, the experiment only focused on price increases because it supports the initial testing with ease to create a significant price difference between the two shopping carts.

Limitations during the writing process were the COVID-19 pandemic, which made it too difficult to conduct an in-store experiment. Based on that, the method of the paper switched from an empirical study (investigation) to a literature review with an empirical experiment design, which serves as a pre-study for subsequent implementation. As a result, this study cannot present any statements regarding the

---

[1] For further information we refer to https://www.microsoft.com/de-at/hololens.

quality of the model or an overall model fit. The literature supports the hypotheses deductively derived from the literature. Still, the hypotheses derived by the authors have not yet been tested and must first be tested for their applicability by a pilot study.

6 Conclusion

Due to the lack of availability of referable studies, we provided an experimental research design, which researches ESLs and DP in a stationary retail environment. The reason is that the technology has not been applied in an experiment yet, and the practical implementation of the ESL technology, still without DP in stores, has just begun. The initial idea came from an experiment by Coca-Cola, which adjusted prices based on temperature and time at a vending machine to maximize profit. This paper intends to provide a design that helps to explore this topic in more detail and gain new insights for academia and the business world. The experiment chose a grocery store setting because these stores were the first ones in Austria, switching to ESL from traditionally price tags.

This pre-study should show the potential of ESL technology. Furthermore, the design, which does not exist in this form, should aim to create a theoretical discussion basis for further research in this area and future design execution, maybe due to the COVID-19 pandemic by using virtual or augmented reality. The experiment addresses the grocery store industry and tries to research which price increases can be made without the customers noticing and dissatisfying them. Therefore, it is described in such detail that third parties can test it for feasibility and replicability.

We developed and used 19 hypotheses to provide a wide range of topics, which can be discussed for further research. Since retail stores are structured relatively the same, the design could be adjusted and extended to different industries or different focus groups. The goal of this design is not only to show stationary grocery stores how to change prices dynamically to improve profit but also to give them feedback about the consumer post-purchase reaction and perception (perceived price fairness) of the new technology and how well the customers accept the technology and the combined price adjustments.

Appendices

Appendix 1

Price Determination

No.	VPI Code	VPI Weight	AK Product	Unit	highest AK 2018	highest AK 2020	MPreis Product	MPreis	Average	Amount	Price (gross)
1	000100	0.08960	Pizza Margherita, frozen	1 Piece	3.32 €	2.45 €	Roncadin Megic Pizza Diavola frisch	3.99 €	3.25 €	2	6.50 €
2	000600	0.17135	Mixed bread	1 Kilogram	1.49 €	1.23 €	Ölz Weizenmischbrot	4.58 €	2.43 €	0.5	1.22 €
3	001900	0.05150	Rice (long grain)	1 Kilogram	0.79 €	0.79 €	JT Jasmin Reis	1.99 €	1.19 €	1	1.19 €
4	002000	0.05784	Flour (wheat)	1 Kilogram	0.45 €	0.45 €	Rauch Superback Mehl mit Dinkel	1.69 €	0.86 €	1	0.86 €
5	002100	0.09301	Pasta Penne	1 Kilogram	0.78 €	0.78 €	JT Penne	0.85 €	0.80 €	2	1.60 €
6	002600	0.14078	Minced meat, beef	1 Kilogram	-	5.75 €	Leichtes Faschiertes	8.00 €	6.88 €	0.5	3.44 €
7	003600	0.06346	Pork tenderloin	1 Kilogram	-	11.13 €	Schweinsfilet	11.00 €	11.07 €	0.5	5.54 €
8	004800	0.10694	Chicken breast meat	1 Kilogram	-	6.34 €	AIA Putenbrust Vac	7.99 €	7.17 €	0.5	3.59 €
9	005661	0.07752	Whole milk	1 Litre	1.05 €	1.04 €	TM Tiroler Berbauern Vollmilch 3.5%	1.29 €	1.13 €	1	1.13 €
10	006200	0.12901	Fruit yoghurt	1 Piece	0.45 €	0.43 €	Salzburger Milch Erdbeer Jogurt	0.59 €	0.49 €	4	1.96 €
11	006500	0.20908	Eggs, barn keeping, size M	1 Piece	0.24 €	0.17 €	Hörmann Eier Bodenhaltung M	0.30 €	0.24 €	10	2.40 €
12	006700	0.12381	Gouda (wrapped)	1 Kilogram	5.53 €	5.73 €	JT Gouda gerieben 48%	7.56 €	6.27 €	0.25	1.57 €
13	007300	0.17973	Tea butter	250 Gram	2.29 €	1.91 €	Gmundnermilch Teebutter 82%	2.59 €	2.26 €	1	2.26 €
14	007800	0.05338	Sunflower oil	1 Litre	1.23 €	1.20 €	ALN Sonnenblumenöl	4.98 €	2.47 €	1	2.47 €
15	008500	0.13461	Apples	1 Kilogram	1.40 €	0.99 €	Gala Apfel	2.47 €	1.62 €	0.5	0.81 €
16	009200	0.10628	Bananas	1 Piece	0.38 €	0.31 €	Banane	0.48 €	0.39 €	4	1.56 €
17	010700	0.05393	Cucumber	1 Piece	0.79 €	1.08 €	Bio Gurke	1.29 €	1.05 €	1	1.05 €
18	010800	0.05005	Regional carrots	1 Kilogram	1.30 €	1.18 €	NFU Bio Karotten Österreich	2.38 €	1.62 €	0.5	0.81 €
19	011400	0.15062	Tomatoes	1 Kilogram	1.49 €	1.49 €	Rispentomaten	2.80 €	1.93 €	1	1.93 €
20	011700	0.05305	Onions	1 Kilogram	-	0.90 €	Bio Zwiebel Netz	2.25 €	1.58 €	0.5	0.79 €
21	011800	0.09940	Potatoes	1 Kilogram	1.30 €	0.71 €	Kartoffel Pfanni Österreich	2.00 €	1.34 €	2	2.68 €
22	013000	0.03824	Jam	1 Kilogram	1.53 €	1.55 €	JT Konfitüre Erdbeere	3.31 €	2.13 €	0.45	0.96 €
23	013200	0.06362	Fine crystal sugar	1 Kilogram	0.89 €	0.80 €	Wiener Gelierzucker	1.49 €	1.06 €	1	1.06 €
24	014100	0.57700	Vinegar	1 Litre	0.45 €	0.39 €	Mautner Markhof Hesperiden Essig	3.18 €	1.34 €	1	1.34 €
25	014200	0.07263	Black tea in infusion bag	1 Piece	-	0.04 €	Twinings Englisch Schwarztee	0.15 €	0.10 €	25	2.50 €
26	014300	0.25906	Bean coffee (ground)	1 Kilogram	4.38 €	4.38 €	Alvorada Wiener Kaffee gemahlen	4.98 €	4.58 €	0.5	2.29 €
27	014800	0.16298	Mineral water	1 Litre	0.17 €	0.17 €	Silberquelle Mineralwasser Mild	0.43 €	0.26 €	6	1.56 €
28	015200	0.14289	Orange juice	1 Litre	0.95 €	0.90 €	Pfanner Orangensaft	1.70 €	1.18 €	1.5	1.77 €
29	015800	0.26690	White wine, glass bottle, quality wine	1 Litre	3.99 €	-	ALN Riesling 2018	6.65 €	5.32 €	1.5	7.98 €
30	016300	0.33513	Bottled beer (glass)	0.5 Litre	0.98 €	-	Zipfer Märzen	1.77 €	1.38 €	6	8.28 €
31	047000	0.09177	Dishwashing detergent	1 Litre	4.30 €	-	Palmolive Spülmittel	3.30 €	3.80 €	1	3.80 €
32	047900	0.18237	Liquid detergent	1 Waschcycle	0.10 €	-	Omo Color Flüssig	0.20 €	0.15 €	35	5.25 €
33	099200	0.08150	Hair shampoo	100 Millilitres	0.20 €	-	Pantene Shampoo	0.98 €	0.59 €	2.5	1.48 €
34	100000	0.07408	Toothpaste	75 Millilitres	0.55 €	-	Elmex Zahnpasta Anti-Karies	1.95 €	1.25 €	1	1.25 €
35	100400	0.10763	Showergel	100 Millilitres	0.25 €	-	Palmolive Duschgel Mineral	0.54 €	0.40 €	10	4.00 €
36	100500	0.07008	Toilet paper	1 Piece	0.22 €	-	JT Toilettenpapier 10x160 4l	0.30 €	0.26 €	15	3.90 €
37	100600	0.05748	Tissues	100 Pieces	0.45 €	-	JT Taschentücher 3lagig	0.55 €	0.50 €	1	0.50 €
									Total price		93.28 €

Appendix 2

Determination of High and Low Prices

No.	VPI Code	VPI Weight	Product	Allergens & Nutrition	Unit	Single Price	Amount	Price (gross)	> 2 €
1	000100	0.08960	Pizza Margherita, frozen	Gluten	1 Piece	3.25 €	2	6.50 €	HIGH
2	000600	0.17135	Mixed bread	Gluten	1 Kilogram	2.43 €	0.5	1.22 €	HIGH
3	001900	0.05150	Rice (long grain)		1 Kilogram	1.19 €	1	1.19 €	LOW
4	002000	0.05784	Flour (wheat)	Gluten	1 Kilogram	0.86 €	1	0.86 €	LOW
5	002100	0.09301	Pasta Penne	Gluten	1 Kilogram	0.80 €	2	1.60 €	LOW
6	002600	0.14078	Minced meat, beef	Non-Vegan	1 Kilogram	6.88 €	0.5	3.44 €	HIGH
	~~003600~~	~~0.06346~~	~~Pork tenderloin~~	~~Non-Vegan, Non-Vegetarian~~	~~1 Kilogram~~				~~LOW~~
7	004800	0.10694	Chicken breast meat	Non-Vegan, Non-Vegetarian	1 Kilogram	7.17 €	0.5	3.59 €	HIGH
8	005661	0.07752	Whole milk	Non-Vegan, Lactose	1 Litre	1.13 €	1	1.13 €	LOW
9	006200	0.12901	Fruit yoghurt	Non-Vegan, Lactose	1 Piece	0.49 €	4	1.96 €	LOW
10	006500	0.20908	Eggs, barn keeping, size M	Non-Vegan, Lactose	1 Piece	0.24 €	10	2.40 €	HIGH
11	006700	0.12381	Gouda (wrapped)	Non-Vegan, Lactose, Histamine	1 Kilogram	6.27 €	0.25	1.57 €	HIGH
12	007300	0.17973	Tea butter	Non-Vegan, Lactose	250 Gram	2.26 €	1	2.26 €	HIGH
13	007800	0.05338	Sunflower oil		1 Litre	2.47 €	1	2.47 €	HIGH
14	008500	0.13461	Apples	Fructose	1 Kilogram	1.62 €	0.5	0.81 €	LOW
15	009200	0.10628	Bananas		1 Piece	0.39 €	4	1.56 €	LOW
16	010700	0.05393	Cucumber		1 Piece	1.05 €	1	1.05 €	LOW
17	010800	0.05005	Regional carrots		1 Kilogram	1.62 €	0.5	0.81 €	LOW
18	011400	0.15062	Tomatoes	Histamine	1 Kilogram	1.93 €	1	1.93 €	LOW
19	011700	0.05305	Onions		1 Kilogram	1.58 €	0.5	0.79 €	LOW
20	011800	0.09940	Potatoes		1 Kilogram	1.34 €	2	2.68 €	LOW
21	013000	0.03824	Jam		1 Kilogram	2.13 €	0.45	0.96 €	HIGH
22	013200	0.06362	Fine crystal sugar		1 Kilogram	1.06 €	1	1.06 €	LOW
23	014100	0.57700	Vinegar		1 Litre	1.34 €	1	1.34 €	LOW
24	014200	0.07263	Black tea in infusion bag		1 Piece	0.10 €	25	2.50 €	HIGH
25	014300	0.25906	Bean coffee (ground)		1 Kilogram	4.58 €	0.5	2.29 €	HIGH
26	014800	0.16298	Mineral water		1 Litre	0.26 €	6	1.56 €	LOW
27	015200	0.14289	Orange juice	Fructose, Histamine	1 Litre	1.18 €	1.5	1.77 €	LOW
	~~015800~~	~~0.26690~~	~~White wine, glass bottle, quality wine~~		~~1 Litre~~				~~LOW~~
	~~016300~~	~~0.33513~~	~~Bottled beer (glass)~~	~~Histamine~~	~~0.5 Litre~~				~~LOW~~
28	047500	0.09177	Dishwashing detergent		1 Litre	3.80 €	1	3.80 €	HIGH
29	047900	0.18237	Liquid detergent		1 Washcycle	0.15 €	35	5.25 €	HIGH
30	099200	0.08150	Hair shampoo		100 Millilitres	0.59 €	2.5	1.48 €	LOW
31	100000	0.07408	Toothpaste		75 Millilitres	1.25 €	1	1.25 €	LOW
32	100400	0.10763	Showergel		100 Millilitres	0.40 €	10	4.00 €	HIGH
33	100500	0.07008	Toilet paper		1 Piece	0.26 €	15	3.90 €	HIGH
34	100600	0.05748	Tissues		100 Pieces	0.50 €	1	0.50 €	LOW
						Total Price		71.48 €	15

Appendix 3

Price Adjustments with a Divider by 6%

No.	VPI Code	VPI Weight	Product	Unit	Single Price	Amount	Price (gross)	>1€	Price Increase	Minor/Large	Increase in %	Adj. Single Price	Increase in €	New Price (gross)	Price Ch.	Min.Lag
1	000100	0.08960	Pizza Margherita, frozen	1 Piece	3.21€	2	6.55€	HIGH	YES	Minor	4%	3.34€	0.36€	6.76€	1	2
2	000600	0.17135	Sliced bread	1 Kilogram	3.43€	0.5	1.13€	LOW	NO					1.32€	2	2
3	001900	0.05150	Rice (long grain)	1 Kilogram	1.19€	1	1.19€	LOW	YES	Minor	2%	1.21€	0.02€	1.21€	2	1
4	002000	0.05784	Flour (wheat)	1 Kilogram	0.86€	1	0.86€	LOW	YES	Large	15%	0.99€	0.13€	0.99€	2	1
5	002100	0.09301	Pasta Penne	1 Kilogram	0.80€	2	1.60€	LOW	NO					1.60€	2	1
6	002900	0.14078	Minced meat, beef	1 Kilogram	6.88€	0.5	3.44€	HIGH	YES	Large	9%	7.50€	0.31€	3.75€	1	1
7	004800	0.10694	Chicken breast meat	1 Kilogram	7.17€	0.5	3.59€	HIGH	YES	Large	12%	8.03€	0.43€	4.02€	1	1
8	003661	0.17252	Whole milk	1 Litre	1.13€	1	1.13€	LOW	YES	Large	12%	1.27€	0.14€	1.27€	1	1
9	006200	0.13901	Fruit yoghurt	1 Piece	0.49€	4	1.96€	LOW	NO					1.96€	2	1
10	006500	0.20908	Eggs, barn keeping, size M	1 Piece	0.24€	10	2.40€	HIGH	YES	Large	10%	0.26€	0.24€	2.60€	1	1
11	006700	0.13381	Gouda (wrapped)	1 Kilogram	6.27€	0.25	1.57€	HIGH	NO					1.57€	2	2
12	007900	0.17973	Tea butter	250 Gram	2.26€	1	2.26€	HIGH	YES	Minor	1%	2.28€	0.02€	2.28€	1	2
13	007800	0.05338	Sunflower oil	1 Litre	2.47€	1	2.47€	HIGH	YES	Minor	6%	2.62€	0.15€	2.62€	1	1
14	008500	0.13481	Apples	1 Kilogram	1.62€	0.5	0.81€	LOW	NO					0.81€	2	2
15	009300	0.06628	Bananas	1 Piece	0.39€	4	1.56€	LOW	YES	Large	13%	0.44€	0.20€	1.76€	1	1
16	010700	0.05393	Cucumber	1 Piece	1.05€	1	1.05€	LOW	NO					1.05€	2	2
17	010800	0.05065	Regional carrots	1 Kilogram	1.62€	0.5	0.81€	LOW	NO					0.81€	2	2
18	011400	0.19062	Tomatoes	1 Kilogram	1.93€	1	1.93€	LOW	YES	Large	11%	2.14€	0.21€	2.14€	2	1
19	011700	0.05505	Onions	1 Kilogram	1.58€	0.5	0.79€	LOW	YES	Large	11%	1.75€	0.09€	0.88€	2	1
20	011800	0.09840	Potatoes	1 Kilogram	1.34€	2	2.68€	LOW	YES	Large	9%	1.46€	0.24€	2.92€	1	2
21	013000	0.03824	Jam	1 Kilogram	2.13€	0.45	0.96€	LOW	NO					0.96€	2	2
22	013200	0.06362	Fine crystal sugar	1 Litre	1.06€	1	1.06€	LOW	NO					1.06€	2	2
23	014100	0.57700	Vinegar	1 Litre	1.34€	1	1.34€	HIGH	NO					1.34€	2	2
24	014200	0.07263	Black tea in infusion bag	1 Piece	0.10€	25	2.50€	HIGH	YES	Large	12%	0.11€	0.30€	2.75€	1	1
25	014300	0.25906	Bean coffee (ground)	1 Kilogram	4.58€	0.5	2.29€	HIGH	YES	Large	10%	5.04€	0.23€	2.52€	1	2
26	014800	0.16298	Mineral water	1 Litre	0.26€	6	1.56€	LOW	YES	Minor	3%		0.05€	1.61€	2	1
27	013300	0.14289	Orange juice	1 Litre	1.18€	1.5	1.77€	LOW	HIGH	Minor	3%	1.22€	0.05€	1.83€	2	1
28	047500	0.09917	Dishwashing detergent	1 Litre	3.80€	1	3.33€	HIGH	YES	Minor	3%	3.99€	0.18€	3.99€	1	1
29	047900	0.11837	Liquid detergent	1 Washcycle	0.16€	35	5.55€	LOW	YES	Large	7%	0.16€	0.17€	5.60€	1	2
30	009200	0.08150	Hair shampoo	100 Millilitres	0.59€	2.5	1.48€	LOW	YES	Minor	4%	0.61€	0.06€	1.53€	1	1
31	100000	0.07498	Toothpaste	75 Millilitres	1.25€	1	1.25€	LOW	YES	Minor	5%	1.31€	0.06€	1.31€	2	1
32	100400	0.10763	Shower gel	100 Millilitres	0.40€	10	4.00€	HIGH	NO					4.00€	2	1
33	100500	0.07008	Toilet paper	1 Piece	0.30€	13	3.90€	HIGH	YES	Large	8%	0.28€	0.31€	4.20€	1	2
34	100600	0.05748	Tissues	100 Pieces	0.50€	1	0.50€	LOW	YES	Large	2%	0.51€	0.01€	0.51€	1	2
						Total Price	71.48€	11	11	13			4.02€	75.38€		
								HIGH	LOW	Large						

=WENN(I5="NO";...;WENN(M5="Minor";RUNDEN(ZUFALLSZAHL()*5+1;0)/100;RUNDEN(ZUFALLSZAHL()*9+6;0)/100))

=ZUFALLSBEREICH(1;2)

Appendix 4

Part I—Introduction

Part I – Introduction

Welcome to the experiment. The experiment will take approximately *1-1,5 hours* to complete. Thank you for your time and your participation!

This experiment is taking place inside a physical grocery store. If you have any questions before the experiment starts, please do not hesitate to ask.

The task of the experiment is straightforward.

1) Read the instructions
2) Take the shopping list
3) Enter the grocery store
4) Do the experiment

Part I – Situation

It is 10:00 on a Tuesday morning on a beautiful day in early summer, and you have the day off at work. You meet up with a friend at noon to go biking to a lake in the afternoon. Before you leave to meet up with your friend, you decided to do your weekly grocery shopping in a local supermarket/discounter. You wrote a shopping list with all the things needed for a household of two, including your partner (*provided on the next page*). Unfortunately, the grocery store of your trust is closed caused by renovation work. You decide to go to the nearest grocery store where you usually do not go that often.

Since you do not visit this grocery store very often, you do not know the layout of the store and where the products are located, which you need to buy.

Your task is to find the products needed on the shopping list and check out with them. Further instructions follow after checkout.

Happy shopping!

Shopping List 1

This is the list of groceries you should buy today.

1	☐	2 Piece	Pizza Margherita, frozen
2	☐	0,5 Kilogram	Mixed bread
3	☐	1 Kilogram	Rice (long grain)
4	☐	1 Kilogram	Flour (wheat)
5	☐	2 Kilogram	Pasta Penne
6	☐	0,5 Kilogram	Minced meat, beef
7	☐	0,5 Kilogram	Chicken breast meat
8	☐	1 Litre	Whole milk
9	☐	4 Piece	Fruit yoghurt
10	☐	10 Piece	Eggs, barn keeping, size M
11	☐	0,25 Kilogram	Gouda (wrapped)
12	☐	250 Gram	Tea butter
13	☐	1 Litre	Sunflower oil
14	☐	0,5 Kilogram	Apples
15	☐	4 Piece	Bananas
16	☐	1 Piece	Cucumber
17	☐	0,5 Kilogram	Regional carrots
18	☐	1 Kilogram	Tomatoes
19	☐	0,5 Kilogram	Onions
20	☐	2 Kilogram	Potatoes
21	☐	0,45 Kilogram	Jam
22	☐	1 Kilogram	Fine crystal sugar
23	☐	1 Litre	Vinegar
24	☐	25 Piece	Black tea in infusion bag
25	☐	0,5 Kilogram	Bean coffee (ground)
26	☐	6 Litre	Mineral water
27	☐	1,5 Litre	Orange juice
28	☐	1 Litre	Dishwashing detergent
29	☐	35 Washcycle	Liquid detergent
30	☐	2,500 Millilitres	Hair shampoo
31	☐	75 Millilitres	Toothpaste
32	☐	1000 Millilitres	Showergel
33	☐	15 Piece	Toilet paper
34	☐	100 Pieces	Tissues

Appendix 5

Invoice 1

Supermarket

Your purchase for invoice 1 includes:

Pizza Margherita, frozen	2 Piece	6.50 €	A
Mixed bread	0,5 Kilogram	1.22 €	A
Rice (long grain)	1 Kilogram	1.19 €	A
Flour (wheat)	1 Kilogram	0.86 €	A
Pasta Penne	2 Kilogram	1.60 €	A
Minced meat, beef	0,5 Kilogram	3.44 €	A
Chicken breast meat	0,5 Kilogram	3.59 €	A
Whole milk	1 Litre	1.13 €	A
Fruit yoghurt	4 Piece	1.96 €	A
Eggs, barn keeping, size M	10 Piece	2.40 €	A
Gouda (wrapped)	0,25 Kilogram	1.57 €	A
Tea butter	250 Gram	2.26 €	A
Sunflower oil	1 Litre	2.47 €	A
Apples	0,5 Kilogram	0.81 €	A
Bananas	4 Piece	1.56 €	A
Cucumber	1 Piece	1.05 €	A
Regional carrots	0,5 Kilogram	0.81 €	A
Tomatoes	1 Kilogram	1.93 €	A
Onions	0,5 Kilogram	0.79 €	A
Potatoes	2 Kilogram	2.68 €	A
Jam	0,45 Kilogram	0.96 €	A
Fine crystal sugar	1 Kilogram	1.06 €	A
Vinegar	1 Litre	1.34 €	A
Black tea in infusion bag	25 Piece	2.50 €	A
Bean coffee (ground)	0,5 Kilogram	2.29 €	A
Mineral water	6 Litre	1.56 €	B
Orange juice	1,5 Litre	1.77 €	B
Dishwashing detergent	1 Litre	3.80 €	B
Liquid detergent	35 Washcycle	5.25 €	B
Hair shampoo	2,500 Millilitres	1.48 €	B
Toothpaste	75 Millilitres	1.25 €	B
Showergel	1000 Millilitres	4.00 €	B
Toilet paper	15 Piece	3.90 €	B
Tissues	100 Pieces	0.50 €	B
Total		**71.48 €**	

Payment cash   71.48 €

	excl.	VAT	incl.
10%	43.60 €	4.36 €	47.96 €
20%	19.60 €	3.92 €	23.52 €

Appendix 6

Part II—Questions

Part II – Questions

Which VAT rates exist in Austria?
- ☐ **10% VAT**
- ☐ 9% VAT
- ☐ **20% VAT**
- ☐ **13% VAT**
- ☐ 19% VAT

Which of these rates is the standard tax rate in Austria?
- ☐ 10% VAT
- ☐ 9% VAT
- ☐ **20% VAT**
- ☐ 13% VAT
- ☐ 19% VAT

Which of these products are charged with 20% VAT in a grocery store?
- ☐ Tomatoes
- ☐ **Mineral water**
- ☐ Bread
- ☐ **Toilet paper**
- ☐ Milk
- ☐ Flowers
- ☐ **Wine**
- ☐ **Coffee**

Which of these products are charged with 10% VAT in a grocery store?
- ☐ **Tomatoes**
- ☐ Mineral water
- ☐ **Bread**
- ☐ Toilet paper
- ☐ **Milk**
- ☐ Flowers
- ☐ Wine
- ☐ Coffee

Which of these products are charged with 13% VAT in a grocery store?
- ☐ Tomatoes
- ☐ Mineral water
- ☐ Bread
- ☐ Toilet paper
- ☐ Milk
- ☐ **Flowers**
- ☐ Wine
- ☐ Coffee

Who collects the VAT?
- ☐ European Union
- ☐ Federation Austria
- ☐ The Provinces (e.g. Tirol, Salzburg, etc.)
- ☐ Districts
- ☐ Communities

Calculate the right prices (round up to 2 digits after the comma):

1 Litre milk costs 1,09€ inclusive VAT. How much do you have to pay without the VAT?

1,09/1,1 = 0.99 €

1 kg of chicken breast cost 9,59€ exclusive VAT. How much do you have to pay at the cashier for 400gram inclusive VAT?

9,59 * 1,1 = 10,55 €
10,55/10 = 1,055 * 4 = 4,22 €

One bottle of wine costs 4,99 exclusive VAT. If you buy two or more bottles, you get a 15% discount on the total purchase of wine (incl. VAT). How much do you pay for one bottle inclusive VAT if you purchase 4 bottles? How much do you save for each bottle inclusive VAT?

4,99 * 1,2 = 5,99 €
5,99 * 4 = 23,96 * 15 /100 = 3,59 €
23,96 – 3,59 = 20,37 / 4 = 5,09 €
5,99 – 5,09 = 0,90 €

Appendix 7

Part III—Introduction

Part III – Introduction

After answering the questions of part II, you can go ahead and read the following instructions.

This experiment is taking place inside a physical grocery store. If you have any questions before the experiment starts, please do not hesitate to ask.

The task of the experiment is straightforward.

5) Read the instructions
6) Take the shopping list
7) Enter the grocery store
8) Do the experiment

Part II – Situation

It is a week later on a Thursday afternoon at 6:00 pm. It is raining the whole day, and you just got out of work and decided to do your weekly grocery shopping because there is hardly anything left from the last purchase. You wrote down a shopping list again with the things needed (*provided on the next page*). The grocery store of your choice still does renovation work. As a result, you go again to the grocery store you went last time to do your grocery shopping.

Your task is again to go pick up the products on your shopping list and check out with them. After checkout, the last part of the experiment takes place in form of a survey, where you will get a tablet to fill it out. When you are done filling out the survey, the experiment is over.

Thank again for your participation and happy shopping!

Shopping List 2

This is the list of groceries you should buy today.

1	☐	0,5 Kilogram	Onions
2	☐	0,45 Kilogram	Jam
3	☐	2,500 Millilitres	Hair shampoo
4	☐	4 Piece	Bananas
5	☐	1 Litre	Dishwashing detergent
6	☐	1 Kilogram	Rice (long grain)
7	☐	1,5 Litre	Orange juice
8	☐	1 Litre	Sunflower oil
9	☐	0,5 Kilogram	Mixed bread
10	☐	1 Litre	Vinegar
11	☐	1 Kilogram	Fine crystal sugar
12	☐	0,5 Kilogram	Minced meat, beef
13	☐	10 Piece	Eggs, barn keeping, size M
14	☐	2 Kilogram	Pasta Penne
15	☐	1 Litre	Whole milk
16	☐	25 Piece	Black tea in infusion bag
17	☐	75 Millilitres	Toothpaste
18	☐	15 Piece	Toilet paper
19	☐	1000 Millilitres	Showergel
20	☐	1 Kilogram	Tomatoes
21	☐	2 Piece	Pizza Margherita, frozen
22	☐	6 Litre	Mineral water
23	☐	1 Piece	Cucumber
24	☐	100 Pieces	Tissues
25	☐	250 Gram	Tea butter
26	☐	0,5 Kilogram	Chicken breast meat
27	☐	0,5 Kilogram	Bean coffee (ground)
28	☐	1 Kilogram	Flour (wheat)
29	☐	35 Washcycle	Liquid detergent
30	☐	2 Kilogram	Potatoes
31	☐	0,5 Kilogram	Apples
32	☐	0,25 Kilogram	Gouda (wrapped)
33	☐	4 Piece	Fruit yoghurt
34	☐	0,5 Kilogram	Regional carrots

Appendix 8

Invoice 2

Supermarket

Your purchase for invoice 2 includes:

Pizza Margherita, frozen	2 Piece	7.08 € A
Mixed bread	0,5 Kilogram	1.22 € A
Rice (long grain)	1 Kilogram	1.31 € A
Flour (wheat)	1 Kilogram	1.08 € A
Pasta Penne	2 Kilogram	1.60 € A
Minced meat, beef	0,5 Kilogram	4.20 € A
Chicken breast meat	0,5 Kilogram	4.27 € A
Whole milk	1 Litre	1.31 € A
Fruit yoghurt	4 Piece	1.96 € A
Eggs, barn keeping, size M	10 Piece	3.00 € A
Gouda (wrapped)	0,25 Kilogram	1.57 € A
Tea butter	250 Gram	2.44 € A
Sunflower oil	1 Litre	2.77 € A
Apples	0,5 Kilogram	0.81 € A
Bananas	4 Piece	1.88 € A
Cucumber	1 Piece	1.05 € A
Regional carrots	0,5 Kilogram	0.81 € A
Tomatoes	1 Kilogram	2.39 € A
Onions	0,5 Kilogram	0.96 € A
Potatoes	2 Kilogram	3.06 € A
Jam	0,45 Kilogram	0.96 € A
Fine crystal sugar	1 Kilogram	1.06 € A
Vinegar	1 Litre	1.34 € A
Black tea in infusion bag	25 Piece	3.00 € A
Bean coffee (ground)	0,5 Kilogram	2.84 € A
Mineral water	6 Litre	1.56 € B
Orange juice	1,5 Litre	1.89 € B
Dishwashing detergent	1 Litre	4.03 € B
Liquid detergent	35 Washcycle	6.30 € B
Hair shampoo	2,500 Millilitres	1.63 € B
Toothpaste	75 Millilitres	1.38 € B
Showergel	1000 Millilitres	4.00 € B
Toilet paper	15 Piece	4.65 € B
Tissues	100 Pieces	0.53 € B
Total		**79.94 €**
Payment cash		79.94 €

	excl.	VAT	incl.
10%	49.06 €	4.91 €	53.97 €
20%	21.65 €	4.32 €	25.97 €

Appendix 9

Plan of Evaluation

Plan of Evaluation

Variable ID	Peculiarity	Question	Statistical implementation	Measurement level	Associated Hypothesis
Recognition		Continuous chronological numbering of the persons interviewed			
cart	0 = No 1 = Yes	Did you recognize a price change between shopping cart 1 and 2?	Frequency, Correlation table with recognition, age	Nominal	H0a Customers do not recognize a price change on the overall amount of the shopping cart
diff	1 = No price difference 2 = 0-2 3 = 2-4 4 = 4-6 5 = 6-8 6 = 8-10 7 = 10-12 8 = 12-14 9 = 14-16	How big was the price difference in Euros?	Frequency, Correlation table with recognition, age	Ordinal	H0a Customers do not recognize a price change on the overall amount of the shopping cart
prod	0 = Pizza Margherita, frozen 1 = Mixed bread 2 = Rice (long grain) 3 = Flour (wheat) 4 = Pasta Penne 5 = Minced meat, beef 6 = Chicken breast meat 7 = Whole milk 8 = Fruit yoghurt 9 = Eggs, barn keeping, size M 10 = Gouda (savaged) 11 = Tea butter 12 = Sunflower oil 13 = Apples 14 = Bananas 15 = Regional carrots 16 = Tomatoes 17 = Cucumber 18 = Onions 19 = Potatoes 20 = Jam 21 = Fine crystal sugar 22 = Vinegar 23 = Black tea in infusion bag 24 = Bean coffee (ground) 25 = Mineral water 26 = Orange juice 27 = Dishwashing detergent 28 = Liquid detergent 29 = Hair shampoo 30 = Toothpaste 31 = Shower gel 32 = Toilet paper 33 = Tissues 34 = None of the products	For which specific products did you recognize a price change? (Multiple choice possible)	Frequency, Correlation table with recognition, age	Nominal	H0b Customers cannot identify the products, which were affected by price adjustments H1a Minor price changes on products up to 2€ (Change A) are more likely to be recognized than major price changes on products above 2€ (Change C) H1b Large price changes on products up to 2€ (Change B) are more likely to be recognized than large price changes on products above 2€ (Change D)
sign	0 = No 1 = Yes	Did you recognize that the price labels where projected digitally?	Frequency	Nominal	H2 The ESL technology is not recognized by the customers

ESL Technology				
	Electronic Shelf Labels (ESLs) are a new price tag technology, which allows prices digitally to the customer instead of classic paper tags. This technology will be used more often in grocery stores but spreads quicker and changes for the retailer is unfold. The information on the price tag			
info	1 = Strongly disagree, 7 = Strongly agree	ESL technology will enhance the communication of product information for the customer	Frequency	Ordinal, Likert Scale	H4b ESLs enhance price information presentation.
imps	1 = Strongly disagree, 7 = Strongly agree	ESL technology will increase the image/reputation of a store.	Frequency	Ordinal, Likert Scale	H4c ESLs positively influence store image perceptions
acce	1 = Strongly disagree, 7 = Strongly agree	ESL technology will be accepted by customers as a replacement of paper price tags	Frequency	Ordinal, Likert Scale	H4d Customers accept ESL technology.
rel	1 = Strongly disagree, 7 = Strongly agree	ESL technology will increase price fairness	Frequency	Ordinal, Likert Scale	H4a ESLs does negatively influence price fairness perceptions
Perception				
	Additionally, the ESL technology gives retailers also the possibility to dynamically adjust prices depending on the circumstances, which you know from the price policy of gas stations. Please choose the one answer that best represents your views, by placing a tick in the appropriate box.			
reco	1 = Strongly disagree, 7 = Strongly agree	If you recognized dynamic prices methods in a grocery store, would that lower your trust towards the supermarket chain?	Frequency	Ordinal, Likert Scale	H6 Exposure to a dynamic pricing event will reduce status overall trust.
incr	1 = Supply increase, 2 = Demand increase, 3 = Retail-only cost increase, 4 = Manufacturer-only cost increase, 5 = Competition increase, 6 = None of them	Which reasons for a price increase are acceptable for you? (Multiple-choice possible)	Frequency	Nominal	H5b A price increase given a demand increase, a supply decrease, or a retailer-only cost increase will be perceived as more unfair than a price increase given a channel or manufacturer-only cost increase
regu	1 = Strongly disagree, 7 = Strongly agree	Is it unfair, when a existing customer pays less for the same products because of loyal card than you as a regular customer?	Frequency; Correlation table with new	Ordinal, Likert Scale	H7 Higher price paid by existing customers relative to new customers triggers stronger negative price fairness judgements than higher prices paid by new customers relative to existing customers
new	1 = Strongly disagree, 7 = Strongly agree	Is it unfair, when a new customer pays less for the same products because the store wants to grow its new customers than you as an existing/loyal customer?	Frequency; Correlation table with exist	Ordinal, Likert Scale	H7 Higher price paid by existing customers relative to new customers triggers stronger negative price fairness judgements than higher prices paid by new customers relative to existing customers
chan	0 = Pizza Margherita, frozen, 1 = Facti (long grain), 2 = Flour (wheat), 3 = Minced meat, beef, 4 = Chicken breast meat, 5 = Whole milk, 6 = Eggs, barn keeping, size M, 7 = Tea bags, 8 = Sunflower oil, 9 = Bananas, 10 = Tomatoes, 11 = Onions, 12 = Potatoes, 13 = Black tea in infusion bag, 14 = Bean coffee (ground), 15 = Orange juice, 16 = Dishwashing detergent, 17 = Liquid detergent, 18 = Hair shampoo, 19 = Toothpaste, 20 = Toilet paper, 21 = None of the products	Which product price change would you perceive as unfair?	Frequency	Ordinal, Likert Scale	H5a Exposure to a dynamic pricing event increases the number of strategic customers.
Communication & Behaviour				
smar	1 = Strongly disagree, 7 = Strongly agree	If you know a grocery stores uses dynamic pricing as a pricing strategy, would you wait to purchase to hope the prices decrease? (Consider there is a possibility that the price can increase.)	Frequency	Ordinal, Likert Scale	H8a The higher the price increase, the lower the perceived price fairness.
purc	1 = Strongly disagree, 7 = Strongly agree	If you found out afterwards that you payed more in an common day, would you purchase at that grocery store again?	Frequency; Correlation table with smar	Ordinal, Likert Scale	

Var	Coding	Question	Analysis	Scale	Hypothesis
sat	0 = Refusal of purchase 1 = Search for Alternatives 2 = Complain at the store 3 = Complain publicly (social media) 4 = Tell your friends/family 5 = Change supermarket chain 6 = Return product	If the price policy of a grocery store in your opinion was unfair, what action would you take? (Multiple-choice possible)	Frequency, Correlation table with pure	Nominal	H3b Exposure to a dynamic pricing event encounters rejection, complaints, negative word of mouth, search for alternatives, decrease satisfaction, and purchase intention
satis	1 = Strongly disagree ... 7 = Strongly agree	Do you think dynamic pricing because of changes in demand or supply is unfair?	Frequency	Ordinal, Likert Scale	
infm	1 = Strongly disagree ... 7 = Strongly agree	Do you find it less unfair if you know in advance the reason (e.g. demand, manufacturer costs) and how much the price is change?	Frequency, Correlation table with trus	Ordinal, Likert Scale	H5b Credible communication has a positive influence on the perceived price fairness
trus	1 = Strongly disagree ... 7 = Strongly agree	Do you trust a grocery store more if you know in advance the reason (e.g. demand, manufacturers costs) and how much the price is changing?	Frequency, Correlation table with satis	Ordinal, Likert Scale	H5b There is a positive relationship between communication and trust
Characteristics Data					
nutr	0 = I am vegetarian 1 = I am vegan 2 = I have another nutritional style 3 = None	Do you have a specific nutritional style?		Nominal	
alle	0 = Lactose intolerance 1 = Histamine intolerance 2 = Fructose intolerance 3 = Gluten intolerance 4 = Other allergy/intolerance 5 = None	Do you have any food allergies?		Nominal	
comp	0 = No 1 = Yes	Are you looking at prices and comparing them to different stores and products?	Frequency	Nominal	
Demographic Data					
sex	0 = Male 1 = Female 2 = Other	Fill out gender	Frequency	Nominal	
age	None	Fill out your birth year (Example 1995)	Frequency, Correlation table with cart, diff prod	Metric	H1b Older customers do not recognise price changes comp ared to younger customers
fam	0 = Single 1 = In a relationship 2 = Divorced 3 = Widowed	Fill out your marital status	Frequency	Nominal	
peop	None	How many people live in your household?	Frequency	Metric	
shop	0 = Me 1 = Someone else	Who normally go grocery shopping in your household?	Frequency	Nominal	
occu	0 = Student 1 = Employee 2 = Worker 3 = Self-employed 4 = Retiree 5 = Unemployed	Fill out your work status	Frequency	Nominal	
inco	1 = No steady income 2 = <=600 3 = 601-1000 4 = 1001-1400 5 = 1401-1800 6 = 1801-2200 7 = 2201-2600 8 = 2601-3000 9 = 3001-3400 10 = 3401-3800 11 = 3801-4200 12 = >=4201	What is your net monthly income (answered in income category)?	Frequency, Correlation table with cart, diff prod	Ordinal	H1a Customers in a higher income level do not recognise price changes because they are less price sensitive

Appendix 10

Survey with soscisurvery.de

Dear participant,

As mentioned before, the last part of the experiment is to fill out this questionnaire. Please answer the questions as honestly as possible.

Information on data protection:
All answers will be kept confidential. The collection and processing of your data is only allowed with your consent. The questionnaire is anonymous, and your data will under no circumstances be used for purposes other than this study. If you have any questions about this privacy policy, please contact me at mm2304@mci4me.at.

By starting this survey, you confirm that you have read the previous information and agree to participate in this study.

Thank you for your participation!

Recognition

1. Did you recognize a price change between shopping cart 1 and 2?

○ No
○ Yes

2. How big was the price difference in Euros?

[Please choose] ▾

3. For which specific products did you recognize a price change? (Multiple-choices possible)

☐ Pizza Margherita, frozen
☐ Mixed bread
☐ Rice (long grain)
☐ Flour (wheat)
☐ Pasta Penne
☐ Minced meat, beef
☐ Chicken breast meat
☐ Whole milk
☐ Fruit yoghurt
☐ Eggs, barn keeping, size M
☐ Gouda (wrapped)
☐ Tea butter
☐ Sunflower oil
☐ Apples
☐ Bananas
☐ Cucumber
☐ Regional carrots
☐ Tomatoes
☐ Onions
☐ Potatoes
☐ Jam
☐ Fine crystal sugar
☐ Vinegar
☐ Black tea in infusion bag
☐ Bean coffee (ground)
☐ Mineral water
☐ Orange juice
☐ Dishwashing detergent
☐ Liquid detergent
☐ Hair shampoo
☐ Toothpaste
☐ Showergel
☐ Toilet paper
☐ Tissues
☐ Non of the products

4. Did you recognize that the price labels where projected digitally?

○ No
○ Yes

New Technology

Electronic Shelf Labels (ESLs) are a new price tag technology, which shows prices digitally to the customers instead of classic paper tags. This technology will be used more often in grocery stores because it is quicker and cheaper for the retailer to switch the information on the price tags.

5. Knowing what ESLs are, please choose in the following the answer that best represents your view by placing a tick in the appropriate box.

ESL technology will enhance the communicatin of product information for the customer.	Strongly disagree	○ ○ ○ ○ ○ ○ ○	Strongly agree
ESL technology will increase the image/reputation of a store.	Strongly disagree	○ ○ ○ ○ ○ ○ ○	Strongly agree
ESL technology will be accepted by customers as a replacement of paper price tags.	Strongly disagree	○ ○ ○ ○ ○ ○ ○	Strongly agree
ESL technology will increase price fairness.	Strongly disagree	○ ○ ○ ○ ○ ○ ○	Strongly agree

Dynamic Pricing

Additionally, the ESL technology gives retailers also the possibility to dynamically adjust prices depending on the circumstances, which you know from the price policy of gas stations.

6. Please choose the one answer that best represents your views by placing a tick in the appropriate box.

	Strongly disagree	Strongly agree
If you recognised dynamic prices methods in a grocery stores, would that lower your trust towards the supermarket chain?	○ ○ ○ ○ ○ ○	
Is it unfair, when a existing customer pays less for the same products because of loyal card than you as a regular customer?	○ ○ ○ ○ ○ ○	
Is it unfair, when a new customer pays less for the same products because the store wants to generate new customers than you as an existing/loyal customer?	○ ○ ○ ○ ○ ○	

7. Which reasons for a price increase are acceptable for you? (Multiple-choice possible)

- ☐ Supply increase
- ☐ Demand increase
- ☐ Retail-only-cost increase
- ☐ Manufacturer-only-cost increase
- ☐ Channel-only-cost increase
- ☐ Competition increase
- ☐ None of them

8. Which product price changes would you preceive as unfair?

- ☐ Pizza Margherita, frozen
- ☐ Rice (long grain)
- ☐ Flour (wheat)
- ☐ Minced meat, beef
- ☐ Chicken breast meat
- ☐ Whole milk
- ☐ Eggs, barn keeping, size M
- ☐ Tea butter
- ☐ Sunflower oil
- ☐ Bananas
- ☐ Tomatoes
- ☐ Onions
- ☐ Potatoes
- ☐ Black tea in infusion bag
- ☐ Bean coffee (ground)
- ☐ Orange juice
- ☐ Dishwashing detergent
- ☐ Liquid detergent
- ☐ Hair shampoo
- ☐ Toothpaste
- ☐ Toilet paper
- ☐ Tissues
- ☐ None of the products

Characteristic data

9. Do you have a specific nutritional style?

○ I am vegetarian.
○ I am vegan.
○ I have another nutritional style.
○ None.

10. Do you have any food allergies?

○ Lactose intolerance
○ Histamine intolerance
○ Fructose intolerance
○ Gluten intolerance
○ Other allergies/intolerance
○ None

11. Are you trying to save money buying groceries?

○ No
○ Yes

12. Are you looking at prices and comparing them to different stores and products?

○ No
○ Yes

Demogrpahic Data

Answer the questions below.

13. Fill out your gender.

○ Male
○ Female
○ Other

14. Fill out your birth year. (Example 1995)

[   ]

15. Fill out your marital status.

○ Single
○ In a relationship
○ Divorced
○ Widowed

16. How many people live in your household?

[   ]

17. Who normally go grocery shopping in your household?

○ Me
○ Someone else

18. Fill out your work status.

○ Student
○ Employee
○ Worker
○ Self-employed
○ Retiree
○ Unemployed

19. What is your net monthly income (measured in income categories)?

○ No steady income
○ <=600
○ 601-1000
○ 1001-1400
○ 1401-1800
○ 1801-2200
○ 2201-2600
○ 2601-3000
○ 3001-3400
○ 3401-3800
○ 3801-4200
○ >=4201

Thank you for completing this questionnaire!

We would like to thank you very much for helping us.
Your answers were transmitted. you may close the browser window or tab now.

References

Adams JS (1965) Inequity in Social Exchange. In: Berkowitz L (ed) Advances in Experimental Social Psychology, vol 2. Academic Press, pp 267–299

Anzenberger J, Busch M, Grabenhofer-Eggerth A et al. (2019) Epidemiologiebericht Sucht 2019

Ayadi N, Paraschiv C, Rousset X (2017) Online Dynamic Pricing and Consumer-Perceived Ethicality: Synthesis and Future Research. Recherche et Applications en Marketing 32:49–70. https://doi.org/10.1177/2051570717702592

Battour M, Ismail MN, Battor M (2011) The Impact of Destination Attributes on Muslim Tourist's Choice. Int J Tourism Res 13:527–540. https://doi.org/10.1002/jtr.824

Bruner GC (2019) Marketing Scales Handbook: Multi-Item Measures for Consumer Insight Research, Library version

Bryman A, Bell E (2011) Business Research Methods, 3rd ed. Oxford University Press, Cambridge, New York NY

Christensen LB, Johnson B, Turner LA (2014) Research Methods, Design, and Analysis, 11th ed. Pearson custom library. Pearson Education Limited, Harlow

Delapina M (2020) Lebensmittel-Warenkorb Wien-Berlin 2020: Warenkorb mit 40 Lebensmitteln - Preisvergleich der preiswertesten Produkten in Supermärkten und bei Diskontern

Den Boer AV (2015) Dynamic Pricing and Learning: Historical origins, current research, and new directions. Surveys in Operations Research and Management Science 20. https://doi.org/10.1016/j.sorms.2015.03.001

Diller H (2008) Preispolitik, 4., vollst. neu bearb. und erw. Aufl. Kohlhammer Edition Marketing. Kohlhammer, Stuttgart

Dütschke E, Paetz A-G (2013) Dynamic Electricity Pricing—Which Programs do Consumers Prefer? Energy Policy 59:226–234. https://doi.org/10.1016/j.enpol.2013.03.025

Evanschitzky H PD Dr., Tönnis S Dipl.-Kffr., Woisetschläger D Dr. et al. (2007) Der Einfluss von Preiserhöhungen auf Konsumenteneinstellungen Eine experimentelle Studie. Thexis 24:7–11

Ecker K, Brem G (2020) Kulturelle Tabus zur alimentären Nutzung von Haustieren / 2. Mitteilung: Persistenz religiöser Nahrungstabus in der studentischen Bevölkerung Österreichs. Wiener Tierärztliche Monatsschrift 107:51–62

Elsbeck G (2018) Digitale Preisschilder leuchten auf. Lebensmittel Zeitung:46

Flier S (2016) Digitale Preisschilder setzen sich durch. Lebensmittel Zeitung:20

Flier S (2019a) Ahold führt digitale Preischilder ein. Lebensmittel Zeitung:37

Flier S (2019b) Rossmann testet Preischilder. Lebensmittel Zeitung:30

Garaus M, Wolfsteiner E, Wagner U (2016) Shoppers' Acceptance and Perceptions of Electronic Shelf Labels. Journal of Business Research 69:3687–3692. https://doi.org/10.1016/j.jbusres.2016.03.030

Garbarino E, Lee OF (2003) Dynamic Pricing in Internet Retail: Effects on Consumer Trust. Psychology and Marketing 20:495–513. https://doi.org/10.1002/mar.10084

Garbarino E, Maxwell S (2010) Consumer Response to Norm-Breaking Pricing Events in E-Commerce. Journal of Business Research 63:1066–1072. https://doi.org/10.1016/j.jbusres.2008.12.010

Grewal D, Hardesty DM, Iyer GR (2004) The Effects of Buyer Identification and Purchase Timing on Consumers' Perceptions of Trust, Price Fairness, and Repurchase Intentions. Journal of Interactive Marketing 18:87–100. https://doi.org/10.1002/dir.20024

Haws KL, Bearden WO (2006) Dynamic Pricing and Consumer Fairness Perceptions. Journal of Consumer Research 33:304–311. https://doi.org/10.1086/508435

Hays CL (1999) Variable-Price Coke Machine Being Tested. The Wall Street Journal

Homans GC (ed) (1974) Social Behavior: Its elementary forms. Harcourt Brace Jovanovich, New York

Huckemann M, Dinges A (1998) Euro-Preis-Marketing: Wie sie mit der richtigen Preisstrategie gewinnen. Luchterhand, Neuwied

Klein R, Steinhardt C (eds) (2008) Revenue Management: Grundlagen und Mathematische Methoden. Springer-Lehrbuch. Springer-Verlag, Berlin

Knotzer D, Delapina M (2018) AK-Preismotiroring Wien - Juni 2018: Warenkorb mit 40 Lebens- und Reinigungsmittel - Preisvergleich der preiswertesten erhältlichen Produkten in Wiener Supermärkten und bei Diskontern

Koschate N (2002) Kundenzufriedenheit und Preisverhalten: Theoretische und empirisch experi- mentelle Analysen, Gabler Edition Wissenschaft. Schriftenreihe des Instituts für Marktorientierte Unternehmensführung Universität Mannheim. Deutscher Universitätsverlag, Wiesbaden, s.l.

Krafft M, Mantrala MK (2010) Retailing in the 21st Century. Springer Berlin Heidelberg, Berlin, Heidelberg

Mak V, Rapoport A, Gisches EJ (2012) Competitive Dynamic Pricing with Alternating Offers: Theory and Experiment. Games and Economic Behavior 75:250–264. https://doi.org/10.1016/j. geb.2011.08.018

McAfee RP, Velde VLt (1978–1983) Dynamic Pricing in the Airline Industry. In: Moullade M, Nairn AEM (eds) The Mesozoic, vol 1. Elsevier, Amsterdam, New York, pp 527–569

McKenzie B, Taylor V (2016) The Use of Electronic Shelf Labels in the Retail Food Sector. International Journal of Economics and Management Engineering 10:627–630

Meyer-Rochow VB (2009) Food Taboos: Their Origins and Purposes. J Ethnobiol Ethnomed 5:18. https://doi.org/10.1186/1746-4269-5-18

Morgan RM, Hunt SD (1994) The Commitment-Trust Theory of Relationship Marketing. Journal of Marketing 58:20–38. https://doi.org/10.2307/1252308

PR Newswire (2019a) Europe Electronic Shelf Label (ESL) Market Industry Outlook and Forecast 2019a–2024

PR Newswire (2019b) The Electronic Shelf Label Market (ESL Market) is Expected to Reach More Than $2 Billion by 2024

Ochs C, Friedewald M, Hess T (eds) (2019) Die Zukunft der Datenökonomie: Zwischen Geschäftsmodell, Kollektivgut und Verbraucherschutz, 1st ed. 2019. Medienkulturen im digitalen Zeitalter. Springer Fachmedien Wiesbaden, Wiesbaden

Reinartz W Prof. Dr., Haucap J Prof. Dr., Wiegand N Dr. et al. (2017) Preisdifferenzierung und -dispersion im Handel

Ratchford M (2014) Perceptions of Price (Un)fairness in a Channel Context. Marketing Letters 25:343–353. https://doi.org/10.1007/s11002-013-9256-z

Research and Market (2017) Electronic Shelf Labels Market in the US 2017–2021

Sevelius A (2019) Die Trends im Lebensmitteleinzelhandel 2019

Solomon PJ, Deeter-Schmelz DR (2015) Electronic Shelf Labeling: An Empirical Investigation of Consumers' Attitudes Toward a New Technology in Retailing. In: Levy M, Grewal D (eds) Proceedings of the 1993 Academy of Marketing Science (AMS) Annual Conference, vol 17. Springer International Publishing, Cham, pp 256–260

Soutjis B, Cochoy F, Hagberg J (2017) An Ethnography of Electronic Shelf Labels: The Resisted Digitalization of Prices in Contemporary Supermarkets. Journal of Retailing and Consumer Services 39:296–304. https://doi.org/10.1016/j.jretconser.2017.08.009

Statista (2014) Einschätzung der Häufigkeit von Lebensmittelunverträglichkeiten in der Bevölkerung in Deutschland im Jahr 2014. https://de.statista.com/statistik/daten/studie/314821/ umfrage/geschaetzte-haeufigkeit-von-lebensmittelunvertraeglichkeit-in-deutschland/. Accessed 06 Aug 2020

Statistik Austria (2020) Warenkorb und Gewichtung des H/VPI 2020

Statista (2018) Geschätzte Anzahl der Vegetarier, Veganer und Flexitarier in Österreich im Jahr 2017. https://de.statista.com/statistik/daten/studie/709815/umfrage/anzahl-der-vegetarier- veganer-und-flexitarier-in-oesterreich/. Accessed 06 Aug 2020

Statista (2019) Pro-Kopf-Konsum von Lebensmitteln in Österreich im Jahr 2018. https://de.statista. com/statistik/daten/studie/674782/umfrage/pro-kopf-verbrauch-ausgewaehlter-lebensmittel-in- oesterreich/. Accessed 01 May 2020

Statista (2020) Anzahl der Gläubigen von Religionen in Österreich im Zeitraum 2012 bis 2019. https://de.statista.com/statistik/daten/studie/304874/umfrage/mitglieder-in-religions gemeinschaften-in-oesterreich/. Accessed 13 May 2020

Theuvsen L, Schütte R (2013) Lebensmittel im Electronic Commerce: Historische Entwicklung und aktuelle Trends. In: Clasen M, Kersebaum KC, Meyer-Aurich A et al. (eds) Massendatenmanagement in der Agrar- und Ernährungswirtschaft: Erhebung - Verarbeitung - Nutzung ; Referate der 33. GIL-Jahrestagung 20.-21. Februar 2013 in Potsdam, Germany. GI Ges. für Informatik, Bonn, pp 339–342

Tillmann TJ, Vogt V (2018) Personalisierte Preise im Big-Data-Zeitalter. Verbraucher und Recht:447–455

Tschunko J (2015) Dynamic Pricing: Die Individualisierung von Preisen im E-Commerce, Kammer für Arbeiter und Angestellte für Wien

Walster EH, Berscheid E, Walster GW (1978) Equity: Theory and Research. Allyn and Bacon, Boston, Toronto

Weisstein FL, Monroe KB, Kukar-Kinney M (2013) Effects of Price Framing on Consumers' Perceptions of Online Dynamic Pricing Practices. Journal of the Academy of Marketing Science 41:501–514. https://doi.org/10.1007/s11747-013-0330-0

Woodcock R (2018) The Efficient Queue and the Case Against Dynamic Pricing. SSRN Electronic Journal. https://doi.org/10.2139/ssrn.3230425

Zelleken H-J, Dellbrügge G (2000) Zur Preispolitik des Lebensmittelhandels. Dynamik im Handel:10–19

The Impact of Quantitative Easing on Stock Market: Evidence from Greece

Sofia Karagiannopoulou, Paris Patsis, and Nikolaos Sariannidis

Abstract In September of 2014, ECB decides the beginning of the first Quantitative Easing (QE) programme called Asset-Backed Securities Purchase (ABSPP) and Covered Bond Purchase Programme (CBPP), in order to face the financial crisis. Next programme was the Public Sector Purchase Programme (PSPP) on 9 March 2015. Finally, on 18 March 2020, the ECB started the third programme called Pandemic Emergency Purchase Programme (PEPP). The goal of this study is to explore the impact of QE programmes on the stock market of Athens, considering the fact that Greece was the only European country to participate only in the third programme. Using daily data from 1/9/2014 to 22/1/2021, 3 GARCH(1,1) models with dummy variables are constructed to incorporate different QE programmes. In addition, 10-year bond, gold, and DAX are used in order to isolate systematic international factors. The empirical results show that the first QE programme has decreased the stock prices, the findings of the second QE programme aren't statistically important, while the third programme has a positive effect on the stock market. The paper concludes that Greek participation on the QE programme played an important role in the stock market and suggests that other researchers investigate the methods in which Greece can utilize the positive climate after the end of PEPP.

Keywords ECB quantitative easing · Stock market · Greece · GARCH

Jel Classification Codes C22 · E44 · E52 · E58

S. Karagiannopoulou · N. Sariannidis
University of Western Macedonia, Kila, Kozani, Greece
e-mail: sof.karag@yahoo.gr

N. Sariannidis
e-mail: nsariannidis@uowm.gr

P. Patsis (✉)
University of Western Macedonia, Grevena, Greece
e-mail: p_patsis@panteion.g

© The Author(s), under exclusive license to Springer Nature Switzerland AG 2022
P. Sklias et al. (eds.), *Business Development and Economic Governance in Southeastern Europe*, Springer Proceedings in Business and Economics,
https://doi.org/10.1007/978-3-031-05351-1_16

1 Introduction

The ECB tried to cope with the global financial crisis of 2008–2009 and the Great Depression by lowering interest rates. When the interest rate reached zero level, it was deemed necessary to take non-conventional monetary policy measures. The purchase of assets, also known as quantitative easing (QE), was elected as the most effective measure. Quantitative easing was first implemented by the Bank of Japan in the 1990s, followed by the US Federal Reserve in 2008 and the Bank of England in 2009. The ECB implemented 3 Quantitative Easing programs. The first program started in September 2014 and involved the purchase of real estate—known as the Asset-Backed Securities Purchase Program (ABSPP)—and, also, the purchase of covered bonds, known as the Covered Bond Purchase Program (CBPP). The 2nd program—Public Sector Purchase Program (PSPP)—was decided on March 9, 2015 and involved the purchase of public-sector bonds, while in March 2020 the Pandemic Emergency Purchase Program was launched regarding the emergency measures that had to be taken to address the effects of the COVID-19 pandemic. It should be noted that not all of the Eurozone countries participated in the Quantitative Easing programs. The ECB set 3 restrictions on government bonds that would be validated. More specifically, the bond market would be able to reach up to 33% per issuer and up to 25% per issue and in addition the national central banks would be able to buy bonds, which would be high-rated ones. Due to these restrictions, Cyprus and Greece did not participate in the 1st program; Cyprus was added as a participant in the 2nd program, while Greece participated, for the first time, in Quantitative Easing in the third PEPP program.

The Greek stock market showed great fluctuations in the period 2014–2021 (Fig. 1). In 2015, the stock market index indicated the largest decline since the beginning of the financial crisis of 2009. The reason lies in the control over the movement

Fig. 1 2014–2021: The course of shares of Athens stock market. *Source* www.investing.com

of capital (capital controls) that led to the interruption of 24 sessions of the stock market (from 29/6/2015 to 3/8/2015) and brought significant losses in the portfolios not only of domestic investors but, mainly, in those of foreign investors; another reason lies in the third recapitalization of the four systemic banks, which saw the value of their shares reaching a historic low, changing the banking nature of the Greek stock market. The following years saw a stabilization of the stock market index, with an upward trend. The next major drop in the index occurred in March 2020, due to the lockdown imposed as a measure to address COVID-19. After the first shock in March, the stock market revealed an upward trend throughout the COVID-19 period.

1.1 The Role of the ECB and Quantitative Relaxation

The ECB is responsible for controlling and guaranteeing the security of the European Banking System. The lack of liquidity that resulted from the global crisis of 2008 forced the ECB to adopt unconventional monetary policy measures, such as the following:

1. Provision of liquidity

   In this case, the ECB provides liquidity to the Eurosystem by facilitating lending capacity, through the reduction of the discount rate and through extensions of lending programs.

2. Management expectations

   In this case, the ECB is committed to keeping the monetary policy rate at zero for a long period of time, aiming to reduce expectations for future short-term interest rates. In this way, a reduction in the long-term interest rate will be achieved and this, in turn, will lead to a reduction in the real interest rate, thus, stimulating the actual economy.

3. Asset Purchase (Quantitative Relaxation)

   With the purchase of assets, also known as Quantitative Easing, the Central Bank expands its balance sheet, providing a large increase in liquidity, with the aim to increase consumption and investment and drive the inflation rate to the desired figure of below but close to 2% in the medium term.

The most important of the 3 measures of non-conventional monetary policy is the purchase of assets. The ECB has developed 3 Quantitative Easing programs (Fig. 2). In September 2014, the 1st Asset-Backed Securities Purchase Program (ABSPP) was launched, which included the Third Covered Bond Purchase and the 1st Asset Purchase Program (APS), for the figure of 10 billion per month. On 22 January 2015, the Board of Directors of the ECB decided to extend the APP to include the asset and public sector market, thus launching the 2nd Public Sector Purchase Program (PSPP) of 50 billion per month. Under this program, the ECB buys investment stocks on the secondary market which are issued by the central governments of the Eurozone

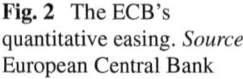

Fig. 2 The ECB's quantitative easing. *Source* European Central Bank

member states, recognized bodies and international organizations established in the Eurozone, as well as multilateral banks with activity within the Eurozone. The first restriction was placed on government bonds which are not traded in the markets, where in order for these bonds to be accepted, the countries in question would have to be subject to a financial assistance program from the European Stability Mechanism. Due to this restriction, Greece did not participate in QE2, while Cyprus participated near the end of QE2. The next limitation addressed the remaining maturity of the eligible bonds—it should be from 2 to 30 years—while their yield to maturity should be higher than the deposit facility rate (−0.2% per day notification of the decision). The volume of QE2 reached 60 billion on a monthly basis; the initial plan was for it to expire on September 30, 2016, with a possibility of an extension until it was ensured that inflation would approach 2% in the medium term. On 18 March 2020, the ECB launched the third € 750 billion Pandemic Emergency Purchase Program (PEPP) to address the serious risks posed by the outbreak of COVID-19 in the monetary policy transmission mechanism and the Eurozone outlook. The restrictions of QE2 were lifted in this program, the result being that, for the first time, Greece was eligible to participate in the program. The Board of the ECB decided to extend the PEPP on 4 June 2020 by 600 billion and by 500 billion on 10 December 2020. The Board will terminate the net asset purchases under PEPP as soon as the COVID-19 crisis is over, but, in any case, not before the end of March 2022.

1.2   The Performance of the Hellenic Stock Exchange During the Quantitative Easing Period

Figure 3 depicts the performance of the Greek stock market during the period of the 1st quantitative easing program. Stock yields have maintained a declining trend throughout QE1 without great fluctuations. The lowest price appears in January 2015, reaching 711.13 points.

   Figure 4 depicts the performance of the Greek stock market during the period of the 2nd Quantitative Easing program. Equity returns show great fluctuation throughout the period. The lowest price is documented in March 2015 reaching 541.7 points,

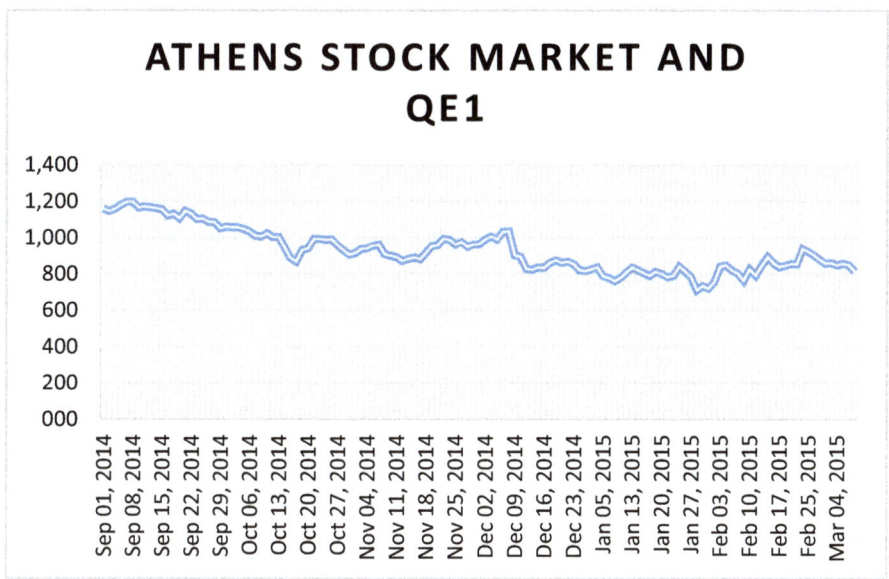

Fig. 3 Athens stock market in the period of QE1. *Source* www.investing.com

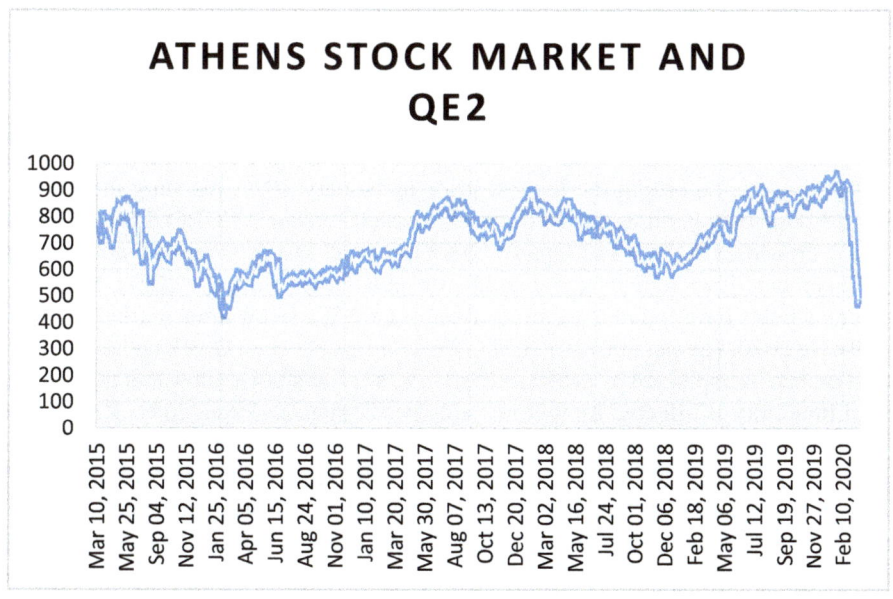

Fig. 4 Athens stock market in the period of QE2. *Source* www.investing.com

Fig. 5 Athens stock market in the period of QE3. *Source* www.investing.com

while the highest performance appears in January 2021 reaching 948.64 points. Let us not forget that Greece was faced with a profound economic and political crisis that drove the country to the brink of exiting the Eurozone, was close to a bankruptcy and resulted in a steep drop in its stock market.

Figure 5 shows the performance of the Greek stock market during the period of the Pandemic emergency program. The performance of the Greek stock market during this period remains stable until October 2020, after which it is characterized by an upward course, recording the highest price in January 2021, reaching the limit of 822.22 points. In contrast to Greek stock market, Europe's EURO STOXX, UK's FTSE, France's CAC 40, and Japan's NIKKEI225 all lost their market values by 30 to 42 percent, down to fears generated by the pandemic (Yarovaya 2021). Similarly, several studies have found a negative effect of COVID-19 on stock markets (Ashraf 2020; He 2020; Hassan 2021; Li 2021). The contrast between Greek and other stock markets can be explained by previous literature, as prior studies show that the market-level immunity is affected by national culture (Fernandez-Perez 2021; Kaczmarek 2021), the level of economic freedom (Erdem 2020), government responses to the pandemic (Narayan 2021), and prepandemic economic conditions (Zaremba 2021).

In our study, we will examine the impact of quantitative easing programs on Greek stock market. In order to isolate systematic international factors, we will use the Greek 10-year bond, gold, and DAX. The rest of the study is organized as follows. Section 2 presents related literature, Sect. 3 outlines the data and methodology, Sect. 4 discusses the results of our analysis, and finally, Sect. 5 concludes the study by providing practical and policy implications and outlining for future research.

2 Literature Review

Financial markets are often called the "barometer" of the national economy and react to monetary policy first, before economic activities. For this reason, it is necessary to explore the effects of monetary policy on financial markets (such as stock market) to assess the monetary policy effect on economy in advance (Wei 2021). Moreover, the "Black Swan" events such as global financial crisis (Karunanayake 2010) and epidemics (Chen 2009; Choi 2020) have an significant adverse effect on stock markets, as these events create sudden shock and fear among investors, which leads to uncertainty (Burch 2016; He 2020). Especially, the global-scale spread of COVID-19 has exerted an unprecedented impact on financial markets (Al-Awadhi 2020; Albulescu 2021; Baek 2020; Zaremba 2021).

A lot of research has focused on the issue of whether Quantitative Easing could stimulate the actual economy of a country (Gagnon 2011; Hamilton 2012; Baumeister 2013; D'Amico 2013). Brunnermeier (2009) indicate that the monetary policy of Central Banks generally tends to affect stock prices. Ueda (2012), Kontonikas (2013), and Ricci (2014) studied the impact of QE policy on the stock markets in advanced industrialized countries. Bernanke (2005) focused on FED's policy and concluded that this unconventional policy led to an increase in stock prices. Similarly, while studying the impact of ECB's unconventional policy on European stock markets, Fernandez-Amador (2011) concluded that QE led to an increase in the German, French, and Italian stock markets and Haitsma (2016) concluded that UMP measures lead to higher stock prices in the euro area.

Zhang (2020) analyzed the potential effects of policy interventions on stock market and feared that the policies such as unlimited quantitative easing adopted by the US government could generate further uncertainties, which could lead to long-run problems. Hudepohl (2021) examine whether QE contributes to exuberance in euro area stock markets and the analysis shows that (the anticipation of) QE is indeed positively related to stock market bubbles. Moreover, even after controlling for macroeconomic fundamentals, periods of QE seem to be the main driver of the exuberance. Newly formed bubbles can give rise to future systemic financial crises when left unchecked by regulators (Brunnemeier 2020).

Hartley et al. (Hartley 2020) find that the impact of QE was more substantial for emerging economies than the developed markets.

In contrast to previous studies, this paper is the first one to use the Greek stock market in order to investigate the impact of QE on it. Due to globalization and increased economic activity, the QE policy implemented by a Central Bank may affect other global markets, such as emerging markets, which have a close economic relationship with developed countries where QE programs have been implemented. The stock markets of these economies are particularly sensitive to changes coming from external factors (Chudik 2011). According to Georgiadis (2016), the impact of the Fed QE was more profound in other economies, rather than in the US economy. According to Tillmann (2016), QE had a significant impact on the financial conditions of emerging market economies. Similar conclusions were reached by Laeven

(2012). The present research will not focus on emerging markets; it will, nevertheless, study the spillover of QE policy in a country that does not take part in the program. Specifically, it will focus on how QE1 and QE2 of the ECB respectively affected the Greek stock market, even though Greece—a member of the Eurozone—did not participate in the first two programs of the ECB.

The period studied in the present research is a period which the Greek stock market is under great pressure, resulting from a double crisis: an economic one and a health one. In times of crisis, the role of Central Banks becomes increasingly critical (Holmstrom 2000; Brunnermeier 2009; Hameed 2010), as these banks have proven themselves inadequate in implementing drastic measures and leading efforts. For example, in the wake of the 2007–2009 global crisis, most Central Banks, such as the Fed, adjusted their monetary policy to reverse the economic damage caused by the crisis (Cecchetti 2009; Goodhart 2008; Rose 2012), while the ECB remained passive and only in 2014 did it turn to non-conventional monetary policy measures to address the effects of the economic crisis.

For the purpose of the research, it was necessary to take into account other control variables, in order to isolate international systemic factors. These variables are gold, 10-year Greek government bond, and DAX. It is worldwide known the traditional role of gold as a hedge against equities in normal times and as a safe haven against equities during stress periods (Baur 2010; Beckmann 2015). According to Shahzad (2020), gold is a strong safe haven for the stock markets of Germany and the USA and acts as a weak safe haven for France, Italy, Japan, and the UK. Shahzad (2017) examine the dependence of gold with ten stock markets, including five larger developed markets (e.g., the USA, the UK, Japan, Canada, and Germany) and five Eurozone peripheral GIPSI countries' (Greece, Ireland, Portugal, Spain, and Ireland) stock markets. The findings suggest that the dependence between stock-gold is not uniform, and this relationship is market state (e.g., bearish, mild bearish, optimistic, or bullish) and country specific. Gold has a negative dependence with major developed (Raza 2016) and GIPSI stock markets across the majority of quantiles, but when both stock and gold markets are pessimistic, i.e., undergoing stress periods, gold shows a positive dependence with stock markets. We use 10-year government bond as a proxy for bond rates generally. The 10-year maturity is often used in academic studies (De Haan 2018; Altavilla 2015; Belke 2021; Hudepohl 2021; Wei 2021). The 10-year Greek government bond reflects the confidence and expectations of the international market participants in the perspectives of the Greek economy. The empirical literature has usually found that the impact of QE programmes on risk-less rates, such as longer-term German rates, or on swap rates, was low and often statistically not significantly different from zero (Altavilla 2019), while the effects of the QE on the three countries (Italy, Spain, France) with the highest risk premiums mentioned above were several times larger (Belke 2021). Andersson (2008), Connolly (2005), and Guiko (2002) found that stock and bond returns were negatively correlated in periods of a highly volatile stock market. DAX index is used in order to isolate the impact of European stock markets on the Greek stock market, as Germany is considered as the leader of the Eurozone. The model used for this study is the GARCH model. It was chosen due to the special characteristics of equity returns. Similarly, Wang (2019) used an

GARCH model to study the impact of FED QE announcements on the mortgage market, while Lee et al. (2020) used a DCC-GARCH to study the effect of FED QE on the Asian stock market.

3 Methodology and Data

In the present survey, daily prices of the Greek stock market were used in order to study the effect of the QE of the ECB on the Greek stock market in the period from 1/9/2014 to 22/1/2021. In addition, 10-year Greek government bond, gold, and DAX are used in order to isolate systematic international factors After the equity returns were calculated, the GARCH model was chosen, as it is in par with the characteristics of equity returns, such as the tendency to be depicted as a slender graph and the volatility clustering. In order to avoid the problem of multicollinearity, 3 GARCH models (1, 1) will be evaluated using dummy variables, so that each model represents a quantitative relaxation program. The dummy variables were defined as follows:

$$i = \begin{cases} 1, \text{ for QE}_1 \\ 2, \text{ for QE}_2 \\ 3, \text{ for QE}_3 \end{cases}$$

where QE_1: from 1/9/2014 to 8/3/2015.
QE_2: from 9/3/2015 to 17/3/2020.
QE_3: from 18/3/2020 to 22/1/2021

$$QE_{it} = \begin{cases} 1, \text{ where } i = 1 \text{ and } 0 < t < 130 \\ 0, \text{ where } i = 1 \text{ and } t \geq 130 \end{cases}$$

$$QE_{it} = \begin{cases} 1, \text{ where } i = 2 \text{ and } 130 \leq t < 1256 \\ 0, \text{ where } i = 2 \text{ and } t < 130 \eta't \geq 1256 \end{cases}$$

$$QE_{it} = \begin{cases} 1, \text{ where } i = 3 \text{ and } 1256 \leq t \leq 1566 \\ 0, \text{ where } i = 2 \text{ and } t < 1256 \end{cases}$$

The equations of the GARCH(1,1) model will be as follows:

Mean equation

$$ASE_{it} = b_0 + b_1 10\_YEAR\ BOND_{it} + b_2 GOLD_{it} + b_3 DAX_{it} + b_4 QE_{it} + u_{it}$$

Variance equation

$$\sigma_{it}^2 = a_1 + a_2 u_{it-1}^2 + a_3 \sigma_{it-1}^2$$

4 Results

The following table depicts the descriptive statistical measures of the stock returns of the Greek stock market.

According to Table 1, 10-year bond has the lowest median (-0.000272), while DAX has the highest price (0.000207). The highest deviation from the mean value based on the standard deviation is 0.034831 and appears to be in 10-year bond. All the variables have a negative asymmetry, while the curvature is positive, which proves it to be slender shaped. According to Jarque–Bera values, the null hypothesis of residual normality is rejected.

Finally, according to Table 2 and the Augmented Dickey–Fuller (ADF) unit root augmentation test, it was concluded that the time series remained stable.

Table 3 presents the GARCH (1, 1) results for the 1st QE program:

The mean equation is:

$$ASE_{1t} = 0.000777 - 0.01502610\_YEAR\ BOND_{1t}$$
$$+ 0.071042\ GOLD_{1t} - 0.026407\ DAX_{1t}$$

Table 1 Descriptive statistics

Variables	ASE	10-year bond	Gold	DAX
Mean	$-4.26e-05$	-0.001321	0.000270	0.000207
Median	0.000647	-0.000272	0.000266	0.000808
Maximum	0.1149606	0.314017	0.046928	0.104143
Minimum	-0.162328	-0.466584	-0.058928	-0.130549
Std. Dev	0.020438	0.034831	0.008603	0.013109
Skewness	-0.710641	-1.764855	-0.115726	-0.749669
Kurtosis	13.39437	52.53816	6.819140	14.23710
Jarque–Bera	7177.027	160,835.6	954.6108	8380.605

Source Authors' results based on the analysis of the variables

Table 2 The results of unit root test augmented Dickey–Fuller

	Level values
Variables	t-statistic
ASE	$-22.20862*$
10-year bond	$-17.20425*$
Gold	$-40.04588*$
DAX	$-39.72983*$

Test critical values: -3.434333, -2.863186, -2.567694 for 1, 5, and 10% respectively

***, **, * Significance level of 1, 5, and 10%, respectively

Source Authors' results based on the analysis of the variables

Table 3 The results of GARCH QE1

Variable	Coefficient	Std. error	z-statistic	Prob
C	0.000777**	0.000352	2.205186	0.0274
10-year bond	−0.015026	0.009639	−1.558969	0.1190
Gold	0.071042*	0.040197	1.767364	0.0772
DAX	−0.026407	0.023925	−1.103754	0.2697
QE1	−0.005738***	0.001346	−4.262056	0.0000
	Variance equation			
C	8.56E–06	1.37E–06	6.246516	0.0000
RESID(−1)^2	0.148753	0.013368	11.12770	0.0000
GARCH(−1)	0.838942	0.012367	67.83772	0.0000

***, **, * Significance level of 1, 5, and 10%, respectively
Source Authors' results based on the analysis of the variables

$$- 0.005738 \, \text{QE}_{1t} + u_{1t}$$

In the period of QE1 programme, gold had a positive impact on Greek stock market at a rate of 7.1% and at a significance level of 10%. On the other hand, the 1st Quantitative Easing program had a negative effect on the Greek stock market at a rate of 0.57% and at a significance level of 1%. The rate of 10-year bond and DAX are not statistically significant at any level of significance.

According to Table 3, the variance equation is:

$$\sigma_{1t}^2 = 8.56\text{E} - 06 + 0.148753 u_{1t-1}^2 + 0.838942 \sigma_{1t-1}^2$$

Table 4 depicts the GARCH (1, 1) results for the 2nd QE program:

Table 4 The results of GARCH QE2

Variable	Coefficient	Std. error	z-statistic	Prob
C	−0.000168	0.000766	−0.218616	0.8269
10-year bond	−0.016651*	0.009688	−1.718661	0.0857
Gold	0.073321*	0.04041	1.831173	0.0671
DAX	−0.027892	0.023947	−1.164932	0.2440
QE2	0.000918	0.000863	1.063535	0.2875
	Variance equation			
C	8.35E-06	1.34E-06	6.246042	0.0000
RESID(−1)^2	0.148136	0.013382	11.06954	0.0000
GARCH(−1)	0.840729	0.012355	68.04727	0.0000

***, **, * Significance level of 1, 5, and 10%, respectively
Source Authors' results based on the analysis of the variables

According to Table 4, the mean equation is:

$$ASE_{2t} = -0.000168 - 0.0166511 0YEAR\_ BOND_{2t}$$
$$+ 0.073321\ GOLD_{2t} - 0.027892\ DAX_{2t}$$
$$+ 0.000918\ QE_{2t} + u_{2t}$$

In the period of QE2 programme, gold had, also, a positive impact on Greek stock market at a rate of 7.3% and at a significance level of 10%. On the other hand, 10-year bond had a negative effect on the Greek stock market at a rate of 1.66% and at a significance level of 10%. The rate of QE2 and DAX are not statistically significant at any level of significance, so no conclusion can be drawn regarding the effect of the 2nd quantitative easing program on the Greek stock market.

According to Table 4, the variance equation is:

$$\sigma_{2t}^2 = 8.35E - 06 + 0.1481369u_{2t-1}^2 + 0.840729\sigma_{2t-1}^2$$

Table 5 depicts the GARCH (1, 1) results for the 3rd QE program:
The mean equation is:

$$ASE_{3t} = 0.000616 - 0.0179401 0YEAR\_ BOND_{3t}$$
$$+ 0.071948\ GOLD_{3t} + -0.026407DAX_{3t}$$
$$+ 0.002784QE_{3t} + u_{3t}$$

In the period of QE3 programme, QE3 and gold had a positive impact on Greek stock market at a rate of 0.27% and 7.19% respectively and at a significance level of 10%. On the other hand, 10-YEAR BOND had a negative effect on the Greek stock

Table 5 GARCH QE3

Variable	Coefficient	Std. error	z-statistic	Prob
C	0.000616*	0.000368	1.676035	0.0937
10-year bond	−0.017940*	0.009553	−1.877912	0.0604
Gold	0.071948*	0.040344	1.783344	0.0745
DAX	−0.026407	0.023925	−1.103754	0.2697
QE3	0.002784*	0.001515	1.837500	0.0663
	Variance equation			
C	8.24E-06	1.32E-06	6.239931	0.0000
RESID(−1)^2	0.145863	0.013114	11.12287	0.0000
GARCH(−1)	0.842919	0.012164	69.29799	0.0000

***, **, * Significance level of 1, 5, and 10%, respectively
Source Authors' results based on the analysis of the variables

market at a rate of 1.79% and at a significance level of 10%. The rate of DAX is not statistically significant at any level of significance.

According to Table 4, the variance equation is:

$$\sigma_{2t}^2 = 8.24\text{E} - 06 + 0.145863u_{2t-1}^2 + 0.842919\sigma_{2t-1}^2$$

5 Conclusion

The purpose of this paper is to study the performance of the Greek stock market during the period of the three Quantitative Easing programs implemented by the ECB. 3 GARCH models (1.1) were evaluated using dummy variables for the QE programmes and 10-year bond, gold, and DAX in order to capture systematic international factors. The conclusions drawn were the following: QE1 had a negative effect on the Greek stock market, QE2 did not have a statistically significant impact, while QE3 had a positive impact on stock prices. In the whole period of QE's programmes gold had a positive impact on stock market, while 10-year bond had a negative impact on stock prices during the 2nd and 3rd QE programme. The index DAX seems not to affect the Greek stock market in any period of QE.

More specifically, during the QE1 period, the results of the research showed that the Greek stock market was negatively affected at a rate of 0.57%. During this period (September 2014 to March 2015), Greece was faced with a profound economic and political crisis that drove the country to the brink of exiting the Eurozone and resulted in a steep drop in its stock market. The QE1 implemented was not able to reverse the negative trend or strengthen the stock market. Let us not forget that Greece did not participate in QE1 and any potential benefits from the program would only become evident as an indirect consequence. Similar conclusions were drawn by Fullwiler (2010) who concluded that the Fed failed to address the 2008–2009 crisis through the adoption of QE programs. According to Mishra (2020) Fed QE2 and QE3 had no effect or even a negative impact on the stock market. Gold had a positive impact on Greek stock market at a rate of 7.1%. Similarly, Shahzad (2017) conclude that, when both stock and gold markets are pessimistic, i.e., undergoing stress periods, gold shows a positive dependence with stock markets.

Regarding the period of the 2nd Quantitative Easing program, the results of the research were not statistically significant, so no safe conclusion could be drawn about the influence of QE2 on stock prices. Similarly, even though Al-Jassar (2019) discovered a positive relationship between QE and European stock exchanges, they argued, however, that it is difficult to decide whether stock markets have indeed been affected by QE; other variables, which can strongly influence prices at the stock market, are not present in this case. In this period, Athens stock market were affected negatively by 10-year bond at a rate of 1.79% and positively by gold at a rate of 7.19%. According to the findings of Shahzad (2017) bonds have a negative dependence with the stock prices, particularly when both markets are under stress.

Several studies conclude that bond and stock prices move in opposite directions (Park 2019; Bekaert 2009; Chondia 2005).

Regarding the 3rd Quantitative Easing program, the conclusion reached by the study is that the Greek stock market was positively affected by QE3 at a rate of 0.27%. This was the first time that Greece was eligible to participate in a quantitative easing program of the ECB; although it was a period of an unprecedented health crisis, with a direct impact on the economy, the country appears to have benefited greatly from QE3 and has managed to reverse the downward trend of the stock market which had resulted from the COVID-19 crisis. Numerous studies have shown that QE policy leads to an increase in stock prices (Miyakoshi 2017; Bernanke 2005; Lenzner 2013; Apergis 2018). In contrast to our findings, Ozili (2020) conclude that monetary policy rates had a significant negative impact on stock index prices during the pandemic period, based on data from leading stock markets in North America, Africa, Asia, and Europe between March 23 and April 23, 2020. Regarding to other control variables, gold had a positive impact on Greek stock market at a rate of 7.19% and at a significance level of 10%. On the other hand, 10-YEAR BOND had a negative effect on the Greek stock market at a rate of 1.79%.

Our study provides valuable implications for international investors and policy makers. For investors, Greek economy appears signs of economic recovery. It seems to get over the fiscal crisis and correspond to health crisis successfully. It is worth noting that, according to Ernst and Young (EΥ) attractiveness Survey 2021, Greece ranks for the first time 8th among the 10 most attractive destinations for foreign direct investment (Papazoglou 2021). For policy makers, the Greek government should utilize the positive climate after the end of PEPP and central banks to confirm how important are the QE programs for a country and consider an expand of these programs. Last but not least, it is suggested to other researchers to expand the research to other countries, such us Cyprus (participate in the end of 2nd QE and in the 3rd QE) or German (considering as the leader of the European economy).

References

Al- Awadhi, A. M.-A. (2020). Death and contagious infectious diseases: Impact of the COVID-19 virus on stock market returns. *Journal of Behavioral and Experimental Finance, 27*, p. 100326.

Al- Jassar, S. A. (2019). The effect of quantitative easing on stock prices: a structural time series approach. *Applied Economics, 51 (17)*, pp. 1817–1827.

Albulescu, C. T. (2021). COVID-19 and the United States financial markets' volatility. *Finance Research Lettetrs, 38*, p. 101699.

Altavilla, C. B. (2019). Measuring Euro Area Monetary Policy. *ECB Working Paper No.2281.*

Altavilla, C. C. (2015, November). Asset Purchase Programmes and Financial Markets: Lessons from the Euro Area. *ECB Working Paper 1864, European Central Bank.*

Andersson, M. K. (2008). Why does the correlation between stock and bond returns vary over time? *Applied Financial Economics, 18*, pp. 139–151.

Apergis, N. (2018). Expectations and quantitative easing in the Eurozone. *Economics and Business Letters, 7 (1)*, pp. 18–23.

Ashraf, B. N. (2020). Stock markets reaction to COVID-19: Cases or fatalities? *Research in International Business and Finance, 54*, p. 1011249.

Baek, S. M. (2020). COVID-19 and stock market volatility: An industry level analysis. *Finance Research Letters, 37*, p. 101748.

Baumeister, C. &. (2013). Unconventional monetary policy and the great recession: Estimating the macroeconomic effects of spread compression at the zero lower bound. *International Journal of Central Banking, 9(2)*, pp. 165–213.

Baur, D. G. (2010). Is gold a hedge or a safe haven? An analysis of stocks, bonds and gold. *Financ. Rev. 45(2)*, pp. 217–229.

Beckmann, J. B. (2015). Does gold act as a hedge or a safe haven for the stocks? A smooth transition approach. *Econ. Modell. 48*, pp. 16–24.

Bekaert, G. E. (2009). Risk, uncertainty, and asset prices. *Journal of Financial Economics, 91*, pp. 59–82.

Belke, A. G. (2021). QE in the euro area: Has the PSPP benefited peripheral bonds? *Journal of International Financial Markets, Institutions &Money 73*, p. 101350.

Bernanke, B. S. (2005). What explains the stock market's reaction to federal reserve policy? *The journal of Finance, 60(3)*, pp. 1221–1257.

Brunnemeier, M. R. (2020). Asset price bubbles and systemic risk. *Rev. Financ. Stud. 33(9)*, pp. 4272–4317.

Brunnermeier, M. K. (2009). Market liquidity and funding liquidity. *Review of Financial Studies, 22(6)*, pp. 2201–2238.

Burch, T. R. (2016). Who moves markets in a sudden marketwide crisis? Evidence from 9/11. *Journal of Financial and Quantitative Analysis, 51(2)*, pp. 463–487.

Cecchetti, S. G. (2009). Crisis and responses: The federal reserve in the early stages of the financial crisis (digest summary). *The Journal of Economic Perspectives, 23 (1)*, pp. 51–75.

Chen, C. C. (2009). The positive and negative impacts of the sars outbreak: A case of the Taiwan industries. *The Journal of Developing Areas, 43(1)*, pp. 281–293.

Choi, Y. L. (2020). The coronovarius (COVID-19) pandemic: Assesing the impact on corporate credit risk. *Moody's Analytics*, pp. 1–17.

Chondia, T. S. (2005). An empirical analysis of stock and bond market liquidity. *Review of Financial Studies, 18(1)*, pp. 85–129.

Chudik, A. &. (2011). Identifying the global transmission of the 2007-2009 financial crisi in a GVAR model. *European Economic Review, 55*, pp. 325–339.

Connolly, R. S. (2005). Stock market uncertainty and the stock-bond return relation. *The journal of Financial and Quantitative Analysis, 40*, pp. 161–194.

D' Amico, S. &. (2013). Flow and stock effects of large-scale treasury purchases: Evidence on the importance of local supply. *Journal of Financial Economics, 108(2)*, pp. 425–448.

De Haan, L. V. (2018). The signalling content of asset prices for inflation: Implications for quantitative easing. *Econ. Syst. 42(1)*, pp. 45–63.

Erdem, O. (2020). Freedom and stock market performance during COVID-19 outbreak. *Finance Research Letters, 36*, p. 101671.

Fernandez- Amador, O. G. (2011, February). Monetary policy and its impact on stock market liquidity: Evidence from the euro zone.

Fernandez- Perez, A. G. (2021). COVID-19 pandemic and stock market response: A culture effect. *Journal of Behavioral and Experimental Finance, 29*, p. 100454.

Fullwiler, S. T. (2010). In Quantitative easing and proposals for reform of monetary policy operations, 645. *Bard College Levy Economics Institute Working Paper*.

Gagnon, J. R. (2011). The financial market effects of the large-scale asset purchases. *International Journal of Central Banking, 7(1)*, pp. 3–43.

Georgiadis, G. (2016). Determinants of global spillovers from US monetary policy. *Journal of International Money and Finance, 67*, pp. 41–61.

Goodhart, C. A. (2008). The regulatory response to the financial market effects of the Federal Reserve's large-scale asset purchases. *International Journal of Central Banking, 7 (1)*, pp. 3–43.

Guiko, L. (2002). Decoupling. *The Journal of Portfolio Mnagement, 28*, pp. 59–67.

Haitsma, R. U. (2016). The impact of the ECB's conventional and unconventional monetary policies on stock markets. *J. Macroecon. 48*, pp. 101–116.

Hameed, A. K. (2010). Stock market declines and liquidity. *The journal of Finance, 65(1)*, pp. 257–293.

Hamilton, J. D. (2012). The effectiveness of alternative monetary policy tools in a zero lower bound environment. *Journal of Money, Credit and Banking, 44*, pp. 3–46.

Hartley, J. S. (2020). An event study of COVID-19 central bank quantitative easing in advanced and emerging economies. *NBER*.

Hassan, M. B. (2021). Spillovers of the COVID-19 pandemic: Impact on global economic activity, the stock market, and the energy sector. *Journal of Risk and Financial Management, 14(5)*, pp. 1–19.

He, Q. L. (2020). The impact of COVID-19 on stock markets. *Economic and Political Studies, 8(3)*, pp. 275–288.

Holmstrom, B. &. (2000). Liquidity and risk management. *Journal of Money, Credit, and Banking*, pp. 295–319.

Hudepohl, T. R. (2021). Quantitative easing and exuberance in stock markets: Evidence from the euro area. *Journal of International Money and Finance, 118*, p. 102471.

Kaczmarek, T. P. (2021). How to survive a pandemic: The corporate resiliency of travel and leisure companies to the COVID-19 outbreak. *Tourism Management, 84*, p. 104281.

Karunanayake, I. V. (2010). Financial crises and international stock market volatility transmission. *Australlian Economic Papers, 49(3)*, pp. 209–221.

Kontonikas, A. M. (2013). Stock market reaction to fed funds rate surprises: State dependence and the financial crisis. *Journal of Banking and Finance, 37*, pp. 4025–4037.

Laeven, L. &. (2012). US monetary shocks and global stock prices. *Journal of Financial Intermediation, 21*, pp. 530–547.

Lee, C.-C. C.-H.-C. (2020). The effects of U.S unconventional monetary policy on Asian stock markets. *The Singapore Economic Review, 65 (4)*, pp. 917–945.

Lee, C.-C. C.-P.-C. (n.d.). The effects of U.S unconventional monetary policy on Asian stock markets. *The Singapore Economic Review, 65(4)*, pp. 917–945.

Lenzner, R. (2013, October 17). " You can Thank Ben Bernanke for 100% of the Stock Mrket Gains since 2009". *Forbes*.

Li, W. (2021). COVID-19 and assymetric volatility spillovers across global stock markets. *The North American Journal of Economics and Finance, 58*, p. 101474.

Mishra, A. K. (2020). Stock market liquidity, funding liquidity, financial crises and quantitative easing. *International Review of Economics and Finance, 70*, pp. 456–478.

Miyakoshi, T. S. (2017). The dynamic effects of quantitative easing on stock price: Evidence from Asian emerging markets, 2001-2016. *International Review of Economics and Finance 49*, pp. 548–567.

Narayan, P. K. (2021). COVID-19 lockdowns, stimulus packages, travel bans, and stock returns. *Finance Research Letters, 38*, p. 101732.

Ozili, P. K. (2020). Spillover of COVID-19: Impact on the global economy. *Available at SSRN 3562570*.

Papazoglou, P. (2021). *Grecce is gaining ground on the investment map. How can we maintain this momentum? EY Attractiveness surcey*. Greece: Ernst and Young.

Park, K. F. (2019). Stock and bond returns correlation in Korea: Local versus global risk during crisis periods. *Journal of Asian Economics 65*, p. 101136.

Raza, N. I. (2016). Gold and Islamic stocks: a hedge and safe haven comparison in time frequency domain BRICS markets. *J. Dec. Areas 50*, pp. 305–318.

Ricci, O. (2014). The impact of monetary policy announcements on the stock price of large European banks during the financial crisi. *Journal of Banking and Finance*.

Rose, A. K. (2012). Cross-country causes and consequences of the 2008 crisis: Early warning. *Japan and the World Economy, 24 (1)*, pp. 1–16.

Shahzad, S. J. (2017). Dependence of stock markets with gold and bonds under bullish and bearish market states. *Resources Policy 52*, pp. 308–319.

Shahzad, S. J. (2020). Safe haven, hedge and diversification for G7 stock markets: Gold versus bitcoin. *Economic Modelling 87*, pp. 212–224.

Tillmann, P. (2016). Unconventional monetary policy and the spillovers to emerging markets. *Journal of International Money and Finance, 66*, pp. 159–179.

Ueda, K. (2012). Deleveraging and monetary policy: Japan since 1990s and the United States since 2007. *Journal of Economic Perspectivesm 63*, pp. 177–202.

Wang, G. (2019, February 3). The effects of Quantitative Easing Announcements on the Mortage Market: An Event Study Approach. *International Journal of Financial Studies.*

Wei, X. H. (2021). The impact of COVID-19 pandemic on transmission of monetary po;icy to financial markets. *International Review of Financial Analysis, 74*, p. 101705.

Yarovaya, L. E. (2021). Determinants of spillovers betwenn islamic and conventional financial markets: Exploring the safe haven assets during the COVID-19 pandemic. *Finance Research Letters, 101979.*

Zaremba, A. K. (2021). The quest for multidimensional financial immunity to the COVID-19 pandemic: Evidence from international stock markets. *Journal of International Financial Markets Institutions and Money, 71*, p. 101284.

Zhang, D. H. (2020). Financial markets under the global pandemic of COVID-19. *Finance Research Letters, 36*, p. 101528.

Pest Analysis of the E-commerce Industry: The Case of Greece

Georgios A. Deirmentzoglou and Evangelos A. Deirmentzoglou

Abstract Electronic commerce (e-commerce) has shown to be a critical driver of economic development and has the ability to boost efficiency and productivity in many countries. In the last years, e-commerce has seen rapid growth, especially during the pandemic of COVID-19. Specifically, Greece saw an increase in the number of Internet users who made online purchases and the total revenues of e-commerce transactions. Despite this growth, Greece still has a slow pace of digital transformation compared to other countries of the European Union. The purpose of this paper was to discuss the future of e-commerce in Greece and investigate the factors of the external macro-environment that can be an opportunity or a threat to Greek e-tailing. PEST analysis was used to examine the political, economic, socio-cultural and technological factors that are related to the digital transformation of Greek retail stores. The analysis showed that the e-tailing industry is facing significant threats, but at the same time, it can take advantage of the opportunities created by the external environment. Although there is a trend towards the digital transition of retailing, the state should support both entrepreneurs and consumers.

Keywords E-commerce · E-tailing · PEST analysis · Digital transformation · Greece

JEL Classification Code L81

G. A. Deirmentzoglou (✉)
Neapolis University Pafos, 2 Danais Avenue, 8042 Pafos, Cyprus
e-mail: g.deirmentzoglou@nup.ac.cy

E. A. Deirmentzoglou
University of Piraeus, 80 Karaoli and Dimitriou St, 18534 Piraeus, Greece
e-mail: edeirme@unipi.gr

© The Author(s), under exclusive license to Springer Nature Switzerland AG 2022
P. Sklias et al. (eds.), *Business Development and Economic Governance in Southeastern Europe*, Springer Proceedings in Business and Economics,
https://doi.org/10.1007/978-3-031-05351-1_17

1 Introduction

E-commerce (electronic commerce) has received increasing attention from the academic community in recent years, as it has made critical changes in the business world and has a significant economic impact (Barutchu and Tunca 2012). It has shown to be a critical driver of economic growth (Humphrey et al. 2003) and has the ability to boost efficiency and productivity in many countries (Kabango and Asa 2015). Moreover, e-commerce can be a business channel that improves the communication between customers, producers and other members of the supply chain (Choshin and Ghaffari 2017).

The e-tailing (electronic retailing) industry has seen rapid growth during the last three decades as it is a radically new way of selling goods and services. Due to many benefits, e.g. cost-effectiveness, 24/7 availability, worldwide reach (Wisker 2020) it became common practice around the world. Moreover, during the years, the number of Internet users is steadily growing. In 2020, there was an annual increase of 7.3% Internet users which results in almost 4.66 billion total Internet users (Johnson 2021). This number means that more than half of the global population uses the Internet actively.

In 2020, e-tailing sales reached 4.28 trillion US dollars, while they are estimated to increase to 5.4 trillion US dollars by 2022 (Chevalier 2021). The pandemic of COVID-19 also played a critical role in the importance of e-commerce. In many countries, online shopping was the only way of purchasing products and services, while physical stores were forced to close by government regulations. Global research by Global Webinex (Hootsuite 2021) conducted during the third quarter of 2020 showed that 90.4% of Internet users had visited the past month an online retail store and 76.8% of the total users had purchased a product online.

In the last years, Greece saw an increase in the number of Internet users who made online purchases and the total revenues of e-commerce transactions (Statista 2020). However, recent surveys (e.g. European Commission 2020) showed that Greece still has a slow pace of digital transformation compared to other countries of the European Union.

The purpose of this paper is to discuss the future of e-commerce in Greece and investigate the factors of the external macro-environment that can be an opportunity or a threat to Greek e-tailing. PEST analysis will examine the political, economic, sociocultural and technological factors that are related to the digital transformation of Greek retail stores.

2 Literature Review

2.1 E-commerce in Greece

The Organization for Economic Cooperation and Development defines e-commerce as "an electronic transaction which is the sale or purchase of goods or services between business, households, individuals, governments and other public or private organizations, conducted over computer-mediated networks" (OECD 2002). E-commerce can be classified depending on the nature of its transactions, with the main types being business-to-consumer (B2C), business-to-business transactions (B2B) and consumer-to-consumer (C2C) (Turban et al. 2018). This paper will examine mainly e-commerce in the retail industry in the Greek context.

In 2018, 10% of the companies made B2C e-commerce sales via a Website; while e-commerce was only 4% of the total turnover of Greek enterprises (Statista 2020). In 2019, B2C e-commerce accounted for 2 billion US dollars (EcommerceDB 2020). Greece in 2020 saw an annual increase of 15.2% (Hellenic Statistical Authority 2020) on the number of Internet users who made an online purchase; while in 2021, e-commerce is estimated to have an annual increase in its revenue by 14%, reaching $3.194 billion total revenue (Statista 2020). Despite this growth, the Digital Economy and Society Index (DESI) by the European Commission (2020) revealed that Greece is in the 27th place of the 28 countries-members of the EU (Commission 2020). However, the new Ministry of Digital Governance has set the objective to transform the country into "digital by default" by the next two years. The factors of the external environment in Greece play a significant role in the issues discussed above; thus, a PEST analysis should be conducted.

2.2 PEST Analysis

PEST analysis can be described as a tool whose main purpose is to identify opportunities and threats of the external macro-environment of an organization or an industry (Wheelen et al. 2017). The name PEST is an acronym that stands for political, economic, sociocultural and technological factors, the main forces of the environment that affect business activities.

- Political factors can be government stability, trade regulations, taxation, prices and wages control, etc.
- Economic factors can be the gross domestic product, economic recession, inflation, interest rates, unemployment rate, income, currency exchange rates, etc.
- Sociocultural factors can be social trends, demographics, cultural characteristics, population size, population distribution, lifestyle changes, income distribution, age distribution, etc.

- Technological factors can be artificial intelligence, innovation, technological trends, etc.

The above factors are interrelated. For example, income can be both an economic and a political factor.

PEST can be found also as PESTEL, PESTLE, PESTEEL or PEST DG. PESTEL or PESTLE has included the ecological/environmental and legal factors, PESTEEL has added the ethical factor, whereas the PEST DG includes demographic and global factors. However, all the extra factors that were mentioned above (ecological, legal, ethical, demographic and global) can be included in the main four factors of PEST (Johnson et al. 2011; Sammut-Bonnici and Galea 2014). For example, demographic can be a sub-category of sociocultural or legal can be a sub-category of political. For the above reason, this paper uses a PEST analysis.

The main purpose of the PEST analysis is to help users focus on each factor and try to find opportunities and threats of the external environment to create a strengths, weaknesses, opportunities and threats (SWOT) analysis (Whittington et al. 2020). Thus, the more factors the users use, the easier to include events that can affect the organization or the industry. By skipping the usage of the PEST analysis, the users may focus only on one category of factors and miss some critical others.

3   Methodology and Findings

PEST analysis will be conducted in order to identify the political, economic, sociocultural and technological factors that are related to the digital transformation of Greek retail stores.

3.1   Political Factors

Political factors play a significant role in business decisions, especially those that are related to business development and further growth (Wheelen et al. 2017). Every company needs a stable political environment in order to form a long-term strategic plan.

- During the decade of 2010–2020, Greece was governed by seven different prime ministers (Papandreou 2009–2011, Papadimou 2011–2012, Pikrammenos 2012, Samaras 2012–2015, Tsipras 2015 and 2015–2019, Thanou, 2015, Mitsotakis, 2019–present) and a combination of six political parties. These events result in an unstable political environment that often takes different decisions and actions regarding business legislation and regulations. This can be a threat to any entrepreneur and investor who wants to start a business in Greece.
- In December 2020, the Greek government announced a new funding program by the National Strategic Reference Framework that will subsidy up to five thousand

euros to retailers of physical stores in order to create an e-shop and 1.500 euros to those that already have an e-shop and need an upgrade (ESPA 2021).
- The strict regulations about COVID-19 have forced many types of businesses to close for several months. The owners of physical stores are facing a big change in their business activities, and the only way to sustain their businesses is to turn to e-commerce. This abrupt change in the external environment has revealed the importance of the digital transformation of enterprises.
- Due to economic globalization and low trade restrictions and tariffs (Geringer et al. 2012), Greek retailers have the opportunity to promote their products to a global environment.

3.2 Economic Factors

Economic factors of the macro-environment influence business viability and profitability (Whittington et al. 2020). Greece seemed to be overcoming the deep economic recession of 2010; however, due to the pandemic of COVID-19, this recession will be sustained. This factor can be translated into the following ways:

- The economic recession will increase the uncertainty of the future, consumers will make fewer purchases, the most economically vulnerable business will shut down, and unemployment will rise. Thus, the economic recession can be seen as a threat to businesses and e-commerce as well.
- Due to this recession, consumers are more likely to turn to e-commerce as they will be able to take advantage of its benefits such as the ability to easily and quickly compare prices and find offers and discounts. A recent survey showed that four out of five Greek consumers do research on Google or other price comparison Websites before their purchase (Krataion Consulting 2020).

3.3 Sociocultural Factors

Sociocultural factors can significantly affect business practices (Deirmentzoglou et al. 2020), and thus, they should be considered when analysing the external environment of an industry.

- Only 51% of Greek individuals have at least basic digital skills, while this percentage in the rest of the EU countries is 58%. Moreover, only 23% has above basic digital skills. This percentage is 10% below the average value of the rest members of the EU (Commission 2020).
- There is a trend in buying from e-shops as it is more convenient and easier than purchasing products and services from physical stores. 16% of consumers made their very first online purchase during the COVID-19 outbreak, while 60% of people claim that they will keep making purchases online (Krataion Consulting 2020).

- Generation Z, the true digital natives, is a mobile-centric generation that became old enough to make their purchases (Menat et al. 2016). According to a survey by Krataion Consulting (2020), during the lockdown, 87% of Greek business saw an increase in sales by a mobile phone (Krataion Consulting 2020).

3.4 Technological

The technological element of the PEST analysis highlights the role of technology in the macro-environment (Johnson et al. 2011).

- During the last years, there is significant progress in fast broadband coverage (2019 DESI value was 66%, while 2020 DESI value is 81%), but still, Greece is below the average of the EU (2020 DESI value is 86%). Regarding 4G coverage, Greece (2020 DESI value is 97%) exceeds the average value of the EU (2020 DESI value is 96%) by one point. In this report, Greece takes zero in the 5G readiness index; however, there is significant progress since the publication of the report (Commission 2020).
- 65% of Greek retailers claim that they have developed digital tools in order to run their business. However, there is a lack of ability to use tools regarding artificial intelligence, mobile apps, electronic pricing, cloud and big data analytics (Krataion Consulting 2020) (Table 1).

Table 1 Opportunities and threats of the e-tailing industry in Greece

Opportunities	Threats
Political • Low /no trade restrictions and tariffs in the EU • Subsidies for creating e-shops • The closure of physical stores makes businesses turn to e-commerce	**Political** • Unstable political environment
Economic • Internet discounts and price comparison	**Economic** • Business shutdown • Rise of unemployment
Sociocultural • New social trend • Generation Z and mobile usage	**Sociocultural** • Low levels of digital skills
Technological • Development of digital tools	**Technological** • Low broadband and 5G coverage

4   Discussion

The Greek state and Greek companies seem to be making rapid strides towards digital transition. This transition is largely due to the changes that COVID-19 has brought to the business environment. During the pandemic, entrepreneurs were forced by the state to close their physical stores for months. As a result, e-commerce was the only solution to maintain their business activities. The above analysis identified the main opportunities and threats of the e-commerce industry in the retail sector.

A major threat to Greek companies and consequently to e-tailing is the frequent change of law. The political environment creates uncertainty for entrepreneurs about future business regulations and policies. Furthermore, the economic recession due to the COVID-19 pandemic will make businesses struggle financially and increase unemployment. Also, a significant threat to Greek e-commerce is technological illiteracy. Recent surveys showed that the Greek population has fewer digital skills than the average of EU countries. Thus, the digital transition of businesses is not enough for the development of the industry. Citizens have to develop the appropriate skills so they can use technology in their daily lives. Finally, Greece is still in a low position compared to other EU countries on issues related to broadband coverage and 5G readiness.

Regarding the opportunities, economic globalization and low regulations and tariffs in the EU and the rest of the world can boost the Greek e-tailing. Moreover, the recent changes in the external environment (e.g. COVID-19) made entrepreneurs realize the importance and identify the benefits of e-commerce, while at the same time they saw an increase in their sales on digital channels. Due to the pandemic, many customers turned to online shopping as the only option to buy products and services. As a result, they became familiar with this way of shopping, while a large percentage of customers stated that they will continue shopping online after the end of the pandemic. Finally, in the last few months, Greece has made great progress in the installation of the 5G network.

5   Conclusion

As mentioned in the above analysis, the e-tailing industry in Greece is facing significant threats, but it can take advantage of the opportunities created by the external environment. The main conclusions drawn from this discussion are that there is a trend towards the digital transition of retailing; however, the state should support both entrepreneurs and consumers. Although there is an increase in online shopping, a recent survey shows that only 47% of online customers are satisfied with online purchases. Notably, they state that improvements should be made in (i) the cost of shipping and return policies, (ii) safety and security transactions, (iii) easy paying process, (iv) next day delivery, (v) loyalty programs, (vi) friendliness of the mobile Website, (vii) the "buy online and pick-up-in-store" process and (viii) mobile app purchase (Krataion Consulting 2020). These results showed that having an online store is not enough; entrepreneurs need the appropriate knowledge, tools and infrastructure to run a digital business. Finally, both the Greek state and every citizen at an individual level should give emphasis on education regarding digital skills, as Greece has lower levels of technological literacy compared to other EU countries.

The present research is limited to secondary data regarding e-commerce in Greece before and during the pandemic. Future research should be conducted after the end of the lockdown on both entrepreneurs and consumers for two purposes. Firstly, to identify which of the factors discussed in this paper had the greatest impact on the e-tailing industry and secondly to discuss the new trends of e-commerce.

References

Barutchu S, Tunca MZ (2012) The impacts of E-SCM on the e-tailing industry - An analysis from Porter's five force Perspectives. Social and Behavioral Sciences 58:1047–1056

Chevalier S (2021) Retail e-commerce sales worldwide from 2014 to 2024. Available at https://www.statista.com/statistics/379046/worldwide-retail-e-commerce-sales/. Accessed 19 Jul 2021

Choshin M, Ghaffari A (2017) An investigation of the impact of effective factors on the success of e-commerce in small- and medium-sized companies. Computers in Human Behavior 66:67–74

Deirmentzoglou GA, Agoraki KK, Fousteris AE (2020) Organizational culture and Corporate Sustainable Development: Evidence from Greece. International Journal of Business and Social Science 11(5):92–98

EcommerceDB (2020) E-commerce in Greece 2020. Ecommerce DB country reports

ESPA (2021) E-λιανικό – Επιχορήγηση υφιστάμενων ΜμΕ επιχειρήσεων του κλάδου του λιανεμπορίου για την ανάπτυξη, αναβάθμιση και διαχείριση ηλεκτρονικού καταστήματος. Available at https://www.espa.gr/el/Pages/ProclamationsFS.aspx?item=5113. Accessed 27 Feb 2021

European Commission (2020) Digital Economy and Society Index – Greece. Available at https://ec.europa.eu/digital-single-market/en/scoreboard/greece. Accessed 23 Dec 2020

Geringer LM, McNett JM, Minor MS, Ball DA (2012) International Business. McGraw-Hill Education

Hellenic Statistical Authority (2020) Survey on the use of information and communication technologies in households and by individuals – e-commerce – privacy and protection of personal data:2020. Available at https://www.statistics.gr. Accessed 3 Feb 2021

Hootsuite (2021) Digital 2021 – Global Overview Report. Available at https://www.hootsuite.com/resources/digital-trends. Accessed 19 Jul 2021

Humphrey J, Mansell R, Paré D, Schmitz H (2003) The Reality of E-commerce with Developing Countries. Media Studies, LSE, London

Johnson G, Whittington R, Scholes K (2011) Exploring Strategy, 9th edn. Prentice Hall

Johnson J (2021) Global digital population as of January 2021. Available at https://www.statista.com/statistics/617136/digital-population-worldwide/. Accessed 19 Jul 2021

Kabango CM, Asa RA (2015) Factors influencing e-commerce development: Implications for the developing countries. International Journal of Innovation and Economic Development 1(1):64-72

Krataion Consulting (2020). Ερευνα για το retail στην Covid-19 εποχή. Available at https://krataionconsulting.com/el/blog-el/έρευνα-για-το-retail-στην-covid19-εποχή/. Accessed 3 Feb 2021

Menat R (2016) Why we're so excited about FinTech. In: Chishti S, Barberis J (ed) The Fintech Book – The Financial Technology Handbook for Investors, Entrepreneurs and Visionaries. Wiley, p 10–12

OECD (2002) Measuring the Information Economy. Available at: http://www.oecd.org/digital/iec onomy/2771174.pdf. Accessed 21 Feb 2021

Sammut-Bonnici T, Galea D (2014) PEST analysis. In: Cooper CL (ed) Wiley Encyclopedia of Management. John Wiley & Sons, Ltd

Statista (2020) E-Commerce – Greece. Available at https://www.statista.com/outlook/243/138/eco mmerce/greece#market-arpu. Accessed 21 Dec 2020

Turban E, Outland J, King D, Lee JK, Liang T-P, Turban DC (2018) Electronic commerce 2018 – A managerial and Social Networks Perspective, 9th edn. Springer International Publishing AG

Wheelen TH, Hunger JD, Hoffman AN, Bamford CE (2017) Concepts in Strategic Management and Business Policy: Globalization, Innovation and Sustainability, 15th edn. Pearson

Whittington R, Regner P, Angwin D, Johnson G, Scholes K (2020) Exploring Strategy – Text and Cases, 12th edn. Pearson

Wisker ZL (2020) Examining relationship quality in e-tailing experiences: a moderated mediation model. Marketing Intelligence & Planning 38(7):863–876

Bibliometric Analysis
of Migration-Tourism-Terrorism Nexus

Daniel Dragičević, Maja Nikšić Radić, and Maja Buljat

Abstract Tourism is considered the most important economic driver of many countries. Employment, inflow of foreign exchange and investment are some of the many channels through which tourism benefits the economy. Tourism faces many problems and terrorism and migrations are undoubtedly one of those. In a broader sense, tourism, terrorism and migration are closely intertwined with the concept of voluntary and involuntary migration. Terrorism has a negative impact on tourism and is considered a major driver of migration flows. Immigrants, after acquiring the necessary economic wealth in a new country of residence, become a part of tourist flows. In this paper, a framework for the migration-tourism-terrorism nexus has been established, and the main areas of current research have been highlighted. Bibliometric analysis was applied to the WOS database for the period from 2001 to 2021. The research implemented a three-tiered approach that identified relevant articles in the area of terrorism and tourism (TT) (138), migration and tourism (MT) (103), and migration, tourism and terrorism (MTT) (2). In addition to the citation and co-authorship analysis, this study analyzed the co-occurrence of keywords. The results show that the USA, UK and China are the most prolific countries, while Tourism Economics, Tourism Management and Annals of Tourism Research are the most relevant journals in the field. The co-keyword analysis identified four distinct research areas for TT and three for MT. At the end of the paper, possible future research directions for each area are clearly indicated, and the limitations of this study are highlighted.

Keywords Tourism · Terrorism · Migration · Bibliometric analysis

JEL Classification L83 · D74 · F22

D. Dragičević · M. N. Radić (✉) · M. Buljat
Faculty of Tourism and Hospitality Management, University of Rijeka, Primorska ul. 46, 51410 Opatija, Croatia
e-mail: majanr@fthm.hr

D. Dragičević
e-mail: danield@fthm.hr

M. Buljat
e-mail: majabuljat1988@gmail.com

© The Author(s), under exclusive license to Springer Nature Switzerland AG 2022
P. Sklias et al. (eds.), *Business Development and Economic Governance in Southeastern Europe*, Springer Proceedings in Business and Economics,
https://doi.org/10.1007/978-3-031-05351-1_18

1 Introduction

Tourism, terrorism and migration are considered a global phenomenon. Tourism is defined as "a social, cultural and economic phenomenon which entails the movement of people to countries or places outside their usual environment for personal or business/professional purposes." (UNWTO 2021).

Tourism affects the economy through channels such as foreign exchange earnings, investment, direct, indirect and induced effects on other sectors of the economy, employment and income (Brida et al. 2016). Empirical research analyzes the impact of tourism on economic growth through the tourism-led growth hypothesis, which states that tourism is one of the most important drivers of economic development. Research on this topic is not homogeneous (Nunkoo et al. 2020; Comerio and Strozzi 2019). Some of the results confirm positive and unidirectional relationship between tourism and economic growth, confirming the tourism-led growth hypothesis in the short run (Bassil et al. 2015; Georgantopoulos 2013) and in the long run (Ertugrul and Mangir 2015; Jalil et al. 2013). Other authors find that economic growth promotes tourism development (Tang and Abosedra 2014; Suryandaru 2020). The heterogeneity of empirical research is even greater, as some results indicate the existence of a bidirectional relationship (Massidda and Mattana 2013; Katircioglu 2009).

There is no internationally agreed and unambiguous definition of terrorism. UNESCO (2017, p.19) defines terrorism as a "particular strategy adopted to achieve a political goal, which is singularly the deliberate creation and exploitation of fear". Similarly, Hudson (1999) stipulates that a terrorist action is unexpected, shocking and unlawful violence against non-combatants and other symbolic targets. The impact of terrorism on tourism is well established through terrorism-led tourism hypothesis. Negative impacts are seen in the reduction of tourism income levels (Schmude et al. 2020; Chen 2011), tourism demand (Muryani and Padilla 2020; Masinde and Buigut 2018) and spatial spillover effects (Seabra et al. 2020; Bassil et al. 2019). Less researched is the tourism-led terrorism hypothesis. Empirical studies suggest a positive relationship between tourism and terrorism (Goldman and Neubauer-Shani 2017; Nikšić Radić et al. 2018). Destination image and visitation intentions are affected by terrorism risk and political instability. Tourism is less sensitive to terrorism than to political instability (Hanon and Wang 2020). Research suggests that the negative influence is lower for tourists who use social networks (Assaker and O'Connor 2021). There is evidence that tourism is resilient to terrorism. Liu and Pratt (2017) found that there is no long-term effect of terrorism on international tourism demand, while the short-term effect is limited from a global perspective. Travelers with strong cosmopolitan beliefs are more resilient to the image of an unsafe destination due to terrorist attacks (Veréb et al. 2020). Short-term negative effects are shorter for developed countries and last only two months after the attack (Zeman and Urban 2019).

Migration is "the movement of persons away from their place of usual residence, either across and international border or within a state," while immigration is "the act of moving into a country other than one's country of nationality or usual residence so that the country of destination effectively becomes his or her new country of usual residence" (IOM 2021). Both tourism and migration represent a movement of people away from their usual place of residence. By extension, tourists and migrants are travelers. Tourism generates migration and vice versa, and migration generates tourism flows (Provenzano 2020). The findings of Marcher et al. (2020) on local tourism destination (South Tyrol) confirm the pull effect that tourism has on migration, but the presence of migrants is also strongly associated with the influx of tourists. The positive influence of migration on tourist flows can be explained by the visiting friends and relatives (VFR) hypothesis. This hypothesis states that immigrants invite their friends and relatives from the countries of origin, thereby increasing overall tourist arrivals in the host country. Relationship maintenance between immigrants and their friends and relatives reflects aspects of social exchange theory and dependence and obligations, especially in terms of relative perspective (Capistrano and Weaver 2017). Empirical research confirms a strong quantitative link between migration and VFR tourism (Dwyer et al. 2014; Provenzano and Baggio 2017). Immigrants are very active hosts to friends and relatives in their new countries and can be seen as ambassadors of the destination (Griffin and Guttentag 2020). The attractiveness of a tourist destination, structural challenges and seasonal fluctuations in tourism makes migration an important source for filling the needed workforce (Joppe 2012). Business opportunities and earning potential in a host country turn immigrants into tourists themselves. Evidence suggests that immigrants' travel habits and leisure activities are linked to domestic (host) tourism (Irimiás 2013). The negative impact of the refugee/migrant influx on the hotel industry is recorded on the example of Greek islands. Ivanov and Stavrinoudis (2018) show that the refugee crisis had a negative impact on the operating statistics of hotels and on the image of the islands themselves. Similarly, the case of Chios and Lesvos (Greek islands) shows a negative attitude of local stakeholders toward the influx of refugees on economic and social life (Tsartas et al. 2020).

Research on the migration-tourism-terrorism nexus is rather sparse. The dynamics between these phenomena have not received enough attention from the research community. To the best of the author's knowledge, there is only one paper, in the WOS database, that substantively examines the relationship between terrorism, tourism and immigration. Harb and Bassil (2019) conclude that the relationship between terrorism and tourism is moderated by the proportion of immigrants in the destination country—a higher number of immigrants offsets the negative impact of terrorism on tourist arrivals.

The main purpose of this article is to classify and identify the most relevant research in this field according to leading articles, authors, journals, countries and institutions. The contribution of this article is to identify key research and future research directions based on the recommendation of the leading articles in the field. The findings will help facilitate future discussions between researchers and policymakers. This article is organized into four sections. After the introduction, the second section explains the data and methodology used. The third section discusses the main findings of the analysis and is followed by the conclusion.

2 Data and Methodology

In this paper, a bibliometric analysis of the articles indexed in the Web of Science database (Web of Science Core Collection) is performed. The main purpose of bibliometrics is to statistically identify important articles and authors based on the number of citations. In addition to citation and co-author analysis, this study analyzed the co-occurrence of keywords. The programs HistCite (Clarivate n.d.) (citation and co-authorship analysis) and VOSviewer (van Eck and Waltman 2020a) (co-occurrence analysis) were used for this purpose. Data mining was performed on March 15 and 16, 2021. A three-step approach was defined to collect the relevant data. First, a Boolean advanced search was performed for articles with the following combination of keywords in Topic: (a) terroris* AND tourism; (b) (immigr* OR migra*) AND tourism; (c) (immigr* OR migra*) AND tourism AND terroris*. The search was also restricted to a time period (2001-March 2021), a language (English) and a document type (article). The first step yielded 520 units for (a), 1718 units for (b) and 11 units for (c). The second step filtered the given results by research area: hospitality leisure tourism, management, economics and business. After the second step, there were 396 articles for (a), 574 articles for (b) and 6 articles for (c). In the third step, the authors identified relevant articles by checking their titles, abstracts and keywords, and the full text was required. At the end 138 articles were analyzed for (a), 103 for (b) and 2 for (c). Literature reviews were excluded from the data mining process, while early access articles were included.

Statistics for each item included Local Citation Score (LCS), Total Local Citation Score (TLCS), Global Citation Score (GCS), Total Global Citation Score (TGCS) and Local Citation Score per year (TLC/t), where Local Citation Score is the number of citations to the paper from the collection (138, 103 and 2, respectively), and Global Citation Score is the number of citations to the paper from all sources, as reported on the Web of Science (WOS) when downloading the data (Clarivate n.d.). Co-occurrence analysis determines the relatedness of keywords based on the number of documents in which they co-occur (van Eck and Waltman 2020b).

3 Results

Descriptive statistics of the annual cumulative number of publications and global citation are shown in Fig. 1. A total of 138 relevant articles were published on terrorism and tourism (TT), 103 on migration and tourism (MT) and 2 on migration, tourism and terrorism (MTT). From 2001 to 2021, the total number of citations to relevant articles from all sources indicated in WOS was: TT = 3288; MT = 1456 and MTT = 5.

Figure 1 shows an increasing publication trend of all subjects with the sharp increase from 2015. The average growth rate of published articles for TT from 2015 to 2020 was 48.6%. The highest TGSC was recorded in 2003 and 2008 (441 and

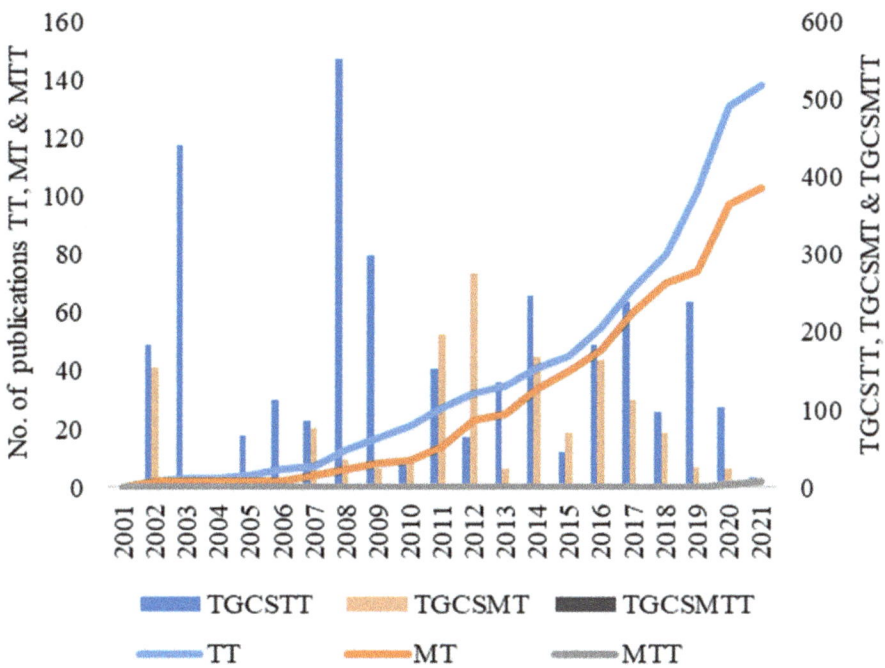

Fig. 1 Number of publications (cumulative) and total global citations from 2001 to 2021

551, respectively). Newly published articles did not receive many citations because it takes time to gain recognition in a field.

Table 1 lists the top five most productive countries in TT, MT and MTT. The top five countries account for 60% of all published articles in the TT research area and

Table 1 Most productive countries in the research field

#	Country	# of Articles	%	TLCS	TGCS	Country	# of Articles	%	TLCS	TGCS
Terrorism and Tourism						*Migration and Tourism*				
1	USA	26	18.8	118	1290	UK	22	21.4	70	494
2	UK	17	12.3	85	503	China	18	17.5	57	391
3	Australia	14	10.1	76	480	USA	16	15.5	19	123
4	China	14	10.1	49	220	Italy	11	10.7	19	78
5	Turkey	12	8.7	30	138	Canada	10	9.7	16	149
Migration, Tourism and Terrorism										
#	Country	# of Articles	%	TLCS	TGCS					
1	Lebanon	1	50	0	4					
2	Ghana	1	50	0	1					

Table 2 Most productive journals in the field

Terrorism and Tourism					Migration and Tourism			
#	Journal	# of Articles	TLCS/t	TGCS/t	Journal	# of Articles	TLCS/t	TGCS/t
1	TE	13	7.08	21.19	ATR	12	4.55	35.99
2	TM	9	12.21	82.99	TG	10	1.46	13.52
3	CIT	8	5.63	21.83	TM	10	6.15	52.38
4	JTR	8	10.7	47.36	IJTR	7	2.1	9.8
5	ATR	6	6.81	58.65	CIT	5	1.75	9.22
Migration, Tourism and Terrorism								
#	Journal	# of Articles	TLCS/t	TGCS/t				
1	TE	1	0	2				
2	THR	1	0	1				

Note TE—Tourism Economics; *TM*—Tourism Management; *CIT*—Current Issues in Tourism; *JTR*—Journal of Travel Research; *ATR*—Annals of Tourism Research; *TG*—Tourism Geographies; *IJTR*—International Journal of Tourism Research; *THR*—Tourism and Hospitality Research

75% in MT. Since there are only two relevant articles in MTT, both are listed in the table. The USA, UK and China are leading countries in the research areas analyzed.

The most active institutions in the field of research are: Bournemouth University (UK), Notre Dame University Louaize (Lebanon), University of Otago (New Zealand), Hong Kong Polytech University (China), Umea University (Sweden) and Cagliari University (Italy).

Leading journals in TT, MT and MTT research are shown in Table 2. Journals are ranked by number of articles published, average local citations (TLCS/t) and average global citations (TGCS/t). The top ranked journal in TT by number of articles is Tourism Economics with 13 published articles, average local citation of 7.08 and average global citation of 21.19. Although the second ranked by number of articles, Tourism Management has the highest TLCS/t (12.21) and TGCS/t (82.99), making it the most relevant journal in TT. Annals of Tourism Research is at the top in MT with 12 published articles, TLCS/t 4.55 and TGCS/t 35.99. Again looking at the citation score, Tourism Management has the highest average citation index with a TLCS/t of 6.15 and a TGCS/t of 52.38. The MTT research topic is perhaps the most novel with the first article published in 2020. Out of two articles analyzed, one is published in Tourism Economics, and one is published in Tourism and Hospitality Research. The analysis shows that Tourism Economics, Tourism Management and Annals of Tourism Research are the most relevant journals.

The co-occurrence analysis of TT was based on a total of 650 keywords, where the minimum number of occurrences of a keyword was set to five. A total of 49 keywords met the set threshold. The most frequently used keyword was terrorism (92 items, total link strength of 379), followed by impact (45 items, total link strength of 253), tourism (53 items, total link strength of 219), international tourism (25 items, total link strength of 156) and political instability (24 items, total link strength of 150). The link strength indicates the number of publications in which two keywords appear together.

In the co-keyword network (Fig. 2a), the size of the circle represents the occurrence of the keywords. As mentioned above, the most frequently used keyword was

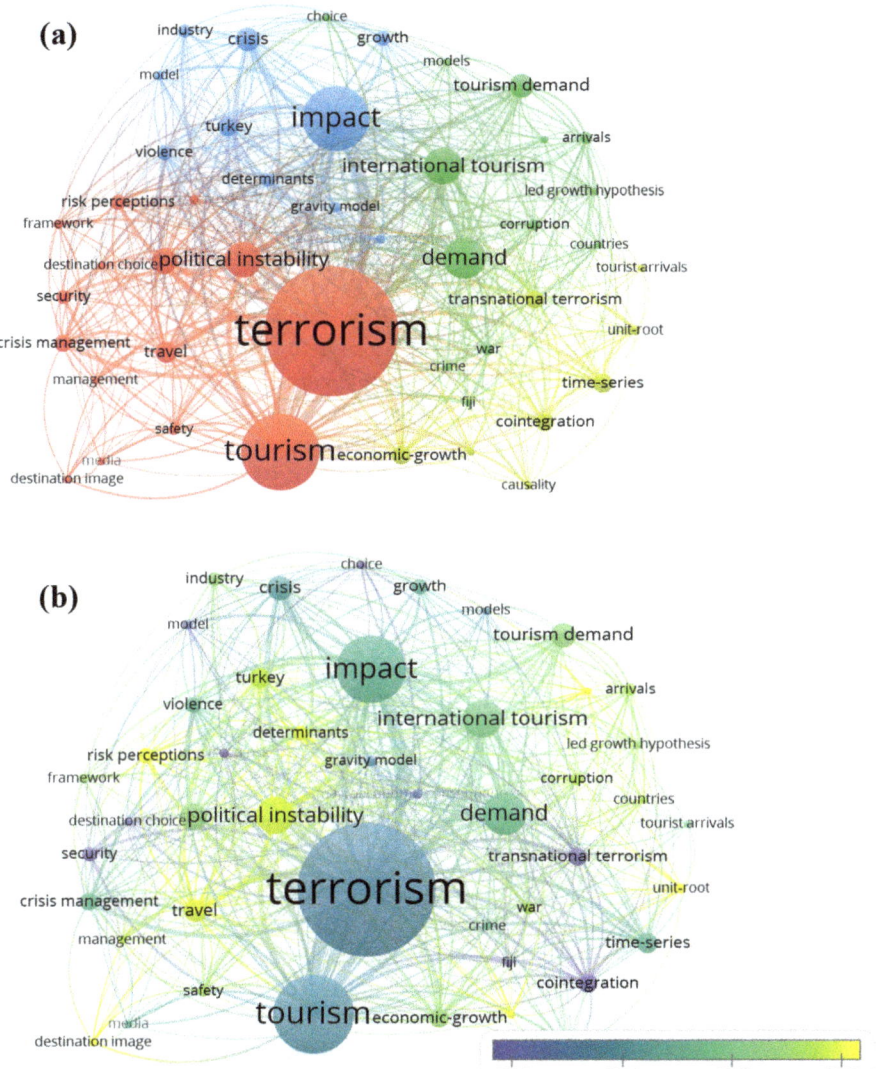

Fig. 2 Keyword co-occurrence analysis in the terrorism and tourism research: **a** co-keyword network visualization based on the occurrences; **b** co-keyword overlay visualization based on the occurrences and average publication per year scores

terrorism. Figure 2a shows the grouping of keywords into four distinct clusters. The red cluster is represented by keywords such as terrorism, tourism, political instability, crisis management, security, risk perception, management and media. This clearly relates to the theme of "destination risk perception and management". The green cluster includes keywords such as international tourism, demand, arrivals, countries and choice. This is the area of "tourism demand". The blue cluster is represented by the term "impact of terrorism", while the yellow cluster contains "models" used in research. The co-keyword overlay visualization (Fig. 2b) shows the most influential keywords over time. Political instability, risk perception and destination image are keywords with high occurrence in recent years.

In the MT co-occurrence analysis, 594 keywords were considered, with the minimum number of occurrences set at five. A total of 27 keywords met the threshold. The most frequently used keyword was migration (43 items, total link strength of 107), followed by tourism (32 items, total link strength of 68), immigration (18 items, total link strength of 55) and experience (10 items, total link strength of 48). Three clusters were formed for the MT. The red cluster is represented by the keywords migration, tourism, destination, visiting friends and relatives, experience, etc. The cluster can be called "VFR travel" because the dominant theme is migration and tourism, which is explained by the hypothesis of visiting friends and relatives. Keywords that emerge in a green cluster are identity, authenticity, diaspora tourism, place attachment, transnationalism, homeland, etc. This could be the theme of "migrant adaptation". The blue cluster deals with "tourism demand and migration" (Fig. 3).

The insufficient number of articles in MTT fields makes co-occurrence unreliable and not meaningful. The most cited paper in the TT field is that of Arana and León (2008) (Table 3). Their results show that the image of a destination is strongly (negatively) affected by terrorist attacks. Risk perception about a destination is undoubtedly important, but it must be taken into account that tourists are not a homogeneous group. Experienced tourists and those seeking familiarity are more likely to be risk averse (Lepp and Gibson 2003). Moreover, research shows that international tourism is more resilient to terrorism in the long run (Liu and Pratt 2017). In the short term, domestic demand, which is insensitive to terrorism, can be seen as a buffer to the decline in foreign tourism (Fleischer and Buccola 2002). The impact of political instability on tourism is greater than the impact of one-time terrorist attacks (Saha and Yap 2014).

The most established author in the MT research area is Neelu Seetaram from Leeds Becket University. This researcher is the author or co-author of four of the five most cited papers in the field. The most influential paper is that of Seetaram (2012b). This paper has been cited 16 times in the field (LCS) and 66 times in the database WOS (GSC). The paper established the relationship between immigration and inward migration with estimated short-run (0.028) and long-run (0.09) immigration elasticities. The data for Australia confirm that immigration is an important determinant of total inbound arrivals (Seetaram and Dwyer 2009) and outbound departures (Seetaram 2012a). A strong quantitative relationship between migration and VFR tourism has been identified for Australia (Dwyer et al. 2014). Employment

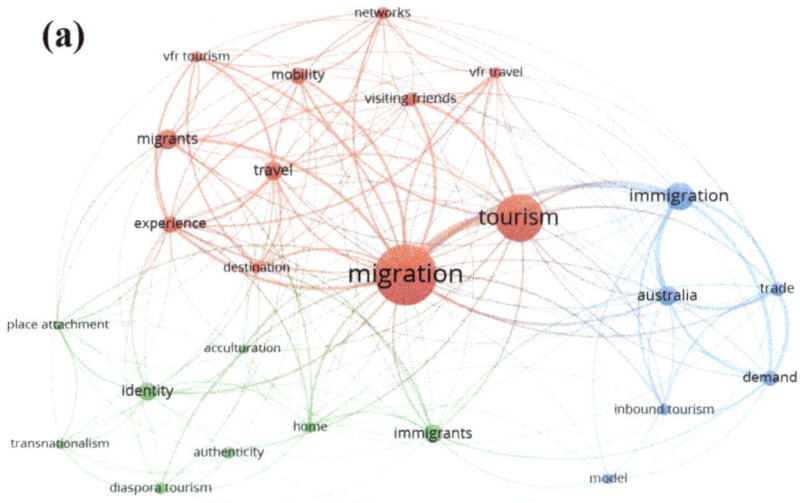

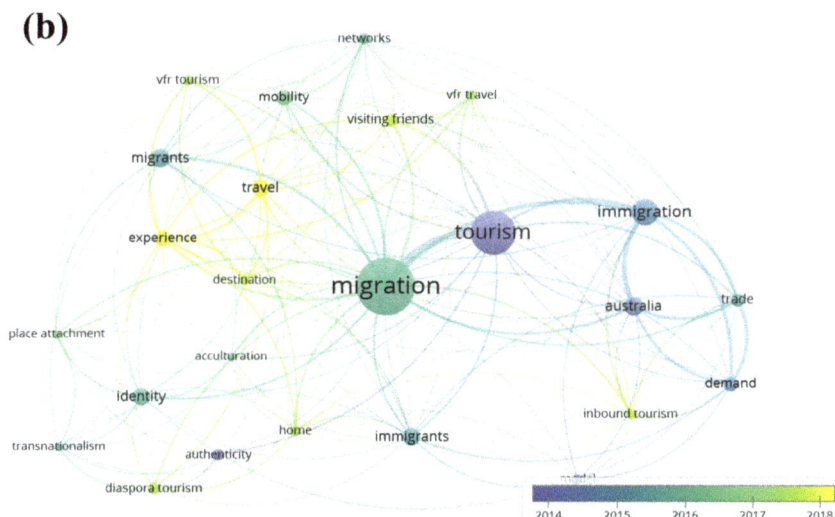

Fig. 3 Keyword co-occurrence analysis in the migration and tourism research: **a** co-keyword network visualization based on the occurrences; **b** co-keyword overlay visualization based on the occurrences and average publication per year scores

in tourism improves migrants' social and cultural skills in the host country (Janta et al. 2011).

As mentioned earlier, there are only two relevant papers published in the field of MTT. The most cited work globally, and perhaps the only one that substantively examines the dynamics of the migration-tourism-terrorism nexus, is Harb and Bassil (2019) (Table 4).

Table 3 Most influential articles in TT and MT field for 2001–2021 period

Terrorism and Tourism

#	Article	LCS	LCS/t	GCS	GCS/t
1	Arana and León (2008)	41	2.93	174	12.4
2	Saha and Yap (2014)	32	4	133	16.6
3	Liu and Pratt (2017)	31	6.2	89	17.8
4	Lepp and Gibson (2003)	25	1.32	441	23.2
5	Fleischer and Buccola (2002)	21	1.05	83	4.15

Migration and Tourism

#	Article	LCS	LCS/t	GCS	GCS/t
1	Seetaram (2012b)	16	1.6	66	6.6
2	Dwyer et al. (2014)	14	1.75	45	5.63
3	Seetaram and Dwyer (2009)	11	0.85	23	1.77
4	Janta et al. (2011)	10	0.91	67	6.09
5	Seetaram (2012a)	8	0.8	29	2.9

Table 4 Articles published in MTT field for 2001–2021 period

Migration, Tourism and Terrorism

#	Article	LCS	LCS/t	GCS	GCS/t
1	Harb and Bassil (2019)	0	0	4	2
2	Preko (2021)	0	0	1	1

The authors use a gravity model to examine the impact of terrorist attacks and the stock of immigrants, as well as other control variables, on tourist flows from country i to country j in year t. They estimated specifications of the gravity model using the Poisson pseudo-maximum likelihood (PPML) estimator on annual data from 35 OECD countries for the period 1995–2015. Their results suggest that the negative impact of terrorism on tourist arrivals can be dampened if the stock of immigrants is sufficiently high.

To formulate important future research directions, an analysis of the recommendations of the top five trend articles for the period 2018–2020 was conducted (Table 5). Some of the future directions in the TT area are to study: (a) how the intensity of terrorism incidents affects different forms of tourism; (b) out-of-sample forecasting and the nature of observed long-term memory behavior; (c) the influence of travel purpose and travel party on travel decisions in response to the threat of terrorism; (d) how the level of disposable income for travel determines the willingness to travel in a terrorism threat situation.

The recommendations from MT research area can be summarized as follows: (a) explore community issues and residents' opinions regarding migrant tourism; (b) identify the extent to which "cultural distance" might influence various aspects of international students' VFR travel; (c) explore the relationship between VFR experiences and permanent residence in a host country; (d) compare different

Table 5 Top five trending articles by LCS in the TT and MT field for the 2018–2020 period

Terrorism and Tourism				Migration and Tourism		
#	Article	LCS	GCS	Article	LCS	GCS
1	Samitas et al. (2018)	12	27	Ndione et al. (2018)	3	4
2	Bassil et al. (2019)	12	25	Tran et al. (2018)	2	3
3	Lanouar and Goaied (2019)	9	39	Choi and Fu (2018)	2	10
4	Walters et al. (2019)	9	22	Huang et al. (2018)	2	16
5	Masinde and Buigut (2018)	5	9	Carson et al. (2018)	1	14

migrant mobilities and their impact on local socioeconomic development in sparsely populated areas.

Finally, MTT recommendations derived from Harb and Bassil (2019): (a) further investigate the nonlinear relationship between terrorism and tourism flows in country-specific studies; (b) test whether the dampening immigrant effect holds for developing countries; (c) further investigate the links between terrorism and immigrants.

4 Conclusion

Tourism, terrorism and migration are the most important issues in the world in the last decade. The purpose of this article was to identify the key research in the mentioned areas. The migration-tourism-terrorism nexus issue is under-researched in the global scientific community. The analysis shows that there are only two relevant articles, but in fact only one that examines the dynamics of migration, tourism and terrorism.

In this paper, a bibliometric analysis was carried out using the database WOS for the period 2001–2021 for the topics TT, MT and MTT. The number of published papers shows an increasing trend in all research areas, especially after 2015. Tourism Economics, Tourism Management and Annals of Tourism Research represent the most relevant journals for the field.

The analysis of TT identified four distinct clusters or areas of research interest. These are: destination risk perception and management, tourism demand, impact of terrorism and models. MT co-occurrence analysis points to three key areas: VFR travel, migrant adaptation, tourism demand and migration.

The article identifies key future research directions for each area. For TT, future research could include examining how the intensity of terrorism incidents affects different forms of tourism, determining the influence of trip purpose and trip party on travel decisions in response to the threat of terrorism, or exploring how the amount of disposable income for travel determines the willingness to travel in a terrorism threat situation. Some of the recommendations for MT are: exploring community issues and residents' opinions regarding migrant tourism, identifying the extent to which "cultural distance" might influence various aspects of international students'

VFR travel, comparing different migrant mobilities and their impact on local socioe-conomic development in sparsely populated areas. As MTT is the least researched, there could be many possible directions. Some of them are: testing whether the dampening immigrant effect applies to developing countries, further investigating the links between terrorism and immigrants.

There are limitations to this study. The analysis only covers the period from 2001 to 2021, and it can be argued that this period was set due to the 9/11 attack in the US and the increasing number of articles in the TT field after this event. On the other hand, TT research is predated to this year. Some of the most cited papers date from the early 1990s. Another limitation is the exclusive use of the database WOS. One of the recommendations for future research is to include more databases such as Scopus. This could provide more comprehensive results. Another limiting factor is the keywords chosen. Synonyms for tourism such as "travel" or "travelers" and for terrorism "violent attacks" can be used.

Acknowledgements This work was supported by the University of Rijeka under Grant ZP UNIRI 8/18.

References

Arana, J.E. and León, C.J. (2008). The impact of terrorism on tourism demand. *Annals of Tourism Research*, 35(2), 299–315.

Assaker, G. and O'Connor, P. (2021). eWOM platforms in moderating the relationships between political and terrorism risk, destination image, and travel intent: the case of Lebanon. *Journal of Travel Research*, 60(3), 503–519.

Bassil, C., Hamadeh, M. and Samara, N. (2015). The tourism led growth hypothesis: the Lebanese case. *Tourism Review*, 70(1), 43–55.

Bassil, C., Saleh, A.S. and Anwar, S. (2019). Terrorism and tourism demand: a case study of Lebanon, Turkey and Israel. *Current Issues in Tourism*, 22(1), 50–70.

Brida, J.G., Cortes-Jimenez, I. and Pulina, M. (2016). Has the tourism-led growth hypothesis been validated? A literature review. *Current Issues in Tourism*, 19(5), 394–430.

Capistrano, R.C. and Weaver, A. (2017). Host-guest interactions between first-generation immigrants and their visiting relatives: social exchange, relations of care and travel. *International Journal of Culture, Tourism and Hospitality Research*, 11(3), 406-420.

Carson, D.A., Carson, D.B. and Eimermann, M. (2018). International winter tourism entrepreneurs in northern Sweden: understanding migration, lifestyle, and business motivations. *Scandinavian Journal of Hospitality and Tourism*, 18(2), 183–198.

Chen, M.-H. (2011). The response of hotel performance to international tourism development and crisis events. *International Journal of Hospitality Management*, 30(1), 200–212.

Choi, S. and Fu, X. (2018). Hosting friends and family as a sojourner in a tourism destination. *Tourism Management*, 67, 47–58.

Clarivate HistCite 12.03.17.

Comerio, N. and Strozzi, F. (2019). Tourism and its economic impact: A literature review using bibliometric tools. *Tourism economics*, 25(1), 109–131.

Dwyer, L., Seetaram, N., Forsyth, P. and King, B. (2014). Is the migration-tourism relationship only about VFR? *Annals of Tourism Research*, 46, 130–143.

Ertugrul, H.M. and Mangir, F. (2015). The tourism-led growth hypothesis: empirical evidence from Turkey. *Current Issues in Tourism*, 18(7), 633–646.

Fleischer, A. and Buccola, S. (2002). War, terror, and the tourism market in Israel. *Applied Economics*, 34(11), 1335–1343.

Georgantopoulos, A.G. (2013). Tourism Expansion and Economic Development: Var/Vecm Analysis and Forecasts for the Case of India. *Asian Economic and Financial Review*, 3(4), 464–482.

Goldman, O.S. and Neubauer-Shani, M. (2017). Does international tourism affect transnational terrorism? *Journal of Travel Research*, 56(4), 451–467.

Griffin, T. and Guttentag, D. (2020). Identifying active resident hosts of VFR visitors. *International Journal of Tourism Research*, 22(5), 627–636.

Hanon, W. and Wang, E. (2020). Comparing the impact of political instability and terrorism on inbound tourism demand in Syria before and after the political crisis in 2011. *Asia Pacific Journal of Tourism Research*, 25(6), 651–661.

Harb, G. and Bassil, C. (2019). Terrorism and inbound tourism: Does immigration have a moderating effect? *Tourism Economics*, 1–19.

Huang, W.-J., Hung, K., Chen, C.-C. (2018). Attachment to the home country or hometown? Examining diaspora tourism across migrant generations. *Tourism Management*, 68, 52–65.

Hudson, R.A. (1999). *The sociology and psychology of terrorism: Who becomes a terrorist and why?* Majeska, Marilyn ed. Library of Congress, Washington D.C. Federal Research Division.

IOM (2021). Key Migration Terms [Internet]. Available from: https://www.iom.int/key-migration-terms#Migration [Accessed 25 February 2021].

Irimiás, A. (2013). Traveling Patterns of Chinese Immigrants Living in Budapest. *Journal of China Tourism Research*, 9(2), 180–190.

Ivanov, S., Stavrinoudis, T.A. (2018). Impacts of the refugee crisis on the hotel industry: Evidence from four Greek islands. Tourism Management, 67, 214-223.

Jalil, A., Mahmood, T. and Idrees, M. (2013). Tourism–growth nexus in Pakistan: Evidence from ARDL bounds tests. *Economic Modelling*, 35, 185–191.

Janta, H., Brown, L., Lugosi, P. and Ladkin, A. (2011). Migrant relationships and tourism employment. *Annals of Tourism Research*, 38(4), 1322–1343.

Joppe, M. (2012). Migrant workers: Challenges and opportunities in addressing tourism labour shortages. *Tourism Management*, 33(3), 662–671.

Katircioglu, S. (2009). Testing the tourism-led growth hypothesis: The case of Malta. *Acta Oeconomica*, 59(3), 331–343.

Lanouar, C. and Goaied, M. (2019). Tourism, terrorism and political violence in Tunisia: Evidence from Markov-switching models. *Tourism Management*, 70, 404–418.

Lepp, A. and Gibson, H. (2003). Tourist roles, perceived risk and international tourism. *Annals of tourism research*, 30(3), 606–624.

Liu, A. and Pratt, S. (2017). Tourism's vulnerability and resilience to terrorism. *Tourism Management*, 60, 404–417.

Marcher, A., Kofler, I., Innerhofer, E. and Pechlaner, H. (2020). Perceptions of and interactions between locals, migrants, and tourists in South Tyrol. *Tourism Geographies*, 1–17.

Masinde, B. and Buigut, S. (2018). Effect of terrorism and travel warning on Kenyan tourism demand. *Tourism Analysis*, 23(2), 283–288.

Massidda, C. and Mattana, P. (2013). A SVECM analysis of the relationship between international tourism arrivals, GDP and trade in Italy. *Journal of Travel Research*, 52, No. 1, 93–105.

Muryani, M.F.P. and Padilla, M.A.E. (2020). Determinants of tourism demand in Indonesia: a panel data analysis. *Tourism analysis*, 25(1), 78–89.

Ndione, L., Decrop, A. and Rémy, E. (2018). Migrants going back homeland for holidays: Rituals and practices of Senegalese migrants in France. *Annals of Tourism Research*, 70, 25–38.

Nikšić Radić, M., Dragičević, D. and Barkiđija Sotošek, M. (2018). The tourism-led terrorism hypothesis-evidence from Italy, Spain, UK, Germany and Turkey. *Journal of International Studies*, 11(2), 236–249.

Nunkoo, R., Seetanah, B., Jaffur, Z.R.K., Moraghen, P.G.W. and Sannassee, R.V. (2020). Tourism and economic growth: A meta-regression analysis. *Journal of Travel Research*, 59(3), 404–423.

Preko, A. (2021). Safety and security concerns at the beach: Views of migrant visitors in Ghana. *Tourism and Hospitality Research*, 21(1), 73–85.

Provenzano, D. (2020). The migration-tourism nexus in the EU28. *Tourism Economics*, 26(8), 1374–1393.

Provenzano, D. and Baggio, R. (2017). The contribution of human migration to tourism: The VFR travel between the EU 28 member states. *International Journal of Tourism Research*, 19(4), 412–420.

Saha, S. and Yap, G. (2014). The moderation effects of political instability and terrorism on tourism development: A cross-country panel analysis. *Journal of Travel Research*, 53(4), 509–521.

Samitas, A., Asteriou, D., Polyzos, S. and Kenourgios, D. (2018). Terrorist incidents and tourism demand: Evidence from Greece. *Tourism Management Perspectives*, 25, 23–28.

Schmude, J., Karl, M. and Weber, F. (2020). Tourism and Terrorism: Economic impact of terrorist attacks on the tourism industry. The example of the destination of Paris. *Zeitschrift für Wirtschaftsgeographie*, 64(2), 88–102.

Seabra, C., Reis, P. and Abrantes, J.L. (2020). The influence of terrorism in tourism arrivals: A longitudinal approach in a Mediterranean country. *Annals of Tourism Research*, 80, p.102811.

Seetaram, N. (2012a). Estimating demand elasticities for Australia's international outbound tourism. *Tourism Economics*, 18(5), 999–1017

Seetaram, N. (2012b). Immigration and international inbound tourism: Empirical evidence from Australia. *Tourism Management*, 33(6), 1535–1543

Seetaram, N. and Dwyer, L. (2009). Immigration and tourism demand in Australia: A panel data analysis. *Anatolia*, 20(1), 212–222.

Suryandaru, R. (2020). Measuring tourism-led growth hypothesis in Indonesia. *International Journal of Culture, Tourism and Hospitality Research*, 14(2), 295–300.

Tang, C.F. and Abosedra, S. (2014). Small sample evidence on the tourism-led growth hypothesis in Lebanon. *Current Issues in Tourism*, 17(3), 234–246.

Tran, M.N.D., Moore, K. and Shone, M.C. (2018). Interactive mobilities: Conceptualising VFR tourism of international students. *Journal of Hospitality and Tourism Management*, 35, 85–91.

Tsartas, P. et al. (2020). Refugees and tourism: a case study from the islands of Chios and Lesvos, Greece. Current Issues in Tourism, 23(11), 1311-1327.

UNESCO (2017). *Preventing violent extremism through education: A guide for policy-makers.* Paris. Available from: http://unesdoc.unesco.org/images/0024/002477/247764e.pdf.

UNWTO (2021). Glossary of Tourism Terms [Internet]. Available from: https://www.unwto.org/glossary-tourism-terms [Accessed 15 March 2021].

Van Eck, N.J. and Waltman, L. (2020a) VOSviewer 1.6.15.

Van Eck, N.J. and Waltman, L. (2020b) VOSviewer Manual [Internet]. Available from: https://www.vosviewer.com/getting-started#vosviewer-manual [Accessed 11 January 2021].

Veréb, V., Nobre, H. and Farhangmehr, M. (2020). Cosmopolitan tourists: the resilient segment in the face of terrorism. *Tourism Management Perspectives*, 33, p.100620.

Walters, G., Wallin, A. and Hartley, N. (2019). The threat of terrorism and tourist choice behavior. *Journal of Travel Research*, 58(3), 370–382.

Zeman, T. and Urban, R. (2019). The negative impact of terrorism on tourism: not just a problem for developing countries? *DETUROPE - The Central European Journal of Regional Development and Tourism*, 11(2), 75–91.

Health Care and the Implementation of Public–Private Partnership (PPP) Instruments in Transition Balkan Countries

Besa Ombashi, Denita Cepiku, and Niccolò Persiani

Abstract The Public–Private Partnership (PPP) phenomenon is enjoying a global revival of popularity, despite much uncertainty on the definitions of partnership and the colorful experience gained from their practical application. While they are being rapidly embraced not only in the free market and developed economies but also in developing countries, uncertainties persist as to what exactly is innovative—or fruitful—about PPP. In developed countries, the evolution of PPP to "state after welfare", reflects a shared experience in systems theory that has evolved substantially, particularly in Western European economies. This article analyzes the dynamics of implementation of PPP in the healthcare sector considered as opportunities for countries in transition, enhancing the case of Albania considered as a typical Balkan transition country of the post-Soviet era. When the course of two decades has almost been completed the changes that countries in transition are facing are significant and have transformed the way of the economic environment. In transitioning or developing economies, despite the potential for PPP arrangements to finance and develop public projects, the use of PPPs has been slow and limited (Yang et al., Public Administration Review 73:301–310, 2013). Currently, Albania boasts a portfolio of more than 222 PPP, 186 in energy with the rest in transport, health, environment, and agriculture. As in the focus of the article, there is an overview of the four PPP in the healthcare sector considering one out of four as the case study based on the importance as well as the changes and needs during Covid-19. The article will highlight a need to adopt a long-term strategy in the field of healthcare as well as applicable standards for the monitoring of the implementation procedures. The healthcare sector in a typical

B. Ombashi
Department of Law, University College Bedër, Tirana, Albania
e-mail: bombashi@beder.edu.al

D. Cepiku
Department of Management & Law, University of Rome Tor Vergata Via Columbia, 2, 00133 Rome, Italy
e-mail: denita.cepiku@uniroma2.it

N. Persiani (✉)
University of Florence, Largo Brambilla, 1, 50129 Florence, Italy
e-mail: niccolo.persini@unifi.it

© The Author(s), under exclusive license to Springer Nature Switzerland AG 2022
P. Sklias et al. (eds.), *Business Development and Economic Governance in Southeastern Europe*, Springer Proceedings in Business and Economics,
https://doi.org/10.1007/978-3-031-05351-1_19

Balkanic transition country, that aspires for European Union membership, such as Albania, was considered as a case study in the research because in the healthcare were introduced reforms aim to improve the public health system, the quality of care provided, and to reduce out-of-pocket healthcare expenses and the application of PPP in this sector were considered as part of this reforms and their success. The case study is based on the data collected from the analysis of the contracts signed between the parties, different reports, interviews and the documentation collection with regard to the management of this contract are going to be used. During the Pandemic moment, the implementation of these contracts became even more important for a country facing a global emergency regarding health care when these contracts were seen as a way of innovation in the management of public services.

Keywords Public–private partnership · Healthcare sector · Outsourcing · Transition Balkan Countries · Long-term strategy

1   Introduction

In Albania, the public health currently receives the second largest budgetary allocation, approximately 36 billion Albanian Lek (ALL), or about US$ 334 million in 2019, accounting for more than 12% of the total budget expenditure and 2,07% of GDP, ranking Albania lower than the average 8.8% of health expenditure in OECD countries (OECD 2020). By this account, governmental and individual spending on health sector amounts to more than eight percent of the country's GDP.

Currently, Albania boasts a portfolio of over 222 PPP, 186 in energy with the rest in transport, health, environment, and agriculture. As in focus of this article there the PPP implemented in the healthcare sector.

Based on the Progress Report of 2017, the demographic profile of Albania is changing, following an aging population with rapidly changing health needs, and it will need to be met by a wider range of capacities and competencies of healthcare providers. Healthcare delivery remains fragmented and will become a growing challenge as Albania develops, society ages, and EU integration accelerates. Political commitment to grow and sustain financing is essential.

Although the access to and quality of health services have been improving, more needs to be done to ensure universal access for all. The Albanian government spends about 2.8% of GDP on healthcare, substantially lower than the amount spent by other countries with comparable income levels. As a result of low public sector spending, out-of-pocket expenditures at the point of service account for about 60% of sectoral funding.

Since 2013 year of the entry into force of the law on PPP, the number of projects requested by contracting authorities has increased, the latter is an indicator of regulating the participation of the private sector in the provision of services/public works. Also, with the entry into force of the Decision of the Council of Ministers no. 50 dated 18.07.2019 "On some additions and amendments to Law no. 125/2013 "On concessions and public–private partnership", the acceptance of unsolicited proposals was limited only to ports, airports, and the energy sector and unsolicited proposals were removed in all areas of concession/PPP provided by Law no. 125/2013, as amended.

The Ministry of Health and Social Protection (MHSP) is responsible for strategies and national health policies and it is also a coordinator of all state and private health institutions. The mission and the values are based on the Albanian Health Strategy 2017–2020: *"The mission of the Albanian health system is to protect, improve and promote health, productivity and the well-being of all people in Albania, providing health and efficient health services and ensuring sustainable progress in public health and medicine".*

The MHSP has adopted the new National Health Sector Strategy—(NH SS) in line with the National Strategy for Development and Integration (NSDI) 2020. The World Health Organization supported the inclusion of health in the NSDI 2020, as tools to achieve Sustainable Development Goals (SDG).

The article attempts to assess the impact of the implementation of PPP in Albania in healthcare as a case of a transition country that initiated to increase private sector participation in order to improve the quality of the services for the citizens.

The findings of the research study indicate that there are different points of view regarding the evaluation and the implementation of PPP from public institutions and from civil society and other professionals in the field. The study highlights a need to adopt a long-term strategy in the field of healthcare as well as applying monitoring standards for the implementation procedures.

This article is related with the studies about the problems and perspectives of introduction of PPP in the healthcare systems of countries in transition, with particular attention paid to the transition countries considering Albania as a case study.

While studying the Albanian healthcare, as Albania aspires for the integration into the European Union and has aligned the domestic legislation according to the European legislation, the introduction of PPP is instead an interesting example of implementation for the following reason:

- The path is at an early stage and considered the Pandemic moment due to Covid 19 the country is on time to reflect and evaluate about the future steps and be considered as a case study as well as an example for the other transition Balkan countries.
- There are diverse extended studies about PPP in the European Countries and there is a gap regarding the research of PPP implementation in the Balkan Countries. This research can be considered as a step to start filling this gap.

The aim of this paper was, therefore, to emphasize the need to foster political will and leadership, requisite legal and regulatory frameworks, promote economic and political stability, and ensure effective PPP adoption and implementation in developing countries considering Albania as a case study. (Ménard and Shirley 2002; Queiroz 2007). Also, such countries must invest in developing adequate market awareness and procedures, incentive mechanisms, institutional acceptance, risk-taking, and contract enforcement to positively impact PPP performance (Snelson

2007). In view of the foregoing, this article seeks to contribute to the literature by conducting a systematic assessment of selected PPP projects in the healthcare system in Albania as a sample of a developing Balkanic country to analyze the factors that influence the successful adoption and implementation of PPP.

The paper is organized as follows. After the overview of the background of PPPs in the Health sector the paper analyzes the healthcare sector in Albania as a case of introducing these contracts in transition countries taking into consideration the four ongoing PPP analyzing the first PPP. Finally, the study settles with the conclusions, limitations, and the future steps for this research.

2 The Research Methodology and Study Approach

The case study methodology has been used as a research methodology in this article (Eisenhardt 1989; Yin 2004). The use of this methodology is appropriate when the object of analysis is complex and the aim is to conduct an in-depth analysis of the phenomenon within its reference context (Yin 2021; Berry and Otley 2004). In fact, the case study offers a variety of data collection and analysis techniques that allow a deep understanding of the phenomena investigated (Parker et al. 2014). Furthermore, one of its main strengths lies in its ability to investigate phenomena from a practical point of view, thus filling one of the most debated points in corporate literature, namely the gap between theory and practice (Chiucchi et al. 2014; Ryan et al 2002). The methodology of the case study is then indicated in the analysis of country systems, with particular reference to countries in transition given the ability of the same to grasp their specificities, extending them, where possible, to similar contexts (Gerring 2006).

Albania has been identified as a significant case study because of the aspiration of becoming the first country in the Balkan to be part of the European Union, as well as it is a country that is particularly related with her border countries such as Kosovo, Montenegro, North Macedonia that are using this instrument in their domestic economies.

The research is also based on secondary and primary data information. Secondary research focused on legislation and other government legal acts. Findings of government and international organizations' reports were also considered, including the government's health sector program, alongside World Bank, IMF as well as the annual Progress Report of the European Commission on the relationship between the health sector and PPP.

The findings of this analysis are based on the first PPP in the healthcare sector in Albania. The study approach involved three primary phases: (1) literature review—reviewing current documentation for PPP projects in the healthcare sector and literature about implementation information, (2) data collection—finding detailed information through interaction with practitioners, and (3) synthesis—synthesizing final results and documentation. The literature review collected data on current and domestic approaches to implementation of the four PPP in the healthcare in Albania.

The literature review included the PPP in Albania in all sectors not only the health sector.

The results of this review provided an understanding of the need for performance-based management systems, a summary of theoretical and applied models, and a basis for developing a comprehensive case study protocol.

Data collection involved the intricate gathering of information from four project case studies and information from the institutions in which they operate giving detailed information for the first as it is considered as a case study. Various detailed findings arise from an arduous content analysis of the PPP documents and the consequent PPP contract signed between the parties. The content analysis of the documents was augmented by discussions about projects and with institutions representative when available.

Meanwhile, looking at the topic and the subject addressed in this study, to understand the nature of the research practice, which should be followed, and the results that would be produced at the end of these practices, at the beginning of the research we tried to identify some assumptions, set out in the hypothesis. Of course, the assumptions are difficult to clarify, as they cannot be directly observed without making an analysis of the facts and conditions that lead to their rise.

3   Background of PPP in the Health Care Sector

Historically, the use of PPP in the healthcare sector can be traced back to the early 1990s, when the UK government recognized the opportunity that existed for using the private sector as a source of financing for major healthcare projects (Allard and Trabant 2007).

PPP has been most promoted as means of enhancing governance effectiveness. While PPP has most commonly been promoted as means of enhancing the effectiveness of governance, for other scholars their benefits extend further becoming as value-laden endeavors that may boost stakeholder and voter appeal, representation, as well as promote conflict resolution.

In just a few decades, the use of PPP in the healthcare sector has grown tremendously in the UK and across Europe. Their popularity in healthcare derives from a basic principle: both the public and private sectors have specific qualities and skills, and by combining those qualities and skills, the result is better (Vaillancourt Rosenau 2000). PPP are regarded as effective and cost-efficient and have become a key mechanism for implementing public and social policy (Osborne 2000). In addition, the role of the public health system is evolving, moving from the direct provision of services to the establishment of partnerships with the private sector aim to improve public health.

In the healthcare sector, PPP is defined as: […] means to bring together a set of actors for the common goal of improving the health of a population based on the mutually agreed roles and responsibilities […] (WHO 1999). The spread in the use of the PPP solution for delivering healthcare services is evident in almost every country. In countries where healthcare is delivered mainly through the public system, many inputs are sourced from the private sector. Moreover, PPP projects are currently being used in the healthcare sector not only to deliver infrastructure projects (e.g., new hospitals, staff accommodations, residences, etc.), but also to provide specific services (e.g., energy management schemes, information technology systems, catering, integrated management system, etc.) (Akintoye and Chinyio 2005; Blanken and Dewulf 2010).

Based on the annual Market Update on the European PPP Expertise Center (EPEC), the number of PPP transactions reaching financial close fell to 29, compared to 38 in 2018. This was the lowest number of transactions since 1996. (EPEC—Review of the European PPP Market in 2019).

By its very scope, covering transactions that reached financial close in EU countries as well as the United Kingdom, Turkey, and countries of the Western Balkans region (i.e., Albania, Bosnia-Herzegovina, North Macedonia, Kosovo, Montenegro, and Serbia), EPEC's annual Market Update constitutes an invaluable source of data to better understand implementation trends of PPP in the healthcare sector. Thus, based on this data, it is possible to observe trends for the 2015–2019 period, both by the number and aggregate value of PPP implemented in these countries, regarding the healthcare sector.

4   PPP in the Health Sector in Albania

Based on the Progress Report of 2017, the demographic profile of Albania is changing, following an aging population with rapidly changing health needs, and it will need to be met by a wider range of capacities and competencies of healthcare providers. Healthcare delivery remains fragmented and will become a growing challenge as Albania develops, society ages, and EU integration accelerates. Political commitment to grow and sustain financing is essential. Although the access to and quality of health services have been improving, more needs to be done to ensure universal access for all. The Albanian government spends about 2.8% of GDP on healthcare, substantially lower than the amount spent by other countries with comparable income levels. As a result of low public sector spending, out-of-pocket expenditures at the point of service account for about 60% of sectoral funding. Since 2013 year of the entry into force of the law on PPP, the number of projects requested by contracting authorities has increased, the latter is an indicator of regulating the participation of the private sector in the provision of services. Also, with the entry into force of the Decision of the Council of Ministers no. 50 dated 18.07.2019 "On some additions and amendments to Law no. 125/2013 "On concessions and public–private partnership", the acceptance of unsolicited proposals was limited only to ports, airports, and the energy sector, and unsolicited proposals were removed in all areas of concession/PPP provided by Law no. 125/2013, as amended. The total number of concessionary/PPP contracts approved for the period 2004–2013 marks the value of 176 in total, while during the period 2014–2019 with the government

Table 1 Case study overview

Project name	Owner	Location	PPP costs (in ALL)	Duration
Package of basic medical examination services for the 40–65 age group	Ministry of Health	Albania	13,833,000,000	10 years Initiation 25.02.2014
Offering a personalized set of surgical instruments, sterile single-use medical material in surgical rooms, treatment of biological waste, and disinfection of surgical halls	Ministry of Health	Albania	10,300,000.00	10 years Initiation 10.04.2019
Provision of hospital laboratory services	Ministry of Health	Albania	13,005,966,000	10 years Initiation 24.04.2017
Provision of hospital laboratory services Hemodialysis service	Ministry of Health	Albania	8,622,931,792.00	10 years Initiation 10.02.2016

Source Author's elaboration

change from Democrats—to the Socialist party—46 concessionary/PPP contracts were approved, or 74% less compared to the period of Democratic Party government. The difference between these two periods consists in the fact that during the Democratic Party government the concessions were approved based on the of green energy policy and were mostly hydropower plants. In the following period starting from 2014 as the law on PPP was approved the number and the typology of the services offered from the private sector changed (Table 1).

4.1 Package of Basic Medical Examination Services for the 40–65 Age Group (Check-Up)

Policy decision. The Council of Ministers Decision[1] nr. 185 dated 2.4.2014 as amended Council of Ministers Decision nr. 721, dated 12.10.2016 launch a 10-year annual program for the health screening of the population initially for the aged 40–65 years to aged 35–70 years.

---

[1] Council of Ministers Decision Nr. 185 of 02.04.2014.

The primary care already adopted by the Council of Ministers on 2014 was introduced as a national program, free to its beneficiaries, aimed at screening of the population for risk factors as well as the most prevalent morbidity for treatment of health problems, prevention of diseases, and complications, detection of disorders, treatment in early stages and improvement of health culture, out of which will benefit all citizens aged 40–65 residing permanently in the Republic of Albania.

Based on the guide of the Ministry of Health for implementation of the national program "Primary care for citizens aged 40–65" created under the direction of Deputy/Minister of Health, was made possible the process of perception, consultation, expertise, elaboration and building of every block for implementation of the national program "Primary care for citizens aged 40–65".

The argumentation of this initiative was as follows: non-communicable chronic diseases, especially cardiovascular and tumor ones are major causes of mortality in Albania. Global scientific evidence has shown that the improvement of healthcare status in a population, has contributed substantially to human and economic development of this population.

The argument in support of this initiative was that: *"Healthcare control to a population has its own advantages for the improvement of public health"*. In order for this primary care to bring benefits, the previously mentioned diseases must meet some criteria. Also, before the application of the respective test, it is necessary to receive the patients' consent. Various countries have created the so-called "screening frames", based on the principles of screening designed by the World Health Organization, aiming at directing the decision-makers where the latter consider issues related to the population screening programs.

There was going to be a new approach that should be based on FD (Family Physician)/HC (Healthcare Center)/Primary Care, via "know how", new healthcare and promoting practices, bringing a new step in providing services, increasing the quality and intensive interdisciplinary communication. This new approach was considered as a new added value in the Albanian healthcare system, aiming at protecting the population from threats to health; it will help people live a longer qualitative life and also protect the society's vulnerable strata.

Detailing government's decision, the Ministry of Health (MoH) specified that screening would include evaluation and counseling for lifestyle factors; a set of physiological tests, such as weight and blood pressure; and a set of standard biochemical tests. The screening would be conducted by public health centers throughout the country, while the private partner would be responsible for transporting and analyzing the blood and urine samples in several laboratories that it had to set up and manage.

Tendering. The Concession's Announcement dated 25–02-2014 organized by the Ministry of Health aims to select the private partner. This project was a proposal requested by the Ministry of Health with a duration of 10 years. The public–private partnership aims at basic medical control which is a national program that aims to screen the population for risk factors and the most prevalent diseases, with the aim of health care, prevention of diseases and complications, early detection of disorders, treatment in the early stages and improvement of health culture.

Important bids evaluation criteria such as previous experience in healthcare or biochemical testing were not part of the criteria-any kind of company could bid, and experience did not carry any weight in the evaluation. Quality of the plan for transportation of samples was assigned 17% of total points, without specifying what it is and how would quality be evaluated. Though specifications required project implementation to start within 45 days of the signing of the contract, deployment time was included in the evaluation criteria and given a 10% weight. Other criteria included *price per unit* (45%), *number of labs planned to be built* (10%), *value of reinvestment in equipment during the last 4 years of the contract* (17%); *social and environment impact* (3%).

Contract. Based on the report of 2019 of the Ministry of Finance: the contract signed in 07.01.2015 has started to be implemented on 31.03.2015 and the implementation of the project has proceeded according to the expected deadlines. Based on this contract, the concessionaire company has undertaken to build, equip the necessary medical equipment, operate, and manage 20 laboratories. Through this control program it becomes possible that, for the medium to long term, diseases can be detected in time and prevented as much as possible, which if not identified in time, would bring significant consequences for themselves. The concession contract established a ten-year period for the service, with a fixed price for the entire period. It also provided a minimum payment guarantee of about 55% of the eligible population, despite the number of persons that would take the annual health check-ups. It also foresaw international arbitration and not Albanian courts for the resolution of disputes.

Implementation. For this public–private partnership contract, 475,000 service beneficiaries are foreseen annually, ie 39,583 cases per month. The risk of demand will be high in the case of this service as in this project through this contract the Contracting Authority guarantees a financial support to the concessionaire up to 475,000 checks per year. Based on the reported data, the number of beneficiaries of this service has increased over the years (see Table 2), marking 365,802 checks for the 9-month period of 2019, or 2.7% more compared to the number planned for this period.

Government data show that about 37% of the eligible population took the health check-up in 2015. This was equal to 52% of the minimum target guaranteed by the government, which means that the private partner was paid for almost twice the number of tests analyzed. In 2016, only about a third of the target population or 44% of the guaranteed minimum took the check-up, which means that the private partner was paid for more than twice the number of tests. In money terms, in 2015 and 2016 the private contractor received, respectively about US$2.2 million and US$2.4 million for tests it did not run, or twice the cost of the tests is carried out.

Table 2 Number of beneficiaries of basic medical check-up

Year	2015	2016	2017	2018	09 quarter 2019
Number of beneficiaries	244,420	329,555	316,601	428,891	365,802

Source Ministry of Finance

In 2016, the number of citizens who have performed a check-up is 329,555, while in 2017 this number is 316,601, means that the number of persons that performed check-ups decreased by 4% (12,954 fewer patients). If we recall that target age group by October 2016 was 40–65 years old and in 2017 it has been extended to 35–70 years, so the number is even lower. So, the demand for this service has come to an end, which means either the checkout package is not properly managed or the civic credentials have come down.

Due to low population turnout, in 2016 the government decided to broaden the target population from 40–65 to 35–70 years, or approximately to increase it by 35%. There is no proper monitoring of the program, and there are no reports published by the government for the progress and results of the program.

Risks. To the competent ministry it results that the authority has reported on contract risks in the prescribed format, specifying the party taking the risk, the fiscal impact if materialized, the probability of occurring in the future, and the expected impact if it occurs. Regarding the risks arising from the implementation of the concession contract, including the construction risk, and the risk of operation and performance, the risk of asset transfer has been transferred to the private party, while the risk of legal changes, material risk from political decisions, and financial risk have been allocated to the public party. Meanwhile, the risk of demand, the risk of force majeure, the risk of renegotiation, the risk of termination of the contract, and the risk of permits and licenses are divided between the parties.

Regarding the demand risk, it is reported to the competent ministry that the Contracting Authority has undertaken awareness campaigns for the population, and has changed the contract regarding the age of the beneficiaries by extending the covered range from 40–65 years to 35–70 years (Fig. 1).

Public and Private Benefits. The very low participation has undermined the program's public benefits. In addition, there are no reports of the impact of the

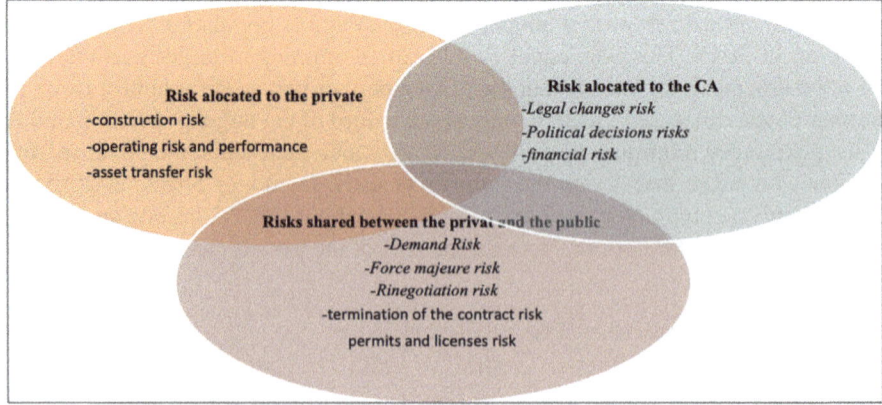

Fig. 1 Risk allocation in the PPP contract *Source* Ministry of Finance

program on detection and prevention of diseases among them that have undergone the screening. From the other side, the private contractor has secured steady profits of over US$2.2 million for 10 years, which are larger than the annual profits of any of the consortium's companies for the past ten years. It is likely that profits are even higher, given the lack of monitoring of the quality of the services and planned investments by the private partner.

Actual situation. Due to the situation of Covid-19 in March 2020 the Albanian government announced that the medical check-up and the medical laboratories contracts will be suspended during 2020 as well as two other PPP contracts.

5 Conclusions and Recommendations

There are already known not only practically, but also theoretically the advantages or disadvantages of Public–Private Partnerships, which are being implemented in the country.

As (Cepiku 2006) argued considering PPPs in this research, the international outsourcing experience shows that the outsourcing of activities and services in public administrations should be evolving, similar to what happened in private companies, toward a greater orientation to the concept of public value. It is a dimension that, unlike costs, needs further specification in order to effectively become a guiding criterion in decision-making processes.

The relationship between government, the private sector, and civil society are considered an important factor in achieving sustainable development and enhances the quality of governance. It is a well-known fact, the partnership is best established through consultation, coordination, participation, and mutual communication. They always remain organized on a constant debate both economic and political, hence these types of connections develop in the arena of political economy, where contracting partners are not equal.

The research came to a concrete conclusion that the civil society should be considered as a factor, because it has a real role in the implementation of the partnership, and actively participates in disseminating information about them, as well as in informing about their results. The increased risk with the termination of contracts also applies to the fulfillment of payments. Tariffs happen to be softened, especially in election years, so that private investment eroded by the government can be easily politicized by the public.

Then it becomes necessary to make a full explanation, regarding the theoretical, legal, and practical reflection, especially on the need for a new remedial approach in the legal framework governing this type of activity. For the debate to be properly understood and interpreted, it is necessary to have all the right *know-how* about this contemporary way of financing the economy.

Also, the Ministry of Finance will not only conduct the evaluation of concessions/PPP but will also monitor the implementation of the respective contracts, based on periodic reports submitted by the contracting authorities, after negotiating the contract with the winning operator and before signing the contract.

Practitioners support the establishment of the Committee for the Selection of Concession/PPP Projects, as a collegial body, with the main object of activity being the selection of concession/PPP Projects, who assist with specialized expertise in drafting the feasibility study. The Committee will be assisted by the Concession Handling Agency, which will analyze the contracting authorities' requests for support with specialized expertise and propose them to the Committee for approval. The establishment of this Committee eliminates the need for specialized expertise, provided by the private sector for drafting and improvement of policy planning and making process. There is an obvious need for establishing clear standards, procedures, and guidelines, and clear responsibilities in the process of designing and drafting policies, in order to avoid arbitrary or illicit interferences, in particular by politics.

Public administration should be trained in policy assessment and evaluation; in particular in cost–benefit analysis, impact analysis, risk assessment, and other advanced policy evaluation techniques. An important element that might be considered to be included in policy-making process is the corruption impact assessment. Access and transparency in the policy-making process should be increased, by instituting mandatory consultations within and beyond government, including hearings with interested parties, civil society, business associations, academia, and media.

Legal framework and PPP practice should be reviewed in order to avoid the use of PPP for creating economic rents and concentration of economic power. Publication and public access of studies, analysis, and other documents related to PPP preparation and contracting should be made public, including evaluation criteria, evaluation reports, winning bids, and contracts. Other improvements should aim at avoiding lengthy PPP contracts, in particular in the field of services; exclusion of inexperienced or financially weak companies, in particular firms leading consortiums; avoiding companies with unidentified or hidden (final) owners, and limiting or conditioning the approval of ownership change during PPP implementation.

Procurement of medication for the public health institutions should be overhauled to increase competition, improve transparency and fight corruption. Specific approaches applied in other developing countries, such as procurement of all medications by international agencies such as UNDP or WHO, can be explored. Another alternative would be procurement from independent bodies, which do not answer to the Ministry of Health or other government agencies that also formulate policies and decisions in the field of medicaments and medical devices.

References

Akintoye, A., & Chinyio, E. (2005). Private Finance Initiative in the Healthcare Sector: Trends and Risk Assessment. Engineering Construction and Architectural Management, 12(6), 601–616.

Allard, G.; Trabant, A. (2007): Public-Private partnership in Spain: Lessons and Op- portunities. IE Business School Working Paper WP10–07.

Amirkhanyan A.A., Kim H.J., Lambright K.T. (2007) Putting the pieces together: A comprehensive framework for understanding the decision to contract-out and contractor performance, International Journal of Public Administration 30(6–7):699–725.

Berry, A.J. and Otley, D.T., 2004. Case-based research in accounting. In The real life guide to accounting research (pp.231–255) Elsevier.

Blanken, A., & Dewulf, G. P. M. R. (2010). PPPs in Health: Static or Dynamic? Australian journal of public administration, 69(1), 35–47.

Cepiku D., (2006), L'esternalizzazione nelle amministrazioni pubbliche. Teorie, politiche ed esperienze a livello internazionale, Aracne, Roma.

Chiucchi, M.S., Giuliani, M. and Marasca, S., 2014. The desing, implementation and use of intellectual capital measurements: A case study. Management and Control.

De Vries J., Huijsman R. (2011) Supply chain management in health services: An overview. Supply Chain Management, International Journal 16(3):159–165.

Eisenhardt, K.M., 1989. Building theories from case study research. Academy of management review, 14(4), pp.532–550.

Gerring, J., 2006. Case study research: Principles and practices. Cambridge university press.

Kakabadse A., Kakabadse N. (2002) Trends in outsourcing: Contrasting USA and Europe, European Management Journal 189–198

Ménard, C. and Shirley, M.M. (2002), Reforming Public Utilities: Lessons from Urban Water Supply in Six Developing Countries, World Bank, Washington, DC.;

Mori A. (2017) The impact of public services outsourcing on work and employment conditions in different national regimes, European Journal of Industrial Relations. 23(4):347–364

Narayanan V., Schoch H.P., Harrison G.L. (2007) The interplay between accountability and management control patterns in public sector outsourcing. International Journal of Business Studies 37–65

OECD (2011) Government Outsourcing. In: Government at a Glance 2011, OECD Publishing, Paris, pp 168–169

OECD (2017) Government Outsourcing. In: Government at a Glance 2017, OECD Publishing, Paris, pp 84–85

OECD (2020) List of variables in OECD health statistics 2020. https://www.oecd.org/els/health-systems/List-ofvariables-OECD-Health-Statistics-2020.pdf

Osborne, S. P. (2000). Public–Private Partnerships: Theory and Practice in International Perspective. London: Routledge.

Parker, R.I., Vannest, K.J. and Davis, J.L., 2014. Non-overlap analysis for single-case research.

Queiroz, C.A.V. (2007), "Public–private partnerships in highways in transition economies: recent experience and future prospects", Transportation Research Record: Journal of the Transportation Research Board, No. 1996, No. 1, pp. 34–40.

Rajabzadeh A., Asghar Anvary Rostamy A., Hosseini A. (2008) Designing a generic model for outsourcing process in public sector: Evidence of Iran, Management Decision 46(4):521–538.

Ryan, B., Scapens, R.W. and Theobald, M., 2002. Research method and metodology in finance and accounting.

Snelson, P. (2007), "Public–private partnerships in transitional countries", Law in Transition, European Bank for Reconstruction and Development, London, pp. 31–37.

Sullivan E.W., Ngwenyama O.K. (2005) How are public sector organizations managing IS outsourcing risks? An analysis of outsourcing guidelines from three jurisdictions, Journal of Computer Information Systems. 45(3):73–87.

Vaillancourt Rosenau, P. (Ed.) (2000). Public–Private Policy Partnerships. London: Cambridge.

Van de Walle S., Hammerschmid G. (2011) The impact of the new public management: Challenges for coordination and cohesion in European public sectors, Haldus kultuur – Administrative Culture. 12(2):190–209.

Yang, Y., Wang, W. and Hou, Y. (2013), "On the development of public–private partnerships in transitional economies: an explanatory framework", Public Administration Review, Vol. 73 No. 2, pp. 301–310.

Yin, R.K., 2004. The case study anthology. Sage.

Yin, R.K., 2021. Case study methods.

The Relationship Between Financing Decision of SMES and Their Performance

Valentina Diana Rusu and Angela Roman

Abstract Access to finance is one of the most important determinants of success and even the survival of a business. Several theoretical and empirical studies argue that small and medium-sized enterprises usually face more problems in obtaining financing compared to larger enterprises. The same happens in the case of enterprises that are in the first years of existence on the market. Thus, through this paper we aim to examine the relationship between the way small and medium enterprises are financed in the first years of existence and their performance. Thus, we want to see if the debt structure of these enterprises plays an important role in obtaining performance. In order to achieve the purpose of the paper, we perform an econometric analysis by choosing a sample of small and medium enterprises from the CEE countries in their first years of existence. Given the fact that start-ups are considered enterprises in the first five years of life, the analysis period considered is 2015–2019. As a method of analysis we use the panel data technique considering as dependent variables a set of indicators that measure the performance of enterprises, and as independent variables indicators that express the degree of indebtedness of enterprises. The data for this analysis are obtained from the financial statements of the companies accessed through the AMADEUS Bureau van Djik database. The results of our research show that the way in which the SMEs financing decisions are based plays a significant role in achieving performance. The use of short and long-term debt can stimulate the performance of enterprises, but an increased gearing ratio hampers this performance. These results can be useful for decision-makers because they emphasize the need for them to focus on formulating policies that facilitate access to finance for SMEs in the first years of life, thus generating an increase in their performance with positive effects at the level of general economy.

V. D. Rusu (✉)
Department of Social Sciences and Humanities, Institute of Interdisciplinary Research, Alexandru Ioan Cuza University of Iasi, Lascăr Catargi Street, no. 54, Iasi, Romania
e-mail: valentinadiana.ig@gmail.com

A. Roman
Faculty of Economics and Business Administration, Alexandru Ioan Cuza University of Iasi, Carol I Boulevard, no. 22, Iasi, Romania
e-mail: aboariu@uaic.ro

Keywords Financing decision · SMEs · Start-ups · Performance · Panel data · CEE
countries

JEL Classification G32 · M13 · C33

1 Introduction

A key element for the survival and functioning of enterprises is represented by the
financial resources to which they have access and which they use in their activity.
These resources can come from own funds or from borrowed resources. Because own
funds are insufficient, most enterprises are forced to use external borrowed resources.
These external borrowed resources are beneficial for enterprises because in order to
grow and develop they need a significant infusion of capital.

The problem that arises is related to the effects that financing decisions have
on the performance of enterprises. Thus, the types and size of external resources
used by enterprises can stimulate or, on the contrary, reduce the performance of
enterprises. Concerns to identify the relationship between indebtedness and business
performance are ongoing in the literature. The empirical results obtained so far are
mixed, because they depend very much on the analysed period, on the sample of
companies considered but especially on the economic particularities of the countries
in which these enterprises operate. Thus, this topic will never become too analysed,
because the new evolutions of the economies will determine the enterprises to adapt.
These adaptations often requiring additional financial resources, but with the risk of
compromising their performance. Or, there is a way for companies to use borrowed
resources and still be able to increase their performance, to ensure their survival on
the market and maintain a competitive environment? This is the main question which
underlines this study.

The challenges regarding access to finance and increasing performance are greater
for small and medium enterprises but also for those at the beginning of the road.
Studies in the literature (Abor, 2005; Akinlo and Asaolu, 2012; Javed et al. 2014;
Robb and Robinson, 2014; Zeitun and Saleh, 2015; Aziz and Abbas, 2019; Hongli
et al. 2019; Nazir et al. 2021) analyse large companies listed on stock exchanges,
because they have access to their financial statements to extract the indicators needed
for analysis. There are also studies that have considered SMEs but smaller in number
(Githaigo and Kabiru, 2015; Yazdanfar and Öhman, 2015; Carvalho et al. 2017;
Ibhagui and Olokoyo, 2018; Mugisha et al. 2020; Rajamani, 2021). Due to their
particularities we decided to choose for our analysis only SMEs. An additional argument for choosing the examination of SMEs is that these enterprises are considered
to be the backbone of entrepreneurship in Europe. Therefore, the main objective of
this study is to identify the relationship between the financing decision of SMEs and
their performance. More, we have chosen a sample of SMEs at the beginning of
their road, i.e. those that are in the first five years of activity. Company level data are
obtained from the AMADEUS database.

Many studies from the literature on this matter focus on developing countries or consider only one country for analysis. The novelty brought by our study consists in the fact that we chose 14 countries from Central and Eastern Europe, and especially that we made a comparison between them on groups with different degrees of development.

Thus, the added value of our study comes from considering almost all the countries from the CEE region and also a large sample of start-ups SMEs. So, through our results we intended to fill this gap in the literature, and also to draw attention to the situation of start-ups.

Our paper is structure as follows: the first part presents a brief literature review; the second part describes the data and the methods used. The third part presents the results of the empirical analysis and discusses them. The study ends with concluding remarks.

2 Literature Review

The findings in the literature are mixed, depending on the sample of enterprises chosen, their size, country but also the analysed period. Thus, in the literature we find studies that highlight the positive relationship of indebtedness and enterprise's performance (Ruland and Zhou, 2005; Robb and Robinson 2014; Tsuruta, 2015; Hongli et al. 2019) but also studies which provide evidence on a negative relationship or mixed results (Akinlo and Asaolu, 2012; Zeitun and Saleh, 2015; Ibhagui and Olokoyo, 2018; Aziz and Abbas, 2019; Mugisha et al. 2020; Nazir et al. 2021).

A significant part of the studies regarding this issue focuses on developing countries. Such as, the study of Akinlo and Asaolu (2012) which found an inverse relation between debt and profitability of Nigerian listed enterprises. The authors show that when the debt increases the profitability of enterprises will decrease, and vice versa. Similar results were obtained by Aziz and Abbas (2019) only that they focused on enterprises listed at Pakistan Stock Exchange, considering a time period of nine years between 2006 and 2014. Also listed enterprises in Pakistan were considered by Nazir et al. (2021) only that their analysed period is 2013–2017 and their results show that both long and short-term debt have negative and significant effect on enterprises performance. This shows that within the same country and on the same type of enterprises the results may be different depending on the analysed period. Another sample of listed companies was analysed by Hongli et al. (2019) only as they are from Ghana. These authors chose only companies from the manufacturing sector and the empirical results obtained by them highlighted the strong and positive effect of financial leverage on enterprises performance, only that 65% of the money from debt is used to finance assets which can really have an important effect on performance. Robb and Robinson (2014) also pointed on the positive effects of indebtedness for the enterprises. They show that using debt financing might increase the market value of the enterprise and also that financial leverage is positively related to return on equity (ROE). Similar results were obtained by Abor (2005).

Javed et al. (2014) also analysed the effects of debt on the performance of enterprises listed from Pakistan and obtained mixed results. Thus, their findings showed that debt has a negative effect on return on equity (ROE) and a positive one on return on assets (ROA).

If the other papers presented above analysed the enterprises from only one country, the study of Zeitun and Saleh (2015) focused on 400 listed enterprises from six countries which are part of the Gulf Cooperation Council. Their results show that the leverage of enterprises is a significant determinant of the performance of enterprises from the considered countries.

Some of the studies also took into account the role that the size of the company plays in investigating the relationship between the indebtedness of enterprises and their performance. Thus, Ibhagui and Olokoyo (2018) claim that for the small enterprises the leverage has a negative effect and this effect is diminishing as the size of the enterprise increases, and may even disappear when the size of the company exceeds a certain threshold. The results obtained by this author are based on a sample of small firms in Japan. A similar result was obtained by the study of Mugisha et al. (2020) which analysed SMEs from Uganda and indicated that short-term debt may hamper the SMEs performance. Other studies (Githaigo and Kabiru, 2015; Yazdanfar and Öhman, 2015; Carvalho et al. 2017; Rajamani, 2021) have also shown, considering samples of SMEs from different countries (like Kenya, Sweden, India, Portugal) that the use of long and short-term loans might reduce the financial performance of this enterprises.

However, although a number of studies have shown more of a negative relationship between the short and long-term indebtedness of SMEs and their performance, we must keep in mind that in order to grow and develop, companies need external financing. They especially need the long-term financing that helps them make investments. So, a certain level of indebtedness is necessary for SMEs, and financial managers should focus on reaching the optimal level (Pervan et al. 2017).

In addition to these mentioned negative effects, there are also studies that highlight the benefits of increased indebtedness for small enterprises, pointing out that high leverage can make SMEs management more efficient (Tsuruta, 2015). Saidi et al. (2019) also found that debt financing is positively associated with SMEs performance, expressed by business expansion and outputs.

3   Data and Method

For creating the database for our study we selected the Central and Eastern European region countries (Albania, Bosnia and Herzegovina, Bulgaria, Croatia, Czech Republic, Estonia, Hungary, Kosovo, Latvia, Lithuania, Montenegro, North Macedonia, Poland, Romania, Serbia, Slovakia and Slovenia). The data were obtained from AMADEUS database created by Bureau Van Djik. For creating the sample of enterprises, we used the search strategy from the database and we selected active small and medium enterprises, by excluding the micro firms (which have less than

10 employees). Also we chose to focus only on start-up enterprises, thus we only considered enterprises founded 5 years ago or less. For this reason, the period selected for the analysis is 2015–2019. With these search criteria we have extracted 8.074 enterprises from Amadeus database belonging to different sectors of activity. Next, we performed a database processing, starting from the availability of data for performance indicators but also those regarding indebtedness. The final sample includes 7.294 enterprises from 14 CEE countries (for Albania, Kosovo and Slovakia we did not had enough data for the considered indicators, so these countries were excluded from the sample). See the distribution of sample in Table 1.

Around 32% of the enterprises from the sample are from Romania followed by Bulgaria with 18%. Poland and Hungary were also countries whose companies accounted for more than 10% of those chosen for analysis. This can be explained by the fact that these countries generally have a higher total number of SMEs than the other countries included in the sample (see the data offered by the European Commission (2021), SBA Fact sheets).

Moreover, in order to perform a more in-depth analysis, depending on the degree of development of the countries in which the enterprises operate, we chose to group them according to World Economic Situation and Prospects 2020 Report realized by the UNCTAD (UN DESA, 2020). This report realizes a classification of countries according to the per capita GNI in June 2019. According to this classification the CEE countries are included into two groups: High-income countries (Croatia, Czech Republic, Estonia, Hungary, Latvia, Lithuania, Poland and Slovenia) and Upper

Table 1 Number and percentage of start-up SMEs by country

Country	Number of start-up SMEs	Percentage of start-up SMEs in total sample (%)
Bosnia and Herzegovina	215	2.95
Bulgaria	1351	18.52
Croatia	381	5.22
Czech Republic	40	0.55
Estonia	100	1.37
Hungary	844	11.57
Latvia	229	3.14
Lithuania	114	1.56
Montenegro	69	0.95
North Macedonia	46	0.63
Poland	1088	14.92
Romania	2398	32.88
Serbia	175	2.40
Slovenia	244	3.35

Source processed by the authors

middle income countries (Bosnia and Herzegovina, Bulgaria, Montenegro, North Macedonia, Romania and Serbia) (UN DESA, 2020, pp. 168).

Considering the findings from the literature review we formulated a model for testing the relationship between financing decision of SMEs and their performance. The general equation that we used for the econometric model that we tested in this analysis is:

$$\text{Performance}_{it} = \beta_1 indebtedness_{it} + \beta_2 Z_{it} + \mu_{it} \tag{1}$$

where: i represents the country and t is time (2015–2019); *Performanceit* represents the dependent variable and is measuring the SMEs performance; *indebtednessit* represents the indicators measuring the level of SMEs indebtedness; Z_{it}: represents the control variables; β_1 and β_2: are the coefficients whilst μit is the error term.

Because the performance of SMEs can be measured by different indicators, and following the tendency from the studies in the literature (Hongli et al. 2019; Forte and Tavares, 2019; Nazir, et al. 2021; Rajamani, 2021) in our analysis we use three alternative measures for the performance: return on assets (ROA), return on equity (ROE) and profit margin. These are the most commonly used and also the most accessible indicators of performance. Therefore, we use three specific models expressed by the following equations:

$$\text{ROA}it = \beta_1 indebtedness_{it} + \beta_2\text{RGDP}_{it} + \beta_3\text{INFL}_{it} + \mu_{it} \tag{2}$$

$$\text{ROE}it = \beta_1 indebtedness_{it} + \beta_2\text{RGDP}_{it} + \beta_3\text{INFL}_{it} + \mu_{it} \tag{3}$$

$$\text{PROFITM}it = \beta_1 indebtedness_{it} + \beta_2\text{RGDP}_{it} + \beta_3\text{INFL}_{it} + \mu_{it} \tag{4}$$

The variables included in our analysis are presented with their definition and measurement in Table 2.

Data on control variables were obtained from the International Monetary Fund (2021) for real GDP growth rate and World Bank (2021) for the inflation rate.

Starting from the findings of other studies analysed in the literature review and also based on our expectations, we defined a couple of hypotheses:

Hypothesis 1: Long-term debt of start-up SMEs is negatively related to their performance.

Hypothesis 2: Short-term debt of start-up SMEs is negatively related to their performance.

Hypothesis 3: Higher gearing ratio of start-up SMEs is negatively related to their performance.

The next steps of our empirical analysis are: first we performed a test of the variables to identify the presence of a unit root. Only the variable measuring inflation resulted to have a unit root, thus we calculated the first difference of this variable. There were no problems with the other variables in this regard. Then, we transformed the variables that express long-term indebtedness and current liabilities by applying

Table 2 Variables description

Variable (abbreviation)	Definition (Measurement)
Dependent variables	
Return on Assets (ROA)	Shows how profitable is a firm reported to its total assets. Is calculated by dividing the net income of the firm by its total assets (annual, %)
Return on Equity (ROE)	Is calculated by dividing the net income of the firm by its shareholders equity (annual, %)
Profit margin	It shows what percentage of the sale was turned into profits. Shows how many cents of profit have been generated by each monetary unit of sales (annual, %)
Independent variables	
Long-term debt	Is the amount of debt of a firm, which has the maturity in more than one year (annual, thousand euro)
Current liabilities	Are the short-term financial obligations of a firm, that are due within one year or within a normal operating cycle. (annual, thousand euro)
Gearing ratio	Is the measurement of the firm's financial leverage, and shows the degree to which a firm's activities are funded by shareholders' funds versus creditors' funds (annual, %)
Control variables	
Real GDP growth rate	Is measured by the changes of GDP rate from one year to another
Inflation rate	Is measured by the consumer price index and shows the annual percentage change in the cost to the average consumer of acquiring a basket of goods and services that may be fixed or changed at specified intervals, such as yearly (annual, %)

Source processed by the authors

the natural logarithm, because these variables were initially measured in absolute size. Following, we analysed the descriptive statistics and the correlation matrix. Finally, we applied the panel data regression models for testing the relations between the variables included.

4   Results and Discussions

Our first step in the empirical investigation is the analysis of the descriptive statistics of the variables because it helps us understand the behaviour of the indicators considered (see Table 3). The variables measuring the performance and the indebtedness are significantly different between firms, fact highlighted by both high standard deviation and high amplitude of the variables.

From the results highlighted for the indicators that measure performance, we notice that we have in our sample both enterprises that have a very high performance and enterprises with very low performance. We also notice large differences between ROE and ROA. These differences may be related to how the two rates are calculated,

Table 3 Descriptive statistics of the variables

Variable	Mean	Max	Min	Std. Dev	Obs
ROA	14.141	100.000	−100.000	29.164	33674
ROE	56.766	1000.000	−995.170	98.977	28837
Profit margin	7.768	100.000	−100.000	21.133	33044
Long-term debt	95.074	61,071.82	−1.113	653.398	19479
Logarithm of Long-term debt	4.375	11.019	−4.843	1.838	5243
Current liabilities	335.285	37,012.23	−271.467	903.086	33405
Logarithm of Current liabilities	4.335	10.519	−6.907	2.145	31694
Gearing ratio	3.846	6.907	−6.907	1.843	8794
Real GDP growth rate	4.074	7.300	1.100	1.185	36401
D Inflation rate*	0.804	3.286	−2.249	1.511	29176

*Note * the first difference of this variable*
Source authors own calculations

so ROE is reporting the net income to equity and ROA to the assets. The average ROA of the SMEs included in the sample is higher than profit margin.

The different number of observations obtained for the analysed variables is due to the availability of data in the database.

From the analysis of the descriptive statistics we also observe that start-up SMEs included in our sample use mainly short-term financing. This finding is consistent with the literature which shows that small firms usually develop more strong short-term relations with third parties (Gibson, 2004) and use mainly trade credit and short-term loans to finance their working capital (Bańkowska et al. 2020).

For identifying the correlation coefficients between variables we analyse the correlation matrix. The results summarised in Table 4 indicate that ROA has a significant and inverse association with long-term debt and gearing ratio. The value of correlation coefficient of 26.4% confirms the presence of a week negative relationship between ROA and long-term debt. In the same time the value of 41.5% for the coefficient of correlation shows a medium negative relationship between ROA and gearing ratio. The same type of relationships with the same sign, only weaker (correlation coefficients of 0.9% and 27.9%) are obtained between Profit margin, on the one hand, and long-term debt and gearing ratio, on the other hand. ROE has a significant and positive association with long-term debt, but is a week one (16.1%).

However, Long-term debt, Current liabilities and Gearing ratio have a very low and low correlation with each other (correlation coefficients smaller than 70%) confirming the lack of multicollinearity amongst variables.

For estimating the results of the regression analysis we used panel data models. We tested three estimation models: OLS adapted to panel data, fixed effects and random effects. The results of the Hausman tests and the Redundant fixed effects tests showed that the best model fitted to our data is the fixed effects model. Thus the centralized results in Table 5 show the coefficients and standard errors (in parenthesis) for fixed effects models. The main findings of our analysis (see Table 5) show that regardless

Table 4 The correlation matrix of the variables

	(1)	(2)	(3)	(4)	(5)	(6)	(7)	(8)
(1) ROA	1.000							
(2) ROE	0.535*	1.000						
	(0.000)							
(3) Profit margin	0.712*	0.411*	1.000					
	(0.000)	(0.000)						
(4) Logarithm of Long-term debt	−0.264*	0.161*	−0.090*	1.000				
	(0.000)	(0.000)	(0.000)					
(5) Logarithm of Current liabilities	0.003	−0.017	0.021	0.184*	1.000			
	(0.835)	(0.357)	(0.250)	(0.000)				
(6) Gearing ratio	−0.415*	−0.013	−0.279*	0.479*	−0.039*	1.000		
	(0.000)	(0.472)	(0.000)	(0.000)	(0.035)			
(7) Real GDP growth rate	−0.067*	−0.037*	−0.065*	0.187*	0.114*	0.014	1.000	
	(0.000)	(0.044)	(0.000)	(0.000)	(0.000)	(0.429)		
(8) D Inflation rate	0.056*	0.029	0.043*	−0.044*	0.014	0.001	0.036*	1.000
	(0.002)	(0.110)	(0.019)	(0.016)	(0.448)	(0.945)	(0.049)	

Note probability in parenthesis, correlation is significant when p < 0.05 (*)
Source authors own calculations

of the indicator used for measuring SMEs performance, the financing decision of start-up SMEs influences significantly their performance.

Therefore, long-term debt is positively and statically significant related with ROA and Profit margin. Aziz and Abbas (2019) also found a positive relation between long-term debt and performance of the enterprises. Current liabilities are positively and statistically significant related only with Profit margin. These results are in line with those obtained by Abor (2005) and Zeitun and Tian (2007) which found a positive relation between short-term debt and enterprises performance, showing that the use of short-term debt can generate the improvement of enterprises' performance by providing them with the necessary financial resources to carry out their operations

Table 5 The relationship between start-up SMEs indebtedness and their performance

Dependent variable	ROA	ROE	Profit margin
Logarithm of Long-term debt	2.370*** (0.268)	1.322 (1.441)	1.654*** (0.245)
Logarithm of Current liabilities	−0.076 (0.073)	−0.237 (0.180)	0.195** (0.093)
Gearing ratio	−6.803*** (0.284)	−2.566 (1.884)	−3.104*** (0.308)
Constant	30.104*** (0.988)	48.516*** (3.249)	12.461*** (1.838)
Real GDP growth rate	0.698 (0.276)	1.500 (1.263)	0.173 (0.223)
D Inflation rate	−0.503*** (0.136)	−4.805*** (0.749)	−0.255 (0.191)
Obs	1457	3127	3099
R-squared	0.829	0.800	0.804
R-squared adjusted	0.677	0.624	0.629
F-statistic	5.481***	4.554***	4.610***

Note *, ** and *** represents significant values at 1%, 5% respectively 10%; Standard error in parenthesis
Source authors own elaboration

in the early stages, and creating the potential for further development and growth. Therefore, the first and second hypotheses in our study are not supported.

Gearing ratio is negatively and statistically significant related with ROA and Profit margin. This confirms our hypothesis (H3). The negative sign of the coefficient shows that increased leverage of start-up SMEs determines a reduction of their performance. This can be explained by the fact that a high gearing ratio points out that the firm has a larger proportion of debt than equity. Thus, the firm has a greater financial risk, because in case of lower profits and higher interest rates it has a greater risk of loan default or/and bankruptcy. This result is in line with the findings of other studies from the literature (Ibhagui and Olokoyo, 2018) which show that the leverage has a negative effect on firm performance especially for the case of small firms, and as firms grow this effect diminishes. The results of our study are based on the pecking order theory of capital structure because the performance of enterprises is significantly and negatively affected by the level of indebtedness.

The control variables presented the expected impact on performance: positive for Real GDP growth rate (although not statistically significant) and negative for inflation rate.

However, the high value obtained for the constant shows us that there are a number of other indicators that exert a statistically significant influence on the variables chosen to measure the performance of enterprises. This result was to be expected, as there are other factors that exert a stronger and faster influence on performance. This does not influence the objective of our study which was to show if and what relationship exists between the indebtedness of enterprises and their performance. Of course, in future studies we intend to include other factors in the models.

The value of R squared adjusted shows that the variables expressing the indebtedness of start-up SMEs from our models explain above 60% of the variation in the performance indicators. Also, the F statistics shows that our panel data models are significant.

When we analyse the relationship between indebtedness and the performance of start-up SMEs depending on the countries they come from, the results show only small differences (see Table 6). Thus, long-term debt is positively and statistically significant related to ROA, ROE and Profit Margin for high income countries. At the same time, it is also related positively and statistically significant only with ROA and profit margin for Upper middle income countries. Current liabilities are positively and statistically significant related only with Profit margin for the group of high income countries. Gearing ratio is negatively and statistically significant related with all three indicators used for measuring performance for the group of High income countries, and only with ROA and Profit margin for the upper middle income countries.

Thus, the particularities between the two groups of countries are that ROE of start-up SMEs for lower rated countries is not influenced by their indebtedness. Whilst ROE of start-up SMEs in the top ranked countries is positively influenced by long-term debt and negatively by gearing ratio. This can be explained by the fact that countries with high degrees of development offer greater opportunities for business development so that the use of long-term borrowed resources can be seen as a way to stimulate investment and business development. But at the same time, very high indebtedness rates can have negative effects on performance. Here, the problem lies on managers who must find an optimal capital structure so as to adapt to the specific economic conditions of the country in which they operate, but also to use the financial resources they can access in an optimal combination with beneficial effects on performance.

Another difference is the effect of control variables. For high income countries, real GDP growth rate has a positive influence on performance of start-up SMEs, whilst for the other group of countries a negative influence. This may be due to the fact that increasing the level of real GDP for the more developed countries can be seen as a catalyst for business, and especially for those at the beginning of the road, offering them increased opportunities and simulating them to improve their performance.

The same was observed in the case of inflation, negative effects on ROE of start-up SMEs from high income countries, and positive effects on profit margin from upper middle income countries. In high income countries increased inflation determines an increase of prices and of the costs of enterprises, affecting also their investments and generating negative effects on performance. On the other hand, in upper middle income countries inflation reduces the real value of the enterprises debt with positive effects on their performance. These findings are in line with those of Maimunah and Patmawati (2018).

The values of R squared adjusted for the models analysed in Table 6 are between 52 and 96% showing that the variables expressing the indebtedness of start-up SMEs

Table 6 The relationship between start-up SMEs indebtedness and their performance by groups of countries

Dependent variable	ROA	ROE	Profit margin
High income countries			
Logarithm of Long-term debt	2.392*** (0.325)	1.949* (1.094)	1.650*** (0.282)
Logarithm of Current liabilities	−0.073 (0.091)	−0.112 (0.299)	0.154** (0.069)
Gearing ratio	−6.662*** (0.386)	−4.918*** (1.446)	−3.124*** (0.321)
Constant	24.092*** (1.652)	39.025*** (3.591)	9.295*** (0.862)
Real GDP growth rate	1.536*** (0.345)	4.494*** (0.909)	0.668*** (0.144)
D Inflation rate	0.597 (0.367)	−0.403** (0.202)	0.082 (0.124)
Obs	2028	2034	2021
R-squared	0.974	0.829	0.783
R-squared adjusted	0.967	0.684	0.595
F-statistic	15.990***	5.706***	4.183***
Upper middle income countries			
Logarithm of Long-term debt	2.426*** (0.318)	0.890 (2.473)	1.768*** (0.218)
Logarithm of Current liabilities	−0.039 (0.093)	0.013 (0.197)	0.350 (0.212)
Gearing ratio	−7.161*** (0.312)	0.769 (3.035)	−3.175*** (0.410)
Constant	36.669 (1.344)	59.084 (9.810)	16.282*** (2.888)
Real GDP growth rate	−0.074 (0.443)	−4.668*** (0.901)	−0.584** (0.230)
D Inflation rate	−0.308 (0.342)	−2.074 (0.209)	0.689* (0.339)
Obs	1090	1093	1078
R-squared	0.849	0.756	0.824
R-squared adjusted	0.703	0.523	0.654
F-statistic	5.822***	3.240***	4.857***

Note *, ** and *** represents significant values at 1%, 5% respectively 10%; Standard error in parenthesis
Source authors own elaboration

from our models explain in a high proportion the variation of the performance indicators. Also, the F statistics shows that our panel data models are significant.

5 Conclusions

The aim of our research was to determine if exists a relationship between the financing decision of small and medium enterprises start-ups and their performance. The analysis is conducted on start-up SMEs from 14 Central and Eastern European countries for the period from 2015 to 2019. The total number of firms included in the analysis was 7294. This firm belongs to different sectors of activity. For a more in depth analysis we grouped the countries in the sample according to their level of development, and realized a comparative analysis between groups.

The results of the panel data analysis reveal that the financing decision of firms is an important factor in determining their performance. More clearly long-term debt resulted to be positively related with SMEs performance both for total sample and also by groups of countries. Current liabilities resulted to be positively related only with Profit margin for the total sample of countries. Whilst gearing ratio resulted to have a negative relation with performance regardless of the performance measurement method but also of the analysed sample.

Our results are mainly in line with the findings of some studies from the literature but at the same time they are in contradiction with other studies. The results depend on the particularities of the countries analysed in different studies, the periods considered but also the characteristics of the analysed enterprises.

The added value of our study comes from considering almost all the countries from the CEE region and also a large sample of start-ups SMEs. Another element of novelty lies in the grouping of countries according to their degree of development and the comparison of the results obtained for the two groups. We consider that our findings could be of interest both to researchers and policy-makers. On the one hand, because it offers new evidence on the relationship between companies' indebtedness and their performance, with emphasis on enterprises at the beginning of the road. On the other hand, because it shows what financing methods can increase the performance of SMEs at the beginning of activity, thus providing a starting point for policy-makers in decision-making and the adoption of programs to support access to finance for these categories of enterprises.

The limitations of our study come from the availability of the data for the indicators that measure the indebtedness of SMEs. In order to extend the results of this study, we want to include in the analysis all the countries from Europe, but also to group the SMEs according to the sector of activity.

References

Abor J (2005) The effect of capital structure on profitability: an empirical analysis of listed firms in Ghana. J Risk Finance 6(5): 16-30. https://doi.org/10.1108/15265940510633505

Akinlo O, Asaolu T (2012) Profitability and leverage: evidence from Nigerian firms. Global Journal of Business Research 6(1): 17-25

Aziz S, Abbas U (2019) Effect of debt financing on firm performance: a study on non-financial sector of Pakistan. Open Journal of Economics and Commerce 2(1): 8-15

Bańkowska K, Ferrando A, Garcia JA (2020) Access to finance for small and medium-sized enterprises since the financial crisis: evidence from survey data. ECB Economic Bulletin 4: 104-125

Carvalho AF, Lourenço M, Perestrello M (2017) The indebtedness of Portuguese SMEs and the impact of leverage on their performance. Papers presented by the statistics department in national and international fora, Supplement to the Statistical Bulletin, July, Banco de Portugal: 95–108. https://www.bportugal.pt/sites/default/files/anexos/pdf-boletim/suplemento_1_2017_en_2.pdf#page=97

European Commission (2021) SME Performance Review, SBA Fact sheet. https://ec.europa.eu/gro wth/smes/sme-strategy/sme-performance-review_en#sba-fact-sheets

Forte R, Tavares JM (2019) The relationship between debt and a firm's performance: the impact of institutional factors. Manag Finance 45(9): 1272-1291. https://doi.org/10.1108/MF-04-2018-0169

Gibson B (2004) The importance of short term financing sources in small firms. In: Proceedings of the 49th International Conference of the International Council for Small Business (ICSB), South Africa, pp 1–14

Githaigo PN, Kabiru CG (2015) Debt financing and financial performance of small and medium size enterprises: Evidence from Kenya. Journal of Economics, Finance and Accounting 2(3): 473-481

Hongli J, Ajorsu ES, Bakpa EK (2019) The effect of liquidity and financial leverage on firm performance: Evidence from listed manufacturing firms on the Ghana Stock Exchange. Research Journal of Finance and Accounting 10(8): 91-100

Ibhagui OW, Olokoyo FO (2018) Leverage and firm performance: New evidence on the role of firm size. N Am Econ Financ 45: 57-82. https://doi.org/10.1016/j.najef.2018.02.002

International Monetary Fund (2021) International Financial Statistics. https://data.imf.org/?sk=4c5 14d48-b6ba-49ed-8ab9-52b0c1a0179b. Accessed 10 Mar 2021

Javed T, Younas W, Imran M (2014) Impact of capital structure on firm performance: evidence from Pakistani firms. Int J Acad Res Econ Manag Sci 3(5): 28-52

Maimunah A, Patmawati I (2018) Inflation and companies' performance: A cross-sectional analysis. Adv Sci Lett 24(6): 4750-4755. https://doi.org/10.1166/asl.2018.11694

Mugisha H, Omagwa J, Kilika J (2020) Short-term debt and financial performance of small and medium scale enterprises in Buganda Region, Uganda. Int J Financ Bank Stud 9(4): 58–69. https://doi.org/10.20525/ijfbs.v9i4.910

Nazir A, Azam M, Khalid MU (2021) Debt financing and firm performance: empirical evidence from the Pakistan Stock Exchange. Asian J Account Res 6(3): 324-334. https://doi.org/10.1108/AJAR-03-2019-0019

Pervan M, Pervan I, Ćurak M (2017) The influence of age on firm performance: evidence from the Croatian food industry. Journal of Eastern Europe Research in Business and Economics 618681: 1–9. https://doi.org/10.5171/2017.618681

Rajamani K. (2021) Debt Financing and Financial Performance: Empirical Evidence of Indian SMEs Listed in BSE-SME Platform. In: Bilgin M.H., Danis H., Demir E., Vale S. (eds) Eurasian Economic Perspectives. Eurasian Studies in Business and Economics, vol 16/1. Springer, Cham, pp 217–230. https://doi.org/10.1007/978-3-030-63149-9_14

Robb AM, Robinson DT (2014) The capital structure decisions of new firms. Rev Financ Stud 27(1): 153–179. https://doi.org/10.1093/rfs/hhs072

Ruland W, Zhou P (2005) Debt, diversification and valuation. Rev Quant Finan Acc 25(3): 277-291. https://doi.org/10.1007/s11156-005-4768-0

Saidi AA, Uchenna EB, Ayodele MS (2019) Bank loans and small medium enterprises'(SMES) performance in Lagos, Nigeria. *Ilorin Journal of Human Resource Management* 3(1): 52-61

Tsuruta D (2015) Leverage and firm performance of small businesses: evidence from Japan. Small Bus Econ 44(2): 385–410. https://doi.org/10.1007/s11187-014-9601-5

UN DESA (United Nations Department of Economic and Social Affairs) (2020) World economic situation and prospects as of mid-2020. United Nations, New York

World Bank (2021) World Bank Open data. https://data.worldbank.org. Accessed 10 Mar 2021

Yazdanfar D, Öhman P (2015) Debt financing and firm performance: an empirical study based on Swedish data. J Risk Finance 16(1): 102-118. https://doi.org/10.1108/JRF-06-2014-0085

Zeitun R, Saleh AS (2015) Dynamic performance, financial leverage and financial crisis: evidence from GCC countries. EuroMed J Bus 10(2): 147-162. https://doi.org/10.1108/EMJB-08-2014-0022

Zeitun R, Tian GG (2007) Capital structure and corporate performance: evidence from Jordan. Australas Account Bus Finance J 1(4): 40–61. https://doi.org/10.14453/aabfj.v1i4.3

Service-Dominant Logic: The Road Map to Value Co-Creation in Place Marketing

Sofia Daskou, Andreas Masouras, and Anastasia Athanasoula Reppa

Abstract This paper presents a conceptualization of the utility of Service-Dominant Logic (SDL) in theoretically underpinning the value co-creation process that emerges from the interactions and relationships of place visitors with local resource integrators of destinations. Under the SDL of marketing, *service* becomes the ontological content of the place brand and a fundamental mechanism of the exchange of place-branded products. The work is based on the Vargo and Lusch (J Acad Mark Sci 36(1):1–10, 2008) premise, that service is the fundamental basis of exchange, and builds an argument about how operant resources can be deployed by place marketers, as a source of competitive advantage to sustain loyalty to place visitors. It proceeds to explain how to place marketers (i.e., hospitality services, tourist attractions, etc.) co-create value with place visitors (customers) to generate effects that stimulate visitor loyalty and build the place brand. The relationships that develop between the customers and place marketers are embedded in a service ecosystem, which appreciates the phenomenologically determined perceptions of value of the parties and stimulates place visitors to repeat customs. The paper argues in favor of the integration of the roles of the customers and service suppliers in the formation of a value output, which becomes input in the identity of a place.

S. Daskou (✉)
Associate Professor in Business and Customer Management, Department of Economics and Business, Neapolis University Pafos, 2 Danais Avenue, 8042 Paphos, Cyprus
e-mail: s.daskou@nup.ac.cy

A. Masouras
Assistant Professor in Communication and Marketing Communication and Marketing, Department of Economics and Business, Neapolis University Pafos, 2 Danais Avenue, 8042 Paphos, Cyprus
e-mail: a.masouras@nup.ac.cy

A. Athanasoula Reppa
Professor of Educational Administration, Department of Economics and Business, Neapolis University Pafos, 2 Danais Avenue, 8042 Paphos, Cyprus
e-mail: a.reppa@nup.ac.cy

© The Author(s), under exclusive license to Springer Nature Switzerland AG 2022
P. Sklias et al. (eds.), *Business Development and Economic Governance in Southeastern Europe*, Springer Proceedings in Business and Economics,
https://doi.org/10.1007/978-3-031-05351-1_21

Keywords Service-Dominant Logic · Value co-creation · Place marketing · Place branding · Tourism

JEL Classification M

1 Introduction

According to Selimi et al. (2017) tourism has a significantly positive effect on economic growth, in increasing Gross Domestic Product (GDP) per capita by 0.8% (for every 1% increase in tourists) in several Western Balkan countries, constituting place marketing as an imperative contributor to economic development. As such, effective ways of marketing a place are of great interest to this region, and more specifically how visitors themselves (the consumers of the place) augment the process, through their interactive experience with the place. Since "empirical evidence on value co-creation in experience is scarce in the tourism literature" (Liang 2017, p. 363), drawing from the conceptual development of Service-Dominant Logic (SDL), this paper addresses the concept of visitor co-creation of value, as a driver of marketing a place. The paper proceeds to legitimize the suitability of SDL as an ideological foundation of value co-creation and explains how place visitors become resource integrators of marketing a place, via their participatory role of value co-creation with local actors. It also argues that place marketers may benefit from a better understanding of the contributions of place visitors in the co-creation of positive experiences, in the place ecosystem, which contributes to the identity of the place.

2 Fundamental Conceptualization

In order to explain the relationship between place marketing and SDL, the sections that follow present the ontology and key concepts of SDL, the essence of place resource integrators and value co-creation and discuss the nature of place marketing. The relationship between the concepts is also addressed, hereafter.

2.1 Service-Dominant Logic

In 2004, Stephen Vargo and Robert Lusch published a seminal paper in the *Journal of Marketing*[1] that transformed marketing thinking. In their article, Vargo and Lusch (2004) introduced and coined the concept of SDL, a theory that asserts that companies and their customers become co-creators of value, which is an outcome of their

---

[1] *Italics* adopted in the paper are used to indicate emphasis.

interactions and explains that service (rather than goods) provision is the fundamental unit of economic exchange. Over the years, their theory evolved into a paradigm of marketing (Lusch et al. 2010), which recognizes the relational nature of market exchanges and the role of customer-firm interactions. Consequently SDL, theoretically underpinned several conceptual and empirical works, including: the examination of the influence of seller resources on buyer satisfaction in business to business contexts (deLeon and Chatterjee 2017); the radicalization of service innovation of manufacturing firms (Goduscheit and Faullant 2018); the identification of the antecedents and consequences of service innovation (Ordanini and Parasuraman 2011); the conceptualization of servicescape (Nilsson and Ballantyne 2014); an understanding of co-production of public service (Alford 2016) and the development of public services (Westrup 2018); the co-creation of value in healthcare (Joiner and Lusch 2016); an understanding of the effect of B2C and C2C co-created digital communications on perceptions of service (Peltier et al. 2020); the enhancement of e-commerce of wine (Festa et al. 2019); the modeling of the effects of motivational sources on value in use and brand equity of branded apps (Tran et al. 2021); the exploration of the antecedents of loyalty to branded applications (app) and brands (Fang 2019); the co-creation of value in the festival experience (Van Winkle and Bueddefeld 2016); the design of agritourism activities that enhance tourists' experience (Rong-Da Liang 2017); and the development of tourist destination image (Añaña et al. 2018).

The original (2004) paper, oriented marketing thinking on *process* rather than on *outputs*. It identified issues that consistently emerged from relationship, services, and business-to-business marketing and emphasized value (co)creation as the cohesive theme of these steams/subdisciplines of marketing, in a narrative that was developed around the micro-level of marketing (Vargo and Lusch 2004). The authors later developed their theory further, by positioning service as the *basis*, rather than the *unit* of exchange, between *actors* (rather than firms and their customers), and added more fundamental premises, recognizing actors' *phenomenological* perspective of value, and their characteristics as resource integrators (Vargo and Lusch 2008). In 2011, Vargo and Lusch clarified that in the value co-creation process, actors integrate resources and engage in service exchange. In 2016 they modified foundational premise 4, into "Operant resources are the fundamental source of strategic benefit" (Vargo and Lusch 2016, p. 8), replacing the term competitive advantage with *strategic benefit*, to highlight the role of service providers as beneficiaries or reciprocal service. Furthermore, they developed an additional premise according to which "value co-creation is coordinated through actor-generated institutions and institutional arrangements" (Vargo and Lusch 2016, p. 18).

2.1.1 The SDL Lexicon

The evolution of SDL offers several lessons to marketing academia and practice. The theory comprises of several foundational premises (see Table 1), which explain the central role of operant resources, as sources of strategic benefit (Vargo and Lusch

Table 1 Foundational premise development

Foundational premise	2004	2008	Update
FP1	The application of specialized skills and knowledge is the fundamental unit of exchange	Service is the fundamental basis of exchange	*No Change* **AXIOM STATUS**
FP2	Indirect exchange masks the fundamental unit of exchange	Indirect exchange masks the fundamental basis of exchange	*No Change*
FP3	Goods are distribution mechanisms for service provision	*No Change*	*No Change*
FP4	Knowledge is the fundamental source of competitive advantage	Operant resources are the fundamental source of competitive advantage	Operant resources are the fundamental source of strategic benefit
FP5	All economies are service economies	*No Change*	*No Change*
FP6	The customer is always the co-producer	The customer is always a co-creator of value	Value is co-created by multiple actors, always including the beneficiary **AXIOM STATUS**
FP7	The enterprise can only make value propositions	The enterprise cannot deliver value but only offer value propositions	Actors cannot deliver value but can participate in the creation and offering of value propositions
FP8	Service-centered view is customer-oriented and relational	A service-centered view is inherently customer-oriented and relational	A service-centered view is inherently beneficiary oriented and relational
FP9		All social and economic actors are resource integrators	*No Change* **AXIOM STATUS**
FP10		Value is always uniquely and phenomenologically determined by the beneficiary	*No Change* **AXIOM STATUS**

(continued)

Table 1 (continued)

Foundational premise	2004	2008	Update
FP11			**New**: Value co-creation is coordinated through actor-generated institutions and institutional arrangements **AXIOM STATUS**

(*Source* Vargo and Lusch (2016, p. 8)

2016). Frempong et al (2020, p. 4.) define *operant resources* as the "individually possessed resources which are generally invisible and intangible, and shaped out of knowledge and capacities". Based on the works of Constantin and Lusch (1994), and Madhavaram and Hunt (2008), Adams et al. (2014) present operant resources as *skill and knowledge* resources, that produce effects on other resources, and can for example be the skills of employees, utilized in pulling firm *capabilities* and other resources, into offerings that better match the needs of customers compared to those of other suppliers in the market. According to Hirscher et al. (2018), knowledge, which constitutes an intangible resource to the firm, impacts on the motivation of actors (i.e., customers) to take part in collaborative, value co-creation activities. The intangible asset of knowledge refers to intelligence of employees, customers, competitors, suppliers, etc. (Ngo and O'Cass 2009), and may also include mental competence, organizational process, and relationships with suppliers, customers, and competitors (Vargo and Lusch 2004).

The useful application of the operant resource of knowledge, produces *value* outcomes (Vargo and Lusch 2004), therefore the capacity to operationalize knowledge is vital to the success of value creation. As such, the capability of the firm to operationalize knowledge is central to the application of a service logic to the marketing approach of the firm. Indeed, an SDL approach recommends marketers to focus on the intangible (operant) resources of customers, which are detrimental to the competitive advantage of the firm (Madhavaram and Hunt 2008). So, the question that arises is *what firm capabilities, lead to strategic competitive benefits?* Morgan et al. (2004, p. 91) define capabilities (in the context of exporting) as the "organizational processes by which available resources are developed, combined, and transformed into value offerings". In a broader context, Day (1994, p. 38) defines capabilities as: "complex bundles of skills and accumulated knowledge, exercised through organizational processes which enable firms to coordinate activities and make use of their assets". Consequently, Ngo and O'Cass (2009) equate capabilities to the glue that binds resources to create value offerings, for customers.

SDL foundational premise 7 specifies that "actors cannot deliver value but can participate in the creation and offering of value propositions" (Vargo and Lusch 2016, p. 8). Economic *actors* are individuals, households, firms, nations, and members of networks who interact and exchange with other actors (Vargo and Lusch 2008). As such, customers are economic actors who interact with providers to co-create value (also a key positioning of foundational premise 6). Firms that provide service, offer value propositions by designing, defining, and creating their offerings (Vargo and Lusch 2004) and although customers may choose not to participate in the co-production of these value positions, they by default contribute to the co-creation value, through their interactions with the firm and other actors (Vargo and Lusch 2016). The principal issue around this foundational premise is the nature of value. So, what is value and how is it co-created by actors?

According to Font et al. (2021), value is determined by actors' perceptions of the benefits of using products and services and is co-created by the customers' interactions with providers (Alford 2016). From a customer perspective, value is perceived as "the trade-off between *what they get* (perceived benefits, quality, or performance) and *what they give*" (Ngo and O'Cass 2009, p. 46), which in effect describes the concept of value in use (Vargo and Lusch 2004). *Value-in-use* represents a customer's judgment (Ballantyne and Varey 2006) of the satisfaction/utility reaped from the consumption of service. From a firm perspective, *value-in-proposition* refers to the "proposed value that the firm builds in its market offering" (Ngo and O'Cass 2009, p. 46). It can be viewed as the promises suppliers make to customers, of the value-in-use they will experience in exchange for the money they will pay, and is conditional to the experienced service quality (or other output) of the customer-firm interaction (Lusch et al. 2007). Font et al. (2021) explain that numerous stakeholders (actors) create value, experienced by customers. As such, in the macro-level context of tourism, it becomes necessary to examine how place marketers (i.e., hospitality services, tourist attractions, etc.) co-create value with place visitors (customers), to generate positive experience (and by consequence loyalty) outcomes.

From a supplier perspective, value can be created by the application of suppliers' operant resources in the market. According to Ngo and o'Cass (2009), firms possess, apply and utilize their innovation-based, marketing-based, and production-based operant capabilities to create value with customers. In other words, the providers exercise their *capacity* (Hurley and Hult 1998) and *organizational intensity* (Weerawardena and O'Cass 2004) to innovate, along with their marketing-based capabilities and production-based capabilities, to create value. Technically speaking, the "integrative process of applying the collective knowledge, skills, and resources of the firm to perform marketing activities" (Ngo and o'Cass 2009, p. 48) which constitutes the market-based capabilities, and "the integrative process of applying the collective knowledge, skills, and resources of the firm to perform production activities (e.g., production adaptability, quality control, productivity, and production scheduling) of the business" (Ngo and o'Cass 2009, p. 48) which constitute the production capabilities of the firm, are the tools/resources organizations have to co-create value with other actors. The Ngo and o'Cass (2009) study demonstrated that in the context of medium and large Vietnamese firms, innovation and marketing-based operant capabilities generate value offerings for customers, which means that innovations offer customers the environment for new co-creation experiences, and the firm's ability to communicate, differentiate and position its offerings, augments value for customers.

2.2 Place Marketing and Place Branding

The literature recognizes marketing a place relevant to: *place brands* (see: Brand America: Anholt and Hildreth 2004; Brand Poland: Florek 2005); *rural communities* (Rausch 2009); *tourist destinations* (see: Tsai 2012, Stephens Balakrishnan 2009); *city marketing and branding* (see: City marketing/branding: Muniz-Martinez 2012; Daskou et al. 2004); *continents* (see: Africa: Abimbola 2006); *regions* (see: Central European: Capik 2007); *nation (country) branding* (see: Anholt 1998; Dinnie 2008); *events* (see: China Olympics: Berkowitz et al. 2007); *municipalities and councils* (see: Birmingham: Virgo and de Chernatony 2006). Therefore, place marketing addresses a place as a product-service, a corporate brand, a geographic location, a destination, and may involve entities such as: groups of countries, cities, boroughs, nations, metro areas, regions, geographic entities, business districts, municipalities, locations of retail agglomerations, markets, and tourist destinations (Daskou 2013). Consequently, due to the numerous stakeholders involved in managing a place brand, and the intricate relationship between (national) identity and culture, Skinner (2008, p. 916) advocates that "places do not have single identities that can be branded as clearly as the products or service brands". Drawing from Brown's (2006) recommendation to investigate brands from a multi-stakeholder perspective, we propose that the interactions and relationships of place visitors with local resource integrators of destinations co-create value that further develop the place-brand.

The concept of *place marketing* is a relatively new field of marketing, although various early approaches to interpret *place* from other scientific fields and approaches such as sociology and geography were used to originally describe the concept (Zenker and Martin 2011). Zenker and Martin (2011) argue that the conceptual interpretation of place-marketing is the whole system of values that defines the characteristics of the place. The promotion of the place, i.e., its characteristics, requires the existence of a toolbox such as the marketing mix, communication designs, marketing management, and branding so that its identity can be communicated to the recipients (target groups), namely tourists, visitors, and other interested parties. The main goal of place-marketing is to promote the values that characterize the place, which then become visible to potential users of the place (e.g., potential visitors) as the elements that differentiate it from other places and its comparative advantages (Kotler et al. 1993). Therefore, branding is the main tool through which the *place* can *communicate* with potential users.

Aitken and Campelo (2011) link the concept of place-marketing with the *community*. Specifically, the authors consider that the particular characteristics of the place and especially the representations of the place, which are highlighted and promoted through the community, are what generate its identity, and enhance the branding of the place. Of particular interest is the approach of these authors (2011) regarding the *brand essence* (i.e., the essential content of the place that shapes and gives its identity which ultimately differentiates it from other places and destinations), and also claim that the *experience of the community* is what ultimately lends itself to building the identity of the place. Warnaby and Medway (2013) follow the same logic, referring to the importance of the place in strengthening the identity of the products related to the place. More specifically, these authors (2013) argue that the commercialization of those products that are based on the image of the place (such as tourism and related services) depends largely on the meaning and value that will give them locus. For example, Masouras et al. (2019) demonstrate that the place gives identity to the product, in the context of the wine industry and argue in favor of the effect of the interconnection of this "mix" to the strengthening of destination marketing. Some of the composites of place marketing mix are the participation and experiences of people in local communities, traditions, and experiences, and myths that are reproduced and enrich the historical history of the place. Thus, cultural and fictional elements are important components of the process.

The basic elements of destination marketing mix are based on human communication, which according to Lichrou et al. (2010), refers to the way communities communicate with other people, as well as the way they convey experiences via storytelling. Furthermore, local culture and cultural peculiarities are elements of the place (Pan et al. 2007), and the place according to Siakalli and Masouras (2020), is an important motivation that influences the section decision of destination, of tourists or travelers. The process of choosing a destination is certainly not simple. It contains many elements the most critical of which is whether the place will meet the needs and requirements of the tourist (satisfaction). The decision for the destination is place-driven and includes several connections with the place (Siakalli and Masouras 2020).

2.3   Resource Integrators

As per the Vargo and Lusch (2016) axiomatic propositions (see axiom 3/ FP9 in Table 1) all social and economic actors are resource integrators. Bruce et al. (2019, p. 174) describe resource integration as the "process by which actors, such as consumers, combine and apply resources in pursuit of value creation" …which consists of "activities to assemble, master, and optimize resources, to plan and fine-tune usage events in real-time, and to reflect upon previous activities" (p. 182). Clearly, place visitors become resource integrators who participate in the value co-creation of the service experience of the place they visit. During the process, visitors contribute their time, disposable income, energy, and interactions, to experience the place, via episodic interactions with various actors such as local service staff (i.e., restaurants, museums, hotels, spas, etc.), other social actors (operators of transportations, local citizens and other tourists) and the operand resources of the place-brand (accommodations, museums, restaurants, etc.). Therefore, we propose that the dialectic communication between the actors becomes content in the visitors' international experience of the place service. As per the SDL paradigm of marketing, reciprocal service is exchanged between local actors and places visitors, in the form of the operant resources they invest in the experience. In other words, the visitors experience the place through the encounters with place actors. These encounters are according to Gronroos and Voima (2013, p. 140) "situations in which the interacting parties are involved in each other's practices. The core of interaction is a physical, virtual, or mental contact, such that the provider creates opportunities to engage with its customers' experiences and practices and thereby influences their flow and outcomes". The outcomes, in this case, represent the visitors' perceptions of the place brand.

In terms of a place as a destination, and in addition to the operand resources (i.e., infrastructure, tourist attractions, hotels, and entertainment-leisure venues, etc.) required, the investment of the place-brand is human capital. Especially in the case of tourism development, which requires specialized personal skills to approach and attract customers, as well as, process management, the design and implementation of adult and lifelong learning programs can be a useful tool for the development and specialization of the human capital invested. In this context, soft skills of service staff will be extremely supportive in the development of tourism services, especially as research of CEDEFOP (2020b), predicts possible continuous increase in demand for sellers and service providers (including tourism), public and private sector and technical and assistant professionals, by 2030. In the context of a place-brand, as staffing of new services and organizations will be an urgent priority (CEDEFOP 2020a), adult education programs focus on adult skills relevant to upgrading and re-skilling individuals, who interact with visitors of the place. These skills are augmented capabilities and become operant resources of the place-brand.

3   Road-Mapping Value Co-Creation in Place Marketing

Research investigations in the tourism industry indicate that co-creation is related to customer satisfaction, loyalty, and service spending (Grissemann and Stokburger-Sauer 2012), supporting the relevance of considering visitors' experience of co-creation of value in the context of place brands. More recent studies have demonstrated that combining an SDL approach with the specific characteristics of the type of touristic service, intensifies tourist intention to revisit (Liang 2017). In the context of visitors' experiences, Van Winkle and Bueddefeld (2016) argue that value is experienced from service in use in a social context, where social systems are part of the value co-creation process, in which actors bring meaning to the experience. In applying these views to the context of a place brand and by further building on the SDL lexicon and pre-submitted literature on place-marketing, we propose the instrumental role of actors' operant resources in cocreating value that affects the place-brand. More specifically, place brands are complex entities, created by value generation outputs of several actors, who operate in a network. This view agrees with Vargo and Lusch (2008) position that value is created in networks of networks. In this case, the *place* is the *context* where value is created, by resource integrators that interact and co-create experiences and stories. In that sense, *the service encounters between actors become* as much a *part of the place,* as are the venues, the heritage, the monuments, and all other elements of the servicescape of the place. Therefore, the place servicescape is a component of a service ecosystem. Vargo and Lusch (2016 p. 10) define a service ecosystem as a "relatively self-contained, self-adjusting system of resource-integrating actors connected by shared institutional arrangements and mutual value creation through service exchange". Indeed, the place ecosystem includes resource integrators (actors) who co-operate in the coordination and integration of operant resources to brand the place. Consequently, individual resource integrators should understand their place in the ecosystem and continuously contribute to the identity formation, by sharing knowledge and information.

The place ecosystem functions as a cluster (or clusters) of unique experiences of interactions of various resource integrators, which in a sense concurs with the views of Binkhorst and Den Dekker (2009, p. 311) who argue that visitor co-creation experiences are suited in tourism contexts "especially during free time people express their quest for ever more unique experiences reflecting their own personal stories". From a marketing perspective, we propose that place marketers may wish to contemplate, *how and when* to engage the visitors in value co-creation processes, as the intensity of visitor desire for co-creation may vary (i.e., see: Van Winkle and Bueddefeld 2016). Indeed Van Winkle and Bueddefeld (2016, p. 250) recommend marketers to "consider how enabling people to cultivate existing experiences and meanings will add depth to their experience", which can be the conceptual foundation of the communication practices (see O'Malley and Patterson 2010), of the place branding campaigns.

Place marketers can develop value propositions, which according to Baldassarre et al. (2017) are inherent in the interactions between actors that include shared hedonic values. Font et al. (2021) recommend that visitors may prefer positively framed messages that agree with and augment their personal values, which in the case of place branding may include hedonic aspects. These aspects could emerge from the promotion of the adaptive, absorptive and innovative capabilities of service providers (Wang and Ahmed 2007), which offer a brand competitive advantage (Evans 2016), and reflect all the operant resources of the resource integrators of the place-brand. This way, through value co-creation, the integration of the roles of the customers and service suppliers in the formation of a value output, becomes input in the identity of a place. Place identities (the basis of place-branding) thus include the application of operant resources of place visitors and other place actors, in a system of interactions that co-create: (a) the value proposition of a place and (b) the satisfaction utility that visitors reap from the service experience of the place. Jointly, (a) and (b) co-create the place-brand.

4 Conclusion

The paper conceptualized the utility of Service-Dominant Logic in theoretically underpinning the value co-creation process that emerges from the interactions and relationships of place visitors with local resource integrators of destinations. SDL serves place marketing by explaining the role of actors (visitors and local resource integrators) in shaping the identity of a place, as the outcome of actors' interactions in an ecosystem that facilitates actors to apply their operant resources. In the place ecosystem, operant resources can be deployed by place marketers, as a source of competitive benefit, to sustain the loyalty of place visitors. To market a place, marketers should examine how the interactions and relationships of place visitors with local resource integrators of destinations co-create value, since the engagement between the actors, becomes the essence of visitors experience of the place service. As such, place marketers will wish to identify how and when to engage the visitors in value co-creation practices that define their phenomenological perception of a place. SDL offers several possible applications in place-marketing, in that it can be used to identify typologies of operant resources that enhance the value proposition of a place. This argument corroborates with the views of Hunt (2000), that improved collaborative and absorptive competencies, can be deployed by organizations to reduce the relative resource cost and augment their relative value propositions.

The utility of SDL in addressing place marketing has so far been relatively underexplored since a phenomenological approach to the perceptions of the actors requires complex qualitative approaches to study the phenomenon which normally take a lot of time investment of possible actor samples. Nevertheless, we urge researchers to further investigate the nature of value expectations place visitors have, prior to selecting a destination. In addition, more research is required to explore the role of place-visitors in the experience and actors' engagement of other visitors, and how these outcomes affect place identities and the design of a place brand.

References

Abimbola T (2006) Market access for developing economies: Branding in Africa. Place Branding 2(2):108–117, https://doi.org/10.1057/palgrave.pb.5990049 .

Adams FG, Richey RG Jr, Autry CW, Morgan TR, Gabler CB (2014) Supply Chain Collaboration, Integration, and Relational Technology: How Complex Operant Resources Increase Performance Outcomes. Journal of Business Logistics 35 (4): 299–317. https://doi.org/10.1111/jbl.12074.

Aitken R, Campelo A (2011) The Four Rs of Place Branding. Journal of Marketing Management 27 (9/10): 913–933.

Alford J (2016) Co-Production, Interdependence and Publicness: Extending Public Service-dominant Logic. Public Management Review 18 (5):673–691. https://doi.org/10.1080/14719037.2015.1111659.

Anholt S.(1998) Nation-brands of the Twenty-first Century. Journal of Brand Management 5 (6): 395–406.

Anholt S, Hildreth J (2004) Brand America: The Mother of All Brands. UK, Cyan Books.

Baldassarre B, Calabretta G, Bocken, NMP, Jaskiewicz T (2017) Bridging Sustainable Business Model Innovation and User-driven Innovation: A Process for Sustainable Value Proposition Design. Journal of Cleaner Production 147: 175–186.

Ballantyne D & Varey RJ (2006) Creating Value-in-use Through Marketing Interaction: The Exchange Logic of Relating, Communicating and Knowing. Marketing Theory 6 (3): 335–348.

Berkowitz P, Gjermano G, Gomez L. Schafer G (2007) Brand China: Using the 2008 Olympic Games to Enhance China's Image. Place Branding and Public Diplomacy 3 (2): 164–178.

Binkhorst E, Den Dekker T (2009) Agenda for Co-creation Tourism Experience Research, Journal of Hospitality Marketing & Management 18 (2/3): 311–327.

Brown J (2006) Attitudes and Experiences of the Rebranding of Liverpool: The Liverpool 08 Local Experience, In: Proceedings of the Contemporary Issues in Retail Marketing Conference, Destinations and Locations: Exploring the Multiple Identities of Place, Manchester Metropolitan University 2006.

Bruce HL, Hugh N, Wilson HN, Macdonald EK, Clarke B (2019) Resource Integration, Value Creation and Value Destruction in Collective Consumption Contexts. Journal of Business Research 103:173–185.

Capik P (2007). Organising FDI Promotion in Central–Eastern European Regions, Place Branding and Public Diplomacy 3 (2): 152–163.

CEDEFOP (2020a) Empowering Adults Through Upskilling and Reskilling Pathways - Volume 1: Adult Population with Potential for Upskilling and Reskilling (2/2020a) CEDEFOP/EU.

CEDEFOP (2020b) Empowering Adults Through Upskilling and Reskilling Pathways - Volume 2: Cedefop Analytical Framework for Developing Coordinated and Coherent Approaches to Upskilling Pathways for Low-skilled Adults (7/2020b) CEDEFOP/EU.

Constantin JA, Lusch RF (1994) Understanding Resource Management. Oxford, OH: The Planning Forum.

da Silva Añaña E, Dos Anjos FA, de Lima Pereira M (2018) Touristic Destination Image in Light of the Service Dominant Logic of Marketing. Tourism & Management Studies 14 (3): 7–18.

Daskou S, Thom C, Boojihawon DK (2004) Marketing a City: Glasgow, City of Architecture and Design. The Global Business & Economics Review 6 (1): 22–37.

Daskou S (2013) A Service Dominant Logic (SDL) Approach to Place Marketing: Conceptual Considerations. Business & Economics Society International 2013 Conference, Monte Carlo, Monaco, (6–9 July).

Day GS (1994) The Capabilities of Market-Driven Organizations. Journal of Marketing 58 (4): 37-52. https://doi.org/10.1177/002224299405800404.

de Leon AJ, Chatterjee SC (2017) B2B Relationship Calculus: Quantifying Resource Effects in Service-dominant Logic. Journal of the Academy of Marketing Science 45: 402–427.

Dinnie K (2008) Nation Branding: Concepts, Issues and Practice, Elsevier, Amsterdam.

Evans NG (2016) Sustainable Competitive Advantage in Tourism Organizations: A Strategic Model Applying Service Dominant Logic and Tourism's Defining Characteristics. Tourism Management Perspectives 18:14–25.

Fang YH (2019) An App a Day Keeps a Customer Connected: Explicating Loyalty to Brands and Branded Applications Through the Lens of Affordance and Service-dominant Logic. Information & Management 56 (3): 377–391, https://doi.org/10.1016/j.im.2018.07.011 .

Festa G, Cuomo MT, Metallo G (2019) The Service-dominant Logic Perspective for Enhancing the E-commerce of Wine - A test/application on the Italian Wine Sector. Journal of Business Research 101:477–484, https://doi.org/10.1016/j.jbusres.2018.12.077.

Florek M (2005) The Country Brand as a New Challenge for Poland. Place Branding, Vol. 1, No. 2, pp. 205–214.

Font X, English R, Gkritzali A, Tian W (2021) Value Co-creation in Sustainable Tourism: A Service-dominant Logic Approach. Tourism Management 82:104-200, https://doi.org/10.1016/j.tourman.2020.104200 .

Frempong J, Chai J, Ampaw EM, Amofah DO, Ansong KW (2020) The Relationship Among Customer Operant Resources, Online Value Co-creation and Electronic-word-of-mouth in Solid

Waste Management Marketing. Journal of Cleaner Production 248: 119–228, https://doi.org/10.1016/j.jclepro.2019.119228 .

Goduscheit RC, Faullant R (2018) Paths Toward Radical Service Innovation in Manufacturing Companies—A Service-Dominant Logic Perspective. Journal of Product and Innovation Management 35 (5): 701–719.

Grissemann US, Stokburger-Sauer NE (2012) Customer Co-creation of Travel Services: the Role of Company Support and Customer Satisfaction with the Co-creation Performance. Tourism Management 33 (6):1483–1492.

Gronroos C, Voima P (2013) Critical Service Logic: Making Sense of Value Creation and Co-creation. Journal of the Academy of Marketing Science 41 (2): 133–150.

Hirscher AL, Niinimaki K, Armstrong CMJ (2018) Social Manufacturing in the Fashion Sector: New Value Creation Through Alternative Design Strategies? Journal of Cleaner Production 172: 4544–4554. https://doi.org/10.1016/j.jclepro.2017.11.020.

Hunt SD (2000) A General Theory of Competition: Resources,Competences, Productivity, and Economic Growth, California, Thousand Oaks: Sage Publications.

Hurley RF, Hult GTM (1998) Innovation, Market Orientation, and Organizational Learning: An Integration and Empirical Examination. *Journal of Marketing* 62 (July): 42−54.

Joiner K, Lusch R (2016) Evolving to a New Service-dominant Logic for Health Care. Innovation and Entrepreneurship in Health 3: 25–33.

Kotler P, Haider DH, Rein I (1993) Marketing Places: Attracting Investment, Industry, and Tourism to Cities, States, and Nations. New York: The Free Press.

Liang AR (2017) Considering the Role of Agritourism Co-creation from a Service-dominant Logic Perspective. Tourism Management 61: 354–367.

Lichrou M, O'Malley L Patterson M (2010) Narratives of a Tourism Destination: Local Particularities and Their Implications for Place Marketing and Branding. Place Branding and Public Diplomacy 6 (2): 134–44.

Lusch RF, Vargo SL, O'Brien M (2007) Competing Through Service: Insights from Service-dominant Logic". Journal of Retailing, 83 (1): 5–18.

Lusch RF, Vargo SL, Tanniru M (2010) Service, Value-networks, and Learning. Journal of the Academy of Marketing Science 38 (1): 19–31.

Madhavaram S, Hunt SB (2008) The Service-Dominant Logic and a Hierarchy of Operant Resources: Developing Masterful Operant Resources and Implications for Marketing Strategy. Journal of the Academy of Marketing Science, 36 (1): 67–82.

Masouras A, Komodromos I, Papademetriou C (2019) Cyprus's Wine Market: Influencing Factors of Consumer Behaviour as Part of Destination Marketing. In: Kavoura A., Kefallonitis E., Giovanis A. (eds) Strategic Innovative Marketing and Tourism. Springer Proceedings in Business and Economics. Springer, Cham. https://doi.org/10.1007/978-3-030-12453-3_73 .

Morgan NA, Kaleka A, Katsikeas CS (2004) Antecedents of Export Venture Performance: A Theoretical Model and Empirical Assessment. Journal of Marketing, 68 (1): 90−108.

Muñiz Martinez N (2012) City Marketing and Place Branding: A Critical Review of Practice and Academic Research, Journal of Town & City Management 2 (4): 369–394.

Ngo LV O'Cass A (2009) Creating Value Offerings via Opernat Reserource-based Capabilities. Industrial Marketing Managment. 38: 45–59.

Nilsson E, & Ballantyne, D. 2014. Reexamining the Place of Servicescape in Marketing: A Service-dominant Logic Perspective. Journal of Services Marketing 28 (5): 374–379.

Ordanini A, Parasuraman A (2011) Service Innovation Viewed Through a Service Dominant Logic Lens: A Conceptual Framework and Empirical Analysis. Journal of Service Research, 14 (1): 3–23. https://doi.org/10.1177/1094670510385332.

Pan B, MacLaurin T, Crotts JC (2007) Travel Blogs and the Implications for Destination Marketing. Journal of Travel Research, 46 (1): 35–45.

Peltier JW, Dahl J, Swa EL (2020) Digital Information Flows Across a B2C/C2C Continuum and Technological Innovations in Service Ecosystems: A Service-dominant Logic Perspective. Journal of Business Research 121: 724-734, https://doi.org/10.1016/j.jbusres.2020.03.020 .

Rausch A (2009) Capitalizing on Creativity in Rural Areas: National and Local Branding in Japan. Journal of Rural and Community Development 4 (2): 65–79.

Selimi N, Sadiku L, Sadiku M (2017) The Impact of Tourism on Economic Growth in the Western Balkan Countries: An Empirical Analysis. International Journal of Business and Economic Sciences Applied Research 10 (2):19–25.

Siakalli M, Masouras A. (2020) Factors That Influence Tourist Satisfaction: An Empirical Study in Pafos. In: Kavoura A., Kefallonitis E., Theodoridis P. (eds) Strategic Innovative Marketing and Tourism. Springer Proceedings in Business and Economics. Springer, Cham. p. 459–466 https://doi.org/10.1007/978-3-030-36126-6_51 .

Skinner H (2008) The Emergence and Development of Place Marketing's Confused Identity. Journal of Marketing Management, 24 (9/10): 915–928.

Stephens Balakrishnan M (2009). Strategic Branding of Destinations: A Famework. European Journal of Marketing 43 (5/6): 611–629.

Tran TP, Mai ES, & Taylor EC (2021) Enhancing Brand Equity of Branded Mobile Apps via Motivations: A Service-Dominant Logic Perspective. Journal of Business Research 125: 239–251.

Tsai S (2012) Place Attachment and Tourism Marketing: Investigating International Tourists in Singapore. International Journal of Tourism Research 14: 139–152.

Van Winkle CM, Bueddefeld JNH (2016) Service-dominant logic and the Festival Experience. International Journal of Event and Festival Management 7 (3): 237–254.

Vargo SL, Lusch RF (2004) Evolving to a New Dominant Logic for Marketing. Journal of Marketing 68 (January): 1–17.

Vargo SL, Lusch RF (2008) Service-dominant Logic: Continuing the Evolution. Journal of the Academy of Marketing Science 36 (1): pp. 1–10.

Vargo SL Lusch RF (2016) Institutions and Axioms: an Extension and Update of Service-Dominant Logic. Journal of the Academy of Marketing Science 44 (1): pp. 5–23.

Virgo B, de Chernatony L (2006) Delphic Brand Visioning to Align Stakeholder Buy-in to the City of Birmingham Brand. Journal of Brand Management 13 (6): 379–392. https://doi.org/10.1057/palgrave.bm.2540280 .

Wang CL, Ahmed PK (2007) Dynamic Capabilities: A Review & Research Agenda. International Journal of Management Reviews 9 (1): pp. 31–51.

Warnaby G, Medway D (2013) What About the 'Place'in Place Marketing? Marketing Theory 13(3): 345–363.

Weerawardena J, O'Cass A (2004) Exploring the Characteristics of the Market-driven Firms and Antecedents to Sustained Competitive Advantage. Industrial Marketing Management 33 (5): 419–428.

Westrup U (2018) The Potential of Service-dominant Logic as a Tool for Developing Public Sector Services A Study of a Swedish Case. International Journal of Quality and Service Sciences 10 (1): 36-48.

Zenker S, Martin N (2011) Measuring Success in Place Marketing and Branding. Place Branding and Public Diplomacy 7 (1): 32–41.

Degree of Personal Income Taxation Convergence in the Eurozone

Dimitra Ntertsou, Christos Galanos, and Konstantinos Liapis

Abstract **Purpose**: The purpose of this article is to assess tax regime similarities among Eurozone countries in the field of Personal Income Tax, given that human capital is highly mobile and thus affected by the design of a country's tax code. **Design/Methodology/Approach**: Using information on the Central government personal income tax rates and thresholds, available on the OECD Tax Database, this article employs dendrograms to present similarities of tax regimes and clustering of homogeneous Eurozone countries for four different years (2003–2008–2013–2018), in order to capture the effects of the 2008 economic crisis in the design of personal income tax systems. **Findings**: Our findings suggest a great degree of divergence in the design of personal income tax systems, especially regarding the degree of progressivity as well as top income brackets and marginal rates. It is interesting to observe how clusters of groups of countries with similar tax regimes are differentiated through time. **Originality/Value**: Most of the literature, when comparing different tax regimes, focuses on tax revenues and average tax burdens. The value of this research stems from the fact that it provides a similarity analysis, based on the actual design of the tax schedule. Results can be indicative of the degree of convergence in Eurozone countries, thus providing tax authorities with a transparent methodology to assess the level of fiscal harmonization.

D. Ntertsou
Faculty of Sciences of Economy & Public Administration, Economic & Regional Development Department, Panteion University of Social & Political Sciences, 136, Sygrou Ave., 17671 Athens, Greece
e-mail: d.ntertsou@panteion.gr

C. Galanos (✉)
Department of Agricultural Business Administration and Supply Systems, Agricultural University of Athens, Thiva, Greece
e-mail: christos.galanos@gmail.com

K. Liapis
Accounting and Business Administration, Faculty of Sciences of Economy & Public Administration, Economic & Regional Development Department, Panteion University of Social & Political Sciences, 136, Sygrou Ave., 17671 Athens, Greece
e-mail: konstantinos.liapis@panteion.gr

P. Sklias et al. (eds.), *Business Development and Economic Governance in Southeastern Europe*, Springer Proceedings in Business and Economics,
https://doi.org/10.1007/978-3-031-05351-1_22

Keywords Personal tax · Convergence · Eurozone · Clustering

JEL Classification E63 · H20 · H24

1 Introduction

Governments in designing their personal income tax systems, face a series of complicated choices between different—often competing—policy objectives. Besides
raising revenues, three additional features of personal income taxation are especially
important (OECD 2006). First, since income taxes affect incentives, they inevitably
distort economic behaviour in ways that economic efficiency is adversely affected.
Second, the distribution of the impact of income taxes across population raises issues
of both horizontal and vertical equity. Finally, simplicity and compliance costs are
important considerations, since they both affect economic efficiency, as well as the
public perceptions of the fairness of the tax system.

When designing tax systems, policymakers have to weigh up the different goals
they try to achieve. This often implies that difficult trade-offs will have to be made.

The choice of a country's personal income tax schedule depends on how the
trade-off between equity and efficiency is reconciled (OECD 2010a, b).[1] Governments impose progressive income tax to redistribute income and achieve vertical
equity. However there is a trade-off. A progressive income tax may result in a loss
in economic efficiency where it reduces incentives to work more. Taxation affects
the choice of jobs, whether an individual enters the labour force, whether spouses
enter the labour force, whether the individual takes a second job and the effort put
into the job, the amount that the individual saves and the forms savings take, the age
of retirement and whether he or she will continue to work part-time beyond the age
of retirement (Stiglitz 2000).

In practice, governments may build tax systems substantially around broad income
and expenditure bases to minimize differences in tax rates applied to different bases
(OECD 2006), so as to ensure a level of equity and reduce distortions.

Another trade-off involves the introduction of personal tax allowances, exemptions or credits, so as to increase vertical equity. These measures apart from giving
rise to complexity (e.g. where they depend on some measure of income and expenditures) they also hinder economic efficiency as taxpayers use more resources to
understand how to minimize their taxes, within the framework of the tax law.

Within the European Union, the principles of income taxation have not constituted
such an important area of harmonization as indirect taxes, as the differences found
in direct taxations are less dangerous for the functioning of the common market. As
a result, direct tax regulations in the EU are left at the discretion of Member States.

In its Communication of 23 May 2001 on "Tax policy in the European Union—
Priorities for the years ahead" the Commission reiterated its belief that there is no

---

[1] OECD (2010a, b), page 19.

need for an across the board harmonization of Member States' direct tax systems. The Commission underlined that "in many tax fields, harmonization is neither necessary nor desirable in view of the widely differing characteristics of Member States' tax systems and different national preferences". There should only be action at EU level where action by individual Member States could not provide an effective solution.

Specifically, in the field of personal income tax, the Commission pointed that taxes are a matter for the Member States to determine and acknowledged that coordination at EU level is important to ensure the removal of obstacles to the exercise of EC Treaty freedoms (free movement of workers, services, capital and the freedom of establishment) and to cross-border activities, as well as to prevent double taxation or non-taxation.

The 2008 financial and economic crisis resulted in severe challenges for public finances in many EU countries. Regarding tax policy, an important question emerged. Whether it would be possible to transform the tax system in order to yield additional revenues, while minimizing the distortionary effects on growth.

The European Commission in its Communication of March 2010 on "Europe 2020: A Strategy for smart, sustainable and inclusive growth", called for growth-oriented tax policy reforms in order to mitigate the negative effects of deep recession. It stressed that raising taxes on labour, which in the past had resulted to increased unemployment, should be avoided and that the burden on labour should be progressively shifted to energy and environmental taxes.

At the same time though, the majority of the peripheral Member States of the Eurozone (Portugal, Spain and Greece) which were more severely hit by the economic crisis, had to resort to bailout agreements, which entailed the implementation of comprehensive economic adjustment programmes. These agreements involved among others the increasing of the tax burden on individuals. Even Italy, which did not enter a financing agreement, came under intense pressure to adjust its economy. Even though the bailout recipe had some common characteristics, the outcome was not the same for these countries and the time needed for the consolidation was different.

The current research attempts to assess tax regime similarities among Eurozone member countries and to classify them into separate groups. The aim is to draw conclusions on whether there was a harmonized approach among Eurozone countries regarding the design of personal income taxes during this deep economic recession. General conclusions are drawn on the level of personal income taxes divergence within the Eurozone. Dendrograms are employed to present similarities of tax regimes and clustering of homogeneous Eurozone countries for four different years (2003, 2008, 2013, 2018).

2 Literature Review

Mirrlees (1971) conceptualized the classic trade-off between equality and efficiency that governments face in direct taxation. In his work, which is considered to be the modern analysis of Optimal Taxation, he argued that the marginal tax rate schedule must be tailored to the shape of ability distribution. He concluded that optimal tax rates should lie between 0 and 1 and that an approximately linear income-tax schedule would maximize the social welfare function (which is expressed as the sum of individual utilities). Seade (1977) related the analysis of optimal taxation to the shape of tax schedules and argued that the marginal tax rate should be zero at the income level of the top earner for bounded income distributions. Tuomala (1990), in early numerical simulations of the Mirrlees model, found that "the marginal tax rate falls as income increases, except at income levels between the bottom decile". Diamond (1998) argued that the implications for policy derived from the optimal taxation theory have been somewhat limited. He emphasized the importance of the shape of distributions of skills and used labour supply elasticities to derive optimal income tax rates. His findings challenged the suggestion for tax rates to decline slowly towards zero as one approaches the absolute top of the skill distribution. Saez (2001), building on the work of Diamond, showed that marginal rates should increase between middle and high-income earners and that at high incomes they should be at least 50% and as high as 80%. Piketty and Saez (2012) recognized that optimal taxation literature identifies tax schemes that do reduce distortions conditional on equity objectives but argued that their policy implications are difficult to implement in practice.

The Mirrlees Review in its final report "Tax by Design" (2011) concluded that optimal tax theory is a powerful tool and that the desirable characteristics of a good tax system are more likely to be achieved within a simple, neutral and stable tax system. The core of their proposal is for a progressive, neutral tax system, i.e. a single tax on income with an allowance and two or three rates, combined with a single benefit to support those with low income and/or high needs. The design of the rate schedule should reflect the best available evidence on how responsive people at different income levels and with different demographic characteristics are.[2]

The OECD, in its Tax Policy Study on Fundamental Reform of Personal Income Tax (2006) concluded that dual and flat personal income tax reforms are options for further tax reform.[3] It is argued that flat tax systems, which are simpler and achieve a certain degree of progressivity through a tax free personal allowance, can minimize income shifting and thus achieve efficiency by turning into (semi-) dual income tax systems with lower tax rates for capital income and proportionality instead of progressive taxation of labour income.

In its "Tax Policy Reform and Economic Growth" (2010) study, the OECD concluded that progressive income tax schedules have sizable adverse effects on GDP per capita and that there is a negative relationship between top marginal personal income tax rates and the long-run level of total factor productivity. Therefore reducing progressivity and lowering top statutory rates are more growth-oriented personal income tax policy reforms.

Mankiw et al (2009) by comparing theory with practice, observed a worldwide trend towards tax systems with flatter tax rates. Also, top marginal personal income

---

[2] The Mirrlees review, page 474.

[3] OECD (2006), page 135.

tax rates in the EU followed a downward path since 2000. This downward path though was reversed in several countries with the outbreak of the financial crisis. Nevertheless, they still remain at lower levels compared to the beginning of the century, in the majority of EU countries.

There is little evidence in literature that this downward trend is the direct outcome for competition for skilled labour or savings. Kleven et al. (2014) examine the relationship of top Personal Income Tax (PIT) rates on international mobility of high-earning individuals and their findings suggest a very strong impact. On the contrary, Conway and Rork (2012) do not confirm any significant relation. Egger et al. (2007) find a positive relationship between neighbouring top PIT rates and domestic top PIT rates. Specifically they find that a cut in neighbouring top PIT rates by 1 pp results in a 0.37 pp cut in the domestic top PIT rate. For personal taxation, it is difficult to disentangle the effect of international competition from that of social preferences and the evolution of policy thinking (Benassy et al. 2014).

At the same time, harmonization of these taxes is much more difficult than indirect taxes, both from the political, technical and legislative points of view (Wolowiec and Szybowski 2017).

Wolowiec and Sobon (2011) find that despite the lack of directives to regulate the rules of taxing personal income, there is a "quite harmonization" taking place, as a consequence of tax competition, and thus several common personal income tax characteristics can be found in the EU.

Still, despite this "quite harmonization", personal income tax systems within the European Union, are strongly differentiated, regarding the number and the size of tax brackets, the number and level of marginal tax rates, the tax credits as well as tax allowances.

There are annual publications that provide comparative analysis of personal income taxation systems in different countries, notably the OECD Taxing Wages Report (2003 – 2020) which provides unique information on income tax paid by workers and social security contributions levied on employees and their employers in OECD countries. Amounts of taxes and benefits are calculated for eight household types which differ by income level and household composition and only standard personal income tax reliefs are taken into consideration. Results include the marginal and effective tax burden for one and two-earner families, and total labour costs of employers.

The EU Taxation Trends Reports, mostly focuses on the evolution of labour tax revenues at EU level, as well as the evolution of the Top PIT Rate, the Implicit Tax Rate on labour and the Tax Wedge on low wage earners.

The published literature in assessing similarities in the field of personal income taxation is limited. Velichkov and Stefanova (2017) use cluster analysis to study similarities between EU countries with respect to tax systems. More specifically, regarding personal income taxation, they use indicators such as Taxes on Labour as a percentage of Total Taxation, Implicit tax rates on Labour and Top Statutory Personal Income Tax Rates.

Liapis and Ntertsou (2020) also assess tax systems similarities in the EU, using variables such as the personal income tax revenues as a percentage of GDP, the Top

Statutory Personal Income Tax Rates and the Shadow Economy as a percentage of GDP.

Research so far has focused on comparing different countries' personal income tax systems by using as criteria the average tax rate, the implicit tax rate or the top PIT rate. Calculation of average rates though is often complicated, as it depends on the level of wage and other characteristics of the tax system, such as personal allowances, family allowances, tax credits, exemptions etc. The implicit tax rate on labour is an overall aggregate indicator, based on macroeconomic variables in the national accounts and therefore only gives an indication of the overall tax burden on labour, taking into consideration the whole income distribution. Top PIT rates alone don't say much since it is much different to apply the top PIT rate at a rather low-income threshold, compared to a rather high-income threshold. In practice, the design of the income tax schedule, the breadth of the income thresholds, the level of the marginal rates affect work incentives, employment or relocation decisions economic agents have to take. Taking that into consideration, the current paper broadens previous work by incorporating in the analysis specific characteristics of the actual design of the countries' personal income tax schedule. Results are indicative of the degree of convergence in Eurozone countries.

This paper is organized as follows; Sect. 3 focuses on the design of personal income tax system in Greece during the fiscal consolidation period (up until year 2018). Section 4 describes the tax data and methodology used for the assessment of personal income tax similarities among Eurozone countries and Sect. 5 describes the results of our analysis.

3   Personal Income Tax Reforms in Greece During the Fiscal Consolidation

In the first seven years that followed Greece's accession to the EMU 2001–2007, the Greek economy grew at an average annual rate of 4.2%. The driving forces behind this significant GDP growth was on the one hand domestic demand, driven mainly by private consumption, due to the increase in incomes and the expansion of consumer credit and on the other hand fixed capital investment, mostly on housing, due to low-interest mortgages and rising income expectations.

Unfortunately, the productive base did not expand as much as needed and it remained introverted. As domestic production could not meet increasing domestic demand, the gap was filled by imports, which gradually widened the current account deficit to unsustainable levels. The country was borrowing to consume more and more products and services that it did not produce. As a result, the growth path of the Greek economy was rather distorted and for sure not sustainable.

When the financial and economic crisis erupted in 2008, it was made clear that in order for the Greek economy to survive, a multi-annual programme had to be implemented to reduce the government deficit, control the debt dynamics and carry out extensive structural changes.[4] In early 2010, the government deficit could not be financed from the markets any more. Thus, in April 2010, the Greek government addressed the countries of the Euro area and the IMF with a request for financial support and the following month, the Memorandum of Economic and Financial Policies was signed. This marked the beginning of a long period of sharp and painful economic adjustment.

As part of the restrictive economic policy pursued, a number of tax measures were legislated on the revenue side. The present research focuses on the direct tax measures adopted in Greece during the fiscal adjustment period in the field of personal income tax.

The current section briefly describes the main changes introduced in Greece in the personal income tax schedule and tax base from 2008 and up to 2018. We use 2008 as a starting point, despite the fact that officially the fiscal adjustment in Greece started in May 2010, when the First Memorandum of Understanding with the EU and the IMF was signed, for comparability reasons with the pre-crisis period.

The Income Tax Code (Law 2238/1994), as amended and stood up until 2013 defined six categories of taxable income: income from immovable property, i.e. land and buildings; income from movable property, i.e. investment income; from business; from agriculture; from employment; and from professional activities and other sources.

In the period preceding the economic crisis, Greece simplified the personal income tax code, reduced the progressivity of the tax system by cutting the top statutory personal income tax rate and at the same time increased the tax-free personal income. The progressive personal income tax schedule further to its amendment in 2006 (Law 3522) had as follows for years 2008 and 2009:

2008		2009	
Salaried/Pensioners			
Income bracket	Tax rate (%)	Income bracket	Tax rate (%)
12.000	0	12.000	0
18.000	27	18.000	25
45.000	37	45.000	35
>75.000	40	>75.000	45
Non Salaried–Entrepreneurs			
Income bracket	Tax rate (%)	Income bracket	Tax rate (%)
10.500	0	10.500	0
1.500	15	1.500	15

(continued)

[4] Even though economic factors contributed to the crisis, they were not the root causes. Sklias and Maris (2013) found that the root causes can be found within the political and institutional model of development and the mode of governance and highlighted as key factors the development of statism, the failed Europeanization, the high level of corruption, the impact of syndicates and interest groups on the formation of economic policies, the skewed model of governance, populism and the unstable political and parliamentary regime for the past 30 years preceding the economic crisis.

(continued)

2008		2009	
18.000	27	18.000	25
45.000	37	45.000	35
>75.000	40	>75.000	40

The tax reform enacted in 2008 (Law 3697) foresaw a gradual reduction of the personal income tax rate applied to the central tax bracket (25%) by one percentage point per year, for the years between 2010 and 2014 where the central tax rate would be down to 20%.

Since then, revenue-raising objectives motivated the adoption of fiscal measures, in response to the economic crisis, so as to finance growing fiscal deficits. The gradual decrease of the tax burden for middle incomes was repealed by the provisions of **Law 3842/2010**, approved in April 2010, shortly before the signing of the First Memorandum of Understanding. Several amendments were introduced according to the new tax law, which went in the opposite direction compared to the reforms enacted in the early 2000s. These involved the elimination of the different treatment of employment income and pensions and of other income, increase in the number of income brackets, increase of the top statutory tax rate and increase of the income threshold on which the top statutory tax rate applied., broadening of the tax base through the abolition of several tax exemptions.

Overall, the aim of the reform was "to introduce a fairer and more efficient tax system intended to simultaneously improve or even eradicate the weaknesses and defects in the tax system which has prevailed in Greece over many years in the past".

The Personal Income Tax system, overhauled in 2010, was further modified in 2011. Under **Law 3986/2011** and **Law 4024/2011** the personal income tax schedule was further restructured. The number of income tax brackets was reduced by merging the four central brackets to two and the base was broadened through the dramatic decrease of the first tax-free income bracket. Also, the tax base was further broadened with the abolition of several deductions from taxable income and their replacement with tax credits. Also, an annual special solidarity contribution was imposed on individuals whose income exceeded €12.000.

A comprehensive income tax reform was legislated in January 2013, that broadened the tax base and shared more equally the tax burden. The main elements of the tax reform introduced with **Law 4110/2013** were the simplification of the personal income tax schedule with three income brackets (instead of eight) and the replacement of the tax free income bracket with a system of tax credits. A separate tax schedule for income earned by professionals and self-employed was introduced where neither a tax free income bracket nor a tax credit were granted to professionals and self-employed. As the European Commission reported in the First Review of the Second Adjustment Programme for Greece in December 2012 "The elimination of the tax allowance for the self-employed is expected to generate substantial additional revenues, given that well over half the self-employed declare incomes less than the standard allowance of the personal income tax of EUR 5 000 per year". The remaining of tax reliefs, such as the principal home rent, educational expenses, mortgage interest and life or medical insurance premiums were eliminated. Social security contributions of self employed which were previously partially deductible (10%) from the tax, qualified with this new law as expenses of the self employed and as a result were fully deducted from the gross income.

A major reform of the tax system was undertaken in the second half of 2013, complementing the Income Tax Reform adopted earlier in 2013. **Law 4172/2013** replaced the Income Tax Code (Law 2238/1994) as it stood at that time. According to the European Commission, with this reform "numerous tax loopholes have been closed to consolidate the tax base and reduce the potential for erosion". With this reform, four new categories of income were introduced for individuals (instead of six): employment and pension income, business activity income (such as self-employment), capital income (dividends, interest etc.), capital gains income (sale of real estate property, shares, bonds etc.), and each category of income triggers a different tax treatment.

Finally, **Law 4387/2016**, for income earned from 1/1/2016 reduced the opportunities for tax avoidance by pooling together income from salaries, pensions and business activities under a single rate schedule, further broadened the tax base by reducing the amount of tax credit, increased the number of tax brackets from three to four and increased the top statutory PIT rate, applicable to a lower income threshold. The solidarity surcharge was fully integrated into the Income Tax Code, changing from average to marginal rates and was levied on all income (whether subject to personal income tax or not). The income brackets were partly harmonized with those for personal income tax.

The above mentioned changes on personal income tax schedules and solidarity surcharge rates are summarized in the following tables (Tables 1, 2 and 3).

4 Data and Methodology

In order to assess similarities of personal income tax systems among Eurozone countries, data on the main characteristics of the personal income tax systems were extracted from the OECD Tax Database—Table I.1,[5] which summarizes information provided by member countries for the Taxing Wages annual publication.

Specifically, this table reports statutory central government personal income tax rates for wage income plus the taxable income thresholds at which these statutory rates apply. The table also reports basic/standard personal allowances, tax credits and surtax rates. The information is applicable to a single person without dependents.

---

[5] Which is the source table for our data in the analysis. https://stats.oecd.org/index.aspx?DataSetCode=TABLE_I1.

Table 1 Personal income tax schedule for income from employment/pensions 2008–2018

	2008	2009	2010	2011	2012	2013	2014	2015	2016	2017	2018
Tax rate (%)	0	0	0	0	0	22	22	22	22	22	22
Income Bracket (%)	12.000	12.000	12.000	5.000	5.000	25.000	25.000	25.000	20.000	20.000	20.000
Tax rate (%)	27	25	18	10	10	32	32	32	29	29	29
Income Bracket (%)	30.000	30.000	16.000	12.000	12.000	42.000	42.000	42.000	30.000	30.000	30.000
Tax rate (%)	37	35	24	18	18	42	42	42	37	37	37
Income Bracket (%)	75.000	75.000	22.000	16.000	16.000				40.000	40.000	40.000
Tax rate (%)	40	40	26	25	25				45	45	45
Income Bracket (%)			26.000	26.000	26.000						
Tax rate (%)			32	35	35						
Income Bracket (%)			32.000	40.000	40.000						
Tax rate (%)			36	38	38						
Income Bracket (%)			40.000	60.000	60.000						
Tax rate (%)			38	40	40						
Income Bracket (%)			60.000	100.000	100.000						
Tax rate (%)			40	45	45						
Income Bracket (%)			100.000								
Tax rate (%)			45								

Table 2 Personal income tax schedule for non-salaried–entrepreneurs, 2008–2018

	2008	2009	2010	2011	2012	2013	2014	2015	2016	2017	2018
Tax rate (%)	0	0	0	0	0	26	26	26	22	22	22
Income bracket (%)	10.500	10.500	12.000	5.000	5.000	50.000	50.000	50.000	20.000	20.000	20.000
Tax rate (%)	15	15	18	10	10	33	33	33	29	29	29
Income bracket (%)	12.000	12.000	16.000	12.000	12.000				30.000	30.000	30.000
Tax rate (%)	27	25	24	18	18				37	37	37
Income bracket (%)	30.000	30.000	22.000	16.000	16.000				40.000	40.000	40.000
Tax rate (%)	37	35	26	25	25				45	45	45
Income bracket (%)	75.000	75.000	26.000	26.000	26.000						
Tax rate (%)	40	40	32	35	35						
Income bracket (%)			32.000	40.000	40.000						
Tax rate (%)			36	38	38						
Income bracket (%)			40.000	60.000	60.000						
Tax rate (%)			38	40	40						
Income bracket (%)			60.000	100.000	100.000						
Tax rate (%)			40	45	45						
Income bracket (%)			100.000								
Tax rate (%)			45								

Table 3 Solidarity surcharge rates, 2011–2018

	2011	2012	2013	2014	2015	2016	2017	2018
Tax rate (%)	0	0	0	0	–	–	–	–
Income bracket (%)	12.000	12.000	12.000	5.000	12.000	50.000	50.000	50.000
Tax rate (%)	1	1	1	10	0,7	2,2	2,2	2,2
Income bracket (%)	20.000	20.000	20.000	12.000	20.000	20.000	20.000	20.000
Tax rate (%)	2	2	2	18	1,4	5	5	5
Income bracket (%)	50.000	50.000	50.000	16.000	30.000	30.000	30.000	30.000
Tax rate (%)	3	3	3	25	2	7	7	7
Income bracket (%)	100.000	100.000	100.000	26.000	50.000	40.000	40.000	40.000
Tax rate (%)	4	4	4		4	8	8	8
Income bracket (%)					100.000	65.000	65.000	65.000
Tax rate (%)					6	9	9	9
Income bracket (%)					500.000	220.000	220.000	220.000
Tax rate (%)					8	10	10	10

Since data in Table I.1 are expressed in national currencies, our sample includes the 16 Eurozone countries which are at the same time members of the OECD.[6] Germany is not included in our sample, as a unique feature of German personal income tax is the use of a mathematical formula (instead income thresholds and respective marginal rates) in tax progression. Cyprus and Malta are not included in our sample, as they are not OECD member countries and therefore no comparative information was available for these countries.

The similarity analysis is conducted for four different years (2003, 2008, 2013 and 2018) for comparability purposes with the pre-crisis period. The aim is to observe how clusters of groups of countries with similar tax regimes are differentiated through time by capturing possible effects of the economic crisis.

In order to generate homogeneous groups of countries, we perform Hierarchical Agglomerative Clustering by the average linkage as linkage rule using the Palisade software. Personal Income Tax systems similarities are assessed using as criteria the top PIT rate and the level of income at which the top PIT rate applies. Criteria are then broadened to include in the standard PIT reliefs (personal allowances and tax credits) provided in the personal tax systems in our sample. In order to address the fact that not all of our variables are expressed in the same units of measurement, the Mahalanobis

---

[6] Austria, Belgium, Estonia, Finland, France, Greece, Ireland, Italy, Latvia, Lithuania, Luxembourg, Netherlands, Portugal, Slovak Republic, Slovenia, Spain.

Table 4 Top PIT rates in years 2003, 2008, 2013, 2018

Country	2003	2008	2013	2018	Dif 2018–2003
Lithuania	33.00	24.00	15.00	15.00	−18.00
Estonia	26.00	21.00	21.00	20.00	−6.00
Spain	29.16	27.13	30.50	22.50	−6.66
Latvia	25.00	25.00	24.00	23.00	−2.00
Slovak Republic	38.00	19.00	25.00	25.00	−13.00
Finland	35.00	31.50	31.75	31.25	−3.75
Luxembourg	38.00	38.00	40.00	38.00	0.00
Ireland	42.00	41.00	41.00	40.00	−2.00
Italy	45.00	43.00	43.00	43.00	−2.00
France	48.09	40.00	45.00	45.00	−3.09
Greece	40.00	40.00	42.00	45.00	5.00
Portugal	40.00	42.00	48.00	48.00	8.00
Belgium	50.00	50.00	50.00	50.00	0.00
Slovenia	50.00	41.00	50.00	50.00	0.00
Netherlands	52.00	52.00	52.00	51.95	−0.05
Austria	50.00	50.00	50.00	55.00	5.00
Average	40.08	36.54	38.02	37.67	

distance metric is used, as it takes into account variances and covariances among the variables. The end product for each stage of this cluster analysis is a tree diagram (Dendrogram).

5 Results

5.1 Top PIT Rates

The following table provides an illustration of the trend of top PIT rates in each country. Top PIT rates for each year reviewed (2003, 2008, 2013 and 2018) are reported in the first four columns. In the last column, the difference between the rate applied in 2018 and the rate applied in 2003 is shown. Countries are ranked from the lowest to the highest rate applied in 2018 (Table 4).

The level of the top PIT rate differs greatly between EU member-states in all years examined. There is though a clear downward trend during the period examined. This decrease in labour taxation was in response to the need to put in place more employment—friendly tax systems.[7]

---

[7] European Commission (2009), Tax Policy Reforms, page 27.

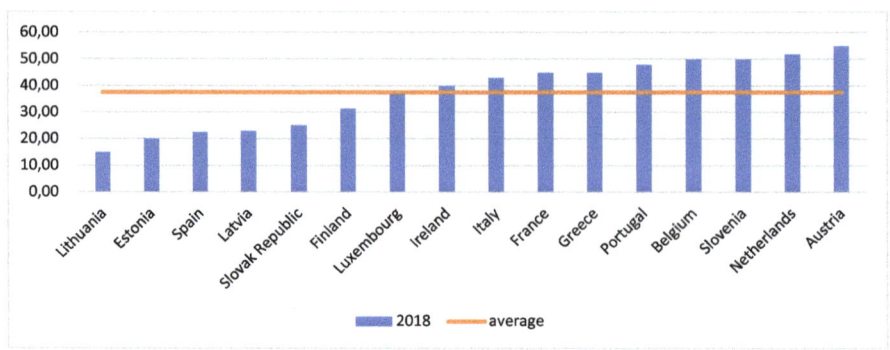

Fig. 1 Top PIT rates in year 2018

On average, the top PIT rate in our sample went down by 2.41 percentage points. Ten out of sixteen countries have reduced the top PIT rate, with the biggest cuts having taken place in Lithuania and the Slovak Republic.

Only three out of sixteen Eurozone countries in our sample have increased the top PIT rates, compared to 2003. Not surprisingly, Greece and Portugal, both severely hit by the economic crisis are among these countries. Revenue needs as well as public perception that higher incomes should bear the burden of fiscal consolidation have been the drivers of these tax policy reforms.

In Luxembourg, Belgium and Slovenia the top PIT rates are at the same level as 2008 (some fluctuations took place during this period for Luxembourg and Slovenia).

What is impressive is the distance between the lowest top PIT rate applied in Lithuania and the highest top PIT rate, applied in Austria. This difference of 40 percentage points is indicative of the great degree of divergence among Eurozone countries regarding the personal income taxation systems.

The following figure provides a graphical illustration of the ranking of the top PIT rates in 2018 and how they compare with the average top PIT rate of our sample (Fig. 1).

5.2   Top PIT Rates and Top Income Thresholds

The picture given by the top PIT rates is incomplete. The top PIT rate alone does not say a lot about the PIT structure as this rate is applicable from different income levels in different member countries. Therefore, we incorporate in our analysis the income level at which the top PIT rate applies, with the aim to better assess tax systems similarities among the countries included in our sample. The results of clustering are shown in the following dendrograms (Fig. 2).

The agglomerative method is a "bottom-up" approach, where each observation starts in its own cluster, and pairs of clusters are merged as one moves up the hierarchy.

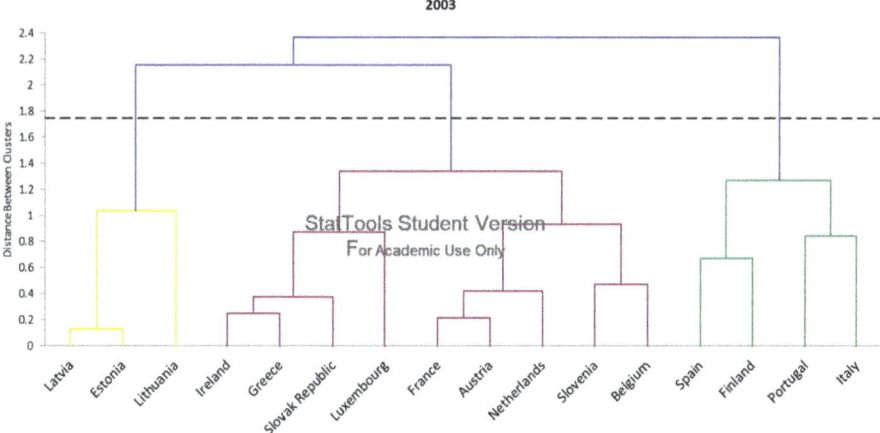

Fig. 2 Dendrogram year 2003—Top PIT rate and top income threshold

At the bottom level, Latvia and Estonia are clustered together, since they both apply flat tax rates of 25% and 26% respectively. Lithuania, which also applied a flat tax rate of 33% at that time, is also clustered with Latvia and Estonia.

In 1994, after the collapse of the Soviet Union, Estonia radically reformed its tax system and replaced the progressive personal income tax schedule with a single flat tax rate. Estonia's paradigm was followed by Lithuania in the same year and Latvia the following year.

Ireland and Greece are clustered together since they apply a similar level of top PIT rates (42% and 40% respectively) to similar levels of top income thresholds (28.000 € and 23.400 € respectively). The Slovak Republic which applies a slightly lower top PIT rate of 38% to an income threshold of 18.721 € is clustered with Ireland and Greece. Luxembourg, which also applies a top rate of 38% but to a much higher income threshold, is clustered at a third stage with the Slovak Republic.

France, Austria and the Netherlands are clustered together since they all apply top PIT rates around 50% above income thresholds of approximately 50.000 €.

Slovenia and Belgium are clustered together since they both apply a top PIT rate of 50%. They form a separate homogeneous group though, because they apply the top PIT rate to much lower income levels (37.770 and 29.740 € respectively) compared to France, Austria and the Netherlands.

Spain and Finland are clustered together, since the personal income tax burden in these countries seems rather low compared to other countries. They both apply rather low top PIT rates of 29.16% and 35% respectively on comparatively rather high-income thresholds of 45.000 and 55.200 €. It should be noted though that both countries apply personal income tax at a sub-central level and as a result the final tax burden is ambiguous, as it depends on which municipality/autonomous community the taxpayer is located.

Finally Portugal and Italy are clustered together as they apply top PIT rates of 40% and 45% to rather high-income thresholds of 52.276 and 70.000 € respectively (Fig. 3).

In 2008, the Baltic countries remained clustered together. The over performance of tax revenues and the significant annual growth rates enabled the lowering of top PIT rates in Estonia and Lithuania.

The Slovak Republic is also clustered with the Baltic countries. In the context of its accession to the European Union and strong economic growth, the Slovak Republic had adopted a fundamental tax reform in 2004 which abolished the five-band rate schedule on labour income and introduced a flat rate of 19% (OECD 2015).

The second group of similar countries consisted of the five southern Euro countries (Spain, Greece, Italy, Portugal and France) and Finland. At the second stage they are clustered with the rest of the southern euro countries. Greece at that time applied the same top PIT rate of 40% but to a much higher income threshold of 75.000 €. It resembled France (40% over 69.505 €), Italy (43% over 75.000 €) and Portugal (42% over 62.546 €).

The third group of countries consisted of central Eurozone countries (Austria, Belgium, Ireland, Luxemburg, Netherlands, Slovenia). Compared to 2003, Austria and the Netherlands remained clustered together, with Belgium sharing some common characteristics, especially regarding the top PIT rate of 50%.

Slovenia, reduced the 50% top PIT rate to 41% and was clustered at a second stage with Luxembourg and Ireland, which both apply rates close to 40%.

Taking the above into consideration, we could conclude that new EU countries, in the period preceding the crisis, had adopted growth-friendly personal income tax reforms by applying a flat tax rate to personal income and by lowering the tax rate. On the contrary, the old central and southern Eurozone countries had not followed the Commission's general recommendations of shifting tax burden away from labour to

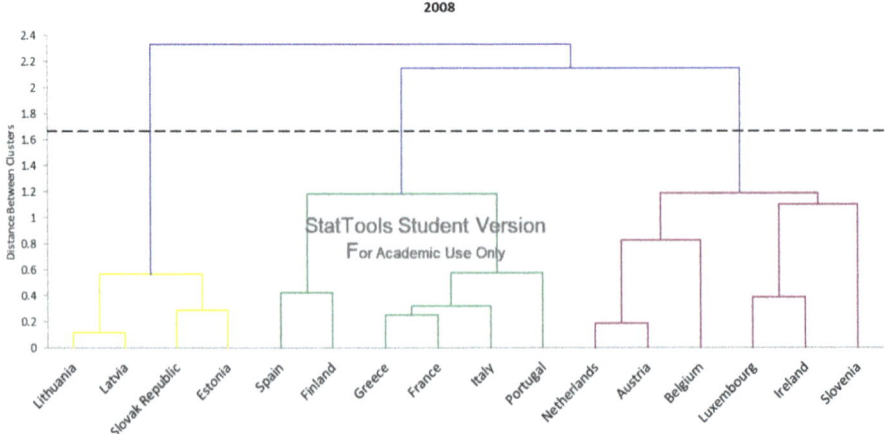

Fig. 3 Dendrogram year 2008—top PIT rate and top income threshold

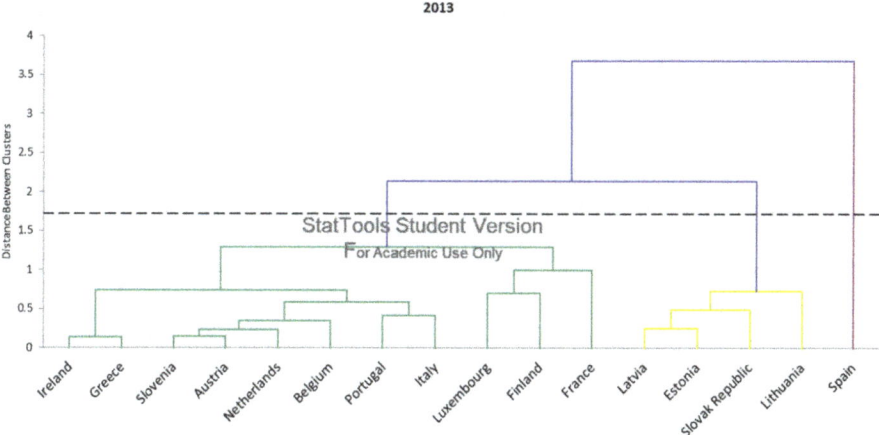

Fig. 4 Dendrogram year 2013—top PIT rate and top income threshold

tax bases which are less detrimental to growth. Even though the personal income tax burden does not depend only on the level of top PIT rate and top income threshold, it gives an indication of the Governments' priorities and perceptions on how labour and specifically higher income should be taxed (Fig. 4).

Since the end of 2008, and in order to limit the negative effects of the economic crisis, a coordinated budgetary stimulus has been adopted in the context of the European Economic Recovery Plan (EERP). The EERP called for Member States to adopt temporary and targeted fiscal stimulus measures in the course of 2009–10. These measures had to be consistent with each country's room for fiscal manoeuvre.

In October 2009, the ECOFIN Council agreed on the principles for a coordinated exit from the fiscal stimulus adopted earlier. The pace of adjustment would be different for every country, due to specificities of country circumstances, but nevertheless it was agreed that fiscal consolidation in all euro area countries should start by 2011 at the latest ECB (2013).[8]

Compared to 2008, there has been an overall upward trend in top personal income tax rates (the average rate in our sample was increased from 36.54% to 38.02%) which is indicative of a growing tendency toward steeper progressivity and greater fairness of the taxation system.

It is interesting to see how clusters of countries have differentiated compared to 2008. In 2013, the Baltic countries, along with the Slovak Republic remained clustered together. In the Slovak Republic, as of 2013, the 19% flat PIT was replaced by a progressive tax with two marginal rates (19% and 25%). This change was in part driven by a growing consensus among the population that the government should play a more active role in income redistribution (OECD 2015). Even if the flat personal tax system was abandoned, the top PIT rate did not increase dramatically.

---

[8] ECB Monthly Bulletin, December 2013, page 88.

The Latvian economy was among the hardest hit by the global financial crisis and it was the first country to receive financial assistance from the Eurozone in 2008. Tax measures adopted were motivated by the need to increase revenues. The personal income tax rate (which had been reduced from 25 to 23% in 2009), was increased again to 26% (European Commission 2010). But since 2011, previous reductions were reversed and in 2013 the personal income tax rate was 24%.

Although the economy of Estonia was severely affected by the recession, the government adopted a prudent fiscal policy stance. The foreseen reduction of the personal income tax rate by one percentage point annually was temporarily frozen and the tax rate was kept at 21% (European Commission 2010).

Lithuania was the only country to dramatically reduce its personal income tax rate from 24 to 15%.

Regarding central Eurozone countries, the core group of Austria, Netherlands and Belgium remained clustered together, with Slovenia joining the cluster, since it restored the top PIT rate back to 50% and increased the top income threshold at similar levels.

The southern euro area economies are no longer clustered together. Ireland, Greece, Portugal and Spain had to resort to bailout agreements, which entailed the implementation of comprehensive economic adjustment programmes. Only in the case of Spain the economic adjustment programme was targeted to recapitalization and restructuring of the Spanish financial sector. Even Italy, which did not enter a financing agreement, came under intense pressure to adjust its economy (Manasse and Katsikas 2018).

In all these countries the tax burden on labour was increased, either through raising the tax rate, or reducing the top income threshold, or both.

Greece increased the 40% top PIT rate to 42%, while at the same time the top income threshold in Greece was reduced dramatically. As a result, Greece was clustered with Ireland, which kept the 41% top PIT rate change but reduced the income threshold from 35.400 euros to 32.800 euros.

Portugal, increased the top PIT rate by 6 percentage points, but at the same time increased the top income threshold and as a result, it was clustered with Italy.

In Spain in 2011 a personal income tax reform was adopted, where two additional brackets were added and the top central personal income tax rate was applicable at an income threshold of 300.000 euros. It is the strong differentiation in income thresholds that ends up in Spain not being clustered with any other country.

France, Luxembourg and Finland increased the top PIT rates but at the same time dramatically increased the top income thresholds and as a result are clustered together.

We could conclude that tax policy in the Baltic countries and the Slovak Republic is broadly consistent with the plan to shift the tax burden away from labour and towards consumption and the environment. In central Eurozone countries, the tax burden, as depicted by top PIT rates and top income thresholds, remained rather high, even in the aftermath of the economic crisis. The southern economies, which were more severely hit by the recession followed fiscal consolidation programmes which envisaged higher rates on high-income earners (Fig. 5).

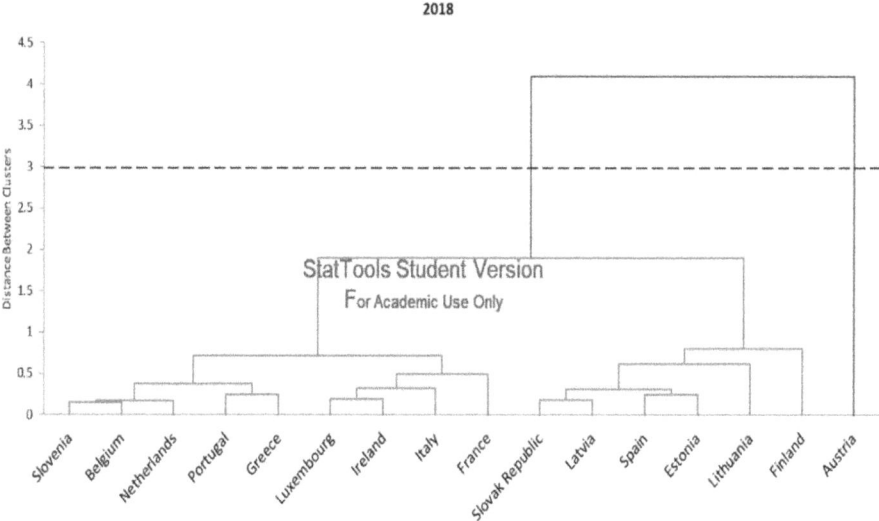

Fig. 5 Dendrogram year 2018—top PIT rate and top income threshold

Since 2013, the overall developments in personal income taxation were in the direction of lower rates, although major reforms were limited in number.

Both Estonia and Latvia further reduced the top personal income tax rate. The Baltic countries remained clustered together but it is observed that Spain, which had again radically reformed its personal income tax system, related more with Baltic countries and the Slovak Republic, since it applied a top PIT rate of 22.5% over an income threshold of 60.000 €. We should be cautious though with the interpretations of these results, as the sub-central PIT rates are not taken into consideration.

The central euro area countries (Slovenia, Belgium and the Netherlands) remain clustered as their top PIT rates and income thresholds remain to a large extent the same.

In Austria, a comprehensive tax reform came into force on 1 January 2016. The new personal income tax schedule was the centrepiece of the reform. The number of brackets was increased from four to seven resulting in a slower and more gradual progression. The top PIT rate of 50% used to apply on income exceeding 60.000 euros. With the tax reform, three more brackets were added, with the top PIT rate of 55% applying to income exceeding 1.000.000 euros. The top income tax rate introduced was planned to be a temporary measure until 2020 (Ivaskaite et al. 2017). As a result, Austria formed a cluster by itself.

In 2018, Greece was the only country still under a bailout programme and prolonged austerity. It was the only country which increased both the PIT rate (45%) and the top income threshold (40.000 €). It was clustered with Portugal which applied a top PIT rate of 48% over the income threshold of 80.640 €. On the contrary, Ireland, which was clustered with Greece back in 2013, decreased its PIT rate by 1 percentage point and only moderately increased its income threshold and as a result was clustered with Italy and France, which have kept top PIT rates unchanged and slightly increased the top income thresholds.

In general though, we could conclude that the southern euro area economies still share common characteristics, especially regarding the top PIT rate. The top income thresholds vary considerably, which results in total different tax burdens in these countries.

5.3 Personal Allowance and Tax Credit

Cross-country differences in their personal income tax systems stem not only from the different tax rates and income thresholds, but also, because countries typically define taxable income differently as most tax systems contain numerous allowances and exemptions. There are also several countries, which provide tax credits in order to reduce the tax burden of individuals. In the OECD Taxing Wages model and as a result in Table I.1, for comparability reasons, only standard PIT reliefs are reported and these take the form of either a Personal Allowance or a Tax Credit.

A standard personal allowance reduces taxable income and is automatically available to all taxpayers and unrelated to expenditures incurred by the taxpayer. As such, it can be compared to a tax-free (zero-rate) threshold, incorporated in the tax schedule. From now on, when referring to a personal allowance, we as well refer to tax-free thresholds.

A tax credit reduces the final income tax obligation and is also automatically available to all taxpayers and unrelated to expenditures incurred by the taxpayer. Tax credits are typically available as fixed amounts. Where a PIT relief is provided in the form of a tapered tax credit (which means that the amount of tax credit is targeted at lower income taxpayers and is decreasing as taxable income rises) the maximum tax credit is shown and therefore included in our analysis.

It is interesting to see how different Eurozone countries are clustered together, if the level of personal allowance and/or tax credit are included in our similarity analysis, along with the top PIT rate and the top income threshold. The results of clustering are shown in the following dendrograms (Fig. 6).

When more characteristics of the personal income tax design are factored in, it is observed that the Baltic countries along with the Slovak Republic were clustered together in 2013.

The central euro area countries were divided in two different groups. Slovenia was clustered with France and Belgium since they all applied rather high top PIT rates and provided less generous PIT reliefs. Ireland was clustered with the Netherlands and Austria.

The southern euro area economies (Spain, Portugal and Italy) with the exception of Greece were clustered together. Greece, which at that period of time had a more generous personal income tax system, shared common characteristics with Luxembourg and Finland (Fig. 7).

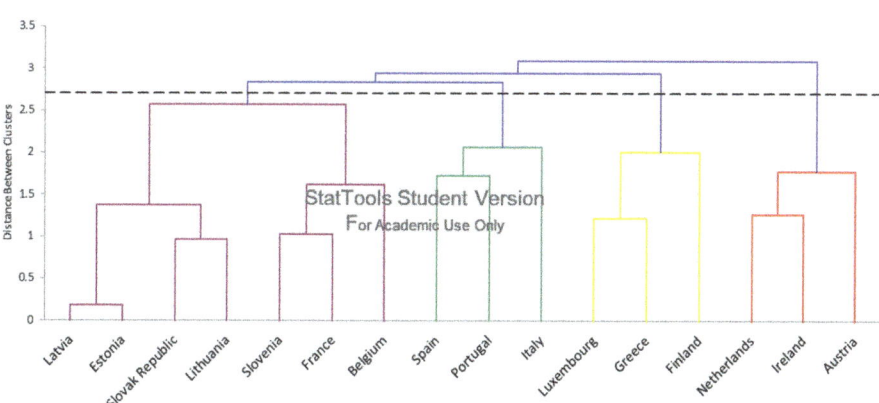

Fig. 6 Dendrogram year 2003

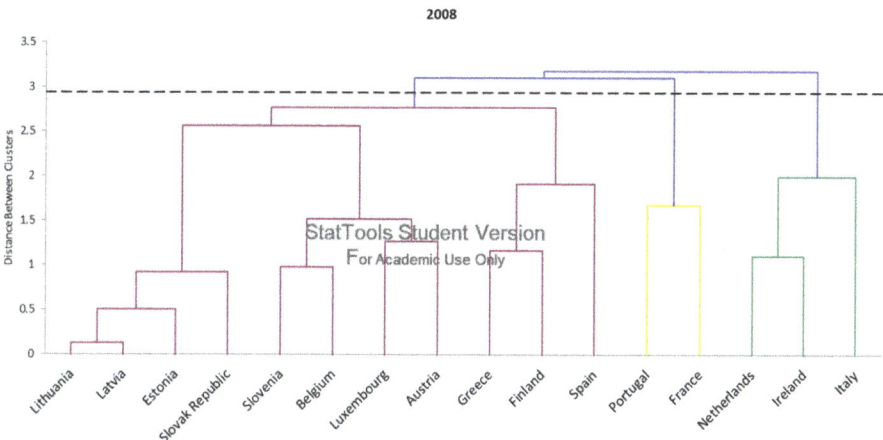

Fig. 7 Dendrogram year 2008

What changed in 2008, compared to 2003, was that Italy was no longer clustered with other southern European economies, since it had changed the design of its personal income tax system and provided relief in the form of a tax credit. As a result, it was clustered together with Ireland and the Netherlands.

Greece remained clustered with Finland, and Spain was clustered with them at a second stage. Portugal was now clustered with France (Fig. 8).

The major change in 2013 compared to 2008 was that Greece, which as already mentioned increased the tax burden on labour, was now clustered with Italy, Ireland and the Netherlands. Greece introduced a new Income Tax Code, where no generous personal allowance was provided any more. On the contrary, the PIT relief took the

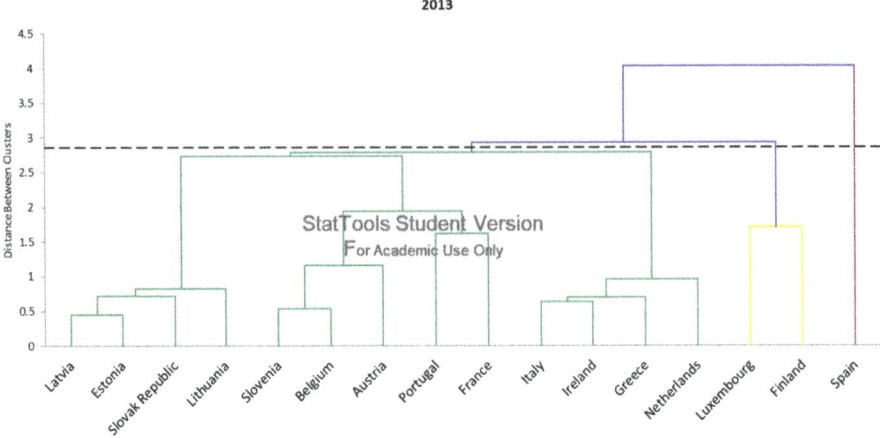

Fig. 8 Dendrogram year 2013

form of a tapered tax credit, which means that the tax burden on those who earn higher income increased. As a result, Greece was clustered with countries which provided tax credits. Luxembourg, Austria which both have introduced generous tax policy reforms were clustered together (Fig. 9).

The main change observed in 2018 was that Spain was clustered with the Baltic countries and Slovak Republic, which means that the personal income tax system has become more generous. Austria, which used to be clustered with other central European countries such as Belgium and Slovenia, has a personal tax system heterogeneous compared to the rest of the countries included in the sample, following its major tax reform in 2016.

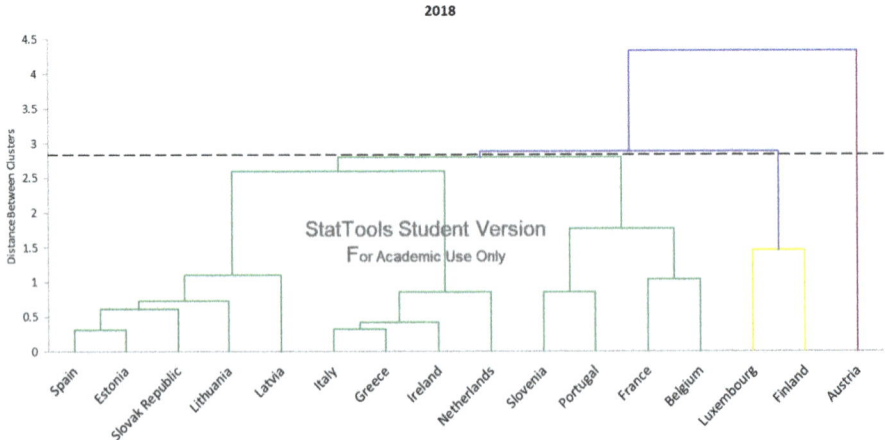

Fig. 9 Dendrogram year 2018

6   Conclusions

The current research confirms that there is a significant degree of divergence of personal income tax systems among Eurozone countries. The European Commission's invitation to shift the taxation burden from labour to other tax bases, less detrimental for growth, can be hardly seen as a universal recipe for all member countries, in designing and implementing their personal income tax systems reforms. Tax structure is country specific and depends on particular circumstances and society's preferences (Trasberg 2010).

However, the economic crisis triggered academics to propose a re-examination of the EU's tax policy strategy. Baimbridge et al. (2012), suggested a common European tax system as a complement to national tax systems. Similarly, Sklias et al. (2014) suggested that the EU should follow the American paradigm where taxes are imposed both from the federal state, the autonomous states and the local governments, with the aim to effectively diffuse regional risks and asymmetries.

The results indicate that personal income taxation similarities between Eurozone countries can be assessed through clustering analysis of some basic design features.

When personal income tax systems' similarities were assessed by taking into consideration not only the top PIT rate, as the majority of research in this area, but also the income level at which this rate applied, some broad conclusions can be drawn:

- New member countries, and more specifically, the three Baltic countries and the Slovak Republic, are all clustered together. These countries apply one or two rather low personal income tax rates, which do not exceed 25%. The personal income tax design in these countries seems aligned with the pro-growth tax policy recommendations of the European Commissions. Also, it is aligned with the personal tax system suggested with optimal tax theory and the 2011 Mirrlees review as it increases simplicity and minimizes trade-offs.
- The Eurozone consists of two speed economies, which is reflected in their personal income tax systems.
- Coordinated Market Economies (CMEs) which form the core of the Eurozone and which in our sample consist of the Netherlands, Belgium, Austria and Finland, have similar top PIT rates and income thresholds. No clear conclusion can be drawn for Finland, since sub-central PIT rates also apply.
- Mixed Market Economies (MMEs) which were the late-comers both politically and economically, and which in our sample consist of Greece, Italy, Spain and Portugal. All four countries, severely hit by the economic crisis, adopted austerity policies. Even though tax policy reforms were in the same direction, the end product diverges. Despite the fact that the level of top PIT rate is similar, it is the top income threshold that differentiates significantly.
- Finland and Luxembourg both apply relatively low top PIT rates to relatively high top income thresholds.

The overall personal income tax burden is determined not only by the tax rates and income thresholds, but also by PIT reliefs, which can take the form of personal allowances, exemptions, tax credits. When these two additional design features of the tax systems are included in our similarity analysis, clusters of countries differentiate to a large extent.

In a globalized world, international tax competition induces several countries to be more "aggressive" in lowering top PIT rates and income thresholds so as to attract high-income individuals. But the results of the current research indicate that the top PIT rate is not sufficient criteria to draw conclusions on the attractiveness of a personal income tax system.

Further research on this topic could incorporate in the analysis more criteria, such as the degree of progressivity of personal income tax codes.

References

Baimbridge, M. & Burkitt, B. & Whyman, P. B. (2012). The Eurozone as a Flawed Currency Area. The Political Quarterly, Vol. 83, No. 1, 1–13

Bénassy-Quéré, A., Trannoy, A. & Wolff, G. (2014). Tax Harmonization in Europe: Moving Forward, *Notes du conseil d'analyse économique,* 14, 1–12.

Conway, K.S. and Rork, J., (2012). No country for old men (or women) - Do state tax policies drive away the elderly *National Tax Journal*, Vol. 65, Issue 2, 313–356

Diamond, A. P., (1998). Optimal Income Taxation: An Example with a U-Shaped Pattern of Optimal Marginal Tax Rates, *The American Economic Review* , Mar., 1998, Vol. 88, No. 1 pp. 83–95

Delgado, F.J. (2013). Are Taxes Converging in Europe? Trends and Some Insights into the Effects of Economic Crisis. *Journal of Global Economics*, 1(1), 24–26

ECB (2013). Monthly Bulletin, December 2013

Egger, P., Pfaffermayr, M. and Winner, H., (2007). Competition in Corporate and Personal Income Taxation, *Mimeo*, 18th April

European Commission Annual Publication, Taxation Trends in the European Union (2008–2018)

European Commission (2009). Monitoring revenue trends and tax reforms in Member States 2008, *European Economy Series*, 4

European Commission (2010). Monitoring revenue trends and tax reforms in Member States 2010, *European Economy Series*, 6

European Commission Annual Edition. Tax Reforms in the EU States, (2011–2018)

European Commission. The Economic Adjustment Program for Greece. Quarterly Reviews (2010–2017)

European Commission Communication (2001). Tax policy in the European Union—priorities for the years ahead, (2001/C 284/03)

European Commission Communication (2010). A strategy for smart, sustainable and inclusive growth, (COM 2010/2020 final)

European Commission Communication (2015) A Fair and Efficient Corporate Tax System in the European Union: 5 Key Areas for Action (COM 2015/302 final)

EU Annual Edition (2005, 2010, 2015 and 2020). Taxation trends in the European Union, Data for the EU Member States, Iceland and Norway

Ivaškaitė-Tamošiūnė V., Leodolter A. and Schmitz M-L, (2017). Personal Income Taxation in Austria: What do the Reform Measures Mean for the Budget, Labour Market Incentives and Income Distribution?, *Economic Brief 030*, July 2017

Kleven, H.J., Landais, C., Saez, E. and Schulz, E. (2014). Migration and Wage Effects of Taxing Top Earners: Evidence from the Foreign Tax Scheme in Denmark, *The Quarterly Journal of Economics,* 129(1), pp. 333–378

Liapis, K.J., Ntertsou, D., (2020). Tax Competitiveness between EU countries. The role of tax rates and the shadow economy in the determination of tax revenues, Presentation at 2020 HFAA Conference.

Manasse P., and Katsikas D., (2018). Economic crisis and structural reforms in Southern Europe: Policy lessons, *VoxEU*

Mankiw, N.G., Weinzierl, M. and Yagan, D. (2009). Optimal Taxation in Theory and Practice, *National Bureau of Economic Research*, Working Paper 15071

Mirrless, J.A., (1971). An Exploration in the Theory of Optimal Income Taxation, *Review of Economic Studies* 38: 175–208

OECD (2015). Moving Beyond the Flat Tax - Tax Policy Reform in the Slovak Republic, *OECD Taxation Working Papers* No. 22

OECD Annual Publication (2003 – 2020), *Taxing Wages*

OECD (2006). Fundamental Reform of Personal Income Tax, *OECD Tax Policy Study* No. 13

OECD (2010a). Choosing a Broad Base - Low Rate Approach to Taxation, *OECD Tax Policy Studies*, No. 19, OECD Publishing, Paris

OECD (2010b). Tax Policy Reform and Economic Growth, *OECD Tax Policy Studies*, No. 20, OECD Publishing, Paris

Piketty T., and Saez E., (2012). Optimal Labor Income Taxation, *NBER Working Paper Series*, 18521

Saez, E. (2001). Using Elasticities to Derive Optimal Income Tax Rates, *Review of Economic Studies* 68, 205–229

Seade, J.K.(1977). On the Shape of Optimal Tax Schedules, *Journal of Public Economics*, 7, 203–236

Sklias, P. and Maris, G., (2013). The Political Dimension of the Greek Financial Crisis, Perspectives on European Politics and Society", 14:1, 144–164

Sklias, P., Roukanas S., Maris, G. (2014). Keynes and the Eurozone' s Crisis: Towards a Fiscal Union?, *Procedia Economics and Finance* 9 (2014), 66–73

Stiglitz, J.E., (2000). Economics of the Public Sector, 3rd Edition, W.W. Norton & Company, New York/London

Trasberg, V., "Dynamics of European Tax Structures"

Tuomala, M. (1990). Optimal Income Tax and Redistribution, *New York: Oxford University Press*

Velichkov, N. and Stefanova, K., (2017). Tax Models in the EU: a Cluster Analysis, *Economic Alternatives,* Issue 4, pp. 573–583

Wolowiec, T. and Sobon, J., (2011). EU Integration and Harmonisation of Personal Income Taxation, *Contemporary Economics,* Vol. 5 Issue 1, pp. 36–46

Wolowiec, T. and Szybowski, D., (2017). Economic Dimension of Harmonizing Personal Income Taxation in the European Union Countries, *International Journal of New Economics and Social Sciences,* No 2 (6), pp. 9–27

Greek Taxation Revenues Before and After the Economic Crisis

Aikaterini Tsisinou and Giannoula Florou

Abstract Taxation is a basic revenue source for a state. In this paper we present the essential characteristics of Greek taxation system. We analyze the taxes from different income categories, from business taxes and non-business taxes, from different Greek regions. We compare revenue data of the year 2019 with corresponding revenue data from the year 2011, before the economic crisis. Our aim is to find how economic crisis influenced the Greek taxation system and its efficiency. We present our findings and our proposals for optimal taxation.

Keywords Greek taxation system · Economic crisis · Revenue categories

JEL Classification H21 · H24 · H25

1 Introduction

The financial crisis which erupted in the US in 2008 (mainly due to the large openings of its banks in the real estate market in a very short period of time) took the form of a fiscal crisis in the European Union, manifested through huge deficits and significant public debts. Since Greece is a country with substantial structural problems in its economy and has a high amount of public debt, it inevitably was extremely vulnerable to the global crisis of 2008 (GSEBEE 2019).

A severe social and economic crisis developed from 2010 onwards. Greece was the only country in the EU that went through three Economic Adjustment Programs and lost more than 25% of its GDP. Sklias et al (2014) declare, "The state should intervene through the expansion of fiscal policies in order to maintain the appropriate effective

A. Tsisinou · G. Florou (✉)
Accounting and Finance Department, International Hellenic University, Kavala, Ag Loukas, Thessaloniki, Greece
e-mail: gflorou@ihu.gr

A. Tsisinou
e-mail: tsisinou@af.ihu.gr

demand in the economy… In good times, the states should maintain budget surpluses but during financial turmoil should intervene to market economy by creating deficits in order to give the necessary impetus for growth". In order to cover the budget deficits and the amortization of the public debt, in Greece, it was necessary to increase the tax revenues, which occurred with frequent changes in the exercise of tax policy. Various researchers analyze the Greek tax system in the years of financial crisis, about corporate effective tax rates (Stamatopoulos et al 2016) or about tax behavior with quantitative research of new aspect of reforming the financial management system. (Varotsis and Katerelos 2020). This paper analyzes the amount of income taxes of individuals at the beginning of the crisis, in 2011 and then in 2019, after 8 years of financial crisis. In the economic year 2011, "the first program of financial rescue and economic adjustment of Greece was implemented by the European Commission (EU), the International Monetary Fund (IMF) and the European Central Bank (ECB), in order to avoid bankruptcy and to correct macroeconomic imbalances" (Stournaras 2020). In summer of 2018 the third financial adaptation program was smoothly completed, and so, we select to analyze income taxes of next year 2019.

At the beginning of 2010, the tax policy in Greece exhibits the trend followed by the rest of the EU countries, introducing the reduction of tax rates. In 2011 the tax rates were reduced compared to 2010 and the tax-free limit was increased (up to 12000 thousand Euros) for all individuals. To cover the revenue deficit, 2 new taxes were put forward, the solidarity tax and the performance tax. In the year 2012, the tax-free limit was reduced and in 2013 it was completely abolished for the freelancers and the self-employed, whose income was fully taxed. Solely for employees and pensioners there was still a tax-free limit and in the subsequent year it was also applied to professional farmers. Tax rates are rising, while almost all tax exemptions are being abolished, living expenses are rising, while wages and pensions are falling.

All this combined with the instability of the economy, the blow-up of unemployment, the lack of job opportunities and lack of investment opportunities lead to reduced incomes and the economic migration of companies and individuals. Analysis of tax revenues at regional and national level for 2011 was done by Stamatopoulos and Karavokyris (2012). Comparing the tax incomes of Greeks in detail by regions, between 2011 and 2018, one can notice a decrease in incomes with the added burden of high taxation. (AADE 2020, IOBE 2018, Alifragkis 2018, Mparmpas 2020).

2 Income and Tax Revenues

We will include some general information regarding the taxation system and its purpose and we will describe the focus points of this paper. We use data for the economic year 2011 and 2019, which are about the tax years 2010 and 2018 correspondingly. When we refer to the economic year 2011 we mean the fiscal year or the management period of 2010, meaning that for the overall income of 2010 the tax year is 2011 (Ministry of Economy, 2012). From 1/1/2014, the law 4172/2013 defines the meaning of the tax year which coincides with the calendar year. The calendar year cannot exceed the 12-month period and replaces the terms "management period" and "financial year", which were used by the old code. Thus, the tax year 2018 indicates the period between 1/1/2018 and 31/12/2018 and the taxes that will be paid by natural or legal persons will refer to the tax year 2018, regardless of the time the payment was executed.

2.1   The Income Tax Scale for the Financial year 2011

The income tax scale is described in terms of tax rates depending on the size of the income. In Greece, this constantly changes by law instatements. For the year 2011, this was established by the law 3842. The scale varies from 18 to 45% (8 different rates). It is presented in Table 1 and applies for all sources of (year 2010) income.

2.1.1   The Main Characteristics of 2011 Tax System

Since 2011 is a year characterized by financial crisis, with a decrease in the incomes of Greek people, there is special care for the ones with low incomes, so that they are not burdened with taxes, as well as for young people up to the age of 35, who start their own businesses. Taxpayers are also encouraged to ask for proof of purchase of goods and services, in order to reduce the tax evasion of self-employed professionals.

Tax-free income

Regarding the tax-free limit of twelve thousand Euros (12,000 €), it is applied to all the taxpayers, if some of the conditions described below can be applied. The tax-free limit of 12,000€ increases by one thousand five hundred (1500€) Euros if the taxpayer has a child who is financially dependent on him, by three thousand (3000€)

Table 1 Tax scales for 2011

Income (in Euros)	Tax rate %	Sliding-scale tax (in Euros)	Total income (in Euros)	Total tax (in Euros)
12,000	0	0	12,000	0
+4,000	18	720	16,000	720
+6,000	24	1440	22,000	2160
+4,000	26	1040	26,000	3200
+6,000	32	1920	32,000	5120
+8,000	36	2880	40,000	8000
+20,000	38	7600	60,000	15,600
+40,000	40	16,000	100,000	31,600
Excess	45			

Euros if he has two children who are financially dependent on him, by eleven thousand five hundred (11,500€) Euros if he has three children who are financially dependent on him and by two thousand (2000 €) Euros for each child over the third one who is financially dependent on him. For the inhabitants of small islands (population less than 3100 inhabitants) the tax-free amount of the scale (12,000 Euros) is increased by 50% and becomes 18,000 Euros.

There is also special care, in terms of taxation, in order to facilitate young entrepreneurs, people who are self-employed and people running their own business. In particular, income up to 30,000 € is not under taxation, if these people begin working for the first time from 01/01/2010 onwards and at the time of starting they have not completed the thirty-fifth year of their age. The exemption is valid for three years: the year of commencement and the following two years.

Tax-free conditions with receipts

In order to combat the tax evasion of the people who are self-employed, so that taxpayers with an income of more than 6000 Euros can be tax-free, they must provide receipts issued in accordance with the provisions of the Hellenic Code of Accounting Books and Records for expenditure on goods and services. Expenditures for the acquisition of assets, telecommunications, energy, water, etc., transport tickets are excluded.

The minimum amount of receipts required to be submitted, by submitting the tax return to the Hellenic Tax Office is: (a) at a rate of ten percent (10%) for personal income up to twelve thousand (12,000) Euros and (b) at a rate of thirty percent (30%) for individual income above twelve thousand (12,000) Euros. If the amount of the receipts of expenses submitted by the taxpayer is less than the above mentioned percentage, a tax on the difference of ten percent (10%) is imposed. On the contrary, if the amount of the receipts of expenses submitted exceeds this percentage, it is deducted from the total tax, a tax calculated at a rate of ten percent (10%) on the difference. The amount of expenses can in no case exceed the amount of fifteen thousand (15,000 €) Euros for the debtor and thirty thousand (30,000 €) Euros for the spouses. Expenses are calculated only if they have been included in the original income tax declaration.

Expenses that are deductible and result in reductions in the total tax or income

Incentives are also given to provide receipts for service costs, in which there has been a great deal of tax evasion in the previous years. Thus, each of the following expenses is deducted at a rate of 20% of the overall tax.

- The cost of the rent, which cannot exceed 1200 Euros.
- The cost of life and death insurance, which cannot exceed 1200 € for a single person and 2400 € for a married person.
- The cost of tuition for private lessons and tutoring cannot exceed 1200 €.
- The cost of donations-sponsorships to the State, the local authorities, the holy temples, etc. This reduction is made if the amounts of donations and sponsorships exceed a total of € 100 Euros and cannot exceed 10% of the total income.

- Hospital care costs. The amount of the reduction cannot exceed 6000 €.
- Cost of installation of natural gas—photovoltaic systems—district heating etc. A percentage of 10% of this cost is deducted from the overall tax up to the amount of 6000 € Euros and lastly, the costs of medical care, where the total annual amount is deducted from the income.
- The reduction for the cost of interest on mortgages continues to apply only if the loans concern a first home up to 120 sqm, just like in 2010.

Expenses for presumptive income

Another way to control tax evasion is to institutionalize maintenance presumptions and tax according to these presumptions. The objective costs that are taken into account for the determination of the total annual cost of the taxpayer are costs such as owner-occupied or rented dwellings or free main and secondary residences. Passenger car expenses (annual objective cost does not apply to Antiques and Wheelchairs), expenses for private schools, expenses for domestic helpers, car drivers, etc., expenses for yachts, aircraft, helicopters, gliders, swimming pools. The annual objective expenses for pensioners over the age of sixty-five (65th) are reduced by thirty percent (30%).

It must be noted that, an amount is added to the above objective costs as a minimum objective cost of living (3000 € for a single, divorced or widowed person and 5000 € for spouses who submit a joint declaration).

2.1.2 Special Additional Taxation of 2011

In order to increase tax revenues and cover deficits, two special taxes were institutionalized in 2011, a solidarity contribution and a performance fee.

Those who have an annual income over 12,000 €, in the financial year 2011, are obliged to pay the special solidarity levy for the very first time (article 29 of the law 3986/2011), which is calculated on the basis of the total net personal income or of the imputed income according to the scales shown in Table 2.

For the financial year 2011 in particular, in addition to the imposition of the special solidarity levy, a new special tax is imposed for the tradesmen and for those who

Table 2 Solidarity levy rates

Solidarity levy Income	Rate of solidarity levy (%)
0.00–12,000	0
12,000.01–20,000	1
20,000.01–50,000	2
50,000.01–100,000	3
100,000.01-	4

practice a free profession, the "performance fee", which is set at three hundred (300 €) Euros (article 31 of law 3986/2011).

2.2 Analysis of Tax Revenues for 2011

For the total number of taxpayers, legal persons constitute the 11%, and natural persons the 89%. The number of taxpayers results from the number of tax returns, where it amounted to 5,681,066 for the fiscal year 2011. The legal persons that submitted tax returns amounted to 223,989. Table 3 shows the total income of natural and legal persons and their respective taxes. Greece's total taxable income is about 116.5 billion Euros and the amount of direct taxes is 10.4 billion Euros. We observe that legal entities that constitute 11% of the total income are charged with 29.5% of the total tax.

In Greece in 2011, the total declared income (excluding the application of presumptions) amounted to 97,944,878,220 Euros, which is divided into its sources of origin, as described in Table 4. Surely, the total taxable amount of physics persons in the country is calculated with the application of presumptions and it reached the total of 103,699,371,550 Euros.

Table 3 Statistical report of tax data 2011

	Income	%	Tax	%
Physics persons	103,699,371,550	89	7,337,456,339	70.5
Legal entities	12,811,081,880	11	3,065,604,359	29.5
Total	116,510,453,430	100	10,403,060,698	100

Source Ministry of Economy

Table 4 Income per category

Income from:	amount	%
Real estate	8,876,174,090	8.6
Transferable securities	16,488,050	0.0
Commercial-industrial enterprises	8,610,339,950	8.3
Agricultural enterprises	1,564,968,100	1.5
Paid services	73,850,536,150	71.2
Liberal professions	4,605,747,120	4.4
Other foreign income	420,624,760	0.4
Declared income	97,944,878,220	94.5
Additional presumptive difference	5,754,493,330	5.5
Total taxed income	103,699,371,550	100.0

Source Ministry of Economy

Table 5 Income and tax of spouse

	Income	%	Tax	%
Debtor	81,562,638,950	78.7	6,031,019,039	82.2
Spouse	22,136,732,600	21.3	1,306,437,300	17.8
Total	103,699,371,550	100.0	7,337,456,339	100.0

Employees and pensioners constituted the category with the highest income in our country in 2011 (percentage 75.4%). Natural persons engaged in business, commercial, industrial and liberal professions participate in the total income of the country with a percentage of 13.49%. Additionally, in the total income of Greece, those who have income from agricultural enterprises participate with a percentage of 1.6% and natural persons who declare income from real estate, or rent, or imputed income from the possession of real estate participate with a significant percentage of 9.06%.

The distribution of taxable income as well as the tax paid between the debtor and the spouse, is described at Table 5. The spouses file a joint tax return (mainly the man is indebted in the case of a married couple). Almost 1/5 of the total taxable income and the corresponding tax comes from the spouse of the debtor.

Table 6 presents the distribution of taxpayers by region in Greece, with the taxable income per region, the corresponding tax per region as well as the percentage of tax paid by each region to the total taxable income of the country. In the last column, we calculated the average tax rate of each region by dividing the tax amount by the total income of the region. This percentage is called the "average weighted rate". In total, it is 7.08% of the total taxable income of Greece.

As shown in Table 6, the largest district of the country, the region of Athens, has the largest number of taxpayers in the whole country, 38.05%. Its taxable income amounts to 44.52% of the total taxable income while its contribution to the total tax is 58.46%. That is, 38.05% of taxpayers pay 58.46% of the total taxes. We have an average weighted rate of 9.29% of total taxable income.

The second largest region is Central Macedonia with 15.34% of the total taxable income. We can observe that the two largest districts of the country gather the 55.03% of taxpayers of the country with a taxable income of 59.86% and contribute the significant percentage of 70.41% of the total annual tax. Double weighted average rate of 14.80% of the total taxable income, from the average rate with which the country is taxed as a total of 7.08% on taxable income.

We can observe that the region of Western Macedonia was taxed with the third highest average rate of 6.15% of the total taxable income, with a number of taxpayers 2.57% share in the income 2.37% and with a contribution to the total tax of 2.06%.

We also notice that the region of Eastern Macedonia and Thrace was taxed with the lowest average rate of 4.45% of the total taxable income, with a number of taxpayers 5.22% share in the income 4.42% and with a contribution to the total tax of 2.78%.

In depth, in the country as a whole, the declared income, the taxable income, the total number of taxpayers, and finally the paid tax, are presented in Table 7. It becomes clear that 7.5% of taxpayers, despite the declaration of real annual income

Table 6 Taxpayers, income and tax per region 2011

Region	Number of Taxpayers	% of total taxpayers	Declared income	Taxed Income	% of total income	TAX	% of total tax	% tax on region taxed income
ATTICA	2,161,410	38.05	44,469,832,998	46,170,321,090	44.52	4,289,781,992	58.46	9.29
THESSALY	369,852	6.51	5,602,107,001	6,003,202,020	5.79	281,551,020	3.84	4.69
PELOPONNESE	299,676	5.28	4,394,654,010	4,772,042,100	4.60	262,045,896	3.57	5.49
CENTRAL GREECE	268,928	4.73%	4,239,930,020	4,497,712,120	4.34	234,582,035	3.20	5.22
WEST GREECE	327,928	5.77	4,926,485,028	5,295,664,008	5.11	282,599,700	3.85	5.34
CRETE	295,411	5.20	4,626,535,033	4,957,328,030	4.78	264,542,120	3.61	5.34
EASTERN MACEDONIA -THRACE	296,501	5.22	4,218,746,005	4,582,757,005	4.42	204,010,099	2.78	4.45
CENTRAL MACEDONIA	964,619	16.98	14,778,031,040	15,903,075,010	15.34	876,901,950	11.95	5.51
WEST MACEDONIA	145,814	2.57	2,276,412,020	2,458,905,099	2.37	151,174,083	2.06	6.15
EPIRUS	167,012	2.94	2,623,387,002	2,812,562,007	2.71	145,997,880	1.99	5.19
NORTHERN AEGEAN	103,620	1.82	1,625,249,005	1,742,653,040	1.68	91.967.910	1.25	5.28
SOUTHERN AEGEAN	166,732	2.93	2,598,155,008	2,782,971,083	2.68	163.972.010	2.23	5.89
IONIAN ISLANDS	113,563	2	1,565,354,050	1,720,178,938	1.66	88.329.644	1.21	5.14
TOTAL	5,681,066	100	97,944,878,220	103,699,371,550	100	7.337.456.339	100	7.08

Table 7 Taxpayers, income and tax per family income 2011

2011	Taxpayers		Declared income		Taxed income		Total tax	
Family income scales in Euros	number	% Total	Euros	% Total	Euros	% Total	Euros	% Total
= 0	426,255	7.50		0.00	2,012,553,943	1.94	15,220,973	0.21
UP TO 1.000	153,890	2.71	67,997,144	0.07	814,484,613	0.79	5,924,951	0.08
≫2.000	129,675	2.28	193,781,649	0.20	703,641,402	0.68	3,363,269	0.05
≫3.000	136,835	2.41	342,843,804	0.35	756,893,478	0.73	3,390,119	0.05
≫7.000	857,817	15.10	4,448,019,277	4.54	5,587,637,152	5.39	14,986,902	0.20
≫10.000	627,931	11.05	5,298,700,351	5.41	5,698,169,186	5.49	10,273,186	0.13
≫12.000	449,885	7.85	4,942,723,109	5.03	5,113,031,099	4.9	6,890,959,	0.01
≫15.000	573,707	10.17	7,719,808,960	7.9	7,877,535,936	7.63	29,575,626,	0.49
≫20.000	684,821	12.05	11,855,791,260	12.10	11,990,279,770	11.56	199,836,669	2.72
≫28.000	642,845	11.32	15,175,258,270	15.49	15,250,203,649	14.71	664,959,971	9.06
≫36.000	364,425	6.41	11,541,596,908	11.79	11,559,003,666	11.14	771,518,559	10.51
≫45.000	255,677	4.50	10,264,696,306	10.48	10,265,570,386	9.90	861,989,161	11.75
≫55.000	160,382	2.82	7,927,739,786	8.09	7,924,404,231	7.64	886,081,240	12.08
≫65.000	82,247	1.45	4,892,832,052	5.00	4,889,439,538	4.72	710,833,202	9.69
≫75.000	45,167	0.80	3,140,999,033	3.21	3,137,818,356	3.02	541,679,312	7.38
≫85.000	27,313	0.48	2,174,129,343	2.22	2,171,512,751	2.09	422,519,055	5.76
≫110.000	33,136	0.58	3,163,010,530	3.23	3,158,888,985	3.05	701,648,003	9.56
≫150.000	17,667	0.31	2,221,746,904	2.27	2,218,730,523	2.14	592,509,333	8.08
≫170.000	3,435	0.06	546,334,651	0.56	545,149,961	0.53	165,330,224	2.25

(continued)

Table 7 (continued)

2011	Taxpayers		Declared income		Taxed income		Total tax	
Family income scales in Euros	number	% Total	Euros	% Total	Euros	% Total	Euros	% Total
≫250.000	5,444	0.10	1,089,078,305	1.11	1,087,720,558	1.05	363,648,563	4.96
≫500.000	2,225	0.04	715,248,051	0.73	713,927,925	0.69	271,124,709	3.70
≫900.000	236	0.01	149,634,031	0.15	150,044,245	0.14	62,435,189	0.85
More than 900.000	51	0.00	72,908,496	0.07	72,730,196	0.07	31,717,164	0.43
Total	5,681,066	100.00	97,944,878,220	100.00	103,699,371,549	100.00	7,337,456,339	100.00

of zero (0) Euros, are taxed on the basis of imputed income and thus their taxable income amounts to 1.94% of total taxable income at a national level, while their contribution to the total tax is 0.21%.

10.21%, i.e. 580,145 taxpayers, have an income of less than 1000 Euros and their contribution to the total tax is of the order of 0.29%.

48.90%, i.e. 2,782,288 taxpayers, out of the total of 5,681,066 taxpayers, have an income of up to 12,000 Euros, which is the tax-free limit according to the income tax scale with a contribution to the total tax of 0.73%.

71.12% of taxpayers, i.e. 4,040,816 taxpayers out of the total of 5,681,066 taxpayers have an annual family income of less than 20,000 Euros and their contribution to the total tax is of the order of 3.95%.

93.35% of the taxpayers, i.e. 5,303,763 taxpayers out of the total of 5,681,066 taxpayers, belong to family income scales which are lower than 45,000 Euros per year and constitute the 35.3% of the total tax.

Another 6.60% of the 374,791 taxpayers belong to family income scales over 45,000 and less than 250,000 Euros; they constitute the 59.76% of the total tax. Furthermore, 0.05% of the taxpayers, i.e. 2,512 taxpayers, have taxable incomes over 250,000 Euros and their contribution to the total tax is of the order of 4.98.

Out of the total of 5,681,066 taxpayers, only 51 taxpayers in the whole country have family incomes that annually amount to levels greater than 900,000 Euros, while their contribution to the total tax is of the order of 0.43%.

We observe that 48.90% of the taxpayers essentially have a tax-free income since their income is up to 12,000 Euros, which also constitutes the tax-free limit and the minimum tax, that resulted from the 0.73% of the total tax, is because of the taxation due to presumptions and not because of the net income.

71.12% of taxpayers, i.e. 4,040,816 out of a total of 5,681,066, with incomes of less than 20,000 Euros, contribute a tax percentage of 3.95% of the total tax.

22.23% of the taxpayers, i.e. 1,262,947 taxpayers, with incomes greater than 20,000 Euros and less than 45,000 Euros, contribute a tax percentage of 31.32% of the total tax.

Lastly, 6.65% of the 377,303 taxpayers with incomes greater than 45,000 and above contribute a tax of 64.74% to the total tax.

2.3 Characteristics of 2018 Tax System

2.3.1 The Income Tax Scale for 2018

The income tax scale for 2018 was determined by the provisions of KFE (law 4172/2013). The need to increase tax revenues to cover the budget deficit has led to frequent changes in income taxation. The changes in rates and scales were intended to increase the tax burden. In 2018 we have a significant reduction in the number of scales from 8 to 4 and at the same time we have the abolition of the tax-free for

Table 8 Tax scales for 2019

Scale of income	Tax rate %	Tax scale € (in Euros)	Total of income	Total of tax
20,000	22	4,400	20,000	4,400
10,000	29	2,900	30,000	7,300
10,000	37	3,700	40,000	11,000
Excess	45			

Table 9 Tax scales for 2019 for income from properties

Income from properties of natural persons	Rate (%)
0.00–12,000.00	15
12,000.01–35,000.00	35
More than 35,000.01	45

incomes originating from business activity, which offered the possibility of collecting tax from the very first Euro of income (Table 8).

The basic tax scale concerns income from individual business activity, from paid work and pensions. In the case that income derives from more than one of the above mentioned sources, the income is added up and taxed at the same rate.

The same scale will be applied to the calculation of the tax on income from agricultural activities. However, the profits from an individual agricultural enterprise are taxed independently, that means they are not added to the income from salaries, pensions, companies so that they can be taxed according to the scale.

Real estate is taxed independently with the tax scale presented in Table 9. All real estate income is taxed, and with a higher tax rate than other incomes of natural persons for amounts over 12,000 Euros. The annual income of natural persons from the short-term rental property that is usually serviced through the international online platform Airbnb will be taxed at the same rate. In the past few years, many property owners have turned to the exploitation of real estate with short-term leases, due to the increase of tourism and the use of electronic reservations directly by citizens. A special tax has been introduced for this source of income.

We notice a differentiation in comparison to 2011 in the single income taxation category. The scale varies from 22 to 45% (4 different coefficients). In 2011, there were 8 different rates in order to expand the distribution of tax burdens and enhance the progressiveness of the system. The tax-free income in 2011 was set at 12,000 Euros without differentiations between paid pensioners and professionals. We can infer that, in 2019 compared to 2011, the tax burden increased at all income levels.

In terms of imputed income, the objective costs taken into account in determining the taxpayer's total annual expenditure remain the same as in 2011.

Table 10 Percentage of minimum expenditure through an electronic transaction and payment by card

Income	Percentage of minimum expenditure through an electronic transaction and payment by card
1–10,000	10%
10,000,01–30,000	15%
More than 30,000.01	20% and up until 30,0000 Euros

2.3.2 Tax Reduction for Electronic Payments

The use of electronic payments was instituted for the first time by the law 4446/2016, putting an end to the collection of receipts, except for certain exceptions, now linking electronic transactions with the tax-free. It was implemented from 1/1/2017. The aim of the measure was the tax compliance of professionals and companies by encouraging taxpayers to make use of electronic transactions.

In order to be entitled to the tax deduction from 1900 to 2100 Euros, every paid, retired and professional farmer, is required to make expenses for the purchase of goods or services of an amount equal to 10–20% of the total income, as shown in Table 10. In the case of the taxpayer not being able to cover the minimum amount between the required and the declared, the difference will be taxed at 22%.

Exempted from the obligation to use electronic means of payment for the realization of expenses are taxpayers of the age of seventy (70) years old and above, individuals with a disability rate of eighty percent (80%) and above, those who are in legal aid and EU tax residents. The above taxpayers are required to collect handwritten receipts and submit them to the competent tax authorities in case they are needed for a check-up.

2.3.3 Expenses that Are Deductible and Result in Reductions in Total Tax or Income

Almost all tax exemptions that were effective in 2011 were gradually abolished. Even the tax exemption for medical and pharmaceutical expenses from 2017 onward has been abolished. The only tax exemption that remains, from 2016 onward, except for the cost of donations-sponsorships to the State, the local authorities, the holy temples, is the tax deduction for money donations to members of the Parliament and political parties. The tax deduction in this case is 10%, provided that the donation rate cannot exceed 5% of the taxpayer's income and the annual donation cannot exceed 5000 Euros to a member of the Parliament and 20,000 Euros to a political party.

Instead of the tax-free income that was abolished, tax reductions are introduced for special categories. The tax deductions for employees, pensioners (and mainly farmers) based on the tax scale are as follows:

(a)   by 1900 Euros for a taxpayer who has no children who are financially depen-
        dent on him, when the taxable income does not exceed the amount of 20,000
        Euros. This amount is equivalent to a tax-free income limit of 8,636.36. In
        the case of having financially dependent children, the tax is reduced by 1950
        Euros for a taxpayer with one (1) financially dependent child (equivalent to a
        tax-free limit of 8,863.64), by 2000 Euros for a taxpayer with two (2) finan-
        cially dependent children (equivalent to a tax-free limit of 9,090.91), by 2100
        Euros for a taxpayer with three (3) financially dependent children and more
        (equivalent to a tax-free limit of 9,545.45). If the amount of the resulting tax is
        less than these amounts then the tax reduction is limited to the amount of tax
        concerned.
(b)   The amount of tax reduction in the above case is reduced by 1% per 1000 Euros
        of taxable income (by 10 Euros per 1000 Euros of income) for taxable income
        from paid services and pensions, over the amount of 20,000 Euros.

We should stress that the above tax reductions apply to professional farmers, as
they are defined in paragraph 1 of article 65 of the law 4389/2016. That is, for those
who at least 50% of their income comes from agricultural activities and remain
employed for at least 30% of their total annual working time.

If income has been obtained from a sole proprietorship in parallel with income
from employment and pensions or along with income from other categories, the tax
reduction will only be proportionate to the part of the income derived exclusively from
paid work and pensions or from a sole proprietorship. We can observe an existing
discrimination and a greater burden on incomes besides salaries and pensions.

For young entrepreneurs, based on the provisions of article 29, par.2 of the law
4172/2013, referring to natural persons who start a business, the tax rate of the first
step of the above scale (22%) is reduced by fifty percent (50%), provided that their
annual gross income from business activity does not exceed ten thousand (10,000)
Euros, for the first three years in which they are professionally active.

2.3.4   Special Extraordinary Taxation

The solidarity contribution continues to exist with a differentiated percentage ratio,
as shown in Table 11. The solidarity contribution is levied on the taxable income,

Table 11 Solidarity contribution rate

Solidarity contribution income	Solidarity contribution rate (%)
0–12,000	0
12,000–20,000	2.2
20,000–30,000	5.0
30,000–40,000	6.5
40,000–65,000	7.5
65,000–220,000	9.0

real or imputed, over 12,000 Euros. There is an exception for pensioners over the age of 65. In this category the imputed income resulting from the application of the living presumptions is reduced by 30% for the calculation of the special solidarity contribution. Essentially, it significantly increases the real tax burden of taxpayers, for incomes over 20,000 Euros in particular. The solidarity contribution confirmed in 2019 amounted to 610,972,597 Euros.

This tax measure was implemented for the first time in 2011. It was included in the urgent measures for the implementation of the medium-term Framework Strategy 2012–2015 (Law 3986/2011) and was expected to be implemented until 2014. Its enforcement was deemed necessary to address the consequences of the financial crisis and was temporary. However, with the law (n.4305/2014) it was extended to tax 2015. Eventually, with the law 4387/2016, it was incorporated in the "Tax Revenue Code" which constitutes one of the most mnemonic obligations of Greece.

Taxpayers who carried out individual business activities also paid the annual performance fee for 2019, which amounted to 650 Euros paid individually and an additional 600 Euros, paid for each branch. The performance fee certified for 2018 amounted to 376,674,517 Euros.

2.4 The Analysis of Tax Revenues for 2019

In the total of taxpayers, in 2019, legal persons constitute the 14.48% and natural persons the 85.52% (Table 12). The number of taxpayers results from the number of tax returns, which amounted to 6,469,044 in 2019. Additionally, in 2019, more legal persons and legal entities submitted declarations compared to previous years (2010–2018), an overall total of 268,752.

This may be due to the fact that the establishment of certain legal entities has become easier and more appealing. In 2016, with the law 4387/20165 (known as Katrougalos law), the insurance contributions of the self-employed were linked to the amount of their taxable income, creating a high operating cost for entrepreneurs. In order to reduce the amount of insurance contributions, many young and old entrepreneurs founded Private Capital Companies (IKE). The main advantage that IKE offers is the optional insurance of the partners while, at the same time, only the manager is compulsorily insured. In the case the manager is a partner and does not get paid, he is insured with the lowest possible amount, namely 167.95 Euros, while if he does receive a fee then he is insured with a percentage of 26.95% on the overall fee he receives. In addition, the set-up cost is limited to a fee of 70 Euros, a minimum capital of 1 Euro is required and the establishment of IKE becomes easier and faster with the use of online one-stop service from mid-2018 onward. This resulted in the creation of 4449 new companies in the first semester of 2018 and 55.34% of the new companies were IKE within the whole year, according to the data collected by ΓΕΜΗ.

At a national level, the total income (excluding the application of presumptions) amounted to 75,224,524,468 Euros, which was divided in the way it is described in

Table 12 Statistical report of tax data 2019

	Income	%	Tax	%
Physics persons	81,629,294,848	85.52	8,451,275,017	65.94
Legal entities	13,817,106,149	14.48	4,365,015,330	34.06
Total	95,446,400,997	100	12,816,290,347	100

Source Ministry of Economy

Table 13 Income per category 2019

Income category	Income amount
Real estate	6,473,869,068
Business activity	3,325,593,781
Agricultural business activity	1,251,411,812
Paid services	61,480,835,451
Transferable securities	2,692,814,356
Declared income	75,224,524,468
Additional presumption Difference	6,404,770,380
Total taxed income	81,629,294,848

Table 13. The total taxable amount of natural persons of the country is calculated by the application of presumptions and amounts to a total of 81,629,294,848, depending on the source which is presented in Table 13.

Employees and pensioners belonged to the category with the highest income rate in Greece in the tax year 2018, with a rate of 81.73%. Physics persons engaged in business activity participate in the total income of the country with a percentage of 4.42%. Those who have income from agricultural enterprises participate with a percentage of 1.66% and those who have income from real estate participate with a percentage of 8.61% in the total income of the country.

The total income of 2018 was decreased by 23.24% in comparison to the total income of 2010. The income of employees and pensioners decreased by 16.75%, due to the dramatic decrease of income on salaries and pensions during the period of the economic crisis and signed memoranda. Income deriving from the business activity of individuals decreased by 9.07%.

The distribution of the taxable income and total tax between the debtor and the spouse is described in Table 14.

The Table 15 includes data of the number of taxpayers per district, as well as the percentage of taxpayers per district in the total number of taxpayers in the country.

Table 14 Debtor and spouse income

Taxed income	Combined	Debtor	Spouse
	81,629,294,848	64,640,254,313	16,989,040,535
Total tax	8,451,275,017	6,858,051,508	1,593,223,509

Table 15 Taxpayers, income and tax per region 2019

Region	Number of taxpayers	% of taxpayers	Declared income	Taxed income	% of total income	Tax	% of total tax	% tax on region taxed income
Attica	2,403,286	37.15	34,131,439,727	36,235,179,996	44.39	4,575,949,731	54.15	12.63
Thessaly	418,600	6.47	4,201,895,611	4,650,753,111	5.70	366,660,566	4.34	7.88
Peloponnese	345,380	5.34	3,327,673,835	3,718,370,057	4.56	309,391,034	3.66	8.32
Central Greece	298,031	4.61	3,087,538,362	3,404,179,116	4.17	279,926,742	3.31	8.22
West Greece	384,629	5.95	3,555,552,188	4,014,126,062	4.92	318,832,515	3.77	7.94
CRETE	364,237	5.63	3,936,819,561	4,296,672,675	5.26	378,363,496	4.48	8.81
Eastern Macedonia & Thrace	343,891	5.32	3,283,419,555	3,627,468,505	4.44	284,358,744	3.36	7.84
Central Macedonia	1,103,735	17.06	11,421,505,108	12,571,531,301	15.40	1,119,171,431	13.24	8.90
West Macedonia	163,685	2.53	1,668,600,771	1,835,162,041	2.25	160,947,394	1.90	8.77
Epirus	192,669	2.98	1,986,689,559	2,182,259,651	2.67	178,337,435	2.11	8.17
Northern Aegean	118,447	1.83	1,224,561,549	1,349,993,052	1.65	119,102,300	1.41	8.82
Southern Aegean	191,880	2.97	2,102,220,652	2,287,374,012	2.80	233,973,341	2.77	10.23
Ionian Islands	140,574	2.17	1,296,607,990	1,456,225,269	1.78	126,260,290	1.49	8.67
Total	6,469,044	100	75,224,524,468	81,629,294,848	100%	8,451,275,017	100%	10.35

Table 15 shows the distribution of taxpayers in each Greek district, including the taxable income per district, the corresponding tax and the tax rate that each district paid to the total taxable income of the country. The Weighted Rate was calculated by dividing the country's total tax for the fiscal year 2018 by the corresponding level of taxable income.

It becomes clear that the largest district of the country, namely Attica, has the greatest number of taxpayers in the whole country, 37.15%. Its taxable income amounts to 44.39% of the total taxable income while its contribution to the total tax is of the order of 54.15%. That is, 37.15% of the taxpayers pay 54.15% of the total taxes. The weighted average income of Attica was taxed at the highest rate of 12.63% of the total taxable income. The weighted average rate corresponding to the total tax of the country is 10.35% of the taxable income.

The second largest district of taxable income is Central Macedonia. We observe that, in the two largest districts of the country, 54.21% of taxpayers with a taxable income percentage 59.79% of the total, contribute 67.39% in tax. They were taxed weighted average with a double rate of 21.53% on the total taxable income, than the weighted average rate that the country is taxed with as a total of 10.35% on the total taxable income. We also notice that the South Aegean region was taxed at the third highest weighted average rate of 10.23% of the total taxable income with a taxpayer rate of 2.97%, contribution to the total income 2.8% and a total tax contribution 2.77%.

2.5   Distribution of Tax and Taxpayers According to Income in 2019

Table 16 presents in detail the declared income, the taxable income, the total number of taxpayers and finally the tax paid.

We observe that 9.9% of the taxpayers, namely 639,860 thousand taxpayers, despite the declaration of real annual income of zero (0) Euros, are taxed on the basis of imputed income and thus their taxable income amounts to 1.75% of the total taxable income at a national level, while their contribution to the total tax is of the order of 0.17%.

20.99%, i.e. 1,357,165 taxpayers, have an income of less than 1000 Euros and their contribution to the total tax is 0.58%.

58.89% have incomes below 10,000 Euros, i.e. 3,810,064 taxpayers, and their participation in the total tax is 4.78%.

83.38% of taxpayers, 5,394,312 taxpayers out of a total of 6,469,044, have annual family incomes of less than 20,000 Euros and their contribution to the total tax is of the order of 25.60%. 97.53% of the taxpayers, i.e. 6,309,273 out of a total of 6,469,044 taxpayers who belong to family income scales below 45,000 Euros annually, pay 64.18% of the total tax.

Table 16 Taxpayers, income and tax per family income 2019

2019 Scales of family income in Euros	Taxpayers		Declared income		Taxable income		Total tax	
	Number of tax returns	% of total	Euros	% of total	Euros	% of total	Euros	% total
= 0	639,860	9.90	0		1,431,238,712	1.75	14,655,433	0.17
Up to 1.000	717,305	11.09	161,109,502	0.21	2,363,053,257	2.89	31,569,764	0.41
≫2.000	274,147	4.23	409,492,185	0.54	1,074,547,438	1.32	24,520,527	0.29
≫3.000	248,735	3.84	620,039,327	0.82	1,082,627,076	1.33	31,679,544	0.37
≫7.000	1,214,982	18.78	6,112,732,078	8.13	7,193,362,624	8.81	150,289,786	1.78
≫10.000	715,035	11.05	6,019,630,144	8.00	6,301,253,476	7.72	149,149,093	1.76
≫15.000	922,044	14.25	11,468,285,564	15.25	11,644,045,033	14.26	697,820,351	8.26
≫20.000	662,204	10.24	11,432,007,523	15.20	11,499,885,470	14.09	1,062,263,064	12.57
≫28.000	499,744	7.73	11,703,909,440	15.56	11,730,325,961	14.37	1,297,398,435	15.35
≫36.000	264,403	4.09	8,378,625,368	11.14	8,384,898,756	10.27	1,057,338,657	12.51
≫45.000	150,814	2.33	5,998,085,616	7.97	6,000,725,277	7.35	904,940,653	10.71
≫55.000	66,739	1.03	3,291,933,436	4.38	3,293,026,766	4.03	602,339,413	7.13
≫65.000	32,865	0.51	1,954,722,234	2.60	1,955,216,879	2.40	413,628,774	4.89
≫75.000	18,070	0.28	1,257,596,748	1.67	1,257,980,452	1.55	294,982,845	3.49
≫85.000	11,100	0.17	883,567,018	1.17	883,851,239	1.08	221,126,520	2.62
≫110.000	13,856	0.21	1,324,705,323	1.76	1,324,880,219	1.62	358,913,245	4.25
≫150.000	8,322	0.13	1,052,184,686	1.40	1,052,341,212	1.29	313,296,791	3.71
≫170.000	1,927	0.03	307,434,529	0.41	307,466,575	0.38	96,569,638	1.14
≫250.000	3,562	0.06	720,087,952	0.96	720,137,350	0.88	225,490,215	2.67
≫500.000	2,319	0.04	774,576,358	1.03	774,627,526	0.95	222,915,671	2.64

(continued)

Table 16 (continued)

2019	Taxpayers		Declared income		Taxable income		Total tax	
Scales of family income in Euros	Number of tax returns	% of total	Euros	% of total	Euros	% of total	Euros	% total
≫900.000	604	0.01	389,327,789	0.52	389,327,789	0.48	100,182,053	1.19
More than 900.000	407	0.01	964,471,648	1.28	964,475,761	1.18	180,204,547	2.13
Total	6,469,044	100,00	75,224,524,468	100,0	81,629,294,848	100.00	8,451,275,017	100.00

2.42% of the taxpayers, i.e. 156,441 taxpayers of the total number of taxpayers who belong to family income scales over 45,000 and less than 250,000 thousand Euros participate in the tax at a rate of 29.9% of the total tax.

Furthermore, 0.06% of taxpayers, i.e. 3,330 taxpayers, have taxable incomes over 250,000 Euros and their contribution to the total tax is of the order of 5.96%.

Out of the total of 6,469,044 taxpayers, only 407 taxpayers in the whole country have family incomes that annually amount to levels greater than 900,000 Euros, while their contribution to the total tax is of the order of 2.13%.

We can infer that 2.48% of the taxpayers, i.e. 160,178 thousand out of the total of 6,469,044 taxpayers, with incomes over 250,000, contribute 35.86% to the total tax.

83.38% of the taxpayers, i.e. 5,394,312 taxpayers with an annual family income of less than 20,000 Euros, contribute 25.60% to the total tax.

Finally 14.15% of the taxpayers, i.e. 904,960 taxpayers with annual family incomes greater than 20,000 and less than 45,000 Euros, contribute 38.57% to the total tax. It becomes clear that 16.63% of taxpayers, i.e. 1,065,138, pay 74.43% of the total tax.

2.6   Comparison Between 2011 and 2019

In 2011, the system's strategy was the reduction of the financial charges for middle-incomes and the financial burdening of incomes over 40,000 Euros. With the tax-free limit for all natural persons at 12,000, 48.90% of taxpayers did not pay tax while 71.12% of taxpayers with incomes less than 20,000 Euros contributed a percentage of 3.95% to the total tax. 6.65% of taxpayers with incomes greater than 45,000 Euros contributed 64.74% to the total tax.

In 2011, in order to redistribute the tax burden and enhance the progressiveness of the tax scale, the number of tax revenue scales was increased to 8 tax scales. In 2009 the corresponding number was 3 for employees and pensioners and 4 for the self-employed and professionals. Also in 2011 a single tax scale was introduced for all citizens, and the maximum tax rate was increased from 40 to 45%. The tax-free income limit was of 12,000 Euros for all individuals, employees, pensioners, the self-employed and freelancers, which increased according to the number of dependent children in the taxpayer's family.

A chronic problem of the Greek economy was tax evasion and, as an incentive to reduce it, the presentation of receipts corresponding to 10% of income was introduced, so that there is tax-free income for the taxpayer. Additionally, for the exact same reason the minimum annual objective expenditure was introduced. Two new special taxes were imposed in 2011. The solidarity tax burdened incomes over 12,000 Euros and the achievement tax for entrepreneurs and freelancers. As a relief to the taxpayers the possibility of tax exemptions with reductions in the total tax or in the taxable income was also offered.

For 2011, the number of taxpayers was 5,681,060 and the total declared income was 97,944,878,220 Euros (Table 17). With the application of the living presump-

Table 17 Comparison between 2011 and 2019

	2011	2019	Change
Taxpayers	5,681,060	6,469,044	+787,984
Declared income	97,944,878,220	75,224,524,468	−23.2%
Total tax	7,337,456,339	8,451,275,017	+15.2%
Income of salaried-pensioners	73,850,536,150 (75.5%)	61,480,835,451 (81.7%)	−12,369,700,699 −16,75%
Income from businessmen	13,216,087,070 (13.5%)	3,325,593,781 (4.42%)	−9,890,493,289 −67.23%
Taxpayers with an income over 28.000 and below 45.000 Euros	10.91% Total tax 22%	6.42% Total tax 23,2%	Taxpayers −41.15% Total tax +5.41%
Taxpayers with an income below 28.000	82.5% total tax 13%	91.10% total tax 40.9%	Taxpayers +10.42% Tax increased +214.61%
Taxpayers with an income above 45.000	6.6%	2.5%	−62.71%
Income tax over 45.000	65% total of tax	35.9% total of tax	−44.6%

tions, the taxable income was calculated at 103,699,371,550 Euros and a total tax of 7,337,456,339 Euros was paid. Employees and pensioners declared 75.45% of the total income, 73,850,536,150 Euros and natural persons with business activity 13.49% of the total income 13,216,087,070 Euros.

The two largest regions of the country, Attica and Central Macedonia, comprised 55.03% of taxpayers and declared income corresponding to 60.49% of the total income of the country. These two districts contributed 70.41% of the total tax. 64.74% of the total tax was paid by 6.65% (namely 377,303) of the taxpayers with incomes over 45,000 Euros. 93.35% were taxpayers with incomes below 45,000 Euros and 82.44% were taxpayers with incomes below 28,000 Euros, who contributed 13% of the total tax (Table 17). We can safely conclude that the change in the income tax scale that took place in 2011 reduced the median income (up to 28,000 Euros) and increased the tax burden for incomes over 45,000 Euros.

From the following year, the tax-free limit was reduced and in 2013 it was abolished. Tax rates have risen, almost all tax exemptions have been abolished, pensions and salaries have been cut down. The changes were mainly aimed at increasing tax revenues to cover the country's budget deficits.

In 2018 the number of tax scales decreased from 8 to 4, almost as much as in 2010. The number of taxpayers was 6,469,044 people, 787,984 more taxpayers than in 2011. However, the declared income was reduced by 23.20% compared to 2011 while the tax paid was increased by 15.18%. It can be seen that natural persons with lower incomes pay more taxes. Income coming from paid services continues to be the category with the highest income in the country but decreased by 16.75% due to a great number of wage cuts.

Table 18 Change of tax rates from 2011 to 2020

Income	2011 + solidarity levy (%)	2018 + solidarity levy (%)	2020 (%)
0–10.000	0 + 0	22 + 0	9
10.00 to 20.000	18–24 + 1	22 + 2.2	22
20.000 to 30.000	26–32 + 2	29 + 5.2	28
30.000 to 40.000	36 + 2	37 + 6.5	36
over 40.000	38–45 + 4	45 + 9	44

In the two largest regions of the country, Attica and central Macedonia, the number of taxpayers slightly increased, the declared income decreased by 23.11%, but the tax contributed to the total tax of the country increased by 10.23%.

At a national level, in 2018, revenues shifted downward. Individuals who declared income over 45,000 Euros constitute only 2.48%, having suffered a decrease of 62.71%. They contributed to the total tax at a rate of 35.86% with a lower tax by 44.61%. The tax burdens shifted to the middle classes. The number of taxpayers with incomes below 20,000 Euros increased by 17.24% and contributed 25.60% of the total tax, which was increased by 548.10% compared to 2011. Taxpayers with incomes higher than 20,000 and less than 45,000 decreased at a rate of 36.35% but paying a higher tax at a rate of 23.15%.

To correct this distribution of taxation, in 2020, for the first time since the beginning of the 10-year memorandum period of the economic crisis, reliefs in income tax were introduced and no tax increase was put forward. The new tax scale has reduced tax rates (Table 18). Specifically, the minimum rate became 9% from 22% for an annual income of up to 10,000 Euros. The tax rate for annual income from 20,000 Euros to 30,000 Euros became 28% instead of 29%. The rate for incomes was reduced from 30,000 to 40,000 Euros, to 36% from 37%. The maximum tax rate was slightly reduced from 45 to 44% for incomes over 40,000 Euros.

3 Conclusions

The main source of revenue for financing government expenditures and the provision of public goods is taxation, with the personal income tax (P.I.T) being an important part of the state tax revenue. The present work focused on the analysis of tax revenues of the financial years 2011 and 2019 during the period of the economic crisis in Greece.

For 2020, the solidarity tax will be temporarily suspended for incomes from business activities, dividends, interest and real estate. For income earned from paid employment exclusively in the private sector there will be a temporary exemption from the special solidarity contribution in 2021. The presumptions will not apply under certain conditions for taxpayers affected by the Covid 19 pandemic. The future analysis of tax revenues of 2021 will determine whether the distribution of the tax actually became more just for Greek taxpayers.

References

AADE (2020). https://aade.gr/menoy/statistika-deiktes/eisodima/etisia-statistika-deltia.

Alifragkis El. (2018). *Income tax code for natural and legal persons.* Publisher Vroteas.

GSEBEE (2019). *Report on Small and Medium Enterprises. IME.*

IOBE (2018). *Income taxation in Greece.* IME.

Ministry of Economy (2012*). Statistical Report of Tax Data 2011.* Available at https://www.gsis. gr/dimosia-dedomena/forologikon-dedomenon-statistika-prin-2011

Mparmpas N. (2020). *Income tax code per article interpretation (n.4172/2013).* Editions Sakoula SA.

Sklias P., Roukanas S., Maris G. (2014). Keynes and the Eurozone's Crisis: Towards a Fiscal Union? *Procedia Economics and Finance 9, 66 – 73.*

Stamatopoulos D. and Karavokyris An. (2012). *Income taxation of natural and legal persons.* Eleforin tax institute, Athena.

Stamatopoulos I., Hadjidema S., Eleftheriou K. (2016*). Explaining Corporate Effective Tax Rates Before and During the Financial Crisis: Evidence from Greece.* MPRA Paper No. 73787. Availiable at https://mpra.ub.uni-muenchen.de/73787/

Stournaras G. (2020). *Lessons from the Greek financial crisis, the challenges and opportunities for the future.* Speech by Governor of the Bank of Greece.

Varotsis N. and Katerelos I. (2020). Tax behaviour relating to the review of a revised regional tax policy: a study in Greece. *Journal of Economic Structures (2020) 9:7* Availiable at https://doi. org/10.1186/s40008-020-0181-z

The Impact of COVID-19 on Firm Stock Price Volatility

Marinela Chamzallari, Antonios Chantziaras, and Christos Grose

Abstract Our study investigates the impact of the COVID-19 external shock on the stock return volatility of global firms. Using a sample of 30,516 firms, accounting for 60% of listed firms globally, scattered across 63 countries, we evidence that COVID-19 cases (fatalities) have a positive and significant impact on stock return volatility of global firms, measured at different estimation intervals (windows of 30, 60, 90, 180, and 250 days). In particular, a one standard deviation increase in COVID-19 cases (fatalities) is associated with 0.79% (0.86%) increase in firm volatility. Additionally, we inform that the effect of COVID-19 is amplified for companies from Oceania and Asia. Our insights are advantageous to a wide spectrum of stakeholders, including managers, market participants, and policy makers.

Keywords COVID-19 · Volatility · Return stability

JEL Classification G01 · G15 · G32

M. Chamzallari · A. Chantziaras (✉)
School of Humanities, Social Sciences and Economics, International Hellenic University, 14th klm Thessaloniki-Moudania, 57001 Thessaloniki, PC, Greece
e-mail: antonios.chantziaras@durham.ac.uk; a.chantziaras@ihu.edu.gr

M. Chamzallari
e-mail: m.chamzallari@ihu.edu.gr

A. Chantziaras
Durham University Business School, Durham University, Mill Hill Lane, Durham DH1 3LB, UK

C. Grose
School of Economics and Business Administration, International Hellenic University, 65404 Agios Loukas, Kavala, PC, Greece
e-mail: c.grose@ihu.edu.gr

© The Author(s), under exclusive license to Springer Nature Switzerland AG 2022   433
P. Sklias et al. (eds.), *Business Development and Economic Governance in Southeastern Europe*, Springer Proceedings in Business and Economics,
https://doi.org/10.1007/978-3-031-05351-1_24

1 Introduction

> The COVID-19 pandemic has triggered the deepest economic recession in nearly a century, threatening health, disrupting economic activity, and hurting well-being and jobs.[1]

The COVID-19 has battered the global market and had drastic consequences for trade, supply chains, and economies, while it has triggered a "massive spike in uncertainty" across the globe (Baker et al. 2020, 2). By evaluating the remarkable transmissibility of the virus and the velocity of its global spread, the World Health Organization (WHO) declared the COVID-19 outbreak a global pandemic on 12 March 2020.[2] The COVID-19 threat inevitably led to tremendous health and economic damages, since more than 100 million people have been infected worldwide with a total cumulative death of around 2.3 million.[3] The pandemic has reverberated across economies. In the first quarter of 2020, China proclaimed a drop in GDP of 6.3% compared to the first quarter of 2019 (Hofman 2020), the US economy shrank by 4.8% (Erdem 2020), while Eurostat estimated a 3.8% decrease in GDP of EU member states.[4] Consequently, the world is expecting to face budget cuts as the total cost of COVID-19 is estimated at $8.8 trillion, while International Monetary Fund's Fiscal Monitor projects global fiscal deficits to reach 10% of global GDP (Hofman 2020) and the expected growth rate to be -3% in 2020 (Erdem 2020).

To the extent of the damage, equities drastically plummeted, while market volatility soared upward globally. Stock markets in the US, Europe, and Asia were particularly sensitive. During March 2020, the value of G7 countries' main indices reached their 20-year lows (Yousef 2020), even at lower levels as compared to the Global Financial Crisis (GFC) of 2008. It is only recently since scholars started investigating the effect of COVID-19 on capital markets in general, and on stock price volatility in particular (e.g., Al-Awadhi et al. 2020; Erdem 2020; Heyden and Heyden 2021; Yousef 2020). Analyzing stock market indices of 75 countries, Erdem (2020) evidence that the pandemic resulted in an increase of volatility and a decrease of index returns. Heyden and Heyden (2021) reveal significant negative market reactions to COVID-19 cases across the US and Europe, while a similar pattern is also evident for China (Al-Awadhi et al. 2020) and Japan (Takahashi and Yamada 2020).

Despite sharing similarities with the aforementioned studies, our study diverges in several fonts. First, we offer insights into the impact of COVID-19 on stock return volatility using firm-level data, and thus deviate from studies concentrating on stock market indices (e.g., Erdem 2020; Yousef 2020). Second, our sample considers

---

[1] See https://www.oecd.org/coronavirus/en/themes/global-economy (Accessed 10 February, 2021).

[2] https://www.euro.who.int/en/health-topics/health-emergencies/coronavirus-covid-19/news/news/2020/3/who-announces-covid-19-outbreak-a-pandemic (Accessed 10 February, 2021).

[3] Further details on Covid-19 infections and fatalities can be found in https://coronavirus.jhu.edu/map.html (Accessed 10 February, 2021).

[4] https://ec.europa.eu/eurostat/statistics-explained/index.php?title=Impact_of_COVID-19_on_main_GDP_aggregates_including_employment#GDP_estimates_published_for_2020-Q1 (Accessed 10 February, 2021).

firms from 63 countries and thus extends the findings of single-country studies (Al-Awadhi et al. 2020; Takahashi and Yamada 2020). Third, we further understandings at a global scale by engaging a sample that covers around 60% from approximately 51.000 active listed global firms.[5] Fourth, we capture the effect of COVID-19 on stock return volatility both at the short- and at the long-term, by using a moving variance approach within estimation windows spanning from 30 to 250 days. Finally, we enlighten the reader on the differences of COVID-19 impact across regions, by clustering our analysis, and reveal that the effect of COVID-19 is amplified for companies from Oceania and Asia.

This study contributes to prior literature in the following ways. First, the analysis adds to the existing studies in regards to the impact of external shocks (natural disasters, financial crises) on the stock markets. Second, it extends the existing limited literature examining the impact of COVID-19 across various aspects, including the volatility of stock returns in financial markets. Third, we employ large scale data that capture 60% of global listed firms, and thereby we add to prior literature on the impact of COVID-19 at a global scale. Finally, we conduct regional analyses and inform that the effect of COVID-19 is amplified for companies from Oceania and Asia.

The rest of this paper is organized as follows: Sect. 2 provides the theory and hypothesis development. Section 3 presents the research methodology. Section 4 presents the data and empirical tests, while Sect. 5 concludes the study.

2 Theory and Hypothesis Development

Volatility in financial markets is critical to a wide spectrum of decision makers, including individual and institutional investors, portfolio managers, industry regulators and policy makers. Managing volatility and understanding its determinants is very important for investors, as often portfolio expected returns and volatility are negatively correlated (Li et al. 2005). Prior research suggests that most investors do not hold "fully" diversify their portfolio for several reasons such as (a) transactions costs (Ang et al. 2006), (b) heterogeneity in their preferences (e.g., preferences for stocks with higher volatility) (Goetzmann and Kumar 2008), (c) financial constraints (Xu and Malkiel 2003) etc. Therefore, understanding the drivers of stock price volatility is essential for enhancing investor's wealth, since under-diversification may result in higher risk (Abdelsalam et al. 2021).

Prior literature has put emphasis on examining how various external shocks (i.e., weather events, earthquakes, recession, and diseases) impact volatility in global financial markets. Empirical evidence indicate sharp movements in stock prices (i.e.,

---

[5] See the World Federation of Exchanges https://webcache.googleusercontent.com/search?q=cache:oWYsB4yZzRIJ:https://focus.world-exchanges.org/storage/app/media/statistics/WFE%2520H1%25202019%2520Market%2520Highlights%2520press%2520release%2520draft%25205%252016.08.2019.pdf+&cd=5&hl=en&ct=clnk&gl=gr (Accessed 10 February, 2021).

higher volatility) during periods of financial distress and recession (e.g., the Great Recession of 1929 (e.g., Romer 1990); the Dotcom bubble of 1999–2001 (e.g., Bakshi and Wu 2010); and the GFC of 2008 (e.g., Kotkatvuori-Örnberg et al. 2013)). On top of these, in recent years we observe an increasing interest on how different types of natural disasters (e.g., hurricanes, earthquakes, floods, bushfires, cyclones, tsunamis) affected the global marketplace (e.g., Bourdeau-Brien and Kryzanowski 2017; Valizadeh et al. 2017).

Bourdeau-Brien and Kryzanowski (2017) find that major natural disasters have a significant impact on stock returns and volatilities of U.S. firms. In the same direction, Worthington and Valadkhani (2004) find similar results when considering the effect of severe disaster shocks (e.g., floods, wildfires, earthquakes, storms, cyclones) on the Australian stock market from 1982 to 2002. They highlight that market returns are more sensitive to shocks provided by natural events like cyclones, bushfires, and earthquakes. Significant negative impact on stock returns have been also shown to pertain in the periods following the California Earthquake of 1989 (Shelor et al. 1990), the occurrence of back-to-back 2005 hurricanes (Katrina and Rita) (Gangopadhyay et al. 2010), and the Great East Japan earthquake of 2011 (Hood et al. 2013; Takao et al. 2013).

In addition to the aforementioned shocks, financial markets have been impacted by an ascending number of infectious diseases such as Ebola virus, MERS CoV, SARS, Lassa fever, Nipah virus, Zika virus etc. The spread of these contagious diseases not only affects people's health and life but also induces a decline in economic growth (Liu et al. 2020). For instance, Chen et al. (2007) indicate a negative impact of the impact of the SARS outbreak in 2003 on the stock returns Taiwanese tourism firms.

The outbreak of COVID-19 is one of the most recent events on the international scene. Consequently, there is scarce literature examining the stock market behavior during this period. However, various studies emphasized that the spread of the virus is causing great fear or shock to the financial markets that need further investigation. Baek et al. (2020) examined the stock market volatility of 30 industries operating in the U.S. They observe that volatility is affected by different economic indicators and is sensitive to COVID-19 news. In addition, they document that systematic risk is higher for defensive industries (e.g. utilities, telecom) and lower for aggressive industries (e.g., business equipment, automobiles). Heyden and Heyden (2021) investigate the short-term market reactions of US and European stocks to the public information about COVID-19. While the first case of the COVID-19 does not have a significant impact, the announcement of the first death stimulates a negative stock price reaction to the COVID-19.

Liu et al. (2020) analyze the impact of the COVID-19 outbreak on 21 major stock market indices and suggest that stock markets in most vulnerable countries and areas faced higher negative abnormal returns relative to other countries. In another study, Bash (2020) sheds light into the effect of the first registered case of COVID-19 on stock market returns of 30 countries. Results reveal that COVID-19 has a significant negative impact on index return. This finding is in line with Zhang et al. (2020) estimation. They examine the volatility of ten stock markets in the countries with the highest number of confirmed cases between January and February 2020 and find that volatility increased substantially in February due to COVID-19. Baker et al. (2020) used textual analysis of news mentions and found that the COVID-19 pandemic has resulted in the highest stock market volatility among all recent infectious diseases including the Spanish Flu of 1918. Additionally, Zaremba et al. (2020) reveal that governmental interventions (lock-downs and prevention measures) have significantly increased daily stock market volatility.

Building on the work of Al-Awadhi et al. (2020), which reveals that stock markets around the world have reacted to the COVID-19 pandemic with strong volatility, as well as on the aforementioned literature, we form the following hypothesis:

H: The number of COVID-19 cases (fatalities) is positively associated with stock return volatility of global firms.

3 Research Design

3.1 Empirical Model

We conduct our investigations using panel data analysis, in line with relevant studies and due to the daily frequency nature of our data (Zaremba et al. 2020). We evaluate the impact of COVID-19 cases (fatalities) on stock return volatility of global firms by relying on model the specification outlined in the following equation:

$$
\begin{aligned}
\text{VOLATILITY}_{i,t} = {} & \beta_0 + \beta_1 \text{COVID}_{i,t,c} + \beta_2 \text{ROA}_{i,t} + \beta_3 \text{LnASSETS}_{i,t} \\
& + \beta_4 \text{LEVERAGE}_{i,t} + \beta_5 \text{MB}_{i,t} + \mu_d + \mu_c + \varepsilon_{i,t}
\end{aligned}
\tag{1}
$$

The dependent variable (VOLATILITY) is a vector representing the volatility of daily stock returns at different estimating windows. Following prior studies (e.g., Dutt and Humphery-Jenner 2013), we estimate return volatility using a moving variance approach within estimation windows of 30, 60, 90, 180, and 250 days. COVID represents the COVID-19 related measures employed in our study,[6] namely (a) the total number of COVID-19 cases in each day (LnCASESTOT) and (b) the total number of COVID-19 related fatalities (LnDEATSHSTOT). Both COVID-19 measures are in daily frequency, while in our analyses we transform them into natural logarithms so as to obtain better distributional properties and to reduce the impact of outliers.

Our model also considers several firm-level variables, all measured on a quarterly basis, to control cross-sectional differences in firm characteristics that may influence return volatility. We control for profitability and size using the ratio of earnings before interest and taxes (EBIT) to total assets (ROA) and the natural logarithm of total

---

[6] Data on COVID-19 cases and fatalities are available through the World Bank, and in particular through "Our World in Data" (see https://github.com/owid/covid-19-data/blob/master/public/data/README.md (Accessed 10 February, 2021).

assets (LnASSETS), respectively, since larger and more profitable firms are more likely to experience lower return volatility (Pastor and Veronesi 2003). As a measure of financial leverage, we use the ratio of total debt over total assets (LEVERAGE) because financially distressed firms are more likely to be leveraged and have higher return volatility (Rajgopal and Venkatachalam 2011). Previous studies provide an association between volatility and firm growth opportunities, since growing firms exhibit more fluctuations in their returns (Cao et al. 2008; Pastor and Veronesi 2003). Therefore, we consider for firm growth opportunities, operationalized as the market-to-book value of equity (MB). The standard errors of all the regression estimates are adjusted using heteroskedasticity-corrected and clustered robust standard errors, clustered on firms.

Finally, we winsorize all continuous variables at the 1st and 99th percentiles to mitigate the effect of outliers, while we also include industry and country indicators in all our estimates to alleviate any concerns for unobserved industry and country effects. μ_d denotes indicator variables with a value of one for industry d, and zero otherwise; μ_c denotes indicator variables with a value of one for country c, and zero otherwise; and $\varepsilon_{i,t}$ is the error term. We present the variable definitions in Appendix.

3.2 Data

Our estimation period considers the date the WHO declared COVID-19 as global pandemic (i.e., 12 March 2020) and spans up to 30 September 2020.[7] Our sample selection considers the entire universe of active and listed firms in the DataStream database, which is the primary source for stock price information and accounting data. We consider the country of the stock exchange as the relevant company location (similar to Dutt and Humphery-Jenner 2013), and match the number of COVID-19 cases and/or fatalities reported each day, available through the World Bank. At this stage, our sample comprises of 31,649 firms (translated into 818,532 observations). Our data requirements for control variables for model (1) further drop 1105 firms, due to missing data. Following previous studies (e.g., Abdelsalam et al. 2021), our sample selection criteria require at least four firms in one country, and thus we eliminate 24 firms. Table 1 describes the sample selection process.

Our final sample comprises 30,516 firms (translated into 783,241 observations; see Table 1 for a description) scattered across 63 countries (see Table 2). Drawing upon Table 2 reveals that companies from three countries predominate, namely Japan (26.01), Australia (19.95), and India (19.51). Additionally, the right part of Table 2 informs on the average number of daily cases and fatalities across our in sample firms. In particular, we observe that the US, Turkey, Brazil, Italy and UK belong to the top five countries in terms of the total number of COVID-19 cases (CASESTOT) and the total number of COVID-19 fatalities (FATALITIESTOT).

---

[7] Since our volatility measures are estimated at windows spanning up to 250 days, we collect stock price data for 250 days trailing the declaration of COVID-19 as global pandemic by the WHO.

Table 1 Sample selection process

Sample selection stages	No. firms	No. firm-years
Companies with return volatility data available through DataStream and COVID-19 data available through World Bank	31,649	818,532
Delete: Companies with missing financial data for our empirical model	1105	34,177
Delete: Observations of companies don't meet the four companies per country criterion	28	1114
Final sample	**30,516**	**783,241**

4 Empirical Results

4.1 Univariate Analysis

The descriptive statistics for the main variables used in our analysis are provided in Table 3. The results show that volatility is higher in the short term, as compared to the long-term, as indicated by the mean, median, and max values of the Vol30, Vol60, Vol90, Vol180, and Vol250. Indicatively, the mean (max) of Vol30, Vol60, and Vol90 are 0.039 (0.205, 0.194, and 0.187 respectively), as compared to Vol180 and Vol250 which values are 0.037 (0.178 and 0.174, respectively). Moving to the rest of the control variables, the average firm exhibits negative profitability (the mean of ROA is −0.095) and has an average leverage of 0.235, both on a quarterly basis.

Table 4 presents the Pearson correlation coefficients between the sample variables. We observe that all volatility measures are positively correlated with each other, while the same also applies to the COVID-19 measures. Hence, we consider each of them separately in our analyses. Additionally, both COVID-19 measures are positively and statistical significantly correlated with firm return volatility measures. With regards to the remaining pairwise correlation coefficients, none of them is higher than 0.53 (in absolute terms) and thus suggest no serious problem of multicollinearity. This is also verified by the low values of the mean–variance inflation factors (VIFs), which do not exceed 1.4 across all models and are even lower than the conservative cut-off value of 5 (Studenmund 2016).

4.2 Multivariate Analysis

We conduct a multivariate analysis to investigate further the association between COVID-19 and firm return volatility. Table 5 reports the panel data analysis of the effect of COVID-19 cases on firm return volatility. The first row shows the dependent variable employed in each model, measured at different estimation windows (30, 60, 90, 180 and 250 days). The empirical results confirm a positive and statistically significant impact of COVID-19 cases (LnCASESTOT) on firm returns volatility, as all

Table 2 Country distribution of observations

No	Country	Region	Firms	Obs	Percent	CASESTOT	FATALITIESTOT
1	Australia	Oceania	1370	156,268	19.95	3613.19	45.01
2	Austria	Europe	52	755	0.10	3247.93	100.04
3	Bahrain	Asia	31	48	0.01	0.00	0.00
4	Belgium	Europe	106	886	0.11	12,002.58	1750.07
5	Bermuda	Americas	7	251	0.03	89.74	5.39
6	Botswana	Africa	4	260	0.03	36.20	0.99
7	Brazil	Americas	263	718	0.09	70,411.73	3685.29
8	Canada	Americas	1604	30,614	3.91	17,146.53	1226.99
9	China	Asia	4124	7244	0.92	24,401.47	1033.32
10	Croatia	Europe	62	62	0.01	0.00	0.00
11	Czech Republic	Europe	12	12	0.00	0.00	0.00
12	Denmark	Europe	105	1341	0.17	4730.30	215.65
13	Egypt	Africa	149	3575	0.46	9445.83	400.72
14	Estonia	Europe	16	142	0.02	802.18	23.56
15	Finland	Europe	131	131	0.02	0.00	0.00
16	France	Europe	526	3573	0.46	21,546.95	3556.49
17	Germany	Europe	496	2186	0.28	41,079.58	1595.40
18	Greece	Europe	157	157	0.02	0.00	0.00
19	Guernsey	Europe	36	938	0.12	170.67	7.63
20	Iceland	Europe	16	81	0.01	88.04	0.17
21	India	Asia	2385	152,837	19.51	224.33	5.93
22	Indonesia	Asia	474	710	0.09	39.69	3.18
23	Iraq	Asia	25	89	0.01	43.61	3.44
24	Ireland	Europe	62	1406	0.18	9664.24	592.33
25	Israel	Asia	396	585	0.07	1839.24	25.60
26	Italy	Europe	262	973	0.12	59,770.08	8070.75
27	Jamaica	Americas	10	400	0.05	288.25	5.21
28	Japan	Asia	3270	203,753	26.01	2483.56	83.80
29	Jersey	Europe	5	170	0.02	216.14	16.97
30	Kenya	Africa	5	125	0.02	856.86	26.57
31	Kuwait	Asia	138	518	0.07	2161.80	16.55
32	Lithuania	Europe	27	149	0.02	640.97	22.58
33	Luxembourg	Europe	45	285	0.04	145.90	1.31
34	Malaysia	Asia	781	32,981	4.21	2831.76	41.87
35	Mexico	Americas	121	121	0.02	0.00	0.00

(continued)

Table 2 (continued)

No	Country	Region	Firms	Obs	Percent	CASESTOT	FATALITIESTOT
36	Monaco	Europe	10	66	0.01	3.55	0.00
37	Netherlands	Europe	121	641	0.08	12,545.17	1504.05
38	New Zealand	Oceania	107	8781	1.12	455.69	6.80
39	Nigeria	Africa	91	913	0.12	1625.20	43.96
40	North Macedonia	Europe	27	27	0.00	0.00	0.00
41	Norway	Europe	165	165	0.02	0.00	0.00
42	Oman	Asia	78	326	0.04	1997.83	8.86
43	Pakistan	Asia	224	18,099	2.31	31,712.75	640.73
44	Philippines	Asia	201	571	0.07	1717.22	86.43
45	Poland	Europe	12	541	0.07	11,149.63	486.03
46	Qatar	Asia	43	43	0.01	0.00	0.00
47	Romania	Europe	83	83	0.01	0.00	0.00
48	Russia	Europe	169	169	0.02	0.00	0.00
49	Saudi Arabia	Asia	5	95	0.01	388.74	1.16
50	Singapore	Asia	500	14,631	1.87	8895.19	6.43
51	South Africa	Africa	135	6065	0.77	19,464.87	383.37
52	South Korea	Asia	1943	4218	0.54	2661.26	46.58
53	Spain	Europe	163	487	0.06	33,360.36	3406.37
54	Sri Lanka	Asia	203	9483	1.21	16.01	0.03
55	Sweden	Europe	581	3638	0.46	13,788.42	1385.09
56	Switzerland	Europe	227	1854	0.24	7770.70	328.66
57	Taiwan	Asia	1760	1760	0.22	0.00	0.00
58	Thailand	Asia	591	2960	0.38	812.31	13.05
59	Turkey	Asia	5	200	0.03	85,231.79	2252.36
60	United Arab Emirates	Asia	103	103	0.01	0.00	0.00
61	United Kingdom	Europe	1018	35,513	4.53	53,768.40	7607.10
62	United States Of America	Americas	3848	65,830	8.40	625,540.95	29,776.66
63	Vietnam	Asia	830	1635	0.21	47.78	0.00
Total			30,516	783,241	100	–	–
Average			–	–	–	19,094.812	1119.786

This table presents the country distribution of the companies included in our sample. The last four columns depict the average number of: (a) the total number of COVID-19 cases (CASESTOT); and (b) the total COVID-19 fatalities (FATALITIESTOT), as per country. COVID-19 data capture the period from 12 March 2020 up to 30 September 2020, and are derived on a daily frequency through the World Bank (https://github.com/owid/COVID-19-data/blob/master/public/data/README.md)

Table 3 Descriptive statistics

Variable	Obs	Min	25th	Mean	Median	75th	Max	StDev
Vol30	783,241	0	0.016	0.039	0.029	0.049	0.205	0.035
Vol60	783,241	0	0.017	0.039	0.03	0.048	0.194	0.034
Vol90	783,241	0	0.018	0.039	0.03	0.048	0.187	0.033
Vol180	783,241	0.004	0.018	0.037	0.029	0.044	0.178	0.03
Vol250	783,241	0.004	0.018	0.037	0.028	0.043	0.174	0.029
LnCASESTOT	783,241	0	0.693	4.495	3.434	7.937	14.443	3.951
LnFATALITIESTOT	783,241	0	0	2.012	0	3.784	11.592	2.861
ROA	783,241	−3.486	−0.048	−0.095	0.022	0.061	0.332	0.474
LnASSETS	783,241	4.754	9.933	11.629	11.667	13.325	17.826	2.563
LEVERAGE	783,241	−4.489	0.016	0.617	0.235	0.767	9.406	1.549
MB	783,241	−12.64	0.59	2.102	1.1	2.32	27.58	4.314

This table presents the descriptive statistics of the variables employed in our analyses. The continuous variables are winsorized at the 1st and 99th percentiles. All variables are defined in the Appendix

Table 4 Pearson correlation matrix

Variable	1	2	3	4	5
1. Vol30	1.00				
2. Vol60	0.91***	1.00			
3. Vol90	0.85***	0.96***	1.00		
4. Vol180	0.79***	0.89***	0.94***	1.00	
5. Vol250	0.76***	0.86***	0.91***	0.98***	1.00
6. LnCASESTOT	0.30***	0.33***	0.33***	0.26***	0.22***
7. LnFATALITIESTOT	0.24***	0.28***	0.30***	0.25***	0.21***
8. ROA	−0.35***	−0.40***	−0.42***	−0.47***	−0.49***
9. LnASSETS	−0.38***	−0.43***	−0.46***	−0.51***	−0.53***
10. LEVERAGE	−0.07***	−0.08***	−0.08***	−0.09***	−0.09***
11. MB	−0.04***	−0.05***	−0.05***	−0.05***	−0.05***
Variable	6	7	8	9	10
6. LnCASESTOT	1.00				
7. LnFATALITIESTOT	0.92***	1.00			
8. ROA	−0.08***	−0.07***	1.00		
9. LnASSETS	−0.00***	0.01***	0.47***	1.00	
10. LEVERAGE	−0.02***	−0.01***	0.10***	0.21***	1.00
11. MB	0.01***	0.02***	0.03***	0.01***	0.32***

This table correlation coefficients of the variables used in our main analysis. All variables are winsorized at the 1st and 99th percentiles. Values with asterisks *, **, and *** indicate significance at the 10, 5, and 1% levels, respectively (2-tailed). All variables are defined in the Appendix

coefficients of LnCASESTOT attain positive and statistically significant coefficients at 1%. The effect is economically significant, as one standard deviation increase in the number of COVID-19 cases (3.951) is associated with a 0.79% (0.40) increase in firm volatility (calculated as 3.951×0.002 (3.951×0.001)), within estimating windows of 30, 60, and 90 (180 and 250) days.

The mean–variance inflation factors (VIFs), do not exceed 1.4 across all models and are even lower than the conservative cut-off of 5 (Studenmund 2016), inferring that multicollinearity is not likely to be of concern. It is worth noting that all control variables have also proven to be important determinants of return volatility. The negative coefficients of ROA and LnASSETS are affirmative to the notion that larger and more profitable firms exhibiting lower return volatility (Pastor and Veronesi 2003); whereas the positive coefficient of LEVERAGE suggests that financially

Table 5 The impact of COVID-19 cases on firm return volatility

	(1)	(2)	(3)	(4)	(5)
Dependent variable	Vol30	Vol60	Vol90	Vol180	Vol250
LnCASESTOT	0.002***	0.002***	0.002***	0.001***	0.001***
	(58.62)	(56.21)	(54.27)	(44.44)	(42.05)
ROA	−0.013***	−0.011***	−0.009***	−0.010***	−0.011***
	(−15.11)	(−14.04)	(−11.10)	(−12.91)	(−14.39)
LnASSETS	−0.003***	−0.004***	−0.005***	−0.005***	−0.005***
	(−28.49)	(−39.09)	(−41.58)	(−36.30)	(−31.82)
LEVERAGE	0.001***	0.002***	0.003***	0.002***	0.002***
	(5.16)	(10.98)	(12.19)	(9.41)	(9.11)
MB	−0.000***	−0.001***	−0.002***	−0.001***	−0.001***
	(−2.68)	(−8.98)	(−9.12)	(−5.65)	(−5.33)
(intercept)	0.065***	0.085***	0.099***	0.102***	0.100***
	(27.32)	(35.92)	(38.35)	(38.90)	(36.31)
Industry dummies	Yes	Yes	Yes	Yes	Yes
Country dummies	Yes	Yes	Yes	Yes	Yes
R^2	0.335	0.413	0.441	0.477	0.495
Mean VIF	1.261	1.302	1.326	1.337	1.345
Observations	783,172	783,172	783,172	783,172	783,172

This table reports the panel data analyses of the effect of COVID-19 cases on firm return volatility. The dependent variables are: (a) the variance of daily stock returns over the past 30 days—Vol30 (Column 1); (b) the variance of daily stock returns over the past 60 days—Vol60 (Column 2); (c) the variance of daily stock returns over the past 90 days—Vol90 (Column 3); (d) the variance of daily stock returns over the past 180 days—Vol180 (Column 4); and (e) the variance of daily stock returns over the past 250 days—Vol250 (Column 5). The t-statistics in parentheses are based on heteroskedasticity corrected robust standard errors, clustered on firms. All continuous variables are winsorized at the 1st and 99th percentiles. The statistical significance at the 10, 5, and 1% levels are indicated by *, **, and ***. All variables are defined in the Appendix

distressed firms are exposed to higher return volatility (Rajgopal and Venkatachalam 2011).

Beyond the total number of cases, we also consider the number of COVID-19 fatalities (LNFATALITIESTOT) as our main variable of interest. Table 6 indicates that (LNFATALITIESTOT) attains positive and significant coefficients, at 1%, across all estimation windows of return volatility. The effect of COVID-19 fatalities is higher as compared to COVID-19 cases, as a one standard deviation increase in the number of COVID-19 fatalities (2.861) is associated with a 0.86% (0.57%) increase in firm volatility (calculated as 2.861 × 0.003(2.861 × 0.002)) within estimating windows of 30, 60, and 90 (180 and 250) days. Moving to the rest of the control variables, we observe that they remain qualitatively similar as previously described.

Table 6 The impact of COVID-19 fatalities on firm return volatility

	(1)	(2)	(3)	(4)	(5)
Dependent variable:	Vol30	Vol60	Vol90	Vol180	Vol250
LnFATALITIESTOT	0.003***	0.003***	0.003***	0.002***	0.002***
	(42.10)	(45.00)	(46.48)	(41.42)	(39.58)
ROA	−0.013***	−0.011***	−0.009***	−0.010***	−0.011***
	(−14.33)	(−13.72)	(−11.26)	(−13.30)	(−14.70)
LnASSETS	−0.003***	−0.004***	−0.005***	−0.005***	−0.005***
	(−30.07)	(−39.21)	(−40.18)	(−33.65)	(−29.28)
LEVERAGE	0.001***	0.002***	0.002***	0.002***	0.001***
	(6.36)	(10.75)	(11.43)	(8.34)	(7.95)
MB	−0.000***	−0.001***	−0.002***	−0.001***	−0.001***
	(−4.07)	(−8.60)	(−8.27)	(−4.59)	(−4.22)
(intercept)	0.067***	0.087***	0.099***	0.101***	0.098***
	(28.04)	(36.07)	(37.80)	(37.18)	(34.40)
Industry dummies	Yes	Yes	Yes	Yes	Yes
Country dummies	Yes	Yes	Yes	Yes	Yes
R^2	0.315	0.402	0.440	0.480	0.497
Mean VIF	1.244	1.289	1.317	1.334	1.342
Observations	783,172	783,172	783,172	783,172	783,172

This table reports the panel data analyses of the effect of COVID-19 fatalities on firm return volatility. The dependent variables are: (a) the variance of daily stock returns over the past 30 days—Vol30 (Column 1); (b) the variance of daily stock returns over the past 60 days—Vol60 (Column 2); (c) the variance of daily stock returns over the past 90 days—Vol90 (Column 3); (d) the variance of daily stock returns over the past 180 days—Vol180 (Column 4); and (e) the variance of daily stock returns over the past 250 days—Vol250 (Column 5). The t-statistics in parentheses are based on heteroskedasticity corrected robust standard errors, clustered on firms. All continuous variables are winsorized at the 1st and 99th percentiles. The statistical significance at the 10, 5, and 1% levels are indicated by *, **, and ***. All variables are defined in the Appendix

5 COVID-19 and Return Volatility—Regional Analyses

In this section we extend our analyses and we attempt to reveal potential differences across regions, attributable to the spillover of the COVID-19 across the globe. For this reason, we separate our sample as per region (namely companies listed in Africa, Americas, Asia, Europe, and Oceania) and repeat our empirical tests for all estimation windows (30, 60, 90, 180, and 250 days). We focus on the effect of COVID-19 fatalities, as our main results reveal that its magnitude on return volatility is higher as compared to the number of cases (Table 7).

6 Sensitivity Analyses

We perform additional robustness exercises to probe robustness of our results. First, we use alternative specifications of COVID-19 measures and instead of the total number of cases (fatalities), we use the new number of cases (fatalities). Re-estimating our analyses reveal that both alternative measures attain positive and significant coefficients, while its magnitude is higher and thus reveal that market participants perceive the escalation of COVID-19 cases (fatalities) as more breaking news and thereby increase market volatility. Second, we moderate concerns related to high representation of certain countries in our sample, since Japan (26.01), Australia (19.95), and India (19.51) account for more than 65% of our sample. Therefore, once concern is that our results are an artifact of this disproportionate representation. Although we employ country-fixed effect across all our estimates, we repeat our analysis after excluding firms from the aforementioned countries and observe that our results remain unchanged.

7 Conclusions

This study provides concurrent evidence in regards to the impact of COVID-19 on global markets. The empirical results suggest that both COVID-19 cases and fatalities have a positive and significant effect on stock return volatility of global firms. The magnitude of COVID-19 fatalities is higher as compared to COVID-19 cases, within estimating windows of 30, 60, 90, 180, and 250 days. In particular, regression results indicate higher stock market reaction during the early days of confirmed cases (i.e., Vol30, Vol60, and Vol90). Beyond these, our further investigations reveal that COVID-19 fatalities have a stronger impact among firms from Oceania and Asia, as compared to firms from the Americas and Europe.

Our results add to existing studies exploring the impact of external shocks (natural disasters, financial crises) on the stock markets. Second, we inform on the significant positive effect of COVID-19 cases (fatalities) on the volatility of global firms, via

Table 7 The impact of COVID-19 fatalities on firm return volatility of different regions

	(1)	(2)	(3)	(4)	(5)
Panel A—Daily stock returns over the past 30 days					
Region	Africa	Americas	Asia	Europe	Oceania
LnFATALITIESTOT	0.000	0.002***	0.004***	0.002***	0.004***
	(0.53)	(16.78)	(38.59)	(19.58)	(23.76)
Control variables	Yes	Yes	Yes	Yes	Yes
Industry dummies	Yes	Yes	Yes	Yes	Yes
Country dummies	Yes	Yes	Yes	Yes	Yes
R^2	0.307	0.325	0.178	0.206	0.255
Mean VIF	1.158	1.527	1.097	1.242	1.325
Observations	10,938	97,866	452,888	56,431	165,049
Panel B—Daily stock returns over the past 60 days					
Region	Africa	Americas	Asia	Europe	Oceania
LnFATALITIESTOT	0.000	0.002***	0.003***	0.002***	0.006***
	(0.32)	(18.21)	(39.41)	(21.98)	(29.09)
Control variables	Yes	Yes	Yes	Yes	Yes
Industry dummies	Yes	Yes	Yes	Yes	Yes
Country dummies	Yes	Yes	Yes	Yes	Yes
R^2	0.329	0.425	0.251	0.300	0.350
Mean VIF	1.159	1.600	1.117	1.280	1.379
Observations	10,938	97,866	452,888	56,431	165,049
Panel C—Daily stock returns over the past 90 days					
Region	Africa	Americas	Asia	Europe	Oceania
LnFATALITIESTOT	0.001***	0.002***	0.003***	0.002***	0.006***
	(4.20)	(19.07)	(42.69)	(22.84)	(31.27)
Control variables	Yes	Yes	Yes	Yes	Yes
Industry dummies	Yes	Yes	Yes	Yes	Yes
Country dummies	Yes	Yes	Yes	Yes	Yes
R^2	0.332	0.478	0.277	0.359	0.404
Mean VIF	1.171	1.651	1.129	1.308	1.416
Observations	10,938	97,866	452,888	56,431	165,049
Panel D—Daily stock returns over the past 180 days					
Region	Africa	Americas	Asia	Europe	Oceania
LnFATALITIESTOT	0.001***	0.002***	0.002***	0.002***	0.004***
	(3.91)	(17.35)	(39.95)	(23.91)	(25.06)
Control variables	Yes	Yes	Yes	Yes	Yes
Industry dummies	Yes	Yes	Yes	Yes	Yes

(continued)

Table 7 (continued)

	(1)	(2)	(3)	(4)	(5)
Country dummies	Yes	Yes	Yes	Yes	Yes
R^2	0.325	0.539	0.282	0.369	0.439
Mean VIF	1.150	1.730	1.126	1.302	1.432
Observations	10,938	97,866	452,888	56,431	165,049

Panel E—Daily stock returns over the past 250 days

Region	Africa	Americas	Asia	Europe	Oceania
LnFATALITIESTOT	0.001***	0.001***	0.001***	0.001***	0.002***
	(5.72)	(18.55)	(35.95)	(21.87)	(19.32)
Control variables	Yes	Yes	Yes	Yes	Yes
Industry dummies	Yes	Yes	Yes	Yes	Yes
Country dummies	Yes	Yes	Yes	Yes	Yes
R^2	0.361	0.564	0.281	0.351	0.463
Mean VIF	1.151	1.771	1.124	1.288	1.451
Observations	10,938	97,866	452,888	56,431	165,049

This table reports the panel data analyses of the effect of COVID-19 fatalities on firm return volatility across different regions. The dependent variables are: (a) the variance of daily stock returns over the past 30 days—Vol30 (Panel A); (b) the variance of daily stock returns over the past 60 days—Vol60 (Panel B); (c) the variance of daily stock returns over the past 90 days—Vol90 (Panel C); (d) the variance of daily stock returns over the past 180 days—Vol180 (Panel D); and (e) the variance of daily stock returns over the past 250 days—Vol250 (Panel E). Control variables have been included in all models, but they are omitted for brevity. The t-statistics in parentheses are based on heteroskedasticity corrected robust standard errors, clustered on firms. All continuous variables are winsorized at the 1st and 99th percentiles. The statistical significance at the 10, 5, and 1% levels are indicated by *, **, and ***. All variables are defined in the Appendix

engaging large-scale data that capture 60% of global listed firms. In this light, the study might be advantageous to a wide spectrum of investors, portfolio managers, and decision-makers, since results confirm a significant positive impact on return volatility. Although the COVID-19 external shock has been extended worldwide, not all countries have reacted in the same way. Hence, investigating the impact of COVID-19 on the most affected countries such as Italy, Spain, France, the UK, or the United States, would be a worthwhile contribution to the existing literature.

Acknowledgements This paper is based on Marinela Chamzallari's dissertation for the MSc in Banking and Finance, at the International Hellenic University, under the supervision of Dr. Antonios Chantziaras. We acknowledge the helpful comments by two anonymous referees. The paper has also benefited from the comments of participants at the 13th International Conference on Economics of the Balkan and Eastern European Countries (Pafos) who provided valuable feedback.

Appendix—Variable Definitions

Variable	Definition
Panel A: Volatility measures	
Vol30	The variance of daily stock returns over the past 30 days (Data source: DataStream)
Vol60	The variance of daily stock returns over the past 60 days (Data source: DataStream)
Vol90	The variance of daily stock returns over the past 90 days (Data source: DataStream)
Vol180	The variance of daily stock returns over the past 180 days (Data source: DataStream)
Vol250	The variance of daily stock returns over the past 250 days (Data source: DataStream)
Panel B: Main independent variable—COVID-19 measures	
LnCASESTOT	Natural logarithm of the total number of COVID-19 cases reported in the country the company is listed (Data source: World Bank)
LnFATALITIESTOT	Natural logarithm of the total number of COVID-19 fatalities reported in the country the company is listed (Data source: World Bank)
Panel C: Firm fundamentals	
ROA	Return on assets, measured as the ratio of income before extraordinary items over total assets (Data source: DataStream)
LnASSETS	Natural logarithm of total assets (Data source: DataStream)
LEVERAGE	Leverage ratio, measured as total debt over total assets (Data source: DataStream)
MB	Market-to-book value of equity (Data source: DataStream)

References

Abdelsalam, O., A. Chantziaras, J. A. Batten, and A. F. Aysan. 2021. "Major shareholders' trust and market risk: Substituting weak institutions with trust." *Journal of Corporate Finance* 66: 101784. https://doi.org/10.1016/j.jcorpfin.2020.101784.

Al-Awadhi, A. M., K. Al-Saifi, A. Al-Awadhi, and S. Alhamadi. 2020. "Death and contagious infectious diseases: Impact of the COVID-19 virus on stock market returns." *Journal of Behavioral and Experimental Finance* 27: 100326. https://doi.org/10.1016/j.jbef.2020.100326.

Ang, A., R. J. Hodrick, Y. Xing, and X. Zhang. 2006. "The cross-section of volatility and expected returns." *The Journal of Finance* 61 (1): 259–299. https://doi.org/10.1111/j.1540-6261.2006.00836.x.

Baek, S., S. K. Mohanty, and M. Glambosky. 2020. "COVID-19 and stock market volatility: An industry level analysis." *Finance Research Letters* 37: 101748. https://doi.org/10.1016/j.frl.2020.101748.

Baker, S. R., N. Bloom, S. J. Davis, and S. J. Terry. 2020. "COVID-induced economic uncertainty." *National Bureau of Economic Research*. https://doi.org/10.3386/w26983.

Bakshi, G., and L. Wu. 2010. "The behavior of risk and market prices of risk over the Nasdaq bubble period." *Management Science* 56 (12): 2251–2264. https://doi.org/10.1287/mnsc.1100.1256.

Bash, A. 2020. "International evidence of COVID-19 and stock market returns: An event study analysis." *International Journal of Economics and Financial Issues* 10 (4): 34–38. https://doi.org/10.32479/ijefi.9941.

Bourdeau-Brien, M., and L. Kryzanowski. 2017. "The impact of natural disasters on the stock returns and volatilities of local firms." *The Quarterly Review of Economics and Finance* 63: 259–270. https://doi.org/10.1016/j.qref.2016.05.003.

Cao, C., T. Simin, and J. Zhao. 2008. "Can growth options explain the trend in idiosyncratic risk?" *The Review of Financial Studies* 21 (6): 2599–2633. https://doi.org/10.1093/rfs/hhl039.

Chen, M. H., S. S. Jang, and W. G. Kim. 2007. "The impact of the SARS outbreak on Taiwanese hotel stock performance: An event-study approach." *International Journal of Hospitality Management* 26 (1): 200–212. https://doi.org/10.1016/j.ijhm.2005.11.004.

Dutt, T., and M. Humphery-Jenner. 2013. "Stock return volatility, operating performance and stock returns: International evidence on drivers of the 'low volatility' anomaly." *Journal of Banking and Finance* 37 (3): 999–1017. https://doi.org/10.1016/j.jbankfin.2012.11.001.

Erdem, O. 2020. "Freedom and stock market performance during Covid-19 outbreak." *Finance Research Letters* 36: 101671. https://doi.org/10.1016/j.frl.2020.101671.

Gangopadhyay, P., J. D. Haley, and L. Zhang. 2010. "An examination of share price behavior surrounding the 2005 hurricanes Katrina and Rita." *Journal of Insurance Issues* 33: 132–151. http://www.jstor.org/stable/41946307.

Goetzmann, W. N., and A. Kumar. 2008. "Equity portfolio diversification." *Review of Finance* 12 (3): 433–463. https://doi.org/10.1093/rof/rfn005.

Heyden, K. J., and T. Heyden. 2021. "Market reactions to the arrival and containment of COVID-19: An event study." *Finance Research Letters* 38: 101745. https://doi.org/10.1016/j.frl.2020.101745.

Hofman, B. 2020. "The global pandemic: How COVID-19 has changed the world." *Horizons: Journal of International Relations and Sustainable Development* (16): 60–69. https://doi.org/10.2307/48573749.

Hood, M., A. Kamesaka, J. Nofsinger, and T. Tamura. 2013. "Investor response to a natural disaster: Evidence from Japan's 2011 earthquake." *Pacific-Basin Finance Journal* 25: 240–252. https://doi.org/10.1016/j.pacfin.2013.09.006.

Kotkatvuori-Örnberg, J., J. Nikkinen, and J. Äijö. 2013. "Stock market correlations during the financial crisis of 2008–2009: Evidence from 50 equity markets." *International Review of Financial Analysis* 28: 70–78. https://doi.org/10.1016/j.irfa.2013.01.009.

Li, Q., J. Yang, C. Hsiao, and Y.-J. Chang. 2005. "The relationship between stock returns and volatility in international stock markets." *Journal of Empirical Finance* 12 (5): 650–665. https://doi.org/10.1016/j.jempfin.2005.03.001.

Liu, H., A. Manzoor, C. Wang, L. Zhang, and Z. Manzoor. 2020. "The COVID-19 outbreak and affected countries stock markets response." *International Journal of Environmental Research and Public Health* 17 (8): 19. https://doi.org/10.3390/ijerph17082800.

Pastor, L., and P. Veronesi. 2003. "Stock valuation and learning about profitability." *The Journal of Finance* 58 (5): 1749–1789. https://doi.org/10.1111/1540-6261.00587.

Rajgopal, S., and M. Venkatachalam. 2011. "Financial reporting quality and idiosyncratic return volatility." *Journal of Accounting and Economics* 51 (1): 1–20. https://doi.org/10.1016/j.jacceco.2010.06.001.

Romer, C. D. 1990. "The Great Crash and the onset of the Great Depression." *The Quarterly Journal of Economics* 105 (3): 597–624. https://doi.org/10.2307/2937892.

Shelor, R., D. Anderson, and M. Cross. 1990. "The impact of the California earthquake on real estate firms' stock value." *Journal of Real Estate Research* 5 (3): 335–340. https://doi.org/10.1080/10835547.1990.12090623.

Studenmund, A. H. 2016. *Using econometrics: A practical guide.* 7th ed. Boston, MA: Pearson.

Takahashi, H., and K. Yamada. 2020. "When Japanese stock market meets COVID-19: Impact of ownership, trading, ESG, and liquidity channels." *SSRN Electronic Journal.* https://doi.org/10.2139/ssrn.3577424.

Takao, A., T. Yoshizawa, S. Hsu, and T. Yamasaki. 2013. "The effect of the Great East Japan earthquake on the stock prices of non-life insurance companies." *The Geneva Papers on Risk and Insurance. Issues and Practice* 38 (3): 449–468.

Valizadeh, P., B. Karali, and S. Ferreira. 2017. "Ripple effects of the 2011 Japan earthquake on international stock markets." *Research in International Business and Finance* 41: 556–576. https://doi.org/10.1016/j.ribaf.2017.05.002.

Worthington, A., and A. Valadkhani. 2004. "Measuring the impact of natural disasters on capital markets: An empirical application using intervention analysis." *Applied Economics* 36 (19): 2177–2186. https://doi.org/10.1080/0003684042000282489.

Xu, Y., and B. G. Malkiel. 2003. "Investigating the behavior of idiosyncratic volatility." *The Journal of Business* 76 (4): 613–645. https://doi.org/10.1086/377033.

Yousef, I. 2020. "Spillover of COVID-19: Impact on stock market volatility." *International Journal of Psychosocial Rehabilitation* 24 (6): 18069–18081. https://doi.org/10.37200/IJPR/V24I6/PR261476.

Zaremba, A., R. Kizys, D. Y. Aharon, and E. Demir. 2020. "Infected markets: Novel coronavirus, government interventions, and stock return volatility around the globe." *Finance Research Letters* 35: 101597. https://doi.org/10.1016/j.frl.2020.101597.

Zhang, D., M. Hu, and Q. Ji. 2020. "Financial markets under the global pandemic of COVID-19." *Finance Research Letters* 36: 101528. https://doi.org/10.1016/j.frl.2020.101528.

Turkey's International Economic Relations: The Nature and the Scope of Turkish Economic Ties with Africa

Victoria Pistikou

Abstract The aim of the paper is to assess the tendency and dynamics of Turkey's economic relations with selective countries in Africa. The research question is whether these economic ties rely upon economic or political incentives and to what degree. Current literature examines Turkish economic relations focusing on China, the Western Balkans, the Gulf, and the Middle East, while little has been said about Turkey's rising role in Africa as an economic power. In addition, most of the studies approach this issue from a geostrategic perspective rather than the economic one. In order to answer the research question, it is necessary to examine the correlation between macroeconomic and political variables in order to assess whether high levels of Turkish economic connectivity with African states emerge as a result of market operation or emerge as a consequence of political goals or is a combination of both of them. From 2000 onwards I will examine the dynamics and the tendencies of Turkish economic relations with selective African countries in terms of indicators including trade relations, FDIs, development, and humanitarian assistance. I will then assess to what extent those international economic relations tendencies coincide with Turkish political and geostrategic considerations.

Keywords International Economic Relations · Turkey · Africa

JEL Classification F50 · F59

1 Introduction

The aim of the paper is to assess the tendency and dynamics of Turkey's economic relations with selective countries in Africa in order to assess whether these economic ties rely upon economic or political incentives and to what degree. Current literature

V. Pistikou (✉)
Department of Economics, Democritus University of Thrace, University Campus, P.C.69100, Komotini, Greece
e-mail: vpistiko@econ.duth.gr

© The Author(s), under exclusive license to Springer Nature Switzerland AG 2022
P. Sklias et al. (eds.), *Business Development and Economic Governance in Southeastern Europe*, Springer Proceedings in Business and Economics,
https://doi.org/10.1007/978-3-031-05351-1_25

has not focused that much on the economic aspect of Turkey's rising role in Africa as an economic power. In this paper, the analytical framework in order to answer the research question relies upon economic variables, such as the development aid, trade, and foreign direct investments as well as the economic dynamics of selected African countries.

According to the literature, Turkey's presence in the African continent is mainly correlated with development cooperation. According to the theoretical perspectives, donor countries seem to be more selective regarding aid allocation and favor recipient countries that can carry out developmental projects and are more functional in policies and institutions, especially when the rule of low is concerned (Tikuisis and Carment 2017; Winters and Martinez 2015; Dollar and Levin 2006). Moreover, another significant determinant of aid allocation is trade relations. In particular, donors use aid in order to promote their export interests and their comparative advantage favoring recipients who are also trading partners and create new markets for their products (Hoeffler and Outram 2011; Younas 2008; Berthélemy and Tichit 2004) although Nowak-Lehmann et al. (2009:1199) question this claiming that "exports are caused by aid and not vice versa."

However, it is more likely for recipients to be offered a Preferential Trade Agreement in order to foster donor's utility and continue receiving aid (Bermeo 2018). On the other hand, large donors' competition in trade is reflected in aid allocation, since they provide more aid "in trade-related sectors to important export-market recipients" (Barthel et al. 2014:362) resulting to a serious challenge for aid coordination (Fuchs et al. 2015).

In this context and given that Turkey has emerged as one of the most generous donors in Africa, I will examine the further economic ties which have been developed due to development aid between Turkey and selected African countries. First I analyze Turkey's development aid and then I assess trade relations as well as the economic dynamics of selected African countries. Foreign Direct Investments are not omitted, however, due to insufficient data, they cannot be taken into account in order to examine their correlation with trade, GDP, and other macroeconomic indexes. Instead, a reference is made where appropriate.

2 Literature Review

Up to now, current studies have focused on Turkey's economic and political relations with China, the Western Balkans, the Gulf, and the Middle East, while little has been said about Turkey's rising role in Africa as an economic power. More specifically, many scholars analyze the rising role of Turkey in the Western Balkans (Hake and Radzyner 2019; Koppa 2020; Türbedar 2011; Vračić 2016; Önsoy and Udum 2015), Gulf and Middle East (Hürsoy 2013; Martin 2009; Lochery 1998; Kardaş and Macit 2015; Barkey 2011; Habibi 2012) due to the Islamic factor as well as security, energy and economic interests which allow Turkish influence in these regions. In addition, other global players such as the EU, China, Russia, and the US also play significant role in the mentioned areas, raising competition among great as well as regional powers, such as Turkey (Özcan 2008; Barkey 2008; Kim and Eom 2008; Besenyő and Oláh 2012; Aghaie Joobani and Mousavipour 2015; Mamedov and Lukyanov 2018).

Turkish-African relations have been developed since 1998 and they are based on diplomatic infrastructure and institutional cooperation, increasing the number of Turkish embassies, arranging summits and along with Turkish NGO's paved the way for establishing Turkey as a soft power in the African continent, (Ozkan and Orakci 2015; Haşimi 2014; Davutoğlu 2013; Baird 2016), especially addressing problems such as food insecurity and poverty. Therefore, most of the studies attribute Turkey's involvement in Africa to political motives, based on peace and stability, rather than economic ones.

More specifically, according to the literature, Turkish strategic engagement in Africa is based on four pillars: politics, security and diplomacy, trade and investment, aid as well as humanitarian NGO's (Shinn 2015; Wheeler 2011; Besenyő and Oláh 2012; Bacik and Afacan 2013). Turkey has engaged selectively in territorial conflicts either providing humanitarian assistance or contributing to peacekeeping operations in Africa, especially in Somalia (Shinn 2015; Ozkan and Orakci 2015; Akpınar 2013). In addition, providing Somalia with humanitarian and development aid upgrades Turkey's impact and influence, promoting the "Turkish formula" through the Ankara consensus and thus emerging as a soft power in the region (Ozkan and Orakci 2015; Kirişçi 2009; Donelli and Gonzalez-Levaggi 2016; Donelli 2018).

Other scholars argue that Turkey's engagement in Africa has to do with its attempt to promote its interests from an institutional perspective, as part of its wider strategy through development banks using its ability to exercise influence within regional organizations, such as the African Union and other sub-regional African Organizations and create new opportunities in political, economic and military level (Celik et al. 2014; Sıradag 2020). More specifically, Turkey *"obtained observer status at the African Union"* (Bilgic and Nascimento 2014:1) and along with the Turkey-Africa Cooperation Summit, Turkey managed to be considered as a strategic partner for the African states (Korkut and Civelekoglu 2013; Ozkan 2010; Bilgic and Nascimento 2014). In addition, Turkish embassies have been accredited to the Economic Community of West African States (ECOWAS) and Turkey became member of the Common Market for Eastern Southern Africa (COMESA), the Intergovernmental Authority on Development (IGAD), and the Economic Community of Central African States (ECCAS). In addition, Turkey became a non-regional member of the African Development Bank (Ozkan 2010). In this context, Turkey provides development aid and technical assistance through TIKA (Turkish Cooperation and Coordination Agency) increasing its development projects and activities in the continent and became one of the most important donors, especially in Somalia (Bilgic and Nascimento 2014; Ozkan and Orakci 2015; Shinn 2015; Tepeciklioglu et al. 2017; Bacik and Afacan 2013).

However, other studies stress that Turkey mainly promotes its economic interests, since it maintains a comparative advantage over most of the African states (Chabi and Saygili 2020; Enwere and Yilmaz 2014), therefore, economic motives are those which define Turkish strategy in Africa (Ozkan 2010; Tepeciklioglu et al. 2017).

More specifically, bilateral trade between Turkey and sub-Saharan Africa has been raised as well as the FDIs (Ozkan 2010; Hammoura 2016; Shinn 2015; Bacik and Afacan 2013). In addition, Turkey needs the African market for its products and multinationals since it seeks ways to diversify its international economic relations (Ozkan 2012; Enwere and Yilmaz 2014). Increased trade and business activities not only did they have significant impact on trade volume between Turkey and African states but also allowed Turkey to have access to raw materials, oil and gold from Africa (Ozkan 2012).

Summarizing, Turkey's involvement in Africa has to do with political, security as well as economic reasons, however, is not clear from the literature which sector appears to be the most significant or defines Turkey's interests in the African continent. In particular, most of the scholars argue that domestic political changes in Turkey created a new strategy toward Africa in addition to the past, where little attention had been given in that region, suggesting that today's presence on the African continent emerged due to the new government's strategy. On the other hand, other studies examine Turkish-African relations from the Turkish perspective and its role as a soft power, focusing on development aid, diplomatic cooperation, and trade, without mentioning the gains or the patterns that Turkey may follow in implementing such policies in sub-Saharan Africa. Therefore, this paper intents to contribute to the literature by assessing whether high levels of Turkish economic connectivity with African states emerge as a result of market operation or emerge as a consequence of political goals or is a combination of both of them.

3 Turkish-African Relations: The Economic Dimension

3.1 International Development Cooperation

Turkish objectives over Africa are carried out through different channels of foreign policy and especially through development cooperation, by the Turkish Development Assistance (TiKA). The Turkish development agency, TiKA, established in 1992 and since then provides development aid and technical assistance in least developed countries, mainly focusing on humanitarian assistance although Turkey's first attempt to have access in the African continent began in 1985, focusing on institutional capacity (OECD 2021d). Turkey is among the most generous donors since its ODA corresponds to 1.15% of its GNI which is very high among traditional donors, such as Sweden, Finland, and Norway.

In particular, according to the OECD report in 2019 Turkish ODA accounted for 1.15% of the GNI and in absolute numbers, Turkey's ODA was 8.6 billion USD. Compared to other OECD countries, such as Germany or the United Kingdom, which spent 23.8 and 19.3 billion USD, respectively, the total amount seems low, however, as a percentage of GNI, Turkey is one of the most generous countries, corresponding to the UN ODA objective, which is 0.7% of GNI (Table 1).

Table 1 Total ODA and ODA/GNI in selected countries, 2019

Country (OECD DAC members)	Total ODA (mil.USD)	ODA/GNI (%)
Luxembourg	474	1.05
Norway	4292	1.02
Sweden	5397	0.99
Denmark	2546	0.71
United Kingdom	19,365	0.70
Germany	23,806	0.60
Netherlands	5292	0.59
Switzerland	3093	0.44
France	12,176	0.44
Belgium	2177	0.42
Turkey (OECD non-DAC member)	*8652*	*1.15*

Source OECD (2021a)

It is also noticeable that Turkish ODA as a share of GNI increased through a decade from 0.1 to 0.95%, according to the OECD (2021d). This reveals Turkey's intention to increase its presence and impact on this field. In addition, most of the total Turkish ODA was spent in bilateral rather than on multilateral level, which is something that most of the countries follow in terms of effectiveness (Alesina and Dollar 2000; Barder 2012; Schraeder et al. 1998; Biscaye et al. 2017) and most of the contributions of multilateral aid were made in Regional Development Banks (OECD 2021d)

From 2010 to 2019 the Turkish contribution to international institutions raised from 47 to 197 million USD, which is approximately by 321%, however, it remained low compared to the amount spent in bilateral level (TiKA 2021). Furthermore, according to the OECD (2021b) Turkey provides most of development aid in lower-middle-income countries, accounted for 7.1 billion USD. Approximately 1 billion was unallocated and only 137.68 million USD was distributed to LDCs (OECD 2021b). In particular, Middle East and North Africa is the region that received most of the Turkish aid, approximately 7.2 billion USD while the sub-Saharan region received only 100 million USD. Countries from the sub-Saharan Africa which are among the top ten recipients of the Turkish ODA are Somalia and Sudan in the 7th and 9th place with 29 and 19 million USD, respectively. Given that most of the total aid was distributed in Syria, the 88% concerned humanitarian aid while only 1.2% concerned economic infrastructure and other sectors.

Regarding the sub-Saharan Africa, the most benefiting LDCs, according to TiKA (2021), are Niger, Sudan, Chad, Djibouti, Guinea, and Somalia. As for North-Sahara Africa, most of the Turkish aid goes to Algeria, Tunisia, Libya, and Egypt. However, Turkey is not among the top ten donors, apart from Libya, thus most of the ODA is provided mainly by the US, the UK, Saudi Arabia, Japan, Germany, and multilateral actors such as the EU or international institutions, such as UNICEF.

As it is set out in Fig. 1, humanitarian aid is the dominant sector for countries such as Sudan, Somalia, Chad, and Libya, while in other African states, such as Egypt, Tunisia, Guinea, and Djibouti, most of the aid is distributed in the economic and social infrastructure. Therefore, although the Turkish ODA is characterized humanitarian does not neglect other sectors. In this context, within a decade, the Turkish ODA in LDCs raised from 108 million USD to 2.4 billion USD (TiKA 2021a). As it is illustrated in Fig. 2, only Somalia among the LDCs received most of the aid from 2014 to 2018, while the rest of the countries remained at the same level. As far as

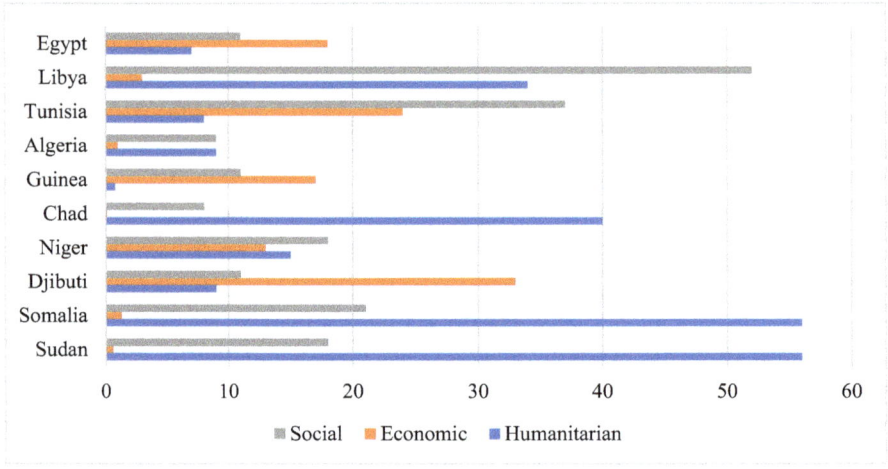

Fig. 1 Turkish ODA by sector in selected countries (% of total aid). *Source* OECD (2021c)

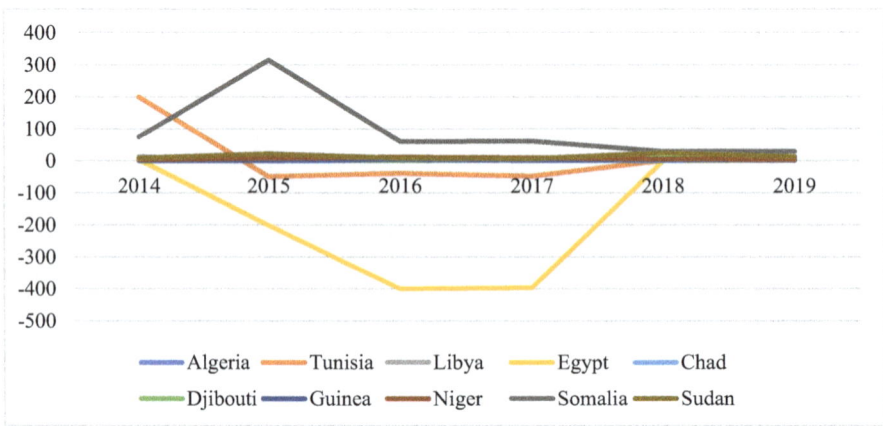

Fig. 2 ODA distribution by selected countries (mil. USD). *Source* TiKA 2021b

the northern Africa is concerned, the Turkish ODA to Egypt and Tunisia decreased, while in Algeria remained at the same levels.

3.2 Trade Relations

Regarding trade relations, Turkey's exports are higher with north African states, such as Egypt, Algeria, and Tunisia in addition to sub-Saharan states, such as Somalia, Sudan, and Niger. In particular, the value of Turkish exports in Egyptian market reached in 2020 3.1 billion USD and the exports in Libya 1.6 billion USD. On the other hand, Somalia and Niger accounted for 272 and 58.8 million USD, respectively. It is also important to notice that exports concern intermediate and consumer goods while Turkish imports from these countries concern fuels, raw materials, and minerals (WITS 2021) (Fig. 3).

It is also noticeable that the Turkish ministry of foreign relations provides economic data and economic cooperation only for the north African countries, such as Algeria Tunisia, Libya, and Egypt, while evidence for outward foreign direct investments to these countries is insufficient.

In particular, Tables 2, 3, 4, and 5 show exports, imports, volume, and balance, respectively, between Turkey and the selected countries in northern Africa. There are no data regarding Turkish FDI flows to Algeria, according to CEIC (2021), however, trade balance is positive for Turkey for the years 2016 and 2018 but there is a reduction in trade volume, which decreased by 32.8%.

In addition, the same can be said for Tunisia regarding the Turkish FDI flows. Trade balance is also positive for Turkey while trade volume slightly decreased within four years.

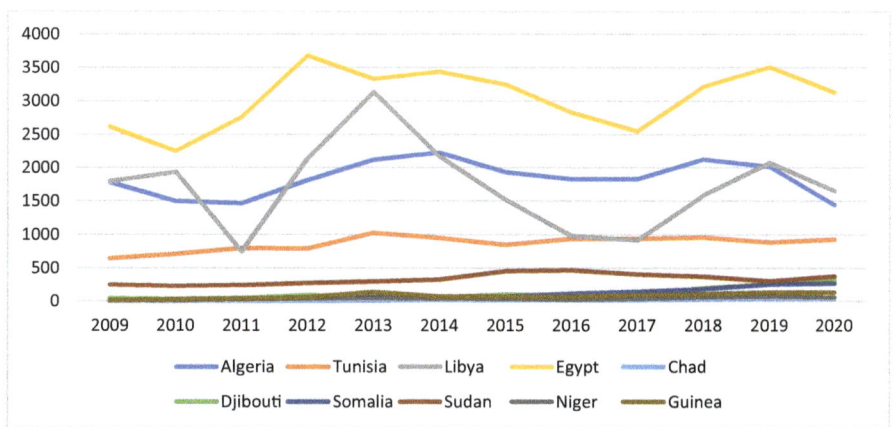

Fig. 3 Turkey's exports to selected African countries 2009–2019 (mil.USD). *Source* IMF (2021)

Table 2 Turkey's exports in Africa (selected countries)

Exports (mil.USD)	2014	2015	2016	2017	2018
Algeria	2,083	1,826	1,737	1,713	2,031
Tunisia	915	820	910.7	915	904
Libya	2.060	1.420	906	880	1.498
Egypt	3.301	3.129	2.733	2.360	3.055
Chad	–	–	–	–	–
Djibouti	–	–	–	–	–
Somalia	–	–	–	–	–
Sudan	–	–	–	–	–
Niger	–	–	–	–	–
Guinea	–	–	–	–	–

Source Turkish Ministry of Foreign Affairs (2021)

Table 3 Turkish imports from Africa (selected countries)

Imports (mil.USD)	2014	2015	2016	2017	2018
Algeria	2,642	1,919	1,347	1,762	1,137
Tunisia	197	144	214.3	206	182
Libya	249	196	161	248	367
Egypt	1.437	1.216	1.443	1.997	2.190
Chad	–	–	–	–	–
Djibouti	–	–	–	–	–
Somalia	–	–	–	–	–
Sudan	–	–	–	–	–
Niger	–	–	–	–	–
Guinea	–	–	–	–	–

Source Turkish Ministry of Foreign Affairs 2021

On the other hand, Turkish FDI flows to Egypt in 2018 accounted for 2 mil. USD and in Libya 1 mil. USD in 2010 (CEIC 2021). Trade balance was positive for Turkey regarding the mentioned partners and the trade volume although decreased with Libya it increased with Egypt, showing a more active market.

Moreover, Turkey's strategy was to enrich its economic cooperation with other countries through regionalism. According to the WTO *«total trade in goods and services grew from the equivalent of 48% of GDP in 2010 to 60% in 2014; and, since 2010, exports increased by 38% to US$157.7 billion in 2014 (current prices) [...] It is noted that many of Turkey's FTA partners are relatively small trade partners of Turkey.»* (WTO 2021a). As it is illustrated in Fig. 4, Turkey's regional trade agreements increased remarkably from 1990 onwards, which shows that Turkey's

Table 4 Volume of trade (Turkey and selected African countries)

VOLUME (mil.USD)	2014	2015	2016	2017	2018
Algeria	4,721	3,745	3,083	3,475	3,168
Tunisia	1.112	964	1.125	1.121	1086
Libya	2.309	1.616	1.067	1.128	1.865
Egypt	4.738	4.345	4.177	4.357	5.245
Chad	–	–	–	–	–
Djibouti	–	–	–	–	–
Somalia	–	–	–	–	–
Sudan	–	–	–	–	–
Niger	–	–	–	–	–
Guinea	–	–	–	–	–

Source Turkish Ministry of Foreign Affairs 2021

Table 5 Balance of Trade (Turkey-selected African countries)

Balance (mil.USD)	2014	2015	2016	2017	2018
Algeria	−0.563	−0.93	0.388	−0.049	0.894
Tunisia	718	676	696.3	709	722
Libya	1.811	1.224	745	632	1.131
Egypt	1.864	1.913	1.290	363	865
Chad	–	–	–	–	–
Djibouti	–	–	–	–	–
Somalia	–	–	–	–	–
Sudan	–	–	–	–	–
Niger	–	–	–	–	–
Guinea	–	–	–	–	–

Source Turkish Ministry of Foreign Affairs 2021

regional expansion was not accidental or opportunistic but part of a wider economic strategy in order to foster its foreign economic relations and increase its exports.

In this context, Turkey negotiates trade agreements with Somalia, Democratic Republic of Congo, Djibouti, Cameroon, Chad, Libya, and others (Turkish Ministry of Trade 2021). However, Turkey has already trade agreements with Egypt, Morocco, and Tunisia. In particular, a Free Trade Agreement entered into force in 2007 between Egypt and Turkey, eliminating tariff and non-tariff barriers, especially in agricultural products. As it is mentioned, *"Turkey and Egypt granted each other unlimited tariff elimination or reduction and/or tariff reduction or elimination in the form of tariff quotas for some agricultural products originating in the other Party"* (Turkish

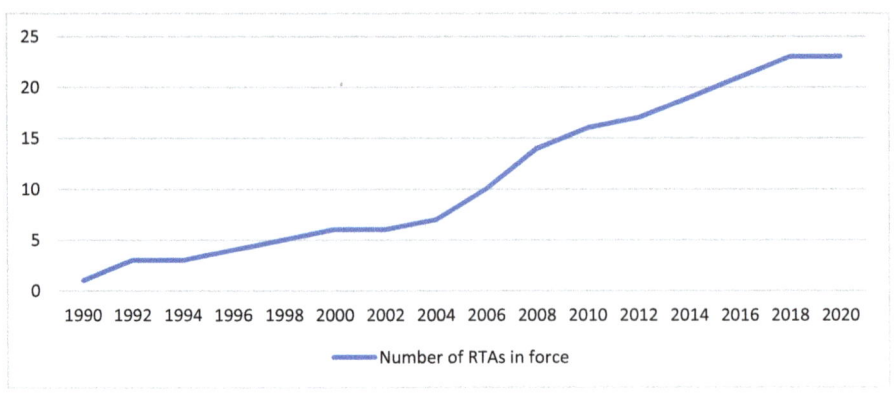

Fig. 4 Turkey's evolution of RTAs. *Source* WTO (2021)b

Ministry of Trade 2021). The FTA with Morocco signed in 2004 *"regulates numerous subjects such as sanitary and phytosanitary measures, state monopolies, intellectual property rights, balance of payments, anti-damping"*, etc. as well as duty reduction or elimination in agricultural products (Turkish Ministry of Trade 2021). In addition, the Association Agreement with Tunisia signed in 2004 eliminates tariffs and non-tariff barriers in trade and industrial products between the two partners while in agricultural products *"Turkey and Tunisia granted each other tariff reduction and/or elimination in the form of tariff quotas for certain agricultural products originating in the other Party"* (Turkish Ministry of Trade 2021). Turkey also signed a Preferential Trade Agreement (PTA) in 2006 with Malaysia, Iran, and Nigeria as members of Developing 8 (D-8). Undoubtfully, regional agreements contributed to Turkish trade surplus and increased Turkish exports. In particular, according to Fig. 5, despite some

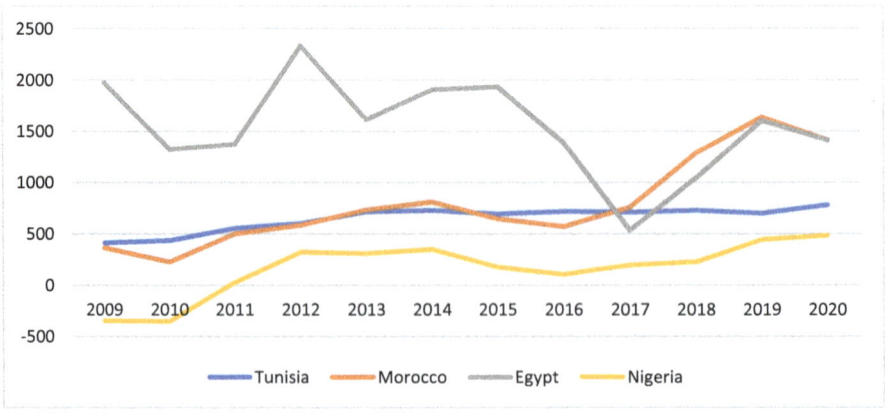

Fig. 5 Turkish trade balance with selected African countries (mil.USD). *Source* author's calculations based on data from the IMF (2021)

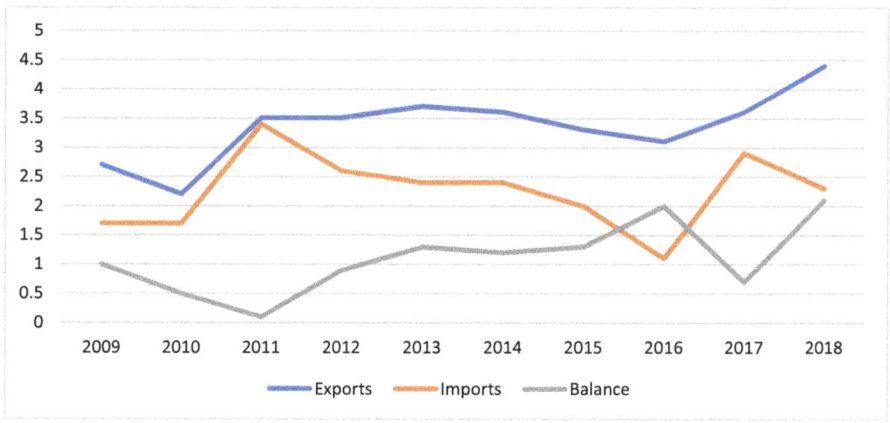

Fig. 6 Turkish—Sub-Saharan Trade (billion USD). *Source* WITS (2021)

fluctuations during the decade, there was a positive balance of Turkish trade with Tunisia, Morocco, Egypt, and Nigeria, and the Turkish exports increased by 110% on average.

In addition, Turkish exports to sub-Saharan Africa increased, especially from 2016 onwards and as it is set out in Fig. 6, there was a trade surplus through the decade and the highest rate was in 2016 where Turkish exports in sub-Saharan African accounted for 3.1 billion USD and imports only for 1.1 billion USD.

Regarding Foreign Direct Investments, there are many Turkish firms operating in the African continent. Turkish investments concern construction, infrastructure, wholesale and retail trade, manufacture of textile and clothing, and main metal industry and the project value reached 55 billion USD (Mondaq 2018). According to analysts, Turks prefer less competitive markets when they have to make up for losses or they cannot achieve their objectives in very competitive markets, such as the EU (Financial Times 2016). The value of the Turkish investments in Algeria are approximately 3.5 billion USD and it is a critical partner for Turkey since it is the fourth natural gas supplier after Russia, Iran, and Azerbaijan (Daily Sabah 2020).

In addition, Turkish investments mainly concern infrastructure and construction sector. There are many Turkish firms that carry out projects in African countries such as Algeria, Ethiopia, Senegal, Libya, Tunisia, Cameroon, etc. (Mondaq 2018). Moreover, 148 Turkish companies have invested 2,084 billion USD in Ethiopia and employ 959 Turkish and 27,710 Ethiopian citizens (DEIK 2021). Moreover, Burkina Faso had the highest amount of Turkish investments in 2018 in the region and in 2017, Turkish investors accounted for 760 million USD. Most of the investments concerned the textile sector (64%), tourism (27%), energy (5%), real estate (3%), and machinery (1%), and African countries which received most of the Turkish investments were, among others, Burkina Faso, Morocco, and Tunisia (DEIK 2019).

On the other hand, the economic environment supports the development of Turkish trade relations and investments with Africa. According to Fig. 7, the African Gross

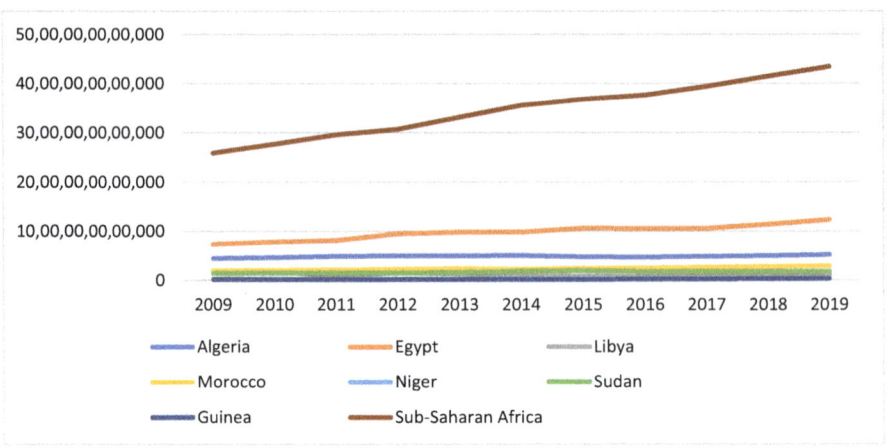

Fig. 7 GDP (PPP) in selected African countries and the region (USD). *Source* World Bank (2021)

Domestic Product, based on purchasing power parity, shows a stable and increasing trend. More specifically, the GDP in most of the mentioned countries has not been increased in addition to the Egyptian economy. It is also remarkable the fact that the real GDP in the sub-Saharan Africa has been increased by almost 70%, which indicates the economic perspectives of the region to policymakers and investors.

4 Conclusions

The aim of the paper was to assess the tendency and dynamics of Turkey's economic relations with selective countries in Africa in order to assess whether these economic ties rely upon economic or political incentives and to what degree. Current literature has not focused that much on the economic aspect of Turkey's rising role in Africa as an economic power. In this paper, the examined economic variables, such as the development aid, trade, and foreign direct investments as well as the economic dynamics of the African countries were the analytical basis in order to answer the research question.

The first conclusion is that the development of Turkish-African relations relies upon domestic political factors. Most of the scholars argued that it was the Turkish government's strategy to create further and deeper economic ties with Africa and it did not follow market needs. On the contrary, the Turkish government paved the way for opening new markets and creating new opportunities for Turkish products and firms.

Second, competition with other great powers in Africa, such as China, the EU, Russia, and the US should not be ignored. As it mentioned, *"all of the counties, whether they are big or small, try to get a share from the richness that considered*

*will be in the African continent in the future. But the continent is more uncompan-
ionable to the Western countries"* (DEIK 2019). That is to say that Turkey considers
its involvement in Africa a positive-sum game due to the fact that, in contrast to
other actors, does not have a colonial past, therefore, it can develop its economic
partnerships from a clear basis. Therefore, the African market is considered as a new
opportunity land for Turkish products and firms in order to have a competitive impact
against other traditional economic powers.

Third, Turkey's involvement in Africa relies upon development assistance, trade
and investments. Apart from the political aspects of foreign aid and the donors'
motives, development assistance combined with trade agreements opens new markets
for Turkish firms and especially for small and medium enterprises. As it is mentioned
"In order to improve foreign trade with Africa, support to SMEs is highly important"
(DEIK 2019).

Fourth, Turkey has developed a long-term economic relationship with Africa,
since does not count only on market operation but also creates institutional frameworks for deepening economic cooperation, such as the African Business Council
and Turkey-Africa Partnership Summit. Therefore, its close partnership with the
African Union and other sub-regional African Organizations, shows that Turkey's
motives are mainly economic with political aspects, since it aims to establish its
presence and economic cooperation in the region.

Last but not least, Turkey's involvement in Africa promotes both political and
economic objectives, however, the dominant element is economic, since a more
competitive Turkish economy in Africa will create the conditions for exercising
political influence in the wider region and perhaps challenging the traditional powers
and the status-quo. Therefore, the economic expansion is the main objective that
may allow Turkey to turn economic gains into political and Turkey imitates the
Western countries' strategies in Africa. As Turkish foreign policy analysts mention,
*«Turkey aims to become an economic, humanitarian and military power in sub-
Saharan Africa"* (ISS 2021). Once again, the significance of the analytical framework
provided by the International Political Economy for analyzing such complex issues
is remarkable.

References

Aghaie Joobani, H., & Mousavipour, M. (2015). Russia, Turkey, and Iran: Moving Towards Strategic
    Synergy in the Middle East?. *Strategic Analysis, 39*(2), 141–155.
Akpınar, P. (2013). Turkey's peacebuilding in Somalia: The limits of humanitarian diplo-
    macy. *Turkish Studies, 14*(4), 735–757.
Alesina, A. and D. Dollar, "Who Gives Foreign Aid to Whom and Why?," Journal of Economic
    Growth 5 (2000):33–63.
Bacik, G., & Afacan, I. (2013). Turkey discovers Sub-Saharan Africa: The critical role of agents in
    the construction of Turkish foreign-policy discourse. *Turkish Studies, 14*(3), 483–502.
Baird, T. (2016). The geopolitics of Turkey's 'humanitarian diplomacy'in Somalia: a
    critique. *Review of African Political Economy, 43*(149), 470–477.

Barder, O., "Is Multilateral Aid Better," available at http://www.owen.org/blog/6128 (2012).

Barkey, H. J. (2008). The effect of US policy in the Middle East on EU-Turkey relations. *The International Spectator*, *43*(4), 31–44.

Barkey, H. J. (2011). Turkey and Iraq: The making of a partnership. *Turkish Studies*, *12*(4), 663–674.

Barthel, F., Neumayer, E., Nunnenkamp, P., and Selaya, P. (2014). 'Competition for export markets and the allocation of foreign aid: The role of spatial dependence among donor countries' *World Development*, 64 pp. 350–365.

Bermeo, S. (2018). *Targeted development: industrialized country strategy in a globalizing world*. Oxford University Press.

Berthélemy, J. C., & Tichit, A. (2004). 'Bilateral donors' aid allocation decisions—a three-dimensional panel analysis' *International Review of Economics & Finance*, 13 (3) pp. 253–274.

Besenyő, J., & Oláh, P. (2012). One of the new competitors in Africa: Turkey. *ACADEMIC AND APPLIED RESEARCH IN PUBLIC MANAGEMENT SCIENCE*, *11*(1), 135–148.

Bilgic, A., & Nascimento, D. (2014). Turkey's new focus on Africa: causes and challenges. *Norwegian Peacebuilding Resource Centre*.

Biscaye, P. E., Reynolds, T. W., & Anderson, C. L. (2017). Relative effectiveness of bilateral and multilateral aid on development outcomes. Review of Development Economics, 21(4), 1425–1447.

Celik, I. E., Dinçer, H., & Hacioğlu, Ü. (2014). Investment and Development Banks and Strategies in Turkey. In *Globalization and Governance in the International Political Economy* (pp. 131–140). IGI Global.

Chabi, P., & Saygili, F. (2020). The Assessment of South-South Trade Potentialities: The Case of Turkey and ECOWAS Countries. *African Journal of Economic Review*, *8*(2), 190–218.

Davutoğlu, A. (2013). Turkey's humanitarian diplomacy: objectives, challenges and prospects. *Nationalities Papers*, *41*(6), 865–870.

Dollar, D., & Levin, V. (2006). The increasing selectivity of foreign aid, 1984–2003. *World development*, 34 (12) pp. 2034–2046.

Donelli, F. (2018). The Ankara consensus: the significance of Turkey's engagement in sub-Saharan Africa. *Global Change, Peace & Security*, *30*(1), 57–76.

Donelli, F., & Gonzalez-Levaggi, A. (2016). Becoming global actor: The Turkish agenda for the Global South. *Rising powers quarterly*, *1*(2), 93–115.

Enwere, C., & Yilmaz, M. (2014). Turkey's strategic economic relations with Africa: Trends and challenges. *Journal of economics and political economy*, *1*(2), 216–230.

Fuchs, A., Nunnenkamp, P., and Öhler, H. (2015). 'Why donors of foreign aid do not coordinate: The role of competition for export markets and political support' *The World Economy*, 38 (2) pp. 255–285.

Habibi, N. (2012). Turkey and Iran: Growing economic relations despite western sanctions. *Middle East Brief*, *62*.

Hake, M., & Radzyner, A. (2019). Western Balkans: Growing economic ties with Turkey, Russia and China.

Hammoura, J. (2016). Turkey expending to Africa: A case of strategic diversification. *Middle East institute for Research and Strategic Studies*, 1–5.

Haşimi, C. (2014). Turkey's humanitarian diplomacy and development cooperation. *Insight Turkey*, *16*(1), 127–145.

Hoeffler, A., & Outram, V. (2011). 'Need, merit, or self-interest – What determines the allocation of aid?' *Review of Development Economics*, 15 (2) pp. 237–250.

Hürsoy, S. (2013). Turkey's Foreign Policy and Economic Interests in the Gulf. *Turkish Studies*, *14*(3), 503–519.

Kardaş, Ş., & Macit, F. (2015). Turkey-Azerbaijan relations: The economic dimension. *Journal of Caspian Affairs*, *1*(1), 23-46.

Kim, Y., & Eom, G. H. (2008). The Geopolitics of Caspian Oil: Rivalries of the US, Russia, and Turkey in the South Caucasus. *Global Economic Review*, *37*(1), 85–106.

Kirişçi, K. (2009). The transformation of Turkish foreign policy: The rise of the trading state. *New Perspectives on Turkey*, *40*(1), 29–57.

Koppa, M. E. (2020). Turkey, Gulf States and Iran in Western Balkans: more than the Islamic factor?. Journal of Contemporary European Studies, 1–13.

Korkut, U., & Civelekoglu, I. (2013). Becoming a regional power while pursuing material gains: The case of Turkish interest in Africa. *International Journal*, *68*(1), 187–203.

Lochery, N. (1998). Israel and Turkey: Deepening ties and strategi

Mamedov, R., & Lukyanov, G. (2018). Russia and Turkey: Approaches to Regional Security in the Middle East. *Perceptions: Journal of International Affairs*, *23*(2), 51–71.

Martin, L. G. (2009). Turkey and Gulf cooperation council security. *Turkish Studies*, *10*(1), 75–93.

Nowak-Lehmann D, F., Martínez-Zarzoso, I., Klasen, S., & Herzer, D. (2009). 'Aid and Trade–A Donor's Perspective' *The Journal of Development Studies*, 45 (7) pp. 1184–1202.

Önsoy, M., & Udum, Ş. (2015). The role of Turkey in western Balkan energy security. *Asia Europe Journal*, *13*(2), 175–192.

Özcan, M. (Ed.). (2008). Harmonizing foreign policy: Turkey, the EU and the Middle East. Ashgate Publishing, Ltd..

Ozkan, M. (2010). What drives Turkey's involvement in Africa?. *Review of African Political Economy*, *37*(126), 533–540.

Ozkan, M., & Orakci, S. (2015). Turkey as a "political" actor in Africa–an assessment of Turkish involvement in Somalia. *Journal of Eastern African Studies*, *9*(2), 343–352.

Schraeder, P. J., S. W. Hook, and B. Taylor, "Clarifying the Foreign Aid Puzzle: A Comparison of American, Japanese, French, and Swedish aid flows," World Politics 50 (1998):294–323.

Shinn, D. (2015). Turkey's Engagement in Sub-Saharan Africa.

Sıradag, A. (2020). Turkey's Engagement with the African Organisations: Partner or Competitor?. *India Quarterly*, *76*(4), 519–534.

Tepeciklioglu, E. E., Tok, M. E., & Basher, S. (2017). Turkish and BRICS Engagement in Africa. *J. Sustainable Dev. L. & Pol'y*, *8*, 48–51.

Tikuisis, P., & Carment, D. (2017). 'Categorization of states beyond strong and weak' *Country Indicators for Foreign Policy* (CIFP) https://ir.library.carleton.ca/pub/14302 [accessed 5 February 2020].

Türbedar, E. (2011). Turkey's New Activism in the Western Balkans: Ambitions and Obstacles. *Insight Turkey*, *13*(3).

Vračić, A. (2016). Turkey's role in the Western Balkans.

Wheeler, A. T. (2011). Ankara to Africa: Turkey's outreach since 2005. *South African Journal of International Affairs*, *18*(1), 43–62.

Winters, M. S. and Martinez, G. (2015). 'The role of governance in determining foreign aid flow composition' *World Development*, 66 pp. 516–531.

Younas, J. (2008). 'Motivation for bilateral aid allocation: Altruism or trade benefits' *European journal of political economy*, 24 (3) pp. 661–674.

Internet References

CEIC (2021) "Balance of Payments", available at https://www.ceicdata.com/en/indicators, (accessed 3 October, 2021)

Daily Sabah, (2020) "Turkey, Algeria eye $5 billion in bilateral trade, expand mutual investments" available at https://www.dailysabah.com/economy/2020/01/26/turkey-to-increase-bilateral-trade-volume-with-algeria-to-5-billion (accessed 3 May, 2021)

DEIK, (2019), "Outbound Investment Index 2019", available at https://www.deik.org.tr/information-center-publications (accessed 3 May, 2021)

DEIK, (2021), "Ethiopia", available at https://www.deik.org.tr/uploads/etiyopya-infografik-eng.pdf (accessed 3 May, 2021)

Financial Times (2016) "The reasons behind Turkey leader Recep Erdogan's Africa tour" available at https://www.ft.com/content/aaf3981a-27e5-11e6-8ba3-cdd781d02d89 (accessed 3 May, 2021)

International Monetary Fund (IMF), (2021). Turkey: exports of goods to its partners, available at https://data.imf.org/?sk=9D6028D4-F14A-464C-A2F2-59B2CD424B85&sId=1515619375491 (accessed 3 May, 2021)

ISS (2021) "Is Turkey's expanding African footprint also a proxy battleground for Erdoğan's Middle East and European rivalries?" available at https://issafrica.org/iss-today/making-turkey-great-again (accessed 3 May, 2021)

Mondaq, 2018 "Turkey: Commercial Relations Between Turkey And African Countries" available at https://www.mondaq.com/turkey/inward-foreign-investment/741414/commercial-relations-between-turkey-and-african-countries (accessed 3 May, 2021)

OECD (2021a), available at https://www.oecd.org/dac/financing-sustainable-development/development-finance-data/ODA-2019-detailed-summary.pdf (accessed 3 May, 2021)

OECD (2021b), Gross Bilateral ODA 2018–2019, available at https://public.tableau.com/views/AAAA_nonDAC/Dashboard2?:embed=y&:display_count=yes&:showTabs=y?&:showVizHome=no#1 (accessed 3 May, 2021)

OECD (2021c), Interactive summary charts by aid (ODA) recipients, available at https://public.tableau.com/views/OECDDACAidataglancebyrecipient_new/Recipients?:embed=y&:display_count=yes&:showTabs=y&:toolbar=no?&:showVizHome=no (accessed 3 May, 2021)

OECD (2021d), Turkey, available at https://www.oecd-ilibrary.org/sites/714276e8-en/index.html?itemId=/content/component/714276e8-en#section-d1e40401 (accessed 3 May, 2021)

TiKA, (2021a) "Turkish Development Assistance Report 2019", available at https://www.tika.gov.tr/upload/sayfa/publication/2019/TurkiyeKalkinma2019WebENG.pdf (accessed 3 May, 2021)

TiKA, (2021b) "Turkish Development Assistance Reports", available at https://www.tika.gov.tr/en/publication/list/turkish_development_assistance_reports-24 (accessed 3 May, 2021)

Turkish Ministry of foreign Affairs, (2021) "Regions", available at https://www.mfa.gov.tr/sub.en.mfa?59f21ff8-791d-4e37-9f39-b4513dfe9399 (accessed 3 October, 2021)

Turkish Ministry of Trade, (2021) "Trade Agreements" available at https://www.trade.gov.tr/free-trade-agreements (accessed 3 May, 2021)

World Bank (2021) GDP PPP available at https://data.worldbank.org/indicator/NY.GDP.MKTP.PP.CD?locations=DZ-TD-DJ-LY-GN-EG-MA-NE-ZG-SD (accessed 3 May, 2021)

World Integrated Trade Solutions (WITS) (2021) available at https://wits.worldbank.org/CountryProfile/en/Country/TUR/Year/2010/TradeFlow/Import/Partner/SOM/Product/all-groups (accessed 3 May, 2021). https://wits.worldbank.org/CountryProfile/en/Country/TUR/Year/2012/TradeFlow/EXPIMP/Partner/by-region

World Trade Organization (WTO), (2021a) "Turkey: summary" available at https://www.wto.org/english/tratop_e/tpr_e/s331_sum_e.pdf (accessed 3 May, 2021)

World Trade Organization (WTO), (2021b) "Turkey: Evolution of RTAs, 1948 – 2021" available at http://rtais.wto.org/UI/charts.aspx (accessed 3 May, 2021)